DEVELOPMENT, TRADE, AND THE WTO

A Handbook

Bernard Hoekman, Aaditya Mattoo, and Philip English, editors

THE WORLD BANK
Washington, D.C.

Cover and interior design by W. Drew Fasick, Serif Design Group, Washington, D.C.

Cover photographs: background image, U.S. National Aeronatics and Space Administration. Inset images, clockwise from upper left: Edwin G. Huffman, the World Bank; Curt Carnemark, the World Bank; the World Bank; Edwin G. Huffman, the World Bank; PhotoDisc; Francis Dobbs, the World Bank.

ISBN 0-8213-4997-X

Library of Congress Cataloging-in-Publication Data

Development, trade, and the WTO: a handbook / Bernard Hoekman, Aaditya Mattoo, and
Philip English, editors.
      p. cm.
   Includes bibliographical references.
   ISBN 0-8213-4997-X
  1. World Trade Organization—Handbooks, manuals, etc. 2. International economic
relations— Handbooks, manuals, etc. 3. International trade—Handbooks, manuals, etc. I.
Hoekman, Bernard M., 1959- II. Mattoo, Aaditya. III. English, Philip.

HF1385 .D48 2002
382- -dc21   2002066398

Contents

Figures

Boxes

the globe. It aims to provide a summary of the economics of sound trade policy and to be a guide to many of the behind-the-border regulatory issues that confront countries in the contexts of both domestic reform and international negotiations. Views and approaches to many of the issues that are dealt with in this volume differ substantially, and these differences are reflected here. All are motivated by the question of how the global trade architecture might be made more supportive of development, and the question of how developing countries can use international negotiations and cooperation as an instrument to further domestic reform and access to export markets.

The Handbook is intended to be a source of information and guidance for all practitioners, defined as those with either a responsibility for, or a strong interest in, real-world trade policy making, rather than the theory of international trade. Such practitioners will be in ministries of trade, industry, and finance; parliaments; private sector associations such as chambers of commerce; consumer organizations, and policy institutes.

The diversity and pragmatism of the views represented contribute to the richness of this Handbook and make it a very worthwhile resource for all trade practitioners. It will help us "seize the moment" and fulfill Doha's promise to focus on the need for trade to bring about greater growth and poverty reduction.

NICHOLAS STERN
SENIOR VICE PRESIDENT AND
CHIEF ECONOMIST
THE WORLD BANK

A Tribute to J. Michael Finger

FIFTEEN YEARS AFTER THE PUBLICATION OF THE WORLD BANK'S FIRST HANDBOOK on trade policy and multilateral negotiations (Finger and Olechowski 1987), the development dimensions of trade policy and trade negotiations often seem to be neglected. This is especially the case as regards trade agreements, where negotiations are frequently driven by interest groups in high income countries and where outcomes can have significant costs for developing countries, both in a monetary or resource-use sense and—since these obligations may deflect attention and resources away from other, more important, tasks—in opportunity costs. The focus of much of the advice and assistance that is offered to developing country policymakers centers on enhancing their understanding of the rules of the international trading game, as opposed to determining what type of trade policy makes the most sense from a development perspective. The latter is crucial, as only on that basis is a national "bottom-up" approach to the design of multilateral rules possible. As noted by J. Michael Finger (1991a, 1991c), when it comes to the relationship between the multilateral trading system and development, there is a widespread tendency to "think about GATT only in the GATT way." Finger made this observation before the creation of the WTO and, characteristically, well before it became conventional wisdom in the development community. Subsequent experience has reinforced his insight.[1]

This Handbook continues a series that Finger launched in 1987. Mike Finger, who retired from the World Bank in 2001, has been a source of inspiration, a guide, and a mentor to several generations of trade policy analysts. Many of the contributors to this volume have been inspired by his writings, and a significant number have also been colleagues and friends. This Handbook is dedicated to him both as a practical tribute to his work and influence and in the belief that his clear-sighted approach to trade policy will motivate researchers, analysts, and commentators who have never had the opportunity to meet him.

Finger has noted that "trade theory is about identifying whose hand is in whose pocket. Trade policy is about who should take it out" (Finger 1981). Both are important. Good policymaking requires a solid grounding in fact and analysis—an understanding of the processes that are taking place—and a frank recognition that, at least for international trade, there will be winners and losers from virtually any policy decision. Trade policy advice needs to provide this grounding, but it must also understand and internalize how the potential conflicts between winners and losers are played out in actual decision-making institutions. Merely wringing one's hands and bemoaning the fact that policy advice is ignored is not satisfactory; one needs to see why and ask how institutions can be designed to produce better policy outcomes.

Five components of good trade policymaking can be distinguished: economic analysis, information and data, political economy, operationalization of policy advice, and a contestable market for policy research. Each is discussed below.

Economic Analysis

Economic analysis is perhaps the most obvious and most easily provided input into the policy cocktail. Many academic economists are active in this area, and theory is cheap. Getting concepts clear and showing how one thing implies another, and under what conditions, are necessary first steps toward any

countries must address their own needs directly via their own policy and should not view the multilateral system as providing a shortcut to good trade policy or good trade outcomes; it just does not do that (Finger and Winters 1998).

These political-economy problems figure prominently in this Handbook, for it is only by recognizing their force that they can be overcome. Thus, for example, Chapter 52, by Tarr, stresses the political-economy advantages of uniform tariffs, which are much more robust to lobbying than tailor-made tariffs. Rodrik, in Chapter 1, emphasizes the importance of developing local institutions as local solutions to local problems rather than adopting uniform institutions imposed by the international community, and this analysis is consistent with Finger's point about the costs of certain Uruguay Round institutions (Finger and Schuler 2000). In Chapter 22, Finger explores the political economy of safeguard provisions, and in Chapter 7 Finger and Winters explore what reciprocity means in the current broad agenda of the WTO. (It has no "external" definition; it is whatever deal the parties are willing to agree on.)

Operationalization of Policy Advice

Policy analysis is ultimately sterile if it does not change behavior. How to present and package the findings of analysis in ways that both strike chords with decisionmakers and are (relatively) easy to apply is critical. Again, Mike Finger leads the way. The clarity and directness of his writing is a model for all researchers. And it is substantially achievable by them too, for while it certainly requires talent, it mostly relies on thinking hard—and with brutal objectivity—and on working hard (spending time refining one's prose). Finger also has a talent for the memorable phrase or metaphor: "Antidumping is ordinary protection with a great public relations program" (Finger 1993); "Where the WTO got it wrong, it was perhaps because the World Bank did not get it at all" (Finger and Nogués 2002, on the inappropriateness of certain Uruguay Round outcomes for development); "Half of domestic interests have no chance to score" (on antidumping, in Chapter 22 below, with a picture of a soccer field of which only one end has a goal).

The discussion of political economy in the preceding section covered some aspects of operationalizing trade policy advice: recognizing reactionary

forces and shining a light on them (Jagdish Bhagwati's "Dracula principle"); redressing the balance of forces in trade debates to promote consumer interests; and making transparent the winners and losers from any action (or inaction); see, for example, Finger (1982, 1986). It also illustrates the dangers of complexity, suggesting a second aspect of operationalization: the use of rules of thumb in policymaking. Among the rules of thumb advocated in this Handbook by some authors are the use of uniform tariffs as a robust antidote to sectoral special pleading and rent-seeking, and promotion of effective competition as the single most important objective in services markets.

A Contestable Market for Policy Research

An important dimension of such beneficial competition relates to policy analysis. The social function of such research is to improve policy outcomes by basing them on the best possible understanding of the effects of policy. De facto, its political function is to smooth the path of decisionmaking by ensuring that relatively minor issues do not destroy social consensus and impose huge costs in the form of strife. This second function is not unimportant (as Rodrik notes in Chapter 1), but it is often at variance with the first. The tension between the two roles of policy research is felt most immediately in official policy research centers. If analysts there stick to the objective side of their brief, they are ignored, abused for being irrelevant or obstructionist, and often, as happened to Finger's unit in the U.S. Treasury, closed down. If they stress the political aspects, they discredit themselves and, ultimately, their institutions as purveyors of information; indeed, they may even discredit analysis itself. And by giving a politically convenient compromise a gloss of spurious intellectual respectability, analysts can sow the seeds of further problems by establishing the wrong basis for thinking about future decisions. The fallacy that trade liberalization creates jobs (perpetrated, for example, in the debate on the North American Free Trade Agreement), and its refutation by experience, have made rational trade policy more difficult to achieve. The fallacy that reductions of tariffs on a developing country's exports are more important than reductions of tariffs on its imports has led to the waste of huge resources on instruments such as trade preferences, the Generalized System of Preferences (GSP), and the New International Economic

Order and, ultimately, to the false notion that the GATT/WTO process and good trade policy are coterminous (see Finger 1975, 2001; Finger and Kreinin 1976).

How can this tension be resolved? In his valedictory speech to the U.S. Treasury (Finger 1981), Mike Finger observed that "political responsibility is the ultimate intellectual vasectomy." What is the answer? It is to ensure that the market for policy research is open and contestable. Governments and international organizations require research arms, but it is vital that others, outside government, are also able to participate fully in this market. Governments thus have to make data and information easily available publicly, accept criticism, and be prepared to justify distributive judgments and decisions.

Finger has shown by example what type of analysis is necessary for better policy choices and outcomes. We hope that this Handbook, and the kind of collaborative, research capacity–building effort on which it draws, will help stimulate others to emulate the "Finger approach" to policy research and analysis.

BERNARD HOEKMAN
L. ALAN WINTERS

Notes

1 Similar arguments are made in Finger and Kreinin (1976) and Finger (1982).

2 This is not to decry basic economic science but merely to place it outside the box of policy research.

3 The actual collection was mostly (and continues to be) done by the UNCTAD, but the presentation and use of the data for policy analysis was pursued more vigorously by the World Bank.

4 Another example was Finger and DeRosa (1980), which showed with the simplest of tools that the IMF's Commodity Compensatory Fund might not have the desired effect of stabilizing developing countries.

5 A CD-ROM that replicates the country schedules is available, but it is not an electronic file of data.

participants. The Trade and Production Database CD-ROM included with the Handbook is the result of the painstaking work of Marcelo Olarreaga and Alessandro Nicita. Miroslava Zervoudakis and Faezeh Foroutan were key contributors to the project's Website, <www.worldbank.org/trade>, which has become the major dissemination vehicle for the output generated by team members.

The chapters included in the Handbook benefited from comments and feedback obtained from participants in workshops, conferences, and seminars, who are too numerous to be mentioned by name here. We are very grateful to the people and institutions that hosted and helped arrange these meetings, in particular Richard Eglin, Sam Laird, and Peter Tulloch of the WTO secretariat, who organized a major conference in September 1999 and a day-long review seminar of the first draft of the Handbook in May 2001. Members of the WTO delegations in Geneva provided invaluable suggestions that helped improve the final product. We thank those who acted as readers and discussants of chapters and the handbook as a whole, including Claude Barfield, Paul Collier, Richard Eglin, Alan Gelb, Joe Francois, Jacob Kol, Patrick Messerlin, Douglas Nelson, David Palmeter, Garry Pursell, Jayanta Roy, Alan Winters, Luc de Wulf, Jamel Zarrouk, and Ambassador B. K. Zutshi.

Finally, we acknowledge the considerable time and effort that has been devoted to the preparation of the second CD-ROM included with this Handbook, "Applied Trade Policy for Developing Countries: Outline, Content, and Readings for a Short Course." Our thanks go to the principal authors, Jaime de Melo, Centre d'Etudes et de Recherches sur le Développement International (CERDI), and Marc Bacchetta, WTO, and to their organizations, as well as to Olivier Jammes (CERDI) for CD-ROM development.

Contributors

Rudolf Adlung	World Trade Organization
Kym Anderson	Adelaide University, Australia, and CEPR
Marc Bacchetta	World Trade Organization
Bijit Bora	World Trade Organization
Antonia Carzeniga	World Trade Organization
Rupa Chanda	Indian Institute of Management
Philippe Chauvet	World Trade Organization
Rafael Cornejo	Inter-American Development Bank
Valentina Delich	FLACSO/Argentina and LATN
Jaime de Melo	University of Geneva, CERDI, and CEPR
Luc De Wulf	Independent Consultant
Liam Ebrill	International Monetary Fund
Philip English	World Bank
Simon J. Evenett	World Trade Institute, Berne, and CEPR
J. Michael Finger	American Enterprise Institute, Washington, D.C.
Carsten Fink	World Bank
Joseph F. Francois	Erasmus University, Rotterdam, and CEPR
Carlo Gamberale	World Trade Organization
Luis Jorge Garay S.	Inter-American Development Bank
Reint Gropp	International Monetary Fund
James Hodge	University of Cape Town
Bernard Hoekman	World Bank and CEPR
Peter Holmes	University of Sussex, U.K.
Gary N. Horlick	O'Melveny & Myers, Washington, D.C.
Robert E. Hudec	Tufts University, Boston.
Stefano Inama	UNCTAD
Veena Jha	UNCTAD
Hanaa Kheir-El-Din	Cairo University
Masamichi Kono	Financial Services Authority (Japan)
Sam Laird	UNCTAD and University of Nottingham, U.K.
Miguel F. Lengyel	FLACSO/Argentina and LATN
David F. Luke	Organization for African Unity
Catherine L. Mann	Institute for International Economics, Washington, D.C.
Will Martin	World Bank
Keith E. Maskus	University of Colorado
Aaditya Mattoo	World Bank
Andreas Maurer	World Trade Organization

Constantine Michalopoulos	Independent consultant
Francis Ng	World Bank
Alessandro Nicita	University of Geneva
Marcelo Olarreaga	World Bank and CEPR
T. Ademola Oyejide	University of Ibadan, AERC, and the Development Policy Center, Ibadan, Nigeria
Arvind Panagariya	University of Maryland
Mari Pangestu	Centre for Strategic and International Studies, Jakarta
Frank J. Penna	The Policy Sciences Center, Inc., New Haven, Conn.
Francisco Javier Prieto	Organization of American States
Garry Pursell	Independent consultant
Vinod Rege	International trade consultant
Dani Rodrik	Harvard University
Kamal Saggi	Southern Methodist University, Dallas, Tex.
Pierre Sauvé	OECD
Maurice Schiff	World Bank
Philip Schuler	University of Maryland
Howard J. Shatz	Harvard University
Eleanor Shea	O'Melveny & Myers, Washington, D.C.
Beata K. Smarzynska	World Bank and CEPR
Brian Rankin Staples	Trade Facilitation Services, Ottawa
Sherry M. Stephenson	Organization of American States
Robert M. Stern	University of Michigan
Janet Stotsky	International Monetary Fund
Arvind Subramanian	International Monetary Fund
David G. Tarr	World Bank
Simon Tay	Member of Parliament, Singapore
Diana Tussie	FLACSO/Argentina and LATN
Lee Tuthill	World Trade Organization
Coenraad J. Visser	University of South Africa
Jayashree Watal	World Trade Organization
John S. Wilson	World Bank
L. Alan Winters	University of Sussex, U.K. and CEPR

Abbreviations

ACIS	Advance Cargo Information System
ACP	African, Caribbean, and Pacific (Cotonou Convention, formerly Lomé)
ACWL	Advisory Centre on WTO Law
AD	antidumping
AERC	African Economic Research Consortium
AGOA	African Growth and Opportunity Act (U.S.)
AMS	aggregate measure of support
APEC	Asia-Pacific Economic Cooperation
ASEAN	Association of Southeast Asian Nations
ASYCUDA	Automated System for Customs Data and Management (UNCTAD)
ATC	Agreement on Textiles and Clothing (WTO)
ATPA	Andean Trade Preferences Act
BDV	Brussels Definition of Value
BIT	Bilateral Investment Treaty
BTN	Brussels Tariff Nomenclature
CAP	Common Agricultural Policy (EU)
CBD	Convention on Biological Diversity
CCC	Customs Cooperation Council (now the WCO)
CCCN	Customs Cooperation Council Nomenclature
CEFACT	Center for Facilitation of Procedures and Practices for Administration, Commerce, and Transportation (UN)
CGE	computable general equilibrium (model)
c.i.f.	cost, insurance, and freight
CRM	customs reform and modernization
CRTA	Committee on Regional Trade Agreements (WTO)
CTE	Committee on Trade and Environment (WTO)
CTH	change in tariff heading
CVD	countervailing duty
DSB	Dispute Settlement Body (WTO)
DSP	dispute settlement procedures (WTO)
DSU	Dispute Settlement Understanding (WTO)
EBA	Everything but Arms (EU initiative for LDCs)
EC	European Community
EDI	electronic data interchange
EDIFACT	Electronic Data Interchange for Administration, Commerce, and Transport (UN)
EEC	European Economic Community
EFTA	European Free Trade Association

EPZ	export-processing zone
ERP	effective rate of protection
EU	European Union
FAO	Food and Agriculture Organization of the United Nations
FDI	foreign direct investment
f.o.b.	free on board
FSC	foreign sales corporation
FTA	free trade area
FTAA	Free Trade Area of the Americas
GATS	General Agreement on Trade in Services (WTO)
GATT	General Agreement on Tariffs and Trade (WTO)
GDP	gross domestic product
GMO	genetically modified organism
GNP	gross national product
GPA	Agreement on Government Procurement (WTO)
GSP	Generalized System of Preferences
GTAP	Global Trade Analysis Project
HCC	Heads of Customs Conference (NAFTA)
HS	Harmonized Commodity Description and Coding System
ICC	International Chamber of Commerce
ICTSD	International Centre for Trade and Sustainable Development
IDB	Integrated Data Base (WTO)
IECC	International Express Carriers Conference
IF	Integrated Framework for Technical-Related Assistance, Including Human and Institutional Capacity Building to Support Least-Developed Countries in Their Trade and Trade-Related Activities
IFIA	International Federation of Inspection Agencies
ILO	International Labour Office
IMF	International Monetary Fund
IPRs	intellectual property rights
ISIC	International Standard Industrial Classification
ISO	International Organization for Standardization
ITC	International Trade Centre (UNCTAD and WTO)
ITC	International Trade Commission (U.S.)
ITCB	International Textiles and Clothing Bureau
ITO	International Trade Organization
LATN	Latin American Trade Network
LDC	least-developed country (UN classification)
MAI	Multilateral Agreement on Investment
MEA	Multilateral Environmental Agreement
MENA	Middle East and North Africa
MERCOSUR	Common Market of the South
MFA	Multifibre Arrangement
MFN	most-favored-nation
MRA	mutual recognition agreement
MTA	multilateral trade agreement
MTN	multilateral trade negotiation
NAFTA	North American Free Trade Agreement
NATO	North Atlantic Treaty Organization
NGO	nongovernmental organization
NRP	nominal rate of protection

NTB	nontariff barrier
NTM	nontariff measure
OAU	Organization of African Unity
OECD	Organisation for Economic Co-operation and Development
OMA	orderly marketing arrangement
PPM	production and processing method
PSI	preshipment inspection
PTA	preferential trading agreements
Quad	Canada, European Union, Japan, and the United States
QR	quantitative restriction
R&D	research and development
RCA	revealed comparative advantage
RIA	regional integration agreement
ROO	rules of origin
SADC	Southern African Development Community
SCM	subsidies and countervailing measures
S&D	special and differential (treatment)
SDR	Special Drawing Right
SGS	Société Générale de Surveillance
SITC	Standard International Trade Classification
SPS	sanitary and phytosanitary
STE	state trading enterprise
TABD	Transatlantic Business Dialogue
TBT	technical barriers to trade
TMB	Textiles Monitoring Body (WTO)
TPO	trade promotion organization
TPRB	Trade Policies Review Body (WTO)
TPRM	Trade Policies Review Mechanism (WTO)
TRIM	trade-related investment measure
TRIPS	Trade-Related Aspects of Intellectual Property Rights (WTO agreement)
TRQ	tariff rate quota
UNCITRAL	United Nations Committee on International Trade Law
UNCTAD	United Nations Conference on Trade and Development
UNDP	United Nations Development Programme
USTR	U.S. Trade Representative
VER	voluntary export restraint
WCO	World Customs Organization
WHO	World Health Organization
WIPO	World Intellectual Property Organization
WITS	World Integrated Trade Solution (World Bank)
WTO	World Trade Organization

Introduction

ANY COUNTRIES HAVE BEEN LESS THAN SUCCESSFUL IN INTEGRATING INTO THE world economy and benefiting from trade reform programs. The reasons are multifaceted and comprise a mix of domestic and international factors. Barriers to trade and investment remain high in many nations, with policy regimes implying significant anti-export bias. Numerous countries have been affected by civil strife and war. And in spite of the trade preferences granted by member countries of the OECD, industrial country tariff structures are still characterized by escalating tariffs, with high tariff peaks for agricultural products and for labor-intensive products such as clothing.

There is general agreement that many complementary policies and institutions are needed to support trade policy reforms in order to create an enabling environment for supply-side responses that generate employment and economic growth. As Dani Rodrik argues in Chapter 1 of this Handbook, if trade policy reform is to be successful, it must be embedded in and supported by an effective institutional setting, and it must be complemented by other reforms. A large and complex "behind-the-border" agenda has to be addressed if trade reform is to have its intended effect. Much depends on complementary policies that define the business environment—on policies regarding investment in human capital (education), infrastructure, and the quality of public and private sector governance. The Handbook focuses on a number of the elements of that agenda, as well as on more "traditional" trade policy issues such as the design of the tariff regime.

Trends in the Multilateral Trading System

Although the challenges confronting developing countries primarily concern domestic policies and institutions, trade policies, narrowly defined, are still important in today's international economic landscape. Barriers to exports of some products in which developing countries have a comparative advantage remain high—tariffs on some agricultural products are over 100 percent. Agricultural subsidies in OECD countries exceeded US$300 billion in 2000, contributing to global price instability and impeding the ability of developing countries to compete on export markets.

Trade between developing countries began to grow rapidly in the 1990s, increasing the significance of their own trade barriers for export interests in these countries. Antidumping actions are no longer limited to OECD economies but have come to be used intensively by a number of developing countries. Barriers to trade in services are many times those that apply to trade in merchandise, especially where movement of the service provider is necessary. In many cases these barriers and detrimental policies can be removed only through international negotiations.

International trade agreements, in particular the WTO agreement, have become the focal point for many discussions on trade and investment policy. As a result, policymakers and citizens of developing countries are confronted with demands that a number of trade policy–related issues be addressed in the context of multilateral or regional negotiations. This offers opportunities to pursue what are regarded as desirable domestic reforms, but it also poses risks associated with agreements or rules that may not be supportive of development prospects.

The traditional mechanism driving trade agreements has been the reciprocal exchange of commitments to reduce trade barriers. This mechanism results in greater welfare improvements than can be obtained through unilateral reform, as it generates liberalization both at home and abroad and makes politically feasible domestic trade reforms that otherwise might be blocked by powerful vested interests. International cooperation can also be a useful device for pursuing domestic reforms that are indirectly linked to trade. As tariff barriers have fallen and quantitative restrictions have disappeared, the focus of trade agreements has increasingly shifted toward regulatory regimes that can have an impact on trade and investment.

Multilateral negotiations on nonborder policies, administrative procedures, and domestic legal regimes have proved much more complex than talks on traditional market access. Because it is more difficult to trade "concessions," the focus tends to be on the identification of specific rules that should be adopted. Given the disparities in economic power and resources among countries, the outcome often reflects the status quo in high-income countries. These may be fully consistent with the development priorities of low-income countries, but there is no presumption that this will be the case.

Developing country misgivings regarding the rule-making dimensions of the WTO became increasingly prominent in the 1990s. These concerns centered on the costs required for implementing some WTO agreements, the lack of adequate financial assistance, and the failure of high-income countries to grant "special and differential" treatment to developing countries. (Most of the provisions in the WTO agreements calling for such treatment are "best endeavor" commitments that are not binding on high-income countries.) A more fundamental concern was that the rules of the game were not always compatible with national efforts to reduce poverty and increase economic growth.

For the rules to make sense for all members, stakeholders in developing countries must participate in the domestic policy formation process, be able to inform national representatives of their views, and hold their representatives accountable for outcomes. If WTO agreements were unambiguously seen by constituencies in developing countries as being conducive to (or consistent with) the attainment of development objectives, these agreements could play a much more beneficial and effective role. In the run-up to the 1999 WTO ministerial meeting in Seattle, a number of prominent observers and policymakers called for the launch of a "Development Round" of negotiations under WTO auspices to address developing country concerns. Similar calls were put forward in the preparations for the 2001 ministerial meeting in Doha.

The Doha Development Agenda that emerged from the meeting clearly reflects the increased prominence of development concerns in WTO deliberations—in turn, the result of increased participation by developing countries in the trading system. All that was done, however, was to define an agenda. Achievement of a prodevelopment outcome remains a major challenge. Resistance to liberalization of "hard-core" sectors such as agriculture and textiles that are of key interest to developing countries is very strong; conversely, many low-income countries are unwilling to extend the reach of the WTO to cover new issues. Implicitly, if not explicitly, much of the discussion and debate at Doha concerned defining the limits of the WTO. Developing countries played a central role in this debate, with many resisting the further expansion of the WTO into the territory of domestic regulation.

The Doha Ministerial Declaration launches negotiations on market access for manufactures, dispute settlement, WTO rules, disciplines on regional integration, environment, and intellectual property rights (geographical indications). These talks will complement ongoing negotiations on agriculture and services, as mandated by the Uruguay Round agreements. Negotiations are to be concluded by 2005. At the next WTO ministerial meeting, in 2003, negotiations will be launched on four "Singapore issues"—competition, investment, trade facilitation, and transparency in government procurement—if agreement on modalities can be obtained by explicit consensus at that time.

Whether the end result will be prodevelopment will depend to an important degree on the extent to which developing *and* industrial country trade barriers are lowered, and on the rules that emerge. A key determinant of the outcome of the negotiations will be effective and proactive developing country participation. This, in turn, requires a good understanding of where national interests lie and a good understanding of the substantive issues, not just by government officials but also by the private sector and civil society. There is clearly a need to strengthen capacity to undertake analysis and to identify national reform priorities, market access constraints, and the potential merits and implications of multilateral disciplines. This Handbook is intended as a contribution to that effort—as a useful resource for analysts and stakeholders engaged in the design of trade-related policies.

Objectives of the Handbook

A major challenge confronting developing countries is to use international negotiations and cooperation as instruments for improving their terms of trade and their access to export markets and as mechanisms for adopting and implementing domestic policy reforms that will raise living standards and reduce poverty. The design of trade policy reform is a complex matter that extends far beyond tariffs and quotas applied at the border. It must be complemented by policies designed to ensure that enterprises can compete on world markets. There is no "one size fits all" package of policy reform, and no magic bullet. Approaches will and must differ across countries, reflecting different circumstances, endowments, legal systems, and cultures.

One goal of this Handbook is to provide information on the implications of—and options offered by—international trade agreements, especially the WTO, for developing countries that seek to use trade as a vehicle for development. Contributors were asked to write relatively short chapters on a variety of trade policy–related topics that are important from a development perspective and that are subject to or affected by multilateral rules, or may become so. The chapters assess the economics of the issues, survey what cross-country experience suggests are good practices, and consider the pros and cons of the possibilities for using international cooperation as an instrument for improving both domestic policy and access to export markets. Although there is an emphasis on the WTO, many of the issues addressed also arise in the context of regional integration agreements.

Notwithstanding its length, this Handbook can only partially address the many policy issues that arise in the course of efforts to integrate into the world economy. The focus is on trade policy, broadly defined to cover both traditional instruments of commercial policy—tariffs, customs administration, and so on—and "new" issues such as services, intellectual property, and the behind-the-border regulatory agenda that has implications for market access conditions. The approach is one of multiple voices; the contributors include many authors who have no connection to the World Bank. In all cases, contributors wrote in a personal capacity, and their views do not necessarily reflect those of the institutions with which they are affiliated.

Not everyone will necessarily agree with all the policy recommendations made by the authors. After all, as we noted above, on a number of issues there is no "one size fits all" answer, and this is especially true of regulatory policies. What matters most is to ask the right questions and to determine the status quo in a given area. It is important to obtain as much information as possible regarding alternative policy options, to understand what type of analysis is needed to provide policy guidance, and to have a good understanding of the prevailing multilateral rules of the game.

Although much of what is contained in the Handbook is motivated by the fact that the issues are on the agenda of international negotiations, the emphasis of many contributors is on economic and development dimensions. The institutions and policies that are important for development and economic growth extend far beyond the subject areas that the WTO deals with or can deal with. Although the WTO can be useful in helping countries address specific bottlenecks and constraints that impede trade, most of the trade policy agenda is domestic. It is therefore vital that policymakers and civil society have a good understanding of what their national priorities are and what makes for good policy, informed by the experiences of other countries, in order to determine what types of multilateral cooperation can help countries benefit from trade integration.

Relatively little emphasis is given in the Handbook to an enumeration of WTO disciplines. There are many readily available resources that can provide the interested reader with such information, starting with the WTO Website, <www.wto.org>. The CD-ROM provided with this Handbook, "Applied Trade Policy for Developing Countries," contains all of the major agreements and many other WTO documents. Therefore, only key aspects of WTO rules are discussed. Relatively more attention is given to the General Agreement on Trade in Services (GATS) and the Trade-Related Aspects of Intellectual Property Rights (TRIPS) agreement than to General Agreement on Tariffs and Trade (GATT) disciplines, since a wealth of analysis and information exists on "traditional" trade policy instruments. The chapters in the Handbook dealing with merchandise trade issues focus primarily on those subjects that are of greatest interest to develing against foreign providers (suppliers) of goods, services, and production factors (knowledge, labor, and capital), and it takes in the functioning of institutions that affect the investment climate in a country. The recognition that trade policy has a much wider ambit than border policies implies that governments and civil society must have a broad focus and must consider the interrelationships between different policy areas and the operation and effectiveness of existing institutions. Kym Anderson, in Chapter 2, emphasizes the need for an economy-wide perspective on trade policy reform.

Key complementary factors that often determine the success of trade policy reform are the real exchange rate and the ability of the government to maintain revenue collection objectives. As Howard J. Schatz and David G. Tarr document in Chapter 3, although countries may maintain different types of exchange rate regimes, allowing the real exchange rate to appreciate significantly over time has often led to the failure of trade reforms. Chapter 4, by Liam Ebril, Janet Stotsky, and Reint Gropp, examines the fiscal implications of trade liberalization. Tariff revenue remains important for many low-income countries. In pursuing further tariff reform, efforts have to be made to develop alternative domestic tax bases and to ensure that reliance on tariff revenues does not needlessly distort resource allocation incentives. Cross-country experience suggests that policy reforms can be designed so as to maintain or increase revenue collection.

Although the available research indicates that trade liberalization reduces poverty overall, segments of the poor may be hurt by it, and in Chapter 5, L. Alan Winters looks at the interactions between trade reform and poverty alleviation. Reform programs supporting liberalization must be complemented by efforts to strengthen social safety nets. Since some of the poor are likely to be so destitute that any decrease in incomes will impose extreme hardship, it is important to identify which of them may be adversely affected by reforms and to determine the most appropriate set of policies to complement trade reform.

A key message that emerges from the chapters in this part is the need for analysis that focuses not only on trade policy narrowly defined but also on the complementary reforms and institutions that are required if trade reforms are to benefit society. Such analysis should include a diagnosis of the current situation, benchmarking in relation to good practice and competitors, determination of the incentive and redistributional implications of status quo policies and possible changes, and identification of the complementary actions that are needed to make trade reform an effective component of a poverty-reducing growth strategy.

Further Reading

Jeffrey Sachs and Andrew Warner, "Economic Reform and the Process of Global Integration," *Brookings Papers on Economic Activity*, 1 (1995): 1–118, is a widely read and influential empirical study that finds an unambiguous positive relationship between openness and economic performance. Dani Rodrik, *Has Globalization Gone Too Far?* (Washington, D.C.: Institute for International Economics, 1997), provides a skeptical view of the benefits of globalization for growth and welfare in the absence of the institutions and policies needed to manage downside risks. An accessible account of the effects of the inward-looking, import-substituting development strategies popular in the 1960s and 1970s, as well as the shift toward more outward-looking policies in the 1980s, is given by Jagdish Bhagwati in *Protectionism* (Cambridge, Mass.: MIT Press, 1988). Edward Buffie, *Trade Policy in Developing Countries* (Cambridge, U.K.: Cambridge University Press, 2001), analyzes trade policy in an integrated framework that allows for economic dynamics and incorporates the structural features of developing countries. Neil McCulloch, L. Alan Winters, and Xavier Cirera, *Trade Liberalization and Poverty: A Handbook* (London: Centre for Economic Policy Research, 2001), provides a comprehensive treatment of the links between trade and poverty in the context of the WTO.

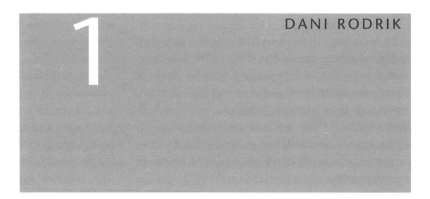

DANI RODRIK

TRADE POLICY REFORM AS INSTITUTIONAL REFORM

ECONOMISTS ARE TRAINED TO THINK ABOUT TRADE POLICY REFORM IN TERMS of changes in the levels of tariffs and quantitative restrictions (QRs) and the shifts in relative prices brought about by these alterations. They use economic models, supplemented by quantitative estimates of elasticities, to analyze the implications of changes in tariffs and QRs for production, consumption, and trade. By tweaking their models sufficiently, they can predict the likely impacts on employment, poverty and distribution, macroeconomic balances, and the government budget. If they are ambitious (reckless?), they will also pass judgment on dynamic efficiency, technological progress, and long-run economic growth.

Policymakers often have a different perspective on trade reform. For them, the actual changes in tariff schedules are typically only a small part of the process. What is at stake is a deeper transformation of the patterns of behavior within the public sector, and of the government's relationship with the private sector and the rest of the world. The reform goes beyond particular levels of tariffs and QRs: it sets new rules and expectations regarding *how* these policy choices are made and implemented, establishes new constraints and opportunities for economic policy more broadly, creates a new set of stakeholders while disenfranchising the previous ones, and gives rise to a new philosophy (alongside a new rhetoric) on what development policy is all about. Hence, trade reform ends up being much more than a change in relative prices: it results in institutional reform of a major kind.

In the language of economics, institutional reform changes not only policy parameters but also behavioral relationships. Correspondingly, the resource-allocation and dynamic consequences of trade reform become harder to discern using the type of analysis that is the applied economists' stock in trade. Household behavior and investment decisions get altered in ways that are difficult to track in the absence of knowledge about the "deep parameters" of the economy. When the reform is well designed and consistent with the institutional needs of the economy, it can spur unexpected levels of entrepreneurial dynamism and economic growth. When it is not, it can result in a stagnation that will appear surprising.

Viewing trade reform as institutional reform helps clarify the criteria by which trade reform should be evaluated. My main argument in this chapter is that the relevant criterion is neither openness to trade nor consistency with existing WTO rules.[1] The yardstick that matters is the degree to which trade reform contributes to the construction of a *high-quality institutional environment* at home. My working hypothesis, supported by empirical evidence to which I will refer below, is that a high-of stabilizing the macroeconomy through monetary and fiscal policies. There is also a sense in policy circles, particularly in Latin America, that fiscal and monetary institutions, as currently configured, have added to macroeconomic instability, rather than reduced it, by following procyclical rather than anticyclical policies. These developments have spurred the trend toward central bank independence and have helped open a new debate on designing more robust fiscal institutions. Some countries (Argentina being the most significant example) have given up on a domestic lender of last resort altogether by replacing their central bank with a currency board. The debate over currency boards and dollarization illustrates the obvious, but occasionally neglected, fact that the institutions needed by a country are not independent of that country's history.

Institutions for Social Insurance

One of the liberating effects of a dynamic market economy is that it frees individuals from their traditional entanglements—the kin group, the church, the village hierarchy. The flip side is that it uproots them from traditional support systems and risk-sharing institutions. Gift exchanges, the fiesta, and kinship ties—to cite just a few of the social arrangements for equalizing the distribution of resources in traditional societies—lose many of their social insurance functions. And as markets spread, the traditional ways of managing the risks that have to be insured against become much less effective. A modern market economy is one where idiosyncratic (individual-specific) risk to incomes and employment is pervasive.

The huge expansion of publicly provided social insurance programs during the 20th century is one of the most remarkable features of the evolution of advanced market economies. In the United States it was the trauma of the Great Depression that paved the way for major institutional innovations in this area: social security, unemployment compensation, public works, public ownership, deposit insurance, and legislation favoring unions. In Europe the roots of the welfare state reached in some cases to the tail end of the 19th century. But the striking expansion of social insurance programs, particularly in the smaller economies most open to foreign trade, was a post–World War II phenomenon. Social insurance need not always take the form of transfer programs paid out of fiscal resources. The East Asian model,

represented well by the Japanese case, is one in which social insurance is provided through a combination of enterprise practices (such as lifetime employment and enterprise-provided social benefits), sheltered and regulated sectors (mom-and-pop stores), and an incremental approach to liberalization and external opening.

Social insurance legitimizes a market economy because it renders it compatible with social stability and social cohesion. But the existing welfare states in Western Europe and the United States engender a number of economic and social costs—mounting fiscal outlays, an "entitlement" culture, long-term unemployment—that have become increasingly apparent. Partly because of this experience, developing countries, such as the countries in Latin America that adopted the market-oriented model following the debt crisis of the 1980s, have not paid sufficient attention to creating institutions of social insurance. The upshot has been economic insecurity and a backlash against the reforms. How these countries will maintain social cohesion in the face of large inequalities and volatile outcomes, both of which are being aggravated by the growing reliance on market forces, is an important question that has no obvious answer.

Institutions of Conflict Management

Societies differ in their cleavages. Some are made up of an ethnically and linguistically homogenous population marked by a relatively egalitarian distribution of resources. Others are characterized by deep cleavages along ethnic or income lines. These divisions often hamper social cooperation and engender social conflict. Economists have used models of social conflict to shed light on questions such as: Why do governments delay stabilizations when delay imposes costs on all groups? Why do countries rich in natural resources often do worse than countries that are resource-poor? Why do external shocks often lead to protracted economic crises that are out of proportion to the direct costs of the shocks themselves?

Healthy societies have a range of institutions that make such colossal coordination failures less likely. The rule of law, a high-quality judiciary, representative political institutions, free elections, independent trade unions, social partnerships, institutionalized representation of minority groups, and social insurance are examples of such institutions. What makes these arrangements function as institutions of conflict management is that they entail a double "commitment technology": they warn the potential "winners" from social conflict that their gains will be limited and assure the "losers" that they will not be expropriated. They tend to increase the incentives for social groups to cooperate by reducing the payoff to socially uncooperative strategies.

Trade Policy and Institutional Reform

What is the link between trade policy reform and these institutions? Trade reform often entails the importation of institutions from abroad. Sometimes this is the outcome of deliberate policy actions to "harmonize" a country's economic and social institutions with those of its trading partners. Membership in the WTO, for example, requires the adoption of a certain set of institutional norms: nondiscrimination in trade and industrial policies, transparency in the publication of trade rules, WTO-consistent patent and copyright protection, and so on. Similarly, membership in the European Union (EU) requires the adoption of wide-ranging legal and bureaucratic requirements set down in Brussels.

At other times, institutional arbitrage is the result of the working out of market forces. Mobility of employers around the world, for example, makes it harder to tax corporations and tilts national regimes toward the taxation of nontraded goods and factors, such as labor. Financial integration raises the premium for macroeconomic stability and makes central bank independence look more desirable. Finally, openness can change national institutions by altering the preferences that underlie them. Civil liberties and political freedoms are among the most important imported concepts in the developing world; the demands for democracy to which these ideas give rise are a direct product of openness in this broad sense.

Arbitrage in markets for goods and capital, in the absence of second-best complications, is associated with normatively desirable outcomes; it increases efficiency. One cannot make the same presumption where arbitrage in institutions is concerned. There are no theorems stating that institutional convergence, harmonization, or "deep integration" through trade is inherently desirable. While many of the examples cited above involve outcomes that are desirable (greater democracy, for instance), this is not true of all *possible* outcomes. Think of the countries that face the prospect of adopting the EU's Common Agricultural Policy or its antidumping regime. It all depends on the circumstances and on how national governments are able to use such circumstances.

One way that governments can use institutional arbitrage to good effect is to enhance the credibility of domestic institutions. For example, the new disciplines imposed on developing country governments by the WTO—in the areas of tariff bindings, quantitative restrictions, services, subsidies, trade-related investment measures (TRIMs), and intellectual property—can be viewed as helping these governments overcome traditional weaknesses in their style of governance. These disciplines impose a certain degree of predictability, transparency, rule-bound behavior, and nondiscrimination in areas of policy often subject to discretion and rent-seeking. In the same vein, perhaps the greatest contribution of the North American Free Trade Agreement (NAFTA) to the Mexican economy was the element of irreversibility and "cementing" that the agreement has contributed to Mexico's economic reforms. In Europe the accession of Greece, Portugal, and Spain to the EU has made return to military dictatorship in those countries virtually unthinkable.

Imported institutions, however, can also turn out to be ill suited or counterproductive. Many of the labor standards that some labor groups in the North would like developing countries to adopt—such as higher minimum wages or restrictions on some kinds of child labor—may fit in this category. The new patent restrictions called for by the Trade-Related Aspects of Intellectual Property Rights (TRIPS) agreement of the WTO are at best a mixed blessing for countries such as India that have so far benefited from cheap pharmaceuticals. A similar argument can be made about pressures for tightening environmental standards in developing countries.

Successful institutional reforms typically combine imported blueprints with local flavor. A good example of this in the area of trade comes from Mauritius, where superior economic performance has been built on a peculiar mix of orthodox and heterodox strategies. This economy's success derives in large part from an export-processing zone (EPZ), which operates under free trade principles. The EPZ has enabled a boom in exports of garments to European markets and an accompanying investment boom at home. Yet the island's economy has combined the EPZ with a domestic sector that was high

outstanding cases—East Asia, China, India since the early 1980s—involve partial and gradual opening up to imports and foreign investment.

The appropriate conclusion to draw from the evidence is not that trade protection should, as a rule, be preferred to trade liberalization. There is no evidence from the past 50 years that trade protection is systematically associated with *higher* growth. The point is simply that the benefits of trade openness should not be oversold. When other worthwhile policy objectives are competing for scarce administrative resources and political capital, deep trade liberalization often does not deserve the high priority it typically receives in development strategies. This is a lesson that is of particular importance to countries, such as those in Africa, that are in the early stages of reform.

Conclusion

A high-quality policy environment is one that sends clear signals to producers and investors, precludes rent-seeking, does not waste economic resources, is consistent with the administrative capabilities of the government, and maintains social peace. Trade policy reform contributes to economic development insofar as it helps build high-quality institutions along these lines. I have argued here that the first question policymakers contemplating trade reform should ask is not whether the reform will result in higher volumes of trade, render their trade regime more liberal, or increase market access abroad but whether it will improve the quality of institutions at home. The results of trade negotiations—whether bilateral, regional, or multilateral—should be judged by the same yardstick.

Notes

This chapter draws heavily on several earlier papers, in particular Rodrik 1999, 2000a, and 2000b.

1 It should go without saying that openness to trade and adherence to WTO rules are not the same thing. A country can follow free trade policies without being a member of the WTO, and many WTO rules are at variance with free trade (as in the cases of antidumping, safeguards, and regional agreements).

2 See Hoff and Stiglitz (2000) for a useful survey and discussion.

3 See Kapur and Webb (2000) and Pistor (2000) for useful discussions of the limitations of importing legal and institutional forms from abroad.

4 Our detailed analysis covers the five papers that are probably the best known in the field: Dollar (1992); Sachs and Warner (1995); Ben-David (1993); Edwards (1998); and Frankel and Romer (1999).

KYM ANDERSON

2

ECONOMYWIDE DIMENSIONS OF TRADE POLICY AND REFORM

taking an economywide perspective when considering the effects of actual policies at home or abroad or of potential policy reforms. Given the significance of agriculture in low-income countries, the chapter focuses primarily on the possible direct and indirect effects of policies on this sector, emphasizing the need to consider the impact of input as well as output price distortions on producer incentives.

EVERY COUNTRY HAS AN INTEREST IN TRADE POLICY REFORM. THIS IS TRUE even for the most open of economies because, although that government may not be distorting incentives, government policies of many other countries are distorting the prices received by the open economy's exporters in international markets. Moreover, it is *relative* prices that matter: the incentives facing producers or consumers of a particular product can be distorted not only by policies directly affecting the price of that product but also, and sometimes even more strongly, by policies affecting the prices of products that are substitutes or complements in production or consumption. Government intervention in currency markets also can have nontrivial distortionary effects on incentives. Farmers, for example, may receive the international price for their produce and yet be harmed by having to convert from foreign to domestic currency at an artificially low exchange rate.

This chapter explores not just the direct but also the various indirect ways in which trade and trade-related policies affect the welfare of people in developing countries. Its purpose is to identify the importance of

Direct Effects of Policies: A Single-Sector Perspective

Historically, the governments of poor agrarian economies have taxed farmers in one way or another (Krueger, Schiff, and Valdés 1988). Sometimes it has been an in-kind tax, such as a proportion of grain output. In other settings, where a cash crop was being exported, producers often have been required to sell to a statutory marketing authority that paid them only a fraction of the export price. Either way, farmers receive less than the free-market price for their produce. Except in the unlikely event that all of those taxes come back to farmers in the form of government goods and services they otherwise would have purchased with that taxed income, the incentive to produce and market farm products is reduced.

Governments of such agrarian economies typically return little of the proceeds of those taxes to farm families, especially at early stages of the country's development. Rather, the taxes tend to be used to develop urban infrastructure, pay officials relatively high wages, subsidize food consumption, and so on.

ers. In this sample of developing countries, the latter enjoyed direct nominal protection of 20 percent in that decade, so even the most favored farmers in those countries were being disadvantaged by the dominance of the adverse indirect effects of non-agricultural policies on agricultural incentives.

What would be the economywide implications of reducing import tariffs in the above case? Reducing the food import restrictions alone would probably boost production of exported farm goods, which would improve resource allocation *within* the farm sector. But it would also free mobile resources that could then move to nonfarm activities, which, on average, are more protected than farming. Hence, whether the overall efficiency of national resource use would rise or fall is an empirical question if only a subset of import restrictions and exchange rate distortions is to be removed. Only if the most protected industries were to be liberalized first would resources necessarily move to less protected industries and sectors and thereby guarantee an improvement in the efficiency of the use of these resources in producing tradables. Even then, there is the possibility that those mobile resources would move into the production of more nontradables if the currency remained overvalued. This is the reason for the value of comprehensive reform that simultaneously frees trade in goods, services, and currencies.

What about Markets for Factors of Production?

An economywide perspective on trade reform would be incomplete unless it also extended to restrictions on factor flows. Theorists in the 1950s pointed to the possibility that trade in goods could be a complete substitute for trade in productive factors in terms of both the volume of product trade and the welfare gains from trade (Mundell 1957). That theoretical possibility holds only under fairly restrictive conditions, however. More recently, attention has been drawn to the possibility that trade in some productive factors complements rather than substitutes for trade in products (Markusen 1983). That can happen when other productive factors are sector-specific and goods trade is thus insufficient to equalize factor prices across countries. In that case trade in internationally mobile factors can generate further welfare gains from trade. It can also happen when there are differences in technologies across countries; then each country should import the factor

used intensively in the industry in which it has a technological advantage.

For nationalistic and cultural reasons, permanent immigration of labor has not been made easy in recent decades, but numerous countries have tolerated temporary movements of labor, bringing mutual gains to the countries involved. Much more important in the past two decades, however, has been the growth in movement of capital across national borders. Foreign direct investment can bring with it not just financial capital but also managerial and marketing skills, technological knowledge, and intellectual property—forms of capital that foreign firms might not be willing to see exported if they were unable to retain control over them. Developing countries seeking to exploit fully their comparative advantages therefore need to relax their restrictions on foreign investment inflows. By the same logic they also need to allow foreign investment outflows so that domestic owners of capital also can earn the highest rewards possible.

The Dynamic Consequences of Trade Reform

Freeing up trade in goods, services, currencies, and capital not only improves the efficiency of national resource use and consumer welfare at a point in time but also contributes to economic growth. The mechanisms by which openness contributes to growth are gradually becoming better understood, thanks to the pioneering work of such theorists as Grossman and Helpman (1991) and Rivera-Batiz and Romer (1991). In a helpful survey of the subsequent literature, Taylor (1999) identifies several channels through which openness to trade can affect an economy's growth rate. They include the scale of the market when knowledge is embodied in the products traded, the effect of knowledge spillovers, and the degree to which redundant creation of knowledge is avoided through openness. More important from a policymaker's viewpoint, the available empirical evidence strongly supports the view that open economies grow faster (Edwards 1993; USITC 1997).

What if Trade Reform Harms the Environment?

Ideally, in adopting an economywide perspective, all significant influences of trade reform on human welfare should be considered. That could include a whole range of so-called noneconomic policy objectives, as well as standard economic effects such as those on the natural environment, poverty, unemployment, food security, and distribution of income and wealth across regions and households. Space is not available to discuss each of these here, but excellent treatments are available in such books as Corden (1997). The main conclusion to be drawn from that literature is that whatever the domestic policy objectives one has in mind, trade policy instruments are virtually never first-best ways of achieving those objectives.

This conclusion does not mean that trade reform can be undertaken without regard for society's other objectives. Welfare improvement via trade liberalization cannot be guaranteed if optimal domestic policies are not in place. There is no better illustration of this than with respect to the natural environment. Reducing restrictions on exports of logs, for example, in the absence of any other forest resource policies is likely to lead to excessive deforestation. Another example is the reduction in Mongolia's export tax on cashmere, which encouraged the excessive grazing of common pastures. In these and in many other such cases overexploitation was the result of property rights being poorly defined or poorly policed. Clearly, better resource and environmental policies are required before optimal social welfare can be achieved.

Note, however, that those resource and environmental policies are warranted, regardless of the degree of openness of the economy. All that trade reform requires in addition is that the levels of environmental policy intervention be adjusted when trade is liberalized to ensure that any additional environmental damage which accompanies opening up is matched in value terms with the marginal gains from trade expansion. Of course, trade reform need not cause additional environmental damage; at least equally possible is the prospect that the changes in production and consumption that accompany trade liberalization will actually reduce pollution or resource depletion (Anderson 1997).

Implications for Reform-Minded Producers and Trade Policymakers

A clear implication of this economywide perspective for producers seeking to influence government policy is that their focus should not be confined to measures directly affecting their own industries. As the Krueger, Schiff, and Valdés (1988) study shows, the indirect effect of nonagricultural and macroeconomic policies on farmers' welfare can be several times as large as the direct influence on incentives of agricultural polices affecting export-oriented farmers. This is also true within a sector, and even more so to the extent that productive factors are more readily substitutable within than between sectors.

In lobbying for trade reform, care is needed to ensure that trade liberalization is not accompanied or followed by "re-instrumentation" of support. There are numerous ways to support producers other than through trade policy, and many of them are even more inefficient than trade measures. It would be counterproductive to lobby for the removal of a trade restriction if it led to such an inferior replacement.

A major aspect of exporters' lobbying activities often involves encouraging the removal of impediments to market access abroad. Here again, an economywide perspective is needed (as is vigilance in preventing re-instrumentation). Consider, for example, the interests of developing countries with a strong comparative advantage in agriculture. They would be likely to benefit directly from reduction in agricultural protectionism in advanced industrial countries, but they could also benefit, albeit indirectly, from a reduction in manufacturing protection in those same countries. The most obvious example is a reduction in the very high barriers to imports of textiles, clothing, and footwear. Greater global production and trade in those products would result from reduced protection, with the output expansion concentrated in newly industrializing countries. A direct consequence would be an expanded demand for cotton, wool, and leather inputs—but that is only part of the impact on agrarian developing countries. Probably more important is that such reform would speed the industrialization of the more densely populated developing countries, which would attract resources away from their farm sectors. An indirect consequence, therefore, would be increased demand for food imports by those newly industrializing countries. This suggests there is scope for agrarian and newly industrializing developing countries to act collectively in pushing hard for greater market access for farm and textile products in advanced economies. In return, developing countries would be expected to provide more access to their markets for the goods and services exported by advanced

the devaluation, the exchange rate will reach a new equilibrium and that the equilibrium is strongly influenced by the policies of the central bank and the government.

The Problems of an Overvalued Exchange Rate

Countries that attempt to maintain overvalued exchange rates significantly impede their growth in the medium to long term. Theory, cross-country statistical studies, and case histories all reinforce the basic findings that exchange rate overvaluation can reduce economic efficiency, misallocate resources, increase capital flight, and, most perniciously, lead to exchange and trade controls.

The Theory

Theory suggests that there are many channels through which an overvalued exchange rate hurts the economy and growth:

- It discriminates against exports. Since a significant portion of the costs of production is paid in domestic currency, the overvalued exchange rate results in a reduction of exporters' incentives and ability to compete in foreign markets. This chokes foreign exchange receipts and damages a country's ability to purchase the imports needed for economic activity.
- Import-competing industries are faced with increased pressure from foreign companies, resulting in calls for protection against imports from industrial and agricultural lobbies. The political pressures for protection eventually prove to be overwhelming, and governments yield to lobbying and impose higher tariffs on imports. This closes the economy to international competition and reduces access to needed imported inputs and technology. As a result, growth falls. Devaluation serves the dual purpose of uniformly protecting import-competing industries and increasing incentives for exporters.
- Productivity advances are less rapid because the export sectors and the import-competing sectors, where productivity advances are often fastest, are disadvantaged by an overvalued exchange rate (Cottani, Cavallo, and Khan 1990).
- Overvaluation induces capital flight among domestic citizens anticipating a devaluation. As a

result, less foreign exchange is available for needed imports.
- Foreign exchange may be rationed and allocated inefficiently by the government.
- Efforts to defend an overvalued exchange rate through very tight monetary policy can plunge the country into severe recession.

The Need to Restore Internal Balance

When a country experiences a deficit in its trade balance, it is not in "external" balance. It follows from a national income accounting identity that a trade deficit means the country is spending more than its income. That is, the trade deficit allows the country to consume or spend beyond its income (or beyond the value of what it is producing). When a country's expenditure does not equal its income, it is not in "internal" balance. These external and internal imbalances can severely impede country economic performance, and it is these imbalances that countries suffering from external shocks often face.

Although a nominal devaluation is designed to correct the problem of external balance, it will also be important to ensure internal balance; otherwise, the trade deficit may not be corrected by the nominal devaluation. For many developing countries the trade deficit reflects the government's fiscal deficit, which is often financed by monetary expansion. The monetary expansion in turn leads to inflation. In this environment the impact on the real exchange rate of a nominal devaluation is likely to be eroded by inflation, since high inflation tends to appreciate the real exchange rate, making elimination of the trade deficit problematical.

In general, monetary or fiscal policies will have to be combined with exchange rate policies to achieve both internal and external balance simultaneously. This is a special case of a more general principle of economics: multiple policy targets typically require multiple policy instruments. In this chapter, however, we focus on the experience of countries that have limited the use of exchange rate adjustment as an economic policy instrument.

Problems with "Automatic" Adjustment Mechanisms

Unless the central bank takes offsetting action, a trade deficit will result in a decline in the domestic money supply. Thus, one response to an overvalued exchange rate is to hold the nominal exchange rate fixed and assume that domestic prices and wages will fall and so help bring tradable goods prices back to internationally competitive levels. This is the "specie flow mechanism" described by David Hume in the 18th century. The problem with this strategy is that in most modern economies, prices and wages tend to be sufficiently inflexible downward that sustained and substantial periods of unemployment must be endured if the strategy is to have a chance of succeeding. Most countries are unwilling to endure these high costs. (See Sachs and Larraín 1999 for a further discussion.) For example, as is described below, Chile endured a deep recession in 1982–83 before it devalued in 1984, and the francophone African countries in the CFA zone experienced disastrous consequences from overvaluation; in some, the economic contractions were comparable to the Great Depression in the United States.

The CFA zone experience also casts doubt on the claim that countries should avoid devaluation in order to retain international investors. The zone certainly had stable prices and exchange rates, but its failure to solve the problems brought on by the overvalued real exchange rate substantially decreased its attractiveness to foreign investors. Capital flight increased in anticipation of an eventual devaluation (Clément and others 1996).

Cross-Country Economic Performance

Cottani, Cavallo, and Khan (1990) investigated the effects of real exchange rate misalignment and variability on the economic performance of 24 developing countries between 1960 and 1983. They found that exchange rate misalignment was strongly related to low growth of per capita GDP. Misalignment was also related to low productivity (capital did not go to the companies or sectors that could make the best use of it), slow export growth, and slow agricultural growth.

A study of growth in 12 countries between 1965 and 1985 (Edwards 1989) reinforced these findings.[4] The greater the misalignment, the lower the growth during the period. Furthermore, exchange controls and trade impediments, proxied by the black-market exchange rate premium, were negatively related to growth.

There is strong evidence that overvaluation of real exchange rates was greatly implicated in Africa's poor economic performance. Among other studies with similar results, Ghura and Grennes (1993) analyzed the relationship between the real exchange rate and macroeconomic performance in 33 Sub-Saharan African countries between 1972 and 1987. They found that misalignment, or overvaluation, was associated with lower levels of growth of real GDP per capita, lower levels of exports and imports, lower levels of investment, and lower levels of savings, even when they corrected for other causes.

Case Studies of the Effects of Overvaluation

The economic histories of developing countries that followed a classic import-substituting industrialization strategy after World War II provide good illustrations of the negative effects of an overvalued exchange rate combined with trade controls. Latin America, more than any other region, followed this strategy, but it was not alone. We select illustrative episodes from Argentina, Chile, Uruguay, Turkey, and the CFA zone of Africa.

Argentina, Chile, and Uruguay

Argentina, Chile, and Uruguay all followed import-substituting industrialization policies that led to a bias against exports, extremely uneven rates of trade protection across sectors, and controlled financial systems. They also experienced recurrent balance of payments crises and slow growth (Corbo, de Melo, and Tybout 1986). By the early 1970s, all three had accelerating inflation, bottlenecks in production, slow export growth, and balance of payments difficulties (Corbo and de Melo 1987). In response, they went through two phases of stabilization and reform, one in the mid-1970s and the other during 1979–82. The second phase is most relevant for evaluating the effects of an overvalued exchange rate and import controls on economic performance.

In the second phase all three countries used a nominal exchange rate anchor to halt inflation. The exchange rate appreciated, and when it became apparent that the nominal rate could not be sustained, capital flight resulted. In Uruguay and Argentina, where there were no capital controls, major capital outflows occurred. In Chile, where there were capital controls, people engaged in capital flight by buying imported consumer durables. This capital flight occurred in all three countries well before the onset of the debt crisis in 1982.

number of countries became insolvent or illiquid as a result of private sector inability to repay debts, government and public enterprise arrears, and capital flight. Export earnings collapsed in response to the adverse terms of trade shocks and the overvaluation of the real exchange rate. The contractionary macroeconomic policies adopted by most CFA countries reduced import levels, and inflation remained low, but budgetary and external deficits rose. The fixed nominal rate and various policy-induced rigidities in domestic prices, particularly in wages and nontradable goods prices, meant that adjustment had to come through reduced employment, output, and growth.[6]

Constrained by their fixed exchange rates, at least two of the CFA zone countries tried to carry out "mock devaluations," with subsidies to exports and increases in import tariff rates. In Côte d'Ivoire the scheme collapsed after a short trial because of administrative difficulties, inability to give the export subsidy plan a sufficient budget, and lack of support by the government. In Senegal administration of the plan proved difficult, and the scheme encouraged overinvoicing by exporters and smuggling and underinvoicing by importers. The plan also proved costly to the budget, as tariffs were already high and the increases could not generate much more revenue.

Finally, on January 12, 1994, the countries held a "maxi-devaluation," changing the rate to the French franc from 50:1 to 100:1.[7] The CFA devaluation had excellent intermediate-term effects on growth. For the 12 CFA countries in Devarajan's sample, World Bank data showed that real GDP growth between 1990 and 1993 averaged almost minus 0.3 percent annually, weighted by GDP (World Bank 1999). From 1994 to 1997, however, growth in the sample countries averaged 5.1 percent annually, according to the same data source.[8] Cameroon, the largest country in the CFA zone, grew at an annual rate of minus 3.4 percent in the first period but by 4.5 percent in the second period (World Bank 1999). Devarajan (1997) found that a year after the devaluation, the average undervaluation for the group was 2 percent, but with significant variance.

Conclusion

Worldwide experience has shown that defending the exchange rate has no medium-run benefits. In a classic pattern, once reserves are drawn down,

countries often apply high or prohibitive trade protection on selected products or vis-à-vis selected countries. Even given a limited objective of reducing the demand for foreign exchange, an increase in imports will occur through informal channels, depending on how porous the borders are. With diverse protection, while some sectors will be protected, the burden of the costs of adjustment to the overvalued exchange rate will be borne by the unprotected sectors, by those sectors that are more susceptible to informal or illegal imports, and by the export sectors. Countries typically eventually devalue, but it is better that the devaluation be accomplished without debilitating losses in reserves and lost productivity due to import controls.

As the experience cited here shows, governments must avoid policies that contribute to an overvalued exchange rate. Although we do not advocate any particular type of exchange rate regime in this chapter, we emphasize that whatever regime is employed, policies should be aimed at maintaining a competitive real exchange rate.

Notes

The authors thank Arup Banerji, Julian Berengaut, Dominique Desruelle, Lawrence Hinkle, Fred King, Kiyoshi Kodera, Albert Martinez, Will Martin, Francis Ng, Paul Ross, Maurice Schiff, and seminar participants at the World Bank for helpful comments on earlier drafts of this paper.

1 As of the beginning of 1999, the IMF (1999: app. I) reported arrangements for 185 countries. The exchange rate regimes can be categorized as pegged (84 countries), floating (75 countries), and limited flexibility (26 countries). Of the 84 countries with pegged exchange rates, 37 have no separate legal tender, 8 use a currency board arrangement, 24 peg to another currency, and 15 peg to a composite of currencies. Of those using a floating rate, 27 maintain a managed float and 48 an independent float.

2 See *Global Currency Report* (1999). Of 160 countries listed, 38 had black market premiums of more than 10 percent at the end of 1998. Of the 38, 19 had premiums of more than 25 percent, 13 had premiums of more than 50 percent, and 10 (Afghanistan, Algeria, Angola, Iraq, the Democratic Republic of Korea, Liberia, Libya, Myanmar, São Tomé and Principe, and Somalia) had premiums of more than 100 percent. The black-market exchange rate is likely to be overly depreciated in relation to an equilibrium long-run real exchange rate, since an actual real depreciation would increase the supply of and reduce the demand for foreign exchange. See Ghei and Kamin (1999) for a detailed explanation and econometric evidence.

3 Ghei and Pritchett (1999) call this the "import compression syndrome." Since devaluations (which reduce imports) are often accompanied by reductions of trade barriers (which increase

imports), econometric evidence on the import-reducing impact of devaluation has been weak. Ghei and Pritchett argue that devaluations significantly reduce imports if there is proper adjustment for the simultaneous reduction of trade protection.

4 The 12 countries studied were Brazil, Colombia, El Salvador, Greece, India, Israel, Malaysia, the Philippines, South Africa, Sri Lanka, Thailand, and Yugoslavia.

5 The countries in the study were Benin, Burkina Faso, Cameroon, Central African Republic, Chad, Congo, Côte d'Ivoire, Gabon, Mali, Niger, Senegal, and Togo.

6 For example, both Senegal and Côte d'Ivoire had rigid labor laws that kept wages high throughout the predevaluation period (Foroutan,1997). Clément (1994) noted that throughout the CFA zone, rising wage costs contributed to substantial drops in public enterprise profitability, expanding the public sector financing requirement. Extensive controls over both producer prices and retail prices, particularly nontradable goods prices, added to the price rigidities in many countries.

7 The Western and Central African monetary unions (comprising Benin, Burkina Faso, Cameroon, Central African Republic, Chad, Congo, Côte d'Ivoire, Equatorial Guinea, Gabon, Mali, Niger, Senegal, and Togo) changed their rates from 50 CFA francs: 1 French franc to 100 CFA francs: 1 French franc. At the same time, Comoros changed its rate from 50 Comoros francs: 1 French franc to 75 Comoros francs: 1 French franc.

8 The unweighted averages are 0.1 percent for 1990–93 and 4.7 percent for 1994–95.

LIAM EBRILL
JANET STOTSKY
REINT GROPP

4

FISCAL DIMENSIONS OF TRADE LIBERALIZATION

D ESPITE SUBSTANTIAL TRADE LIBERALIZA-
TION OVER THE PAST DECADE, MANY
developing countries continue to have restrictive
trade regimes characterized by high tariffs and pervasive nontariff barriers (NTBs). Given the now
well-established nexus between open trade regimes
and improved export and growth performance, further trade liberalization to promote sustainable
growth and integration into the global trade system
remains essential. Because trade liberalization has
implications for fiscal revenues, and because many
low-income countries continue to rely to a significant extent on trade taxes as a source of revenue,
attention must center on the fiscal dimension of
trade reform in designing a strategy for trade liberalization.

The Revenue Impact of Trade Liberalization

Trade liberalization has often been delayed by concerns that it will have a negative impact on fiscal
revenues and contribute to macroeconomic instability. In fact, the impact of trade liberalization on
revenues is generally ambiguous and depends on

the reforms undertaken and the
initial circumstances of the particular country.

Table 4.1 shows a taxonomy of
trade reform measures and their
expected effect on the government's fiscal position. As noted
above, the impact can be positive,
negative, or neutral, depending on
the nature of the restrictions and
the characteristics of the particular country. For the most part,
however, the reforms will generally enhance revenue collections or
will have an ambiguous effect. The sequencing of trade
liberalization in programs supported by the IMF and
the World Bank normally gives the highest priority to
the removal of nontariff barriers, which tend to be the
most distortionary, followed by measures to rational-
ize the tariff structure. Below, we take a brief look at
some of these measures and their implications for the
country's fiscal position.

Nontariff barriers encompass a whole range of
practices, including quotas, bans, export and import
licensing, and state trading monopolies. In addition
to the economic efficiency arguments, the initial focus
on removing NTBs has the advantage of also increasing fiscal revenues. Quotas and bans provide no revenue to the budget and offer ample opportunities for
rent-seeking behavior or for smuggling. Accordingly,
the conversion of quotas into equivalent tariffs (normally accompanied by a scheduled timetable for further reduction in tariff rates) or the removal of bans
will, other things being the same, have an immediate
positive effect on fiscal revenues as rents are transferred to the government in the form of trade tax revenues. For these reasons, removal of NTBs should be
addressed early in the reform process.

Table 4.1 Revenue Impact of Trade Liberalization

Trade reform	Expected revenue impact
Replace nontariff barriers with tariffs	Positive
Eliminate tariff exemptions	Positive
Eliminate trade-related subsidies	Positive
Reduce tariff dispersion	Ambiguous/positive
Eliminate state trading monopolies	Ambiguous/positive
Reduce high average tariffs	Ambiguous
Lower maximum tariff	Ambiguous
Reduce moderate or low average tariffs	Negative
Eliminate export taxes	Ambiguous/negative

Sources: IMF and World Bank staff estimates.

Eliminating tariff exemptions (excluding export duty drawback schemes) and trade-related subsidies should have a direct positive effect on the government's fiscal position. Moreover, not only does the existence of tariff exemptions, especially discretionary exemptions, provide an incentive for importers to seek additional exemptions, but their proliferation also increases the incentive for classifying taxable products as exempt, which has a negative impact on revenues. Thus, in addition to their direct positive fiscal effect, eliminating discretionary exemptions and other complexities can contribute to improved governance.

The fiscal impact of reducing tariffs depends on their initial levels and coverage and on the extent to which they are reduced. In principle, given an unchanged level of imports, lowering tariffs will reduce trade taxes. Since, however, the lower rates are also likely to increase the demand for imports, the net impact on revenues will depend on the price elasticity of import demand. The higher the elasticity is, the more likely it is that a reduction in tariffs will have a net positive impact on fiscal revenues.

In countries with prohibitively high tariffs, there is a strong incentive for tax evasion, either through misclassification or by smuggling and avoiding paying the tax altogether. Therefore, lowering such tariffs is likely to generate higher revenues because it reduces the cost of compliance and increases the volume of recorded trade subject to taxation as smuggling activities subside. More generally, a reduction in tariff dispersion will tend to bolster revenues by reducing incentives for tax evasion.

The reform of the trade regime in the direction of a more uniform tariff structure could increase fiscal revenues as a result of increased transparency and simplification of tax administration. A uniform structure, or one with few tariff bands, will minimize tax evasion and ease the task of customs administrators by reducing opportunities for misclassification and valuation mistakes.

If a country has already implemented substantial trade reforms, at some point further reductions in rates (other things being the same) will result in lower revenue collection, at least in the short run. Given the longer-term growth benefits of trade reform, however, the appropriate response would be to offset any potential revenue loss by using other, less distorting, broader-based taxes (for example, a value-added tax), applied equally to both domestically and foreign-produced goods. The distortion to the economy from taxing both imports and domestic substitutes at equivalent tax rates is generally less than that of taxing imports alone, and taxing both yields larger revenues.

For developing countries in which trade taxes are an important source of revenue, a further reduction in the average tariff could be perceived to have a negative effect on revenues and to inhibit the pace of further reforms. In these cases mobilizing alternative sources of revenue and diversifying tax sources away from trade taxes is critical but is likely to be a long-term process requiring an early start toward a broader-based tax. Since such a process takes time to prepare and implement, technical assistance from the IMF should be sought at an early stage of the liberalization process and should also be used to support the trade reform measures by improving customs administration. But even in countries that are highly dependent on trade taxes, there is no reason to delay implementing trade reform measures that have a positive or neutral impact on revenues. In fact, heavy reliance on such taxes strengthens the case for proceeding more rapidly with the revenue-increasing elements of trade reform, especially the tariffication of NTBs and the curtailment of exemptions.

Significant progress has been made in reducing the role of export taxes, in part because their elimination is now generally accepted as a way of enhancing growth prospects and strengthening a country's external position. The effect on revenues from lowering export taxes will depend on how much and how rapidly the reduction expands total trade and reduces illegal activities such as smuggling. Since export taxes are often claimed to be substitutes for some form of income tax on hard-to-tax sectors such as agriculture, their reduction or elimination is likely to be accepted by the country authorities if it is implemented as one element of an overall tax reform package for broadening the tax base. Elimination of export taxes will also have a positive impact on the producers of the commodities that are affected. In the case of agricultural products, these producers may be among the poorer segments of society (Box 4.1).

Finally, in many programs supported by the IMF or the World Bank, substantial trade liberalization has been accompanied by a devaluation of the exchange rate in order to, among other things, provide incentives for exporters so that they can take advantage of the more liberal trade regime. In general, the effect of devaluation on trade taxes is ambiguous (Tanzi 1989) and will depend on the price elasticity of import demand; if import demand is inelastic, the devaluation will result in a higher value of imports in local currency terms and will increase revenues at any given level of tariffs.

Case Studies and Other Empirical Evidence

Several studies (for example, Ebrill, Stotsky, and Gropp 1999; Sharer and others 1998) have examined the actual impact on fiscal revenues following the implementation of trade reforms. These studies strengthen the observation noted above that the sequencing of trade reforms can be done in a way that minimizes its adverse effect on revenues. Some of the main conclusions from these studies follow.

- For countries that initially started with highly restrictive trade regimes, trade reforms were implemented with a view toward protecting budgetary revenues, and for the most part countries were able to achieve significant liberalization without compromising their fiscal objectives. Empirical evidence suggests that liberalization of quantitative restrictions tended to bolster revenues and that tariff reforms did not result in revenue losses.
- Fiscal considerations were the main factors cited as limiting the extent of targeted trade reforms. Greater trade liberalization could have been targeted and achieved if more attention had been given to supportive fiscal policies and to revenue-neutral trade measures.
- The effects of trade reform on revenues also depend significantly on the accompanying macroeconomic policies and, in particular, on an appropriate exchange rate policy.

Lessons for the Design of Trade Policy

The discussion in this chapter suggests that there is scope for so tailoring the pattern of trade liberalization as to avoid adverse consequences for revenues. Accordingly, adjustment programs supported by the IMF and the World Bank should, at the start of the reform process, focus on broad-based trade liberalization measures, with a front-loading of those elements that are likely to have a positive impact on revenues. The discussion also underscores the importance of sound macroeconomic policies and, in particular, the need for an appropriate exchange rate and for efforts to broaden the domestic tax base.

Nevertheless, the problems posed by trade liberalization in cases where it is perceived to have an initial negative effect on revenue (especially in countries that rely significantly on trade taxes) should not be minimized. Even if alternative revenue and expenditure measures are readily available, there are likely to be political and economic challenges. In addition, the consideration of fiscal alternatives will take place in the context of program design, which usually involves fiscal pressures in many areas of both revenue and expenditures, including outlays in support of structural reform other than trade policy.

Since sustained trade liberalization could eventually lead to a reduction in the share of trade tax revenues in total receipts, maintaining revenue performance will require compensating domestic tax reforms. Given the long gestation period of tax policy and administrative reforms, it is critical that the reform of domestic taxes be considered at the very outset of the trade reform exercise and that technical assistance be sought at an early stage of the liberalization process.

BOX 4.1 EXPORT TAXES

Developing countries often impose export taxes on primary commodity exports. Export taxation is one policy instrument that is not subject to WTO disciplines, reflecting WTO members' focus on import policies. This makes it particularly important to determine the economic effects of such policies. In some cases taxes are imposed in lieu of royalties for the extraction of minerals; in others they are used to provide protection to industries that process primary commodities. In the latter case they can have adverse impacts on the poor that need to be carefully monitored and analyzed. The export taxes mean that primary producers and farmers receive a price below that prevailing in world markets for their commodities. Elimination of the tax will raise their incomes but may bankrupt established processing facilities that are viable only if they pay lower-than-world prices for their inputs. Such plants may employ poor urban labor, giving rise to a policy conundrum. In such cases a careful analysis of the appropriate trade regime for poverty alleviation and the provision of safety nets is needed.

Sometimes export taxes are used in an attempt to exercise market power, and in such cases the policy can have a very adverse effect on the poor. An example is Madagascar's marketing board for vanilla.

In 1960 Madagascar, the world's lowest-cost producer of high-quality bourbon vanilla, accounted for 60 percent of world exports of natural vanilla. From its dominant position, Madagascar organized a bourbon vanilla cartel, with Comoros and Reunion, which set high export prices. Madagascar restricted supply by regulating its domestic market through a marketing board (CAVAGI) that fixed low producer prices and required licenses for growing, preparing, and exporting vanilla.

If this strategy were to be assessed by the effect it had on export prices of vanilla from Madagascar, it was a clear success. The export price of vanilla increased from US$10 per kilogram in the late 1960s to more than US$65 in the early 1990s. However, Madagascar's share of world markets declined to 30 percent as Indonesia, which was outside the cartel, took advantage of high world prices to develop its export capacity. The entry of Indonesia into world markets left the total value of Madagascar's exports constant throughout the 1970s and 1980s. CAVA-

GI's interventions in the domestic market had a similar depressing effect on producer prices, which fluctuated around US$5 per kilogram during the 1980s.

Who benefited from the bourbon vanilla cartel and CAVAGI's domestic policies? Indonesian producers were clearly the winners. The losers were Madagascar's producers—mainly smallholders, numbering about 60,000, with an average production of 130 kilograms and an average income of US$650 per plantation.

A recent study provides estimates of the producer prices that would have prevailed in Madagascar had the marketing board been abolished. These are close to US$26, well above the US$5 price fixed by CAVAGI. Taking into account the increase in production that such a change in prices would have generated, laissez-faire policies would have increased the vanilla producer surplus eightfold. Perhaps surprisingly, given the market power that Madagascar had in international markets, free trade (no intervention) would have also increased Madagascar's welfare, by 0.5 percent of GDP—the outcome of a major gain equivalent to 2.2 percent of GDP for producers, partially offset by a 1.7 percent of GDP loss to the marketing board.

An alternative to free trade would have been for CAVAGI to eliminate its interventions in the domestic market but to continue to exploit its market power in international markets through an export tax. Estimates suggest that the optimal export tax would have been close to US$25 per kilogram instead of the US$61 implicit tax that CAVAGI was imposing on producers. This would still have resulted in a doubling of the vanilla producers' surplus and, when combined with the tax revenues, would have generated a welfare gain close to 1 percent of GDP.

A likely explanation as to why these alternative policies were not pursued is that the marketing board's revenue would have declined under both scenarios. This suggests that Madagascar's marketing board pricing policies had objectives other than welfare maximization and that the heavy implicit taxation of small producers generated an important income redistribution from the rural poor to the urban elite.

Source: Prepared by the volume editors, based on de Melo, Olarreaga, and Takacs (2000).

BOX 5.1 (CONTINUED)

Does the reform depend on or affect the ability of poor people to take risks? The very poor cannot bear risk easily. Because the consequences of even small negative shocks are so serious for the poor, they may be unwilling to take opportunities that increase their average income if the chance of losses also increases. This might leave them with only the negative elements of a reform package. Similarly, if a reform makes it more difficult for the poor to continue their traditional risk-coping strategies, it may increase their vulnerability to poverty even if it raises mean incomes.

If the reform is broad and systemic, will any growth it stimulates be particularly unequalizing? Economic growth is the key to sustained poverty reduction. Only if it is very unequalizing will it increase absolute poverty.

Will the reform imply major shocks for particular localities? Large shocks can create qualitatively different responses from smaller ones; for example, markets can seize up or disappear altogether.

Thus, if a reform implies very large shocks for particular localities, mitigation through phasing, or, better, through compensatory and complementary policies, could be called for. There is a trade-off, however, because, typically, larger shocks will reflect bigger shortfalls between current and potential performance and hence larger long-run gains from reform.

Will transitional unemployment be concentrated on the poor? The nonpoor typically have assets that carry them through periods of adjustment. The situation might be unfortunate for them, but it is not poverty strictly defined. The poor have few assets, so even relatively short periods of transition could induce a descent deep into poverty. If the transition impinges on the poor, there is a strong case for using some of the long-run benefits of reform to ease their adjustment strains.

Source: Winters (2000a).

real policy question: should we automatically condemn a trade reform because it means that one poor person loses or one person is pushed into poverty? I believe very strongly that we should not. Rather, the identification of hardship arising from a generally desirable policy reform should stimulate the search for complementary policies to minimize the adverse consequences and reduce the hurt that they cause. Rejecting any reform that adversely affects any poor person is a recipe for long-run stagnation and for an ultimate increase in poverty. Even the requirement that no household fall temporarily into poverty is likely to be extremely restrictive in poor countries. The more utilitarian view that the number of households (or persons) in poverty should not increase is more appropriate, although even then, consideration of the depth of poverty is required.

All judgments ultimately must be quantitative, not just qualitative. In practical circumstances, it is easier to identify losers from trade policy than potential gainers. Losers are identifiable, concrete, and personified (see Krueger 1990), whereas the gains are diffuse and appear merely prospective and

theoretical. For this and other reasons, losers will usually be better able to articulate their interests than gainers, and so the volume of opinion is not a sufficient indicator of the relative strengths of the pluses and minuses of a policy change. This is particularly true given that the poor are generally much less able to advertise and defend their interests than are wealthier groups.

In what follows, I explore three responses to the possibility that trade reform can create poverty: manipulating trade policy itself, compensating the losers or the poor, and pursuing complementary policies to try to ensure that as few people as possible are net losers.

Can Trade Policy Be Managed to Alleviate Poverty?

One natural response to the possibility that trade liberalization could exacerbate poverty in certain sections of a society is to "manage" liberalization in a way that eliminates or at least reduces the problems. At the conceptual level, this is just common sense: poverty alleviation is arguably our highest priority, whereas trade policy is just a means to an end. It makes sense to marshal all the tools we have toward achieving our principal goals, and indeed, it would be perverse to do anything different.

But on a practical level, the question is *how* to use trade policy to achieve poverty objectives. First, there is the possibility that we do actually have goals other than poverty alleviation—for example, as regards average incomes, security, foreign policy, or environmental sustainability—and these would need to be factored in. Second, even leaving aside additional objectives, we need to decide which measure of poverty we are aiming at: there are choices even among income- or consumption-based measures, let alone among the various concepts and dimensions that characterize modern views of poverty. Third, there may be questions about trading poverty in one region against that in another, and there will certainly be, fourth, tradeoffs between poverty today and poverty tomorrow. Fifth, what else figures in the policy packages among which we are deciding? Are other policy instruments frozen at current levels, so that the question is only one of how trade reform impinges directly on the real incomes of the poor? Or can we presume that other policies will be optimized, so that, say, boosting incomes in the top decile at the expense of higher prices for the poor is acceptable because it will permit a redistribution via the tax-benefit system that more than offsets the initial growth in the income gap? These questions illustrate that saying "manage trade policy" is not helpful until one specifies *how* to manage it.

Don't Do It

One response to the fear that a trade liberalization will cause poverty is, "don't do it." But even if the direct effect of a reform might be to worsen poverty overall, this is not generally a satisfactory response. Although it has proved difficult to isolate the effects of trade liberalization on economic growth empirically, the predominant view is that it has an important role. The well-publicized cross-country studies that supported this view in the 1990s (for example, Dollar 1992; Sachs and Warner 1995; Edwards 1998) have recently received rough treatment from Rodriguez and Rodrik (2001). The latter argue, with some justification, that these studies' measures of openness are flawed—in particular, because they either are endogenous (at least as much due to

growth as a cause of growth) or include much more than just trade policy—and that their econometrics are weak. But Rodriguez and Rodrik do not argue that trade liberalization is harmful to growth, nor do they deal with other evidence for a beneficial relationship, such as the manifest failure of closed economies and the findings of a number of case studies (see, for example, Srinivasan and Bhagwati 1999). Thus while Rodriguez and Rodrik should certainly inspire greater modesty in policy advice and renewed research efforts, they have not (yet) reversed the presumption that openness is likely to boost long-run growth.

The difficulty of establishing an empirical link between liberal trade and growth arises at least partly from two difficulties, both of which should inform our policy attitude. The first is the difficulty of measuring trade stances once one comes inside the boundary of near autarchy: tariffs need to be aggregated, quantitative restrictions assessed and then aggregated, and the degrees of credibility, vulnerability to lobbying, and enforcement measured (see Winters 2000b). This suggests that while one should staunchly recommend openness, one needs to be cautious about declaring particular regimes open or not. Which was the more open in 1997, Brazil, or Chile? Both had average most-favored-nation (MFN) tariffs of around 11–12 percent, but in Chile there appeared to be little discretion and little sensitivity to industrial lobbying, whereas in Brazil political pressures could be observed almost every day.

The second difficulty is that, although liberal trade policies are likely to be beneficial under any circumstances (because they enlarge the set of opportunities), a quasi-permanent effect on growth almost certainly requires combination with other good policies as well. The latter point is made repeatedly by the IMF and the World Bank in their policy advice.[2] Krueger (1990) has argued that openness is likely to be correlated with better policy in a number of dimensions, and supporting evidence for this assertion might be detected in Ades and Di Tella (1997, 1999), on corruption, and in Romer (1993), on inflation. Thus, openness brings advantages not only on its own but also as part of a constellation of policies designed to ensure efficiency and competition in markets, and transparency and predictability in policymaking.

The second part of the openness-poverty link concerns the connection from growth to poverty.

Official retraining has mixed success under any circumstances, and, what is worse, it is difficult to separate those cases where trade is to blame from those where it is not. Unless one is willing to underwrite almost any adjustment, identification of cases is a major difficulty. Making a general commitment, however, is not attractive because of the potentially huge cost and because doing so shifts private risk to the public sector, with all the attendant moral hazard problems. It is not the role of the state, nor is it feasible, to absorb every negative shock that might afflict individuals. Yet it is difficult to make a moral case as to why trade shocks warrant adjustment assistance while other shocks do not.[4]

A further complication arises in giving compensation in a way that encourages rather than discourages adjustment. European agricultural policy is essentially designed to protect farmers from the consequences of declining comparative advantage, yet it has the effect of rewarding current, not former, farmers. Compensation may be decoupled from current output but not from farming as an activity.

In cases where liberalization leads to the loss of jobs, government can insist on, and perhaps help finance, redundancy payments. These payments can help some people avoid poverty, if they use their money productively, but they are not guaranteed to do so. (See Winters 2000a on the "new poor" in Zimbabwe.)[5] Moreover, redundancy payments typically reward past service, not current need, and so they are not particularly well targeted for poverty alleviation purposes.

General compensatory policies, including safety nets, are designed to alleviate poverty from any source directly. They replace the problem of identifying the shock with the task of identifying the poor. Ideally, countries should already have such programs in place. Indeed, a major part of the effect of these programs arises from their mere existence rather than their use: they facilitate adjustment by assuring the poor that there is a minimum (albeit a barely acceptable one) below which they will not be allowed to fall. Such schemes, if trade-adjusting countries do already have them, offer the advantages over tailor-made schemes of automaticity, immediacy, and a degree of "road-testing," and they also avoid the problems associated with targeted trade adjustment assistance. If they are sensibly constructed, they need not entail huge expenditure; there is little chance of moral hazard problems if the thresholds are set low enough; and, since relieving poverty is more or less universally recognized as a responsibility of the state, there is little argument about the legitimacy of such interventions.

Targeting is a major problem for safety nets, not only technically but also because the middle classes are often better able to access them than the poor. Sustainability is another difficulty; a major trade shock could put severe financial pressure on a scheme just at a time when it is most needed. Ravallion (1999) offers some useful thoughts on setting up safety nets. Workfare is a good start, provided that the wage is low enough, that there is little or no administrative discretion in its application, and that the tasks set are seen to be of communal interest. In fact, Ravallion suggests that local communities select the projects to be undertaken under workfare and that better-off communities should be asked to cofinance the projects. Workfare has to be supplemented, however, by schemes to provide food to people such as the elderly and infirm who cannot work and to children (through, for example, food-for-education schemes). These supplementary schemes may be tripped on and off according to need, but they should have a permanent infrastructure and sensitive and quick triggers. Expenditure on safety nets is almost by definition countercyclical, and so a firm commitment by government is required to ensure that the money does not dry up in times of greatest need.

Examples of useful safety nets can be found in Bangladesh. According to the Consumer Unity & Trust Society,

> It is generally recognized that programs such as Food for Education (FFE), Vulnerable Group Development (VGD), Test-Relief, and Food for Work positively induce alleviation of poverty. For example, during the unprecedented floods of 1998, about 4.5 million VGD cards were distributed in Bangladesh, which provided crucial help at a critical time. The FFE program has helped increase school attendance of poor children by 21%. (CUTS 1999: 110)

The safety nets in Zambia and Zimbabwe, by contrast, are currently regarded as too poorly run and underfunded to be able to offer serious assistance to losers from trade liberalization.

Safety nets are not the only answer to the threat of increasing poverty from trade liberalization, but they are an important part of the response. They can generally be targeted better than other policies, and they are not very distortionary of market forces. If countries do not have safety nets already, they should consider setting them up as part of the context for a trade liberalization that may create short-term poverty. The safety nets should not, however, be trade shock–specific.

Complementary Policies for Better-Functioning Markets

A critical issue concerning the poverty impacts of trade liberalization, especially for surprises connected with it, is the functioning of markets. Trade liberalization must be accompanied by monitoring to determine whether any markets are failing. Policies designed to ensure that markets continue to function or to develop, where required, will have high payoffs for both aggregate income and poverty alleviation. Some important circumstances are discussed next.

Infrastructure Support

Potential opportunities for poor producers to benefit from a more open trading regime have been lost because critical infrastructure was either absent or had deteriorated. In both Zimbabwe and Zambia remote farmers found their opportunities constrained by inability to reach major market centers. In the same way, many of the benefits from relaxed retailing regulations and from availability of new or cheaper goods have been confined to urban and periurban areas.

Market Institutions

The poor frequently seem unable to attain the economic mass required for the establishment of markets that, once in place, may be viable. Policy should aim at the creation of the market as an institution, not at the ongoing subsidization of market activity. One aspect of facilitating the participation of the poor in markets may be to find means to allow them to combine very small consignments of inputs or outputs into reasonably sized bundles and so reduce transactions cost sufficiently to make dealing with poor producers worthwhile. Horticulture in Zimbabwe offers an illustration of a successful policy of this kind (Winters 2000a). Although horticulture is

relatively underdeveloped in most of the smallholder areas, increasing numbers of resettled and communal households are now becoming involved as producers of the main crops. This has primarily been the result of "outgrower" schemes and of sourcing or subcontracting by large-scale commercial farms. The Horticultural Promotion Council (HPC) estimates that around 3,000 small-scale farmers are now growing for export on a contract basis, accounting for approximately 10 percent of Zimbabwe's exports.[6] In January 1999 the HPC established the Small-Scale Linkage Programme, designed to provide communal and resettled farmers with the knowledge and skills to produce high-value, off-season export crops.

Credit Markets

Development economics affords many examples of how missing credit markets have prevented development, and the same phenomenon is visible in responses to trade liberalization. Thus, for example, achieving minimum consignment size might entail hiring draft power or seasonal labor, but this is not possible without credit. Similarly, establishing informal businesses in areas such as trading may require more capital than the poor can raise. These cases in which the poor are not able to respond to incentives as strongly as the less poor replicate the results of López, Nash, and Stanton (1995) in their panel study of Mexican agriculture.

Labor Mobility

The secret of spreading the benefits of increasing labor demand widely is labor mobility. If markets are segmented for cultural or geographic reasons, breaking down these barriers through information and facilitating physical mobility will have an equalizing effect.

Establishing Businesses

If the regulations for establishing new businesses are cumbersome, if the businesses' ability to obtain inputs (especially utilities) is weak, or if regulations on expansion and on labor recruitment and separation are restrictive, this could curtail the willingness of entrepreneurs to start or expand operations. A success story of business deregulation is the growth of maize hammer milling in Zimbabwe. Following

THE WORLD TRADE ORGANIZATION

T he WTO was created in 1995 as one of the outcomes of the Uruguay Round of multilateral trade talks. The Uruguay Round, which concluded in 1994 after eight years of complex and sometimes contentious negotiations, was a landmark in the history of the trading system. Agriculture and textiles and clothing became subject to stronger multilateral disciplines, and the trading system was extended to include intellectual property and trade in services. The WTO establishes the rules of the trade policy game for its members, which increasingly include developing countries. (Membership at the time of writing stood at 144, but more than 50 developing countries have yet to join the WTO.) A good understanding of how the WTO works and what it does is a necessary condition for maximizing the benefits of membership.

The chapters in this part discuss some of the major features of the WTO that are relevant to developing countries. A brief summary of the basic rules and the institutional mechanisms of the WTO (Chapter 6, by Bernard Hoekman) is followed by

discussions of the "engine" of the WTO—the principle of reciprocity (Chapter 7, by J. Michael Finger and L. Alan Winters); the accession process (Chapter 8, by Constantine Michalopoulos); and the dispute settlement mechanism (Chapters 9, by Valentina Delich, and 10, by Robert E. Hudec). The last is the aspect of the WTO that attracts most attention. The WTO is unique among international organizations in that it has a well-functioning, binding dispute settlement mechanism. This is of great importance to developing countries, which generally will not be able to induce compliance with negotiated rules in bilateral disputes with large industrial economies. In practice, because countries value the trading system, the large and powerful tend to abide by the rulings of dispute settlement panels, providing an incentive for developing countries to ensure that they are able to use the system.

The ability to use the WTO system is a function of many factors. Among the necessary conditions are that countries participate in the negotiations on the rules of the game and that they use the WTO in a

governments. These codes emerge from the exchange of trade policy commitments in periodic negotiations. The WTO can be seen as a market in the sense that countries come together to exchange market access commitments on a reciprocal basis. It is, in fact, a barter market. In contrast to the markets one finds in city squares, countries do not have access to a medium of exchange: they do not have money with which to buy, and against which to sell, trade policies. Instead they have to exchange apples for oranges: for example, tariff reductions on iron for foreign market access commitments regarding cloth. This makes the trade policy market less efficient than one in which money can be used, and it is one of the reasons that WTO negotiations can be a tortuous process. One result of the market exchange is the development of codes of conduct. The WTO contains a set of specific legal obligations regulating trade policies of member states, and these are embodied in the GATT, the GATS, and the TRIPS agreement.

Basic Principles

The WTO establishes a framework for trade policies; it does not define or specify outcomes. That is, it is concerned with setting the rules of the trade policy game, not with the results of the game. Five principles are of particular importance in understanding both the pre-1994 GATT and the WTO: nondiscrimination, reciprocity, enforceable commitments, transparency, and safety valves.

Nondiscrimination

Nondiscrimination has two major components: the most-favored-nation (MFN) rule, and the national treatment principle. Both are embedded in the main WTO rules on goods, services, and intellectual property, but their precise scope and nature differ across these three areas. This is especially true of the national treatment principle, which is a specific, not a general commitment when it comes to services.

The MFN rule requires that a product made in one member country be treated no less favorably than a "like" (very similar) good that originates in any other country. Thus, if the best treatment granted a trading partner supplying a specific product is a 5 percent tariff, this rate must be applied immediately and unconditionally to imports of this good originating in all WTO members. In view of the small number of contracting parties to the GATT (only 23 countries), the benchmark for MFN is the best treatment offered to any country, including countries that are not members of the GATT.

National treatment requires that foreign goods, once they have satisfied whatever border measures are applied, be treated no less favorably, in terms of internal (indirect) taxation than like or directly competitive domestically produced goods (Art. III, GATT). That is, goods of foreign origin circulating in the country must be subject to taxes, charges, and regulations that are "no less favorable" than those that apply to similar goods of domestic origin.

The MFN rule applies unconditionally. Although exceptions are made for the formation of free trade areas or customs unions and for preferential treatment of developing countries, MFN is a basic pillar of the WTO. One reason for this is economic: if policy does not discriminate between foreign suppliers, importers and consumers will have an incentive to use the lowest-cost foreign supplier. MFN also provides smaller countries with a guarantee that larger countries will not exploit their market power by raising tariffs against them in periods when times are bad and domestic industries are clamoring for protection or, alternatively, give specific countries preferential treatment for foreign policy reasons.

MFN helps enforce multilateral rules by raising the costs to a country of defecting from the trade regime to which it committed itself in an earlier multilateral trade negotiation. If the country desires to raise trade barriers, it must apply the changed regime to all WTO members. This increases the political cost of backsliding on trade policy because importers will object. Finally, MFN reduces negotiating costs: once a negotiation has been concluded with a country, the results extend to all. Other countries do not need to negotiate to obtain similar treatment; instead, negotiations can be limited to principal suppliers.

National treatment ensures that liberalization commitments are not offset through the imposition of domestic taxes and similar measures. The requirement that foreign products be treated no less favorably than competing domestically produced products gives foreign suppliers greater certainty regarding the regulatory environment in which they must operate. The national treatment principle has often been invoked in dispute settlement cases brought to the GATT. It is a very wide-ranging rule: the obligation applies whether or not a specific tariff commitment was made, and it covers taxes and other policies, which must be applied in a nondiscriminatory fashion to like domestic and foreign products. It is also irrelevant whether a policy hurts an exporter. What matters is the existence of discrimination, not its effects.

Reciprocity

Reciprocity is a fundamental element of the negotiating process. It reflects both a desire to limit the scope for free-riding that may arise because of the MFN rule and a desire to obtain "payment" for trade liberalization in the form of better access to foreign markets. As discussed by Finger and Winters in Chapter 7 of this volume, a rationale for reciprocity can be found in the political-economy literature. The costs of liberalization generally are concentrated in specific industries, which often will be well organized and opposed to reductions in protection. Benefits, although in the aggregate usually greater than costs, accrue to a much larger set of agents, who thus do not have a great individual incentive to organize themselves politically. In such a setting, being able to point to reciprocal, sector-specific export gains may help to sell the liberalization politically. Obtaining a reduction in foreign import barriers as a quid pro quo for a reduction in domestic trade restrictions gives specific export-oriented domestic interests that will gain from liberalization an incentive to support it in domestic political markets. A related point is that for a nation to negotiate, it is necessary that the gain from doing so be greater than the gain available from unilateral liberalization. Reciprocal concessions ensure that such gains will materialize.

Binding and Enforceable Commitments

Liberalization commitments and agreements to abide by certain rules of the game have little value if they cannot be enforced. The nondiscrimination principle, embodied in Articles I (on MFN) and III (on national treatment) of the GATT, is important in ensuring that market access commitments are implemented and maintained. Other GATT articles play a supporting role, including Article II (on schedules of concessions). The tariff commitments made by WTO members in a multilateral trade negotiation and on accession are enumerated in schedules (lists) of concessions. These schedules

establish "ceiling bindings": the member concerned cannot raise tariffs above bound levels without negotiating compensation with the principal suppliers of the products concerned. The MFN rule then ensures that such compensation—usually, reductions in other tariffs—extends to all WTO members, raising the cost of reneging.

Once tariff commitments are bound, it is important that there be no resort to other, nontariff, measures that have the effect of nullifying or impairing the value of the tariff concession. A number of GATT articles attempt to ensure that this does not occur. They include Article VII (customs valuation), Article XI, which prohibits quantitative restrictions on imports and exports, and the Agreement on Subsidies and Countervailing Measures, which outlaws export subsidies for manufactures and allows for the countervailing of production subsidies on imports that materially injure domestic competitors (see Chapter 17, by Pangestu, in this volume).

If a country perceives that actions taken by another government have the effect of nullifying or impairing negotiated market access commitments or the disciplines of the WTO, it may bring this situation to the attention of the government involved and ask that the policy be changed. If satisfaction is not obtained, the complaining country may invoke WTO dispute settlement procedures, which involve the establishment of panels of impartial experts charged with determining whether a contested measure violates the WTO. Because the WTO is an intergovernmental agreement, private parties do not have legal standing before the WTO's dispute settlement body; only governments have the right to bring cases. The existence of dispute settlement procedures precludes the use of unilateral retaliation. For small countries, in particular, recourse to a multilateral body is vital, as unilateral actions would be ineffective and thus would not be credible. More generally, small countries have a great stake in a rule-based international system, which reduces the likelihood of being confronted with bilateral pressure from large trading powers to change policies that are not to their liking.

Transparency

Enforcement of commitments requires access to information on the trade regimes that are maintained by members. The agreements administered by the WTO therefore incorporate mechanisms designed to facilitate communication between WTO members on issues. Numerous specialized committees, working parties, working groups, and councils meet regularly in Geneva. These interactions allow for the exchange of information and views and permit potential conflicts to be defused efficiently.

Transparency is a basic pillar of the WTO, and it is a legal obligation, embedded in Article X of the GATT and Article III of the GATS. WTO members are required to publish their trade regulations, to establish and maintain institutions allowing for the review of administrative decisions affecting trade, to respond to requests for information by other members, and to notify changes in trade policies to the WTO. These internal transparency requirements are supplemented by multilateral surveillance of trade policies by WTO members, facilitated by periodic country-specific reports (trade policy reviews) that are prepared by the secretariat and discussed by the WTO General Council. (The Trade Policy Review Mechanism is described in Box 6.1.) The external surveillance also fosters transparency, both for citizens of the countries concerned and for trading partners. It reduces the scope for countries to circumvent their obligations, thereby reducing uncertainty regarding the prevailing policy stance.

Transparency has a number of important benefits. It reduces the pressure on the dispute settlement system, as measures can be discussed in the appropriate WTO body. Frequently, such discussions can address perceptions by a member that a specific policy violates the WTO; many potential disputes are defused in informal meetings in Geneva. Transparency is also vital for ensuring "ownership" of the WTO as an institution—if citizens do not know what the organization does, its legitimacy will be eroded. The trade policy reviews are a unique source of information that can be used by civil society to assess the implications of the overall trade policies that are pursued by their governments. From an economic perspective, transparency can also help reduce uncertainty related to trade policy. Such uncertainty is associated with lower investment and growth rates and with a shift in resources toward nontradables (Francois 1997). Mechanisms to improve transparency can help lower perceptions of risk by reducing uncertainty. WTO membership itself, with the associated com-

mitments on trade policies that are subject to binding dispute settlement, can also have this effect.

Safety Valves

A final principle embodied in the WTO is that, in specific circumstances, governments should be able to restrict trade. There are three types of provisions in this connection: (a) articles allowing for the use of trade measures to attain noneconomic objectives; (b) articles aimed at ensuring "fair competition"; and (c) provisions permitting intervention in trade for economic reasons. Category (a) includes provisions allowing for policies to protect public health or national security and to protect industries that are seriously injured by competition from imports. The underlying idea in the latter case is that governments should have the right to step in when competition becomes so vigorous as to injure domestic competitors. Although it is not explicitly mentioned in the relevant WTO agreement, the underlying rationale for intervention is that such competition causes political and social problems associated with the need for the industry to adjust to changed circumstances. Measures in category (b) include the right to impose countervailing duties on imports that have been subsidized and antidumping duties on imports that have been dumped (sold at a price below that charged in the home market). Finally, under category (c) there are provisions allowing actions to be taken in case of serious balance of payments difficulties or if a government desires to support an infant industry.

From GATT to WTO

Over the more than four decades of its existence, the GATT system expanded to include many more countries. It evolved into a de facto world trade organization, but one that was increasingly fragmented as "side agreements" or codes were negotiated among subsets of countries. Its fairly complex and carefully crafted basic legal text was extended or modified by numerous supplementary provisions, special arrangements, interpretations, waivers, reports by dispute settlement panels, and council decisions. Some of the major milestones are summarized in Table 6.1.

The GATT's early years were dominated by accession negotiations and by a review session in the mid-1950s that led to modifications to the treaty. Starting in the mid-1960s, recurring rounds of mul-

BOX 6.1: TRANSPARENCY: NOTIFICATION AND SURVEILLANCE

Transparency at both the multilateral (WTO) level and the national level is essential to ensure ownership of commitments, reduce uncertainty, and enforce agreements. Efforts to increase the transparency of members' trade policies take up a good portion of WTO resources. The WTO requires that all trade laws and regulations be published. Article X of the GATT, Article III of the GATS, and Article 63 of the TRIPS agreement all require that relevant laws, regulations, judicial decisions, and administrative rulings be made public. More than 200 notification requirements are embodied in the various WTO agreements and mandated by ministerial and council decisions. The WTO also has important surveillance activities, since it has a mandate to periodically review the trade policy and foreign trade regimes of members. The WTO's Trade Policy Review Mechanism (TPRM), established during the Uruguay Round, builds on a 1979 Understanding on Notification, Consultation, Dispute Settlement, and Surveillance under which contracting parties agreed to conduct a regular and systematic review of developments in the trading system. The objective of the TPRM is to examine the impact of members' trade policies and practices on the trading system and to contribute to improved adherence to WTO rules through greater transparency. The legal compatibility of any particular measure with WTO disciplines is not examined, this being left for members to ascertain.

The TPRM was originally motivated in part by concerns stemming from the fact that the only available review of global trade policies at the time was produced by the United States (Keesing 1998). The TPRM is an important element of the WTO because it fosters transparency and enhances communication, thereby strengthening the multilateral trading system. Country-specific reviews are conducted on a rotational basis, and the frequency of review is a function of a member's share in world trade. The four largest players—the European Union, the United States, Japan, and Canada—are subject to review by the WTO General Council every two years. In principle, the next 16 largest traders are subject to reviews every four years, and the remaining members are reviewed every six years. A longer periodicity may be established for least-developed countries. The trade policy review (TPR) for a country is based on a report prepared by the government concerned and on a report by the WTO Trade Policies Review Division. TPRs are supplemented by an annual report by the Director-General of the WTO that provides an overview of developments in the international trading environment.

By subjecting the trade policies of the largest industrial country markets to regular public peer review, the TPRM shifts the balance of power in the WTO ever so slightly in favor of the developing countries (Francois 2001). Equally important, the TPRM provides domestic interest groups with the information necessary to determine the costs and benefits of national trade policies. The reports are not analytical in the sense of determining the economic effects of various national policies—the size of the implied transfers and the beneficiaries and losers under the prevailing policies. This task is left to national stakeholders (think tanks and policy institutes).

Sources: Hoekman and Kostecki (2001); Francois (2001).

tilateral trade negotiations gradually expanded the scope of the GATT to take in a larger number of nontariff policies. Until the Uruguay Round, however, no progress was made on agriculture or on textiles and clothing. The deal that finally allowed these sectors to be subjected to multilateral disciplines included the establishment of rules for trade in services and enforcement of intellectual property rights (IPRs), as well as the creation of the WTO.

There are many similarities between the GATT and the WTO, but the basic principles remain the same. The WTO continues to operate by consensus and to be member driven. There were, however, a number of major changes. Most obviously, the coverage of the WTO is much wider. A change of great importance is that in contrast to the GATT, the WTO agreement is a "single undertaking"—all its provisions apply to all members. Under the GATT there was great flexibility for countries to "opt out" of new disciplines, and in practice many developing countries did not sign specific agreements on issues such as customs valuation or subsidies. This is no longer the case, implying that the WTO is much more important for developing countries than the GATT was. Also important were changes in the area of dispute settlement, which became much more "automatic" with the adoption of a "negative consensus" rule. (All members must oppose the findings in a dispute settlement to block adoption of reports.) Finally, the secretariat acquired much greater transparency and surveillance functions through the creation of the Trade Policy Review Mechanism.

Scope, Functions, and Structure of the WTO

The WTO is headed by a ministerial conference of all members that meets at least once every two years. By contrast, under the GATT a decade could pass between ministerial meetings. The more frequent participation by trade ministers under the WTO was intended to strengthen the political guidance of the WTO and enhance the prominence and credibility of its rules in domestic political arenas. Article II of the Marrakech Agreement that established the WTO charges the organization with providing a common institutional framework for the conduct of trade relations among its members in matters to which agreements and associated legal obligations apply.

Four annexes to the WTO define the substantive rights and obligations of members. Annex 1 has three parts: Annex 1A, Multilateral Agreements on Trade in Goods, which contains the GATT 1994 (the GATT 1947 as amended by a large number of understandings and supplementary agreements negotiated in the Uruguay Round); Annex 1B, which contains the GATS; and Annex 1C, the TRIPS agreement. Annex 2 contains the Understanding on Rules and Procedures Governing the Settlement of Disputes (DSU)—the WTO's common dispute settlement mechanism. Annex 3 contains the Trade Policy Review Mechanism (TPRM), an instrument for surveillance of members' trade policies. Finally, Annex 4, Plurilateral Trade Agreements, consists of

Table 6.1 From GATT to WTO: Major Events

Date	Event
1947	The GATT is drawn up to record the results of tariff negotiations among 23 countries. The agreement enters into force on January 1, 1948.
1948	The GATT provisionally enters into force. Delegations from 56 countries meet in Havana, Cuba, to consider the final draft of the International Trade Organization (ITO) agreement; in March 1948, 53 countries sign the Havana Charter establishing an ITO.
1950	China withdraws from the GATT. The U.S. administration abandons efforts to seek congressional ratification of the ITO.
1955	A review session modifies numerous provisions of the GATT. The United States is granted a waiver from GATT disciplines for certain agricultural policies. Japan accedes to the GATT.
1965	Part IV (on trade and development) is added to the GATT, establishing new guidelines for trade policies of and toward developing countries. A Committee on Trade and Development is created to monitor implementation.
1974	The Agreement Regarding International Trade in Textiles, better known as the Multifibre Arrangement (MFA), enters into force. The MFA restricts export growth in clothing and textiles to 6 percent per year. It is renegotiated in 1977 and 1982 and extended in 1986, 1991, and 1992.
1986	The Uruguay Round is launched in Punta del Este, Uruguay.
1994	In Marrakech, on April 15, ministers sign the final act establishing the WTO and embodying the results of the Uruguay Round.
1995	The WTO enters into force on January 1.
1999	Ministerial meeting in Seattle fails to launch a new round.
2001	A new round of trade talks (the Doha Development Agenda) is agreed on in Doha, Qatar.

Source: Hoekman and Kostecki (2001).

Tokyo Round codes that were not multilateralized in the Uruguay Round and that therefore bind only their signatories. Together, Annexes 1 through 3 embody the multilateral trade agreements. Article II of the WTO specifies that all the agreements contained in these three annexes are an integral part of the WTO agreement and are binding on all members. All of these instruments are discussed further in this chapter or in other chapters of this volume.

The WTO is charged with facilitating the implementation and operation of the multilateral trade agreements, providing a forum for negotiations, administering the dispute settlement mechanism, exercising multilateral surveillance of trade policies, and cooperating with the World Bank and the IMF to achieve greater coherence in global economic policymaking (Art. III WTO). Between meetings of the ministerial conference, which is responsible for carrying out the functions of the WTO, the organization is managed by the General Council, at the level of diplomats. The General Council meets about 12 times a year. On average, about 70 percent of all WTO members take part in its meetings, at which members are usually represented by delegations based in Geneva. The General Council turns itself, as needed, into a body that adjudicates trade disputes (the Dispute Settlement Body, or DSB) or that reviews members' trade policies (the Trade Policy Review Body, or TPRB).

Three subsidiary councils, on goods, on services, and on intellectual property rights, operate under the general guidance of the General Council. Separate committees deal with the interests of developing countries (Committee on Trade and Development); surveillance of trade restriction actions taken for balance of payment purposes; surveillance of regional trade agreements; trade-environment linkages; and WTO finances and administration. Additional committees or working parties deal with matters covered by the GATT, the GATS, or the TRIPS agreement. There are committees, functioning under the auspices of the Council on Trade in Goods, on subsidies, antidumping and countervailing measures, technical barriers to trade (product standards), import licensing, customs valuation, market access, agriculture, sanitary and phytosanitary measures, trade-related investment measures, rules of origin, and safeguards. In addition, working groups have been established to deal with notifications, with state-trading enterprises, with the relationships between trade and invest-

ment and between trade and competition policy, and with the issue of transparency in government procurement. Specific committees address matters relating to the GATS or the TRIPS agreement. All WTO members may participate in all councils, committees, and other bodies, with the exceptions of the Appellate Body, dispute settlement panels, the Textiles Monitoring Body, and committees dealing with plurilateral agreements.

About 40 councils, committees, subcommittees, bodies, and standing groups or working parties functioned under WTO auspices in 2000, more than twice the number under the GATT. Such bodies are open to all WTO members, but generally only the more important trading nations (less than half of the membership) regularly send representatives to most meetings. The degree of participation reflects a mix of national interests and resource constraints. The least-developed countries, in particular, tend not to be represented at these meetings; often, they do not have delegations based in Geneva. All of these fora, plus working parties on accession (averaging close to 30 in the late 1990s), dispute settlement panels, meetings of regional groups, meetings of heads of delegations, and numerous ad hoc and informal groups add up to 1,200 events a year at or near WTO headquarters in Geneva. Most WTO business is conducted in English, but many official WTO meetings require French and Spanish interpretation.

The main actors in the day-to-day activities are officials affiliated with the delegations of members. The WTO—like the 1947 GATT—is therefore something of a network organization (Blackhurst 1998). The WTO secretariat is the hub of a very large and dispersed network comprising official representatives of members based in Geneva, civil servants based in capitals, and national business and nongovernmental groups that seek to have their governments push for their interests at the multilateral level. The operation of the WTO depends on the collective input of thousands of civil servants and government officials who deal with trade issues in each member country.

Initiatives to launch multilateral trade negotiations and to settle disputes—the two highest-profile activities of the WTO—are the sole responsibility of WTO members themselves, not the secretariat. The member-driven nature of the organization puts a considerable strain on the national delegations of members. Many countries have no more than one

J. MICHAEL FINGER
L. ALAN WINTERS

7

RECIPROCITY IN THE WTO

Reciprocity: Mutual or correspondent concession of advantages or privileges, as forming a basis for the commercial relations between two countries.

—The Oxford English Dictionary[1]

RECIPROCITY HAS BEEN A MOTIVATING PRINCIPLE OF THE GATT/WTO SYSTEM. Although the *economics* of import restrictions recognizes that the losses from a country's own restrictions exceed domestic gains, the *politics* has not found a way to enfranchise the domestic interests that bear these domestic losses—users and consumers of imports. When trade policy involves an exchange of domestic restrictions for foreign restrictions, this amplifies the voice of export interests. The success of the GATT/WTO system manifests the ingenuity of reciprocally agreed liberalization as a means of transferring political power over domestic import restrictions to export interests, and it also manifests the power of these interests.

In this chapter we explore the role of reciprocity in GATT/WTO negotiations and in the processes of making adjustments and settling disputes under or within an agreement. We look at the role of reciprocity in past agreements, and we present evidence suggesting that reciprocity is not the only force that shapes the outcome of a negotiation. We then turn to two issues that relate to reciprocity: "credit" in reciprocal negotiations for unilateral liberalization by developing countries, and an "apples versus oranges" problem that arises because the WTO spans both border trade restrictions (tariffs, quotas, and the like) and within-border regulatory structures such as standards and intellectual property. Failure to recognize the apples versus oranges problem, we argue, has led to a troublesome Uruguay Round outcome.

Reciprocity in GATT Rules

The thrust of the GATT/WTO system is that agreement defines reciprocity (or balance), not the other way around. An agreed outcome from a negotiating round, the system presumes, is an outcome that each member considers advantageous, by whatever standard the *member* chooses to apply. Beyond that, various provisions for adjustment, such as renegotiation and safeguard actions, attempt to *maintain* the balance that the agreement has established. The same holds for dispute settlement. In this section we look at how reciprocity enters into each of these parts of the system.

Negotiations

Reciprocity serves to motivate negotiations. Participants and commentors use reciprocity, or its functional equivalent, "balance," as a standard against which to evaluate an outcome. The rules, however, do not define that standard; determining the standard is part of the evaluation itself.[2]

The GATT, and the Marrakech Agreement that established the WTO, refer in their preambles to "entering into reciprocal and mutually advantageous arrangements directed to the substantial reduction of tariffs and other barriers to trade." GATT Article XXVIII bis, the article that provides for negotiations to be held, refers also to "negotiations on a reciprocal and mutually advantageous basis." Neither the GATT nor the WTO provides further specification of what is "reciprocal" or of what is "mutually advantageous." The logic of the GATT/WTO is that in the negotiations each member is sovereign to determine for itself whether a proposed agreement is to its advantage—to decide the criteria by which to identify the pluses and minuses, and to apply those criteria by whatever formula the member considers appropriate. The GATT's tradition of decision by consensus reinforces the idea that an agreement is an outcome that each member considers to be to its benefit. If any one member does not find the outcome advantageous, the proposed agreement does not go into effect.

GATT Elaboration on Reciprocity in Negotiations. An early (1955) GATT working party, in response to a proposal to establish rules for how concessions should be measured, concluded that "governments participating in negotiations should retain complete freedom to adopt any method they might feel most appropriate for estimating the value of duty reductions and bindings . . ." The working party went on to note that "there was nothing in the Agreement, . . . to prevent governments from adopting any formula they might choose, and therefore considered that there was no need for the Contracting parties to make any recommendation in this matter" (GATT 1994a: 912–13). Similarly, Arthur Dunkel, Director-General of the GATT from 1980 to 1992, observed, "Reciprocity cannot be determined exactly; it can only be agreed upon" (GATT Press Release 1312, March 5, 1982).

Since the GATT and the Marrakech Agreement are silent on how a member might measure the advantage it draws from the agreement, they say nothing about how much one country should gain from the negotiations relative to another. The word "balance" does not appear in the GATT/WTO text on negotiations. An agreement (the outcome of a negotiating round) defines balance, not the other way around. Although the GATT/WTO rules make no demands as to what reciprocity means in a negotiation, there remains the practical political-economy question of what it means in negotiating practice—what countries have interpreted as equivalent concessions, and what they have not. We take up this topic below.

Treatment of Developing Countries in Negotiations. Part IV of the GATT provides elaborate commitments to the developing countries. For example, Article XXXVI.8 states, "The developed contracting parties do not expect reciprocity for commitments made by them in trade negotiations to reduce or remove tariff and other barriers to the trade of less-developed contracting parties." The commitments of Part IV, however, are not legally binding. Exhortations such as the one quoted are qualified by other phrases: for example, "The developed countries shall to the fullest extent possible—that is, except where compelling reasons, including legal reasons, make it impossible . . ."(Art. XXXVII.1), and "The adoption of measures to give effect to these principles and objectives shall be a matter of conscious and purposeful effort on the part of the contracting parties both individually and jointly" (Art. XXXVI.9). The operational meaning of such phrases is to make clear that they are not legal commitments. The commitment is to a nonmeasurable "conscious and purposeful effort," not to a measurable result.

Although such statements do not express legal obligations, they do have behind them the weight of moral suasion; they are intended to *influence* behavior without going so far as to *regulate* it. This moral suasion has not delivered much. For example, the Trade-Related Aspects of Intellectual Property Rights (TRIPS) agreement, the customs valuation agreement, the Sanitary and Phytosanitary (SPS) agreement, and several other Uruguay Round agreements suggested that industrial country members furnish technical assistance to developing country members that request it. This provision, however, is not a binding commitment; the developing countries undertook to implement *bound* commitments in exchange for *unbound* commitments for assistance. Although developing countries pressed hard at the WTO for delivery on such promises, bilaterally or through an increased WTO technical budget, the high-income countries have done little. The stalemate has prompted Rubens Ricupero (2000) to suggest that in the future, negotiations on topics that will involve expensive implementation be accompanied by an "implementation audit" that

a formula approach did lead to broader reductions—U.S. cuts applied to 44 percent of imports. Exclusion of free riders took the form of negotiation over "exclusion lists" and, as the figures show, did limit spillover to free riders to only 9 percent of concession imports.

Fewer Concessions Given, Fewer Received

Table 7.2 provides another indication that to receive concessions, a country has to give concessions. The message is obvious: the lower the degree of participation in the negotiations, the lower the share of exports affected by the concessions of other participants.

Domestic Reciprocity

At the same time, there is more to the liberalization process than concessions given over the international table versus concessions received. The bargaining process ties access to foreign markets to the granting of access to the domestic market and thereby mobilizes export interests to favor import liberalization. But the domestic politics of setting gains for export industries against losses for import-competing industries is not frictionless. For a government motivated toward trade liberalization, the tough tradeoffs are not between it and foreign governments but between domestic winners and losers.

Overcoming such frictions has been, in practice, partly a matter of power—in the simple case in which negotiating authority must be specifically granted, using export industries to win more congressional votes than the opposition can rally. It has also been partly a matter of compensation. Adjustment assistance is the straightforward example,

although public works and other benefits have also been used.[6]

Another way in which governments attempt to minimize the problem of compensating losers is by taking advantage of the large volume of intraindustry trade that characterizes the modern trading system. To the extent that concessions given by an industry can be offset by concessions received on the products exported by the same industry, the government need not develop interindustry mechanisms for balancing losers against winners. Gilbert Winham (1986: 65) notes that from the Kennedy Round forward, there has evolved a tendency to look for such "self-balancing sectors." In regional agreements such balancing can be increased through the use of rules of origin. An example is the way in which the North American Free Trade Agreement (NAFTA) and other regional agreements in which the United States participates condition access to the U.S. market for textile products on the use of U.S.-made fibers or fabrics.

Noneconomic Objectives

War, according to Clausewitz, is the pursuit of diplomacy through other means. Often, so is trade policy. Freedom of international commerce was the third of U.S. President Woodrow Wilson's Fourteen Points. To Cordell Hull, secretary of state for President Franklin D. Roosevelt, the link was straightforward: "Unhampered trade dovetailed with peace; high tariffs, trade barriers and unfair economic competition with war" (Hull 1948: 81). After World War II, leadership in Europe and in the United States saw economic union in Europe and the construction of an open global trading system more as strategic objectives than as economic ones. A government that can mobilize noneconomic motives

Table 7.2 U.S. Imports Covered by Kennedy Round Tariff Concessions (Reductions plus Bindings) as a Share of Total U.S. Imports from the Country Group
(percent)

Country group	Share (percent)
Major participants	70
Other industrial country participants	49
Active developing country participants	33
Other developing countries	5

Note: Data are for 1994 imports.
Source: Finger (1979): 435.

into significant support for trade liberalization will be in a position to play a hegemonic role (as the United States did in early GATT rounds) and to make larger concessions than it receives in exchange.

Locking In

Developing countries that have unilaterally liberalized sometimes view binding such liberalization internationally as a defense against the risk of backsliding should political authority shift or popular support wane. Such an objective, like a noneconomic one, can motivate a government to accept what a calculation based strictly on considerations of mercantilist market access would view as a bad bargain.

Individual Sacrifice for the Common Good

Many of the participants in the initial ITO and GATT negotiations viewed their task as the construction of a system from which all countries would derive significant noneconomic benefits (perhaps economic gains as well, but the emphasis was usually on noneconomic considerations). This view of reciprocity differs from the mercantilist bargaining model in that the benefits a participant gets are not unequivocally identified with the particular market access concessions that the country receives; the link between contribution and benefit is amorphous, resulting from the collective nature of the system rather than from any particular element of it.

Robert E. Hudec, in his 1987 book *Developing Countries in the GATT Legal System*, builds on the common-good view to provide a convincing interpretation of how GATT members came to accept "special and differential treatment" as the appropriate attitude toward developing countries. In constructing any system from the contributions of its members, Hudec notes, it is difficult to ask the less well off to contribute proportionally with the better-off members.

The Uruguay Round Tariff Reductions Scorecard: What We Learn from It

Reciprocity—"get what you pay for," or, more aggressively, "pay for what you get!"—was clearly the motivating principle of the Uruguay Round negotiations. For example, developing countries would not negotiate in "new areas" such as services

and intellectual property rights unless high-income countries negotiated on agriculture and on textiles and clothing.

Equal Sacrifice, Softly Applied

When, however, the time came for totting up, the equal sacrifice concept was the one that delegations used.[7] Particularly in the last month of the negotiations (the mopping-up phase) the negotiators devoted significant attention to ensuring that each participating country had made an appropriate contribution to the tariff reduction exercise. Delegations widely but informally accepted that the targets were average reductions of one-third for industrial countries and one-fourth for developing countries.[8] The negotiating guidelines lacked precision; for example, was the one-third cut to be a weighted or an unweighted average? Over all products, or only over dutiable items?

Tied up with achievement of these targets was the question of how countries would receive "credit" for unilateral tariff reductions and for extensions of bindings that did not imply tariff cuts. The agricultural negotiations established formal negotiating guidelines, not only on the amounts by which import restrictions and other agricultural supports were to be reduced by each country but also for how agricultural nontariff barriers were to be converted to tariffs.

These percentages were negotiating *guidelines,* not bound commitments. Even in agriculture, where the negotiating guidelines were circulated as a GATT document (GATT 1993b), legal commitments were the rates notified on each country's schedule. The GATT/WTO members seem to have policed these guidelines rather softly. Interviews with more than a dozen delegations after the round found none that had attempted to calculate the depth of cut by each country, or even for major trading partners. Likewise, no delegation had tabulated concessions received—that is, the coverage of its exports by concessions scheduled by other countries. A number of developing country delegations pointed to the agriculture and the textiles and clothing agreements as evidence that they had paid attention to what they would receive, but in agriculture, too, although the guidelines were more precise, either the numbers were checked only casually or disregard of the guidelines was widely accepted. After-the-fact examination has turned up a lot of "dirty tariffication"—tariff rates considerably in excess of those that the guideline formulas generate (Hathaway and Ingco 1996).

The interviews revealed that as the negotiations were being completed, selling the agreement at home—that is, gaining approval—was an important consideration. The issue was not the overall balance of concessions; it was to make sure that powerful domestic constituencies were accommodated. The focus was on the effect on the big trees, not the forest.

Concessions Given versus Concessions Received: Great Differences among Countries

"Concessions given" is a familiar concept. Its complement, "concessions received," refers to the concessions made by trading partners that apply to a given country's exports.[9] In Table 7.3, columns (1) through (3) show the depth of tariff reductions, and columns (4) through (6) attempt to introduce the scope as well as the depth of tariff changes.

It is hard to find equal sacrifice in this subpart of the Uruguay Round outcome. If all the reductions were equal, column (2) would show identical numbers for each country, as would column (5). It is also hard to find mercantilist balance. If such balance had been achieved—that is, if each country received concessions roughly in line with the concessions it gave—all the numbers in column (6) would be zero, which is clearly not the case. The summary statistic in the last row reports that, on average, a country's imbalance (positive or negative) was over half as large as the value of the concessions the country received.[10]

Credit for Unilateral Liberalization

Many developing countries undertook unilateral liberalization in the 1980s and 1990s. Credit in the reciprocal negotiations for this liberalization was part of the informal guidelines for meeting the equal sacrifice criterion. From what delegations told us in interviews, informal practice was more or less to calculate tariff cuts from the rate prevailing in 1988 to the rate bound at the Uruguay Round. Developing countries were given credit for unilateral liberalization by allowing them to count from the rates applied earlier, at the beginning of the 1980s. In any case, no tabulation of country-by-country tariff cuts was made, either by the GATT secretariat or by individual countries, and no formal target was

ever established for what any country should "give" or could expect to "receive." It is hence impossible to measure the extent to which credit for unilateral liberalization was given.

On the question of how to take into account bindings that did not imply tariff cuts, such as ceiling bindings, not even an unofficial approach evolved. Toward the end of 1990 the Mexican delegation circulated a nonpaper arguing that credit should be given for expansion of the scope of bindings, but it did not offer a method for measuring the "tariff cut equivalent."[11] Later, the chair of the GATT Market Access Group provided guidelines for such measurement, including a matrix of suggested equivalents between depth of tariff cut and scope of expansion of bindings. The view of the negotiators with whom we spoke was that there never emerged even notional agreement on how to convert extension of bindings into a tariff cut equivalent.

Giving credit for unilateral liberalization by developing countries is part of the standard pro–developing country list of what a negotiation should do. But the fact that what is an "appropriate" outcome is defined by the agreement and not by an exogenous standard means that calls for credit for unilateral liberalization are an exercise in moral suasion, not an application of economic or accounting science. Finger, Reincke, and Castro (2002: table 2) found that the suasion did have an effect. Bindings of unilateral tariff cuts (but not unbound unilateral cuts) do seem to have been counted toward developing countries' fulfillment of their "obligation" to reduce tariffs by one-fourth.

In sum, calls for credit for unilateral liberalization—where that liberalization has then been bound under the GATT/WTO—have been effective. Calling for a "credit rule," however, reveals a misunderstanding of how the GATT/WTO works.

Apples versus Oranges

The "grand bargain," as Sylvia Ostry (2000) has labeled it, that was struck at the Uruguay Round was that the developing countries would take on significant commitments in "new areas" such as intellectual property and services, where industrial country enterprises saw opportunities for expanding international sales. The industrial countries, in exchange, would open up in areas of particular export interest to developing countries: agriculture, and textiles and clothing.

Table 7.3 Tariff Concessions Received and Given at the Uruguay Round

Economy	Percentage tariff reduction[a]			Mercantilist balance (percentage point dollars)[b]		
	Received (1)	Given (2)	(1) – (2) as percentage of (1) (3)	Concessions received (4)	Concessions given (5)	(4) – (5) as percentage of (4) (6)
High-income						
Australia	0.76	3.35	–341	21,032	88,162	–319
Austria	2.64	3.74	–42	74,602	108,820	46
Canada	0.22	0.89	–305	5,291	26,205	–395
European Union	1.94	2.19	–13	578,816	627,939	–8
Finland	3.47	2.52	27	63,924	44,021	31
Hong Kong (China)	2.36	0.00	100	60,258	0	100
Iceland	1.59	0.20	87	2,151	299	86
Japan	2.06	1.06	49	481,006	143,142	70
New Zealand	0.84	0.83	1	5,126	4,155	19
Norway	1.15	2.17	–89	24,250	44,263	–83
Singapore	1.96	0.85	57	50,294	32,741	35
Switzerland	2.15	0.89	59	100,659	46,829	53
United States	1.21	1.07	12	214,791	283,580	–32
Transition						
Czech and Slovak Union	2.06	1.05	49	9,773	7,312	25
Hungary	1.82	1.69	7	7,755	13,727	–77
Poland	1.36	1.26	7	8,609	7,112	17
Developing						
Argentina	0.98	0.00	100	6,331	0	100
Brazil	1.37	0.00	100	38,037	98	100
Chile	0.50	0.00	100	3,291	0	100
Colombia	1.25	0.02	98	6,323	81	99
India	1.22	6.16	–405	14,380	67,172	–367
Indonesia	0.87	0.25	71	16,222	3,355	79
Korea, Rep. of	1.87	5.99	–220	100,809	262,918	–161
Malaysia	1.46	1.97	–35	36,108	28,966	20
Mexico	0.16	0.00	100	960	3	100
Peru	0.57	0.03	95	1,586	58	96
Philippines	2.43	1.29	47	19,748	12,847	35
Sri Lanka	1.36	0.01	99	1,595	33	98
Thailand	1.33	5.93	–346	20,564	95,953	–367
Tunisia	1.42	0.02	99	2,506	72	97
Turkey	1.72	3.00	–74	12,557	32,661	–160
Uruguay	0.52	0.00	100	772	6	99
Venezuela, R. B. de	0.21	0.13	38	2,051	806	61
Summary statistics	Sum of absolute differences/ sum of received = 86 percent			Sum of absolute differences/ sum of received = 58 percent		

a. Weighted average of change measured as $dT/(1 + T_{avg}) * 100$, where T_{avg} is the average of the before- and after-change rates, calculated across all tariff lines, including those on which there was no reduction. Why this formula? Whereas cutting by half a tariff of 2 percent saves the importer only 1 cent, cutting by half a tariff of 50 percent saves the importer 25 cents. As a part of what the importer pays, the tariff reduction relates to the tariff charge plus the price received by the seller—to $P_s(1 + T)$ rather than simply to T. Finger, Ingco, and Reincke (1996) provide a more detailed explanation.

b. Tariff cut as measured in column (1) or (2) multiplied by the value (in millions of dollars) of the imports or exports to which the importing country applies MFN tariff rates. A percentage point dollar is a 1 percent tariff change on 1 dollar of exports or imports.

What the North gave in this exchange was traditional market access, reduction of import restrictions, and in agriculture, reduction of export subsidies and production subsidies. What the South gave in the new areas was different. WTO obligations on services, on intellectual property rights, and on standards basically have to do with the structure of the domestic economy. The industrial countries that wanted these areas to be covered by the WTO rationalized their inclusion by reference to their "trade-related" attributes (although the actual motivation was the trade interests of their enterprises). Whatever the fig leaf, regulation here is, figuratively speaking, nine-tenths concerned with the domestic economy and one-tenth about trade.

The two sides of the grand bargain have fundamentally different economics. In real economics, giving away an import restriction is not a cost; it is something that *enhances* the national economic interest. GATT bargaining is a response to the difficult *politics* of liberalization, not to the good sense of its economics. The economics of new area responsibilities are different in two respects (see also Chapter 48, by Finger and Schuler):

- Implementing such responsibilities will cost money—for example, for laboratories to develop and enforce standards.[12]
- The result can be a substantial net cost rather than a benefit. For many developing countries the economics of TRIPS is the same as the economics to oil importers of oil price increases. Just the patent changes required by TRIPS will cost some countries more than they gain from the whole of the market access liberalization package (see Finger 2001).

The problems that developing countries face in the new areas largely have to do with project design and cost-benefit analysis—with development economics, not market access. The World Bank and the GATT/WTO are different institutions that work in different ways. These differences are not arbitrary; they reflect what the international community knows about how to deal with trade issues versus how to deal with development issues (see Finger and Nogués 2001).

The Uruguay Round Scorecard

The outcome of the Uruguay Round was a good one for the North. Not only did the industrial countries gain from the concessions they received; the economics of the concessions they gave was also positive, through the opening up of their own agriculture and textiles sectors. And for the South? On the gain dimension—market access—developing countries did not achieve a mercantilist surplus (Table 7.4). Their tariff reductions covered as large a share of their imports as did those of the industrial countries, and their tariff cuts, measured by how these reductions will affect importers' costs, were deeper than those of the industrial countries. This is true even when we take into account the tariff equivalent of the Multifibre Arrangement (MFA) quotas that the industrial countries have committed themselves to remove.

For developing countries as well as industrial countries, concessions made in the grand bargain make for difficult domestic politics. For developing countries, these concessions will also mean real economic costs. The scorecard on the Uruguay Round grand bargain? The South's concessions in the new

Table 7.4 Uruguay Round Tariff Concessions, All Merchandise

	Industrial economies		Developing economies	
	Percentage of imports	Depth of cut[a]	Percentage of imports	Depth of cut[a]
Includes tariffication and bound reductions on agricultural products	30	1.0	29	2.3
Includes the above plus the tariff equivalent of elimination of the Multifibre Arrangement	30	1.6	29	2.3

a. Depth of cut, $dT/(1 + T)$, is a weighted average across all products, including those on which no reduction was made.
Source: Finger and Schuknecht (2001): table T-1, based on Finger, Ingco, and Reincke (1996).

areas are, as mercantilism, unrequited—and as real economics, they are costly.

Conclusions

Reciprocity in negotiations is a motivation and an objective, not a criterion. Within an agreement, reciprocity—better known in this context by its other name, balance—comes closer to having an operational meaning. Still, it is to a large extent something that can be agreed on but not measured. "Credit" is moral suasion—a useful rallying cry for driving a better deal for the South. It is, however, futile, and a basic misunderstanding of the GATT/WTO, to think that credit can be converted into the "shall" language of obligation.

Mistaking clean clothes for dirty was acceptable when that was what both sides brought to the table. Each took home what its politics saw as the other's dirty laundry. In economics, each was doubly better off; trading market access "concessions" was good economics for the giver as well as for the receiver. Bringing in the new areas changed things. What the developing countries are now asked to put on the table can have domestic economic costs as well as domestic political costs. Reciprocal bargaining over the political dimension may not be enough. Progress in these areas may require management of their economic dimensions, as well.

Notes

1 According to the *Oxford English Dictionary,* the first recorded use of "reciprocity" in this sense can be found in the Preliminary Articles for the Peace between the United States and Great Britain, in 1782.

2 Finger, Hall, and Nelson (1982) sort decision processes into "political" versus "technical" ones. At the technical end of the spectrum, the criteria are given, and the decision turns on whether or not the criteria are met. Examples are an antidumping determination or a jury's decision in a court trial. At the other end of the spectrum, a "political" decision involves debate over what the criteria are, as well as about whether the criteria are met. A legislative decision on tax reform might be an example. In this framework, reciprocity in a negotiation is a political concept. What it means operationally is not specified by the rules of the negotiation.

3 Finger (1998) discusses in more detail GATT/WTO safeguards and other pressure valve provisions.

4 There are time limits as well as notification and consultation requirements.

5 The WTO Dispute Settlement Understanding (Art. 3.7) establishes explicit priorities among different outcomes: "The aim of the dispute settlement mechanism is to obtain a positive solution to a dispute; A solution mutually acceptable to the parties to a dispute and consistent with the covered agreements is clearly to be preferred; Withdrawal of the measures concerned if they are found to be inconsistent with . . . the covered agreements; Compensation . . . only if the immediate withdrawal of the provision is impractical . . . a temporary measure pending the withdrawal of the measure . . . inconsistent with the covered agreements; and, the last resort . . . suspending . . . concessions or other obligations . . ."

6 Zeiler (1992) provides examples of the trades U.S. President John F. Kennedy made to win congressional approval of the authority to negotiate in what came to be called the Kennedy Round. Providing quota protection for the textile industry was one; another was an extensive waterways project for the state of Oklahoma.

7 Provided that each country's trade is balanced (that is, exports equal imports) and that there are uniform cuts with complete coverage (of goods and countries), "equal sacrifice" comes to the same arithmetic as "get what you pay for."

8 These guidelines were cited by many of the Geneva delegations that were interviewed by Finger and colleagues as part of the research published as Finger, Reincke, and Castro (2002). As to the origin of the figures, at the July 7–9, 1993, G-7 summit in Tokyo, the "Quad" (Canada, EU, Japan, and the United States) trade ministers announced a substantial market access agreement, as well as their goals for what they hoped to achieve overall: reductions to zero for selected products or harmonization at low levels; a 50 percent cut in tariffs 15 percent and above; and, for other tariffs, a negotiated reduction of at least one-third. The one-third reduction for industrial countries may thus have come from this agreement; we have not identified the origin of the one-fourth target for developing countries.

9 The formula $dT/(1 + T)$, not dT/T, was used to measure tariff change. Concessions given for a country are the familiar sum for the country of all its MFN tariff cuts across all tariff lines, weighted by imports. For concessions received, if D_{ij} is the reduction of the MFN tariff rate of country i on tariff line (that is, "product") j, and W_{ijk} is the share or weight (by value) of country k's total exports of product j to country i, then the "reduction received" (column 1 of Table 7.3) by country k is the sum, across countries and across products, of D_{ij} multiplied by W_{ijk}. To calculate percentage point dollars of concessions received, for W_{ijk} in that formula we substitute V_{ijk} the value of k's exports of product i to country j. The countries in the table are those for which data were available from the WTO Integrated Database. See Finger, Ingco, and Reincke (1996) for a description of the database and a more detailed explanation of the calculations.

10 For some of these countries, counting only the concessions made at the Uruguay Round leaves out the unilateral liberalization they implemented in the 1980s. If, however, we drop from the table all the Latin American countries plus Sri Lanka and Tunisia, the average (absolute) imbalance is still 36 percent.

11 In GATT/WTO usage, a nonpaper is a way of circulating an idea for discussion without proposing that the idea be adopted; it is a means of promoting preliminary discussion. The nonpaper was cosponsored by 19 other developing countries.

12 Although considerable amounts of money will flow in different directions as a result of a tariff reduction and the political fallout may be severe, implementing the reduction costs nothing. The signature of an executive or ratification by a legislature does it.

8

CONSTANTINE
MICHALOPOULOS

WTO ACCESSION

ACCESSION TO THE WTO IS A COMPLEX, DIFFICULT, AND LENGTHY PROCESS. In May 2001 it was a process being faced by 28 countries, 9 of them transition economies and about half of the remainder, least-developed countries (LDCs). This chapter analyzes the WTO accession process and identifies the main issues and challenges faced by acceding countries.

Benefits of Membership

There are three main benefits of WTO membership: (a) strengthening of domestic policies and institutions for the conduct of international trade in both goods and services, which is required before accession into the WTO can be accomplished; (b) improvements in the ease and security of market access to major export markets; and (c) access to a dispute settlement mechanism for trade issues.

Policies and Institutions

Although there are significant differences in the institutional and policy environment of the various countries applying to join the WTO, many developing countries and economies face very similar challenges in establishing the institutions needed to implement WTO commitments. Perhaps the most important of these challenges is the need to introduce laws and institutions for the operation of private enterprises and markets free from government controls—other than those explicitly provided under WTO regulations—regarding, for example, standards, sanitary and phytosanitary (SPS) provisions, intellectual property rights, and state-trading practices.

Equally important to a country's economy is the introduction of greater stability in commercial policy, which is a consequence of adherence to WTO rules and legally binding agreements. Stability is important both to domestic producers and to exporters from other countries wishing to access these economies' markets. Adherence to WTO provisions—for example, by binding tariffs and by specifying conditions for foreign direct investment (FDI) in the services agreement—would improve the efficiency and productivity of acceding countries.

WTO membership also offers the opportunity for new members to lock in existing, relatively liberal trade regimes. Although the trade regimes in acceding economies vary considerably, many have established regimes with relatively low tariffs and no significant formal nontariff barriers. For these countries, membership provides the opportunity to lock in these regimes by assuming legally binding obligations regarding tariff levels. This not only permits them to enjoy the benefits of liberal trade but also gives them a first line of defense against the domestic protectionist pressures that are present in all market economies.

Market Access

Two main dimensions of market access are of importance to acceding economies. The first is the extension of permanent and unconditional most-favored-nation (MFN) status, which comes with WTO membership. At present, economies that are not members of the WTO have been granted MFN treatment voluntarily by major trading partners, but there is nothing to guarantee that they will continue to be accorded such treatment. For example, in the United States extension of MFN to Russia and several other economies in transition is contingent on the economies' adherence to the provisions of the Jackson-Vanik amendment to the 1974 Trade Act regarding freedom of emigration.[1] The second point is the substantial evidence that the incidence of antidumping actions (both investigations and definitive measures) is much higher against non-WTO members than against members.

Dispute Settlement

Access to an impartial and binding dispute settlement mechanism, the decisions of which have a significant chance of being enforced, is an important potential benefit for the acceding economies, many of which are small and heavily dependent on international trade. The WTO's dispute settlement mechanism has proved successful in providing opportunities for members to obtain satisfaction regarding grievances stemming from practices of other members that cause trade injury. Although developing countries face some problems in accessing this mechanism, membership provides an opportunity that, with proper assistance, can be beneficial to new members, especially in their relationships with large trading partners.

The Accession Process

The process of accession to the WTO is demanding and lengthy. It can be divided into an introductory phase of formalities and three substantive phases. The three substantive phases are (a) the applicant's preparation of a memorandum on the foreign trade regime (hereafter referred to as the "memorandum"), which describes in detail the country's poli-

cies and institutions that have a bearing on the conduct of international trade; (b) the members' fact-finding phase; and (c) the negotiation phase. The last two phases, while conceptually separate, tend to overlap in practice. Throughout, the applicant is faced with meeting WTO requirements and provisions, as well as demands by existing members. With very few exceptions, negotiation is in one direction only: the applicant is asked to demonstrate how it intends to meet the existing WTO provisions—it cannot change them. Existing members can ask the applicant to reduce the level of protection in its markets, but the reverse does not usually occur.

The Formalities

After a country sends a letter to the Director-General of the WTO expressing its desire to accede to the organization, the request is considered by the WTO General Council, which consists of representatives of all members and which meets frequently during the course of the year. The General Council routinely decides to set up a working party, with appropriate terms of reference, to consider the accession application, and it nominates a chairman of the working party.[2] Membership in the working party is open to all members of the WTO. In the case of applications by large countries such as China or Russia, many countries participate; in the case of smaller countries, the working party is usually made up only of the "Quad" (Canada, the European Union, Japan, and the United States) plus a number of other members, including neighboring countries that are significant trading partners of the applicant. The formalities phase can be quite short—no more than a few months.

The Memorandum

The preparation of the memorandum on the foreign trade regime by the applicant explaining its policies and institutions can be a demanding task because of the range of issues that the memorandum has to address and the degree of detail required. The issues include much more than simply trade in goods and services, although describing the trade regime for services, which encompasses the financial sector, insurance, telecommunications, professional services, and the like, is a large task in itself. Relevant subjects also include various aspects of foreign exchange management and controls, investment and competition policy, protection of intellectual and other property rights, and enterprise privatization. The preparation of the memorandum is solely the responsibility of the applicant, and so is any delay in its preparation.

Even if the original memorandum is prepared quickly, if it is incomplete in its details or if the legislation and practices described are inconsistent with WTO provisions, the subsequent question-and-answer period can be protracted. At times, members have asked the WTO secretariat to review draft memoranda before their circulation to prevent incomplete documentation from being disseminated. The secretariat, however, assumes no responsibility regarding the contents of the memorandum.

Questions and Answers

Once the memorandum has been circulated to WTO members, the accession process enters the second stage, in which members ask questions and obtain clarifications on the applicant's policies and institutions. This typically takes several months. (In the case of Russia, it took more than a year.) The working party usually does not meet until the memorandum and the initial questions and answers have been distributed.

The purpose of the detailed review that takes place during this phase and that may involve several working party meetings is to make sure that the legislation and institutions of the applicant are in conformity with WTO provisions. The applicant is requested to submit for the consideration of the working party members relevant legislation on a variety of issues covered by the WTO. Delays during this phase are frequent; if a member feels that the answers submitted to a question or the actions taken to remedy an inconsistency are inadequate, it simply resubmits the question for the next round.

Although the issues raised in each accession working party vary somewhat depending on the country, some common themes emerge in the discussions of accession, especially, but not exclusively, in the case of countries in transition.

- Within the context of laws and the operations of government institutions, two broad issues typically receive special attention: the degree of privatization in the economy, and the extent to which government agencies involved in the regulation of economic activity do so on the basis of transparent rules and criteria, as opposed to administrative discretion. A key issue for enterprises that are expected to remain state owned is whether they operate under market conditions or enjoy special monopoly rights and privileges.

- Some issues relate to the jurisdiction and capacity of national agencies to implement policies on which commitments are being made. The fundamental concern is one of governance: do the agencies have the authority and capacity to implement the commitments that they are making in the context of WTO accession regarding the laws and regulations that affect the conduct of international trade? A related concern has to do with the role and jurisdiction of local authorities and whether they have the right and opportunity to nullify commitments made by the national authorities in the context of accession negotiations.

Negotiations

At some point during the question-and-answer phase—after most, but frequently not all, the points raised by working party members have been answered—the applicant is requested to submit its so-called initial schedule of offers in goods and services. This consists of (a) the detailed schedule of tariffs the applicant proposes to impose on goods and the level at which the tariffs are "bound," and (b) the commitments it makes (and the limitations it sets) on providing access to its market for services.[3] In addition, the applicant is requested to make commitments regarding the level of support it plans to provide to its agriculture in relation to a base reference period (usually three representative years before the application for accession), as well as other aspects of its support for agricultural trade, such as export subsidies.

Once these offers are tabled, the accession process enters its final phase, which involves specific bilateral negotiations between the applicant and each WTO member that wishes to hold such talks regarding the tariff level or the degree of openness of the services sector proposed by the prospective member. The actual timing of the original offers varies considerably, and sometimes they are tabled very early in the question-and-answer phase, as happened, for example, in the case of Georgia. Often, bilateral negotiations take place in parallel with formal meetings of the working party that

Countries thus have a strategic choice to make during the negotiations phase: how liberal their trade regime will be, consistent with overall WTO disciplines.

A strategy that some countries have pursued in their accession negotiations is to try to liberalize as little as is necessary to ensure accession. Since such applicants cannot negotiate significant improvements in their access to other markets, they try to maintain significant levels of protection to use as bargaining chips for obtaining improved access in future negotiating rounds. Some of the countries that are using this strategy, such as China and Russia, also feel that significant levels of protection are necessary during a transition period when inefficient state-owned enterprises are being restructured (see Gabunia 1998). These countries have typically presented initial offers that propose to bind tariffs at rates much higher than those currently applied.

Similar issues arise in services. Many transition and developing economies feel that their services sectors are underdeveloped and would like to limit the commitments they make to open these sectors to foreign competition. This is especially an issue in such areas as financial services and telecommunications, in which countries frequently face requests from WTO members to establish liberal policies regarding commercial presence. Such policies would permit foreign services suppliers to establish subsidiaries or joint ventures based on the principle of national treatment, which prohibits discrimination against foreign services providers and thus has a direct bearing on foreign direct investment.

There are significant dangers to a "minimum liberalization" accession strategy. Individual countries, especially small developing economies, have little leverage in market access negotiations, and so the potential benefits they may be able to obtain through such a strategy may be very small. At the same time, maintaining protection through relatively high tariffs and protected agriculture and services sectors imposes costs on the applicants' own economies: they forgo the benefits of a more liberal trade regime, which, in the first instance, accrue to the country itself. If countries bind tariffs at levels higher than those applied and assume few commitments regarding agriculture and services (both of which are possible under WTO rules), they are subject to another risk: they create an opening for domestic interests to exert political pressure for additional protection in the future, and they produce uncertainty about trade policy among the country's trading partners.

Several transition countries that have recently become WTO members, such as Albania, Estonia, Georgia, the Kyrgyz Republic, Latvia, and Mongolia, pursued a different strategy. In most respects their governments adopted a liberal trade strategy as part of the process of accession.[4] This entails (a) binding tariffs at the usually low currently prevailing levels or agreeing to reduce and bind tariffs at low levels as part of the accession negotiations; (b) agreeing to a liberal trade regime in agriculture and services; and (c) at an early date after accession, participating in such agreements as the government procurement code, which increases competition and transparency in the operation of their markets.

The fundamental benefits of such a strategy are economic: these countries reap the benefits of liberal trade and investment. But the strategy has a number of other advantages as well: it tends to facilitate negotiations for accession; it provides governments with political cover against domestic protectionist interests that may otherwise succeed in subverting an existing liberal trade regime; and the legally binding WTO commitments lock in reforms by making it more difficult for future governments to reverse the liberalization. Increased protection to "safeguard" against serious injury to domestic industry is permitted under WTO rules, but it is based on a detailed and transparent investigation to demonstrate injury, which is then notified to the WTO and subjected to the scrutiny of other members. This is far more difficult than for a powerful domestic industry to simply seek government support for raising tariffs beyond the applied level but below the higher bound level, which a government can do almost without any constraint. The point about the WTO is not that it prohibits protection but, rather, that it permits it only according to certain rules; obeying these rules makes protection more transparent as well as more difficult to initiate and expand.

The Chinese accession, concluded in 2001, has combined elements of both strategies and has raised a number of additional issues. First, China has used the process of WTO accession to stimulate and make irreversible substantial trade liberalization and more broadly based reforms. Second, China, in many ways an economy in transition, considers itself a developing country and has been seeking to obtain transition periods and other special and differential treatment that WTO agreements extend to developing countries. The latter includes nonreciprocity, preferential market access, and different commitments and time limits in the implementation of the provisions of various aspects of the agreements, ranging from agriculture to subsidies and trade-related intellectual property rights (TRIPS). China, because of its position as a large market, has also bargained on certain aspects of market access, such as on textiles and on issues related to its designation as a nonmarket economy.

Attitudes and Policies of WTO Members

The demands made on newly acceding countries are greater than WTO disciplines on existing members. Based on recent accession experience, the areas discussed below are ones in which members typically request that acceding countries make more far-reaching commitments than those made by many existing members at similar levels of development.

Tariffs. Acceding countries are requested to bind all tariffs, whereas many developing countries continue to have a large portion of their tariff schedule outside agriculture unbound. Ceiling bindings have been accepted, but there is pressure to bind close to applied rates.

Agriculture. In addition to binding the tariff schedule, commitments are expected on aggregate measures of support (AMS), export subsidies, and the like. Since many acceding countries did not provide substantial support to agriculture but, rather, penalized it, the requests they face for reductions in AMS may not be warranted, and in any case meaningful calculation of commitments in this area is subject to serious statistical difficulties.

Rules and Disciplines. Acceding countries are typically requested to meet all commitments at entry with regard to, for example, TRIPS, customs valuation, standards, and SPS regulations, without time limits such as those available to existing members at similar levels of development, and regardless of whether institutional weaknesses make it difficult for them to fulfill such commitments. Such weaknesses relate broadly to the operations of a market economy; it takes time to establish the institutional infrastructure that would enable the applicants to discharge their responsibilities properly under the WTO agreements. When such weaknesses are brought out in negotiations, members suggest that the applicant seek technical assistance, available from a variety of bilateral and multilateral donors, and that it present a detailed plan regarding the particular aspects of the relevant WTO provisions in which weaknesses exist and how and within what time period it proposes to remedy them.

UNCTAD, the World Bank, the European Union, Switzerland, and the United States, as well the WTO, have programs that provide technical assistance on various aspects of the accession process, especially in the preparation of the initial country memorandum. Anecdotal evidence about these programs suggests a somewhat uneven performance. Most countries report very helpful contributions by foreign consultants and advisers in the preparation of the memorandum. In some cases, however, it appears that advice provided by outside experts has actually slowed the accession process because the consultants suggested, and the country agreed to, a "bargaining" strategy of tariff binding at high levels and limited offers on services. In addition, there have been problems of coordination among the various donors, as well as between the bilateral aid agencies providing the assistance and their colleagues in the trade ministries who negotiate the accession.

Plurilateral Agreements. There is pressure for countries to begin examining the provisions of the plurilateral agreements (for example, on government procurement and civil aviation) at the time of accession and to commit to a timetable for completing negotiations soon after accession.

"Market Economy" Issues. Although there is no explicit requirement in the WTO agreements that a member have a market economy, a requirement that acceding countries have, fundamentally, such an economy is being pushed de facto by existing members as part of their leverage in the accession process.[5] The pressures have been felt by all acceding countries, including China, where explicit understandings were reached with regard to the existence of state trading in specific sectors. At the same time the Quad countries have been unwilling to modify their own antidumping procedures regarding the designation as "nonmarket economies" of transition countries that have become WTO members. Under this designation, different, less transparent, and potentially discriminatory practices can be applied in the determination of whether dumping has occurred and, in the case of EU safeguard actions, against imports from a number of these countries, including all the members of the Commonwealth of Independent States (CIS) and China (Michalopoulos and Winters 1997). For this reason, the nonmarket economies label has been a major cause of trade friction between many transition economies, on the one hand, and the United States and the European Union, on the other.

Legal justification for using such procedures can be found in GATT provisions that permit different treatment "in the case of imports from a country which has complete or substantially complete monopoly of its trade and where all domestic prices are fixed by the State" (Palmeter 1998: 116). These practices were perhaps fully justified when practically all trade was controlled by state trading enterprises or ministries and prices were fixed by the state. Countries in transition, however, have made great progress in introducing market forces in recent years. It would be difficult to argue that, say, China or Russia has at present "a substantially complete monopoly on trade" or that *all* domestic prices in these countries are fixed by the state. Thus, continuation of the traditional EU and United States antidumping practices no longer appears justified in the new setting (Michalopoulos and Winters 1997).[6] Because the GATT antidumping provisions accept national legislation and practices as decisive, the odd situation can arise in which countries become new WTO members but are still designated as nonmarket economies for antidumping purposes.

Lessons of Experience and Issues for the Future

The first important lesson of experience is that each accession case involves a different negotiation, with different dynamics. This makes it difficult to generalize. Nevertheless, the cases of a number of small countries that have recently concluded the accession process suggest that the smaller the country and the more liberal its regime, the faster the accession process. There are two reasons for this: smaller countries realize that the costs of protection are high for them, and the small size of their economies poses fewer market access issues for major WTO members.

It is politically difficult to adopt a liberal trade strategy at accession, especially when major trading partners, which are WTO members, take advantage of opportunities that are perfectly legal under the WTO to limit market access—for example, by maintaining high levels of protection in agriculture. Even recognizing the political difficulties involved, a strong argument can nonetheless be made that if developing countries and transition economies currently applying for WTO accession adopt a liberal trade strategy at entry, they will maximize the benefits and opportunities for integration in the international community that WTO membership offers and will accede more quickly, as well.

It is fair to ask whether countries should not maintain some flexibility in their initial offers, as they are bound to face demands to liberalize by existing members almost irrespective of the level of protection they initially propose. Although there is merit in this point, it probably should not be pushed too far. Experience in recent accession negotiations suggests that countries which make initial offers to bind their tariffs at levels significantly different from the applied level encounter serious difficulties in accession—even though the practice is widespread among existing developing country members, many of which have not bound large portions of their tariff schedule. When such an initial offer is put on the table (as has happened with several countries of the former Soviet Union, as well as other applicants for accession), working party members basically refuse to consider it or to enter negotiations on that basis. They simply ask the country to submit a revised offer with bound rates closer to the applied ones before serious negotiations take place.

China's accession is unique, for both political and economic reasons, and lessons from it have to be drawn with extreme care. Undoubtedly, China has used WTO accession to promote and lock in wide-ranging reforms. China differs from most recently acceding countries in that it has been able to negotiate a number of transition periods—for example, for eliminating quantitative restrictions, licensing, and state trading—as well as the maintenance of tariff quotas in agriculture. It probably has much more bargaining power than all the recently acceding countries taken together. It is a moot point whether the time limits and extensions obtained by China (which were much less than it requested) are compatible with its economic interests or whether a faster liberalization of its trade regime would have been more conducive to the country's longer-term development. To WTO members negotiating China's accession, it is almost irrelevant what Chinese protection does to China's economy; they are concerned about the impact of such protection on their exports to the Chinese market and its large potential.

At the same time, China has had to accept limitations on its market access that other developing countries have not. For example, it has agreed to be subject to product-specific selective safeguards; it accepted three more years of restrictions in the implementation of the Agreement on Textiles and Clothing (ATC), from which it had been completely excluded; and it agreed to be designated a nonmarket economy for 15 years. In this context, the more exceptions and the longer transitions a large country such as China seeks to obtain, the more WTO members will strive to maintain provisions that inhibit full access of the acceding country's products in their markets.

It can be argued that WTO members' insistence on a liberal commercial policy at entry is likely to serve the acceding countries' long-term development interests, as well as WTO members' commercial objectives. But insistence on adherence to all WTO commitments at entry and without transition periods in areas (such as customs valuation, TRIPS, standards, and SPS) where there are obvious institutional weaknesses in LDCs and transition economies raises serious problems. That is, acceding countries, motivated by their strong desire for membership, may agree to obligations that they cannot implement, leaving them open to subsequent complaints. Alternatively, providing generous transition periods at a time when the transition periods for other countries that are already members are expiring would create inequities between existing and new members. The solution to this problem may be the substantial extension of some of these transition periods both for existing low-income members of the WTO and for acceding LDCs and transition economies; after all, these transition periods were arbitrarily set in the first place.

Conclusion

For a variety of reasons, the process of WTO accession has been and is likely to continue to be lengthy,

complex, and challenging for all countries, especially the LDCs. The process is inherently time consuming, but there are a number of steps that acceding countries and WTO members could take which would facilitate and expedite accession.

Governments seeking accession need, first, to establish a central coordination point to provide direction and manage the multiplicity of legislative and regulatory changes in their foreign trade regime that are necessary for accession. Second, they need to adopt liberal trade policies, which will both contribute to their effective integration into the international economy and facilitate WTO entry. Third, governments need to focus on and identify those areas of the WTO agreements in which weaknesses in their institutional infrastructure require that they delay implementation of WTO provisions. They should actively solicit technical assistance, prepare a realistic plan for implementing remedial actions, and seek agreement to obtain suitable delays in the implementation of the agreements as part of the accession process (despite the apparent reluctance of members to agree to such extensions so far).

WTO members can also take steps to help expedite the accession process. It is in their interest that the organization achieve universal membership sooner rather than later, as current members would benefit if all countries adhered to the rules and provisions of the WTO. In this regard, members should attempt to ensure that accession is not delayed on account of high-income countries' own disagreements or disputes.

WTO members also need to consider the institutional weaknesses of acceding governments and to moderate their demands by agreeing to suitable, time-bound extensions in meeting WTO obligations. This should not mean lowering the requirements but, rather, allowing more time to meet them. If such extensions are not provided, either the negotiations become stalled or the acceding country ends up accepting obligations that it cannot implement. In particular there is merit to extending and standardizing transition periods for acceding countries in the areas of standards, TRIPS, and custom valuation, where countries invariably face serious constraints in meeting requirements at accession.

Industrial countries should continue to provide assistance to developing countries and countries in transition that are not members in order to strengthen their institutional capacities so that they are better able to meet the requirements for WTO accession. Such assistance needs to be better coordinated. The Integrated Program of Trade-Related Technical Assistance to the Least-Developed Countries has the potential to benefit a number of acceding countries. Consistent with preserving the WTO as a member-driven institution, industrial country members should also consider substantially increasing the resources available to the WTO secretariat for assisting acceding governments in the preparation of the original memorandum and in the design of legislation and regulations that would enable the applicants to meet WTO obligations. Channeling more resources through the WTO would permit the secretariat to play a more active role in coordinating assistance efforts in support of accession and would give greater assurance that the outside experts who assist governments with the preparation of the needed documentation and the modification of legislation and regulations do so in ways that more effectively meet WTO requirements. A reasonable objective would be to cut the processing time of accessions to no more than two years, a time frame that is feasible if the above steps are taken. If that schedule were attained by all acceding countries, the WTO would be able to achieve universal membership in the next five years—a worthwhile objective for the international community.

Notes

1 Belarus is subject to annual waivers (as was China, until recently); the other countries have been found to be in full compliance and receive "permanent" conditional MFN treatment. When, however, Georgia, the Kyrgyz Republic, and Mongolia became WTO members, the United States exercised its right of nonapplication under WTO Article XIII; that is, it did not provide these countries with unconditional MFN status and thus, de facto, had not accepted their accession. Subsequently, legislation was enacted permitting the United States to notify the WTO that it has accepted these countries' membership. In the case of China, the United States had to address this important issue through amended legislation before membership negotiations were concluded.

2 Usually the chairman is an ambassador, a permanent representative to the WTO. Countries often request and obtain observer status at the WTO to familiarize themselves with the institution before they make a formal request for accession.

3 Services commitments are typically more general and openended than commitments in the sphere of goods. For a discussion, see Part IV of this volume.

4 The trade regimes in Croatia and Jordan, which also acceded recently, were somewhat less liberal.

5 GATT Article XVII calls for notification of enterprises engaging in state-trading practices. The article, however, was never intended to address problems that come up when the bulk of external trade is controlled by the state. Indeed the GATT accommodated several countries, such as Romania and Czechoslovakia, that at the time had centrally planned economies.

6 In 1997 the European Commission announced proposals for liberalization of EU policy on this issue vis-à-vis Russia and China, which would terminate their designation as nonmarket economies at the country level and would permit determinations to be made case by case, taking into account the market conditions prevailing in each commodity in which dumping had been alleged (Croft 1997). This is similar to U.S. practice.

9

VALENTINA DELICH

DEVELOPING COUNTRIES AND THE WTO DISPUTE SETTLEMENT SYSTEM

AB report. In these instances, only "negative" consensus can stop the process; that is, all members must agree not to proceed or not to adopt panel and AB recommendations or rulings. This reversal of the consensus rule led to a radical change in the dynamics of dispute settlement, making it more automatic and less dependent on the power of the countries involved in a dispute. Since there is an extensive literature comparing the GATT and WTO systems, we confine ourselves to briefly summarizing the salient features of the DSU before turning to developing country experience and concerns.[1]

The WTO Dispute Settlement System

The Dispute Settlement Body (DSB), which comprises all WTO members, has the authority to establish panels, adopt panel and AB reports, maintain surveillance of the implementation of rulings and recommendations, and authorize suspension of concessions and other obligations under WTO agreements (Art. 2 DSU). A member must first request bilateral consultations if it considers that a benefit accruing to it directly or indirectly under the WTO agreements is being nullified or impaired (Art. 4 DSU). If consultations fail to settle the dispute, the complaining party may request the establishment of a panel, which must be created unless the DSB decides by consensus not to do so (Art. 6 DSU).

A panel is generally composed of three panelists. Its deliberations are confidential, and the opinions

WITH THE CREATION OF THE WTO, DEVELOPING AND INDUSTRIAL COUNTRIES became subject to the same set of rules and to similar commitments. A new Dispute Settlement Understanding (DSU) was negotiated to enforce multilateral disciplines. The DSU is widely regarded as one of the positive outcomes of the Uruguay Round, marking a move toward a more "automatic" and rule-oriented system (Jackson 1997). This chapter evaluates the functioning of the DSU from a developing country perspective.

Although the cornerstone of the WTO dispute settlement mechanism remains Articles XXII and XXIII of the GATT, the DSU brought about a substantial change in the workings of the system. A major improvement was to remove the consensus requirement at key stages of the process. The DSU states that "where the rules and procedures of this Understanding provide for the Dispute Settlement Body to take a decision, it shall do so by consensus," but this general rule does not apply to the establishment of a panel of experts, the adoption of its report, or, if the report was subject to an appeal before the Appellate Body (AB), the adoption of the

BOX 9.1 (CONTINUED)

India asserted that the EC had not acted consistently with Article 15 of the Agreement on Antidumping, which recognizes that "special regard must be given by developed country members to the special situation of developing country members when considering the application of anti-dumping measures" and calls for exploring constructive remedies before applying anti-dumping duties in instances where they would affect the essential interest of developing country members. India asserted that the EC did not explore any such possibilities prior to the imposition of antidumping duties and did not react to detailed arguments from Indian exporters pertaining to Article 15: "[D]espite repeated and detailed arguments by the Indian parties stressing the importance of the bed linen and textile industries to India's economy, the EC failed to even mention India's status as a developing country, let alone consider or comment on possibilities of constructive remedies." India suggested that "such remedies may consist of, among others, the non-imposition of anti dumping duties or undertakings." India rejected the notion that any procedural mechanism, such as simplified questionnaires or extensions of time, satisfied the requirements of Article 15. The EC agreed in principle and accepted that undertakings could be a remedy, but it argued that Indian exporters did not offer undertakings within the time limits set by the EC regulation.

The United States, a third party in this dispute, argued that Article 15

provides procedural safeguards, and thus, does not require any particular substantive outcome, or any specific accommodations to be made on the basis of developing country status. In the United States' view, [Article 15] does not impose anything other than a procedural obligation to "explore" possibilities of constructive remedies. The word "explore" cannot fairly be read to imply an obligation to reach a particular substantive outcome; it merely requires consideration of these possibilities.

The panel's view was that

the imposition of a lesser duty or a price undertaking would constitute constructive remedies but we come to no conclusions as to what other actions might in addition be considered to constitute constructive remedies as none have been proposed to us. . . . In our view, Art. 15 imposes no obligation to actually provide or accept any constructive remedy that may be identified and/or offered. It does, however, impose an obligation to actively consider, with an open mind, the possibility of such a remedy prior to imposition of an anti-dumping measure that would affect the essential interests of a developing country.

Source: WTO, WT/DSB/M/7 (scallops); WTO, WT/DS/141 (India).

ings are too weak to imply any difference between the possibilities open to industrial and developing countries. Article 21.7, however, mandates that when a matter is raised by a developing country, the DSB is to consider what further action might be appropriate to the circumstances. To date, this provision has not been used by a developing country, perhaps because a precondition is that the country devote resources to analyzing and following cases. This involves checking arguments, issues, and possibilities and comparing experiences and results; exploring new legal as well economic arguments; and, domestically, building up an efficient and

transparent liaison between the state and industry in order to obtain up-to-date information on trade problems in which developing countries have a stake. Developing countries lack the high-level expertise and resources to devote to such activities. International financing for training public officials, screening industrial countries' trade policies, and building a network with other developing countries with the aim of jointly presenting cases could help address some of these problems.

The technical assistance called for in Article 27.2 is provided by only a few consultants and is inadequate, given the large number of cases. In addition, since the WTO secretariat must be impartial, its latitude for helping developing countries with legal strategic issues is limited. In this context, the Advisory Centre on WTO Law (described in Box 9.2) could play an important role in helping developing country governments present and pursue cases. Venezuela has noted the need to increase the number of legal assistants to the secretariat to help developing countries and has called for the creation of a trust fund to establish alliances with private law firms to augment developing countries' legal capac-

ity. These proposals are supported by many developing countries in particular, as there is a common concern regarding the costs associated with submitting, pursuing, and defending cases and the scarcity of human resources for dealing with increasingly complex issues.

Finally, provisions related to least-developed countries have not been invoked at all because no least-developed country has been involved in a dispute, as a complainant or as a respondent.

BOX 9.2 THE ADVISORY CENTRE ON WTO LAW

Claudia Orozco

On the side of the Third WTO Ministerial Conference, held in Seattle in 1999, ministers from 29 WTO member countries signed an agreement establishing the Advisory Centre on WTO Law (ACWL). The establishment of the ACWL is a concrete action toward addressing the needs of developing countries for advice and training on WTO law. The contractual nature of the WTO requires that members have a full understanding of the content and scope of their rights and obligations and that they are able to access the dispute settlement mechanism. Otherwise, the ever-growing complexity and breadth of the system, coupled with the relative scarcity of specialized human resources in developing countries and the costs of specialized external legal counsel, would marginalize many members.

To help address these needs, a legal aid facility was proposed, with two goals: (a) training government officials in WTO jurisprudence, and (b) providing specialized legal advice on WTO law, to include support throughout legal proceedings. The response was the establishment of the Advisory Centre as a small, independent international organization based in Geneva and open to all WTO members. By March 31, 2000, the final date for becoming a founding member, the treaty had been signed by 9 industrial and 22 developing countries. The 38 least-developed countries that are members of the WTO are priority beneficiaries of the ACWL's services. The agreement entered into force in July 2001, after the requisite number of countries completed the

ratification process, and the Advisory Centre became operational in October 2001.

The Advisory Centre provides legal advice on WTO law to developing countries and to economies in transition. This legal advice might take the form of advisory opinions on particular questions of law, analysis of situations involving trade concerns, or legal advice provided throughout a dispute settlement proceeding. In recognition of the differences among developing countries, the extent of the support to be provided will depend on the needs and requirements of each member in each case. Examples might include outlining the legal questions of a case, drafting submissions, and commenting on drafts prepared by government officials. In addition, the ACWL holds regular in-house seminars on jurisprudence for Geneva-based officials and regional yearly seminars for officials based in capitals. Finally, and most important, the ACWL offers on-the-job training for government officials in charge of a particular case and internships for government lawyers responsible for WTO issues.

Note: Claudia Orozco was minister counselor at the mission of Colombia to the WTO between August 1994 and July 2000. She served as legal counselor and was a panelist in several cases. On February 1998 she submitted the project proposal for the Advisory Centre on WTO Law to the Netherlands, the United Kingdom, and Norway and led consultations with an informal group of WTO members. The result was a proposal that was offered to all WTO members.

Developing Country Participation in the DSU

As of September 2000, 207 complaints had been notified to the WTO (Table 9.1). Of these, 16 were active, 40 had concluded with the adoption of either an AB or a panel report, 34 had been settled bilaterally or were inactive, and 12 were being implemented (WTO 2000).[4] Industrial countries brought the most cases, and their share of total complaints (74 percent) was greater than their share of world exports. Among the different categories of cases, those brought by industrial countries against developing countries appear to have increased the most between the GATT period and the WTO era, from 10 to 31 percent. Over 40 percent of industrial country cases were against developing countries—higher than the developing countries' 27 percent share of industrial countries' exports in 1998. The proportion of cases by developing countries against industrial countries was also higher than might have been expected (66 percent of all developing country complaints) and was higher than the share of industrial countries in developing country exports, 57 percent (Weston and Delich 2000).

Latin America and Asia are the developing country regions most involved in the dispute settlement process. To date, African countries have not initiated or been respondents in any case, although several, including Nigeria and Zimbabwe, have made presentations as third parties.

No single theme dominates the substance of the cases involving developing countries. "As respondents, developing countries have been involved in matters ranging from patent protection under the [Trade-Related Aspects of Intellectual Property Rights, or TRIPS] Agreement, to balance-of-payments restrictions, safeguard measures, and the taxation of alcoholic beverages" (Lacarte-Muro and Gappah 2000). The exception is intellectual property rights (IPRs), with many complaints alleging violation of the TRIPS agreement by both developing and industrial countries. As of 1999, the number of TRIPS cases had already reached 16, equivalent to 10 percent of all filings under the DSU. Eleven of these filings were brought by the United States (Geuze and Wager 1999). As regards developing countries, Correa (2001) notes that "although the adoption by another Member of unilateral trade sanctions would be incompatible with the multilateral rules, developing countries have continued to be under unilateral demands by some developed countries, notably the United States in the area of IPRs, in some cases aiming at ensuring protection of such rights beyond the minimum standards set forth by the Agreement" (Correa 2001: 22).

Although developing countries are likely targets for intellectual property rights cases, IPRs may also become their most effective means of exerting pressure and eventually retaliating. Ecuador's threat to suspend its TRIPS concessions in the *Bananas* case (see Chapter 10, by Hudec, in this volume) and the strategy used by Brazil with regard to public health and patents would appear to be the first steps in this direction (Dyer 2001; see also Chapter 36, by Maskus, in this volume).[5] Subramanian and Watal (2000) have proposed that "developing countries convert their TRIPS obligations into instruments of

Table 9.1 Number of Dispute Settlement Cases, 1995 through September 2000

	Complaint by		Total complaints	Share of total cases (percent)
	Industrial countries	Developing countries		
Complaint against:				
Industrial countries	89	35	124	60
Developing countries	65	18	83	40
Total	154	53	207	100
Share of total cases (percent)	74	26		
Memorandum:				
Share of cases under				
GATT (percent)	84	16		

Note: Based on number of cases brought by each country. The European Union and its member countries are counted jointly.
Source: Weston and Delich (2000); WTO (2000b); IMF, *Direction of Trade Statistics,* various issues.

multilateral enforcement embodying the retaliation possibilities in domestic legislation" (p. 415). According to these authors, "domestic legislation implementing the TRIPS agreement must clearly specify that the country's executive reserves the right to revoke or dilute these rights in the event that partner countries are found to be in non-compliance with commitments that affect the country's interest" (p. 411). In addition, they hold that "if designed with care, retaliation in TRIPS can be feasible, effective, and legal. Further, it has one really attractive attribute that distinguishes it from conventional trade retaliation in the area of goods: retaliation in TRIPS can be genuinely welfare enhancing in a way that conventional retaliation—a case of shooting oneself in the foot to shoot at the other person's foot—is not" (p. 405).

Proposals for Reforming the Dispute Settlement System

A number of proposals have been made by developing countries and by scholars to improve the functioning of the dispute settlement system. This section briefly summarizes these suggestions.

On Implementation of Recommendations and Rulings and Suspension of Concessions

Three proposals have been made: amend the system to resolve procedural problems such as the sequencing issue described earlier; allow financial compensation for developing countries; and turn retaliation into a collective action.

A large number of WTO members have made a joint proposal that Article 21.2 of the DSU be reformed to address the sequencing problem.[6] The proposal foresees the creation of Article 21 bis, entitled "Determination of Compliance," that would establish the following procedures. A complaining party may request the establishment of a compliance panel (a) any time after the member concerned states that it does not need further time for compliance; (b) any time after the member concerned has submitted a notification that it has complied with the recommendations or rulings of the DSB; or (c) 10 days before the date of expiration for the "reasonable period of time" to comply. While consultations between the member concerned and the complaining party are desirable, they are not required prior to a request for a compliance panel.

The compliance panel would comprise the members of the original panel, if its report had not been appealed, or the members of the Appellate Body that considered the appeal if the report of the original panel had been appealed. The compliance panel would be required to circulate its report within 90 days of the date of its establishment, after which any party to the compliance panel proceeding would be permitted to request a meeting of the DSB to adopt the report within a period of 10 days. The report would be subject to the negative consensus rule: it would be automatically adopted unless the DSB decided by consensus not to adopt.

Compliance panel reports would not be subject to appeal. If the compliance panel found that the member concerned had failed to bring its measures into compliance within the reasonable period of time determined by the original panel, the complaining party could request authorization from the DSB to suspend the application of concessions to the member concerned or to suspend other obligations under the covered agreements.

The joint proposal also modifies Article 22.2 to entitle the complaining party to request authorization to suspend concessions if a compliance panel report pursuant to Article 21 bis finds that the member concerned has failed to bring its measures into compliance with the ruling of the DSB. If the member concerned objects to the level of suspension proposed, the proposal states that "the matter shall be referred to arbitration. The arbitration shall be completed and the decision of the arbitrator shall be circulated to Members within 45 days after the referral of the matter. The complaining party shall not suspend concessions or other obligations during the course of the arbitration."

In regard to financial compensation, Pakistan has commented that "[i]t would be useful to clarify that the term 'compensation' used in Article 22 includes grant of financial compensation to the complaining party by the country which has been found to be in violation of the rules. Panels should be authorized to recommend payment of such financial compensation in disputes between developed and developing countries where they find that as a result of WTO inconsistent measures taken by developed countries, the developing country has lost its trade in the affected product" (WT/GC/W/162). It is not the first time that a developing country has called for the inclusion of financial compensation in the dispute settlement system: a similar proposal was made during the GATT era (see Chapter 10, by Hudec, in this volume).[7]

Proposals have also been made to make violation of WTO rules a collective problem and, accordingly, to require collective retaliatory actions. Pauwelyn (2000: 6), for instance, argues that

> with the advent of the WTO—its legal refinement, quasi-judicial dispute settlement system, and, in particular, major expansion into new fields that directly affect individuals—it may be time to move away from the idea of the GATT/WTO only as a package of bilateral balances between governments. Has the time not come to introduce the WTO as a truly multilateral construct providing legal rules as public goods that merit collective enforcement for the good of governments and economic operators? . . . [T]he enforcement of WTO rules can and should be seen as a collective rather than a mainly bilateral exercise.

In addition, Pauwelyn has proposed that "coupled with countermeasures, a broad scheme of compensation—additional market access offered by the losing party to WTO members—would provide genuine leverage to induce compliance, a move beneficial to all WTO members, and not just 'compensation' to the one or few that brought the case" (p. 9).

Finally, Pakistan has presented a proposal that Article 22.3 be amended to eliminate the possibility of cross-retaliation by industrial against developing countries. This would impede, for instance, retaliation against trade in goods if a developing country has been found to be in violation of the TRIPS agreement (WT/GC/W/162, p. 3).

On the Appellate Body

The role of the Appellate Body—in particular, the extent to which it has gone beyond its mandate and undertaken to "make rules" through interpretation of WTO agreements—has been severely questioned by developing countries.[8] Pakistan has called for an interpretation of "the relevant provisions in the DSU to make it clear that the responsibility for clarifying or modifying the provisions of the WTO Agreements clearly rests with the WTO member countries and that it would not be appropriate for the Appellate Body to usurp these functions under the guise of interpreting law on the basis of contem-

porary developments." In particular, Pakistan proposed that such clarification make clear that panels or the Appellate Body were not permitted to take into account "unsolicited information" including "*amicus curiae* briefs from private parties" (WT/GC/W/162).

In November 2000, at a special WTO General Council meeting, developing countries called for the Appellate Body to exercise extreme caution in inviting *amicus curiae* briefs from nongovernmental organizations (NGOs). (The context was the developing countries' reaction to the AB ruling on the *Asbestos* case.) Developing countries sought to limit the Appellate Body's "interpretation powers" and to prevent NGOs from participating in the dispute settlement system. Brazil, Egypt, India, Pakistan, Uruguay, and the Association of Southeast Asian Nations (ASEAN) countries argued that a decision to admit *amicus curiae* briefs was a substantive and not a procedural one and was therefore something for WTO members to decide. Moreover, "developing countries took the view that non-governmental organizations are not accountable to sovereign parliaments and have no contractual rights and obligations in the WTO. The AB had let itself be unduly influenced by the campaign of NGOs of major trading entities. In effect, NGOs were being accorded privileges greater than those enjoyed by WTO Members."[9]

As for the composition of the Appellate Body, India has proposed that, to promote an atmosphere conducive to impartial and independent functioning of the Appellate Body, all future appointments of AB members should be for a nonrenewable fixed term of five or six years, to ensure that members have no incentive to seek support for their reappointment (WT/DSB/W/117).

On Time Lines

The joint proposal mentioned earlier would shorten the consultation period from 60 to 30 days; the period could be extended by up to 30 additional days if one or more of the parties in the dispute were a developing country and the parties agreed. In addition, in the Working Procedures, the proposal would reduce the time for receipt of the complaining party's first written submissions to three–four weeks (currently, it is three–six weeks), while increasing the time for the party complained against to respond to four–five weeks instead of two–three weeks, as at present. Since the proposal unifies the reports (there would be a single report, including the descriptive sections and the panel's findings and conclusions), it eliminates the period during which parties submit their comments on the descriptive report and, consequently, the possibility that at the request of a party the panel would hold a further meeting on the issues identified in the written comments. After making other adjustments on time lines, the proposal states that "the total reduction of time is up to approximately 47 days, and the time frames in Article 20 (the reference to 9 months and to 12 months), and the periods in Art. 21.4 (the reference to 15 months and to 18 months) shall be reduced by one month" (WT/MIN[99]8, p. 7).

On Third Parties

In relation to third parties, the joint proposal retains the obligation contained in Article 10 that a copy of all documentation submitted in a case be given to third parties. It allows exclusion, however, of certain factual confidential information (designated as such by the disputing party) and sets a period of 15 days for the party to provide a nonconfidential summary that can be disclosed to the public of the information contained in the confidential submission.

A Special Prosecutor, "Light" Procedures, and Customs Unions

Hoekman and Mavroidis (2000) have proposed a kind of "special prosecutor," able to act on an ex officio basis, to detect illegalities. They also suggest "light" procedures for cases involving less than US$1 million of exports; in such cases a single panelist would be asked to address the dispute within three months. Turkey has proposed amending Article 10 of the DSU to grant all parties to customs unions the right to participate in panel and AB proceedings in disputes concerning measures introduced pursuant to a common trade policy of the union (WT/MIN[99]/15).

Conclusion

The Dispute Settlement Understanding brought about a positive and beneficial change for developing countries. Weaker states have a better chance to defend their interests in a rule-oriented than in a power-oriented system. However, since the DSU

provisions relating to enforcement of S&D language in WTO agreements are ineffective, developing countries do not enjoy a "neutral" playing field. Although the DSU is not biased against any party in a dispute, developing countries are less well equipped to participate in the process: they have fewer people with the appropriate training, they are less experienced, and they can bring fewer financial resources to bear. Therefore, although the DSU is an asset, developing countries must work to obtain international financing for training and capacity building and for the establishment of a joint mechanism among developing countries to screen industrial country trade policies of interest to them—not only to reduce the costs of the screening but also to coordinate the submission of joint cases. In addition, developing countries could use cases in which they are involved as a way to identify gaps in WTO agreements that need to be addressed through negotiations.

Reform of the dispute settlement system does not appear to be a priority on the negotiating agenda of developing countries. Their efforts are mainly directed toward defending their interests as best they can in current cases, bridging the gap with industrial countries in terms of legal expertise, and establishing more effective enforcement and retaliatory devices.

Notes

1 See for example, Komuro (1995); Lafer (1996); Jackson (1997); Montaña Mora (1997).

2 On the sequencing problem, see the *Salmon* dispute between Austria and Canada; the U.S.-Australian dispute over leather subsidies; and the *Bananas* case. See also O'Connor and Vergano (2000); Rhodes (2000); Valles and McGivern (2000).

3 Cases in which S&D clauses were invoked by a party in a dispute were *European Communities: Antidumping Duties on Imports of Cotton-Type Bed Linen,* complaint by India; *Korea: Measures Affecting Imports of Fresh, Chilled, and Frozen Beef,* complaint by the United States; *India: Quantitative Restrictions on Imports of Agricultural, Textile and Industrial Products,* complaint by the United States; *Brazil: Export Financing Programme for Aircraft,* complaint by Canada; *Canada: Measures Affecting the Export of Civilian Aircraft,* complaint by Brazil; and *Indonesia: Certain Measures Affecting the Automobile Industry,* complaints by the United States, the European Communities, and Japan. There were also cases in which S&D clauses were invoked by a third party or some kind of statement was made about a developing country's preferential treatment on the basis of its status as a developing country. Examples include *Guatemala: Antidumping Investigation Regarding Imports of Port-*

The entire system was based on consensus decision-making, which meant that the consent of the defendant was required before the procedure—creating a panel, defining its terms of reference, appointing its members, adopting its ruling, and authorizing retaliation—could move forward at all. The central reform made by the WTO Dispute Settlement Understanding (DSU) was to make the procedure go forward automatically on the request of the complainant, with or without the consent of the defendant.

In addition to its central weakness, the formal remedies provided by the GATT legal system when legal violation was found were also rather limited. A ruling of violation entitled the complaining government to a rather general "recommendation" calling on the defendant government to comply with its obligations. The recommendation was directed only toward future conduct, with no compensation for harm done while the violation was in force. There was no time limit on the order to comply, and the process of seeking compliance could drag on for years. The complaining government could at some point request authorization to retaliate by imposing approximately equal trade barriers in return, but the request could be vetoed by the defendant. In modern GATT practice, only two requests for retaliation authority were made, both against the United States, and both were vetoed.[1]

Despite the defendant's ability to block the procedure, the GATT disputes procedure produced a considerable number of dispute settlement complaints during its almost 50-year history. My own study of GATT cases from 1948 to the end of 1989 counted 207 cases filed during that period, of which 88 produced legal rulings; of the 88, 68 were rulings of violation. In the decade of the 1980s, when the GATT system had matured, there were 115 complaints yielding 47 legal rulings, of which 40 were rulings of legal violation (Hudec 1993: 277–78). Provisional data from a continuation of that study list 71 more complaints in the final five years of GATT operations (1990 to 1994), with 22 legal rulings, 20 of which were rulings of legal violation.[2]

Notwithstanding the defendant's ability to block adoption of adverse rulings, the great majority of the violation rulings were in fact adopted. Moreover, the bulk of these violation rulings, including many of those not adopted, did produce a satisfactory correction of the practice at issue. In its first three decades the GATT system achieved almost a 100 percent success rate in producing a satisfactory

response to legal rulings. In the 1980s, when governments began to use the dispute settlement system to deal with more politically controversial matters, the success rate dropped to about 81 percent—not up to the standards of most domestic legal systems, but still a very impressive performance for an international legal regime, especially in the politically sensitive area of trade policy (Hudec 1993: 285–94).

Although complaints by developing countries did not achieve the same level of success as those brought by larger countries, the results were still favorable in a significant percentage of the cases. Over the GATT's entire history, 28 complaints were brought by developing countries. Of these, 17 ended in legal rulings, 11 of which were rulings of legal violation, and 10 of the 11 (91 percent) had a successful outcome. Of the 22 complaints known to be based on a valid legal claim, satisfaction was achieved in 18 of the cases (82 percent). Even in the more contentious cases of the 1980s, legally valid complaints by developing countries achieved a 73 percent success rate (Hudec 1993: 315–26).

The paradoxical contrast between the voluntary procedures and weak remedies of the GATT dispute settlement system, on the one hand, and its rather strong record of success, on the other, contains a lesson. It teaches that the enforcement of international legal obligations cannot be explained by superficial analysis of dispute settlement procedures and remedies. Enforcement requires that governments be persuaded to reverse decisions they have taken in violation of the agreement. Governments are not private litigants. They are complex institutions that make decisions in their own peculiar, often irrational, manner, which we call "politics." Even smaller governments are strong enough to be able to resist coercive forces that would move private litigants. Governments, however, usually have a longer-term interest in the efficacy of the legal relationships they have established with other governments, and so they are more inclined to act in ways designed to preserve those relationships. Ultimately, the compliance decisions of governments are determined more by calculated self-interest than by force.

In my view, government compliance with legal rulings is usually the product of at least three interrelated factors that influence the way in which governments make trade policy decisions. First, some parts of the defendant government's decisionmaking apparatus usually want the conduct called for by GATT legal obligations to be pursued for its own sake, simply because it is good policy. Such officials, and the private interest groups that share this view, constitute an existing political force within the defendant government, and the effect of GATT legal rulings is to give them greater influence in the national decisionmaking process. Second, many officials and private interest groups within the national government's decisionmaking process perceive a value in the legal system itself, believing that both they and their country will gain more over the long term from an effective legal system than they will gain from noncompliance in this or that individual case. Although these actors may not want to tie their country's hands through rigid commitments to a particular legal system—or may not have enough political support to go that far—they will nonetheless argue strongly against noncompliance in individual cases that would damage respect for the system. Finally, one should not underestimate the influence of active pressure by other governments. If a majority of member governments believes in the value of an existing legal system, those governments will have the same incentive to discourage noncompliance with legal rulings and will express their views in the form of collective condemnation of noncompliance.

But even if all three factors existed in cases where no legal rulings were provided, legal rulings sharpen the focus on the issue of compliance, and the normative force of such rulings increases the power of those participants who favor compliance. This is so whether or not the ruling is enforced by coercive sanctions.

As noted above, the GATT dispute settlement procedure almost never employed retaliation as an enforcement device. The fact that the GATT nonetheless produced a large number of successful legal rulings indicates, therefore, that the internal government forces just described frequently did play a significant role in bringing about successful outcomes. This is not to say, of course, that enforcement would not have been even more effective if more retaliation had been employed. Other things being equal, one would expect a better chance of compliance with a retaliation tool than without it. The key point, however, is that a legal ruling without retaliation can still be an effective policy tool for a developing country seeking to reverse a legal violation by a larger country. Although not invariably effective, in many cases it may well be more effective than the other practical alternatives. Policy decisions that focus only on the availability of retaliation thus run the risk of ignoring the other, quite valuable, gains that can be achieved from a legal ruling alone.

The WTO Reforms

In the Uruguay Round, WTO member governments agreed to establish a more rigorous dispute settlement system. As noted above, they began by making the disputes procedure move forward automatically. The automaticity of the procedure makes it more difficult for larger countries to bully smaller countries into giving up their legal complaints. If developing countries want to have a legal ruling, it will now require less diplomatic confrontation to get one.

The remedies granted for enforcing a binding ruling were also strengthened. In addition to making retaliation more readily available, the Uruguay Round reforms adopted a number of reforms intended to strengthen the effect of the ruling itself. The primary remedy set forth in the DSU is still the legally binding "recommendation" ordering the defendant to bring its conduct into compliance. Although the recommendation is still only future-directed (it provides no remedy for the harm done by the violation so far), some steps were taken to make that future-directed order more effective.[3] Panels were given explicit power to make nonbinding suggestions for how compliance can be achieved—a power that, if used, could sharpen the focus of compliance pressures. Quite a bit more was added to the procedure for following up a recommendation after it has been issued. There is now a procedure for establishing a time limit for compliance, which, so far, has ranged from 6 to 15 months. During that period, the illegal measure is under periodic review, and it remains under periodic review, without further action by the complainant, as long as noncompliance lasts. For the government that does not, or cannot, retaliate, these changes make it easier for the complainant to focus and maintain community pressures for compliance.

Retaliation is still the final remedy for eventual noncompliance. In contrast to the GATT disputes procedure, under which retaliation was a vague and seldom-used remedy, the new WTO procedure appears to make retaliation the central objective of

it were to extend to refunds of such things as GATT-illegal tariff charges. Developing countries themselves might wish to think twice about whether they wish to shoulder such a refund responsibility. Meanwhile, the weight of joint U.S.-EU opposition to refunds in AD/CVD cases promises to be formidable, especially since U.S. opposition is now required by statute.

Other Forms of Trade Retaliation

The standard complaint of developing countries about the remedy of trade retaliation is that it is too weak to be effective against large countries. The amount of retaliation is limited to the trade loss caused by the illegal trade measure in question. Since individual developing countries tend to have only a small share of the defendant country's market, their retaliation measures can affect only a small amount of that country's trade—usually not enough, the argument runs, to cause any significant hardship for the large industrial country or its producers.

Academic discussions of GATT/WTO remedies usually arrive at the question of whether GATT/WTO trade retaliation should not be measured according to a scale that would make certain that the amount of retaliation is large enough to be meaningful against larger countries. Such proposals are usually justified by arguments that the law must have sanctions large enough to accomplish its task.

Two objections are usually interposed against such proposals for proportional retaliation. The most important is the assertion that the purpose of retaliation has never been to serve as a punitive sanction; on the contrary, the right to retaliate has always been viewed as a right to maintain the balance of reciprocity in GATT obligations. The starting assumption has been that the obligations undertaken by each country involve a balance of benefits—the benefits granted to others in the form of a country's own obligations, balanced against the benefits that country obtains from the obligations undertaken by others. The theory is that a breach of legal obligations reduces the benefits being received by the complaining country and that, if the breach is not cured, the complaining country must be allowed to reestablish the balance by withdrawing obligations of its own. Such balancing, however, requires only retaliation equal to the amount of the benefits lost.

This compensatory theory of trade retaliation has run through GATT law since the days of the negotiations on the International Trade Organization (ITO) in 1947–48.[14] That theory is, of course, a policy choice; GATT governments could always adopt a different standard if they wanted to. The significance of the history of the compensatory theory is simply that it shows a steadfast desire on the part of leading GATT members not to have a law with stronger sanctions.

The second objection to proportional retaliation is a practical one: an individual developing country usually does not have a large enough market to assemble the amount of trade retaliation that would be needed to cause noticeable pain in a large industrial country—at least not without shutting down most of its own economy. The only way to achieve significantly greater retaliation would be to develop some form of collective retaliation by many countries at the same time. Thus, the proposal usually shifts to one for collective retaliation, asking that the GATT put aside both the compensatory limit to retaliation and the notion that only the complainant is entitled to retaliate.

In 1965 the developing country proposals for reform of the GATT dispute settlement remedies included a proposal calling for collective retaliation.[15] The justification for the proposal was the same as the one advanced today: individual developing countries could not impose sufficient retaliation to cause noticeable pain in larger industrial countries. The idea was that in such cases a number of countries would be authorized to deny market access to the large-country defendant. By definition, this retaliation would also have been punitive in amount, although there were some arguments that higher retaliation levels could be based on a "development multiplier" that inflated the measurement of the harm developing countries suffered from GATT-illegal trade restrictions.

Industrial countries strongly resisted this proposal. Beyond the objections based on unwillingness to change the "compensatory" limit to retaliation, there were also objections based on an assertion that multiple retaliations would soon produce so many new restrictions that they would choke the channels of commerce. In informal conversations, industrial country delegates tried to point out that, solidarity notwithstanding, countries not involved in the dispute would soon tire of being asked to harm their own citizens for this purpose. Even farther behind the scenes, of course, was the awareness by industrial countries that the existing limitations on remedies suited them quite well, for the very same reasons that developing countries did not like them. Viewing things from the perspective of their role as potential defendants, industrial countries were quite content with membership in a legal system in which they could hurt others but some of the others could not really hurt them.

Cross-Retaliation under the TRIPS Agreement

In 1999 the several strands of argument claiming that trade retaliation is not a practical policy instrument for developing countries were brought together in a new type of retaliation proceeding initiated by Ecuador in the *Bananas* case (Box 10.1).[16] Ecuador tried to take advantage of the "cross-retaliation" provisions found in Article 22.3 of the WTO

BOX 10.1 THE *BANANAS* CASE

The European Union (EU) import regime for bananas has long been a bone of contention. In effect, the EU maintains a system that gives preferential market access to bananas produced by African, Caribbean, and Pacific (ACP) countries. As a result Caribbean producers have always had a substantial share of the EU market, to the detriment of Central and South American countries. Preferences predated the formation of the European Economic Community (EEC) and, in fact, caused problems between France and Germany during the negotiations leading to the creation of the EEC in 1957; Germany had a free trade regime for bananas and imported from Latin American countries, while France maintained very high barriers to support French colonial producers (Messerlin 2001). These differences led to the imposition of national intra-EU trade barriers, reserving the U.K., French, and Spanish markets for former colonies. The policies were a very inefficient way of assisting the former colonies: every dollar transferred cost EU consumers US$5, of which US$3 went to distributors and US$1 was wasted (Borrell 1997).

In 1993 the EU adopted a complex import licensing and distribution system for the union as a whole, as part of its effort to create a single market. The common market organization that was imposed was based on historical trading relationships and was designed to continue to provide preferential access for ACP countries (signatories of the Lomé Convention). It involved two tariff quotas—one for traditional ACP suppliers and one for nontraditional ACP and Latin American growers—and four categories of suppliers. Out-of-quota imports were subject to high specific tariffs.

Operators that traditionally exported bananas from former British and French Caribbean colonies were granted 30 percent of all import licenses for non-country-specific quotas. These licenses could be used to import ACP bananas or could be sold to firms desiring to import from Latin America. In the latter case, which often occurred, the quota allocation system resulted in a transfer of rents from the (mostly U.S.-based) firms buying the licenses to those granted the quota rights. Borrell (1997) estimated that the new regime was worse than the national ones it replaced: total costs to EU consumers were about US$2 billion, while ACP suppliers obtained US$150 million—a cost per consumer of over US$13 for each dollar transferred.

Latin American producers brought two cases to the GATT contesting the national systems (in 1992) and the new common EU regime (in 1993). They won both. In 1994 the EU concluded a Banana Framework Agreement with four countries (Costa Rica, Colombia, Nicaragua, and Venezuela) under which these countries were allocated specific quotas on the understanding that they would not bring a case to the WTO before 2002. In 1996 four Latin American producers that had been left out of this agreement (Ecuador, Guatemala, Honduras, and Mexico), joined by the United States on behalf of U.S. multinational fruit firms, contested the EU import regime in the WTO, claiming that it discriminated against their producers and banana marketing companies. The object of the attack was not so much the tariff preferences that were granted to ACP countries—for which the EU had obtained a waiver—but the allocation of quotas.

(continued)

against such industrial inputs would be *ineffective* "given the fact that Ecuador, as a small developing country, only accounts for a negligible proportion of the EC's exports of these products" (para. 95). With regard to consumer goods, the panel ruled that Ecuador had failed to demonstrate that retaliation against such goods would be ineffective, without explaining why Ecuador's similarly "negligible" proportion of the EC market for consumer goods was not as probative in that case (para. 100).

The rather superficial and inconsistent answers on this point suggest that the panel did not have enough time to develop a fully coherent analysis of the long-standing developing country claims about the inadequacy of trade retaliation. But the answers do show the panel's inclination to support those claims of inadequacy, and they also show that the support may be limited to the clearer case of retaliation against industrial inputs. It would not be wise to read much more into the decision than this, especially since, in the absence of appellate review, the next panel will not be bound by anything said in this report. On balance, the panel's rather unclear response was encouraging enough to make it worthwhile for developing country officials to think about the possibility of cross-retaliation in dispute settlement cases involving uncured violations.

Potentially, the most significant aspect of Ecuador's retaliation proposal was the possibility that retaliation under TRIPS could be both more "practicable" and more "effective" than trade retaliation. In theory, at least, denying the intellectual property rights of foreign owners results in assets being made available to developing countries at cheaper prices, which is usually a benefit to economic development rather than a burden on it. Likewise, although the amounts of retaliation in most cases will still be "negligible," at this time in the WTO's history the ripple effects of even small-scale denial of intellectual property protection could cause considerably more political discomfort than the usual small-scale case of trade retaliation. As the arbitration panel itself made clear, however, TRIPS retaliation will involve a number of distinctive legal, practical, and economic problems for the retaliating state.[18] Ecuador's retaliation request in the *Bananas* case is therefore only a very tentative first step in a much longer journey. A great deal more analysis, and considerably more practical experience, will be needed before it is clear whether TRIPS retaliation is the key to this long-troubling problem.

I would end on a note of caution with regard to TRIPS retaliation. As pointed out earlier in this chapter, there is considerable evidence that the power of retaliation, although helpful, is not really the key ingredient in enforcement of GATT/WTO legal rulings. To reiterate the point, enforcement of legal rulings is a political process involving the cultivation of a government decision to change a previous decision. The U.S. Congress was wrong to insist on retaliation as the key to its enforcement demands. The U.S. negotiators were wrong to play up to that misconception by trying to persuade the Congress that easier retaliation would make WTO enforcement as effective as the Congress wanted. Developing countries would be just as wrong to think that practicable TRIPS retaliation will bring about a decisive change in the political fundamentals of WTO enforcement. More effective retaliation will make the system work somewhat better for developing countries, but it is not wise to invest all the eggs in that basket.

Notes

1 Both requests came in the Superfund case, *United States: Taxes on Petroleum and Certain Imported Substances*, GATT, BISD, 34th Supp. 136–66 (1988). The follow-up proceedings are discussed in Hudec (1993): 210–11, 535–37.

2 The continuation study has not yet been published.

3 The next section discusses the single exception to the statement that the recommendation provides no remedy for harm incurred in the past: the effort in several cases to make defendant governments refund antidumping and countervailing duties imposed in violation of GATT law. See text at notes 7–14, below.

4 See GATT, BISD, 14th Supp. 18 (1966). The procedures call for mediation and fact-gathering by the secretariat, the automatic establishment of a panel (a significant advance in those days), and a considerably accelerated time schedule.

5 For a brief description of the negotiations, see Hudec (1990): 242–43. The GATT document series recording the negotiations is COM.TD/F. The main proposals are COM.TD/F/W.1 (April 27, 1965) and COM.TD/F/W.4 (October 11, 1965). I participated in these negotiations as a U.S. delegate, and some of the information given here is based on my personal recollections.

6 Normally, the only way to secure refunds is to try to persuade national authorities to revise their interpretation of national law in light of the GATT/WTO ruling so that *as a matter of national law* the refund is owing. The refunds carried out after adverse panel rulings made under the North American Free Trade Agreement (NAFTA) Chapter 19 review of AD/CVD occur only because national legislation makes dispute settle-

ment under Chapter 19 part of the domestic AD/CVD proceeding and thus binding on national authorities as a matter
of domestic law.

7 See the explanation in note 6.

8 *New Zealand: Imports of Electrical Transformers from Finland,*
GATT, BISD, 32nd Supp. 55–70 (1986).

9 The two cases are as follows. (1) *United States: Countervailing
Duties on Fresh, Chilled and Frozen Pork from Canada,* GATT,
BISD, 38th Supp. 30–47 (1992). After the U.S. CVD had been
withdrawn, the United States agreed not to block adoption of
the panel ruling, but it reserved its position on the merits. (2)
*United States: Measures Affecting Imports of Softwood Lumber
from Canada,* GATT, BISD, 40th Supp. 358–517 (1995). The
United States announced that it would be refunding deposits
and bonds for other reasons, but it expressly reserved its position on the validity of the panel's order that deposits and
bonds be refunded; GATT, SCM/M/67 (meeting of October
27–28, 1993).

10 The four cases were as follows. (1) *Canada: Countervailing Duty
on Boneless Manufacturing Beef,* GATT, SCM/85 (October 13,
1987); panel report not adopted. The case is discussed briefly
in Hudec (1993): 221–22, 533–34. (2) *United States:
Antidumping Duties on Stainless Seamless Pipes and Tubes from
Sweden,* GATT, ADP/47 (August 20, 1990); panel report not
adopted. The impasse over remedies in this case is discussed
briefly in Hudec (1993): 253–54, 572–73. (3) *United States:
Antidumping Duties on Gray Portland Cement and Cement Clink-
er from Mexico,* GATT, ADP/82 (July 7, 1992); panel report not
adopted. (4) *European Communities: Antidumping Duties on
Audio Tapes in Cassettes Originating in Japan,* GATT, ADP/136
(April 28, 1995); panel report not adopted.

11 The European Community appears to have shifted toward the
U.S. position during a 1993 complaint against Brazilian coun-
tervailing duties; it initially asked for a refund order in its com-
plaint but withdrew its request during the panel proceeding.
See *Brazil: Imposition of Provisional and Definitive Duties on Milk
Powder and Certain Types of Milk from the European Economic
Community,* GATT, SCM/179 (December 27, 1993), para. 200.
The EC opposed a request for refunds in the *Audiocassette* case
(see note 10).

12 Section 129 of the Uruguay Round Agreements Act, 108 Stat.
4813, 4836, 19 U.S.C. 3501, 3538 (1994), provides partial
authority to revoke AD/CVD and safeguards measures in order
to comply with WTO panel rulings. Although this is an
advance over prior law, subsection (c)(1) limits the effect of
such revocations to "unliquidated" entries that enter or are
withdrawn from the warehouse on or after the date of the
order revoking the measure.

13 *Guatemala: Antidumping Investigation Regarding Portland
Cement from Mexico,* WTO, WT/DS60/R (June 19, 1998) (panel
report), reversed on appeal WT/DS60/AB/R (November 2,
1998) (Appellate Body report).

14 The text of GATT Article XXIII.2, based on the August 1947 draft
of the ITO Charter, states that the contracting parties may
authorize such retaliation "as they deem to be appropriate in
the circumstances." The final ITO Charter text adopted in March
1948 changed this passage to read "appropriate *and compensatory, having regard to the benefit which has been nullified or
impaired,*" to make clear that retaliation was not to exceed the
amount needed to compensate for the harm done (ITO Charter,
Article 95.3). See also *Havana Conference, Reports of Committees
and Principal Subcommittees,* UN, ICITO 1/8 (September 1948),
p. 155.

During the history of the GATT, the only GATT panel to discuss
the issue was the 1952 panel that adjudicated the level of the
Netherlands retaliation against U.S. dairy restrictions. The panel
claimed that the word "appropriate" in the (1947) text of Article
XXIII.2 gave the panel a certain flexibility to take into account
other factors that might aggravate the harm. But the panel
found it "appropriate" to *reduce* the level of retaliation by 20 percent from the amount submitted by the Netherlands, suggesting
that flexibility cut in both directions. See *Netherlands: Action
under Article XXIII:2,* GATT, BISD, 1st Supp. 32, 62–64 (1953), discussed in detail in Hudec (1990), ch. 16. A similar interpretation
of "appropriate" was offered by the GATT secretariat's legal
adviser during discussions of the Superfund case. See GATT,
C/M/220 (GATT Council meeting of April 8, 1988), p. 35.

In the WTO Dispute Settlement Understanding, para. 22.4
clearly states that the retaliation shall be equivalent to the
amount of the nullification and impairment caused by the measure at issue. Thus, it returns to the original meaning of the ITO
Charter. The WTO arbitration panels that have ruled on the
amount of retaliation have all followed this instruction. See *European Communities: Regime for the Importation, Sale and Distribution of Bananas—Recourse to Arbitration by the European
Communities under Article 22.6 of the DSU,* WT/DS27/ARB/USA
(April 9. 1999) (U.S. retaliation); id., WT/DS27/ARB/ECU (March
24, 2000) (Ecuador retaliation); see also *European Communities:
Measures Concerning Meat and Meat Products (Hormones —
Recourse to Arbitration by the European Communities under Article
22.6 of the DSU,* WT/DS26/ARB (July 12, 1999) (U.S. retaliation);
id., WT/DS48/ARB (July 12, 1999) (Canada retaliation).

15 See sources cited in note 5.

16 *European Communities: Regime for the Importation, Sale and Dis-
tribution of Bananas — Recourse to Arbitration by the European
Communities under Article 22.6 of the DSU,* WT/DS27/ARB/ECU
(March 24, 2000) (decision by panel of arbitrators).

17 The objection to the possibility of GATS retaliation by Ecuador
in other services sectors was based on essentially different
arguments, resting primarily on the nature of Ecuador's limited
GATS obligations (WT/DS27/ARB/ECU, paras. 103–20). The
issues raised by this defense, and the panel's response, are not
treated in this chapter.

18 The panel delivered a lengthy lecture on the prospective perils
of such retaliation (WT/DS27/ARB/ECU, paras. 130–65).

Much attention has centered recently on granting least-developed countries (LDCs) duty- and quota-free access to industrial country markets. This is important for these countries because existing patterns of protection discriminate against them, as is demonstrated in Chapter 12, by Olarreaga and Ng. Preferential access to markets will be beneficial to LDCs, but it comes at a cost to other developing countries. This cost, however, is limited, given the small size of most LDC economies. Of greater significance is the evidence that preferences are of limited value. One reason is that they are generally conditional on stringent rules of origin. Chapter 13, by Luis Jorge Garay and Rafael Cornejo; Chapter 14, by Stefano Inama; and Box 13.1, by Gomi Senadhira (on the U.S. African Growth and Opportunity Act) show that rules of origin can be restrictive and can give rise to high compliance (red tape) costs.

Red tape is also an important factor in customs clearance procedures in general. Developing countries therefore confront a large and important trade facilitation agenda. In part, this agenda has to do with market access—for example, with simplifying rules of origin, which can be pursued through the WTO (see Chapter 14)—but it is mostly domestic. The domestic part of the agenda is the most important and requires institutional strengthening, as well as policy change. Of particular relevance for the discussion in Part III are customs administration reform and trade facilitation. These are areas in which numerous international bodies are active and in which the private sector can become part of the solution—for example, through the provision of certification or inspection services.

Country experience suggests that strengthening customs regimes and their administration to reduce transaction costs, antiexport bias, and corruption is important in harnessing trade reform for development. Transactions costs related to customs clearance can be a major impediment to investment in tradable sectors, especially in activities that are time-sensitive or where it is important to be integrated into global production networks that operate on the basis of just-in-time supply chain management. Streamlining customs procedures and eliminating red tape require a concerted effort that involves exploiting potential partnerships and synergy with organizations that have expertise in this area, including the private sector (for example, express carriers). Vinod Rege, in Chapter 15, reviews international efforts to standardize customs valuation

and looks at how these might be made more responsive to the needs of developing countries. In Chapter 16 Brian Rankin Staples examines the organizations and instruments involved in trade facilitation initiatives and summarizes the lessons from cross-country experience in this area.

Many countries have sought to use export-promoting policies either as a vehicle to offset the anti-export bias created by other policies (overvalued exchange rates, transactions costs, and so on) or as a way of supplementing trade reform efforts. Industrial policies of various types are common in many countries: examples include subsidies, export promotion, and creation of export-processing zones (EPZs). Two issues arise: What makes sense from a development viewpoint? And to what extent does the WTO restrict the use of efficient policies for promoting industrialization and export development?

There may, in fact, be a good case for pursuing EPZs and promoting exports; these mechanisms can be effective ways of offsetting the high transactions costs that prevail in developing economies and that inhibit investment. It is important, however, to design such schemes in ways that limit the scope for rent-seeking and reduce the likelihood of investment occurring in sectors in which the country does not have a potential comparative advantage. As Mari Pangestu explains in Chapter 17 in the East Asian context, WTO rules do not significantly constrain the ability of developing countries to pursue welfare-enhancing policies. The agreements do, however, have implications for industrial policies, especially export subsidies and local content requirements.

Philip English and Luc De Wulf, in Chapter 18, examine experiences with trade promotion organizations, EPZs, subsidies, duty drawbacks, and other export promotion policies and mechanisms and review the options for developing countries. In countries where tariff revenues continue to be needed, it is crucial that exporters have access to imported intermediate inputs at world market prices in order to be competitive. This requires well-functioning customs regimes that efficiently refund duties paid on imported inputs or, preferably, allow exporters to import inputs duty-free without running afoul of WTO subsidy rules. Implementing such systems requires training and institutional strengthening. For example, many African countries lack well-functioning drawback regimes, and this increases antiexport bias.

Trade-related investment measures (TRIMs) are sometimes used in an effort to promote industrial development. Among them are local content requirements, which, as Bijit Bora notes in Chapter 19, have become controversial following the adoption of WTO rules that apply to developing countries. (These rules were already embodied in the GATT but were not enforced against this country group.) Although, in principle, a case for such policies can be made—they may be appropriate for offsetting specific distortions—experience in many countries reveals that great care must be taken in their use. The case study on Australia in Chapter 20, by Garry Pursell, illustrates that the use of TRIMs can mean a very high cumulative cost to society.

The final chapters in this part look at the elimination of remaining quotas on imports of apparel and textiles and at the use of safeguard actions. These topics are closely linked: many observers expect the incidence of safeguard measures to increase once quotas under the Multifibre Arrangement (MFA) are fully eliminated, as required by the WTO Agreement on Textiles and Clothing (ATC). Hanna Kheir-El-Din, in Chapter 21, discusses the implications of the ATC for developing countries.

The so-called instruments of contingent protection—antidumping and emergency measures—that are permitted under the WTO if imports are deemed to injure domestic industries are a major source of uncertainty regarding market access conditions. Antidumping, traditionally used by industrial countries, is increasingly being employed by developing nations. As J. Michael Finger explains in Chapter 22, some of these instruments, especially antidumping, make no economic sense and are best avoided by developing countries. More efficient instruments are available that are preferable from a development perspective. A key element of such a mechanism is that it takes into account the interests of all parts of society, not just a subset of the domestic industry that confronts competition from imports. This is a policy area in which further multilateral rule making can be important for developing countries. However, as Finger notes, domestic actions to improve the economic content and rationality of these measures are likely to be more beneficial. In the meantime, exporters have to live with the threat of being confronted with contingent protection. In Chapter 23 Gary N. Horlick and Eleanor Shea, two practicing trade lawyers, discuss the relevant U.S. trade law

provisions and outline how firms should respond to the various stages of the trade litigation process.

Although this Handbook is not a legal reference to the WTO, many of the chapters in this part refer to GATT provisions. For ease of reference for those who are not familiar with the WTO, the Glossary provides a summary of key GATT rules and articles.

Further Reading

UNCTAD, *Duty and Quota Free Market Access for LDCs: An Analysis of QUAD Initiatives* (Geneva, 2001), is a comprehensive and detailed discussion of current initiatives to provide LDCs with preferential access to major industrial country markets. Rolf Langhammer and André Sapir, *Economic Impact of Generalized Tariff Preferences* (London: Trade Policy Research Centre, 1988), although somewhat dated, is a useful analysis of the economic effects of Generalized System of Preferences (GSP) schemes. The authors argue that these schemes largely benefit countries which pursue export-oriented policies and, for the most part, do not need preferences to compete. Edwin Vermulst, Jacques Bourgeois, and Paul Waer, *Rules of Origin in International Trade: A Comparative Study* (Ann Arbor: University of Michigan Press, 1994), provides a comprehensive discussion of origin rules. John Raven, *Trade and Transport Facilitation: An Audit Methodology* (Washington, D.C.: World Bank, 2000), is a useful set of tools for those seeking to identify trade facilitation bottlenecks and priorities. Gerald K. Helleiner (ed.), *Non-Traditional Exports and Development in Sub-Saharan Africa: Experience and Issues* (Helsinki: World Institute for Development Economics Research, 2001), provides surveys and assessments of the instruments used to promote exports in low-income countries and reviews experience with them. Theodore Moran, *Foreign Direct Investment and Development* (Washington, D.C.: Institute for International Economics, 1998), offers an extensive discussion of experience with TRIMs and related policy measures. J. Michael Finger (ed.), *Antidumping: How It Works and Who Gets Hurt* (Ann Arbor: University of Michigan Press, 1993), brings together case studies illustrating how antidumping is applied in practice and assessing the implications for users and targets. Neil Vousden, *The Economics of Trade Protection* (Cambridge, U.K.: Cambridge University Press, 1990), is a good academic textbook on the instruments of trade policy.

about 3.5 percent when Uruguay Round commitments are fully implemented. But the devil is in the details; there is considerable variation across countries and across sectors. Simple average tariffs can be twice as high as import-weighted rates—the higher the tariff, the less tends to be imported. On the other hand, the existence of various preference schemes means that even applied MFN rates may overstate the tariffs on much trade.

Particularly high tariffs and tariff peaks (several times the average and, in some cases, well over 100 percent) prevail in some sectors. Many of these high rates are in areas of export interest to developing countries—textiles and clothing, footwear, and agriculture (Table 11.1). Agricultural tariffs are generally higher than those on manufactures. The impact of tariffication of agricultural nontariff barriers (NTBs) in the Uruguay Round was so great in some cases as to increase average tariffs.

Industrial countries' tariff escalation, by which tariffs are increased at later stages of processing in order to encourage domestic processing, may negatively affect industrialization in developing countries. Table 11.2 provides a picture of tariff

escalation in industrial countries at the completion of Uruguay Round implementation. Developing countries also have relatively high tariffs on labor-intensive manufactures and agriculture. In general, their tariffs are typically higher than those of industrial countries and also show a pattern of escalation (Michalopoulos 1999a).

As mentioned in Chapter 6, by Hoekman, in this volume, what matters in the WTO is the level at which tariffs are bound. In the case of developing countries, bound rates are often much higher than the applied rates. For example, WTO members from North Africa and the Middle East have bound rates that average 26.8 percent, whereas applied rates average 14.4 percent (Table 11.3). This creates a degree of uncertainty about market access in such countries.

The stylized facts are, therefore, sectoral patterns of tariffs that remain highly dispersed, with significant gaps between applied and bound tariff rates. The reasons for this relate partly to evolution in sectoral policy and partly to the participation of WTO members in negotiations. Agricultural policy in many countries is rooted in the history of food

Table 11.1 Post–Uruguay Round Applied and Bound Rates of Industrial and Developing Economies by Major Product Group
(percent)

Product group	Industrial economies		Developing economies	
	Applied	Bound	Applied	Bound
1. Agriculture, excluding fish	5.2	7.2	18.6	19.9
2. Fish and fish products	4.2	4.9	8.6	25.9
3. Petroleum	0.7	0.9	7.9	8.4
4. Wood, pulp, paper, and furniture	0.5	0.9	8.9	10.3
5. Textiles and clothing	8.4	11.0	21.2	25.5
6. Leather, rubber, and footwear	5.5	6.5	14.9	15.4
7. Metals	0.9	1.6	10.8	10.4
8. Chemical and photographic supplies	2.2	3.6	12.4	16.8
9. Transport equipment	4.2	5.6	19.9	13.2
10. Nonelectrical machinery	1.1	1.9	13.5	14.5
11. Electrical machinery	2.3	3.7	14.6	17.2
12. Mineral products; precious stones and metals	0.7	1.0	7.8	8.1
13. Manufactures, not elsewhere specified	1.4	2.0	12.1	9.2
Industrial goods (rows 4–13)	2.5	3.5	13.3	13.3
All merchandise trade	2.6	3.7	13.3	13.0

Note: Weighted averages, excluding trade within free trade areas. The applied rates are those for the base period; the bound rates are those applying after implementation. In some instances this means that the applied rates are higher than the bound rates.
Source: Finger, Ingco, and Reincke (1996).

Table 11.2 Tariff Escalation on Products Imported by Industrial Economies from Developing Economies

Product	Post–Uruguay Round bound tariff (percent)
All industrial products (excluding petroleum)	4.3
Raw materials	0.8
Semimanufactures	2.8
Finished products	6.2
All tropical products	1.9
Raw materials	0.0
Semimanufactures	3.5
Finished products	2.6
Natural resource–based products	2.7
Raw materials	2.0
Semimanufactures	2.0
Finished products	5.9

Source: GATT (1994a).

Table 11.3 Post–Uruguay Round Import-Weighted Applied and Bound Tariff Rates
(percent)

Country group or region	Applied tariff rate	Bound tariff rate
Industrial economies	4.0	4.7
Developing economies	13.1	20.8
Latin America and the Caribbean	10.1	18.6
East Asia and Pacific	9.8	16.6
South Asia	27.7	56.1
Other Europe and Central Asia	9.6	14.9
Middle East and North Africa	14.4	26.8
Sub-Saharan Africa	16.5	19.8

Note: Unweighted averages, excluding trade within free trade areas. The applied rates are those for the latest year available, generally 1997, 1998, or 1999. The data on applied rates cover 96 developing countries and 23 industrial countries. Data on bound rates were available for only 65 developing countries. See Appendix A, Table A.2, of this Handbook for country details on applied tariffs.
Sources: WTO, IDB CD-ROM 2000; WTO, *Trade Policy Review,* various issues; World Bank (2000e).

security and a perceived need for self-sufficiency. As a result, agriculture was effectively excluded from negotiations before the Uruguay Round. In developing countries high tariffs reflected import-substitution industrialization policies. By virtue of provisions for special and differential treatment, these countries were not required to make concessions in the early GATT rounds. As a result, they received little in return, so that many of their exports continue to face high tariffs.

The gap between bound and applied rates has much to do with autonomous reform programs

undertaken by developing countries in the 1980s and 1990s. It is also an outcome of the increasing prevalence of regional trade agreements (Crawford and Laird 2000), as well as the application of unilateral preferences such as those under the Generalized System of Preferences (GSP), the Cotonou Agreement (successor to the Lomé Convention), the Caribbean Basin Initiative, and special preferences to improve market access for the least-developed countries. When MFN bound rates are reduced in multilateral negotiations, the value of such preferences is decreased, and this may have led some

Table 11.4 Patterns of Protection in Manufacturing, 1995

| | Importing region | |
| | High-income economies | Developing economies |
Exporting region		
Import-weighted average tariffs (percent)		
High-income economies	0.8	10.9
Developing economies	3.4	12.8
World	1.5	11.5
Implied tariff paid (billions of U.S. dollars)		
High-income economies	16	93
Developing economies	23	57
World	40	150

Source: Hertel and Martin (2000).

negotiating power. Formula approaches that call for proportionately higher cuts on high tariff rates can help reduce tariff peaks and escalation (see Laird, 1999b; see also Chapter 53, by Panagariya, in this volume). A formula approach can also help overcome difficulties related to how to grant credit. Another option may be to carry out early reductions (that is, before the conclusion of a negotiating round) and to make deeper cuts in MFN tariffs on products of particular export interest to developing countries or to the least-developed countries, as was done on tropical products in the Uruguay Round. Prior to the Seattle Ministerial, some Asia-Pacific Economic Cooperation (APEC) countries proposed an "early harvest" of products for accelerated liberalization (see the analysis by Dee, Hardin, and Schuele 1998). Proposals have been made to reduce very low rates (nuisance tariffs) to zero. But deeper tariff cuts on raw materials and components than on finished goods can increase effective protection, producing a perverse result for resource allocation.

Simplification of the structure of tariff rates can increase transparency and help reduce distortions in trade and production, so that a negotiation can be used to restructure sectoral and fiscal policy. Most WTO members have a range of tariff rates—typically, zero for raw materials, a low to moderate rate for intermediate products, and higher rates for finished goods—but some countries have hundreds of different rates.

If agreed average cuts are import-weighted, as has been the case for industrial products in the past, countries may be able to avoid cutting rates on products subject to prohibitively high rates or

NTBs. One way to prevent such exceptions is to agree on a minimal cut on each tariff line. In the Uruguay Round agriculture tariff cuts were made on the basis of simple averages. Import-weighting was not a practical proposition because prohibitive nontariff barriers mean that some products are not imported.

Many tariff types are legitimate under the WTO. In addition to percentage or ad valorem rates, duties may be specific (for example, US$1.00 per kilogram), alternative (US$1.00 per kilogram or 10 percent, whichever is higher), or mixed (US$1.00 per kilogram plus 10 percent). Switzerland is exceptional in that all its rates, other than zero rates, are expressed in specific terms. Specific tariffs are often designed to offset low international prices for the affected product, in lieu of variable levies, which are prohibited under the WTO Agreement on Agriculture.[1] This practice is sometimes said to impart a bias against imports from low-cost suppliers—in most cases, developing countries. Ad valorem tariffs would be more transparent. Requiring members to provide information on the ad valorem incidence of other rate types would be useful.

Tariff quotas or tariff-rate quotas are tariffs that increase above a certain value or volume of imports. They are used for agricultural imports of commodities subject to minimum import requirements. For example, the duty for the first 1,000 tons of a product imported in a fiscal year may be 10 percent, but the duty after the first 1,000 tons might be 50 percent.[2] Some duties of this kind are also expressed as specific rates. The WTO Agriculture Agreement does not stipulate how tariff quotas are to be administered—that is, who gets to import at the in-quota or lower rate and who must pay the higher rate. To put the issue in perspective, among all WTO members 1,371 tariff quotas are in operation. Although in some instances the out-of-quota rate is not being applied even when imports exceed the quota amount, and average quota fill rates in 1999 were only about 50 percent, there are estimates that the out-of-quota rate exceeds 100 percent for some affected products (Elbehri and others 1999).

Nontariff Barriers

Strictly speaking, market access negotiations in the WTO are concerned only with tariffs. In the case of NTBs, which certainly affect market access, the main focus of negotiations is in the area of rules, which set conditions for the use of such measures. Examples include contingency protection (safeguards, antidumping, and countervailing measures), technical barriers (including sanitary and phytosanitary measures), local content requirements, subsidies, import licensing, state trading, and rules of origin.[3]

Under the WTO Agreement on Safeguards, voluntary export restraints were to be eliminated in return for some flexibility in the use of safeguards. There remain, however, some measures with very similar effects: production restraints (e.g., on aluminum and petroleum), sectoral consultations (automobiles), and the use of price restraints ("undertakings") as the outcome of antidumping investigations. Technically, any discussion of these cases would also come under the rules negotiations, one of the functions of which is to ensure that tariff liberalization is not undermined by NTBs.

There are a number of areas in which negotiations are designed specifically to reduce or eliminate NTBs rather than establish how they may be used. In the case of industrial products, the main NTBs are currently in the textiles and clothing area, and these are being eliminated as the sector is progressively integrated into GATT 1994.[4] In principle, no further negotiations on quota elimination should be required in this sector, but the fact that the main liberalization has yet to take place has given rise to fears that the industrial countries may be unable to meet their obligations under the WTO Agreement on Textiles and Clothing (ATC). (For further discussion on textiles and clothing, see Chapter 21, by Hanna Kheir-El-Din, in this volume.)

Agriculture

The main NTBs that directly affect market access primarily concern the agricultural sector and involve subsidies and tariff rate quotas (TRQs). Formally, under Article IV of the WTO Agreement on Agriculture, market access negotiations are strictly defined as the tariff negotiations, but market access will also be directly affected by further reductions in the use of domestic subsidies, which are already covered in the negotiations mandated by the Uruguay Round agreement.

To put the mandated negotiations into context, it is important to understand that before the Uruguay Round there had been little discipline in the agricultural sector. As a result of the round, agriculture was largely brought under the main WTO disciplines. Import measures had to be eliminated or converted to tariffs ("tariffied"), and the tariffs were then subject to progressive reduction commitments, except for rice and some staples that were subject to minimum access commitments—that is, TRQs. It was also agreed to reduce the level of domestic support, except for exempted "green-box" policies and de minimis amounts. Industrial countries were to reduce domestic support (the aggregate measure of support, or AMS) by 20 percent over 6 years, while developing countries were to reduce their domestic support by 13 percent over 10 years. The agreement also included reductions in outlays on export subsidies (for industrial countries, a reduction of 36 percent over 6 years, and for developing countries, one of 24 percent over 10 years) and in the volume of subsidized exports (reductions of 21 percent over 6 years by industrial countries and 14 percent over 10 years by developing countries). Special safeguards (increased duties) can be triggered by increased import volumes or price reductions (by comparison with average 1986–88 prices expressed in domestic currency). A peace clause, intended to constrain the use of countervailing measures until 2003, is sometimes seen as setting a time limit on the current negotiations.

Before the official launch of the mandated negotiations in agriculture, work had already begun in the WTO under an exercise on the analysis and exchange of information. The formal negotiations are conducted in special sessions of the WTO Committee on Agriculture, which was established by the WTO General Council in February 2000. The terms of the negotiations are laid out in Article 20 of the

Europe, 2.6 in Japan, and 2.9 in the United States (OECD 1997a). These NTBs, however, apply to clothing—a sector that is of great interest to developing countries, and one that will remain constrained by quotas until 2005 (see Chapter 21, by Kheir-El-Din, in this volume). In the case of agriculture, although the Uruguay Round led to tariffication of all NTBs (with the exception of rice in Japan), tariff rate quotas are often used; these involve two-tier tariff systems with out-of-quota imports subject to higher tariffs.

This chapter provides a brief description of the extent and importance of existing tariff peaks in the Quad, the preferential treatment granted to devel-oping countries for these tariff peak products, and the prevailing pattern of developing country exports.[1] It concludes with an assessment of the impact on developing countries of the elimination of tariff peaks by the Quad and with an evaluation of the initiatives by some OECD members to grant least-developed countries duty- and quota-free access to their markets. Examples include the EU "Everything but Arms" initiative discussed in Box 12.1 and U.S. actions to provide improved access to U.S. markets to Caribbean and Sub-Saharan African countries. The challenge will be to extend such initiatives to a broader set of poor countries.

BOX 12.1 THE EUROPEAN UNION'S "EVERYTHING BUT ARMS" INITIATIVE

In February 2001 the European Union (EU) granted duty- and quota-free access for all goods originating in least-developed countries (LDCs), with the exception of armaments. The "Everything but Arms" (EBA) initiative was enacted by Council Regulation 416/2001—amending European Community (EC) Regulation 2820/98—which applied a multiannual scheme of generalized tariff preferences for the period July 1, 1999, to December 31, 2001. The amendment extended duty-free access without any quantitative restrictions to 919 agricultural products originating in LDCs; more than half of these items were meat and dairy products, beverages, and milled products. The EBA entered into force on March 5, 2001.

The EBA was adopted as an amendment to the existing Generalized System of Preferences (GSP) scheme to ensure its compatibility with WTO rules. The basis for the EBA under the WTO is paragraph 2(d) of the Enabling Clause of 1979, which allows special treatment to be granted to LDCs in the context of any general or specific measures in favor of developing countries. Thus, at least from this legal point of view, the EBA initiative is tied to the existing GSP scheme. This fact, however, does not impose any constraint on the EU with regard to the scope and nature of the LDC preferential trade regime.

The EU also had to ensure the WTO-compatibility of the EBA by avoiding a constraint imposed by Article 174(2)(b) of the Lomé Convention. This article, which enjoined nondiscrimination among African, Caribbean, and Pacific (ACP) states, was eliminated by the Cotonou Agreement. The EU can now offer better market access to least-developed ACP states without extending it to ACP countries that are not in the least-developed category, as Article 174(2)(b) would have required. The EBA, like the existing GSP scheme, also allows for diagonal cumulation of origin between the LDCs, on the one hand, and, on the other, Association of Southeast Asian Nations (ASEAN) members, South Asian Association for Regional Cooperation (SAARC) members, and the EU.

There are several ways in which the EBA differs from the EU's GSP scheme. First, in contrast to the GSP, the EBA is not subject to renewal and revision and has no time limitation. The European Commission will review the functioning of the EBA in 2005, when amendments can be introduced if necessary. Second, new provisions allow the EU to introduce safeguard measures when imports of products originating in the LDCs increase massively in relation to the usual levels of production and export capacity. Specific safeguard measures apply especially with regard to sensitive products such as bananas, rice, and sugar should imports cause serious disruptions to the EU mechanisms regulating these products, in particular, the Common Agricultural Policy (CAP) and the ACP-EU protocols.

Product Coverage

All products are included in the EBA initiative. Only three products are not liberalized immedi-

BOX 12.1 (CONTINUED)

ately: bananas, rice, and sugar. Duty-free access for these products will be phased in as follows:

- *Bananas.* Duties are to be eliminated gradually over five years in equal 20 percent annual reductions starting in January 2002. All duties are to be eliminated by January 1, 2006.
- *Rice.* Liberalization will occur over four years, starting in September 2006 with a 20 percent reduction, to be increased to 50 percent on September 1, 2007, and to 80 percent on September 1, 2008. Elimination of duties is to be complete by September 2009. During the transition period, LDC rice exports will benefit from a tariff rate quota (TRQ). The initial quantities of this quota are to be based on best LDC export levels to the EU in the recent past, plus 15 percent. The quota will grow every year by 15 percent, from 2,517 tons (husked-rice equivalent) in the 2001/02 September-to-August marketing year to 6,696 tons in 2008/09.
- *Sugar.* The arrangements for sugar are similar to those for rice. Full liberalization will be phased in between July 1, 2006, and July 1, 2009. During the transition period, LDC raw sugar can be exported duty-free to the EU within the limits of a tariff quota, which will be increased from 74,185 tons (white sugar equivalent) in 2001/02 to 197,355 tons in 2008/09. The provisions of the ACP-EC Sugar Protocol will remain valid.

Safeguard Provisions

While the EBA initiative clearly breaks new ground in granting full market access for the least-developed countries, it also provides for mechanisms to avoid disruptions to the EU market. Under the EU's current GSP scheme, preferential tariff treatment may be temporarily withdrawn, in whole or in part, in the case of certain activities such as slavery, forced labor, export of goods made by prison labor, manifest shortcomings in customs controls on export or transit of drugs, failure to comply with international conventions on money laundering, fraud, or failure to provide the cooperation required for the verification of certificates of origin. Other circumstances qualifying for such a

withdrawal are manifest cases of unfair trading practices on the part of a beneficiary country or manifest infringements of the objectives of international conventions concerning the conservation and management of fishery resources.

A safeguard clause in Article 28 states that MFN duties on a product may be reintroduced if that product originating from a developing country is imported on terms that cause or threaten to cause serious difficulties to a EU producer of like or directly competing products. In examining the possible existence of such *serious difficulties,* the European Commission takes the following factors, among others, into account: reduction in market share of EU producers, reduction in their production, increase in their stocks, closure of their production capacity, bankruptcies, low profitability, and low capacity utilization, employment, trade, and prices. The EBA initiative modifies this scheme by:

- Adding to the grounds for the possible temporary withdrawal of preferences massive increases in imports into the EU of products originating in LDCs, in relation to their usual levels of production and export capacity. This addition will allow the European Commission to "react swiftly when the Communities' financial interests are at stake."
- Inserting a new paragraph in Article 28 of the GSP allowing for the suspension of the preferences provided by this regulation for bananas, rice, and sugar "if imports of these products cause serious disturbance to the Community markets and their regulatory mechanisms." Here it becomes clear that while the EU is generally ready to extend preferential market access to sensitive products, it also wants to provide for special safeguards regarding the three most sensitive ones. The Commission announced that whenever LDC imports of bananas, rice, and sugar exceed or are likely to exceed the previous year's level by more than 25 percent, the Commission will automatically examine whether the conditions for applying GSP safeguard measures are met.

Source: European Commission (2001); UNCTAD (2001).

Table 12.2 Tariff Peaks and Preferential Duty Rates, Quad Economies, 1999

Preferential trade agreements/GSP	Number of countries	Average unweighted preferential duty rate (percent)	
		Tariff peak products	All goods at HS six-digit level
Canada			
United States	1	7.1	1.6
Australia	1	28.2	7.8
New Zealand	1	28.2	7.8
Mexico	1	15.9	3.1
Chile	1	12.2	2.4
Israel	1	11.8	2.5
Caribbean countries[a]	18	23.3	4.3
GSP-only beneficiaries[b]	108	28.2	6.2
Least-developed countries[c]	47	22.8	4.4
Other countries (MFN rate)		(30.5)	(8.3)
European Union	15		
Eastern Europe and Middle East[d]	30	20.1	1.8
GSP-only beneficiaries[e]	42	19.8	3.6
Least-developed ACP countries[f]	37	11.9	0.8
Other ACP countries[g]	32	12.4	0.9
Other least-developed countries[h]	11	12.6	0.9
Other countries (MFN rate)[i]		(40.3)	(7.4)
Japan			
GSP-only beneficiaries[j]	127	22.7	2.3
Least-developed countries[k]	42	19.0	1.7
Other countries (MFN rate)		(27.8)	(4.3)
United States			
Canada	1	0.6	0.1
Mexico	1	1.6	0.3
Israel	1	0.6	0.1
Andean Pact[l]	4	14	1.7
Caribbean Community[m]	22	13.5	1.6
GSP-only beneficiaries[n]	80	16	2.4
Least-developed countries[o]	38	14.4	1.8
Other countries (MFN rate)		(20.8)	(5.0)

a. Includes 18 Caribbean countries or territories under Commonwealth Caribbean Countries Tariff.
b. Excludes eight developing countries: Albania, Aruba, Bosnia and Herzegovina, FYR Macedonia, Mongolia, Oman, Saudi Arabia, and Yugoslavia.
c. Excludes Myanmar.
d. Includes countries with reciprocal and nonreciprocal trade agreements with the EU.
e. Includes most developing economies in Latin America and Asia; excludes Hong Kong (China), Republic of Korea, and Singapore, which are non-GSP economies.
f. Includes 37 ACP and least-developed countries under the Lomé Convention.
g. Includes 32 ACP countries under the Cotonou Convention but not under the group of least-developed countries.
h. Includes 11 least-developed countries that are not ACP members.
i. Includes all industrial countries as well as Hong Kong (China), Korea, Singapore, and 14 transition countries.
j. Includes 127 countries; excludes Albania, Bosnia and Herzegovina, Estonia, Latvia, Lebanon, Lithuania, FYR Macedonia, Moldova, Vietnam, and Yugoslavia.
k. Excludes three LDCs: Comoros, Djibouti, and Tuvalu. Three others (Democratic Republic of Congo, Kiribati. and Zambia) are included in the GSP group.
l. Includes Bolivia, Colombia, Ecuador, Peru, and República Boliviariana de Venezuela under the Andean Trade Preference Act.
m. Twenty Caribbean countries covered by the Caribbean Basin Economic Recovery Act, as well as The Bahamas and Nicaragua.
n. Includes 80 developing countries or territories under the GSP scheme but excludes 29 other developing economies.
o. Based on the UN list of 48 least-developed countries but excludes 10 countries, including Senegal.
Source: WTO files.

granted to LDCs is quite small; their exports face an average tariff of 29 percent.

LDC exports to the world that are affected by Japanese tariff peaks include sugar (HS 17), raw hides and skins (HS 41), and footwear (HS 64). Of these three products, sugar is the only one for which almost no preference is granted. The 5 percent LDC preference margin for sugar brings the tariff faced by LDC exporters to 66 percent. Full duty-free access is granted for raw hides and skins, while for footwear an 80 percent preference margin is granted to LDCs, bringing the tariff down to less than 8 percent.

Effects of Eliminating Tariff Peaks in the Quad

Tariff peaks are important for all developing countries, but, as explained above, they are relatively more restrictive for LDCs. Unilateral initiatives to grant duty- and quota-free access have focused primarily on LDCs. Such preferential access will be beneficial to recipients but comes at the cost of greater discrimination against non-LDC developing countries. That is, there is likely to be trade diversion (see Chapter 55, by Hoekman and Schiff, in this volume). Studies of the impact of granting full, unrestricted access to LDC exports in Quad markets suggest that the increase in export revenue could be as large as US$2.5 billion, or 11 percent (see Table 12.3). Most of the increased export revenue for LDCs would be earned in Canada and the United

States. Exports from other developing countries would fall by some US$1.1 billion, which represents 33 percent of the total increase in LDC exports but only 0.05 percent of developing country exports. Thus, diversion is significant but does not add up to much, given the small share of LDCs in world trade.

The distribution of changes in export revenue across products and countries will vary across markets (Figure 12.1). In the case of the European Union, 65 percent of the increase in LDC export revenue is concentrated in sugars and confectionery (HS 17), with the primary beneficiaries being Malawi, Zambia, and Mozambique. The EBA initiative, however, will be applied to LDC exports of sugar only in 2009. In Japan, as well, most of the increase (90 percent) is in sugars and confectionery. For Canada and the United States most of the increase in exports occurs in apparel and clothing (HS 61 and 62) and, to a much smaller degree, in footwear, with Bangladesh expected to be the main beneficiary, given its large export potential in these sectors.

Conclusion

The gains from preferential access are conditional on the ability to redirect and expand exports, which requires the establishment of strong business relationships and a good reputation as a supplier in new markets. The benefits of preferential access are also heavily dependent on the extent to which other policies that affect market access constrain exports from LDCs. Rules of origin and the threat of contin-

Table 12.3 Effects of Granting Duty- and Quota-Free Access to Quad Markets to LDC Exporters
(millions of U.S. dollars)

	Canada	European Union	Japan	United States	Quad economies
Change in LDCs' exports	1,602	185	496	1,107	2,497
	(7.20)	(0.83)	(2.23)	(4.97)	(11.22)
Change in GSP beneficiaries' exports	558	–100	–292	–387	–929
	(–0.03)	(–0.01)	(–0.02)	(–0.04)	(–0.05)
Change in all developing country exports	1,013	72	204	654	1,362
	(0.03)	(0.00)	(0.01)	(0.02)	(0.04)
Change in imports by Quad economies	15	2	3	108	117
	(0.01)	(0.00)	(0.00)	(0.01)	(0.01)
Change in LDC welfare	1,159	122	332	915	1,694
	(0.67)	(0.07)	(0.19)	(0.53)	(0.99)

Note: Figures in parentheses are percentages of values at the base year (1996–98 averages).
Source: Authors' calculations.

13

LUIS JORGE GARAY S.
RAFAEL CORNEJO

RULES OF ORIGIN AND TRADE PREFERENCES

THE APPLICATION OF TRADE PREFER-ENCES, WHETHER UNILATERAL (SUCH AS the Generalized System of Preferences, or GSP) or granted as the result of free trade agreements (FTAs), requires guidelines that enable the origin of goods to be defined so as to ensure that preferences benefit only those products originating in the beneficiary countries. Preferential trade agreements therefore include origin regimes that stipulate the provisions and procedures for determining country of origin.

Commercial exchanges involve goods that are wholly obtained or produced in the exporting nation or that contain components from third countries. For the second type of merchandise, it is necessary to define the conditions, types, and amounts of imported components that these goods can contain and still be considered as originating inside the country or region to which preferences have been granted. The general approach taken in most jurisdictions is that the origin of a product is determined by the location where the last substantial transformation took place; that is, the country in which significant manufacturing or processing

occurred most recently. "Significant" or "substantial" is defined as sufficient to give the product its essential character.

Rules of origin aim at preventing what is technically known as *trade deflection*. This may arise when goods from third countries confront different tariffs in FTA member countries, creating an incentive to bring merchandise into the FTA through the member country with the lowest tariffs and then ship it as a duty-free item to countries in the FTA with higher tariffs. The same incentive is created by GSP regimes for firms located in nonbeneficiary countries. Requiring a minimum level of substantial transformation aims to prevent such practices by limiting the applicability of trade preferences to those goods that satisfy rules of origin.

Origin regimes can result in inefficient production and discrimination (by favoring the companies that are best able to adapt to and satisfy the requirements); an unequal distribution of benefits among factors of production, activities, and countries; and administrative and transactions costs.[1] Stringent rules of origin can severely restrict the sourcing of inputs from outside an FTA, thereby leading to investment diversion—decisions by multinational firms to locate production facilities within the region. If the region is not large and dynamic, this may negatively affect firms' efficiency and competitiveness (Barfield 1996; Winters 1997). The operational and administrative costs of certifying and verifying origin are potentially large and can increase efficiency losses. Net operating costs can be expected to rise with increased administrative complexity, lack of transparency, multiple qualification criteria, and the proliferation of "rules of origin families." In Europe the costs of collecting, managing, and storing the information needed for origin verification and administration equal about 3 percent of product prices (Garay and Quintero 1997).[2] The complexity of rules of origin regimes is illustrated in Box 13.1.

BOX 13.1 THE U.S. TRADE AND DEVELOPMENT ACT OF 2000

Gomi Senadhira

The U.S. Trade and Development Act of 2000 contains two important sections providing for preferential access to the U.S. market. Title I of the law consists of the African Growth and Opportunity Act (AGOA), which extends significant trade benefits to Sub-Saharan African countries. Title II contains similar preferences for Caribbean countries; these are not discussed here.

The AGOA recognizes that trade and investment can be powerful tools for promoting sustainable economic growth, and it provides a number of market access concessions to the countries of Sub-Saharan Africa (SSA). To be eligible to receive benefits, an SSA country has to be designated a beneficiary country by the president of the United States. Necessary conditions for this are that the SSA country has established (or is making progress toward) a market-based economy, the rule of law and political pluralism, economic policies to reduce poverty, a system to combat corruption and bribery, protection of internationally recognized workers' rights, and elimination of barriers to trade and investment. Beneficiary countries may not engage in activities that undermine U.S. national security or grossly violate human rights.

Under the AGOA, beneficiary countries receive preferential access for 1,835 tariff line items, in addition to the standard GSP list of approximately 4,600 items available to all GSP-eligible countries. This additional list includes a number of important products that were previously excluded from GSP benefits such as footwear, luggage, handbags, watches, and flatware. These benefits for AGOA-eligible countries would continue to September 30, 2008, seven years longer than the present extension of GSP benefits to the rest of the world. In recent years U.S. GSP benefits have been renewed every two years. The eight-year duration of GSP benefits

for SSA countries therefore provides greater security for potential investors. The act also eliminates the competitive-need limitations in the GSP program for AGOA beneficiaries. Finally, the AGOA countries receive significant benefits for apparel exports.

Apparel Provisions of the AGOA
Under the apparel provisions, SSA countries would get duty- and quota-free access for:

- Apparel assembled in SSA from U.S. fabric, formed from U.S. yarn cut in the United States.
- Apparel cut and assembled in the SSA from U.S. fabric formed from U.S. yarn and stitched with U.S. thread.
- Apparel made from African regional fabric (fabric formed in one or more SSA countries from U.S. or SSA yarn), subject to a tariff rate quota set at 1.5 percent of total U.S. apparel imports in the 12 months preceding October 1, 2000, to be increased over the next seven years by equal increments to a level of 3.5 percent by October 1, 2007.
- Apparel made in designated "lesser developed" SSA countries with a 1998 per capita income below US$1,500, from fabric of any origin, subject to the same tariff rate quota. This would only apply for a period of four years.
- "Knit to shape" sweaters from third-country yarn such as cashmere and merino wool.
- Apparel made from fabric or yarns not available in commercial quantities in the United States.
- Products that are hand-loomed, handmade, or folklore articles.

AGOA eligibility alone does not provide a SSA country with these benefits. To qualify for these concessions, a country must establish an effective

(continued)

added value and, in addition, a change in tariff heading. When substantial transformation cannot be measured by a shift in tariff classification, the MERCOSUR regime states that the price of third-country inputs, inclusive of cost, insurance, and freight (c.i.f.), shall not exceed 40 percent of the f.o.b. cost of the merchandise. Furthermore, MERCOSUR Decision 16/97 sets specific origin requirements for a list of goods from the chemical, iron and steel, data processing, and communications sectors, and these requirements take precedence over the general criteria. Although the MERCOSUR regime contains no provisions for differential treatment, agreements with Bolivia and Chile do provide for differential treatment in that they set less stringent requirements for goods from Paraguay and Bolivia.

The Andean Community has an origin regime similar to that of Resolution 78, and it also admits special requirements in exceptional cases. In addition, it grants Bolivia and Ecuador preferential treatment. The Andean Community used some special requirements in the 1970s as part of its import-substitution and industrial sector planning strategies. The Andean Community's origin regime, established by Decisions 416 and 417 of July 1997, introduced important provisions regarding origin administration. These stipulated in detail the functions and obligations of the member countries' competent government authorities in this area and specified procedures for requesting the General Secretariat's intervention and guidelines for its decisions. They also detailed the sanctions applicable to certification agencies and officers for issuing improper origin certificates and specified the requirements to be met by nongovernmental agencies empowered to certify the origin of merchandise. Finally, they regulated the criteria and procedures for setting specific origin requirements.

The NAFTA Regime

NAFTA, launched in January 1994, gave rise to a new type of regime for origin rules, with the following elements, among others:

1. It is a system of specific rules at the tariff-item level that are arrived at by combining some or even all of the three qualification criteria described above; frequently, there is more than one rule for determining a good's origin.

2. It applies changes of tariff classifications in a much more versatile fashion than do the other regimes. Classification shifts are not unique for all tariff classifications but are defined according to merchandise type broken down by chapter, heading, and subheading and, in some cases, even by tariff item (the HS eight-digit level of disaggregation). The different levels of tariff liberalization are used both to define the required changes in classification and to limit their scope by providing the option of excluding certain tariff levels from the main requirements. Slightly more than 40 percent of the existing tariff items use a movable classification shift for determining their origin, and a number of these goods also have more than one alternate qualification rule.

3. It uses the regional content criterion for around a third of all items, either alone or, more frequently, in combination with one of the other criteria. It establishes a minimum regional content value of 50 or 60 percent, depending on the method, and calculations use the net cost or transaction value method.

4. It includes concepts not used in earlier regimes, such as the de minimis clause, accumulation, and the introduction of self-certification by exporting companies.[3]

The NAFTA approach exhibits much greater selectivity, specificity, and detail than the general regimes of ALADI or unilateral trade preferences such as the GSP. This NAFTA level of detail can be seen in the official Mexican bulletin *General Rules for the Application of the Customs Provisions of the North American Free Trade Agreement,* in which the rules of origin run to almost 100 pages.

The Central American Common Market Regime (CACM)

The CACM regime is a combination of the ALADI and NAFTA systems. The main criterion is tariff classification change, but it is applied more flexibly than under ALADI Resolution 78. Instead of being applied uniformly at the HS four-digit level, it is measured in terms of changes in chapter, heading, and subheading. In a number of cases the CACM regime allows exceptions to be made to the primary change in tariff heading that is specified. Only with regard to some specific goods does it set additional specific criteria, such as regional content and technical requirements. To date, these have rarely been applied. Use is made of concepts such as the de minimis clause; there is no provision for differential treatment for less-developed countries.

The CACM regime also introduces a series of rules and procedures to ensure correct administration of and due compliance with the rules of origin. The use of tariff shifts as the basic criterion, but applied differently across the full range of tariff classifications, appears to be an attempt to combine administrative simplicity with greater detail and selectivity in the rules of origin applied to different types of goods.

Differences among Systems

The principal differences among origin regimes have to do with whether they follow uniform or differentiated application of the rules, apply multiple criteria, and use value-added tests.

Diversity

The three types of criteria used to determine origin can be employed uniformly or selectively. Thus, the tariff classification change criterion is applied uniformly in the ALADI regime at the HS four-digit level, regardless of the type of merchandise. In contrast, under NAFTA and G3 the required tariff change varies according to the good in question, and in different cases a change in chapter, heading, subheading, or even tariff item may be required.

Multiplicity

Although the regimes in force in the Americas include more than one criterion for classifying origin, they differ in the relative weights they assign to each. The origin regimes in MERCOSUR, the CACM, the Andean Community, and ALADI are basically defined in terms of the tariff classification change criterion or, alternatively, a given level of regional content; in some exceptional cases a combination of criteria is used for specific lists of goods. In contrast, the NAFTA and G3 regimes and some of Mexico's bilateral agreements are based on a multiplicity of criteria, which prevents any one criterion from being singled out as the guiding principle for determining origin. In part, this multiplicity reflects the high degree of detail and selectivity contained in "new-generation" agreements

Alternation

The regimes also differ in their application of the qualification criteria at the level of individual goods. Alternation is to be understood as the application of more than one rule in classifying the origin of a given good. In ALADI, MERCOSUR, the CACM, and the Andean Community alternation is uniform across all tariff classifications, with the additional feature that each rule is based exclusively on a single qualification criterion: for example, the first criterion is based on a change in tariff heading and the alternate one on a specific regional content value. In contrast, NAFTA, the G3, and the Mexican and Chilean bilateral agreements frequently offer a variety of alternate rules for determining a good's origin, without each rule necessarily being based on a single qualification criterion.

The set of alternate rules applicable at the individual item level is defined as a "rules of origin family," which, at least in principle, should stipulate equivalent demands in terms of substantial transformation. In practice, however, the levels of stringency within a family differ as a result of the different requirements of the criteria used to determine origin. If there are goods for which the implied degree of transformation varies between the alternate applicable rules, de facto inconsistencies and inequalities can arise among different types of companies in the FTA and its member countries. Similar consequences tend to arise when different rules of origin families are applied to goods that, in terms of their production techniques or economic nature, are strictly similar, or when a single rules of origin family is used to qualify goods produced through different processes.

Calculation Method

The method used for calculating regional content value varies among regimes. ALADI, MERCOSUR, and the Andean Community require the f.o.b. or c.i.f. transaction value of the merchandise to be used in calculating its regional or national content. These values are well known, clear, and published, and they require neither the exporter nor the customs authorities to keep special records or employ additional controls. NAFTA and some of Mexico's bilateral agreements use two alternate methods for calculating regional content: net cost and transaction value. Estimating the value of regional content

STEFANO INAMA

14

NONPREFERENTIAL RULES OF ORIGIN AND THE WTO HARMONIZATION PROGRAM

R ULES OF ORIGIN HAVE LONG BEEN CON-
SIDERED A TECHNICAL CUSTOMS ISSUE
having little bearing on trade policy. Determinations of origin may, however, have far-reaching
implications, with linkages to domestic disciplines
regulating the marketing of products to final consumers, the geographic denomination of goods, and
the definition of domestic industries. The impact of
rules of origin as a "secondary trade policy instrument" can only be fully grasped when they are considered in association with the primary policy
instruments that they support, such as tariffs, contingency protection measures, trade preferences,
and enforcement of health and safety standards.

Rules of origin are often associated with preferential trade regimes, in that satisfaction of origin
criteria is a precondition for the application of a
preferential tariff. (Preferential trade regimes are
discussed in Chapter 13 in this volume.) Nonpreferential rules of origin apply to trade flows that do
not benefit from tariff or other trade preferences.
One of the main differences between nonpreferential and preferential rules of origin is that the former must provide for an exhaustive method for

determining origin. In the case
of preferential rules of origin, if
the origin criterion is not met,
the preferential tariff will not be
applied; there is no need to fall
back on alternative methods. In
order to administer trade policy
measures in the case of nonpreferential origin rules, if the primary origin criterion is not met,
there must be an alternative
method for determining the
origin of the good. Thus, other
criteria are needed to define ori-
gin when the primary rule has not been met; customs administrations have to be able to determine
where goods come from. Such ancillary rules to
determine origin in cases where the primary rule is
not met are commonly referred to as "residual
rules."

The WTO Agreement on Rules of Origin

The WTO Agreement on Rules of Origin calls for a
Harmonization Work Program (HWP) to create a
common set of nonpreferential rules of origin. Preferential rules of origin are covered by a common
declaration, but they are not subject to the harmonization program. Article 1 of the agreement states
that nonpreferential rules of origin are to be utilized
to determine the origin of goods for the following
purposes:

- MFN tariffs and national treatment
- Quantitative restrictions
- Antidumping and countervailing duties
- Safeguard measures
- Origin marking requirements

- Any discriminatory quantitative restrictions and tariff quotas
- Government procurement
- Trade statistics.

A principal objective of the Agreement on Rules of Origin is to harmonize nonpreferential rules of origin (Art. 9) and ensure that they are applied equally for all purposes (Art. 3). The agreement embodies a built-in agenda for achieving this. Although the work program was to be completed within three years of the entry into force of the WTO (that is, in mid-1998), this did not happen—some say, because of the complexity of the issues.

The HWP is carried out by a technical committee that works under the auspices of the World Customs Organization (WCO) and the WTO Committee on Rules of Origin. As of mid-2001, negotiations were primarily conducted in the latter committee, as most of the technical aspects of the rules had become well understood. Article 9, paragraph 2(c) states that the technical committee is to develop harmonized definitions of:

"(i) wholly obtained products and minimal operations or processes;

"(ii) substantial transformation—based on the product concerned undergoing a change in tariff classification subsequent to being processed (transformed) in the country of export, and

"(iii) supplementary criteria, upon completion of the work under subparagraph (ii), in cases where substantial transformation cannot be determined on the basis of a change in tariff heading alone."

The Issue of "Equally for All Purposes"

Articles 1 and 3(a) of the WTO Agreement specify that on implementation of the HWP, WTO members shall "apply rules of origin equally for all purposes as set out in Article 1." Uniformity contradicts prior practices of some WTO members, and rules of origin are a novelty for most developing country members. To date, only 34 WTO members have notified nonpreferential rules of origin.

The possible implications of common rules of origin for the implementation of other WTO agreements such as that on antidumping have been a factor impeding consensus on the HWP. Concerns arose regarding how to maintain the integrity of certain trade policy measures or regimes pertaining to a particular product or product area. A recent submission by Japan on the relationship between harmonized rules of origin and labeling requirements for foods identified the problems that may arise from the implementation of the HWP, as well as other non-WTO agreements such as the Codex General Standard for the Labeling of Prepackaged Foods. Provisions contained in a non-WTO agreement may exceed what is required for rules of origin purposes, since the objectives are different. In the case of the Codex, the aim is consumer safety—something that goes beyond customs administration purposes.

A possible solution to this impasse suggested by the United States would be to agree that the provision on applying rules of origin "equally for all such purposes" does not necessarily mean members have "to use rules of origin for all such purposes." For some members, this à la carte approach would facilitate agreement on the HWP. For other members, however, such flexibility may greatly diminish the value of the HWP exercise, as it would impair the legal certainty and predictability that the agreement was designed to provide in this area. Developing countries, and especially least-developed countries, may find some attraction in a flexible interpretation, as they would then not be obliged to implement the results of the HWP. (The HWP might turn out to be excessively complicated for their import requirements and burdensome for their customs administrations to apply.) Exports originating in developing countries, however, would remain subject to the disciplines of the HWP when shipped to those WTO members that decide to apply the agreement. An alternative procedure suggested in submissions to the WTO is to conduct an examination of the possible implications of the HWP for other WTO agreements through communication with all the other WTO bodies responsible for the matters outlined in Article 1. This approach, although in principle attractive, would further limit the possibility of concluding the HWP work any time soon.

Impact of Alternative Nonpreferential Rules of Origin

The application of origin rules may have unexpected and unintended consequences for developing country exporters. In many instances, especially in the agriculture and processed foodstuffs sectors, origin may be attributed to another country as a result of relatively simple processing. This can have effects on the application of tariff quotas or of sanitary and phytosanitary measures. For example, if a rule of origin regarding manufacture of shoes from shoe parts is based on where assembly operations are carried out, and if assembly is carried out in many different countries, this will imply the production of "originating shoes" across many countries. Conversely, if origin rules state that origin depends on specific manufacturing operations such as the making of shoe uppers, from an "origin point of view" the production of shoes may become more concentrated, possibly facilitating the invocation of contingent protection measures such as antidumping. Depending on production and industrial strategies, industries will have different incentives in lobbying for alternative rules of origin.

To give another example, if a country is a big producer and exporter of cotton fabrics, which is commonly a "sensitive product" subject to quotas under the ATC, it may have an interest in ensuring that printing and dyeing are origin-conferring operations. In that case, all the cotton fabrics exported to third countries for printing and dying will change origin status once they are shipped out of the country. The fabric-producing country's exports will become less concentrated and specialized, possibly reducing the threat that exports of cotton fabrics will trigger contingent protection. Conversely, if printing and dyeing are not considered to be origin conferring, even if these operations are carried out in third countries this will have no effect on the origin determination of the fabric.

In some other cases, countries may be interested in "obtaining" origin even if the amount of working and processing carried out is minimal. This can occur with agroprocessing and foodstuffs. For instance, in discussions in the technical committee, one delegation argued that the drying and seasoning of imported meat was an origin-conferring operation. The domestic industry involved sold a dried meat product in the domestic market that usually fetched high prices, given consumer perceptions that this product had a distinctive character. Traditionally, the meat used also originated in a particular region. Local manufacturers, however, had begun to use imported meat. If the processing were to confer origin, the dried and seasoned meat obtained from imported fresh meat could legitimately be sold as originating in the region. Thus, domestic producers of dried and seasoned meat could use cheaper imported meat while retaining origin and labeling as high-quality regional products.

There is a close link between rules of origin and geographical indications. (The latter are also covered by Articles 22.1 and 23 of the Agreement on Trade-Related Aspects of Intellectual Property Rights, or TRIPS.) If the HWP applied equally to origin under TRIPS, there might be implications for products that are not produced in a specific region but do meet the origin requirements according to the HWP, and vice versa. For instance, some members have argued that making wine from imported grape must (unfermented juice) should be considered an origin-conferring operation. This proposal, if adopted, could have implications for the protection of geographical indications under TRIPS Article 23, since some wine producers could argue that they are producing originating Bordeaux because they are fulfilling the origin requirement laid down in the HWP. That is, making wine from imported grape must (from France, in this case) would be origin conferring. Not surprisingly, traditional wine producers have opposed this view, arguing that the production of wine is origin conferring only if the wine is made from grapes grown and harvested in the same country where the wine is made. A compromise proposal has been put forward that considers the production of wine an origin-conferring operation only if the whole process, from grapes to wine, is performed in the same country. This would allow grapes (but not grape must) to be imported.

In some cases a country may have an interest in "retaining" origin even if the exported product is processed in a third country before being sold to a final consumer. For example, Colombia argued in the technical committee that the processes of decaffeination and roasting were not origin-conferring operations. The United States, the European Union (EU), and Japan took the opposite view. If roasting and decaffeinating are considered to be origin conferring, most of the Colombian coffee roasted or decaffeinated in the EU and the United States could be marketed as EU and U.S. products. This could severely diminish the image value and marketing potential of Colombian coffee as a quality product with a distinct character and taste.[1]

To sum up, a major issue for countries with respect to harmonization of origin rules is to decide whether to "lose," "retain," or "obtain" origin. The difficulty is that this must be done by product or by categories of product; the best rule for each country may depend on considerations of industrial strategy or structure at the national and global levels.

The relationship between the compilation of trade statistics and harmonized rules of origin is another issue. Applying the same origin rules for both statistical and customs purposes is almost unprecedented in world trade. In most cases, import statistics are classified according to the country of origin as indicated in the invoice. This is, for the most part, the country of exportation and not necessarily the origin of the goods for customs purposes. Moving toward greater consistency between customs origin rules and collection of trade statistics could have significant implications for the measured magnitude of trade flows and trade balances.

There is also a strong linkage between customs rules of origin and marks of origin that are intended to inform consumers of a product's country of origin. The issue of the relationship between marks of origin (how a finished product is to be labeled before being marketed to final consumers) and origin for customs purposes is addressed in Article IX of GATT 1994. A change of the country of origin will also imply a change in the mark of origin. This can have important consequences for consumer choice, especially where brand names or goods of a certain quality are commonly identified with certain countries. Environmental or humanitarian concerns may influence consumer choice toward products from countries that are recognized as respecting human rights, labor laws, or environmental treaties. Although the globalization of production has rendered outdated the notion that a product is wholly produced and obtained in a particular country, consumers may still identify products of a certain quality with specific countries or geographic regions.

Secondary or Residual Rules of Origin

As noted above, nonpreferential rules of origin are aimed at assigning origin to all goods imported into a country. Thus, there must be an origin determination in all cases, as the customs authorities must be able to ascertain the origin of the goods in order to administer trade and other policy instruments. If the primary origin criterion (change in tariff heading or processing requirements) is not met, second-

ary, residual rules should be available to determine origin. Given the existence of multistage, multi-country manufacturing operations, failure to provide exhaustive residual rules would leave a loophole in the predictability of the harmonized set of nonpreferential rules of origin.

The basic question confronted by the technical committee is how to determine the sequence of the application of residual rules and their implementation; that is, how to specify what happens when the goods cannot be subject to the primary rule of origin and the residual rules come into play. Two basic approaches have been discussed. One approach, supported by the United States, is that if the primary rule is not met for a country, then the primary rule should be applied to countries farther up the production chain to ascertain whether the rule has been met in any of them. Only when the primary rule has not been met in any "preceding" country would the use of residual rules be warranted. This can be called the tracing-back option. A second approach, supported by the EU, would limit the utilization of the primary rule to the country where the last production process has taken place. Thus, if the primary rule is not met in the country where the last production process took place, residual rules should be utilized.

The issue, then, is to assess the potential implications of these alternative secondary rules. Under the tracing-back proposal, the customs administration would have to trace back, on the basis of the available documentation, the origin through the preceding countries. In some cases this procedure may be difficult, as it requires that origin certificates be produced for the different manufacturing stages the finished product has undergone. Commercial considerations may also be an impediment to the tracing-back method. For developing country exporters, producers, and administrations, the application of this rule demands a certain degree of customs cooperation. Moreover, the provision of relevant information and documentation may require an extensive knowledge of the rules and awareness of the possible implications on the part of exporters, producers, and customs administrations.

Under the EU approach, origin determination relies to a greater extent on the ability of the customs administration to determine origin at the time of importation. If the primary rule is not satisfied, the customs official will immediately have to resort to general residual rules, that is, value-added criteria. This approach also has significant implications, as it seems to empower the customs authorities to make a final origin determination at the time of importation.

In November 1999 a partial agreement was reached on this issue. The tracing-back approach was rejected for the most part but was retained in the residual rules and, to some extent, in the list of rules on wholly obtained products in Appendix II (that is, as an alternative to a value-added criterion). No final agreement has been obtained on the content and sequencing of the application of these residual rules.

Rules of Origin and Anticircumvention of Antidumping Actions

Once the HWP has been completed, the rules of origin may help resolve the issue of third-country anticircumvention actions in antidumping cases. These measures, which became controversial in the early 1990s, involve actions against imports of products subject to antidumping duties from countries not originally subject to such actions. Such anticircumvention actions were taken on the basis of claims that the firms previously found to be dumping had shifted to production facilities located in third countries. As was pointed out by the Republic of Korea, the WTO Agreement on Antidumping is not clear-cut on the issue of rules of origin since, in Articles 2.2 and 2.5, it refers to both "exporting country" and "origin country" (see G/RO/W/65).

Some countries have argued that the issue could be addressed through the use of harmonized residual rules of origin in cases of alleged third-country circumvention, coupled with Rule 2(a) of the Harmonized System.[2] In the absence of an agreement on the issue of third-country circumvention, a substantial number of WTO members, including not only the United States and the EU but also Latin American developing countries, have unilaterally adopted anticircumvention provisions. Thus, nonharmonized, nonpreferential rules of origin continue to be used to enforce antidumping duties and, consequently, to combat third-country circumvention.

Implementation Issues

Business life evolves at a faster pace than multilateral trade negotiations, yet customs and trade officials will always have to determine origin, apply the rules, and enforce them. This may be one reason why the elaboration of the harmonized rules has involved a level of technical detail and sophistication that is almost unrivaled by other WTO agreements. A basic issue is that the rules of origin that are being negotiated are tailored to the industrial and technological processes used in industrial countries and do not necessarily mirror the needs, abilities, and resources of developing countries and their customs administrations. The benefits of transparency and predictability of harmonized rules are certainly positive for the multilateral trading system. When translated into a WTO commitment, however, they may become an additional burden for administrations that are not adequately equipped.

Moreover, the WTO Agreement is silent on several issues related to implementation, such as certificates of origin. For instance, it is not clear whether, following the implementation of the HWP, WTO members may request certificates of origin for each import transaction, nor is it clear who should be issuing and certifying such certificates. The latter issue has already attracted considerable attention following a U.S. request for information on aspects of the German policy pertaining to certificates of origin. Apparently, release of certain goods in Germany and other EU member states was made subject to the presentation of a certificate of origin issued in the United States or to other related formalities. The United States had no mechanism for certifying determinations made by its local chambers of commerce and did not give legal recognition to these certificates or sanction their issuance. It therefore raised a number of questions concerning the consistency of this practice with the agreement and with the needs of a modern economy.[3]

Conclusions

It is impossible to determine the best rule of origin or the best proposal without being product-, country-, and industry-specific. The fact that the harmonization process involves some 10,000 specific products, each involving a certain industrial process, further complicates matters. That said, some general guidelines can be drawn from efforts to date to agree on rules of origin.

The most important inputs into the formulation of a national position on a specific rule are provided by domestic producers or by importers and exporters. The input of domestic producers is critical, as they are the only ones with detailed information on the use of imported inputs, the structure of the production chain, their own cost structure, and the implications of alternative origin rules for their competitors. Without this input, trade negotiators and customs experts cannot arrive at a sound negotiating position.

The question of the impact of "retaining," "obtaining," or "losing" origin of a product should be carefully evaluated at the country and subregional levels to better define the possible implications as regards other WTO agreements and the implications for origin marking, statistics, and so on.

Early consideration should be given to the implementation aspects of the harmonized rules of origin and especially to the requirement to apply these rules equally for all purposes. This latter requirement may have decisive and different implications, depending on the country and product involved and on the direction of trade (that is, import or export trade flows). As has been emphasized here, applying a harmonized set of rules is a sophisticated and technical affair requiring a highly trained administration and an informed private sector. The rules that will apply will largely be "inherited" from the institutional memory and domestic bodies of laws prevailing in the major trading nations. Most of the implementation burden can therefore be expected to fall on the developing countries. The difficulties in meeting the requirements of preferential rules of origin, especially where the issuance of certificates of origin is concerned, should be duly taken into account. The HWP should not result in a set of unnecessary administrative formalities that conflict with recent initiatives on trade facilitation.

Notes

1 In this specific case, it appears that Café de Colombia is a private trademark owned by a private federation.

2 The first part of Rule 2 (a) extends the scope of any heading referring to a particular article to cover not only the complete article but also that article incomplete or unfinished, provided that, as presented, it has the essential character of the complete or finished article. The second part of Rule 2(a) provides that complete or finished articles presented unassembled or disassembled are to be classified under the same heading as the assembled article. When goods are so presented, it is usually for reasons such as the requirements or convenience of packing, handling, or transport.

3 The matter was discussed at the Committee on Rules of Origin on May 18, 2001.

country of importation (for example, the invoice price), adjusted, where appropriate, to include certain payments made by buyers, such as cost of packaging and containers, assists, royalties, and license fees. Buying commissions may not be included in the transaction value, discounts obtained by sole agents and concessionaires must be accepted, and no add-ins or exclusions other that those provided for in the agreement may be made to the invoice price.

Customs may reject the transaction value by following the procedures laid down in the WTO decision on shifting the burden of proof when they have doubts about the truth or accuracy of the transaction value declared by the importer. In all such cases the agreement limits the discretion available to customs in deciding on the dutiable value, requiring that the value be determined by applying the following five methods, in the hierarchical (sequential) order in which they are listed:

- Value of identical goods sold for export to the same country of importation
- Value of similar goods sold for export to the same country of importation
- Deductive value calculated on the basis of the unit price at which identical or similar imported goods are sold in the domestic market, less applicable deductions for costs incurred within the country of import
- Constructed value computed on the basis of cost of production
- Finally, the "fallback" method described below.

In the case of identical or similar goods, consignments should have been imported at or about the same time as the goods being valued. In cases where value is to be determined on the basis of deductive value, the unit price of goods sold in the domestic market within a period of 90 days of importation has to be taken into account.

Where value cannot be determined under any of the first four approaches, other reasonable methods ("fallback") that rely on information available in the country of importation may be used. These should be consistent with GATT Article VII and with the provisions of the Customs Valuation agreement. For instance, rather than determining the value of goods by comparison with identical or similar goods imported from the same country of exportation, customs could consider the value of goods imported from other countries.

The agreement prohibits the determination of customs value on the basis of the selling price in the domestic market of the goods produced in the importing country; the price of goods in the domestic market of the country of exportation; the price of goods for export to countries other than the country of importation (third-country prices); minimum values; or arbitrary or fictitious values. Because, however, a large number of developing countries use "minimum values" to determine customs duties, particularly for products the prices of which fluctuate widely, the agreement allows developing countries to make a reservation enabling them to maintain these values for a reasonable period of time on a limited and transitional basis.

The agreement requires customs authorities to accept transaction values not only in cases of "arm's-length transactions" but also in instances where transactions are between "related parties." Such relationships may result, for example, from partnership, control by one company of the other, or transactions among parent companies and their subsidiaries or affiliates. In all these cases the agreement urges customs authorities not to reject customs value unless they consider that the relationship has influenced the value declared by the importer. It further provides that customs must accept the declared value if the importer demonstrates, on the basis of prices charged in transactions between "unrelated parties" for identical or similar goods or on the basis of deductive or computed value arrived at in accordance with the provisions of the agreement, that the value declared reflects the correct value of the goods.

Problems and Issues Relating to the Implementation of the Agreement

The Agreement on Customs Valuation allows developing countries to delay application of the agreement for a transition period of five years after the entry into force of the WTO. For developing countries that were not members of the Tokyo Round code, this period expired on January 1, 2000. For countries that have acceded to the WTO since 1995, the five-year period is counted from the date of accession. The agreement provides that the Committee on Customs Valuation may, on request, agree to grant an extension of the transition period. As of early 2001, all industrial countries were applying the agreement. About 23 developing and transition economies that acceded to the WTO after 1995 are in the process of changing over to the transaction-based valuation system, and another 11 countries have been granted an extension or have submitted requests for one. For the remaining 25 or so countries, many of which are in the least-developed group, no definite information is available on their plans to change over from their existing valuation systems to the WTO system, although the transition period has expired.

There are three major reasons for the difficulties developing countries confront in implementing the Customs Valuation agreement. First, many countries do not feel any urgency about changing over, as they have no feeling of ownership toward the agreement. Most countries were not directly involved in the decisions requiring them to abide by the agreement's obligations. As argued by Finger and Schuler (2000), the agreement was "imposed on them in an imperial way with little concern for what it will cost [them to change over from BDV to the new system], how it will be done or if it will support their development efforts."[5]

Second, and more important, not only do developing countries not see any immediate advantages; they are apprehensive that the changeover may result in loss of revenue. Customs revenue still generates a relatively high proportion of total revenue in many developing countries; for some least-developed countries it could be 30 percent or higher.[6] The possibilities of raising additional revenue though other direct or indirect taxes to compensate for the loss are nonexistent or limited.

Third, customs officials are apprehensive that the application of the WTO standards may create practical problems because of the differences in trading environments and the absence in developing countries of computer systems and databases that can be used for price comparison purposes.

These fears are not unfounded. Proposals to make the agreement more responsive to the needs of developing countries have been made in the context of more general discussions in the WTO on the problems of implementing WTO agreements.

To persuade developing countries that have not yet started to apply the valuation agreement to change over to the system, a two-pronged approach at the international level can be considered. First, proposals to improve and further clarify the agreement should be examined and the necessary changes adopted. Second, and more crucial, technical assistance in this area must be broadened and reoriented to create confidence among assistance-receiving countries that the adoption of the system will result in full collection of revenue due and will facilitate rapid clearance of imported goods.

Implementation Issues and Possible Solutions

As noted above, the agreement lays down five standards on the basis of which customs value may be determined when customs authorities decide not to accept the transaction value. The first two methods call for determination of value on the basis of the transaction value of identical or similar goods imported at about the same time. For a number of developing countries, particularly least-developed countries, small economies, and other low-income countries, imports are spaced over time because of the relatively small domestic demand, and there is usually a significant gap between import consignments. Moreover, import trade is often dominated by a few importers that determine the countries and firms from which they want to import. Consequently, there are greater possibilities for collusive deals or informal understandings on prices between importers and the exporting firms.

In many such cases value cannot be based on prices for identical or similar goods, and the customs authorities will have to turn to the other two methods: deductive value (based on price for sale in the domestic market), and constructed value (based on cost of production). The first is costly for customs and is time consuming; from importers' point of view, it could result in delays in customs clearance. The second method requires cooperation by the producer in the exporting country and for this reason will ordinarily be used in transactions between related parties where the price is determined on the basis of transfer pricing.

In most cases, therefore, value must be determined on the basis of the last method—the "fallback" method. Although no definitive information is available, it appears that developing countries applying the agreement use the fallback method to determine customs value for a relatively high proportion of transactions. Some of these countries have suggested that in order to facilitate determination of dutiable value under this method, the "residual restrictions" on the type of prices that could be used should be removed. In particular, they have proposed that the prohibition on determining value on the basis of the

requesting information allege that fraud has been committed, as the industrial country governments are otherwise prohibited by law from furnishing information on prices (WTO, WT/GC/M/56). It has also been argued that because of budgetary constraints on customs departments in industrial countries, it would be difficult to provide the required price information if requests started pouring in from a large number of countries.

The foregoing should not be construed to imply that countries which have not yet taken steps to apply the agreement should wait until solutions are found to these practical problems. All countries are obliged to implement the WTO valuation system, and the transition period that applied to developing countries has expired. However, the difficulties discussed above do point to the need for provision of effective and adequate technical assistance.

Technical Assistance

Technical assistance to help developing countries improve their customs procedures is provided by international organizations and countries on a bilateral basis. Among the international organizations that are most active in the customs area are the WCO, UNCTAD, the IMF, and the World Bank. UNCTAD and the WTO, as well as organizations such as the Asia-Pacific Economic Cooperation (APEC) and the Commonwealth Secretariat, have programs that focus specifically on assisting countries in adopting the WTO agreement. Initially, the emphasis of these programs was almost entirely on explaining the rules, supported by case studies and simulations, and on providing assistance in reforming national legislation. Although such programs were found useful in improving customs officials' understanding of the rules of the system, they were far from effective in allaying apprehensions that the Uruguay Round decision on shifting the burden of proof would not be sufficient to enable customs to deal effectively with undervaluation or other fraudulent practices. Some of the new programs therefore emphasized on-the-job training at customs ports, under which senior customs officials obtained practical training in how to handle such cases effectively.

In addition to assistance provided under these WTO-focused programs, technical assistance for least-developed and small economies must provide support for computerization, modernization, and reform of customs procedures. Building up the comprehensive databases that are required for ascertaining whether goods are undervalued is not possible without computerization. The adoption of the ASYCUDA customs software developed by UNCTAD would also assist these countries in streamlining and reducing customs forms and procedures.

Technical assistance programs should recognize that valuation is only one of the many functions of customs. The emphasis placed on this function in the past in the technical assistance provided by international organizations such as the WTO and the WCO and by the countries providing assistance on a bilateral basis was directed toward enabling countries to fulfill their WTO obligations, not necessarily toward general modernization and reform of customs clearance methods and procedures. Some programs failed even to recognize that without computerization and well-developed databases on prices it would be difficult for customs administrations of countries where undervaluation is widely prevalent to apply the agreement's rules.

This is not the case with the assistance provided by institutions such as the World Bank and the IMF, which have a wider mandate. Such projects, however, can involve high costs. The estimated cost of a project in Tanzania, for example, was US$8 million to US$10 million over three years (Finger and Schuler 2000). Covering all least-developed countries, low-income countries, and small states under comprehensive programs of this kind would involve significant outlays.

A related question that needs to be addressed is whether programs aimed at assisting countries to apply WTO rules should also provide support for these countries to apply the standards and recommendations of the 1999 WCO Kyoto Convention. The convention is expected to provide a blueprint for procedures that customs administrations could adopt for customs control and facilitation of clearance (see Box 15.2). The WCO is arranging seminars and courses to familiarize customs officials with the provisions of the convention and to facilitate its acceptance. Although many developing countries participated in the negotiations to revise the convention, opinion at the national level among both customs and trade associations appears to be divided on the extent to which it is possible for developing countries with entrenched customs corruption to apply all the procedural standards the convention lays down. For instance, it is generally believed that it may be possible for all developing countries to adopt and apply standards relating to the UN layout key for documentation, payment of duties and taxes, cooperation with trade associations, and the establishment of procedures for appealing decisions taken by customs administrations. The same cannot be said of some other standards such as those requiring customs officials to ensure that they carry out physical inspections on or verify the prices of consignments only as warranted by properly conducted risk assessment, or to allow "authorized persons" with a record of compliance with customs requirements to clear goods by providing minimum information and to pay duties on the basis of self-assessment.

BOX 15.2 THE INTERNATIONAL CONVENTION ON THE SIMPLIFICATION AND HARMONIZATION OF CUSTOMS PROCEDURES: 1999 REVISION OF THE KYOTO CONVENTION

In 1999 the WCO completed a full revision of its 1973 Kyoto Convention. The goal of the changes was to provide customs administrations with a modern set of uniform principles for simple, effective, and predictable customs procedures that also achieve customs control. The revised convention is intended to be the blueprint for standard and facilitative customs procedures in the 21st century. This revision was necessary because of the radical changes in trade, transport, and administrative techniques that have taken place since the original adoption of the convention.

General Annex
The General Annex contains the core procedures and practices for clearance of goods that are common to all customs procedures. Acceptance of the annex is an obligatory condition for accession and implementation by contracting parties. The annex, which contains 10 chapters, covers areas relating to:

- Clearance of goods
- Payment of duties and taxes
- Customs cooperation
- Information to be supplied by customs, and appeals in all customs matters
- Areas of concern to both customs administrations and the trading community.

The annex also deals with customs control, including risk management, audit-based controls, administrative assistance between customs administrations and from external organizations, and the use of information technology, which provides the key to keeping procedures simple while ensuring adequate customs control.

No reservations may be entered against the standards and transitional standards set forth in the General Annex. In recognition, however, of the fact that many countries may not be able to apply a number of the standards immediately, the revised convention provides a transition period during which present and new contracting parties are to make any necessary changes in their national legislation. Contracting parties have up to three years to implement the standards and five years to implement the transitional standards.

Specific Annexes
The revised convention has 10 Specific Annexes containing a total of 25 chapters and dealing with the following customs procedures:

- Annex A. Formalities prior to the lodgment of the goods declaration; temporary storage of goods
- Annex B. Clearance for home use; reimportation in the same state; relief from import duties and taxes
- Annex C. Outright exportation
- Annex D. Customs warehouse; free zones
- Annex E. Customs transit; transshipment; cabotage
- Annex F. Inward processing; outward processing; drawback; processing of goods for home use
- Annex G. Temporary admission

(continued)

previously confronted customs administrations in obtaining information from exporting countries.

8 The establishment of such an arrangement would also help countries using preshipment inspection companies secure such information and reduce their dependence on the companies.

9 The relevant GATT articles include Article X, Publication and Administration of Regulations; Article VII, Fees and Formalities connected with Importation and Exportation; and Article V, Freedom of Transit.

BRIAN RANKIN STAPLES

16

TRADE FACILITATION: IMPROVING THE INVISIBLE INFRASTRUCTURE

NATIONAL CUSTOMS AUTHORITIES ARE HAVING TO PROCESS EVER-HIGHER VOLUMES of trade with the same or a declining number of employees, at the same time as traders are demanding faster clearance for their goods and increased administrative efficiency in all programs related to international imports. The Internet and e-commerce are transforming shipments that once would have been transported in a single container and cleared on a single entry into dozens of individualized shipments, each requiring separate customs documents and clearance procedures. This is a major challenge for customs authorities and for express couriers with customers who expect goods to be cleared immediately.

Not only are trade volumes growing steadily; because of foreign direct investment, there is also dramatic growth in trade transactions between related parties. Imports and exports increasingly take place between the same corporate entity. The result is to heighten the visibility of unnecessary transactions costs to transnational corporations that are under intense competitive pressure to reduce these costs, primarily through trade facilita-

tion initiatives. The complexity of international trade is increasing, as well. Whereas previously the primary objective of international corporations was to identify the most cost-effective location for producing a finished product, today the intense pressures of globalization have forced multinationals to identify the most cost-effective locations for the production of the sub-assemblies that go into a final product. These commercial patterns have led to an explosion in regional free trade agreements around the world. Such agreements usually feature complex and confusing rules of origin, placing considerable additional administrative burdens on both the public and private sectors.

In addition to the greater volumes and complexity of trade, there is the issue of trade velocity. Product life cycles are now measured in months, not years, and modern supply chain management techniques have increased the use of "just-in-time" manufacturing, global production sharing, and outsourcing. Trade now moves, and must move, at higher speeds than ever before. In this environment, businesses simply cannot afford to have imported or exported goods tied up for weeks or even days because of unnecessary or antiquated trade formalities. The interaction of all of these issues and factors has led to heightened awareness of the importance of trade facilitation in attracting trade and investment.

Trade Facilitation: The Plumbing

What exactly is trade facilitation? Although initiatives such as improvement of transport infrastructure, trade liberalization, and trade promotion do, in a sense, facilitate trade, they do not constitute what is known today as trade facilitation. Rather, trade facilitation involves reducing all the transactions costs associated with the enforcement, regulation, and administration of trade policies. Trade facilitation, by its nature, is technical and detailed. It has been referred to as the "plumbing" of international trade.

The objective of trade facilitation is to reduce the cost of doing business for all parties by eliminating unnecessary administrative burdens associated with bringing goods and services across borders. The means of achieving this objective are the modernization and automation of import procedures to match established international standards. The meaning and implications of trade facilitation have changed since as recently as a few decades ago. Trade facilitation in previous generations revolved around attempts to harmonize different regimes or to establish an element of mutual recognition between different customs and related policy regimes. Today, the WTO and various World Customs Organization (WCO) conventions set forth a common set of international standards or customs good practices for all countries. The current challenge is, much more than in the past, one of implementation and of convergence in procedures and customs operations based on these international norms. From a trade facilitation viewpoint, asymmetrical customs regimes create uncertainty and, therefore, costs for international traders.

It should be emphasized that use of the term "trade facilitation" does not imply abandonment of efforts to improve trade compliance. On the contrary, trade facilitation, using modern risk analysis techniques, allows compliant importers access to improved, automated import procedures and gives customs authorities the opportunity to concentrate resources on noncompliant traders.

International Agreements and Programs

The World Trade Organization. A number of international agreements have direct implications for trade facilitation. In the WTO these fundamental tools of international trade regulation include the Harmonized Commodity Description and Coding System (HS), the Customs Valuation agreement (discussed in Chapter 15, by Rege, in this volume), and the Agreement on Rules of Origin (discussed in

Chapter 14, by Inama). These agreements determine the tariff classification of an imported product, its country of origin, and its value for duty purposes. The HS is a legal and logical international product nomenclature developed through the Brussels-based WCO and introduced by international convention on January 1, 1988. Contracting parties have committed to apply the HS uniformly at the six-digit level, which covers 1,241 headings. Although the HS is primarily designed for tariff classification purposes, it is also used extensively to determine the goods subject to import and export controls, freight tariffs, the application of (or exemption from) value-added tax regimes, trade statistics, and origin. The HS provides a common "trade language" for all public and private actors in the international trade arena, and the concept of trade facilitation is dependent on a complete understanding and mastery of the HS.

Other WTO agreements that have an effect on the trade facilitation agenda include:

- The Agreement on Import Licensing Procedures, which is designed to ensure that the process of administering import-licensing systems is nondiscriminatory and neutral and does not restrict trade
- The agreements on Technical Barriers to Trade and on Sanitary and Phytosanitary (SPS) Measures, which are discussed in Chapter 41, by Wilson
- GATT Articles V (on freedom of transit), VIII (calling for the simplification of fees and formalities related to the importation and exportation of goods), and X (requiring the timely and comprehensive publication of all laws, guidelines, and decisions that may affect imports or exports and the establishment of judicial or administrative tribunals to review customs administration and decisions)
- The Agreement on Preshipment Inspection (PSI).

Trade facilitation became the subject of WTO discussions in 1997, following the 1996 (Singapore) ministerial meeting. At the Doha ministerial meeting in 2001, it was decided to launch negotiations in 2003, subject to consensus on the modalities of negotiation. Any such negotiations will have to draw on the work of numerous other specialized bodies, the most important of which are discussed briefly below.

The World Customs Organization. Of all the international organizations, the WCO's activities and mandate are the most closely aligned with the issue of trade facilitation. The WCO, founded in 1953, has a membership of 142 economies. Its objective is to increase the efficiency and effectiveness of customs administration around the world by reviewing the technical aspects of customs programs and sharing the results of these studies cooperatively with customs administrations. A major international convention designed to promote the standardization and simplification of customs procedures worldwide is the International Convention on the Simplification and Harmonization of Customs Procedures (the Kyoto Convention), which contains general provisions and special annexes dealing with customs procedures. The convention, originally established in 1973, underwent a major revision in 1999, resulting in improved provisions for automation, electronic commerce, postentry or audit-based reviews, and risk management techniques. The revised Kyoto Convention is the most comprehensive existing instrument for promoting international trade facilitation (see Chapter 15, by Rege). Many in the private sector would like the WTO to eventually incorporate the Kyoto Convention, or at least related principles, into its structure, thereby making such provisions binding and enforceable.

The WCO maintains a customs reform and modernization program (CRM)—an evolving technical assistance product that supports customs reform through training in diagnostic study and in customs needs analysis. The program helps domestic customs authorities implement the required changes that have been identified and evaluate their impact on trade facilitation and customs compliance. Another major instrument is the 1993 Declaration Concerning Integrity in Customs (the Arusha Declaration), which addresses the issue of corruption within customs administrations. The Arusha Declaration is indirectly linked to the CRM and the revised Kyoto Convention in that it promotes standardized customs procedures, electronic commerce, and improved relations between customs brokers and customs.

The WCO is responsible for literally dozens of additional programs, guidelines (such as the Express Consignment Guidelines), resolutions, norms, recommendations, and conventions (including the HS). A particularly important instrument is the Istanbul Customs Convention on Temporary Admission (1993), which deals with temporary admission of goods, means of transport, and animals.

United Nations Agencies. The United Nations Conference on Trade and Development (UNCTAD) is actively involved in trade facilitation and encourages the input and participation of developing economies in trade facilitation initiatives. UNCTAD's Automated System for Customs Data and Management (ASYCUDA), a customs software program, is used in more than 70 developing countries. ASYCUDA simplifies and automates customs functions with a view toward increasing revenue collection, speeding clearance of cargo, and improving data collection and dissemination. Much of UNCTAD's trade facilitation activity has involved the transport sector. Transport initiatives include port development; development of an electronic transport management tool, the Advance Cargo Information System (ACIS); and the concept of national trade and transport facilitation committees that bring together all transport stakeholders within a country to create and promote policies which enhance the efficiency of trade facilitation.

In October 1994 the UN hosted a ministerial-level International Symposium on Trade Efficiency, held in Columbus, Ohio. The focus of the symposium was customs procedures and other microeconomic features that prevent full realization of the potential trading benefits negotiated in the WTO. At the symposium, a set of detailed recommendations, referred to as the Columbus Declaration, was adopted. These recommendations have become critical guidelines in the pursuit of trade facilitation. The symposium also established UNCTAD's Trade Point Global Network, a program that aims to create approximately 180 "trade points" in 109 countries. These trade points will be electronically linked to national centers for trade facilitation and will act as providers of trade-related information and data.

Another relevant UN body is the Center for Facilitation of Procedures and Practices for Administration, Commerce, and Transportation (CEFACT-UN/ECE). Since 1960, this organization has pursued the harmonization and automation of customs procedures and information requirements and it issued the internationally recognized UN/ECE Trade Facilitation Recommendations. CEFACT is perhaps best known for its work on electronic data interchange (EDI), a form of electronic commerce that uses a structured exchange of data between two parties, and for the development of the UN Electronic Data Interchange for Administration, Commerce, and Transport (EDIFACT). EDI and EDIFACT have become important instruments for reducing customs paperwork and exchanging trade-related information between parties that typically handle international trade transactions (for example, insurance firms, customs, freight forwarders, and customs brokers). In addition, the United Nations Commission on International Trade Law (UNCITRAL) has developed significant conventions on the international sale of goods, the carriage of goods by sea, and arbitration rules, as well as the UNCITRAL Model Law on Electronic Commerce.

Regional Integration Initiatives. A number of regional efforts have been undertaken to facilitate trade. Two major trade facilitation initiatives under the North American Free Trade Agreement (NAFTA) are the Canada-U.S. Shared Border Accord and the Heads of Customs Conference (HCC). The Shared Border Accord, signed by Canadian and U.S. customs and immigration agencies, creates a set of common objectives for a joint approach toward trade facilitation and trade compliance. The HCC holds regular trilateral meetings of Canadian, Mexican, and U.S. authorities to review common customs issues, including enforcement cooperation and ways to improve the processing of the cross-border movement of goods. For example, the HCC endorsed the North American Trade Automation Prototype, which uses EDIFACT syntax and is designed to facilitate trade by standardizing data elements and electronic customs procedures.

With the launching of the Osaka Action Agenda in 1996, members of the Asia-Pacific Economic Cooperation (APEC) committed to standardizing customs requirements throughout the region. In 1997 APEC trade ministers agreed to align national norms with international standards and to recognize each other's national standards. Recognizing that simplification and harmonization of customs procedures can make a major contribution to trade facilitation, ministers noted the importance of finding technological solutions to expedite clearance of frequent travelers. An example is the project for an APEC business travel card.

The European Union (EU) has concluded customs cooperation and mutual assistance agreements with several countries. These agreements cover the simplification and computerization of customs operations, the free flow of trade and of enforcement information, and a common approach, wherever possible, to customs valuation. Trade facilitation has also figured on the agenda of the Group of Seven countries; an example is an effort in 1997 to standardize and simplify customs procedures.

Trade facilitation is a major focus of the Free Trade Area of the Americas (FTAA), as well. The FTAA has developed a series of recommendations, known as business facilitation measures, that incorporate trade facilitation principles such as electronic compatibility and risk analysis.

The Private Sector

Most of the nongovernmental entities that actively support trade facilitation programs are, not surprisingly, international transport organizations. They include the International Express Carriers Conference, the International Air Transportation Association, the International Chamber of Shipping, the International Road Transport Union, the International Federation of Freight Forwarders Associations, and the International Federation of Customs Brokers Associations. The International Chamber of Commerce (ICC), based in Paris, is an important nongovernmental actor in trade facilitation and has pursued customs simplification and harmonization since the early 1920s. It promotes harmonized business practices through a variety of instruments, including the Commission on International Commercial Practices, the Standing Committee on Extortion and Bribery, and the ICC Incoterms, which are standard trade terms and definitions for use in international contracts. The ICC, in conjunction with the WCO, also administers the ATA Carnet System for the temporary entry of goods. The ICC has issued a set of 60 international customs guidelines relating to a wide variety of trade facilitation matters. These include the reduction of paperwork and the increased use of electronic commerce; the introduction of risk assessment techniques (preclearance and postclearance audits); and professional training for customs employees.

The ICC was instrumental in having the issue of trade facilitation introduced at the 1996 Singapore ministerial conference of the WTO. There, ministers directed the WTO Council for Trade and Goods to draw on the work of other relevant international organizations in the area of simplification of trade procedures to assess the scope for WTO rules in this area. The ICC has encouraged the WTO to concentrate on customs modernization as an essential complement to WTO rules on customs valuation and to establish a WTO working group on customs modernization. It has also called for harmonization of nonpreferential rules of origin, greater reliance on preshipment inspection (discussed in Box 16.1), and political support for making the revised Kyoto Convention a binding multilateral agreement.

BOX 16.1 INCREASING THE EFFECTIVENESS OF PRESHIPMENT INSPECTION SERVICES

Preshipment inspection (PSI) refers to the verification of unit prices and to the examination and reporting of the quantity and quality of exports before they are shipped to the importing country. PSI can help control over- or underinvoicing of imports, misclassification of imports, undercollection of taxes on imports, and misappropriation of donor funds and can assist with monitoring of origin, compliance with national regulations and tariff exemption schemes, trade facilitation, and consumer protection. PSI services are provided by private companies in the exporting country. Thus, PSI can be thought of as a temporary quasi-privatization or contracting out of selected customs functions to meet specific objectives. It should not be viewed as a substitute for an effective program of customs modernization and institutional reform, which is the proper route to long-term gains in efficiency and growth. Because institution building takes time, PSI can play a useful interim role in three main areas:

Disbursement verification. One motivation for PSI is to monitor the use of donor funds. Where governments have poor statistical capacity, PSI can provide useful evidence.

Revenue collection. Probably the most important reason that governments use PSI is to deal with inefficient or corrupt customs administrations. (Revenue collection shortfalls of up to 50 percent are reported to have occurred in some countries.) The effectiveness of PSI in this regard depends on how well it is implemented. Although reported revenue savings generally exceed PSI fees, which are about 1 percent of the value of inspected goods, case studies suggest that the information provided by PSI companies has often been disregarded; customs administrations often do not want the services because they reduce available rents. Unless governments consistently use a reconciliation system and act on the information generated, PSI will not contribute much to revenue collection. To ensure sustainable revenue collection, customs modernization and institutional reform are also needed, and the strategy should specify how PSI services will be phased out over time (Low 1995).

Trade facilitation. Opponents of PSI often argue that PSI hinders trade by creating additional costly steps for traders that may duplicate control functions imposed by customs administrations. The Indonesian Chamber of Commerce, however, has argued that PSI facilitated trade by speeding up the customs clearance process.

Overall, experience suggests that if PSI is to make a positive contribution, several conditions are essential:

- Transparent procurement rules for the preshipment inspection contract
- Preshipment inspection values and classifications that are an integral part of import documents
- Good use of provided services (with reconciliation by the ministry of finance, at a minimum)
- Arbitration provisions to settle disputes swiftly without holding up goods
- Enhanced competition for service provision and fee setting.

Competition among service providers (split contracts) can reduce fees but could increase transactions costs for users. Serial competition (bidding for a time-bound monopoly franchise, either at the country level or within a certain area) can avoid conflicts of interest by eliminating

(continued)

BOX 16.2 (CONTINUED)

time for export consignments to 10–20 minutes. This dramatic improvement was achieved through three changes:

- The implementation of a single-point clearance mechanism, allowing exporters to go straight to the dockside with their documents instead of having to go to customs offices separately and then having to match documentation to cargo at a later stage.
- The introduction of selective inspection based on risk assessment instead of discretionary physical inspection of consignments. Customs inspects only 10 to 15 percent of shipments, using clearly specified risk criteria. In addition, lack of statistical information is no longer a justification for holding up a consignment.
- The introduction of a binding, comprehensive manual of procedures setting out all customs rights and responsibilities in export clearance. This manual is published, so that exporters and their agents know what the rules of the game are.

Source: Prepared by the volume editors, based on World Bank, "Ethiopia Export Development Strategy" (1997).

- As mentioned earlier, it makes no sense to simply transform outdated and unnecessary customs procedures from a paper format to an electronic format. That is, trade facilitation requires customs reform, and reform implies modernizing and streamlining customs programs to international standards, which are primarily found in the Kyoto Convention.

Common Problems and Rules of Thumb

In June 1994, in a speech before the Customs Cooperation Council (later renamed the WCO), Vito Tanzi, director of the IMF's Fiscal Affairs Department, identified the following major problems in trade facilitation and customs reform:

- *Out-of-date customs procedures* that have not kept pace with developments in transport and technology.
- *Inadequate legislation* that makes it difficult to introduce the changes required to support new ways of doing business, and administrations that often use excuses related to legislation to delay or fail to adopt new systems or procedures instead of working to change the legislation.
- A belief that *computerization is the answer to all problems*, with little thought to understanding the role of computers, the need to simplify procedures, and the use of information produced by computerization to control operations effectively.
- *Inadequate attention to the organization and staffing needs of a modern administration;* many administrations accept passively civil service rules, including controls on organization structure, job classification, and salary levels, instead of striving for control of their own organizations.
- *Lack of understanding of the need for coordination and cooperation between tax and customs administrations.*
- *High levels of corruption* that plague many administrations, causing loss of tax revenue and economic costs.

Tanzi went on to outline solutions and ways forward.

Make customs administrations technology based. The eventual goal is paperless processing systems that include electronic reporting of import and export transactions through electronic data interchange; selective checking based on risk assessment techniques supported by extensive computerized databases; periodic declaration and payment; and increased application of postrelease controls. All of these procedures are already operational in many countries. Countries with less developed infrastructures will encounter difficulties. Yet almost every country has industries such as airlines and banking in which sophisticated technology is already operational. It is, therefore, not unrealistic to expect such technology to be applied in the customs environment.

Rely more on postrelease audits. Experience shows that reliance on postrelease audits yields better results than traditional controls. An IMF technical assistance mission found that an audit office with a staff of 22 had issued assessments totaling US$70 million over a five-year period, whereas there were virtually no results from more than 350,000 physical inspections of containers, employing hundreds of staff, over the same period. Little thought had been given in this case to reallocating staff from the unproductive physical inspection activities to postrelease audit. Of course, countries with a well-developed administration and a more sophisticated trading community will be able to move more quickly to a postrelease audit system of control than countries in which the administration has inadequate human resources or where bookkeeping standards in the trading community are low.

Forge a closer working relationship with the tax department and exchange information and data on the foreign trade activities of importers and exporters. These measures can help improve revenue assessment. The tax department needs to know the amounts of value-added tax (VAT) paid on imports, and it needs to know that export goods have actually left the country. In some cases there are benefits to joint audits by the customs administration and the tax department, particularly for value-added taxation.

Promote service orientation and good relations with the trading community to improve compliance. These goals can be achieved through clear, transparent procedures; regular meetings between customs officials, importers, brokers, freight forwarders, and port and airport authorities; joint training sessions and seminars; establishment of services offices; and dissemination of information. Often, customs administrations in developing countries do not provide sufficient information to the trading community.

Inculcate professionalism and a high level of integrity. Both can be more easily developed through increased autonomy of the customs administration, meaning the ability to control budgets and implement changes, as well as through accountability for performance and the requirement to seek out and remove corrupt officials.

Getting There

An efficient customs administration must be flexible and able to respond quickly to the needs of government. It is not enough to introduce sophisticated technology; this alone will not guarantee success.

For the administration to function well, all its components must be in order: its operational procedures; its organizational structure and management systems, including information systems, supervisory systems, and internal control; its human and financial resources; and its legislative basis.

Comprehensively redefine the operational role and the procedures of customs. It is time for many customs administrations to rethink the way they are doing business. New control strategies need to be introduced that result in minimal interference with trade yet ensure proper enforcement of fiscal and trade laws. Experience has shown that importers are more willing to pay what is due if procedures are efficient and customs has a service-oriented attitude.

Adopt innovative and flexible management systems. This involves decentralization of responsibilities and decisionmaking and more autonomy and accountability for administrators in the field. Headquarters should concentrate on central management functions, including administrative policy, strategic planning, review of the operational systems, analysis of performance, and internal audit.

Strive for autonomy in the management of resources. Decisions related to human, physical, and financial resources should be the responsibility of the administration. Autonomy must, of course, be combined with greater accountability through performance evaluation.

Privatize functions that can be effectively performed at lower cost by the private sector. Laboratory services, receipt of duty and tax payments, and development and operation of computer systems are all activities that could and perhaps should be carried out by the private sector. Warehouses should not belong to or be operated by customs, although this still happens in some countries.

Invest in human resources. Traditional approaches to recruiting and training will have to change. Methods that rely mainly on recruitment at lower levels and on learning on the job need to be altered if the administration is to keep pace with developments. If customs administrations are going to rely in the future on technology- and audit-based systems, different skills will be required.

Establish firm management control, in particular as it relates to integrity. Integrity in an organization requires a clear, well-articulated code of conduct, willingness to take disciplinary action, and effective internal control systems.

Elements of the Trade Facilitation Toolbox

Trade facilitation is an objective; comprehensive reform of customs and related import requirements are the means of achieving this objective. Customs reform does not take place in isolation but in a larger context that includes other considerations, such as transport policies, and other actors, such as importers and carriers. Recently, in an explicit recognition of all these factors, the director general of the International Express Carriers Conference published an audit methodology (Raven 2000) containing detailed questionnaires intended to supplement personal interviews during a trade facilitation audit. Such an audit should be the first step taken by countries concerned with reducing trade costs.[1]

Conclusion

Every year, the private sector spends considerable sums of money to design and develop seamless supply chains for intercompany transactions and for transactions with suppliers and customers. National import and export requirements are a major obstacle to achieving the seamless supply chain. In this sense customs is vital to the flow of international trade in goods, which totals US$6 trillion each year. Pursuing the objectives of trade facilitation on the national level will make the domestic public and private sectors more efficient and will also play an important role in securing and attracting foreign investment. Clearly, for many countries, achievement of trade facilitation objectives will be a long-term process requiring substantial technical and financial assistance. In order to determine what role the WTO could usefully play to attain national facilitation objectives, countries must start by defining these objectives and determining where reforms are needed.

Note

1 Individual questionnaires focus on forwarders/agents/customs brokers/multimodal transport operators; exporters; importers; shipping lines; road carriers; airlines; express operators; ports; airports; border-crossing points; customs; commercial banks; exchange control/central banks; preshipment inspection agencies; chambers of commerce; and departments of trade/external trade. Further information and tools, including the audit, can be obtained from the Trade and Transport Facilitation Website, <wbln0018.worldbank.org/twu/gfp.nsf>.

MARI PANGESTU

17

INDUSTRIAL POLICY AND DEVELOPING COUNTRIES

INDUSTRIAL DEVELOPMENT IS AN INTE-
GRAL PART OF ANY ECONOMY'S GROWTH
strategy. Most countries pursue some kind of industrial policy, although their objectives and approaches may differ radically and may change over time.
Given the changing global and domestic environment, developing countries need to reassess the
options open to them for conducting an effective,
WTO-consistent industrial policy.

Objectives and Scope of Industrial Policy

The economic literature and the lessons from
implementing industrial policy emphasize that an
effective industrial policy or strategy needs well-
defined objectives, justification, and scope. The
World Bank has provided a working definition of
industrial policy as "government efforts to alter
industrial structure to promote productivity based
growth" (World Bank 1992).[1] This definition is useful because it focuses on the objective of economywide factor productivity growth rather than on
merely changing the structure of industrial outputs
or dealing with certain sectors. Industrial policy is
not limited to the manufactur-
ing sector; it also encompasses
the processing of agricultural
and mining products, as well as
services industries, both of
which sectors add value to manufactures.

In practice, industrial policy
often has multiple objectives,
including short-term employment, increased output, more
even income distribution, more
equal regional distribution of
economic activity, and enhanced
technological capacity. There are often also noneconomic objectives, including national pride and
prestige and the perceived need to promote "strategic" domestic industries. These objectives are further confused to the extent that many developing
countries are concerned about foreign ownership
and how it can affect domestic capabilities.[2] It is
important to pursue an industrial policy that has
limited and clearly defined objectives, as there may
not be sufficient policy instruments to meet multiple objectives. Moreover, different objectives may be
inconsistent with each other.

Justifying Industrial Policy

The economic case for government intervention
designed to achieve long-run productivity improvements rests on the need to correct alleged market
failures stemming from externalities, missing markets, or other failures, while taking into account
potential side effects on other sectors in the economy. The traditional economic argument for providing government assistance to certain industries is to
protect infant industries.[3] Import protection in the

form of a tariff or a subsidy based on the output of firms (the two instruments have an equivalent effect on output of a particular industry) is justified on the basis of some dynamic externality such as learning-by-doing or on-the-job training that reduces costs. Under this rationale, only learning processes external to the firm should be assisted, since the firm cannot obtain rents or profits from such training and will thus not invest in it.

There are important qualifications to the infant industry argument. First, the reductions in cost over time should compensate for the higher costs during the period of assistance. Second, the provision is not for blanket assistance to all firms in an industry; the existence of an externality and provision of the assistance should be linked to performance by the recipient (for example, to increased efficiency or cost reduction) and the assistance should be phased out over time. Third, the appropriate instrument for realizing the positive externality from the expansion of domestic industry may not be a tariff or a subsidy, both of which are output based. A more appropriate policy is a subsidy related to the process, job, or product that creates knowledge or learning.

The appropriateness of policy instruments follows a more general theme in the literature on government intervention (see Bhagwati 1971; Corden 1974). Each externality or market failure calls for a tax subsidy whose base is the variable that generates the externality or market failure, and the tax subsidy rate will be the rate that has the optimal effect. Any tax subsidy other than the optimal tax subsidy causes what Corden (1974) called by-product effects, which impose undesired costs elsewhere in the economy.

The economywide effects of intervention in one industry also need to be borne in mind. One way to do this is to focus on the effective rate of protection, which takes account of the impact of a tariff on both inputs and outputs. For instance, a tariff on an input will cause the effective protection of the downstream user to decline (see Box 17.1).

Another economic argument for government intervention—what is known as the second-best argument for tariffs or subsidies for some goods—has to do with the presence of "unremovable" distortions in the form of tariffs or other import protection.[4] In practice, intervention to correct such distortions poses several problems. First, it is not clear why the preferable (first-best) policy of removing the distortion cannot be implemented. Second, the correct determination of the second-

best policy requires the unrealistic requirement of perfect knowledge of all aspects of the economy so that the net effect of the intervention can be known. Third-best interventions made in ignorance of the true values of some behavioral parameters may lead to further distortions and reduce welfare.

Other justifications for industrial policy rest on the rationale of technology development. The appropriate policy under that rationale would call for technology-based intervention, not an output-based intervention such as subsidies, or for assistance for technology development and policies to encourage foreign direct investment (FDI), which is an important vehicle for the transfer of technology. (See Chapter 19, by Bora, and Chapter 34, by Saggi, in this volume.)

Instruments of Industrial Policy

In practice, countries have used a wide range of instruments in the name of industrial policy. These can be categorized as external, product, and factor market interventions.

External market interventions involve protecting domestic industries from imports, using instruments such as import tariffs, quotas, licensing, and local content programs, as well as export promotion measures to assist industries to catch up and break into new markets. Common export promotion instruments are export subsidies, export promotion zones, and subsidized credit (sometimes tied to export targets).

Product market interventions to promote competition in domestic markets include competition policy (to ensure fair competition between domestic players as well as for foreign players) and domestic market entry regulations.

Factor market interventions include policies such as performance requirements and restrictions on FDI designed to influence the operations of foreign affiliates so that the host country realizes a net benefit from FDI (UNCTAD 1999a). Factor market interventions in the capital market and the financial sector are aimed at correcting financial market imperfections, promoting infant industries, and protecting or phasing out declining industries. These measures include setting up development finance institutions, providing direct capital subsidies to selected industrial enterprises, furnishing capital subsidies and capital assistance to declining or mature industries and providing priority access to credit (often at subsidized rates) by requiring financial institutions to lend to

BOX 17.1 NOMINAL AND EFFECTIVE RATES OF PROTECTION

The nominal rate of protection (NRP) can be defined as

$$NRP = (P - P^*)/P^*$$

where P is the domestic tariff-inclusive price of a good and P^* is the free trade price. As the latter cannot be observed in practice, most empirical studies take the world price as a measure of P^*. The effective rate of protection (ERP) can be defined as the proportional increase in value added per unit of a good produced in a country in relation to value added under free trade (no protection). The magnitude of the ERP depends not only on the nominal tariff on the final product concerned but also on the tariffs applied to the inputs used and the importance of those inputs in the value of the final product. A simple formula for calculating the ERP is

$$ERP = (V - V^*)/V^*$$

where V is the domestic value added per unit of the final good (including the tariffs on that good and on its inputs) and V^* is value added under free trade. Value added per unit, in turn, is defined as the gross value of output minus the cost of inputs used in production: $V = t_f P_f - t_i P_i X$, where t_f and t_i equal 1 plus the tariffs on the final good and on inputs, respectively; P_f and P_i are the prices; and X is the amount of input used to produce a unit of the final good. Value added at free

trade prices is the same, except that in this case tariffs do not exist (the value of t is 1).

For example, suppose 1 ton of steel is worth US$1,000 on the world market. To produce it, a factory has to buy 1 ton of iron ore at a world price of US$600. Assume, for simplicity, that nothing more is needed for steel production. Under these circumstances, the value added per ton of steel in the factory will be US$400. If a 20 percent nominal tariff rate is imposed on steel imports and there is no tariff on iron ore, the effective rate of protection in those circumstances will be

$$(1,200 - 600)/400 = 1.5, \text{ or } 50 \text{ percent.}$$

The ERP in this example is more than double the 20 percent NRP on steel. If no tariff is imposed on steel but a nominal tariff of 33 percent is imposed on imports of iron ore, the ERP would be

$$[1,000 - (600 + 200)]/400 = 0.5, \text{ or } -50 \text{ percent.}$$

This example illustrates that an NRP of zero does not necessarily imply that trade is undistorted. As another example, assume that cocoa beans account for 95 percent of the production cost of cocoa butter. The imposition of a 5 percent nominal tariff rate on cocoa butter would then imply an effective rate of protection for the cocoa butter industry of 100 percent.

Source: Hoekman and Kostecki (2001).

particular sectors or types of companies. Intervention in the labor market may have efficiency and equity objectives. The former have to do with human resource development through education and training; the latter include minimum wage requirements and social safety net schemes.

Box 17.2 gives examples of the types of industrial policy instruments used in the Republic of Korea and Japan in the early phase of their industrialization.

Evolution of Industrial Policy

The approach to industrial development and the range of instruments used have evolved over time as a result of changes in development paradigms and

in the external environment. For the sake of concreteness, this section focuses on examples from East Asia, but much of what is said applies to all developing countries.

Industrial policy in East Asia has evolved over the past three decades (Table 17.1) as import substitution has given way to export orientation and, subsequently, to development of a knowledge-based infrastructure. Shifts in policy approaches and instruments have been influenced by internal factors such as the size of the market, the need to adjust to adverse shocks, the ineffectiveness of import-substitution industrialization strategies, and the need to attract FDI for technology and to gain market access. Policy has also been influenced by exter-

and now endeavor to provide an environment conducive to the development of competitive industries and to enhance the economy's flexibility in responding to changes. Table 17.2 provides a summary of the policies pursued by East Asian economies just before the 1997 financial crisis. The response to that crisis reinforced the need for a more comprehensive approach to policy reform, to some extent mandated by IMF reform packages. Countries not supported by IMF programs have also been induced to pursue similar reforms. [5]

Multilateral Rules Regarding Use of Industrial Policy Instruments

An important question concerns the extent to which WTO provisions constrain the policy measures that members can use to protect domestic suppliers and promote exports and transfer of technology. This section contains brief summaries of the major WTO rules regarding industrial policy instruments. Many of these are discussed in greater depth in other chapters of this book.

Tariffs, Antidumping, and Safeguards

Most developing countries have undertaken tariff reduction programs in the past two decades. They have also undertaken to bind many of their tariffs, although frequently at relatively high tariff rates that provide considerable scope for raising applied tariffs (see Chapter 54, by Francois and Martin, in this volume). Although the average level of tariff protection has declined, there continue to be peak tariffs in "sensitive" industries in both industrial and developing countries, and the dispersion of protection remains substantial in many countries.[6]

Import protection can also be imposed through antidumping or safeguard measures, which are often used by industrial countries to protect declining industries. The WTO Antidumping Agreement imposes disciplines on the use of antidumping by countries and contains a number of provisions aimed at reducing the extent to which antidumping can be used against developing countries that are trying to develop their exports.[7]

Export Promotion and Export Subsidies

The Agreement on Subsidies and Countervailing Measures (SCM) prohibits export subsidies by countries with incomes per capita above $US1,000 and lays out rules for the use of countervailing measures to offset injury to domestic industries caused by foreign production subsidies.[8] The SCM agreement covers financial contributions made by or at the direction of a government that provide a benefit to a specific enterprise, industry, or region.[9] Subsidies that are conditional on exports are prohibited, as are subsidies that encourage the use of domestic rather than imported inputs. Taking action against subsidies requires a determination that subsidies exist and have a negative effect on the trade of another member. This is done by showing that there is harm to another member in the form of injury, serious prejudice, or impairment and nullification of benefits.[10] The SCM agreement and its provisions relating to developing countries are discussed in greater detail in Chapter 18, by English and De Wulf, in this volume.

The SCM agreement has important implications for industrial policy. Take, for example, the case of Korea, which has been notorious for its use of targeted subsidies. Before 1995, Korea offered 26 different types of subsidies, totaling about 2.5 trillion won per year. In 1995 it reduced the number to one subsidy to small and medium-size enterprises, only 15.2 billion won in amount (WTO 1996b). In contrast to the voluntary Subsidies Code negotiated during the Tokyo Round, all countries are bound by the WTO agreement, and the SCM agreement extends to subnational governments. It should be noted, however, that the disciplines on subsidies constrain primarily export subsidies; constraints on production subsidies are weak. For developing countries, the SCM agreement is a two-edged sword: it contains a number of loopholes that allow them to continue to use subsidies to promote industrial policy objectives, but these also apply to industrial countries. Thus, developing countries have no prospect of using subsidies to gain a competitive advantage vis-à-vis industrial countries.

The Agreement on Trade-Related Investment Measures

Under the Trade Related Investment Measures (TRIMs) agreement, a number of investment performance–related measures that have an effect on trade were to be notified and eliminated by January 2001 (January 2003 for least-developed countries). The trade-related performance requirements that

Table 17.2 Policies and Measures for Promoting Exports in Asia

Type of measure	India	Malaysia	Bangladesh	Philippines	Thailand	Korea, Rep. of	Singapore	Indonesia	Hong Kong (China)	Japan
1. Measures affecting production										
Industrial development policy										
General	Yes	Yes	No	Yes	Yes	Yes	Yes	No	Yes	Yes
Specific/industry targeting	Yes	Yes	Yes	Yes	Yes	No	Yes	Yes	No	—
Strategic/domestic	Yes	Yes	Yes	Yes	No	No	Yes	Yes	No	—
Export industry	—	—	Yes	Yes	Yes	No	Yes	No	—	—
Support measures										
Import protection	Fall	Yes	—	Yes	Yes	No	No	Yes	No	No
Price controls	Fall	Yes	—	No	—	No	No	Yes	No	—
Investment regulations	Fall	—	—	Fall	—	No	No	Fall	No	—
Credit subsidies/facilities	Yes	Yes	Yes	—	Yes	Yes	Yes	Yes	Yes	Yes
Manpower training	—	Yes	Yes	Yes	—	Yes	Yes	—	Yes	Yes
Investment incentives										
Deregulation	Yes	Yes	—	—	Partly	Yes	—	Yes	—	—
Tax concessions										
Holiday/exemptions	Yes	Yes	Yes	Yes	Yes	Yes	Yes	—	—	—
Reduced rates	Yes	Yes	Yes	Yes	Yes	Yes	Yes	—	—	Yes
Accelerated depreciation	—	Yes	No	No	No	Yes	Yes	—	—	Yes
Production subsidy										
Input subsidy	Yes	Yes	Yes	No	Yes	Yes	No	Yes	—	Yes
Assistance for R&D	Yes	Yes	Yes	Yes	Yes	Yes	Yes	Yes	Yes	Yes
Pricing and marketing arrangements	Yes	Yes	Yes	Yes	Yes	Yes	No	Yes	—	—
Regional assistance	Yes	Yes	Yes	Yes	Yes	Yes	Yes	No	—	Yes
Adjustment assistance	Yes	Yes	No	No	Yes	Yes	Yes	No	Yes	Yes

(continued)

Implications of WTO Rules for Industrial Policy

Some common features of the agreements that discipline the use of government policy to promote particular industries deserve to be highlighted in order to understand the impact on industrial policy instruments under the present agreement, as well as in the future.

First, the agreements take a trade, not a balance of payments, approach to disciplining policies. Since nondiscrimination is the cornerstone of the WTO system, any nonborder policy that affects trade in goods and services (that is, by resulting in discrimination) is subject to discipline or requires an exemption.

Second, the rules are ownership neutral. Apart from the GATS and TRIPS, in which a national treatment standard is applied to covered investments, disciplines on policies such as subsidies and local content protection do not distinguish between foreign affiliates and domestic enterprises. What is important is the "trade effect" of the instrument. This means that countries seeking to apply a particular policy to foreign-owned firms must find a provision in an agreement that allows the use of the policy; they can then apply it to a foreign firm as long as there is no "trade effect."

Third, policies for promoting industries (designed to stimulate investment or export growth) are restricted to generic instead of specific policy instruments. This has the effect of leveling the playing field for international trade by not allowing countries to develop specific industries through specific policy instruments.

Finally, the approach to S&D treatment in the WTO has typically been limited to transitional arrangements, complemented by de minimis provisions (see Chapter 49, by Oyejide, in this volume).

Conclusion

Shifts in development paradigms, technologies, and multilateral rules imply that an effective and WTO-consistent industrial policy for developing countries in the 21st century must be comprehensive, rather than target specific sectors. Recognition of the importance of complementary policies for ensuring competitiveness has shifted the policy focus toward enhancing the efficiency of infrastructure, improving human capital formation, and creating an environment that is conducive to investment and innovation. Moreover, because development of the manufacturing and resource-processing sectors depends on the existence of an efficient services industry, regulatory reform and liberalization must span the services sector.

Multilateral rules are developing in line with the shift toward the use of more generic policies for promoting industrial development. Since export subsidies can no longer be used to promote exports, policy should move in the direction of reducing fiscal and procedural constraints on exports (Laird 1997), trade facilitation, and implementation of non-sector-specific (generic) policies to make the country more competitive. The effect of the WTO rules is not to eliminate the role of government but to shift its emphasis toward the supply side. Policies related to infrastructure, human capital formation, innovation, and diffusion of technology are now critical for export competitiveness. These policies need to be complemented by stable exchange rates that do not penalize or favor exports and by a competition policy that promotes rivalry among producers that contest the domestic market, including foreign companies. These are generic prodevelopment policies that are not confined to—and do not favor—particular industries or producers.

The appropriate response to fears of anticompetitive behavior by foreign companies is not to impose performance requirements and restrictions but to put in place an effective national competition law to ensure fair competition. Many countries have begun to introduce or are preparing to introduce competition laws. The crucial issue here, however, is having the right institutions and mechanisms, able to implement the law objectively and to conduct the necessary investigations. Given capacity constraints, this process will take time in many developing countries. It is therefore important to focus on liberalization of trade in services, domestic regulatory reform, FDI, and other factor markets and to ensure that policies in these areas are subject to WTO rules and disciplines. One advantage of the WTO rules in this context is that they are neutral between foreign and domestic producers, helping to ensure that domestic and foreign producers are able to compete on equal terms.

There is still considerable scope for using industrial policy instruments such as tariffs (within bound rates); subsidies for regional development, R&D, and the environment; and export promotion measures such as credit and insurance schemes at subsidized rates, concessional tax and duty provisions, and export-processing zones. Developing countries intending to use such policies (or seeking to extend transition periods to allow the use of other, WTO-inconsistent policies) need to assess the extent to which policies favoring particular producers are in their national interest. At the same time, the appropriate transition period for changing to a more generic policy stance needs to be based on a realistic assessment that reflects the country's development strategy and the need to build up institutions, capacity, and capability. Finally, the pursuit of industrial policies needs to be subjected to the criteria identified at the beginning of this chapter: clearly defined objectives; a determination that the policy instrument is the most appropriate one for meeting the objective; and implementation that responds to clear criteria and is transparent, preferably with clear performance and exit requirements.

Notes

This chapter draws on Bora, Lloyd, and Pangestu (2000).

1 Martin and Mitra (2001) show that the productivity growth rate in agriculture is higher both on average and for groups of countries at different stages of development.

2 For a discussion of how foreign ownership matters in the context of development, see UNCTAD (1999c).

3 See Kemp (1964) for the first careful statement of the infant industry argument; also see Baldwin (1969).

4 See Lipsey and Lancaster (1956) for the first theoretical exposition; see Lloyd (1974) and Hatta (1977) on the nature of the

second-best set of tax subsidies. Discussion of other second-best instruments such as local content can be found in Rodrik (1987); Greenaway (1992); Chao and Yu (1993); Richardson (1993); Morrissey and Rai (1995); and Moran (1998). For a discussion of export subsidies, see Harris and Schmitt (1999).

5 In the case of the crisis-affected countries that were under an IMF program—Indonesia, Korea, and Thailand—the reforms undertaken have been comprehensive in terms of liberalization of market access in goods and services, and for FDI and competition policy. Implementation is still at issue, but the steps taken have been dramatic.

6 It is useful to distinguish between sunset and infant industries. The former are industries that are declining; the latter are industries that are expanding and, owing to market failures, require protection from competition.

7 See Chapter 22, by Finger, who notes that these instruments are increasingly being used by developing countries; see also Laird (1997).

8 The agreement applies only to nonagricultural products; the WTO Agreement on Agriculture contains separate, and more comprehensive, disciplines on agricultural subsidies.

9 The agreement contains a list of types of measures that would be considered to be *financial contributions*: grants, loans, equity infusions, loan guarantees, fiscal incentives, and the provision of goods and services. Since a *government* is defined to include any public body within the territory of a member, subnational governments, public bodies, and state-owned companies are covered. The definition of a *benefit* has not been fully resolved in cases where indirect financial contributions are involved.

10 *Injury* is defined as harm to a domestic industry caused by subsidized imports into the territory of the complaining member. *Serious prejudice* is defined as adverse effects in the market of the subsidizing member or in a third market. *Nullification of benefits* can arise when improved market access resulting from a bound tariff reduction is undercut by the subsidy.

BOX 18.1   MATCHING GRANT SCHEMES TO PROMOTE EXPORTS

Disillusionment with the performance of trade promotion organizations has led to experimentation with other techniques of export development. Among these are matching grants: projects proposed by individual firms receive grants that have to be matched with the firm's capital. The justification for these schemes is generally that there exist exporting firms that would like to increase their exports and nonexporters that would begin to export were it not for lack of crucial information and services—for example, information about export markets, production techniques, packaging and delivery requirements, and product standards. It is also usually asserted that these firms underestimate the benefits of successful exporting, or overestimate the risks, and therefore are unwilling to undertake the necessary effort and investment. Hence, there is a case for reducing their exposure to risk by supplementing the investment they are willing to make through a grant. The case for a grant (rather than a loan or an equity infusion) is based on the premise that external benefits will accrue to other firms and to the economy in general as a result of the grant-receiving firms' export success. Such benefits operate through demonstration effects, increased awareness of and interest in the country on the part of foreign buyers, and transfer of knowledge and experience acquired by the innovating firm through labor turnover. Another increasingly important objective is to spur the development of specialized services providers that can be beneficial to all sectors of the economy. Some matching grants are therefore made available to these services suppliers, as well as to potential exporters.

Various questions have been raised concerning matching grant schemes. First and most important, it is not clear whether they have actually increased exports *and* generated external benefits. Generally, exports have increased significantly, but this does not justify either the program or the subsidy element; there needs to be evidence of additionality (the firm would not have exported as much without the grant) and of positive externalities (other firms have benefited indirectly). One of the few in-depth evaluations that tried to

examine these questions was conducted for a scheme in Mauritius, which happened to be one of the most successful as measured by its apparent effect on exports (Biggs 1999). The study concluded that nearly half of the firms assisted would have carried out their projects anyway and that the existence of externalities could not be proved. For example, little new demand was generated for local suppliers who might then have been in a better position to serve other exporters. The evaluation called for better targeting of beneficiaries.

This leads to a second issue: the selection process. Some analysts argue that a targeting approach will introduce bureaucracy and increase the scope for discretion, slowing disbursements and undermining the momentum necessary to build a market for services suppliers. They defend the first come, first served approach, which is the one almost always applied in practice. Judging, however, by the rate of disbursement across schemes, the momentum effect has not been good.

A third question concerns the cost-effectiveness of the schemes, including the effect of firm size. The administration and monitoring of grants are easiest when grants are large and few in number. The task becomes almost impossible when there is a very large number of small grants. This creates a dilemma because it is likely that larger firms applying for larger grants are least in need of them and are most likely to undertake the project in any case. This was confirmed in the Mauritius evaluation.

Finally, it is difficult to insulate the grant process from local lobbies and political pressures. There are plenty of anecdotes among practitioners concerning misuse of grants, especially of foreign travel that was, in practice, only marginally devoted to such purposes as contacting foreign buyers and exploring other export opportunities.

In the future, more attention needs to be paid to the economic justification for such schemes, in particular to ensure that there are not bigger policy or institutional obstacles that impede new exporters. When grant schemes are introduced, governments need to have a clearer understanding of their rationale, as well as an appreciation of

BOX 18.1 (CONTINUED)

the need for autonomous and streamlined management. The focus should be on small and medium-size enterprises, and more resources should go to services suppliers. The targeting issue should be addressed in the design stage so

that once the project has begun, its implementation will not be slowed.

Source: Prepared by the volume editors, based on Phillips (2001).

be well targeted with respect to producers, commodities, and markets. In the short term, existing exporters should be targeted, while selective support for potential exports may constitute a good medium-term target. Many TPOs have wasted resources on firms with little or no export potential. In many successful exporting countries, small and medium-size firms have proved to be powerful innovators and exporters, and such firms may benefit the most from well-targeted support.

5. *Quality staffing.* Staffing is crucial for the success of a TPO. A good TPO must be able to pay salaries that are similar to those paid by the private sector to talented staff with business experience. In most cases TPO staff operate under civil service rules that make discipline and accountability difficult and all too often imply unattractive pay and low motivation. Civil service staffing practices bring bureaucracy into the TPO, with the result that staff often do not have the requisite commercial experience to interact efficiently and credibly with the private sector. A partial solution to this problem could be to give TPOs greater autonomy in setting recruitment and salary standards and to draw on the expertise of external consultants.

6. *Adequate funding.* A sustainable TPO should have adequate revenues, derived mainly from domestic sources. Donor support can play a useful role in starting up the TPO, demonstrating the returns to be gained from good TPO work, and bringing best practice to bear, but such support should be temporary and should be followed up with sufficient domestic resources. Much is to be gained by charging fees for services rendered because fees act as a rationing mechanism and ensure that the services provided are valued by the recipient. There are, however, clear limits to levying fees. Some potential exporters will not have the necessary resources or will not fully appreciate the services offered until they succeed in exporting.

Fee-based services may also lead to underprovision of public goods (externalities) that such services may generate: improvement of the country's image abroad, overall quality enhancement of industry, strengthening of the foreign exchange reserve position, and so on. The funding problems of some TPOs have come about because of dwindling budget allocations, requirements to transfer fees raised to the treasury, and piecemeal and badly structured donor financing.

7. *Evaluation of the results.* The effectiveness and efficiency of TPO activities must be periodically evaluated so that policymakers can learn from experience, refine strategies, and avoid self-perpetuating activities. It should be kept in mind, however, that the process of evaluating these services is not an exact science. The impact of TPO activities may well be felt after some delay, and exports are affected by many variables, only some of which are under the control of the TPO. Nonetheless, the export performance of the economy as a whole, as well as that of the enterprises which have benefited from the services of the TPO, can be documented and can be supplemented by client surveys and reviews of the business plans of the enterprises.

Duty Drawback and Temporary Admission

A number of economies that have experienced rapid growth in trade and GDP did so in the context of trade regimes characterized by significant import controls on the domestic market. The Republic of Korea, Taiwan (China), and Japan (in the early stages) are the main examples. The key to understanding these experiences is to look at all the factors that affect competitiveness and the incentives to producers to export or not. Protection creates incentives to sell to the domestic market; that is, it creates a bias against exports. Protection of intermediate products and services seriously handicaps export industries because it raises their costs to levels that are higher than those of their potential competitors in world markets. As Shatz and Tarr discuss in Chapter 3 in this volume, the effect of protection on the real exchange rate also discourages export industries. The East Asian countries managed elaborate systems that offset the bias against exports. A key element of these systems was to allow exporting firms to import inputs and components, including machinery, at world prices through duty drawback or temporary admission schemes.

Benefits and Shortcomings of the Schemes

Duty drawback involves repayment of duties paid on imported inputs that are used in the production of exports (Box 18.2). A problem with duty draw-

---

BOX 18.2 DUTY DRAWBACK FOR DIRECT EXPORTERS: THE CHILEAN CASE

Refunds of duties and indirect taxes on imported inputs used in export production can be made in two ways. Individual drawback systems refund taxes actually paid. Fixed drawback schemes refund taxes on the basis of an estimate of the duties and indirect taxes that enter into the cost of production of exports. Processing of rebate claims is generally based on the ratio of inputs to exported outputs— known as input-output coefficients. These may be self-declared by exporters or predetermined by the authorities, who use standard coefficients uniformly for all exporters. The latter is more appropriate in countries with weak legal regimes and weak administrative capacity. In many countries a major source of delay in granting rebates is that authorities apply ad hoc checks, question the coefficients claimed by exporters, or do not (cannot) apply pretabulated standard input-output coefficients.

The Chilean experience with drawback provides an example that could be replicated in other countries. Since the mid-1980s, two duty drawback systems have been in use: a regular drawback, in force since 1988, under which duties on imported inputs used by exporters are rebated ex post, and the so-called simplified drawback, introduced in 1985 for nontraditional exports. The simplified plan applies to exports of goods that have not yet reached the level of US$20 million for a given tariff line. For such exports, exporters receive a cash subsidy of 3, 5, or 10 percent (depending on the total value of exports for the tariff line concerned) on their export value in lieu of a regular drawback. Although the scheme has been justified on the grounds that it makes life easier for small exporters, it does in fact contain a

subsidy element. The maximum rate of subsidy is around 6 percent, corresponding to the 10 percent drawback rate (which applies if exports are less than US$10 million for the entire tariff line). The magnitude of the subsidy depends on the extent to which imported inputs are used.

This simplified drawback offers moderate and self-extinguishing subsidies for new export products. It is especially valuable for small exporters, who may find it costly to access the regular drawback scheme. It has emerged as an important export incentive: in 1994 the state paid a total of US$150 million under the simplified system, compared with just US$26 million on the regular drawback. Although no careful econometric studies have been done on the impact of the simplified drawback on the emergence of new exports, after its introduction the number of exported manufacturing products and the values exported grew rapidly. Given the construction of the scheme, many of the exports were "new" and were thus likely to be associated with externalities related to information gathering. Over time, as exports grow, such externalities disappear. This makes the automatic elimination of the subsidy, once exports of the item exceed US$20 million, an attractive feature of the scheme.

Although Chile will have to eliminate this subsidy by 2002 to comply with WTO rules (see Box 18.3, below), countries with a per capita income less than US$1,000 would be allowed to implement similar policies under Annex VII of the WTO Agreement on Subsidies and Countervailing Measures.

Source: Agosin (2001).

back schemes is that their administration can be costly and can lead to cumbersome procedures and delays when tariffs are high. The empirical evidence suggests that in countries without well-functioning public administrations, duty drawback is ineffective. Drawbacks are very difficult to administer at tariff rates of more than 15 or 20 percent because of leakage, delays in payment, and fraudulent claims (Mitra 1992). Delays are particularly detrimental to small and medium-size enterprises and small-farmer organizations.

Temporary admission (also called duty suspension) can be more effective in allowing tariff-free access to intermediate inputs for exporters in these situations. Temporary entry regimes do not involve payment of duties on imported inputs; rather, they allow entry on a duty-free basis with a requirement that firms document ex post that the imported inputs have been used in the production of exports. The main potential problem with this approach in low-income countries with weak administrative capacity is leakage of goods into the economy (that is, the goods are not used for export production). A frequently employed option for controlling such leakage is the bonded warehouse or, on a larger scale, an export-processing zone, as described below. These are specific territories that are controlled by customs. Imports into these territories are not taxed on entry, but goods are taxed if they are sold on the domestic market.

Programs such as duty drawback and temporary admission, if properly administered, allow exporters duty-free access to imported intermediates. To avoid antiexport bias more completely, these schemes must be extended to indirect exporters (firms that do not themselves export but that sell to exporters). Administration of such mechanisms is substantially more complicated, however, as most schemes in developing countries exclude small producers and indirect exporters. The experience of many developing countries with drawback and temporary entry has been mixed. Notably, the institutions needed for effective implementation of duty drawback systems have been shown to be ineffective in most Sub-Saharan African countries (World Bank 2000a).

Requirements under WTO Rules

It is important that drawback mechanisms be designed in a WTO-consistent manner to avoid the imposition of countervailing duties by trading part-

ners. Indirect tax rebate and drawback schemes are not considered export subsidies if they do not result in rebates in excess of what was actually levied on inputs consumed in the production of the exported product (see Box 18.2).[1] Normal allowance for waste must be made in findings regarding consumption of inputs in the production of the exported product. Drawback or duty suspension systems on capital goods do, however, constitute an export subsidy if they are conditional on exporting.

On receipt of a complaint that an indirect tax rebate or drawback scheme acts as a subsidy through overrebate or excess drawback of charges on inputs consumed in the production of an exported product, the investigating authorities of the importing country must determine whether the government of the exporting country has in place and applies a system or procedure to confirm which inputs are consumed in the production of the exported product and in what amounts. Where such a system or procedure exists, its reasonableness, effectiveness, and consistency with generally accepted commercial practices in the exporting country must be determined. To the extent that the procedures are determined to meet this test and to be effective, no subsidy should be presumed to exist (Hoekman 1995).

Where there are no monitoring systems, or where these systems are not applied effectively, a determination of the actual inputs involved in the production of the exported good must be made, including a "normal allowance for waste." Determination of whether the claimed allowance for waste is "normal" must take into account the production process, the average experience of the industry in the exporting country, and other appropriate technical factors. The existence of a substitution drawback provision under which exporters are allowed to select particular import shipments on which drawback is claimed cannot of itself be considered to convey a subsidy. Excess drawback of import charges is deemed to exist if governments have paid interest on any monies refunded under their drawback schemes, to the extent of the interest actually paid or payable.[2]

Export-Processing Zones

Export-processing zones (EPZs) are enclaves within which governments attempt to provide a policy environment and associated infrastructure that are conducive to investors seeking to produce for export.[3] In a sense, EPZs are akin to duty drawback and temporary admission customs regimes except that they are limited to a certain geographic location. Many, however, go beyond these customs regimes by addressing infrastructure and related issues. EPZs are generally used to achieve three goals: promotion of investment and employment in export-oriented production; increased foreign exchange earnings from nontraditional exports; and encouragement of foreign direct investment (FDI) in countries where legal, administrative (red tape, corruption), and infrastructure-related weaknesses impede investment in exportables. An added objective is the transfer of technology and know-how from the EPZs to the rest of the economy.

EPZs are a second-best solution compared with generalized economywide reforms, but where countrywide reforms are difficult to implement, they can be a useful instrument in the development arsenal of governments confronting large reform agendas. They allow the public and private sectors to cooperate in creating the preconditions for efficient export production in a small geographic region, as opposed to pursuing reforms and undertaking investment on an economywide basis. One of the most successful examples is Mauritius, where, in the mid-1990s, EPZs generated more than two-thirds of gross exports and employed one-sixth of the work force. Net foreign exchange earnings as a percentage of gross vary widely, from a high of 63 percent in the Republic of Korea and Taiwan (China) in the mid-1980s to a low of 12 percent in Jamaica. The more developed the local economy, the higher the net foreign exchange earnings, since backward linkages are greater.

Effective EPZs combine clear private property rights and investment regulations, no restrictions on foreign exchange, tariff-free imports for export production, moderate levels of taxation, streamlined administrative procedures, and private sector management. Public provision of basic infrastructure outside the zone—telecommunications, roads, and ports—can have positive spillover effects for the local and national economies by facilitating economic activities. However, development of EPZs, including provision of infrastructure and management, should be privately handled.

The success of an EPZ is highly dependent on a hospitable host country economic environment. EPZs have tended to work better when the country pursued sound macroeconomic and exchange rate policies. Experience suggests that investors weigh economic and political stability, labor skill compatibility and productivity, and other similar factors carefully. Incentives such as overgenerous tax packages or legal investment assurances may not attract the right type of investors (or any investors at all). Furthermore, forgoing tax revenues may be expensive, especially if major public investments are made to develop the zone.

When well set up and well managed, EPZs have led to income generation and employment creation, especially opportunities in nontraditional jobs for women in the formal sector. In Bangladesh most employees in EPZs are women; for example, 70 percent of the employees in the Chittagong EPZ are female, a much higher ratio than the national average (ILO 1998). EPZ employment is seen by many as an important factor in reducing the proportion of female poor in the Dominican Republic, from 22.6 percent in 1986 to 15.8 percent in 1993. Wages in EPZs tend to be higher, on average, than wages in the rest of the country.

EPZ experiences range from the success stories of Mauritius and Mexico to several failed zones, as in Senegal. EPZs in Mauritius managed to create more than 90,000 jobs in 1991, or 17 percent of national employment. Mexico's *maquilas* employed about 900,000 workers in 1997, and the sector is among the highest generators of foreign currency (second to oil in 1992). By contrast, the Senegal EPZ employed only 600 workers in 1990 and exported just US$15 million. Most experience with EPZ experiences falls between these two extremes. In the Philippines in 1996 the 4 public and 43 private EPZs had approved investments totaling over US$2.5 billion, employed more than 150,000 people, and exported US$6.5 billion worth of goods. Nonetheless, the high exports have not meant greater backward linkages with the domestic economy; these generally depend on economywide reforms. The consequence has been high import dependency, low net exports (41 percent), and low net foreign exchange earnings.

Attempts to use EPZs in Africa have, except in Mauritius, been much less successful than elsewhere. Some argue that the basic concept is flawed. Blame has also been placed on Africa's lack of adequate infrastructure and services to support the business community, on the timidity or ignorance of investors, and on the lack of indigenous entrepreneurs. Important reasons for the disappointing performance of African EPZs include government interference and the distortions introduced in the operation of free trade and capital regimes. In Senegal excessive administrative red tape and strict labor laws were responsible for the failure of the EPZ. The Gambia, too, has a highly regulated labor market, which raises port loading and unloading costs sharply. These problems are not unique to Africa; similar shortcomings have undermined the EPZs in Jamaica and Panama (although Panama's has succeeded as a free trade zone).

Quality of infrastructure is a major determinant of success. When the Colon Free Zone in Panama was starting up, there was a good port in Colon and a reasonable road to the airport in Panama City. The Dominican Republic developed excellent air, sea, and road transport infrastructure in support of its EPZs. Mauritius also has excellent port and airport facilities. By contrast, with a few notable exceptions, much of Africa's transport infrastructure is in poor condition. Parastatal operating companies often provide poor services; economic conditions have impeded public investments; and budgetary problems have shortchanged basic maintenance.

The establishment of a successful EPZ program requires simultaneous removal of most, if not all, of the bottlenecks in infrastructure, the customs service, and labor regulations. A country must master the creation of a probusiness environment, the provision of infrastructure and services, international marketing, and investor relations— and master them all at the same time. Watson (2000) concludes that the management of the socio-political-economic process of bringing about change on a broad front is the key constraint on success in Africa and elsewhere. The reform process requires the presence of four critical factors: vision, consensus, concerted action, and continuity. Watson goes on to argue that it is typically easier for a weak state to start coordinating its actions on a small scale through an EPZ while it works on nationwide reforms.

EPZs are not defined or referred to in the WTO agreements. To the extent that subsidies are provided through EPZs, however, the rules of the Agreement on Subsidies and Countervailing Measures apply. Restrictions on export subsidies could impinge on countries' ability to employ EPZs in future. This is especially true for countries with income per capita of more than US$1,000 (see Box 18.3, below). Lower tax rates, special credit facilities, and publicly provided infrastructure, all of which

are typical features of EPZs, could, in principle, be contested, to the extent that they represent subsidies to companies that are required to export most, if not all, of their output. Countries currently relying on EPZs would do well to seek clarification on their compatibility with WTO rules and so preempt the possibility of future disputes.

Trade Finance

Export finance is one of the primary constraints inhibiting exports in many low-income developing countries. Inadequacies may result from the overall weakness of the financial sector, or it may reflect difficulties in assessing the creditworthiness of traders or the fact that traders do not have sufficient assets to be judged creditworthy. Small firms and the poor may face special difficulties in obtaining access to the trade credit they need, just as they face difficulties in accessing other parts of the financial sector. Although ensuring the availability of trade finance is a matter that needs to be left to the private sector, governments can use a number of mechanisms to promote access to finance, especially for smaller firms.

Two mechanisms that are sometimes used are foreign currency revolving funds and preshipment export finance guarantee schemes. The revolving funds provide finance for imported inputs needed for export production. An exporter must obtain a letter of credit from a buyer; this letter allows the exporter's bank to access the fund's foreign exchange to pay for the imports. The guarantee schemes cover exporters' manufacturing nonperformance risks and are generally targeted at smaller firms and new entrants into the export area that have difficulty in satisfying banks' collateral requirements but have obtained export letters of credit. Note that preshipment export finance guarantees are not export credit insurance schemes; the latter insure against nonpayment by foreign buyers. Another, more recent mechanism used by a number of countries is grants that are conditional on matching contributions by enterprises (see Box 18.1).

All these mechanisms for alleviating trade finance constraints can be designed to comply with WTO rules. What matters under the WTO is whether provision of the subsidy is conditional on exporting. As discussed in Box 18.3, export subsidies are prohibited for WTO members with per capita incomes above US$1,000. This dimension of WTO rules is

so-called foreign sales corporations (FSCs), under which U.S. firms with exports that have at least 50 percent U.S. content can reduce tax burdens by 15 to 30 percent, and the preferential government loans on noncommercial terms granted by Australia. In both instances dispute panels found that the measures violated WTO rules (Hoekman and Kostecki 2001).

Conclusion

Much has been made of the extent to which some high-performing East Asian economies used export promotion policies to support their impressive export drives and of the fact that some of these measures are no longer available to latecomers. It is true that the rules of the game have evolved. Yet it is also true that many governments have tried and failed to replicate various elements of the East Asian model of export promotion—sometimes at considerable expense in terms of government revenue and misallocated resources. Furthermore, poor countries can ill afford to engage in competitive subsidization of their exports, which will often benefit relatively rich consumers abroad, and they will inevitably lose out in any such contest with richer countries. It is clearly in their interest to discipline the use of export subsidies. Export industries are still often taxed implicitly, if not explicitly, by inefficient government services or poorly functioning markets. There is plenty of work to be done on these fronts, and there is an ample range of instruments compatible with WTO rules that developing country governments have yet to master and that would go a long way toward reducing the antiexport bias in their economies.

In a review of the lessons from East Asia for African trade and industrial policy, five priorities were identified at the project level that are equally relevant to other low-income countries (Harrold, Jayawickrama, and Bhattasali 1996):

- Support for on-the-job training, through payroll tax refunds rather than subsidies, as well as for public training institutions that are demand driven
- Technical assistance to enterprises for access to technology and design skills and for development of external markets
- Export credit support mechanisms, especially preshipment finance
- Development of simple duty-exemption schemes
- Development of industrial parks and export-processing zones.

None of these, with the possible exception of EPZs, currently present problems in the context of the WTO.

More fundamental to replicating the East Asian success are an unequivocal commitment on the part of government to working with the private sector in the pursuit of joint goals and a long-term vision that places export development at the heart of the national development strategy. Many countries have yet to establish these basic preconditions, without which microeconomic interventions are likely to be wasted.

Notes

1 Indirect tax rebate schemes allow for exemption, remission, or deferral of prior-stage cumulative indirect taxes levied on inputs that are consumed in the production of the exported product. Drawback schemes allow for the remission or drawback of import charges levied on inputs that are consumed in the production of the exported product.

2 This rule strengthens the incentive to use temporary admission and duty waiver mechanisms rather than drawback.

3 This section draws on Madani (1999) and Watson (2000).

BIJIT BORA

19

TRADE-RELATED INVESTMENT MEASURES

ALTHOUGH IT IS ONLY FIVE PAGES LONG, THE WTO AGREEMENT ON TRADE-Related Investment Measures (TRIMs) has become a central issue in the debate on the relevance to developing countries of the multilateral trading agreements and the WTO. A combination of factors led to the inclusion of investment in the work program of the Uruguay Round negotiations. These included a changing perception of the role of foreign direct investment (FDI) in development and the intense debate on the linkage between GATT rules and foreign investment policy stemming from the U.S.-Canada dispute on Canada's application of performance measures to foreign firms.[1] Despite an ambitious start to the negotiations, the final text was limited in scope and coverage.

The purpose of this chapter is to assess how well the TRIMs agreement has been implemented and to identify lessons or issues that may be relevant to the mandated review of the agreement and to the future multilateral trade negotiations on investment called for in the 2001 Doha Ministerial Declaration.

The Agreement

The fact that there is a separate text called an "agreement" is a paradox. In essence, all the TRIMs agreement does is to clarify the application of GATT Articles III.4, on national treatment, and XI.1, on quantitative restrictions. It does not even define a trade-related investment measure. Instead the approach that was taken was to include an illustrative list of measures that are inconsistent with these two key paragraphs of the GATT. The list covers both TRIMs that are mandatory or enforceable under domestic law and measures for which compliance is necessary to obtain an advantage. There is no text that specifically addresses issues related to granting national treatment to investors.

The agreement allowed for a notification period of 90 days, beginning January 1, 1995, for WTO members to notify the WTO of measures that were not in conformity with the agreement. After notification, a member was allowed a transition period, the length of which depended on its level of development, to bring its laws into conformity with the agreement. Developing countries were allowed five years; least-developed countries were allowed seven years.

The agreement is a rather modest attempt at disciplining policies that are targeted at foreign enterprises, and it was the outcome of conflicting positions about the extent to which investment issues should be covered by the WTO. In the Uruguay Round, many developing countries resisted the extent to which market access for foreign

negotiations. Six such issues are identified in this section.

Ownership Neutrality

Although the TRIMs agreement presupposed a direct link with the GATT, there was still some confusion regarding whether a policy that violated GATT articles automatically violated the TRIMs agreement. As indicated above, the problem is that the TRIMs agreement did not introduce new language concerning disciplining policies; it merely referred to the GATT articles. This raises a question of how the TRIMs agreement actually fits into the WTO multilateral trade agreements (MTAs) and whether it allows or prevents a measure directly targeted at a foreign enterprise. Part of the confusion lies in the extent to which the TRIMs agreement is actually an instrument related to foreign investment. The term "investment" is used in the title, and there was a general presumption that investment-related policies which affect trade were to be addressed. This perhaps was to be the feature that distinguished the GATT from TRIMs.

One view is that the TRIMs agreement codifies a GATT panel decision on the Canadian Foreign Investment Review Act (FIRA). This, however, is technically wrong because the TRIMs agreement is a stand-alone agreement and needs to be interpreted independent of GATT rules.[4] But since TRIMs is independent, does it have any direct relevance to foreign firms, and does it go beyond GATT rules, especially in the context of Articles III and XI? A number of developing countries have asserted that it does.[5] Yet the 1998 panel report on the TRIMs dispute involving Indonesian policies stated conclusively and clearly, "We note that the use of the broad term 'investment measures' indicates that the TRIMs Agreement is not limited to measures taken specifically in regard to foreign investment. Contrary to India's argument we find that nothing in the TRIMs Agreement suggests that the nationality of the ownership of enterprises subject to a particular measure is an element in deciding whether that measure is covered by the Agreement" (para. 14.73). Therefore, the TRIMs agreement is not confined to policies targeted at foreign firms; it, like the GATT, is ownership neutral. The importance of the Indonesia panel decision and of the subsequent panel decision on Canadian policies is that these findings clarify the relationship between the GATT

articles and the TRIMs agreement. In particular, since the TRIMs agreement is independent, this would imply that any future negotiations would have to take this relationship into account.

Voluntarism and Backsliding

A number of countries have made clear that the central issue in the TRIMs agreement is not the length of time allowed for implementing the obligations but the obligations themselves. For example, a proposal by 12 countries arguing that the text of the agreement should be changed so that commitments to TRIMs are voluntary (WTO, WT/GC/W/354) clearly asked for a derogation of the commitment and, indeed, requested a kind of special and differential treatment that does not exist.[6] Although the proposal is inconsistent with existing rules and with rulings on the application of the rules, it does raise the question of whether some developing countries were adequately prepared for the negotiations.[7] In this context the approach that was taken was to ban outright such policies without any agreed phasing as, in say, the Agreement on Textiles and Clothing. For example, if this approach were adopted, a country that notified a local content scheme would have been required to notify how the scheme was to be implemented and the minimum specified local content. Then a simple phasing-out of 20 percent over five years would have met the transition period deadline while allowing individual members the possibility of being able to monitor the extent of implementation.[8]

In the absence of a well-defined phase-in program, members that notified under the TRIMs agreement were obliged only to bring their laws into conformity with the agreement. Indeed, during meetings of the Committee on Trade and Investment, a number of questions were put to WTO members that notified about their implementation programs, and these members rightly replied that they were under no obligation to respond in detail. Therefore, in simple terms, as with any obligation where the implementation causes difficulty and the implementation program is voluntary, there is no incentive to comply with the obligation. This could be an issue to be taken up in the context of a review of the agreement, especially if new disciplincs are to be considered. Nevertheless, it should be kept in mind that this is a problem for only a third of the countries in less than a quarter of the notifications.

Structural Adjustment as a Defense

The preamble of the TRIMs agreement states that the agreement takes into account the trade, development, and financial needs of developing countries. In this respect, four of the applications for extensions (by Argentina, Malaysia, the Philippines, and Thailand) cited the financial crises that had hit the East Asia and Latin America regions. A fifth (Colombia) cited a particular circumstance of structural adjustment, from illegal to legal farming. These two kinds of cases, without question, are specific to developing countries and appear to be legitimate grounds for an extension.

In the Indonesia panel dispute the arbitrator took up this precise point. In this case he was required to rule on the length of time that it would take Indonesia to implement the panel ruling and bring its laws into conformity with the TRIMs agreement. The complaining parties (the EU, Japan, and the United States) argued that structural adjustment should not be considered a defense because it is part of any obligation to liberalize.[9]

The arbitrator's final ruling was that Indonesia should be allowed 12 months: 6 months for administrative consultations and another 6 months because it was a developing country. Canada was given less time to implement. Thus, the precedent was confirmed that developing countries require more time than industrial countries. The decision also appears to set a precedent regarding structural adjustment as a defense. Indeed, the rulings in this and previous cases indicate unambiguously that without the cover of the TRIMs agreement, any WTO member with policies that are in the TRIMs annex would have to bring these laws into conformity within a 12-month period.[10]

A second issue related to structural adjustment is whether a particular local content scheme is effective. The Philippines has regularly failed to meet its local content targets (Abrenica 2000). Malaysia and Pakistan, by contrast, exceeded their targets by a significant margin, suggesting that any structural adjustment would not pose an immediate problem given that the local content scheme is not affecting the production decisions of firms (Ali 2000; Tyndall 2000).

Timing and Sequencing of Policies: Implementation Plans

Since the transition period for implementation has closed, a number of bilateral question-and-answer sessions have been held between members interested in implementation and members that have requested extensions. Some of these sessions relate to notifying countries' plans to bring their laws into conformity. As a rule, none of the notifying countries had developed an implementation plan or identified alternative policies that could be used to achieve the same objective.[11]

Furthermore, in the cases involving the automotive sector, notifying countries have, in general, not bound most of their tariff lines. This would create an opportunity, given the caveats identified above, for the use of price-based measures to replace quantity-based measures. That avenue does not appear to have been pursued, perhaps because of the incentive compatibility of voluntary schemes and also perhaps because any increase in tariffs would not be interpreted positively by investors (domestic and foreign) or by other WTO members.

An issue related to when a policy should be removed is the sequencing of reform. TRIMs are typically used in conjunction with other policies. Furthermore, given the existence of certain policies, TRIMs could have positive welfare effects. One factor that was not taken into account during the Uruguay Round negotiations was how the removal of certain TRIMs, without addressing companion policies, would affect trade. For example, local content schemes are usually combined with a subsidy. The TRIMs agreement disciplines trade policy instruments but not the subsidy policies. One view would be that liberalization should not proceed, since incentives have not been disciplined. The other view, of course, is that both should be disciplined at the same time.

Nevertheless, the central issue remains: in order to implement obligations, members need to have a solid understanding of what they committed to and a solid vision of how to implement these obligations. This would include the timing and sequencing of liberalization policies to suit countries' own needs.

Interface between Preferential Trade Agreements and Multilateral Trade Rules

The general perception of preferential trading agreements (PTAs) is that they involve a degree of liberalization that goes beyond the obligations at the multilateral level. Indeed, this is precisely the case, especially in the context of tariff and services liberalization. Regarding investment, however, there are a number of cases in which the investment provisions lag behind the TRIMs agreement. The Australia–New Zealand Closer Economic Relations Agreement, which is widely agreed to be one of the most forward-looking preferential trade agreements, does not even have an investment provision, yet it has liberalized services and goods trade (Scollay 1996).

The TRIMs agreement simply specifies a transition period of five years for developing countries without foreshadowing any conflict with PTAs. Argentina, however, in its request for an extension, cites specifically its intention to develop an automotive component in the MERCOSUR trade agreement. Similarly, the transition period provisions in NAFTA are inconsistent with those in TRIMs.

Lack of Criteria for Extensions

Perhaps the most obvious issue that has arisen is the lack of any criteria for an extension of the transition periods. The only possible reference point is the suggestion that the transition period vary with the level of development, with the least-developed countries allowed two more years than developing countries. Clearly, the extension issue would have been much easier to resolve had the criteria for granting extensions been unambiguous and transparent.

Approaches to the Review of the TRIMs Agreement

Article IX of the TRIMs agreement requires a review of the agreement no later than January 1, 2000. Such a review had not begun at the time of writing, in part because of the linkage between the review and a new trade round and also because the agreement has yet to be implemented in its entirety. This section examines some of the options in the context of a review of the agreement.

Full Negotiation on Investment: A New Architecture

The obvious option, given that the TRIMs was a compromise agreement, is to bring the negotiations about investment back full circle to the original mandate provided for in Uruguay in 1986. That wording was broad enough to accommodate an instrument dealing with both market access issues (in the context of right of establishment) and performance requirements. Such an approach would view the existing TRIMs agreement as a basic framework within which to deal with performance requirements that are inconsistent with GATT articles and for which rules on market access would be required. In addition, some attention would also have to be focused on the definition of FDI and the scope of the dispute settlement mechanism. In essence, a new architecture would be required to deal with investment issues.

The EU articulated this view in the context of the preparations for the Fourth Ministerial Conference in Seattle in 1999. Needless to say, some developing countries would be opposed to such an approach. Furthermore, the issue would have to be approached carefully, since commercial presence is already part of the General Agreement on Trade in Services (GATS), and in a positive list manner. It could be argued that, for consistency, if market access issues were to be part of an investment instrument, a similar approach, using a positive list by sector, might be required.

Renovation

Another option would be to renovate the existing architecture by adding an extension or reducing obligations. This option would be preferable to the new architecture option, since it would automatically preclude any discussion of market access issues. Still, it may prove not to be an easy path for negotiation, since the debate about the trade effects of investment measures was not resolved during the Uruguay Round.

To circumvent this problem, one approach might be to adopt a traffic light system as in the SCM agreement. TRIMs that were deemed to be trade distorting and directly inconsistent with the existing provisions of Article 2 would be classified in a red box, those that were not inconsistent would be in a green box, and those on which there is a debate as to their effect would be in a yellow box.

While not novel, the approach could be used to accommodate some of the concerns of developing countries. The traffic light approach could use criteria other than trade effect to determine the allocation of policies among the different boxes. Indeed, the idea of a "development" box separate from the triple-box traffic light approach has been mooted in other negotiations. Perhaps the only caveat is that the criteria for allocating policies, whether trade effects, development dimension, or something else, should be made clear at the outset.

When examining whether the annex list should be extended, high priority should be given to export performance requirements. Currently, the wording allows the use of this policy, since it does not *restrict* trade. It does, however, clearly *affect* trade and should be addressed. Another issue to reexamine is the application of local content policy in light of its use elsewhere. For example, the recent Trade Policy Review for Canada highlighted that these policies are used at the subnational level.

Renovating the existing architecture need not be confined simply to an extension; it could also include cutting back the existing agreement. Indeed, this approach would assume that the existing agreement has gone too far and, given the implementation difficulties, needs to be curtailed. This approach would reduce the policies listed in the annex list or lengthen the transition periods along the lines requested by some members in their Seattle proposals, or both.

No Change

A third approach might be to leave the TRIMs agreement as it is until all WTO members have completed implementing their obligations. This standstill approach would be acceptable to the small number of countries that have requested extensions of the transition period but is unlikely to receive much support from the industrial country members and perhaps a significant majority of developing country members that have conscientiously implemented their obligations.

Conclusions

The debate on the inclusion of investment issues in the multilateral trading system that started in the late 1940s continues today. The TRIMs agreement that was part of the Uruguay Round package was an attempt to address some of the issues related to investment policies. In the end, however (as confirmed by two panel decisions), the agreement simply addresses trade-distorting policies, regardless of whether they are targeted at foreign or domestic enterprises.

The six years of experience with the TRIMs agreement has been an invaluable learning experience for the multilateral trading system on how to deal modestly with issues related to investment. One of the major steps forward has been greater clarity about interpreting GATT rules as they relate to policies aimed at favoring one industry over another. At the same time, a third of the WTO members that were required to implement their obligations failed to do so, suggesting that the agreement is far from perfect. Moreover, as is discussed in Chapter 42, by Hoekman and Saggi, there is no consensus as to how to move investment issues forward in the WTO, if at all.

This chapter has identified a number of key issues that have made implementation of the TRIMs agreement problematic. These issues are divided into two areas: ambiguity in the wording of the TRIMs agreement, which has made interpretation of obligations difficult, and lack of capacity on the part of some developing countries to fully understand the scope and implications of these obligations. These issues have created a tension between the generally accepted notion of efficiency and the broader definition of development. Adherence to the latter may require conceding the former. However, economic theory and a body of empirical evidence provide strong support for the proposition that neutral policies designed to enhance the efficiency of investment are better than targeted government intervention at attracting foreign investment and enhancing its contribution to development (see Chapter 42).

Notes

The chapter has benefited from the comments and discussion of participants at the Special WTO Seminar on Implementation, held on May 20, 2000.

1 Canada: Administration of the Foreign Investment Review Act (BISD 30S/140, 1984).

2 The countries making this argument include Cuba, the Dominican Republic, Egypt, El Salvador, Honduras, India, Indonesia, Malaysia, Nigeria, Pakistan, Sri Lanka, and Uganda.

3 Brazil versus the United States in the context of patent protection (G/TRIMS/D/17).

4 This interpretation was confirmed in the July 1, 1998, report of the panel on *Indonesia: Certain Measures Affecting the Automobile Industry.* Paragraph 162 of the report states, "This reinforces the conclusion that the TRIMs agreement has an autonomous legal existence, independent of that from Article III."

5 Part of this is explained in para. 14.7 of the Indonesia panel decision, which states, "Indonesia also supports the argument put forward by India, a third party, that the TRIMs agreement

is basically designed to govern and provide a level playing field for foreign investment and that therefore measures relating to internal taxes or subsidies cannot be construed to be trade related investment measures."

6 The Uruguay Round Agreement changed significantly the concept of special and differential treatment by allowing for different transition periods. Previously, special and differential treatment applied to market access and measures that would violate the most-favored-nation principle. The proposal by the 12 countries asks for an exemption from an existing obligation—indeed, an obligation that was in the GATT before the Uruguay Round. Furthermore, the request also implies that the panel rulings in both the GATT Canada case and the two WTO cases should be ignored.

7 Another view could be that the outcome was the maximum that some developing countries could accept, given that some industrial countries actually wanted the investment provisions in the Uruguay Round to go beyond existing GATT disciplines.

8 In the implementation of the Agreement on Textiles and Clothing, the flexibility of the wording has allowed some WTO members to back-load their implementation so that the greatest liberalization does not occur until the latest possible date.

9 Bora and Neufeld (2000), in a study of how the five affected Asian countries used tariffs to respond to the financial crisis, found that only Thailand raised tariffs above the bound levels, and only in a few lines. Furthermore, the tariffs that were raised were typically on luxury products, which the authors interpret as evidence that the role of tariffs during the crisis was one of revenue raising as opposed to protection.

10 Canada was awarded eight months as a "reasonable period of time" (WT/DS142/12).

11 This was confirmed through personal interviews with delegates from the notifying countries.

GARRY PURSELL

20

LOCAL CONTENT POLICIES

Australia's Experience with Automobiles

THE AUTOMOBILE INDUSTRY WORLDWIDE IS TECHNOLOGY-INTENSIVE AS REGARDS both its processes and its products, and it is characterized by considerable economies of scale and a high degree of specialization in component manufacture. Largely for these reasons, the global industry has increasingly become internationalized, with component production for individual models located in many countries and assembly concentrated in large domestic markets or in countries that are a base for regional exports. At the same time, consumers demand a large variety of models, at competitive prices. Imports of cars therefore account for high shares of the total supply even in the largest national markets, including the United States and the European Union (EU).

Nevertheless, economic nationalism and the belief that the automobile industry is a transmitter par excellence of the latest industrial technologies have led many countries, at some stage of their economic history, to attempt to become fully or predominantly self-sufficient in car production. In pursuit of this goal, they have sought to persuade international auto firms to establish domestic production facilities and to reduce car imports. The most direct and widely used means of doing so has been to impose quantitative restrictions on imports while at the same time offering international auto producers opportunities to establish local factories, subject to the condition that they go beyond assembly of imported, completely knocked down (CKD) packs and incorporate specified levels of "local content" in the form of domestically produced components.

The experience of many countries reveals that such trade-related investment measures not only involve very high economic costs to consumers, government budgets, and the economy in general but also, on balance, have retarded rather than advanced indigenous technological capabilities. This chapter summarizes the long and well-documented Australian experience with local content plans for autos and draws some lessons from this experience that are relevant for developing countries using or considering similar policies.

Local Content Policies in Australia: A Brief History

Australian policies aimed at creating a domestic auto manufacturing industry started in the mid-1930s, when extra protection against competing imports and a variety of subsidies were offered to induce General Motors to produce a local car, the Holden. Until 1960, production of the Holden and of subsequent cars with substantial Australian content by British Motors and Ford was supported by local con-

Local content, including assembly and marketing costs (percent)	37	60	70	75	80	85
Required import tariff (percent)	19	41	46	51	59	60

Toyota also presented evidence of the costs of producing various components in Australia, compared with production costs of the same components in Japan. These data indicated a cost disadvantage ranging from about 50 percent to more than 500 percent. Mitsubishi and Ford also presented evidence showing a wide range of cost differences, although less marked than those indicated by Toyota.

The Australian experience thus clearly demonstrates the cost of indiscriminate local content rules that require local sourcing of components to meet the requirements regardless of their production cost. In the Australian case, these costs were incorporated in the cost of the finished cars and were reflected in the selling prices of the cars, so that the higher the cost of a component to the car assembler, the more the component contributed to meeting the local content requirement. Depending on how "indigenization" percentages are defined, the same perverse incentive, whereby high-cost components satisfy indigenization requirements more easily than do low-cost components, is likely to be found in developing countries.

3. The local content policies, and the policies that supported them, were strongly countercompetitive. Owing to the local content requirements, many component suppliers had captive markets, and their market power was only limited by the potential ability of the assemblers to set up production in-house. For a number of years even this option was limited by a separate car component manufacturing program. Under this scheme, components produced by independent manufacturers that met a minimum specified local content (usually 85 percent) were deemed to have 100 percent local content when used by a vehicle producer under the plan, even though the same component produced in-house was subject to the general local content requirement applicable to the producer.[2] In this and various other ways, the administering authority (the Federal Department of Business and Consumer Affairs) contributed to the effective cartelization of the domestic auto industry.[3] For example, in the 1970s the department blocked Honda from establishing an assembly plant that would have operated outside the local content plan.

Decisions on the nature of the local content rules and the details of how they were applied to individual firms were crucial for the profitability and survival of the auto firms, and efforts to influence these decisions became a major activity for their managers. In the interest of "fairness," the rules were adjusted to take account of the particular situations of groups of firms or individual firms. As noted earlier, special reduced local content programs were applied to low-volume producers between 1966 and 1975, which gave them considerable cost advantages by allowing them to import components that the larger producers were obliged to buy or to produce domestically. These programs were replaced by provisions that allowed local content to be averaged across a number of models by individual producers. By comparison with new entrants, this gave a decisive advantage to incumbent producers with at least one reasonably large-volume model, if they decided to introduce other, small-volume models. Later, to offset this effect, special low transitional local content arrangements were made for Toyota and Nissan when they joined the local content program and began production.

In 1981 the Industries Assistance Commission noted the "efforts to improve their competitive position by model rationalization and cooperative arrangements between producers" (Australia, Industries Assistance Commission, 1981: 125). Nevertheless, it observed that "manufacturers are continuing to invest in separate and parallel production facilities in what is, by international standards, already a very fragmented industry." All this was made possible by increases in tariffs to accommodate rising industry costs, and for 10 years import quotas were applied to imported cars so as to ensure an 80 percent share of the market to the local industry, regardless of its production costs. The import quotas were extended to include completely and partly knocked down packs. At first, complex rules were established for the allocation of quotas, based primarily on pre-quota imports but with numerous exceptions. Later, the quotas were auctioned, but the auction rules were extremely complex and became the focus of intense lobbying.

4. Contrary to the objectives of the original promoters of these schemes, they retarded rather than promoted technological change in the auto industry. A constant complaint of the local producers was that the local content requirements made it too expensive for them to introduce new components and production techniques in their local operations. They consistently lobbied for lower local content ratios while advocating the same or tighter limits on imports of finished cars. In particular, the local content programs seriously retarded the introduction of smaller, fuel-efficient vehicles into the Australian market (Australia, Industries Assistance Commission, 1981: 125). The industry only began to catch up with the rest of the world after the policy was reversed in 1985 and, especially, after the local content plans were abandoned, in 1989. According to a submission to the Industries Commission by Toyota in 1996, "The Government's car policy since 1984, by reducing protection, has required the car manufacturers to progressively reduce the gaps in their cost, quality and delivery performance" (quoted in Australia, Industry Commission, 1997: 232).

5. Total employment in and associated with the auto industry was reduced rather than increased as a result of the schemes and the policies that supported them. In 1996 total employment in automotive and auto component manufacturing was 70,300, whereas total employment in car retailing, repair, and the sale of auto replacement parts and tires was 295,800, more then four times as great.[4] The Industries Commission cited estimates of own-price elasticities of the demand for private cars in other countries that ranged from about −0.7 to −1.6, and its staff gave a conservative estimate for the Australian market of −0.5. Even using this lower estimate of the demand elasticity, it can be inferred that over time, the reduction in employment in car dealerships, repair shops, and the like as a consequence of the increased protection and higher car prices associated with the local content plan would have far exceeded any plausible estimate of increased employment in auto assembly and auto component production.[5]

6. The addition of "export facilitation" increased rather than reduced the economic costs of the system. Credits that firms received for exports allowed them to reduce their local content. The benefits to the firms of marginal reductions in local content were extremely high—according to Toyota, more than five times the world cost of the components that could now be imported. This made it worthwhile to export at prices that were far below production costs. In 1981 the Industries Assistance Commission pointed out:

There would be little rationale for export facilitation without the inward-looking orientation and high marginal assistance associated with high local content provisions. . . . Export facilitation will increase government direction and control of the industry and add to what is already a complex and administratively costly assistance package. . . . There would be little gain in predicating longer term restructuring of automotive production on the development of high cost exports which would require continuing high subsidy. (Australia, Industries Assistance Commission, 1981: 128)[6]

7. The transactions costs associated with schemes of this kind are likely to be extremely high, both for the government bodies involved in formulating policy and administering the schemes and for the auto and component producers and the many other participants in the automobile market. Defining and administering local content requirements involved the Department of Business and Consumer Affairs in a great deal of micromanagement of the industry and was extremely time- and resource-intensive. For example, the department's responsibilities included:

- Examining the detailed cost and sales records of each producer.
- Making frequent changes to accommodate low-volume and new producers.
- Setting and administering local content conditions for component production.
- Adjusting local content requirements to allow for exchange rate appreciations that affected the various producers in different ways.[7]
- Drawing up and administering rules on "component reversion"—requests for producers to switch from local sourcing to importing particular components.
- Exercising oversight of the prices charged by component suppliers to assemblers to ensure that "local content" was not artificially inflated.
- Monitoring the import prices of components to ensure that assemblers were not underin-

SELECTED TRADE POLICIES AFFECTING MERCHANDISE TRADE

voicing imported inputs to help meet local content requirements.

- Setting the rules for and administering the export facilitation policies adopted in 1979.[8]
- Extending the general auto industry controls to car "derivatives" such as panel vans and small buses using the same engines and other major components as cars and to four-wheel-drive vehicles. These vehicles were initially not subject to local content and related policies, and the import tariffs applied to them were lower than car tariffs. As a result, their prices declined in relation to car prices, leading consumers to choose them instead of cars. To limit this shift, controls were widened to cover the derivatives.

Over the entire history of the local content plans, there were continuing conflicts between the auto producers, the component producers, the trade unions, and many other groups with an interest in the industry and the policies that affected it. These disputes were heard and reported on at length in numerous sessions of the Australian Tariff Board and its successor organizations. Between 1965 and 1996 there were eight major hearings and reports, most of which took more than a year to complete and involved evidence presented by dozens of interested groups. For example, work on the July 1981 report of the Industries Assistance Commission started in March 1979, and evidence for it was presented by 90 different parties—including assemblers, component producers, importers, auto distributors, raw material suppliers, trade unions, trade associations, professional associations, state governments, municipalities, and many others. Special ad hoc bodies were also set up to provide advice on auto industry policies; these included the Car Industry Council, established in 1983, and the Automotive Industry Authority, created in 1985.

In response to these continuous pressures, there was not a year after 1965 in which significant changes were not made in the local content rules themselves or in the tariff and other policies that supported the system. Looking back, it is apparent that, over many years, a great deal of talent, intellectual energy, and administrative and managerial resources—not least in the private sector—was wasted in first creating and building up this economically costly edifice and then in devising ways

of withdrawing from it that were politically acceptable and administratively feasible.

8. Finally, once the local content programs became established and major automobile producers, component suppliers, trade unions, and other groups came to rely on them, it became extremely difficult to remove them. As noted above, detailed critiques by economists and other experts were already being made and were well known in the 1960s, and by the early 1970s these criticisms were consistently reflected in reports on the industry by the Industries Assistance Commission and in numerous press articles. Despite all this, the system had generated its own momentum, and it steadily became more protective and economically costlier. In 1985 policy finally reversed course, and protection began to be wound down, but it took 13 years of sustained effort to reduce it to the present much lower level, which, even in 2001, is still well above the levels found in nearly all other major Australian industries.

There are various explanations for the ability of the auto industry to sustain political support for its special treatment over such a long period:

- The populist appeal of high national content in a well-known and visible consumer product.
- The distinctly nontransparent nature of the protection resulting from the local content programs.
- The development of a strong vested interest in the continuation of the system by the government officials responsible for its administration.
- The determined lobbying of local businessmen and the large international firms allied with them, which entrenched themselves in the Australian market behind the protection of the local content programs. The international auto firms had ample resources that they used to influence the two principal Australian political parties at both the federal and state levels. General Motors, which had a history of support from local content programs going back to the mid-1930s, had a key role in this regard.
- The industry's unionized and influential work force.
- The concentration of most of the investment and employment in the manufacturing side of the industry in a few places—in Melbourne and the nearby town of Geelong, and on the outskirts of Adelaide. Even as late as 1996 the

Victorian and South Australian state governments, the municipalities in which the major auto plants are located, and politicians from these places were still lobbying strongly against further reductions in protection. By contrast, the consumer and general national interest in lower car prices and in a more efficient industry was diffuse and difficult to mobilize.[9]

All of these political-economy reasons for the staying power of the structures created by the local content plans and their supporting policies are likely to be important in other countries that start along similar paths to those traversed in Australia.

Some Implications for Developing Countries

The local content requirements and other aspects of the new auto policies currently being implemented in a number of developing countries have obvious similarities with Australia's past policies. The market for cars in many countries will be too small to allow economies of scale to be captured. For example, India's car market is currently about the same size as that of Australia; 411,000 cars were produced in India in 1996–97, while Australia produced 490,000 in 1996. The potential for costly fragmentation is great, with more than 20 domestically produced models being planned in India, versus 5 models in Australia. More generally, local content regimes involve considerable potential for detailed, complex, ad hoc, and nontransparent government intervention in the industry.

The expensive and economically damaging record of local content policies for automobiles in Australia suggests that the present efforts of a number of developing countries at the WTO to legitimize or indefinitely extend trade-related investment measures (TRIMs) are not in their own economic interest. But the Australian experience also shows the strength of the nationalist and protectionist instincts into which these policies play, as well as the tenacity of the interests that are created by the policies and that would oppose their removal. As became apparent in Australia, because of its transparency, relative simplicity, and relative freedom from lobbying and administrative discretion, tariff-based protection is preferable to TRIMs and would be much more conducive to the economically efficient development of this important industry in developing countries.

Notes

This chapter is based on Pursell (2001).

1 The Tariff Board mutated over time. In 1973 it became the Industries Assistance Commission, in 1989 the Industry Commission, and in 1998 the Productivity Commission. The changing names reflect significant changes in emphasis and coverage, from tariffs and industrial protection in the beginning to, eventually, policies for enhancing productivity and efficiency across all industries (including services industries).

2 This rule deterred in-house production, since any imported parts for the component would reduce the vehicle producer's local content as defined in the plan.

3 The Department of Business and Consumer Affairs was responsible for the administration of the local content plans during the 1970s and 1980s. The Department of Industry and Commerce was responsible for policy aspects.

4 In 1979 employment in auto and auto component manufacturing was 62,368, while employment in motor dealerships and tire retailing alone was 165,700.

5 In 1979, when domestic car prices were about 85 percent above world prices, a cut in protection to 20 percent would have been equivalent to a reduction in car prices of about 35 percent and, assuming a demand elasticity of –0.5, an increase in annual final car demand of 17.5 percent. Over a moderate time span—say, five years—the employment effects from selling more new cars and servicing a larger total stock of cars quickly begin to exceed plausible reductions in employment in auto and component production.

6 Despite the opposition of the Industries Assistance Commission, "export facilitation" was continued by the government and is one element of the early policy package that still exists. However, it lost much of its impact after the local content plan was abolished and, subsequently, as tariffs were reduced.

7 In particular, Japanese producers requested and received special treatment to offset the reduction in their local content ratios that resulted from appreciation of the yen.

8 The export facilitation rules were extremely complex and were changed frequently. For example, initially, local content credits were earned on the basis of the gross value of exports, but this was soon changed to net foreign exchange earnings from exports after deducting the cost of imported components. The concept was further refined to deal with local components that themselves, at first, second, or even further remove, used imported components or materials.

9 After losing out for 13 years, the forces supporting special treatment of the auto industry had a victory in 1997. In a report that year the Industry Commission recommended that the tariff reductions should continue until the tariff reached 5 percent in 2005, but the government rejected this recommendation. Instead, it decided that the reductions would stop in 2000 at 15 percent, with a provision that there would be a further reduction to 10 percent in 2005.

HANAA KHEIR-EL-DIN

21

IMPLEMENTING THE AGREEMENT ON TEXTILES AND CLOTHING

T EXTILES AND CLOTHING ARE IMPORTANT INDUSTRIES IN DEVELOPING COUNTRIES, and they contribute significantly to manufacturing production, employment, and trade in such economies as China, Hong Kong (China), India, the Republic of Korea, and Pakistan. Traditionally, developing countries have protected these industries through tariffs and quantitative restrictions. Until the Uruguay Round, this domestic protection was somewhat justified by the protection accorded to textile and clothing industries in industrial countries. Through a set of bilaterally negotiated agreements under the Multifibre Arrangement (MFA), industrial countries—principally Canada, the European Union (EU), Norway, and the United States—applied widespread and restrictive quotas against imports from developing countries. This violated the fundamental GATT principle of nondiscrimination and the injunction against the use of quantitative restrictions.[1]

In addition, imports of textiles and clothing are restricted by tariffs that in industrial countries are, on average, more than double those on other manufactures (15 percent, as against 6 percent). Tariffs also tend to increase with the stage of processing. Thus, the average tariff on fibers in industrial countries is about 1 percent, but tariffs on clothing often exceed 20 percent, thus enhancing the effective protection to higher value added products in these countries.

In the Uruguay Round developing countries managed to negotiate a compromise agreement to integrate and liberalize trade in textiles and clothing over a period of 10 years, beginning on January 1, 1995. The Agreement on Textiles and Clothing (ATC) is the transitional agreement that regulates trade in textiles over the 10-year MFA phaseout period. Both importing industrial countries and a large number of developing country exporters were in favor of this transition period, to allow domestic industries to prepare for the expected increased competition resulting from freeing of trade in textiles. This chapter reviews the main elements of the ATC, assesses its implementation to date by industrial countries, considers the efficacy of the WTO dispute settlement mechanism as an enforcement device, and discusses the principal concerns of developing countries regarding implementation of the ATC.

Main Elements of the Agreement on Textiles and Clothing

The Agreement on Textiles and Clothing is a multilateral trade agreement under the WTO, but it has distinctive features that differentiate it from other WTO agreements, as well as from the MFA. The

MFA involved separate agreements between certain GATT contracting parties to waive their GATT rights and obligations by applying quantitative restrictions selectively against specified countries, thus violating the nondiscrimination principle. The ATC is an integral part of the multilateral trading system, administered and supervised by the WTO. It applies equally to all WTO members and is binding on all of them. Another difference is that the MFA contained a provision for the accession of non-GATT members such as China. In contrast, accession to the WTO automatically implies membership in the ATC, and non-WTO members are not covered by ATC provisions.

A distinctive feature of the ATC is its fixed time span of 10 years, which cannot be extended. The ATC is therefore a transitional agreement. The agreement's main elements are its product coverage, the program of liberalization, the treatment of existing trade restrictions, the application of transitional safeguards, the fulfillment of commitments under GATT rules, the supervision of ATC implementation, and dispute settlement.

Product Coverage

The product coverage of the ATC is specified in an annex to the agreement in terms of the six-digit level of the Harmonized Commodity Description and Coding System (HS). The ATC covers all of Section 11 of the HS, with the exception of raw fibers. It also covers certain lines from other chapters of the HS that embody textile materials, such as luggage, umbrellas, watch straps, and parachutes. The ATC's product coverage is wider than that of the MFA in that it includes products of pure silk as well as those made from vegetable fibers. The ATC Annex includes both HS lines that were restrained under the MFA and lines that were unrestrained. According to estimates by the International Textiles and Clothing Bureau (ITCB), imports of HS lines that were not restrained under the MFA accounted for 33.6 percent of total imports in 1990. The proportion of HS lines not covered by quantitative restrictions in the United States was 36.8 percent; in Canada and Norway the share was considerably higher.

Liberalization Program

The gradual elimination of quantitative restrictions under the ATC is to be achieved through the step-by-step removal of existing quotas (described by the agreement as "integration") and through accelerated expansion of the remaining nonintegrated quotas ("liberalization"). Integration involves two groups of countries: those that maintained quotas under the MFA (principally, the United States, the EU, Canada, and Norway) and other WTO members that have chosen to retain the right to use the special safeguards provision of Article VI of the ATC.

Integration is to be carried out in three stages. In the first stage, which began on January 1, 1995, WTO members must integrate 16 percent of the total volume of their 1990 imports. In the second stage, which started on January 1, 1998, an additional 17 percent of the total volume of 1990 imports must be integrated, followed by another 18 percent in the third stage, which commences on January 1, 2002. Finally, on January 1, 2005, the remaining 49 percent of the total volume of 1990 imports must be integrated. The choice of products to be integrated is left to the importing country but must include at least one item from each of four major product groups: yarns and tops, fabrics, made-ups, and clothing.

Two comments are in order. First, a more reasonable proposition would have been to choose a reference year as close as possible to the ATC's initiation in 1995 (depending on the availability of import data), rather than 1990. Second, leaving nearly one-half of all imports to be integrated at the end of the transition period does not ensure a smooth and painless process of integration and thereby contradicts one of the purposes of a transition period.

Some avenues of flexibility in exceeding quota limits that applied under the MFA were carried over to the ATC. These include transfer of 6 percent of the unfilled quota volume from the previous year to the current year (carryover), prior utilization of 6 percent of next year's quota (carryforward) and transfer of quotas from one product to the other within the limit of 6 percent of the quota requested to be increased (swing). These flexibility advantages are usually transferred to quota beneficiaries in cases of tight quotas.

Concurrently with the process of integration, products remaining under restriction are allowed an increase in growth rates above those agreed on under the MFA. Quotas for such products are to be increased by an additional 16 percent in the first stage, by 25 percent in the second stage, and by 27 percent in the third. Small suppliers whose restric-

Table 21.2 Number of Quotas Eliminated by Integration in ATC Stages 1 and 2

WTO member	Total number of quotas	Number of quotas eliminated		
		By integration	By early elimination	Total
United States	750	2	11[a]	13
EU	219	14	0	14
Canada	295	29	0	29
Norway	54	0	51	51

a. Quotas eliminated only in respect to Romania.
Source: TMB notifications, reported by ITCB, IC/W/219, July 21, 2000.

Table 21.3 Restrained Trade Freed of Quotas, 1995–97
(percentage of imports)

WTO member	1995	1996	1997
United States			
By volume	6.23	6.03	6.00
By value	6.40	6.14	6.12
EU			
By volume	4.74	4.92	4.77
By value	4.28	4.34	4.18

Source: ITCB, WT/GC/W/283, 2000.

As mentioned, the ATC requires that restraining countries increase the existing growth rates of quotas by no less than 16, 25, and 27 percent successively over the specified three stages. These rates may appear impressive, but in reality they did not yield substantial added access because the base growth rates allowed under the MFA were modest. Table 21.4 reports the additional growth in access for the first two stages (seven years) of the transition period.

With the implementation of the third stage of the ATC, neither the integration proposals nor the proposed additional growth factors significantly improve access or liberalize trade in textiles. For example, under the integration process proposed by the EU, most quotas would be left in place until close to the end of the 10-year transition period. Only 52 of the 219 EU quotas (less than 24 percent) would be dismantled during the three stages—a very modest phaseout indeed! To begin with, in 1990 only 58.3 percent of imports was actually under quota restrictions. This allowed the EU to avoid integrating restrained products that were of any significance. Furthermore, although under its proposal the EU would have integrated 51 percent of the base year imports, this would represent only 12.3 percent of 1995 total imports

Table 21.4 Expanded Market Access Attributable to Increases in Quotas (Stages 1 and 2 Combined)
(percentage of imports)

WTO member	Average pre-ATC growth rate	Total increase in access	Annual average increase in access, 1995–2001
United States	4.61	6.36	1.03
EU	3.44	4.49	0.73
Canada	5.26	7.53	1.22

Source: ITCB, document WT/GC/W/283, 2000.

and 21 percent of overall restrained imports. The bulk of the restrained products (about 79 percent) will have to be liberalized at the end of the transition period. Another indication of the constraining effect of the remaining restrictions is the fact that whereas total EU imports increased by 31 percent between 1995 and 1999, imports from WTO members under quota restrictions expanded by only 20 percent.[2]

The Textiles Monitoring Body

The Textiles Monitoring Body (TMB) has the mandate of supervising the implementation of the ATC. It has a dual function: it examines the conformity of all actions taken with the ATC, and it addresses disputes among members. The ATC requires that changes in rules and procedures, or changes in the category system that affect the implementation or administration of quotas, not upset the balance of rights and obligations between members, adversely affect or impede the access of a member, or disrupt trade under the ATC. Should such changes occur, the parties concerned are to consult. If consultations fail to reach a mutually satisfactory solution, the matter is to be referred to the TMB for decision. The TMB thus acquires the function of resolving disputes among the parties.

The TMB is a standing body made up of a chairman and 10 members drawn from countries that are broadly representative of the WTO. It is almost equally divided between industrial and developing countries. With the exception of four permanent industrial country representatives, membership rotates. This asymmetric treatment favors the industrial country group. The TMB relies principally on notifications by WTO members. Its decisions are taken by consensus, and it has therefore not always been able to resolve disputes. In such cases members may invoke general WTO dispute settlement mechanisms.

ATC Article V.1 requires that members establish the necessary legal provisions and administrative procedures to prevent circumvention by transshipment, rerouting, false declarations, and falsification of documents. When the existence of such circumvention is established through investigation and cooperation among parties, members may agree to deny the entry of goods, to charge the goods to the quota of the true country of origin, or to introduce restraints on the country of transit. If the consulta-

tions do not result in agreement on satisfactory solutions, the problem may be referred to the TMB. The ATC provides for legal action against the exporter or importer under domestic laws in case of false declarations for purposes of circumvention.

Actions taken in fulfilling commitments under the ATC have to be notified to the TMB. (A summary is sufficient if these actions have been notified to other WTO bodies.) If actions have not been taken to fulfill specific commitments, the TMB has to be informed. These commitments are related to the achievement of improved market access for textile products and are entered into to ensure the application of policies in the areas of dumping, subsidies, and piracy of trademarks and designs, with a view to establishing fair and equitable trading conditions and avoiding discrimination against textile imports (ATC Article VII.1).

Developing Country Concerns

Implementation of the ATC to date indicates that little actual liberalization is to be expected before the end of the 10-year transition period. Experience also shows that other policy measures can be easily employed to limit the impact of liberalization. Thus, safeguards and antidumping measures have been used to restrict exports to both the EU and the United States. Some believe that quotas may be a better alternative (see Ozdem and Demirkol 1994), given that industrial countries, especially in the EU, actively use contingent protection to protect their industries. Rules of origin can also be used to restrict trade. Changes in U.S. rules of origin for textile and clothing products, implemented as of July 1, 1996, had adverse effects on sales to countries that produced for export to the American market and created an incentive for such exporters to obtain their materials from countries not subject to quota restraints (ITCB 1999).

The implications of the ATC for developing countries depend principally on the relative importance of restricted markets for their exports, on the significance of textiles and clothing in their external trade, on future trends in competitiveness, and on their own policies in this sector. Industrial country members of the WTO should complement their commitment to phase out quantitative restrictions—whether imposed under the MFA or otherwise—with reductions in most-favored-nation (MFN) tariffs on textiles and clothing.

BOX 21.1 (CONTINUED)

(measured in 1997 ECU, and including indirect efficiency effects). Almost ECU 6.5 billion of these annual gains simply follow from a recapture of ATC quota rents. Other gains stem from increased investment and reallocation of resources to areas with higher returns. The sum of the yearly discounted net income gains from a full 1997 implementation is more than ECU 160 billion.

Recalculating these results (ECU 12.7 billion for consumers, plus ECU 12.3 billion from the gain in efficiency and other factors, for a total of ECU 25 billion) and applying them to an EU family of four, we find that the average gain resulting from accelerated implementation (doing away with quotas and tariffs) amounts to ECU 270 per year per household. Moreover, these figures imply that the annual cost of each job saved in the textile and clothing industries by delayed implementation is, on average, ECU 28,000 for the textile industry and ECU 41,000 for the clothing industry. Since the industry as a whole is contracting, Francois, Glisman, and Spinanger (2000) argue that the cost of EU protection for the textile and clothing industries could well approach the full value added of these industries by the time quotas are removed in 2005.

As for the distribution of the costs of protection across population groups, the quota prices for children's clothing are noticeably higher than for adult clothing, even though adult clothing typically carries higher retail prices. With quota prices for children's clothing in 1997 about 200 percent higher than for comparable adult clothing, the magnified impact on families with children is obvious.

The conclusion to be drawn is that liberalization under the ATC should be effected as quickly as possible and should be comprehensive. Delaying such liberalization to the very end of the ATC transition period (January 1, 2005) would impose continuing significant direct costs on consumers and substantial income losses for the economy as a whole. The resources lost could have been invested in production potential—human or physical capital—in sectors where the EU has clear comparative advantages. Thus, quite apart from the benefits that would accrue to efficient producers of clothing in developing countries, liberalization is in the interest of importing countries.

Source: Prepared by the volume editors, based on Francois, Glisman, and Spinanger (2000).

Notes

1 On the export side, the last incarnation of the MFA (MFA IV) covered Argentina, Bangladesh, Brazil, China, Colombia, Costa Rica, the Czech Republic, the Dominican Republic, the Arab Republic of Egypt, El Salvador, Fiji, Guatemala, Honduras, Hong Kong (China), Hungary, India, Indonesia, Jamaica, Kenya, the Republic of Korea, Macao (China), Malaysia, Mexico, Oman, Pakistan, Panama, Peru, the Philippines, Poland, Romania, Singapore, the Slovak Republic, Slovenia, Sri Lanka, Thailand, Turkey, and Uruguay.

2 EU Integration Plan for ATC Stage 3, ITCB, IC/W/219, July 21, 2000.

3 India filled 107 percent of its yarn quota to the EU in 1994–96, while Pakistan and Indonesia filled 150 and 130 percent of their respective quotas during the same period. Argentina, however, covered only 33 percent of its quota in 1994–95.

The percentage of quota utilization was 6 percent in Brazil, 51 percent in Peru, 56 percent in Thailand, and 77 percent in Korea (see Clément and others 1996).

4 The rates of quota utilization for the main exporters of fabrics to the EU for 1994–96 were as follows: Argentina, 34 percent; Brazil, 28 percent; Bulgaria, 94 percent; Czech Republic, 90 percent; Egypt, 74 percent; Hong Kong (China), 16 percent; Hungary, 37 percent; India, 93 percent; Indonesia, 80 percent; Korea, 46 percent; Malaysia, 101 percent; Pakistan, 98 percent; Peru, 24 percent; Poland, 28 percent; Romania, 34 percent; Singapore, 5 percent; Slovak Republic, 44 percent; Thailand, 108 percent; and Turkey, 71 percent (see Clément and others 1996).

5 It should be noted that the main textile and clothing exports of the CEE countries are wool and man-made fiber products, while the bulk of exports from most Mediterranean countries consists of cotton manufactures.

22

SAFEGUARDS

*Making Sense of
GATT/WTO Provisions
Allowing for Import Restrictions*

TRADE LIBERALIZATION IS NOT ROCKET SCIENCE. ANY PROGRAM THAT SIGNIFICANTLY opens the domestic market to international competition will require a degree of fine-tuning. Any government that maintains a liberal trade policy will be subject to occasional pressures for exceptional treatment—for example, temporary protection for a particular industry. Thus, part of the politics of safeguarding a generally liberal trade policy is to have in place a policy mechanism for managing such pressures; that is, for considering petitions for protection that are exceptions to the general thrust of policy.

This chapter is about such policies. The analytical part reviews the use of GATT/WTO rules that specify how and when a member country may introduce a new trade restriction or replace an old one. (I do not distinguish one instance from the other.)

I draw two major lessons from this analysis:

1. GATT/WTO rules are fungible. At different times, members have used different instruments to handle safeguard issues.
2. GATT/WTO rules do not distinguish economically sensible trade restrictions—those that add

more to the national economic interest than they take away—from ordinary protection.

The prescriptive part of the chapter draws lessons from the GATT/WTO experience—lessons that a government might take into account when deliberating the structure of a safeguard mechanism that would help it manage pressures from particular industries for "exceptional" import protection as the government implements a liberalization program or works to maintain a policy of openness to international competition.

There is more to designing a sensible safeguard mechanism than simply finding what trade restrictions GATT/WTO rules allow. In this regard, these rules are too generous; imposing all the restrictions that are permitted would isolate an economy from the global system. The challenge a government faces is to identify, among the many processes the GATT/WTO allows, a safeguard system that makes economic and political sense—one that distinguishes between restrictions that will and will not advance the national economic interest and one whose political dimensions will help support the government's concern to integrate its economy into the global system.

GATT Experience with Safeguard Provisions

Although the GATT is perhaps best known as the patron of agreements to remove trade restrictions, it includes a number of provisions that allow countries to impose new ones. Twenty of them are listed in Table 22.1, and the list could be longer. Article XX, for example, includes 10 subcategories. *The*

22.1 Renegotiations, Emergency Actions, and Voluntary Export Restraints (VERs), 1948–93

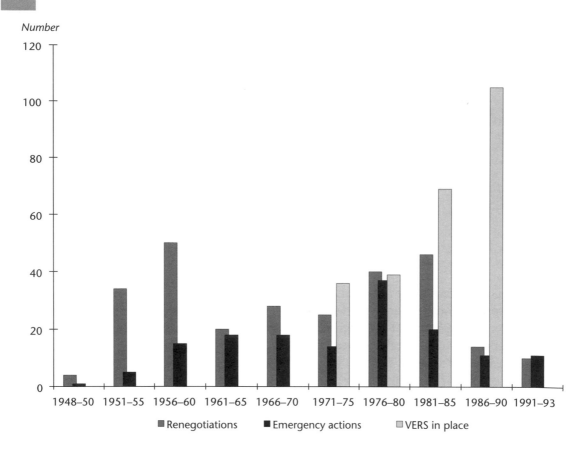

Number

| | Renegotiations | Emergency actions | VERS in place |

least one renegotiation—in total, 110 renegotiations, or almost 4 per country.

In use, Article XIX emergency actions and Article XXVIII renegotiations complemented each other. Of the 15 pre-1962 Article XIX actions that were large enough that the exporter insisted on compensation (or threatened retaliation), 9 were eventually resolved as Article XXVIII renegotiations. Renegotiations under Article XXVIII, in turn, were often folded into regular tariff negotiations. From 1947 through 1961, five negotiating rounds were completed; that is, such negotiations were almost continuously under way. *In the GATT's early years, renegotiations and emergency actions followed by renegotiations were the principal mechanisms for making adjustments.*

Other GATT Provisions That Serve as Pressure Valves

In the GATT's first decade and a half, the renegotiation and emergency action provisions served, for

countries that had reduced and bound their tariffs through the GATT, as the procedures through which the countries would adjust their trade policies to troublesome imports.[5] This was as the GATT's initial framers had intended. In time, however, these mechanisms were replaced by others.

Negotiated Export Restraints. By the 1960s formal use of Article XIX and of the renegotiations process began to wane. Actions taken under the escape clause tended to involve negligible amounts of world trade in relatively minor product categories.[6] Big problems such as textile and apparel imports were handled another way, through the negotiation of "voluntary" export restraint agreements (VERs). The Long-Term Cotton Textile Arrangement, negotiated in 1962, brought GATT sanction to industrial countries' VERs on cotton textiles and apparel. The Multifibre Arrangement (MFA), first negotiated in 1972 and only now being phased out, extended the GATT sanction for such restrictions to virtually all textile and clothing products. Industrial countries used the same device—negotiated export restraints, or VERs—to control troublesome imports into several other important sectors such as steel. *By the 1970s, negotiated or voluntary export restraints (VERs) had become the common mode for dealing with troublesome imports.*

Except for those specially sanctioned by the textile arrangements, VERs were clearly GATT-illegal (GATT 1994a: 494). But although VERs violated GATT legalisms, they accorded well with its ethic of reciprocity:

- They were, at least in form, *negotiations* to allow replacement of restrictions that had been negotiated down. Negotiation was also important to prevent a chain reaction of one country after another restricting its imports, as had occurred in the 1930s.
- A VER did provide compensation, in the form of the higher price that the exporter would receive. Had imports been restricted to the same volume by a tariff, the scarcity value (rent) of the restriction would have been collected by the importing country.
- In many instances the troublesome increase in imports came from countries that had not been the "principal suppliers" with which the initial concession had been negotiated. These new exporters were displacing not only domestic production in importing countries but also the exports of the traditional suppliers. A VER with the new, troublesome supplier could thus be viewed as defense of the rights of the principal suppliers who had paid for the initial concession.

The reality of power politics was another factor. Even though one of the GATT's objectives was to neutralize the influence of economic power on the determination of trade policy, VERs were frequently used by large countries to control imports from smaller countries. *VERs, although GATT-illegal, were more consistent with the GATT's ethic of reciprocity than unilateral actions would have been.*

Just as the renegotiation emergency action mechanism had been replaced by the use of VERs, so VERs in their turn gave way to another mechanism, antidumping. There were several reasons behind this evolution:

- The growing realization in industrial countries that a VER was a costly form of protection[7]

- The long-term legal pressure of GATT rules
- The availability of an attractive, GATT-legal alternative.

The Uruguay Round agreement on safeguards explicitly bans further use of VERs and, along with the Agreement on Textiles and Clothing, requires the elimination of all such measures now in place.

Antidumping. Antidumping was a minor instrument when the GATT was negotiated, and the provision for antidumping regulations was included with little controversy. In 1958, when the contracting parties finally canvassed themselves about the use of antidumping, the resulting tally showed only 37 antidumping decrees in force across all GATT member countries; 21 of these were in South Africa (GATT 1958: 14). Since then, antidumping has become the industrial countries' main safeguard instrument, and it is gaining increasing popularity among developing countries. The scale of use of antidumping is a magnitude larger than that of renegotiations and emergency actions has ever been (Figure 22.2). In the 10 years through 1993, for example, only 30 Article XIX actions were notified to the GATT, an average of 3 a year, as against 164 antidumping cases a year (GATT 1993a: 16, 26).[8] *Antidumping has become the main instrument for dealing with troublesome imports.*

The rise to prominence of antidumping had nothing to do with the logic of a sensible pressure valve instrument. In the United States the shift from other measures to antidumping was propelled by the desire of the Congress to regain control over trade policy from the executive branch, which controlled tariff renegotiations, the implementation of emergency actions, and the negotiation of VERs. By broadening and strengthening the antidumping law and by eliminating the president's discretion to override an affirmative finding, the Congress could give constituents access to import relief that would not be diluted by the president's general foreign policy interests.

The reasons that antidumping emerged as a major policy instrument in the European Union (EU) were similar. Slower growth made European governments sensitive to the displacement of domestic production by emerging Asian exporters. Antidumping was an instrument of the European Union; by the Treaty of Rome, the EU Commission could take antidumping action, but member states

The ITO negotiations never resulted in an agreement, but basically the same set of countries did reach agreement to reduce tariffs. Needing a legal instrument (contract) to give effect to these reductions, the tariff negotiators put together the GATT. With the pressure on to implement the agreed reductions before protectionist interests could block them, the reformers attempted to buy off the protectionists by including in the GATT a number of provisions that would allow countries to impose new trade restrictions. They did not have time to think through the long-run implications of these provisions. Fifty years of experience, however, make evident the following lessons.

1. *GATT provisions are fungible.* Each GATT provision for import restrictions appears to apply only in a specific circumstance: the rationale for a restriction may be to protect national security, to safeguard the balance of payments, to promote an infant industry, to offset dumping, and so on. In practice, these provisions have proved to be quite fungible. The industrial countries' practice shows that action against troublesome imports can be legally packaged as an Article VI antidumping action or, just as conveniently, as an Article XIX emergency action. Similarly, developing countries seeking GATT legality for restrictions that were, in fact, infant industry protection (Art. XVIII, sec. C), found it administratively more convenient—and no legal problem—to declare them as intended to protect the balance of payments (Art. XVIII, sec. B). In the 15 years preceding the Uruguay Round (1973–87), developing countries declared 3,434 restrictions as balance of payment measures and only 91 as infant industry protection. Article XVIII, section C, requires prior notification and compensation and allows retaliation. Actions under Article XVIII, section B, at that time required no compensation, did not permit retaliation, and had no time limit.

2. *GATT provisions impose little discipline.* The drafters of the GATT presumed that discipline would be provided by reciprocity. That is why they established renegotiation and emergency actions as the means by which a country would adjust its tariff rates to troublesome imports. The evolution of the VER evaded the power of reciprocity as pressure against restrictions. Antidumping, today's favorite instrument, is completely outside

the bounds of reciprocity; unilateral action is explicitly permitted.

As to the provisions (listed in Table 22.1) that specify when various restrictive actions may be taken, practice has shown that such action is almost always possible under the rules. In short, GATT allows import relief in every instance in which imports cause or threaten injury—that is, are troublesome to domestic competitors. Import relief is therefore available in every instance in which domestic competitors would complain. The Uruguay Round Antidumping Agreement makes no attempt to correct the weakness of the economic principles on which GATT/WTO treatment of antidumping is based. Its attempts to discipline the imposition of new restrictions depend entirely on procedural, not substantive, constraints.

3. *GATT provisions do not provide a basis for distinguishing between restrictions that would serve the national economic interest and those that would not.* This conclusion follows quickly from the previous two. When import-competing producers would benefit from protection (injury would be avoided), the rules allow protection. The rules do not require that a government, in deciding on a petition for protection, take into consideration the costs that would accrue to domestic users of imports. Box 22.2 elaborates this point.

These conclusions do not mean that the GATT rules cannot be useful to a government that wants to maintain a liberal trade policy. The rules do not *require* protection in every instance in which they *allow* it. As explained in the next section, the procedural and transparency guidelines provided by the GATT/WTO can be the basis for an economically and politically sensible mechanism for determining when requests for exceptional protection will be honored, and when they will not.

An Economically Sensible Safeguard Mechanism

As with trade liberalization, implementing a sensible safeguards policy is not rocket science. In the abstract, good economic policy consists of government interventions that make economic sense—that provide greater benefits than costs to members of the society for whom the government is responsible. In practice, maintaining an economically sensi-

BOX 22.2 THE FLAWED ECONOMICS OF BASING DECISIONS ON AN INJURY INVESTIGATION

More than two centuries ago, economists demonstrated that import restrictions often subtract more from the national economic interest of the country that imposes them than they add to it. There is nothing in such economics to suggest that import competition will be beneficial to *all* domestic interests (or, stated another way, will not be troublesome to *some* domestic interests). On the contrary, there are *net* gains from trade because the benefits to some domestic interests exceed the costs of import competition to others.

An injury investigation acknowledges only half of the familiar economics of international trade. It gives standing to the costs of trade, but it leaves out the gains. It enfranchises the domestic interests that bear the burden of import competition and would therefore benefit from an import restriction, but it disenfranchises the domestic interests that would bear the costs of the import restriction—or, conversely, reap the gains from not imposing it.

As an analogy, one might imagine a soccer pitch with only one goal, like that shown in the figure; the domestic interests that would benefit from the restriction can score, but those that would bear the costs cannot. The investigatory process allows goals only by import-competing interests. In the score that determines the outcome, the interests of users of imports and others that would bear the costs of the import restriction are simply not counted.

A safeguard petition is a request for an action by a government. Correctly deciding when to take or not to take action begins with asking the right questions: *Who in the domestic economy will benefit from the proposed action? Who will lose? And by how much?*

Safeguard investigations should not focus solely on the effect of the proposed restriction on domestic producers of like or competing goods. Rather, they should focus on the national economic interest of the restricting country. National economic interest in this context means the sum of benefits to all nationals who benefit minus the costs to all nationals who lose. Injury, as it is defined in safeguard and antidumping laws, takes into account only one of the two sides that make up the national economic interest. An economically sensible process would allow both sides—those that will benefit from a trade restriction and those that will bear the costs—to score.

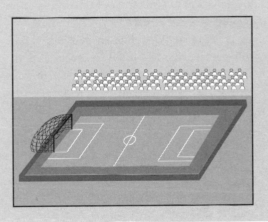

ble international trade policy is often a matter of avoiding interventions that have greater costs than benefits, or, when the realities of domestic politics are taken into account, a matter of minimizing the number or the effect of such interventions.

There will be cases in which other domestic considerations make it impossible to avoid an economically unsound trade intervention. In those instances, good policy becomes a matter of:

- Making restrictions transparent
- Avoiding allowing the restrictions to become precedents for further restrictions

- Managing the restrictions so as to strengthen the politics of avoiding rather than imposing such measures.

Antidumping is not a sensible safeguard mechanism. It focuses on the wrong issue: the nature of the foreign business. The real key issue is the impact on the local economy. Who in the local economy would benefit from the proposed import restriction, and who would lose? On each side, by how much? It is critical that the policy process by which the government decides to intervene or not to intervene give voice to those interests that benefit from open trade and would bear the costs of the proposed intervention. In this spirit, I outline below a policy mechanism that would:

- Help the government distinguish trade interventions that would serve the national economic interest from those that would not
- Even in those instances in which the decision is to restrict imports, support the politics of openness and liberalization.

Guidelines for Procedures

The familiar process of investigating injury from imports to competing domestic producers would be part of an economically sensible safeguard procedure. As explained in Box 22.2, however, an injury investigation captures only half of the impact on the domestic economy. It identifies those domestic interests that would benefit from the proposed restriction, but it fails to take into account those interests that would be penalized by restricted access to imports. Under the revised system, economic analysis of the impact of the restriction on users would proceed in parallel with the analysis of "injury" to competing domestic producers. The concepts and techniques would be much the same as in a traditional investigation, but injury (to users of imports) that would result from reduced access to imports would be measured on the same dimensions as injury (to those who compete with imports) from import competition: lost sales, lost profits, lost jobs, and so on.

A process of the sort suggested makes political as well as economic sense. By giving voice to the interests that would bear the costs of the proposed import restriction, the process will help to fortify the politics of not granting the restriction.

The following are general guidelines:

- *Identify the costs and the losers.* The procedures should bring out the costs of the requested exception and the identities of the persons or groups who will bear these costs. More expensive imports will cost somebody money and—if the imports are needed materials—will eliminate somebody's job. These costs, and the people in the domestic economy who will bear them, should have the same standing in law and in administrative practice as the other side already enjoys.

- *Be clear that the action is an exception.* Public statements should establish that the requested action would be an exception to the principles that underlie the liberalization program and should emphasize that an accumulation of such exceptions would constitute abandonment of the liberalization program and loss of its benefits. Including in the investigation process an expression of the costs that the proposed restriction would impose will help make the point that the action is an exception to the generally beneficial policy of openness to international competition.

- *Don't sanctify the criteria for the action.* The procedures should not presume, as antidumping does, that there is some good reason for granting exceptions. Procedures that compare the situation of the petitioner with preestablished criteria for granting import relief should be avoided. It should be emphasized that the function of the review is to identify the benefits, the costs, and domestic winners and losers resulting from the requested action.

The third guideline is more important than it might seem. The history of antidumping and other trade remedies shows that clever people will always be able to present their situation exactly as the criteria describe. If you start out to find just the few exporters who are being unfair to Mexico, or to the United States, or to Ecuador, you will soon be swamped by evidence that everyone is.

At the technical level, useful concepts for investigation procedures, such as transparency and automatic expiration for any exception that is granted (a sunset clause), can be gleaned from the procedural requirements included in the Uruguay Round Safeguards Agreement.

Notes

1 GATT tariff cuts had to be made on a most-favored-nation basis (applicable to imports from all GATT members). A renegotiation was not conducted with the entire GATT membership but only with the country with which that reduction was initially negotiated, plus any other countries enumerated by the GATT as "principal suppliers."

2 Renegotiation procedures are basically the same under the Uruguay Round agreements as they were before.

3 The Uruguay Round Agreement on Safeguards (but not the initial GATT) requires a formal investigation and determination of injury. It allows, however, a provisional safeguard measure to be taken before the investigation is completed.

4 The Uruguay Round Safeguards Agreement modified the emergency action procedure in several ways. Among other things, no compensation is required, and no retaliation is allowed, in the first three years a restriction is in place; no restriction (including an extension) may be retained for more than 8 years (10 years if the restriction is imposed by a developing country); and all measures in place more than 1 year must be progressively liberalized.

5 Countries that reduced and bound their tariffs did not include most of the developing countries that were members of the GATT.

6 Statistics for 1980 show that actions taken under Article XIX covered imports valued at US$1.6 billion; in that year total world trade was valued at US$2,000 billion (Sampson 1987: 145).

7 For example, Hufbauer and Elliott (1993) found that of the welfare loss to the U.S. economy from all forms of protection in place in the early 1990s, over 83 percent came from VERs.

8 The tally of antidumping orders is partial.

9 During the period 1980–88, 348 of 774 U.S. antidumping cases were superseded by VERs (Finger and Murray 1993). From July 1980 through June 1989, of 384 antidumping actions taken by the European Community, 184 were price undertakings (Stegemann 1992).

GARY N. HORLICK
ELEANOR SHEA

23

DEALING WITH U.S. TRADE LAWS

Before, During, and After

E
XPORTERS TO THE UNITED STATES ARE
CONFRONTED BY A THICKET OF NOT
entirely coordinated U.S. trade laws, administered
by a maze of administrative agencies. From the
perspective of a U.S. industry seeking protection,
however, those laws simply represent different
ways of reaching the same goal—improvement of
the competitive position of the complainant
against other companies.[1] Exporters should disregard any moralistic claims associated with trade
litigation ("dumping," "subsidies," "unfair" access
to raw materials, cheap labor, and so on) and
should view it from that same perspective: how
the dispute will affect their competitive position
in the U.S. market. The only way to be completely
sure of staying out of trade disputes in the United
States is to stay out of the market there. Exporters
can, however, take other action to avoid embroil-
ment in (and to win) U.S. trade disputes—assuming that the necessary action makes sense
commercially.

The First Phase: Before Any Specific Trade Action Is Threatened

What can an exporter do, before
there is any threat of U.S. trade
action, to avoid it? An assessment
of the peculiarities of the major
U.S. trade laws is necessary.

"Nonpolitical" Remedies

The antidumping and countervailing duty laws are the most
important threats to exporters
because they are nondiscre-
tionary [19 U.S.C. secs. 1671–77n (1994 and Supp. IV
1998)]. That means that U.S. companies (or workers)
can file petitions and, if they can prove their cases,
put up import barriers without being stopped by
political intervention.

The imposition of antidumping duties requires a
showing that exports have been sold in the United
States at less than their price in the home or third-
country markets or at less than their cost of production. Thus, theoretically, a company can avoid
antidumping cases by conscientiously checking the
prices of its exports to the United States to ensure that
they are not priced lower than sales at home or to third
countries, or priced below cost. Although such an
"antidumping audit" may well be worth performing if
a trade action is likely, this is not very useful advice if
the result requires that attempts be made to sell in the
United States at above the price the market will pay.

The imposition of antidumping duties also
requires a finding that the imports in question have

caused material injury to the U.S. industry. Certain planning steps probably should be taken in connection with this "injury" question: sales should be monitored to avoid unnecessary "bunching," and careful documentation should be kept showing that one's own company's sales are not price leaders in the U.S. market.

The imposition of countervailing duties requires receipt of a subsidy of some sort. This is not as simple as it sounds; the United States considers as countervailable subsidies some things which may not strike a foreign (or U.S.) businessperson that way, such as government loan guarantees or (perhaps the extreme case) the purchase of inputs from producers who themselves receive subsidies. A company with substantial exports to the United States might want to check its possible liability for government assistance it has received or is contemplating receiving. More important, counseling in advance of receipt of government assistance can be useful, since the form and structure of that assistance could well dictate whether it is countervailable under U.S. laws and WTO rules, and to what extent. It can make a tremendous difference, for example, whether the amount of the government grant is allocated over the output of the entire company or over the output of a single machine bought with the grant. Countervailing duty cases require the same showing of material injury as antidumping cases, and the same precautions would apply.

"Political" Remedies

Section 201, the "escape clause," permits a U.S. industry to seek relief from imports with which it cannot compete effectively [19 U.S.C. secs. 2251, 2252 (1994 and Supp. IV 1998)]. Since Section 201 requires a finding by the U.S. International Trade Commission (ITC) of "serious injury," some advance planning on the injury issue can be done, as with antidumping and countervailing duty cases. Section 201 also requires a decision by the president to grant relief. Because Section 201 proceedings are required to include imports into the United States from all sources, some foreign producers are frequently exposed to the "sideswipe" phenomenon. In the 1984 Section 201 proceeding on steel, for example, the U.S. complainants specifically stated that imports from Canada and Japan were not a prob-

lem, yet Japan wound up with quotas and Canada wound up committing itself not to "surge" (whatever that meant). Thus, one country's exporters frequently can do very little to avoid entanglement in a Section 201 proceeding (although it is advisable to marshal political interest early to get more favorable treatment at the end of the case).

Section 301 provides a remedy that U.S. companies can invoke against unfair foreign trade barriers of almost any description [19 U.S.C. sec. 2411 (1994 and Supp. IV 1998)]. Consequently, it is relatively difficult to plan ahead for application of this section. These disputes, however, rarely arise suddenly. Typically, U.S. willingness to take action will be signaled well in advance and can be planned for. In any event, unilateral action by the United States under Section 301 is now subject to multilateral WTO rules.

Section 337 normally provides a remedy against patent or trademark infringements [19 U.S.C. sec. 1337 (1994 and Supp. IV 1998)]. Consequently, advance planning in this context is similar to normal patent and trademark precautions. Pre-1994 U.S. procedures under Section 337 had been found to violate the GATT, and it remains to be tested whether the 1994 changes make Section 337 consistent with the WTO.

Section 332 investigations by the ITC are purely fact-finding investigations, but they often are instituted in order to build trade cases for a U.S. industry [19 U.S.C. sec. 1332 (1994 and Supp. IV 1998)]. Consequently, they represent a threat, but also an opportunity for exporters to advertise any claims they wish to make about not dumping, not receiving subsidies, or not causing injury. They also can serve as a mechanical device for forcing exporters to focus early on the possibility of trade litigation.

The Second Phase: Notification That a Trade Complaint Is Being Considered

The advice given by specialized counsel in the second phase is inevitably a little murky. The goal is to avoid an unnecessary trade dispute by changing whatever practice is causing the friction, but not if it means giving up a necessary commercial practice. A further complication is the specter of the antitrust laws of the United States (and other countries). The imminence of a trade complaint, whether justified

tion [19 U.S.C. secs. 167lb(d)(1), (2), 1673d(d) (1994)].

In addition, an affirmative preliminary determination by Commerce will trigger a 120-day period within which the commission must make its final injury determination [19 U.S.C. secs. 1671d(b)(2), 1673d(b)(2) (1994)]. Moreover, in certain specified circumstances Commerce can order that the withholding of appraisement be made retroactive for up to 90 days to prevent importers from rushing in, prior to the preliminary determination, merchandise known to be dumped or subsidized [19 U.S.C. secs. 1671b(e), 1671d(a)(2), (b)(4), 1673b(e), 1673d(a)(3), (b)(4) (1994)]. A negative preliminary determination will lead to a continuation of the investigation, with no suspension of liquidation or requirement to post bond. The preliminary determination includes Commerce's first presentation of its policy decisions on issues raised in an investigation. This presentation clarifies the issues of the case and affords both parties an opportunity to develop their strategies.

The preliminary determination is followed within a few days by a disclosure conference at which each side is told separately the details of the calculations leading to the preliminary determination. The purpose of the disclosure conference is to give the parties the detailed knowledge that will enable them to participate effectively in the remainder of the investigation. It is not a good idea to use the disclosure conference to attempt to argue with staff about the results. That is done at a hearing, which may be requested by either party [19 U.S.C. sec. 1677c (1994)]. In addition, the hearing serves the function of getting one's arguments on the record for purposes of possible later judicial or WTO review.

Final AD/CVD Determinations by Commerce. A final determination must be reached by Commerce within 75 days of a preliminary determination in a countervailing duty case, or within 75 days (extendable by 135 days at the request of the party "losing" the preliminary determination) in an antidumping case. If the final determination is negative, the investigation is terminated [19 U.S.C. sec. 1671d(c)(2) (1994 and Supp. IV 1998)]. If the final determination is affirmative, it goes to the ITC for a final determination of the existence of material injury. Cash deposits (which tie up more of the exporter's working capital) are now required instead of bonds [19 U.S.C. sec. 1671d(c)(1) (1994 and Supp. IV 1998)]. During the period between the preliminary determination and the final determination, both parties will be making their best arguments on questions of fact and law/policy. In practice, the ultimate decisionmakers will not have time for anything but the most concise briefs.

Final AD/CVD Determination by the International Trade Commission. In general, the ITC must make a final determination of injury 45 to 75 days after a final affirmative determination of dumping or subsidization by Commerce [19 U.S.C. secs. 1671d(b), 1673d(b) (1994)]. This process involves a full-fledged hearing before the ITC, with pre- and posthearing briefs and use of expert economic and technical witnesses, all within a very short time span. If the ITC's final determination is negative, the investigation is terminated [19 U.S.C. secs. 1671d(b), 1673d(b) (1994)]. If the final ITC determination is affirmative, Commerce must issue an antidumping or countervailing duty order, as appropriate [19 U.S.C. secs. 1671e, 1673e (1994)].

Other Trade Remedies. Affirmative (that is, favorable to the U.S. complainant) findings by the ITC in Section 201 and Section 337 cases cause no direct trade impact. Instead, the affirmative determination triggers a review by the president (in practice, preceded by an interagency review). The president usually accepts Section 337 relief for patent or trademark violations but often rejects relief in Section 201 cases. During the period 1995–2000, however, the president granted trade relief in all Section 201 cases that reached him.

Review

Judicial Review. Judicial review can be sought by one or both parties for almost any final decision in an antidumping or countervailing duty investigation, starting with the initiation of the investigation [19 U.S.C. sec. 1516a (1994 and Supp. IV 1998)]. Judicial review of Section 201 appears to be limited to procedural matters; see *Maple Leaf Fish Co. v. United States,* 566 F. Supp. 899, 570 F. Supp. 734 (Ct. Intl. Trade 1984). Judicial review of Section 337 is limited to the ITC's decision (not the president's); see *Aktiebolaget Karlstads Mekaniska Werkstad v. U.S. Intl. Trade Comm.,* 705 F.2d 1565 (Fed. Cir. 1983).

Administrative Review. Annual reviews of antidumping or countervailing duty orders pursuant to Section 751 of the Tariff Act of 1930, as amended [19 U.S.C. sec. 1675 (1994)] are conducted in much the same way as the original investigation. The annual review represents a chance to raise new facts, including any that may have been missed in the initial investigation, and a less promising opportunity to argue the original points again—at some risk of irritating the staff. In addition, under Section 751(b), Commerce may revoke an order in light of changed circumstances. Commerce has normally refused to use Section 751 as a vehicle for revising recently issued orders; see, for example, *Color Television Receivers from Korea,* 49 *Fed. Reg.* 50420 (Dept. Comm. 1984) (termination).

Section 201 petitions cannot be brought by a losing industry for another year, but the same result can be obtained by having the Senate Finance Committee or the House Ways and Means Committee bring the petition for the losing industry within that one-year period. See, for example, *Non-Rubber Footwear Hearings,* 50 *Fed. Reg.* 4278 (Dept. Comm. 1985). The president must review relief given under Section 201 after four years [19 U.S.C. sec. 2253(e) (1994)]. Commerce and the ITC must review antidumping and countervailing duty orders every five years.

Settlement

Settlement of AD/CVD cases may be obtained by one of two means:

1. *Termination.* Commerce can terminate an investigation on withdrawal of the petition by the petitioner, typically as a result of negotiation of some satisfactory "deal."[5]
2. *Suspension agreements.* In practice, there are three useful types of suspension agreements for countervailing duty cases:

   - Renunciation of the subsidy by the foreign government or recipient company[6]
   - Imposition of an export tax equal to the amount of the subsidy[7]
   - Quantitative restraints.[8]

Antidumping investigations may be suspended upon an agreement by the exporters to revise their prices to eliminate completely any dumping margin [19 U.S.C. sec. 1673c(b)(2) (1994)]. Although there are methods of suspension under the statute that

parallel those for countervailing duty proceedings described above [see 19 U.S.C. sec. 1673c(b)(1), (c)(1) (1994)], they are rarely practicable.

The procedures for AD/CVD suspension agreements are complex. Essentially, they require that an agreement be reached between Commerce and the respondent at least 30 days prior to the date of the final determination in order to allow the domestic petitioner its statutory right of comment [19 U.S.C. secs. 1671c(e), 1673c(e) (1994)]. There are ample provisions for review of suspension agreements.[9]

Settlements under Section 201 in essence turn into political "deals," such as the "voluntary" import restraints imposed in the wake of the Section 201 steel case in 1984. Section 337 cases are frequently settled by consent decrees or licensing agreements between the complainant and the foreign respondent (as is often the case with normal patent and trademark litigation).

The Fifth Phase: After the Case Is Over

A great deal can be accomplished after a case is over to ameliorate the consequences of a negative result. For example, in antidumping cases the method of calculating duties for collection is slightly different from the method used during the initial investigation, and a well-organized company can arrange its sales to minimize duties. Similarly, countervailing duties can be minimized by a review of operations and by decisions as to whether to terminate acceptance of some government assistance, or by payment of export taxes (in which case the foreign government, rather than the U.S. Treasury, in effect collects the duty). Quotas or tariffs under Section 201 or 301 might require changes in business operations; changes in production patterns (the 1983 tariffs under Section 201 on motorcycles with engines larger than 700 cubic centimeters led to a spate of 699 cubic centimeter engines); or diplomatic action, including reprisals or threat thereof.

Notes

1 The complainant may even seek to improve its position in relation to its own subsidiaries, where that is profitable. In recent years cases have been brought by a U.S. subsidiary of a foreign parent against imports from third-country subsidiaries of the same parent—see *Motorcycle Batteries from Taiwan,* 46 *Fed. Reg.* 28465 (Dept. Comm. 1981) (initiation)—and against a U.S. corporation that had signed a supply contract with a foreign company by a second U.S. company that had tried and

their willingness to concede control to the market, and most have a penchant for gradualism. So, in various countries, competition has been introduced, but the number of firms has been fixed by policy; privatization is often partial and limits are set on foreign participation; separate regulators have been created, but they are rarely fully independent.

Even though economic theory is bold in its pronouncements on the extremes, it is more tentative in its prescriptions on the transition path. How much greater are the social benefits if privatization is accompanied by competition? How much competition is desirable—is there no good reason to limit entry? How far should foreign investment be encouraged in concentrated markets? How important is an independent regulator for the emergence of robust competition? What should the regulator regulate? How can any adverse effects of liberalization on income distribution and poverty be best addressed?

A number of questions also arise about the role of the GATS. What have we learned about the interplay between services reform at the national level and negotiations at the multilateral level? Do negotiations simply harvest liberalization that has been achieved unilaterally, or can they actually help eliminate barriers? What is the value of multilateral rules and commitments? Do they foster good policy and help improve economic performance? How much advantage can be taken of the current round of negotiations to encourage desirable policy reform? Is there a need to reform the GATS itself to make it a more effective catalyst for reform of national policies?

A number of basic themes emerge from the contributions in this part and from recent research on services liberalization:

- There are significant potential gains from liberalization within developing countries, especially in key infrastructure services. These gains may, however, not be realized if reform programs are not properly designed.
- Successful domestic liberalization requires a greater emphasis on introducing competition than on changing ownership; effective regulation to remedy market failure and pursue social goals; and credibility of policy reform programs.
- There are substantial potential global gains from the elimination of barriers to services exports by developing countries. Effective access to foreign

markets requires the elimination of explicit (formal) restrictions, as well as multilateral disciplines on implicit regulatory barriers.

The first several chapters in this part provide general background on the current status of international trade in services and the concepts employed in negotiations and agreements on this trade. James Hodge, in Chapter 24, assesses the benefits and costs for developing countries of liberalization of trade in services and outlines the steps involved in negotiating and implementing liberalization. In Chapter 25 A. Maurer and P. Chauvet look at the magnitude of global trade in services and the trends by services sector and describe the difficulties in measuring this trade. Chapter 26, by Robert M. Stern, reviews the literature on the conceptual problems of quantifying barriers to trade and the effects on services trade of reducing those barriers. The key features of the GATS are covered in Chapter 27; Rudolf Adlung, Antonia Carzeniga, Bernard Hoekman, Masamichi Kono, Aaditya Mattoo, and Lee Tuthill contributed sections on particular aspects of the agreement, the state of negotiations, and the implications of the GATS for specific sectors.

The political-economy realities of freeing trade in services and the strategies for using multilateral trade negotiations to bolster domestic liberalization and open markets to developing countries are discussed by Aaditya Mattoo in Chapter 28, with special attention to the movement of individual services providers. Carlo Gamberale and Aaditya Mattoo examine in Chapter 29 the interplay between regulation, liberalization of services trade, and provision of services to the population at large and to the poor, in light of the new multilateral trade disciplines. In Chapter 30, Rupa Chanda focuses on the fourth and perhaps most sensitive mode of trade in services, movement of natural persons. Catherine L. Mann, in Chapter 31, examines the new situations arising from electronic commerce and the Internet and the associated trade issues. Pierre Sauvé, in Chapter 32, discusses important "unfinished business" from the Uruguay Round: the treatment of emergency safeguard measures, subsidies, and government procurement. Finally, Sherry M. Stephenson and Francisco Javier Prieto, in Chapter 33, examine how services trade has been handled in the free trade agreements of the Americas.

Multilateral Engagement: Buttressing Domestic Reforms

Although in principle a country can liberalize its markets and strengthen its regulatory institutions unilaterally, multilateral engagement can aid in this effort, for four reasons. First, liberalization may be constrained by domestic opposition from those who benefit from protection. Second, a country cannot on its own improve access for its exports to foreign markets. Third, a small country may not be able to deal adequately with anticompetitive practices by foreign suppliers. Finally, a country may lack the expertise and resources to devise and implement optimal policy, especially in the area of domestic regulation.

The WTO is the natural forum for pitting the first two elements—opposition to reform at home and barriers to access abroad—against each other constructively through the process of mercantilist negotiations. But there is also a need for complementary multilateral efforts to ensure that the gains from liberalization are not undermined by inadequacies in policy choice and regulation.

Using GATS Negotiations as a Spur to Domestic Liberalization and a Lever for Market Access

The GATS has a deliberately symmetric structure, encompassing the movement of both capital and labor for services provision. In theory, both industrial and developing countries could bargain to exploit their modal comparative advantage, with improved access for capital from industrial countries being exchanged for improved temporary access for individual services providers from developing countries. In practice, countries have been unwilling to grant greater access for foreign individuals (except for the limited class of skilled intracorporate transferees), and a tradeoff between modes of delivery simply has not occurred. Moreover, even the negotiating links across services sectors and between the services and goods sectors do not seem to have been particularly fruitful. And so, since governments have not been able to demonstrate improved access to foreign markets as a payoff for domestic reform, GATS commitments reflect for the most part the existing levels of unilaterally determined policy, rather than liberalization achieved through a reciprocal exchange of "concessions."

This may change with time. With severe shortages of skilled labor in the United States and Europe, and with a powerful constituency of high-technology companies lobbying for relaxation of visa limits, the prospects for serious intermodal tradeoffs—for example, obtaining temporary labor movement in return for allowing greater commercial presence for foreign services providers—are now more promising. The challenges are, first, to devise mechanisms which provide credible assurance that movement is temporary (rather than a stepping-stone to migration) and, second, to devise negotiating formulas that credibly link liberalization across different modes so that we may witness not a bitter round of grudging concessions but a virtuous cycle of mutually beneficial liberalization.

Strengthening GATS Rules and Commitments

In line with the WTO's central concern with securing market access, it would be natural to use the GATS to enhance the credibility of policy at home and security of access to markets abroad through legally binding commitments; to ensure that domestic regulations support trade liberalization; and to prevent discrimination between trading partners by ensuring effective application of the most-favored-nation (MFN) principle.

First of all, the GATS could help secure access to markets that are already open. Trade in electronically delivered products, in which more and more developing countries are beginning to participate, must continue to remain free of explicit barriers—should such barriers ever become feasible (see Chapter 31). The decision by WTO members to impose a moratorium on customs duties on e-commerce achieves little. It would be far more effective to widen and deepen commitments under the GATS on cross-border trade regarding market access (which would preclude quantitative restrictions) and national treatment (which would preclude all forms of discriminatory taxation).

At home, policies that are believed are most likely to succeed. Developing countries themselves could take greater advantage of the opportunity offered by the GATS to lend credibility to reform, by committing to maintain current levels of openness or to achieve greater levels of future openness. In basic telecommunications, the one sector in which countries have been willing to make such commitments, there is evidence that the commitments have facilitated reform.

Developing countries have much to gain from stronger multilateral rules on domestic regulations.

Table IV.1 Summary of Selected GATS Negotiations and Domestic Policy Issues: Current Status and Desirable Outcomes

Issue	Current status	Desirable outcome
Market access commitments under Article XVI of GATS	Numerous restrictions, particularly on entry and foreign equity; in some cases more emphasis on allowing increased foreign ownership and protecting foreign incumbents than on allowing new entry.	Pursue further liberalization, with greater emphasis on eliminating restrictions on entry and promoting increased competition.
	Limited use of the GATS, except in basic telecommunications, to precommit to future liberalization.	Make wider use of the GATS to lend credibility to future liberalization programs.
	Extremely limited market opening commitments on the presence of natural persons.	Widen the scope for the temporary, contract-related presence of natural persons, possibly through the use of formulas linking liberalization across modes (e.g., through the creation of foreign labor content entitlements).
Electronic commerce	Decision not to impose customs duties, which has little meaning since quotas and discriminatory internal taxation are still permitted in many cases.	Widen and deepen the scope of cross-border supply commitments on market access (prohibit quotas) and national treatment (prohibit discriminatory taxation) to ensure that current openness continues.
Procompetitive regulation (Arts. VIII and IX, and the Telecommunications Reference Paper)	Weak basic provisions with limited scope (Art. VIII) and limited bite (Art. IX); commitment to desirable principles in the Reference Paper should, however, contribute to enhanced competition.	Generalize the procompetitive principles in the Reference Paper to other network-based sectors.
		Strengthen disciplines (Art. IX) to deal with international cartels (e.g., in transport).
		Strengthen domestic procompetitive regulation to protect interests of consumers.
Domestic regulation (Art. VI)	Weak current disciplines (Art. VI.5) allow "grandfathering" of protection through certain regulatory instruments; some success in accountancy negotiations in instituting a "necessity test" but disappointing elaboration of disciplines on measures such as qualification requirements.	Generalize the application of a necessity test to regulatory instruments in all sectors, especially where they impede developing country exports.
		Strengthen domestic regulations to remedy asymmetric information–related problems in financial, professional, and other services.
		Choose economically efficient instruments to achieve universal service objectives.

Mutual recognition agreements (MRAs) (Art. VII)	Delicate balance (in Art. VII): MRAs are allowed provided that recognition is not used as a means of discrimination and third countries have the opportunity to accede or to demonstrate equivalence.	Ensure that MRAs do not become a means of discrimination. Improve cuality and uniformity of domestic regulation where socially desirable, to strengthen case for foreign recognition.
Safeguards (Art. X)	Limted progress in current negotiations; no agreement on whether such a mechanism is necessary, desirable, or feasible.	Create an avenue for temporary adjustment-related demands for protection, provided it is subject to strong, enforceable disciplines that prevent protectionist abuse.
Government procurement (Art. XIII)	Limited progress in current negotiations; general reluctance to accept strong disciplines.	Promote transparency and nondiscrimination disciplines but link to the elimination of barriers to mobility of natural persons to fulfil procurement contracts in construction and other services.
Subsidies (Art. XV)	Subject to nondiscrimination requirements where national treatment commitments exist. Little progress in current negotiations.	Ensure freedom for the use of subsidies where they are the best instrument for achieving legitimate economic or social objectives.

Source: Mattoo (2000).

barriers to trade that exist across each mode (Hoekman and Mattoo 2000). Commercial presence tends to be the dominant mode of supply for all but transport and tourism services; cross-border trade is the next most important. Trade through the presence of natural persons is typically small for all sectors, and consumption abroad is only significant for tourism. Barriers to trade are typically regulatory in nature. They include measures that restrict market access by foreign firms (for example, by reserving supply for a public monopoly or through nonrecognition of professional qualifications) or that discriminate against them once they are in the market through, for example, different tax treatment or local borrowing limitations for foreign firms (UNCTAD 1995c).

Liberalization of trade in services therefore involves the reduction of regulatory barriers to market access and discriminatory national treatment across all four modes of supply. This is not to be confused with the process of deregulation that many countries are pursuing. The focus of deregulation is to reduce the total amount of state regulation in a sector, while that of trade liberalization is to ensure that existing regulation does not discriminate against foreign participation in the market. Trade liberalization is consistent with countries' continuing to regulate industries for the purposes of consumer protection, prudential management of the economy, control of natural monopolies, or the achievement of social goals.

Moving to a nondiscriminatory regulatory regime, however, can require significant changes in how some sectors, in particular, public utilities, are currently regulated. Network-based utilities such as electricity, transport, and telecommunications have typically been operated as public monopolies because of the natural monopoly aspects of their production and in order to pursue universal service through cross-subsidization. Changes in technology, increases in demand, and the ability to subdivide the production chain have led to a decline in the importance of the natural monopoly argument in many of these sectors. In this case, continued monopolization for the sake of universal service, when alternative regulatory means of fulfilling these social objectives are available, would clearly fall foul of attempts to give market access to foreign firms.[1] Procompetitive regulatory reform would have to precede liberalization of services.

Another key policy area that comes under the spotlight in services trade liberalization is the treatment of foreign direct investment (FDI). Commercial presence is a key mode of supply for services, and developing countries have historically placed significant restrictions on FDI in order to encourage domestic ownership of capital, limit repatriation of profits, and increase the linkages of the multinational firm with upstream suppliers. Full liberalization of the commercial presence mode of supply would outlaw most of these measures in the services sectors. There is, however, a developmental aspect to the GATS that allows low-income countries to impose limited conditions on FDI, such as training and technology transfer (UNCTAD 2000c).

Gains from Liberalization

The traditionally low tradability of services may create the impression that the gains from services liberalization are small. Because, however, services have a strong intermediate role, the gains from trade include both the direct effect on the sector itself and the indirect effect on all the other sectors in the economy that make use of the service (see Box 24.1). For this reason, Markusen (1989) finds that the potential gains from trade in intermediate services are significantly higher than the gains from trade in final goods. A further reason for the potentially large gains from trade in services is that this trade currently faces very high barriers to trade in comparison with trade in goods. Dee and Hanslow (2001) used a computable general equilibrium (CGE) model to generate rough estimates of the current worldwide gains from services liberalization.[2] They found that the gains are approximately the same as for full liberalization of trade in both agricultural and manufacturing goods.

Standard Gains from Trade

Many developing countries are concerned that most of the gains from trade liberalization will accrue to industrial countries. This perception is based on the observation that many services sectors are human capital–intensive, physical capital–intensive, or both—which means that industrial countries will have a comparative advantage and will dominate any trade after liberalization. This argument, however, ignores the facts that all countries have comparative advantage in *some* area, that services have a key intermediate role in the economy, and that services are largely traded through FDI (Hodge and Nordas 1999).

BOX 24.1 REALIZING THE GAINS FROM FINANCIAL LIBERALIZATION

Argentina. A study of the liberalization of the Argentine banking sector found improved performance in the areas in which foreign banks specialized (Clarke and others 1999). Foreign entry lowered net margins and profits in lending to manufacturing, while margins and profits in consumer lending remained high, as foreign banks had not penetrated that segment. The ratio of operational costs to total assets declined from 1.3 percent in 1990 to 0.5 percent in 1997. Foreign banks also played a role in revitalizing the undercapitalized banking sector with a new infusion of capital.

Colombia. Barajas, Steiner, and Salazar (1999) chronicle the Colombian experience with foreign entry. Colombia followed highly restrictive policies and banned FDI in banking in 1975. In 1991, however, there was a reversal of the restrictive FDI policy, and the rules of entry and exit were significantly liberalized. The deregulation lowered intermediation spreads, reduced administrative costs, and increased loan quality. Intermediation spreads declined almost 8 percentage points between 1991 and 1998 for domestic and foreign banks. Nonperforming loans as a percentage of total loans fell from 7 percent in 1991 to 3 percent in 1998 for foreign banks and stood steady at 6 percent for domestic banks during that period.

Turkey. Denizer (1999) looks at foreign bank entry into the Turkish banking sector, which had been highly regulated and concentrated, dominated by a few large banks with extensive branch networks. Liberalization began in 1980 with a marked decrease in directed credit programs and the elimination of interest rate controls. Commercial presence was liberalized, and large numbers of new foreign banks entered. The number of foreign banks increased from 4 in 1980 to 23 in 1990, and in 1997, after mergers, the number stood at 17. Foreign bank entry had the effect of reducing net interest margins, returns on assets, and overhead expenses of domestic banks. It qualitatively changed Turkish banking by introducing financial and operations planning and improving the credit evaluation and marketing system. Foreign banks also took the lead in

spreading electronic banking and introduced new technologies. The number of ATMs increased rapidly (to 6,500 locations by 1997), and in 1997 Turkey led Europe in new credit card issues.

Africa. The institutional and regulatory framework plays a critical role in realizing the gains from financial liberalization. For example, financial reforms were introduced in many African countries in the 1990s, but they have been less successful than expected (World Bank 2000a). Some of the reasons for the disappointing results are directly related to the financial system, while others pertain to the general economic environment. The restructuring of state-owned banks was not sufficient to change the behavior of the financial institutions; public authorities still pressured these institutions to lend money to loss-making public enterprises; liberalization failed to trigger competition in the banking sector; and governments were mostly reluctant to close down distressed state banks. Liberalization of interest rates in the presence of uncontrolled fiscal deficits had a pernicious effect on domestic public debt, which in turn led to larger deficits. Finally, a crucial shortcoming was the lack of adequate regulatory and supervision mechanisms to monitor the functioning of the financial system.

Republic of Korea. The collapse of the Korean economy in 1997 is another case that reveals the precariousness of financial liberalization in an imperfect policy environment. Korea did liberalize its financial markets substantially, but it encouraged the development of a highly fragile financial structure.* By liberalizing short-term (but not long-term) foreign borrowing, the Korean authorities made it possible for the larger and better-known banks and *chaebols* to assume heavy indebtedness in short-term foreign currency debt. Meanwhile, large *chaebols* in the second tier greatly increased their short-term indebtedness in domestic financial markets (funded indirectly through foreign borrowing by the banks), and the funds borrowed were invested in overexpansion of productive capacity. Financial regulation and supervision were fragmented, with responsibilities

(continued)

223

BOX 24.2 (CONTINUED)

particularly poor, with shippers often unaware of their containers' whereabouts. Shippers attributed this problem to poorly trained staff, the lack of a reliable recovery system, and the inadequate accountability system in government agencies. Finally, the intermodal transport system was seen as poorly integrated, with no streamlined procedures to support the continuous movement of containers between the coast and inland areas.

Another source of inefficiencies is the dominance of state-owned enterprises and the lack of competition in transport services markets. Since pricing in many of the intermediate transport services activities is controlled, the companies have little incentive for aggressively pursuing cost-cutting methods, and, due to lack of competition,

intermediate services providers represent the interests of transport operators. The outcome is that value-added service and reliability, which are essential for winning business confidence in a modern economy, are not priorities for most participants. Investment by foreign enterprises and joint ventures between foreign and domestic enterprises in intermediate transport services are limited in inland regions. Although foreign investment is not prohibited, there are restrictions on their activities, such as requirements that firms carry only the parent companies' products.

Sources: Prepared by the volume editors based on World Bank (1996a); Atinc (1997); Naughton (2001); Graham and Wada (forthcoming).

Services are used intensively in the production and trade of all goods and services in the economy, including in agriculture and mining. Typically, services make up 10–20 percent of production costs and all the costs of trading—communications, transport, trade finance and insurance, and distribution services (Hodge and Nordas 1999). The price and quality of services are therefore crucial in determining the cost of all other products in the economy. The reduction in tariffs on goods to historically low levels and the emergence of global production networks have made services even more important in determining the competitiveness of goods producers. In countries where tariffs are low and the price of services is high, manufacturers may well face negative effective rates of protection. In fact, Limão and Venables (1999) conclude that Africa's poor trade performance is almost exclusively attributable to poor infrastructure-based services. (They find that a 10 percent decrease in transport costs increases trade by 25 percent.) Another consideration is that entry into global production networks requires efficient and timely delivery. Low-quality services that delay production or transport effectively exclude producers from such networks.

The effects extend beyond any one-time gains and may have an impact on the growth rates of countries. Poor-quality, high-priced services not only

affect the current operations of manufacturers but also discourage future investment by locals and foreigners by lowering the profitability of such investment. This partly explains why FDI is limited in the poorest countries despite access to cheap labor. Honglin Zang and Markusen (1999) argue that FDI is unlikely to materialize outside extractive industries if multinationals do not have access to skilled local workers, social infrastructure, utilities, and legal institutions of the necessary quality, at a reasonable price. The result is not just a static loss from poor service delivery but a dynamic growth loss.[4] One reason for low-quality and high-priced services in developing countries is the narrow downstream market for these services. Rodriguez-Clare (1996) argues that small economies may get caught in a development trap because the narrow downstream market constrains the extent of specialization and the exploitation of scale economies in the services sector. This leads to lower-quality and higher-priced services, which in turn limit the ability of the downstream industry to expand.

By expanding the market for intermediate services and by lowering the price and improving the quality of services, trade liberalization should enable poorer countries to better exploit the comparative advantages they do have. Producers of primary and manufacturing goods in developing

BOX 24.3 LESSONS FROM REFORMING ARGENTINA'S PORTS

As part of its overall program of macroeconomic stabilization, liberalization, and public sector reform, the government of Argentina initiated in the 1990s a comprehensive reform of the port sector. The reform was a major success in that it greatly improved the performance of Argentina's largest seaports, facilitating a rapid, more than fourfold expansion in the volume of seaborne trade between 1990 and 2000, from 249,000 TEUs (20-foot-equivalent units) to 1,070 million TEUs.

Before 1990, Argentinean ports were characterized by institutional inadequacies (including a major corruption problem), inefficient cross subsidization, and insufficient investment in the modernization of the sector. Tariffs charged by the publicly operated ports were reportedly among the highest in the world. Total cargo moved in the ports fell by 10 percent between 1970 and 1989, with the port of Buenos Aires alone experiencing a 52 percent reduction in traffic.

The overall reform program consisted of a combination of devolution of most port responsibilities to the provinces, private sector participation, and promotion of service competition. Provinces were given the freedom to operate, concession, or close ports, with the exception of large ports, for which the creation of independent autonomous companies was foreseen. In the case of the port of Buenos Aires, six terminals were competitively concessioned to the private sector, with payment of a leasing fee to the government for use of infrastructure assets, following the landlord port model. To improve the contestability of port operations, the government established free entry into the sector by allowing any operator to build, manage, and operate a port for public or private use. A new regulatory agency, Autoridad Portuaria Nacional, was created under the Ministry of the Economy. Finally, the restructuring process included a significant labor reform that eliminated restrictive work regulations and softened the social impact of labor reductions.

The main economic effect of the overall reforms was to transform Argentina's ports from the most expensive ones in Latin America into the cheapest ones. Private investment picked up in the second half of the 1990s, leading to a substantial expansion in capacity. Productivity has grown sharply, significantly reducing operational costs and duration of stay in ports. Combined with more intense competition between port services providers, this has resulted in a reduction in overall container terminal handling prices, as shown in the table.

Despite these impressive achievements, unresolved issues from the first wave of port reforms and from changes in the competitive environment in the sector, although not pressing, demand solutions in the long run. Intraport competition is working effectively, but the likelihood of future mergers between terminal operators at the port of Buenos Aires raises the risk of collusion. Improved monitoring and benchmarking mechanisms, as well as the fine-tuning of price regulations, may be necessary to ensure that services continue to be provided cost-efficiently. Inefficient customs operations are a key constraint on further productivity gains in the sector and represent a priority for future reform. Finally, some aspects of Argentina's port policy, such as restrictions on the circulation of containers, are reported to restrain intermodal integration. Addressing this issue in the context of the wider policy framework on multimodal transport would contribute to better performance of the transport system nationwide.

Improved Performance in the Port of Buenos Aires

Indicator	1991	1997
Cargo (thousands of tons)	4,000	8,500
Containers (thousands of TEUs)	300	1,023
Capacity (thousands of TEUs)	400	1,300
Cranes (number)	3	13
Productivity (tons per employee)	800	3,100
Average container time at port (days)	2.5	1.3
Charges per container (US$/TEU)	450	120

Note: TEU, 20-foot-equivalent unit.

Source: Prepared by the volume editors, based on Trujillo and Nombela (1999) and Trujillo and Estache (2001).

al benefit of facilitating price reductions that allow larger numbers of low-income households to demand such services and that raise the real income of those households that are already making use of the services (Hodge 2000).

Undertaking Trade Liberalization in Services

In undertaking liberalization in services, it is necessary to lay the institutional foundations for reform, identify a coherent strategy that maximizes the gains while minimizing the adjustment costs, and manage the political consequences of reform to keep the process on track.

Preparing the Institutional Foundations for Liberalization

The institutional foundations for liberalization can include understanding the current trade stance, establishing the governmental process for trade negotiations, and creating the institutions to manage liberalization. The regulatory nature of trade barriers in services makes it difficult to identify the current trade stance in each sector. Instead of merely referring to a tariff schedule, as with goods, policymakers need to examine each piece of regulation in each sector to establish whether it in any way denies market access or discriminates against foreign firms. This is time consuming and is unlikely to result in a clear and quantifiable estimate of the size of the current barriers in each sector.

Putting together a governmental process for devising trade policy is equally problematic. In most countries each services sector has had its own supervisory government department, primarily to oversee the implementation of social goals through public utilities. Although a trade and industry department usually has a mandate to undertake trade negotiations, other departments clearly have a stake in the process and need to be included in the work of devising and implementing a trade liberalization strategy. These other line departments may be "captured" by the industry itself through historical joint planning and may frustrate the reform process. Furthermore, because liberalization is likely to raise revenues from privatization, the process is often captured by the state treasury, which delays the liberalization process to maximize the revenues from the sale of public enterprises. South Africa's

policy on public asset restructuring, which identifies revenue maximization as an explicit goal, has been part of the reason for delays in the privatization process.

In the case of public utilities that are currently state monopolies, there needs to be an initial process of preparing the ground for any future liberalization. At a bare minimum, these state enterprises need to be corporatized, an independent regulatory body has to be established for the industry, and effective antitrust legislation and institutions have to be put in place. Pinheiro (2000) notes that poor sequencing was to blame for some of the unsatisfactory results of regulatory reform in Latin America. Often, regulatory reform was concluded only after firms were privatized. Corporatization entails establishing the enterprise as a distinct business entity with a consolidated asset and liability register that makes it possible to pursue partial or full privatization and competition at a later date. The sector regulator and antitrust authorities are needed to manage competition in a liberalized services sector.

The effectiveness of regulation and competition will, to a large extent, determine the size of the gains from trade and how different groups in society share them (Alexander and Estache 1999).[6] Ineffective regulation and competition will result not in lower prices but in higher profits, benefiting the owners of capital rather than labor or consumers. Furthermore, in a more liberal environment in low-income countries, these owners of capital may well be foreign firms. This applies with equal force to the sector itself and to the downstream producers who will benefit from lower input prices. Sartar (2000) notes that one of the failings of reform in India has been the inability to create effective competition. African countries have found that lack of regulatory capacity is an important barrier to further liberalization in the continent (WTO 2000a).

Putting the regulatory framework in place entails a determination of how the industry will be regulated in a more competitive environment, including how social goals will be met in a competitively neutral manner once monopoly cross-subsidization is prohibited. Much of the focus of trade negotiations in services has been on laying this foundation by establishing clear regulatory principles for opening up network industries in a nondiscriminatory and competitive fashion.[7] Because supply in a liberalized environment will mostly take the form of FDI, it is important that the regulatory framework and process be considered fair and credible to potential investors. This is especially true for telecommunications, electricity, and transport, which involve large sunk investments. Any lack of credibility will result either in lack of entry and competition or in demands by investors for higher returns to cover regulatory risk. Either way, the gains from trade are lowered. Creating a suitable environment for foreign investment extends beyond regulatory certainty; it may include strengthening the legal system, stabilizing the macroeconomic environment, and permitting the repatriation of profits.

Preparing the ground for liberalization is not a public utilities issue alone. For instance, it is widely accepted that liberalization of trade in financial services requires careful preparation so that liberalization will not cause a financial crisis. Such crises can impose significant costs on the economy, from bailing out banks to disruption of real economic activity; they are estimated to cost countries anywhere from 2 to 40 percent of GDP (WTO 1997a). The prerequisites for a successful liberalization are considered to be macroeconomic stability, structural reforms in how banks are regulated, and implementation of effective prudential regulation (WTO 1997a).[8]

Sequencing and Timing of Liberalization

Once the foundation for liberalization has been laid, the next step is to devise a trade liberalization strategy aimed at maximizing the gains and minimizing the adjustment costs. The strategy needs to set out in detail the sequence and timing of liberalization across the different sectors, the modes of supply, and the two groups of barriers (market access and national treatment). It also needs to focus on what concessions are desired from trading partners across these various dimensions. A degree of caution should be observed when designing the liberalization process, as some of the key sectors have a profound impact on the workings of the economy. For example, a rash liberalization of the financial services sector could spark bank failure and might plunge the country into a recession. Once reforms have been carried out, it is difficult to reverse them temporarily to safeguard domestic industries (UNCTAD 2000b). For instance, once a foreign firm has invested infrastructure in services delivery, it is not possible to remove the firm's operating license without imposing severe costs on the firm and losing policy credibility.

The sequencing and timing of liberalization in different services sectors will depend in part on progress in laying the institutional foundations for reform. Complications at this stage may affect the feasibility of going ahead with reform. (For instance, reform of the transport sector in South Africa has been delayed by many years in order to restructure and reduce the excessive debt of the transport public utility.) Ideally, reform should initially be targeted at those sectors that are likely to bring about the most significant gains for the country. These would consist of services that provide important intermediate inputs to the rest of the economy or to specific sectors that the country wishes to promote, or sectors in which protection has resulted in a considerable inefficiency cost to society. (The two are often the same—specifically, in the case of public utilities). The reason for targeting intermediate inputs is that most of the gains from services liberalization are from the downstream effects. Sectors that have an economywide downstream effect, such as communications, transport, finance, and electricity, yield the most gains for liberalization effort. They also serve as inputs into other services sectors whose successful liberalization may well depend on prior liberalization of the intermediate services. For example, success in the tourism sector depends to a large extent on a cheap and efficient transport system (both domestic and international), adequate communications, and widespread foreign exchange trading. Similarly, attraction of foreign FDI and domestic expansion of information technology services will depend on adequate and inexpensive communications services.

The next choice is which modes of supply to open and which barriers to remove. This process can be simplified by eliminating any technically infeasible modes. If liberalization is to have a significant effect on the sector, the dominant mode of supply should be opened up. In most cases this is the commercial presence mode, which is in any case popular as a target for liberalization because of the potentially greater gains and lower adjustment costs. Governments feel they have greater control over the impact of liberalization if the foreign firms are operating within their borders. This is especially true of financial services, where it is feared that consumers cannot be protected when transactions are cross-border. Merely opening a sector to commercial presence

---

BOX 24.5 (CONTINUED)

(China), Pakistan, and the Philippines—the responsibility for establishing interconnection rates lies with the dominant operator, although the regulator is responsible for arbitration of disputes.

Controlling for several economic factors, the study's econometric investigation found that, by themselves, competition for local services, regulation, and privatization of the incumbent operator did not exert any significant influence on main-line penetration but that the interaction of the three had a significant positive impact on telephone availability. Arguably, the three policy variables used capture only imperfectly a multidimensional reform process. The results do, however, indicate that successful liberalization depends on a combination of privatization, competition, and effective regulation.

Source: Fink, Mattoo, and Rathindran (2001).

---

be within the government—for example, a supervisory government department having strong links with incumbents that may well lose from the process. To maintain the momentum of reform, it is important to make common cause with the winners from reform in order to counter political pressures from the losers. This is invariably difficult, since the losers are concentrated and organized firms, while the winners are generally dispersed and unorganized downstream users. To create a balance internally, the government should broaden the decisionmaking process to include the trade and industry department, which represents industrial users, and any other line departments whose users are affected—for instance, the tourism and agriculture departments. Outside the government, industry associations and consumer groups can provide vocal support for reform. Choosing sectors that offer rapid delivery of benefits from liberalization is a means of quickly building widespread support. Finally, the GATS may be used to lock the government into liberalization and prevent future backtracking under political pressure.

Notes

1 Such regulatory measures include a nondiscriminatory universal service tax and direct subsidy to the consumer; equal universal service obligations for new entrants; and competitive bidding for fulfilling universal service orders subsidized by the state.

2 The estimate included only OECD and Asian countries.

3 Water and electricity exports to South Africa form the basis of most of Lesotho's exports (Mochebelele 1998).

4 King and Levine (1993) find that development of the financial sector precedes faster economic growth.

5 Liberalization of financial services in South Africa led to a growing demand for higher-skilled workers, increasing employment and raising the wage premium (Hodge 2001).

6 The reason for the influence of regulation and competition on gains from trade is that many of the gains are concentrated in the category of procompetitive effects.

7 The Reference Paper of the WTO Agreement on Basic Telecommunications is the first to provide regulatory guidelines to signatories of the agreement

8 Structural reforms in bank regulation mainly include ensuring that social policy is not implemented through the banking system by such means as political lending or repression of interest rates on government debt.

A. MAURER
P. CHAUVET

THE MAGNITUDE OF FLOWS OF GLOBAL TRADE IN SERVICES

B ETWEEN 1980 AND 2000, LOW- AND MIDDLE-INCOME ECONOMIES INCREASED THEIR services production by almost 25 percent. The share of services in economic activity (value added) currently ranges from around 38 percent in low-income countries to more than 65 percent in high-income countries (World Bank 2000d: table 4.2). The higher share in industrial countries reflects the fact that demand for services tends to be income-elastic: as people become wealthier, they spend relatively more on services such as tourism, health, and education. In both poor and rich countries the share of services in total activity has been growing, as a result of developments in information and communication technologies and of deregulation and privatization. This chapter provides an overview of the available data on trade in services and discusses some of the methodological problems that arise in this area.

Statistical Measurement of Trade in Services

The growing importance of the services sector in national output has been accompanied by an expan-

sion of the share of commercial services in world exports of goods and services, from 15 percent to almost 20 percent over the past two decades. On average, trade in services grew at an annual rate of 7 percent, whereas merchandise trade grew only by 5 percent. Despite this increase, the share of services in world trade has been smaller than its share in world production.

One reason may be found in the different characteristics of goods and services. Services are more difficult to transport or transfer; that is, they are less tradable and often must be consumed at the place of production. As a consequence, services enterprises are less export-oriented than enterprises in the merchandise sector. The introduction of new technologies, however, has contributed heavily to improving the tradability of services.

Another reason can be found in the statistical measurement of trade in goods and services (see the discussion in Box 25.1). The shares of goods and services in world exports are seriously biased: merchandise trade statistics include reexports and are therefore inflated (general trade system). Trade in services is probably underestimated by the failure to capture important modes of delivery of services. These two factors imply that trade in services may have a much higher share in world exports than the above data suggest.

Methodologically, there exists a reference framework in which international transactions of goods can be identified and measured as regards time, production, transport, and consumption (Schuller 2000: 6). This framework is laid down in the United

BOX 25.1 SERVICES STATISTICS AND THE GATS

Since specific commitments under the GATS are defined on the basis of the four standard modes of supply, services trade statistics should ideally be available on a mode of supply basis. This would enable an assessment both of the relative importance of different modes of supply in a particular sector and of the impact of measures affecting each mode. The breakdown of modes of supply in the GATS diverges, however, from the definition of what constitutes an international transaction in the national accounts. As a result, the only services trade statistics available on a global basis are not reported according to mode of supply.

Balance of payments statistics register transactions between residents and nonresidents. According to balance of payments conventions, if factors of production move to another country for a period longer than one year (which is sometimes flexibly interpreted), a change in residency has occurred. The part of the output generated by such factors that is sold in the host market is then not recorded as trade in the balance of payments. (The GATS definition of trade in services does include local sales by foreign entities that are considered "residents" under conventional statistical criteria.) Thus, transactions involving commercial presence and movement of natural persons remaining in a foreign country for more than one year are not covered by the balance of payments statistics.

The limitations of the existing statistical domains in providing information on trade by different modes of supply are listed in Table 25.1. No clear distinction is made in balance of payments statistics between the modes that are covered (cross-border supply, consumption abroad, and presence of natural persons or commercial presence for less than one year). Consumption abroad of a service could, in principle, come under the balance of payments category "travel." The travel category, however, consists of all expenditures by travelers abroad, including expenditures on goods, and is not subdivided into the different categories of services. Further-

more, some elements of consumption abroad that arise when the property of the consumer moves or is situated abroad, as in ship repair services, are not recorded in travel but in other balance of payments categories.

Commercial presence could be covered by three kinds of statistics: (a) information on flows and stocks of foreign investment that make commercial presence possible; (b) information on market size in service sectors, which may be approximated by using production statistics such as gross output or value added; and (c) information on the activity of foreign companies in domestic markets (for example, data on turnover). The last is to be recorded under the new statistical domain of foreign affiliate trade data. This should remedy some of the deficiencies, but work in this area is only beginning.

The mode "presence of natural persons" includes services suppliers who are present for less than a year in foreign markets and are therefore considered nonresident in the balance of payments context. If such natural persons are themselves service suppliers, their sales are captured in the relevant services categories of balance of payments statistics but are not recorded separately from cross-border sales. Employees are covered by the GATS if they are employed by a services supplier of a WTO member. The earnings of such natural persons are an unidentifiable ingredient of the balance of payments category "compensation of employees," which records the earnings of all natural persons established abroad for less than one year, regardless of the sector of employment. There is no record in the balance of payments statistics of the activities of natural persons who are resident for longer than one year, except that "workers' remittances" and "migrants' transfers" record the transfers they make. Employment data from foreign affiliate trade statistics (such as number of employees and compensation of employees) would be relevant, should they become available, especially if they were broken down between "national" and "foreign" employees.

Nations recommendations on concepts and definitions for international merchandise trade statistics, and a compiler's guide gives recommendations for its implementation.

A similar reference framework for measuring trade in services, the *Manual on Statistics of International Trade in Services* (MSITS), developed by an interagency task force, has only recently been adopted by the U.N. Statistical Commission. When the recommendations in the MSITS are implemented and data are compiled accordingly, that will considerably improve the economic analysis of trade in services and will assist services trade negotiators in trade rounds to come.[1]

At present, the only available statistical framework that provides comprehensive and comparable services trade data across countries is the balance of payments. However, it does not allow for a breakdown of trade flows into the four modes of trade in services described below.

Although methodological constraints and data availability hinder a detailed empirical assessment of services trade (see Table 25.1), proxies derived from balance of payments statistics can be used to estimate trade in services by mode. For example, all major service categories, excluding travel and government services, could be taken as an approximation of mode 1, cross-border trade. This proxy would, however, tend to

Table 25.1 Inadequacies of Statistical Domains with Regard to Modes of Supply

Mode of supply	Relevant data source	Inadequacies
Cross-border supply	BoP service statistics (categories other than Travel)	BoP statistics do not distinguish between Cross-border supply, Presence of natural persons (individual), and Commercial presence for less than one year.
Consumption abroad	BoP statistics (mainly the Travel category)	Travel also contains goods and is not subdivided into the different categories of services consumed by travelers.
		Some transactions related to this mode of supply are also in other BoP categories.
Commercial presence	Production, FDI, and FAT statistics	Production statistics do not distinguish between national and foreign firms.
		FDI statistics do not provide data on output (or sales).
		The definition of FDI does not match the definition of Commercial presence.
		FAT statistics exist only for the United States. Definitions of basic concepts are in the process of being established internationally.
Presence of natural persons (independent)	BoP statistics (mostly categories other than Transport and Travel)	BoP statistics do not distinguish between Cross-border supply, Presence of natural persons (individual), and Commercial presence for less than one year.
		Natural persons who are residents are not covered.
Presence of natural persons (employees)	Employment data from FAT statistics	Not yet available.

Note: BoP, balance of payments; FAT, foreign affiliate transfers; FDI, foreign direct investment.
Source: Prepared by the volume editors, based on Chang and others (1999).

overestimate mode 1, as it would also include trade falling under mode 4, movement of natural persons (Karsenty 2000: 36–37). Travel could be used as an indicator for mode 2, consumption abroad. Outward foreign direct investment (FDI) stocks may be used to estimate commercial presence (mode 3), and the balance of payments category "compensation of employees" gives an initial estimate for mode 4 (Karsenty 2000: 54).

This paper first describes the relative importance of flows of trade in services in comparison with goods. It then analyses bilateral trade flows among the major traders—the United States, the European Union (EU), and Japan—before looking at the relative importance of individual services sectors and at trade in services of foreign affiliates.

Growth of Trade in Services

Between 1990 and 1999, world trade in commercial services increased at an annual rate of 6.2 percent (Table 25.2), with growth rates in the first half of the decade significantly higher than in the second half.[2] Developing countries saw their exports boom in the first part of the 1990s, attaining average annual rates of growth of over 13 percent. In the second part of the decade, services growth fell dramatically, to levels below that for merchandise and below that registered by industrial countries. This reversal in growth is mainly attributable to the Asian financial crisis that erupted in 1997.

Looking at individual geographic regions (leaving aside the Middle East and economies in transition because of lack of comprehensive data), a somewhat different picture emerges. North America's growth in exports of commercial services decreased from 8.1 percent in the first half of the 1990s to 6.6 percent in the second half (Table 25.3). Import growth shows a different trend. In the second half of the decade it grew at a much faster rate, 7.8 percent, contributing to the U.S. current account deficit. Latin America showed strong export and import growth in 1990–95, with imports growing faster than exports. During the second half of the decade the growth of both exports and imports decelerated, but exports were less affected than imports. Growth of trade in services in the EU also decelerated in the second half of the 1990s, down almost to half of the annual growth rates of the 1990–95 period. Intra-EU trade accounts for more than half of the EU's total trade.

Although Africa's export growth in the second half of the 1990s declined, it was still above the world average. By contrast, its imports of services almost stagnated in the second half of the decade. Asia showed strong growth during 1990–95, but because of the financial crisis, growth rates of exports and imports of services fell steeply, to below 1 percent, in the second half of the 1990s. China and India, which were less affected by the crisis, sustained dynamic growth rates. India, in particular, had an average annual growth rate of almost 20 percent for exports, reflecting its specialization in computer and information services.

Looking at the full period 1990–99, one sees that the Americas and Asia were growing at above-aver-

Table 25. 2 Average Annual Growth of Services and Merchandise Trade, 1990–99
(percent)

Economy	Exports			Imports		
	1990–99	1990–95	1995–99	1990–99	1990–95	1995–99
World						
Services	6.2	8.7	3.3	5.8	7.9	3.2
Merchandise	5.5	7.8	2.6	5.7	7.8	3.1
Industrial countries						
Services	5.6	7.1	3.7	5.2	6.6	3.6
Merchandise	4.7	7.0	1.8	5.0	6.3	3.5
Developing countries						
Services	8.2	13.3	2.2	7.2	11.0	2.7
Merchandise	7.4	10.1	4.0	7.4	12.4	1.4

Source: WTO (2000b).

Table 25.3 Trade in Commercial Services by Region, 1990–99
(average annual percentage change in value terms)

Region	Exports			Imports		
	1990–99	1990–95	1995–99	1990–99	1990–95	1995–99
World	6.2	8.7	3.3	5.8	7.9	3.2
North America	7.5	8.1	6.6	6.4	5.3	7.8
Latin America	6.7	8.4	4.6	6.8	9.4	3.5
European Union	5.0	6.5	3.2	5.4	7.1	3.4
Africa	5.0	6.2	3.7	3.0	5.2	0.2
Asia	8.1	14.8	0.2	7.3	12.9	0.7

Source: WTO, *International Trade in Services,* 2000.

age rates, whereas the EU and Africa had below-average growth rates.

Bilateral Trade Flows

The available data do not permit a comprehensive analysis of bilateral trade flows. This chapter therefore considers only trade relations among the United States, the EU, and Japan in 1995 and 1998. In 1998 the combined exports of these economies represented 66 percent of world trade in services, and trade among them amounted to 42 percent of this total (Table 25.4). The EU is the leading trader, accounting for 43 percent of world trade in services, almost twice the share of the value of intra-EU trade. Over one-third of U.S. trade is carried out with the EU; together, the EU and Japan accounted for 47 percent of U.S. exports of services in 1998. More than 70 percent of the EU's trade in services (including intra-EU trade) involves the United States, Japan, or EU member states. The last is the most important market for the EU, as intra-EU trade represents more than half the EU's total trade

in services.[3] Japan represents a relatively small market for U.S. and EU trade but relies heavily on these two countries as export destinations (Table 25.5).

Relative Importance of Individual Service Sectors

The standard presentation of the current account broadly distinguishes the following major service categories: transport; travel; communications; construction; insurance and financial services; computer and information services; royalties and license fees; other business services; personal, cultural, and recreational services; and government services not included elsewhere. Services exercised by the governmental authority are excluded from the GATS and are statistically approximated through the balance of payments component "government services." Within WTO definitions, all services except transport and travel are put in a single category, "other commercial services" or, for short, "other services."

Between 1980 and 1999, the combined share of other commercial services and of travel services in

Table 25.4 Share of Selected Economies in World Trade in Services, 1995 and 1998
(percent)

Origin	Destination					
	United States/Japan/EU			World		
	1995	1998		1995		1998
United States	8	9		17		18
EU	31	31		43		43
Japan	3	2		5		5
Total	42	42		65		66

Source: U.S. Bureau of Economic Analysis (BEA), *Balance of Payments;* Bank of Japan, *Balance of Payments Monthly;* Eurostat, *Geographical Breakdown of the EU Current Account.*

Table 25.8 Trade in Services by Mode of Supply, 1998

Mode	Proxy used	Billions of U.S. dollars	Share (percent)
1	BoP commercial services less travel	860	39.1
2	BoP travel	432	19.6
3	FATS gross output in services +		
	BoP construction services	877	39.8
4	BoP compensation of employees	33	1.5
All modes		2,202	100.0

Note: BoP, balance of payments; FATS, foreign affiliates trade statistics.
Source: Authors' calculations; based on Karsenty (2000).

Foreign Affiliate Trade in Services

Conventional balance of payments statistics underestimate the economic importance of trade in services. Not only do these statistics fail to cover trade in services embodied in goods, but, more important, they do not cover production and sales of services of foreign affiliates—that is, sales made through a commercial presence. The activities of foreign-owned companies are described by foreign affiliates trade statistics (FATS), a conceptual framework developed in the forthcoming *Manual on Statistics of International Trade in Services.* The EU and the OECD are currently developing pilot data collection systems. Until recently, the United States was the only country to regularly publish time-series on these activities.

Foreign affiliates are firms in which the majority of the capital or voting stock is foreign owned.[5] FATS statistics can be developed for both inward and outward FATS. "Inward FATS" refers to the measurement of economic activities of affiliates in the host or compiling country, whereas "outward FATS" refers to activities of affiliates owned by residents of the compiling country and located abroad. Because FATS statistics focus on majority-owned enterprises only, they tend to underestimate the commercial presence mode, as activities of minority-owned enterprises are neglected. (The GATS covers minority-owned enterprises.)

Foreign affiliates are usually established through investment abroad, and their activities are normally recorded in the domestic statistics of their respective resident countries. In the absence of statistics for foreign affiliates, FDI statistics may therefore be used to shed some light on the contribution of foreign affiliates to domestic economic activity. Data on FDI are compiled in the country's balance of payments and international investment position.

Following the assumption that the output level of foreign affiliates is related to foreign investment, outward FDI stocks may give some indication of the activities of foreign affiliates. Although the outward stock of industrial countries decreased by more than 5 percentage points between 1990 and 1999, these countries still represented almost 90 percent of total stocks in 1999 (Table 25.9). During that period the share of Asia in outward stocks increased from 2.9 to 7.3 percent, that of Western Europe increased from 50.5 to 54.1 percent, and that of the EU rose from 46.0 to 49.1 percent. The inward side shows a more balanced distribution, with shares following the same general trends as outward stocks except for Western Europe and the EU, the shares of which dropped dramatically—by 6.9 percentage points for Western Europe (to 36.8 percent), and by 6.5 percentage points for the EU (to 34.6 percent).

Data for the United States show that in 1996 sales through majority-owned foreign affiliates exceeded exports from resident entities (Table 25.10). Because the United States excludes from its FATS data collection sales of foreign affiliates to the country of origin, these data are particularly useful. Balance of payments figures on exports correspond roughly to the cross-border supplies of services, whereas exports by majority-owned foreign affiliates (MOFAs) approximate the commercial presence mode of supply. Although 1996–97 constitutes too short a time period to draw any conclusions, the table nevertheless suggests an increase in the share of MOFA exports, given that these exports grew at a rate twice that of balance of payments exports.

Because FATS time-series are available for only a few countries, it is difficult to generalize these findings. The Statistical Office of the European Communities, however, recently published a study covering Denmark, Sweden, Finland, and the United King-

Table 25.9 Shares in Inward and Outward FDI Stocks, Selected Country Groups, 1990 and 1999

Country group	Outward		Inward	
	1990	1999	1990	1999
World	100.0	100.0	100.0	100.0
Industrial countries	95.2	89.9	78.4	67.7
Other countries	4.8	10.1	21.6	32.3
North America	30.0	27.5	28.8	26.3
Latin America	1.2	2.2	6.7	10.2
Western Europe	50.5	54.1	43.7	36.8
(European Union)	(46.0)	(49.1)	(41.1)	(34.6)
Africa	0.7	0.4	2.5	2.0
Asia	2.9	7.3	12.0	17.7

Source: UNCTAD, World Investment Report 2000.

dom that provides a snapshot of the activity of foreign affiliates in these countries. Such affiliates generated more than 19 percent of total market services, although they accounted for less than 1 percent of the total number of enterprises. Distributive trade activities, especially in the wholesale sector, attracted most of the foreign affiliates. Japanese-owned enterprises accounted for 13 percent of the turnover generated by affiliates, and more than half of the people worked in affiliates owned by companies outside the EU, two-thirds of them being from the United States (Knauth 2000: 1).

Conclusion

Over the past two decades, the share of services in GDP has increased in all economies, yet trade in services, as measured by the balance of payments, accounts for only 20 percent of world trade. Part of the reason for this low share is that services are less tradable than goods. Another factor is that current statistical concepts and methodologies do not allow services trade flows to be measured in line with the GATS classifications.

Trade in services has been growing faster than trade in goods for both industrial and developing economies, with developing countries showing, on average, higher growth rates than the industrial group. Still, more than 40 percent of world trade in services is carried on between the major traders—the United States, the EU, and Japan. Transport services have decreased in importance for both economic groups, whereas exports of travel services have become an important source of receipts, especially for developing countries. The most dynamic service category, however, continues to be "other commercial services," over half of which consists of "other business services."

Table 25.10 Total U.S. Services Trade, 1994, 1996, and 1997
(millions of U.S. dollars, except as indicated)

Indicator	1994	1996	1997	Annual change, 1994–97 (percent)
BOP (exports)	186,001	221,120	240,443	8.9
MOFAs	159,149	223,175	253,253	16.7
BoP (imports)	119,101	137,081	152,447	8.6
MOUSAs	145,414	168,444	205,548	12.2

Note: BoP, balance of payments; MOFA, majority-owned foreign affiliate; MOUSA, majority-owned U.S. affiliate.
Source: Survey of Current Business (October 1999).

Notes

1 A draft version of the MSITS is available at
<http://www.un.org/Depts/unsd/statcom/2001docs/
m86-e.pdf>.

2 "Commercial services" refers to the GATS definition of services
and excludes trade in government services. The terms "services" and "commercial services" are used as equivalent
expressions in this chapter.

3 It should be noted that the bilateral trade figures reported by
each of the two countries may show somewhat different flows.
These discrepancies may be largely attributable to the fact that
imports of services are often more difficult to record than
exports and to methodological differences in the way individual countries compile the data.

4 For methodological explanations concerning the compilation
of these data, see Karsenty (2000); the data presented therein
were updated from IMF balance of payments statistics, and
estimates of foreign affiliate trade statistics (FATS) gross output
were extrapolated using value added in services growth rates
implicitly derived from GDP aggregates.

5 WTO, "Recent Developments in Services Trade: Overview and
Assessment," 1999: p. 4.

ROBERT M. STERN

26

QUANTIFYING BARRIERS TO TRADE IN SERVICES

G IVEN THE SIGNIFICANT GROWTH IN RECENT DECADES OF INTERNATIONAL TRADE IN services (now equal to about 20 percent of global merchandise trade), it is obviously important to consider the barriers that affect this trade and the issues concerning measurement of the barriers. The amount of foreign direct investment (FDI) in both goods and services sectors in and between industrial and developing countries is also increasing. FDI, like services, is subject to a variety of barriers and merits attention in its own right.

The most distinguishing characteristic of services transactions is that their production and consumption occur simultaneously, often requiring direct contact between producers and consumers. Although some services (for example, "separated" services such as telecommunications) are traded internationally across borders in a manner similar to cross-border trade in goods, other services may require the consumer to move to the location of the producer, as in the case of tourism. Furthermore, because of the necessary proximity of consumers and producers, factors of production may have to move across national boundaries to the place of consumption. Thus, FDI may be necessary in order to establish a foreign commercial presence, and temporary cross-border movement of labor may also be required to serve foreign consumers.

Types of Barriers to Trade and FDI in Services

As noted by Hoekman and Braga (1997: 288), as a consequence of the simultaneity of the production and consumption of services, border measures such as tariffs will generally be difficult to apply because customs agents cannot readily observe the service as it crosses the border. Typically, therefore, the restrictive policies followed will be designed to limit the access of foreign services and services suppliers to domestic markets. Hoekman and Braga distinguish the following types of barriers: (a) quantitative restrictions such as quotas, local content, and prohibitions; (b) price-based instruments; (c) standards, licensing, and procurement; and (d) discriminatory access to distribution networks.

• *Quantitative-restriction (QR)–type policies* are commonly applied to services providers. Two prominent examples are bilateral agreements regulating international air transport services, which are usually reciprocal and company-specific, and ocean-cargo-sharing arrangements, which also often rely on reciprocity in providing shipping services in mutual trade. Many countries have outright prohibitions directed against foreign providers of such services as domestic transport, basic telecommunications, and legal, insurance,

Table 26.1 Constructed Ad Valorem Tariff Equivalent "Guesstimates" by One-Digit ISIC Services Sector, Selected Countries
(percentage)

Economy	ISIC 5 (construction)	ISIC 6 (wholesale and retail distribu- tion)	ISIC 7 (transport, storage, and com- munications)	ISIC 8 (business and financial services)	ISIC 9 (social and personal services)
Australia	12.0	7.4	183.4	24.8	25.4
Austria	5.0	4.6	98.7	20.1	13.9
Canada	6.0	9.0	117.7	25.9	40.2
Chile	40.0	34.4	182.2	45.2	42.9
European Union	10.0	10.0	182.0	27.2	23.6
Finland	19.0	14.6	181.0	23.8	31.7
Hong Kong (China)	32.0	31.5	149.8	39.0	42.9
Japan	5.0	4.6	142.0	28.9	32.3
Korea, Rep. of	16.0	21.4	164.9	36.3	40.7
Mexico	24.0	21.3	152.3	40.9	29.8
New Zealand	5.0	13.4	181.5	30.5	36.1
Norway	5.0	13.4	122.2	25.7	24.0
Singapore	12.0	34.4	138.8	35.9	33.7
Sweden	12.0	13.4	184.2	22.5	26.9
Switzerland	5.0	8.0	178.1	27.7	32.3
Turkey	5.0	34.4	31.6	35.4	35.9
United States	5.0	4.6	111.4	21.7	31.7

Note: ISIC, International Standard Industrial Classification.
Source: Hoekman (1995): 355–56.

Table 26.2 FDI Restrictiveness Indices, Selected APEC Economies and Selected Services Sectors
(percent)

Economy	Business	Communication	Distribution	Education	Financial	Transport
Australia	18	44	18	18	45	20
Canada	23	51	20	20	38	24
China	36	82	28	53	45	46
Hong Kong (China)	2	35	5	0	23	9
Indonesia	56	64	53	53	55	53
Japan	6	35	5	20	36	11
Korea, Rep. of	57	69	63	55	88	57
Malaysia	32	42	8	8	61	12
Mexico	29	74	33	45	55	28
New Zealand	9	43	8	8	20	13
Papua New Guinea	30	48	30	30	30	30
Philippines	48	76	48	48	95	98
Singapore	26	52	25	25	38	25
Thailand	78	84	78	78	88	78
United States	1	35	0	0	20	3

Note: APEC, Asia-Pacific Economic Cooperation. The higher the score, the greater the degree to which an industry is restricted. The maximum score is 100 percent.
Source: Adapted from Hardin and Holmes (1997): 112–37.

economies (McGuire 1998); an analysis of impediments to trade in banking services for 23 countries plus the European Union (EU) that distinguished impediments to commercial presence and operations and impediments affecting foreign banks and all banks (McGuire and Schuele 2001); a pilot study of barriers affecting accounting services in Australia, France, the United Kingdom, and the United States (OECD 1997a); an analysis of the commitments of 69 signatories of the February 1997 Agreement on Basic Telecommunications (Marko 1998); indices for measuring the restrictiveness of telecommunications policies in 136 countries (Warren 2001a); and restrictions on foreign maritime services suppliers and all maritime service suppliers, covering 35 economies (McGuire, Schuele, and Smith 2001).

The various frequency-type measures that have been constructed are useful in identifying the types of barrier and the relative degree of protection afforded to particular sectors across countries. But these measures have only limited economic content with regard to assessing the size of service barriers and the consequences of maintaining or eliminating these barriers. As indicated in Table 26.5, below, Hoekman's guesstimates of services tariff equivalents, in particular, have been used in a number of economic modeling studies to represent actual barriers. The results of these studies are problematic, for the reason mentioned above. The question, then, is whether it is possible to construct price-based or quantity-based measures of services barriers that can be used for quantitative assessment of the costs of and benefits from the reduction or removal of the barriers. I next discuss a number of such recent measurement efforts.

Price-Based Measures of Services Barriers

Warren and Findlay (2000) review ongoing efforts to construct price-based measures of services impediments, using estimates of price-cost margins. As they note, Kalirajan and others (2001) have calculated the "net interest margins" for 694 national and state commercial banks in selected economies. The latter authors' "price-wedge" calculations distinguish barriers to establishment and to ongoing operations for foreign and domestic firms. Kalirajan and others show that the price impacts of restrictions on foreign banks are the highest for Chile, Indonesia, the Republic of Korea, Malaysia,

the Philippines, Singapore, and Thailand. Argentina, Australia, Canada, the EU, Hong Kong (China), Switzerland, and the United States appear to have relatively low nonprudential restrictions on foreign banks. Warren and Findlay also discuss (p. 73) work in progress on price-based measures of policy variables for maritime services. Calculations of price-based measures are especially useful because they are derived from observed data. They are, accordingly, well suited for use in economic models designed to assess the effects of banking restrictions on resource allocation and economic welfare. A recent example is the multicountry model of Dee and Hanslow (2001), who use the estimates by Kalirajan and others.

Quantity-Based Measures of Services Barriers

Warren (2001b) has assessed the quantitative impact of barriers in telecommunications services, chiefly mobile telephony and fixed network services, for 136 countries. Combining the quantitative estimates of the effects of removing existing barriers with an estimate of the price elasticity of demand for the telecommunications services involved, he calculated tariff equivalents in the form of price wedges. He shows that the tariff equivalents for domestic and foreign providers of telecommunication services for the advanced industrial countries are relatively low in comparison with the much higher estimates for the newly industrializing countries and developing countries. His estimates have been used in the economic modeling work by Dee and Hanslow already cited.

Francois (1999) fitted a gravity model to bilateral services trade for the United States and its major trading partners, taking Hong Kong (China) and Singapore as free trade benchmarks. He interprets the differences between actual and predicted imports as indicative of NTBs and then normalizes them relative to the free trade benchmarks for Hong Kong and Singapore, which presumably have few barriers. The results for business and financial services and for construction are shown in Table 26.3. As noted in Deardorff and Stern (1998: 24), gravity-model measures of this kind are useful mainly in identifying *relative* levels of protection across sectors and countries. They have, however, some important drawbacks: the attribution to NTBs of all departures of trade from what the included variables can explain places a great burden on the

Table 26.3 Estimated Tariff Equivalents in Traded Services: Gravity Model–Based Regression Method
(percent)

Economy or region	Business and financial services	Construction
North America[a]	8.2	9.8
Western Europe	8.5	18.3
Australia and New Zealand	6.9	24.4
Japan	19.7	29.7
China	18.8	40.9
Taiwan (China)	2.6	5.3
Other newly industrialized countries	2.1	10.3
Indonesia	6.8	9.6
Other Southeast Asia	5.0	17.7
India	13.1	61.6
Other South Asia [b]	20.4	46.3
Brazil	35.7	57.2
Other Latin America	4.7	26.0
Turkey [b]	20.4	46.3
Other Middle East and North Africa	4.0	9.5
Central and Eastern Europe and Russia	18.4	51.9
South Africa	15.7	42.1
Other Sub-Saharan Africa	0.3	11.1
Rest of world	20.4	46.3

a. North American values are derived by assigning numbers for Canada and Mexico to the United States.
b. Turkey and Other South Asia are not separately available in the U.S. data and have been assigned estimated rest-of-world values.
Source: Francois (1999).

model being used. The more imperfect the model, the more likely it is that NTB estimates will have an upward bias. Moreover, since trade cannot be predicted accurately for particular industries and countries, it is not clear how the deviations should be interpreted or to what extent existing trade patterns depart from free trade. As a consequence, the results from modeling studies such as that by Hertel (2000), who used Francois's estimates of services barriers, pose problems of interpretation.

Financial-Based Measures of Services Barriers

Hoekman (2000) has suggested that financial data on gross operating margins calculated by sector and country may provide information about the effects of government policies on firm entry and conditions of competition. He points out,

In general, a large number of factors will determine the ability of firms to generate high margins, including market size (number of firms), the business cycle, the state of competition policy enforcement, the substitutability of products, fixed costs, etc. Notwithstanding the impossibility of inferring that high margins are due to high barriers, there should be a correlation between the two across countries for any given sector. Data on operating margins provide some sense of the relative profitability of activities, and therefore, the relative magnitude (restrictiveness) of barriers to entry/exit that may exist. (Hoekman 2000: 37)

Table 26.4 shows the results for 1994–96 by economy and region, averaged over firms and sectors, for agriculture, manufacturing, and services. Services

Table 26.4 Average Gross Operating Margins of Firms Listed on National Stock Exchanges, 1994–96, by Economy or Region
(percent)

Economy or region	Agriculture	Manufacturing	Services
Australia	8.4	15.5	16.6
Canada	32.1	22.6	32.9
Chile	39.1	40.8	44.0
China	30.6	28.1	49.5
European Union	22.9	23.8	31.6
Hong Kong (China)	25.9	12.8	18.1
Indonesia	41.8	34.3	41.3
Japan	38.4	26.4	28.7
Korea, Rep. of	11.2	25.7	25.8
Malaysia	22.6	6.0	21.6
Mexico	38.4	39.3	37.2
New Zealand	33.3	16.6	26.8
Philippines	18.1	28.6	42.3
Singapore	0.0	11.1	22.0
Taiwan (China)	19.6	25.1	41.3
Thailand	38.2	27.3	52.6
United States	36.6	21.2	42.3
Rest of Cairns Group[a]	36.3	31.1	39.0

a. Includes Argentina, Brazil, and Colombia.
Source: Hoekman (2000), based on calculations using Worldscope (1998) data.

margins are generally higher than manufacturing margins by 10–15 percentage points, and they vary considerably across economies. Australia, Hong Kong (China), and Singapore have the lowest services margins, around 20 percent, while Chile, China, Indonesia, the Philippines, Taiwan (China), Thailand, and the United States have services margins of more than 40 percent. The sectoral results (Hoekman 2000: 38) indicate that the margins for hotels and financial services are relatively high and the margins for wholesale and retail trade are lower. The margins for several developing countries appear to be relatively high in a number of services sectors. Overall, Hoekman suggests that "business services, consultancy, and distribution do not appear to be among the most protected sectors. . . . barriers to competition are higher in transportation, finance, and telecommunications. These are also basic 'backbone' imports that are crucial for the ability of enterprises to compete internationally" (Hoekman 2000: 39).

Financial-based measures of services barriers are especially promising because they can be constructed for a large number of sectors and countries. They need to be interpreted with care, however, because they are indirect measures and do not make allowance for intercountry differences in the quality and variety of services. Nonetheless, these measures are useful as a first approximation of the cost-raising effects of services, and they can be incorporated into economic models, as has been done, for example, in Brown and Stern (2001).

Modeling the Economic Effects of Services Barriers

While the various measures of services barriers noted are of interest, they need to be incorporated into an explicit economic modeling framework in order to determine how the existence or removal of the barriers will affect conditions for competition, production costs, economic welfare, and the intersectoral movement of capital and labor. Most research to date on the modeling of barriers has been focused on international trade in goods rather than on trade in services and FDI. The reasons stem in large part from the lack of comprehensive data on cross-border services trade and FDI and on the associated barriers, together with the difficult conceptual problems of modeling that are encountered. Some indication of pertinent modeling work is provided in Table 26.5. Following Hardin and Holmes (1997: 85), the approaches to modeling can be divided as follows:

- Analysis of services trade liberalization in response to reductions in services barriers (Brown, Deardorff, and Stern 1996; Brown and others 1996; Francois and others 1996; Hertel 2000; Tamms 2001; Robinson, Wang, and Martin 2002)

- Assumption that FDI responds to trade liberalization or other exogenous changes that generate international capital flows in response to changes in rates of return (Martin and Yagashima 1993; Dee, Geisler, and Watts (1996); Donovan and Mai 1996; McKibbin and Wilcoxen 1996; Bora and Guisinger 1997; Adams 1998; Dee, Hardin, and Schuele 1998)[6]

- Modeling of links between parents and affiliates and distinctions between foreign and domestic firms in a given economy or region (Markusen, Rutherford, and Hunter 1995; Petri 1997; Ben-

Table 26.5 Alternative Approaches to Modeling the Impact of Barriers to Trade and Investment

1. Reduction in services barriers

Brown, Deardorff, and Stern (1996); Brown and others (1996)
Based on 8-region, 29-sector, 1990 reference year version of Michigan CGE model, with all goods and services tradable. Uses Hoekman's (1995) "guesstimates" of tariff equivalents covering all modes of providing services, including FDI. Factors involved in FDI assumed to be part of factor markets in country of origin.

Francois and others (1996)
CGE analysis using 1989 reference year and calculation of the effects of price wedges attributable to the Jones Act, which restricts trade in U.S. domestic water transport (cabotage) services.

Australia, Department of Foreign Affairs and Trade (1999)
Based on GTAP model, version 4 (1995) database covering 45 regions and 50 sectors in each region and on the Asia-Pacific G-cubed model with 18 regions and 6 sectors, with inclusion of a financial sector and full (dynamic) macroeconomic closure. Uses modifications of Hoekman's (1995) "guesstimates" of services tariff equivalents.

Hertel (2000)
Based on 19-region, 22-sector CGE model with GTAP 1995 reference year data projected to 2005. Post–Uruguay Round tariff rates are used for agriculture and manufactures. Barriers for business services and construction based on gravity-model estimates in Francois (1999).

Tamms (2000)
Constructs cost functions using data for 50 airlines from 27 countries for 1982–95 and estimates a frontier function to determine the extent to which an airline lies off its frontier.

Robinson, Wang, and Martin (2002)
Based on 10-region, 11-sector, 1995 reference year CGE model, with all goods and services tradable. Uses Hoekman's (1995) "guesstimates" of services tariff equivalents, with allowance for growth in total factor productivity (TFP) stimulated by imports of services by developing countries.

2. Flows of FDI in response to changes in rates of return

Martin and Yagashima (1993)
Analysis of trade liberalization in Asia and Pacific region coupled with assumed changes in inward FDI.

Dee, Geisler, and Watts (1996)
Based on 13-region, 4-sector, 1992 reference year CGE model, with all goods and services tradable; monopolistic competition in the resources, food processing, and manufacturing sectors; allowance for capital accumulation and international factor mobility. Uses Hoekman's (1995) "guesstimates" of services tariff equivalents.

Table 26.5 (continued)

Donovan and Mai (1996)

Uses MEGABARE model to estimate effects of trade liberalization with varying degrees of international capital mobility in response to differential rates of return on investment.

McKibbin and Wilcoxen (1996)

Uses G-cubed model with international capital mobility responding to changes in differential sectoral rates of return to capital.

Bora and Guisinger (1997)

Analysis of investment liberalization in APEC, with allowance for international capital mobility.

Adams (1998)

Based on GTAP model, with 14 regions and 37 perfectly competitive sectors, and on post-NAFTA database. Each region contributes a fixed proportion of its income to a global savings pool. Investment allocation depends on relative rates of return. Focus is on effects of trade liberalization in APEC. FDI is not modeled explicitly.

Dee, Hardin, and Schuele (1998)

Based on same model and data as Dee, Geisler, and Watts (1996), with analysis of APEC sectors selected for "early voluntary sectoral liberalization."

3. Links between parents and foreign affiliates and distinctions between foreign and domestic firms

Markusen, Rutherford, and Hunter (1995)

Analysis of trade liberalization in the automobile industry in the NAFTA countries, using a model with multinational firms or national firms responding to changes in their market shares.

Petri (1997)

Based on 6-region, 3-sector CGE model, using 1992 GTAP dataset, with FDI separated into activities of domestic and foreign-owned firms. Products differentiated by both country of ownership and place of production. Capital allocation between sectors and between domestic and foreign investments responds to changes in rates of return and to investor preferences. Barriers to FDI modeled as a tax on FDI profits.

Markusen, Rutherford, and Tarr (2000)

Conceptual static and dynamic CGE model used to analyze how inward FDI in producer services may complement domestic skilled labor, affect the pattern of trade in goods, and determine the characteristics of the dynamic adjustment path.

Benjamin and Diao (2000)

Based on 10-region, 11-sector CGE model, using data for the early 1990s, with the focus on liberalization of cross-border trade of other private services in APEC. Services providers in the single services sector are imperfectly competitive, have fixed costs, and are able to price-discriminate across countries. Liberalization is modeled as both reducing fixed costs and removing the market segmentation that permits price discrimination. FDI is not modeled explicitly, but it could be.

Dee and Hanslow (2001)

Based on 19-region, 3-sector, 1995 reference year CGE model, with modifications of Petri's (1997) framework and updating of data on FDI stocks, output, and rates of return. Uses averages of services barriers for banking and telecommunications services contained in Kalirajan and others (2001) and in Warren (2001b).

Brown and Stern (2001)

Based on 18-region, 3-sector, 1995 reference year CGE model with features of structure and FDI similar to Dee and Hanslow (2001). Uses estimates of price-cost margins from Hoekman (2000) to estimate services barriers.

Note: APEC, Asia-Pacific Economic Cooperation; CGE, computable general equilibrium (model); FDI, foreign direct investment; GTAP, Global Trade and Analysis Project; NAFTA, North American Free Trade Agreement.
Source: Author's compilation.

Because research on services barriers is so time-intensive, international organizations and government agencies are in the best position to undertake it and underwrite the costs involved. The private sector can also be helpful in providing specialized information and knowledge about different barriers.

Even though measurement of services barriers is imprecise, it does appear that these barriers have significant costs. This is attested by the potential gains in economic welfare that modeling studies suggest would be realized if the barriers were to be reduced or removed. Continuing research, with the use of models incorporating both cross-border services trade and services-related FDI, by members of the academic community and by international and governmental organizations should be encouraged. From what we know to date, services liberalization should remain a central objective in the ongoing WTO services negotiations and as part of a broader WTO negotiating round.

Notes

1 Direct restrictions include limitations on the total size or share of investment in a sector and requirements concernng inputs used (e.g., local content). Indirect restrictions include net benefit or national interest criteria and limitations on membership of company boards. The distinction between rules and case-by-case decisions relates to issues of clarity in specification and transparency as against the exercise of administrative discretion.

2 Hardin and Holmes (1997: 40–43) also provide information on investment incentives, which are widely used and for the most part are not subject to multilateral disciplines.

3 As noted in Hardin and Holmes (1997: 70), the GATS commitments are based on a "positive list" approach and therefore do not take into account sectors and restrictions that are unscheduled. In PECC (1995) it is assumed that all unscheduled sectors and commitments are unrestricted, which would then significantly lower the calculated frequency ratios. It would be useful to determine the accuracy of the PECC assumption.

4 Details on the construction of the indexes and their sensitivity to variations in the restrictive weights are discussed in Hardin and Holmes (1997, esp. 103–11).

5 More recent information on studies completed and in progress in association with the Australian Government Productivity Commission can be accessed at <http://www.pc.gov.au/research/staffres/index/html>.

6 For more recent computable general equilibrium (CGE) modeling studies that focus on issues of international capital mobility, see Ianchovichina, McDougall, and Hertel (1999); Verikos and Hanslow (1999); Walmsley (1999), and selected papers presented at the Third Annual Conference on Global Economic Analysis, Sydney, Australia, June 2000; available at <www.monash.edu.au/policy/conf2000.htm>.

7 See also Dee and Hanslow (2001) for computational results based on a related modeling framework and using estimates of services barriers taken from Kalirajan and others (2001) and Warren and Findlay (2000).

27

RUDOLF ADLUNG
ANTONIA CARZENIGA
BERNARD HOEKMAN
MASAMICHI KONO
AADITYA MATTOO
LEE TUTHILL

THE GATS: KEY FEATURES AND SECTORS

developing a framework of rules for policies related to trade in services.

General Principles

The General Agreement on Trade in Services (GATS) that emerged consists of two main elements: (a) a set of general concepts, principles, and rules that apply to all measures affecting trade in services, and (b) specific commitments that apply to the services sectors and subsectors listed in each member's schedule. The GATS covers all measures imposed by members that affect the consumption of services originating in other members (Art. I). The agreement applies to four modes of supply through which services may be exchanged:

THE FIRST TWO SECTIONS OF THIS CHAPTER PRESENT A BROAD OVERVIEW OF THE General Agreement on Trade in Services (GATS) and the status of negotiations on services. Subsequent sections focus on financial services, telecommunications, maritime services, and air transport services. The sections are the work of individual authors, as listed in a note at the end of the chapter.

The Agreement

The nonexistence of tariffs on services and the importance of regulation greatly complicate the lives of negotiators seeking to agree on the incremental reduction of barriers to services trade. Negotiators require a focal point—some tangible variable enabling parties to set objectives and assess negotiating progress. In merchandise trade negotiations, the focus is on the value of bilateral trade flows and the associated tariff revenues. Lack of data on trade and the complexities associated with identifying and quantifying barriers to trade made this approach impossible for services. In the Uruguay Round negotiators therefore focused primarily on

- Mode 1: cross-border supply not requiring the physical movement of supplier or consumer
- Mode 2: movement of the consumer to the country of the supplier
- Mode 3: services sold in the territory of a member by foreign entities that have established a commercial presence
- Mode 4: provision of services requiring the temporary movement of natural persons.

Trade in services in the GATS context therefore covers both trade in the balance of payments (or national accounts) sense and local sales by foreign affiliates. The GATS does not apply to services supplied in the exercise of government functions. The main provisions of the GATS are summarized in Table 27.1.

Table 27.1 Main Provisions of the GATS

Article	Subject matter
I	Definition. Trade in services covers all four modes of supply.
II	Most-favored-nation (MFN) obligation. Option to invoke exemptions on a one-time basis.
III	Notification and publication. Obligation to create an enquiry point.
IV	Increasing participation of developing countries. High-income countries to take measures to facilitate trade of developing nations.
V	Economic integration. Allows for free trade and similar agreements.
VI	Allows for domestic regulation. Requirements concerning the design and implementation of services sector regulation, including, in particular, qualification requirements.
VII	Recognition of qualifications, standards, and certification of suppliers.
VIII	Monopolies and exclusive suppliers. Requires that such entities abide by MFN and specific commitments (Arts. XVI and XVII) and do not abuse their dominant position.
IX	Business practices. Recognition that business practices may restrict trade. Calls for consultations between members on request.
XIV	General exceptions. Allows measures to achieve noneconomic objectives.
XVI	Market access. Defines a set of policies that may only be used to restrict market access for a scheduled sector if they are listed in a member's specific commitments.
XVII	National treatment. Applies in a sector if a commitment to that effect is made and if no limitations or exceptions are listed in a member's schedule.
XVIII	Allows members to make additional commitments, e.g., regarding qualifications, standards, and licenses
XIX	Calls for successive negotiations to expand coverage of specific commitments (Arts. XVI and XVII).
XXIX	States that annexes are an integral part of the GATS.

Annexes to the GATS allow for one-time most-favored-nation (MFN) exemptions, address the movement of natural persons, exclude air transport services, define commitments on financial and telecommunications services, and clarify the potential coverage of maritime transport commitments.

As in the GATT, the core principle of the GATS is MFN (Art. II). Members are, however, allowed to list MFN exemptions on entry into force of the agreement. MFN exemptions are, in principle, to last no longer than 10 years and are subject to negotiation in future trade rounds.

Specific Commitments

Article XVII.1 contains the basic national treatment obligation, which is a so-called specific commitment: "In the sectors inscribed in its Schedule, and subject to any conditions and qualifications set out therein, each Member shall accord to services and service suppliers of any other Member, in respect of all measures affecting the supply of services, treat-ment no less favorable than that it accords to its own like services and service suppliers."[1] National treatment therefore applies only to those services inscribed in a member's schedule, and then only to the extent that no qualifications or conditions are listed in the schedule.

A second specific commitment is market access. Article XVI stipulates a range of measures restrictive of market access (mostly quotas) that a WTO member cannot maintain or adopt unless specified in its schedule. These measures include restrictions on (a) number of service suppliers allowed, (b) value of transactions or assets, (c) total quantity of services output, (d) number of natural persons that may be employed, (e) type of legal entity through which a services supplier is permitted to supply a service (for example, in banking, branches versus subsidiaries), and (e) participation of foreign capital in terms of limits on foreign equity or on the absolute value of foreign investment. With the exception of (e), the measures covered by Article XVI all take the form of quantitative restrictions.

Article XVI has been interpreted, in "Scheduling of Initial Commitments in Trade in Services: Explanatory Note," as applying to both discriminatory and nondiscriminatory measures.[2] It thus covers both measures of the type "only five new foreign banks will be granted licenses" and measures such as "only 10 new foreign and domestic banks will be granted licenses." Although the six types of measure listed above are in principle prohibited, if a member desires to maintain one or more of them for a scheduled sector, it may do so as long as it lists them in its schedule. To a degree, Article XVI is the equivalent of GATT Article XI, which prohibits the use of quotas. Specific commitments apply only to services sectors listed by members, subject to whatever qualifications, conditions, and limitations are maintained. Since commitments are scheduled by mode of supply as well as by sector, these exceptions may apply either across all modes of supply or for a specific mode.

Members also make horizontal commitments applicable to modes of supply, rather than sector, that are often restrictive in nature. A common example is an "economic needs test." Finally, members have the option of making additional commitments by listing actions to be taken that do not fall under national treatment or market access. Article XVIII of the GATS provides for such additional commitments, stating, "Members may negotiate commitments with respect to measures affecting trade in services not subject to scheduling under Articles XVI or XVII, including those regarding qualifications, standards or licensing matters. Such commitments shall be inscribed in a Member's Schedule." An example of the use to which Article XVIII has been put is the case of a member making an additional commitment in a particular sector to subscribe to international standards.

The specific commitments made by members can be seen as the outcome of a two-step decision. Each member first decides which services sectors will be subject to the GATS market access and national treatment disciplines. It then decides what measures will be kept in place for that sector which violate market access or national treatment. Table 27.2

Table 27.2 Format and Example of a Schedule of GATS Commitments

Commitment type and mode of supply	Conditions and limitations on market access	Conditions and qualifications on national treatment	Additional commitments
Horizontal commitments (across all sectors)			
1. Cross-border	None.	None.	
2. Consumption abroad	Unbound.	Unbound.	
3. Commercial presence (foreign direct investment)	Maximum foreign equity stake is 49 percent.	Unbound for subsidies. Approval required for equity stakes over 25 percent.	
4. Temporary entry of natural persons	Unbound except for intracorporate transfers of senior managers.	Unbound except for categories listed in the market access column.	
Specific commitments (sectoral)			
1. Cross border	Commercial presence required.	Unbound.	
2. Consumption abroad	None.	None.	
3. Commercial presence (foreign direct investment)	25 percent of management to be nationals.	Unbound.	Establishment of an independent regulator.
4. Temporary entry of natural persons	Unbound, except as indicated under Horizontal commitments.	Unbound, except as indicated under Horizontal commitments.	

Note: "None" implies that no exceptions are maintained (a bound commitment).

illustrates the rather complicated format of schedules of commitments. A consequence of the decisions to distinguish between general and specific obligations, to schedule specific commitments by mode of supply, and to allow for MFN exemptions is that much depends on the content of the schedules. The GATS is not a particularly transparent or user-friendly instrument.

The Current Pattern of Commitments

Pursuant to Article XX.1 of the GATS, each WTO member is required to spell out in a schedule the specific commitments on market access and national treatment it undertakes in services. The scope and substance of schedules are not further specified; for example, the agreement does not prescribe any minimum number of sectors to be included or modes of supply to be liberalized. Member governments thus have wide discretion in selecting services from a classification list, which was developed in the Uruguay Round, and in specifying, by way of limitations, trading conditions under any of the four modes of supply of services. The range of scheduling options also includes the possibilities of departing from the common classification list (compliance with which is not mandatory), restricting access to subregions within the national territory, or phasing in commitments at specified later dates ("precommitments").

Given the leeway provided under the agreement, it may prove difficult, if not impossible, to find two identical schedules among the current 140-odd WTO members. Differences in national policy orientation, negotiating strength, and sectoral interests have translated into wide differences in commitments across members, sectors, and modes. Although it might be tempting to use the term "imbalance" in this context, member governments with low levels of commitments would possibly insist that their schedules are a balanced reflection of the Uruguay Round process and of domestic policy constraints that might preclude liberalization of individual areas. Moreover, developing countries, which account for some four-fifths of the WTO's membership, are covered by various flexibility provisions in the agreement allowing them, for example, to open fewer sectors, liberalize fewer types of transactions, and progressively extend access in line with their development situation (Article XIX.2).

Economic Expectations

From an economic perspective, the rationale underlying such provisions may not be immediately evident. Liberal policy bindings under the GATS, not least under mode 3 (commercial presence), could be viewed as a boon rather than a liability for the development process, as they provide an opportunity to enhance, through multilateral access guarantees, a country's attraction for international investment and the associated gains in skills and expertise. In turn, such expectations may have prompted a few developing countries—in particular, transition economies—not to rely on the agreement's flexibility but to undertake commitments comparable in breadth and depth to those undertaken by industrial country members, if not even more ambitious. It would be inappropriate, nevertheless, to consider more hesitant governments insensitive to developmental needs; rather, they may have preferred a more prudent stance because of lack of experience with the agreement or a perceived need for internal legislation to accompany a process of external liberalization. Although adequate competition rules, liability laws, licensing and qualification procedures, and the like may be considered prerequisites for ensuring effective market opening, the ability to develop such legislation may depend in turn on a country's level of social and economic development or the availability of competent technical assistance.

Current Scheduling Patterns

Commitments, by Member. The WTO's current members can be roughly classified into three groups, depending on the number of sectors they have included in their services schedules (see Table 27.3). About one-third of the membership has scheduled 20 or fewer sectors of the 160 or so industries specified in the GATS classification list, one-third has committed between 21 and 60 sectors; and the remaining members, about 50 in number, have included between 61 and about 130 sectors. The last group not only encompasses virtually all industrial countries but also includes some developing and least-developed economies (The Gambia, Lesotho, and Sierra Leone). Among the recently acceding members are such countries as the Kyrgyz Republic and Georgia that have undertaken broader commitments, in terms of sector coverage, than any Uruguay Round participant.

Table 27.3 Number of Committed Services Sectors by Member, July 2000

Number of committed sectors	Number of members	WTO members
≤20	44	Angola, Bahrain, Bangladesh, Belize, Benin, Bolivia, Botswana, Burkina Faso, Cameroon, Central African Republic, Chad, Congo (Dem. Rep), Congo (Rep.), Djibouti, Fiji, Gabon, Grenada, Guatemala, Guinea, Guinea-Bissau, Guyana, Haiti, Honduras, Madagascar, Maldives, Mali, Malta, Mauritania, Mozambique, Myanmar, Namibia, Niger, Paraguay, Rwanda, St. Kitts and Nevis, St. Lucia, St. Vincent and Grenadines, Suriname, Swaziland, Tanzania, Togo, Tunisia, Uganda, Zambia
21–60	47	Antigua and Barbuda, Argentina, Barbados, Brazil, Brunei Darussalam, Burundi, Chile, Colombia, Costa Rica, Côte d'Ivoire, Cuba, Cyprus, Dominica, Dominican Republic, Ecuador, Egypt, El Salvador, Ghana, India, Indonesia, Israel, Jamaica, Kenya, Kuwait, Macau (China), Malawi, Mauritius, Mongolia, Morocco, Nicaragua, Nigeria, Pakistan, Papua New Guinea, Peru, Philippines, Poland, Qatar, Romania, Senegal, Singapore, Solomon Islands, Sri Lanka, Trinidad and Tobago, United Arab Emirates, Uruguay, R. B. de Venezuela, Zimbabwe
≥61	45	Australia, Bulgaria, Canada, Czech Republic, EU (15), Estonia, The Gambia, Georgia, Hong Kong (China), Hungary, Iceland, Japan, Jordan, Korea (Rep.), Kyrgyz Republic, Latvia, Lesotho, Liechtenstein, Malaysia, Mexico, New Zealand, Norway, Panama, Sierra Leone, Slovak Republic, Slovenia, South Africa, Switzerland, Thailand, Turkey, United States

Source: WTO secretariat.

Commitments, by Sector. The positive developmental expectations that may be associated with commitments under the agreement are reflected, to some degree, in the sector structure of current schedules. Among the services most frequently included are not only areas traditionally considered to carry low levels of restrictions, such as tourism, but also core infrastructural services such as finance and communication. If the sectors contained in the classification list are aggregated to a few large clusters, the pattern illustrated in Figure 27.1 emerges: tourism ranks first, having drawn commitments from all but 10 WTO members in at least one subsector, followed by financial services and business services. Commitments in the latter two areas have been scheduled, with varying breadth and depth, by over 100 members. Communications services (with commitments from slightly fewer than 100 members), transport, and construction services rank next. The results for financial

and communications services, including basic telecommunications, are largely influenced by the extended negotiations in these areas, which were conducted beyond the time frame of the Uruguay Round and were successfully concluded in February 1997 (basic telecommunications) and December 1997 (financial services).

At the bottom of the sector hierarchy are the health and education sectors, each with fewer than 50 inclusions in schedules. Governments may have wanted to retain policy discretion (subject to the MFN principle) in these areas, which may be viewed as core public sector responsibilities. Some members may also have felt that, given the organization of their countries' health and education systems, these sectors were beyond the sectoral scope of the agreement. Article I.3 of the GATS provides a general exception for services provided in the exercise of government authority that are not supplied on a commercial basis or in competition.

they were not considered enough to conclude the negotiations. As a result, broad MFN exemptions based on reciprocity remained. The Second Annex on Financial Services to the GATS and the Decision on Financial Services adopted at the end of the Uruguay Round provided for extended negotiations to be held during a six-month period following the entry into force of the GATS—that is, up to the end of June 1995. At the conclusion of this period, WTO members had the possibility of improving, modifying, or withdrawing all or part of their commitments, and they were also able to introduce additional MFN exemptions. Broad MFN exemptions would not be applied until the end of the period.

The Interim Agreement of 1995

The 1995 negotiations, concluded on July 28, 1995, led to an "interim" agreement, since negotiators again decided that the results of the negotiations were not satisfactory. It was agreed that further negotiations would commence after two years, in 1997. As a result of the 1995 negotiations, 29 WTO members (counting the European Union as one member) improved their schedules of specific commitments or removed, suspended, or reduced the scope of their MFN exemptions in financial services, or did both. Those improved commitments were annexed to the Second Protocol to the GATS. Three other countries, Colombia, Mauritius, and the United States, decided not to improve their commitments and took broad MFN exemptions based on reciprocity. As a result of the extended negotiations, and with new accessions to the WTO, 97 members (counting the 15 EU members individually) had made commitments in financial services by mid-1997, compared with some 76 countries at the end of the Uruguay Round.

The 1997 Negotiations

The negotiations were reopened in April 1997. Between November 1 and December 12, 1997, members again had an opportunity to improve, modify, or withdraw their commitments in financial services and to take MFN exemptions in the sector (see the discussion in Box 27.1). As a result of the negotiations, a new and improved set of commitments in financial services under the GATS was agreed to on December 12, 1997. A total of 56 schedules of commitments representing 70 WTO

member governments and 16 lists of MFN exemptions (or amendments thereof) were annexed to the Fifth Protocol to the GATS, which was open for ratification and acceptance by members until January 29, 1999. Fifty-two member governments accepted the protocol by the due date, and those members decided to put the protocol into force on March 1, 1999, in accordance with the terms of the protocol. It was also decided by the Council for Trade in Services that the protocol would be kept open for acceptance until June 15, 1999, for the remaining 18 members. After this deadline expired, each accepting member had to request the council to reopen the protocol for acceptance. As of November 1, 2000, nine Members still had not accepted the Fifth Protocol.

With five countries making commitments in financial services for the first time, the total number of WTO members with commitments in financial services (including the newly acceding countries) will increase to around 105 on the entry into force of the Fifth Protocol. As a result of the negotiations, India, Thailand, and the United States decided to withdraw their broad MFN exemptions based on reciprocity; only a small number of countries submitted limited MFN exemptions or maintained existing broad MFN exemptions. Several countries, including Hungary, Mauritius, the Philippines, and Venezuela, reduced the scope of their MFN exemptions. The United States submitted a limited MFN exemption in insurance, applicable in a circumstance of forced divestiture of U.S. ownership in insurance services providers operating in WTO member countries.

In financial services, WTO members have the option of adopting the Understanding on Commitments in Financial Services (a formula for making advanced commitments under the GATS), and 31 WTO members have adopted it. Among other provisions, the new commitments introduce significant improvements concerning commercial presence of foreign financial services suppliers by eliminating or relaxing limitations on foreign ownership of local financial institutions, on the juridical form of commercial presence (branches, subsidiaries, agencies, representative offices, and so on), and on the expansion of existing operations. Important progress was also made on "grandfathering" existing branches and subsidiaries of foreign financial institutions that are wholly owned or majority-owned by foreigners. Improvements were made in all three major

BOX 27.1 FINANCIAL SERVICES: MARKET ACCESS COMMITMENTS OF DEVELOPING AND TRANSITION ECONOMIES

The approach of many developing and transition countries to the negotiations on financial services was tentative, for perhaps two reasons. First, the negotiations were concluded during the East Asian financial crisis, in a climate of uncertainty and increased awareness of widespread regulatory inadequacies. Second, financial services were being negotiated separately from other goods and services, and countries with export interests in other areas were reluctant to give up negotiating currency by making significant commitments. Therefore, even though the number of countries that participated in the eventual agreement was impressive (all industrial countries and more than 100 developing and transition economies took part), the liberalizing content of commitments was in many cases quite limited (see Tables 27.4 and 27.5). Interestingly, the few African and Eastern European participants made much more liberal commitments than the many Asian and Latin American participants. The Asian countries were more forthcoming in insurance than the Latin American countries, but the converse was true in banking services.

Two other aspects of the commitments were somewhat disappointing. First, in many cases there was less emphasis on the introduction of competition through allowing new entry than on allowing (or maintaining) foreign ownership and protecting the position of foreign incumbents. Second, even where it was deemed not feasible to introduce competition immediately, participants took little advantage of the GATS to lend credibility to reform programs by precommitting to future liberalization.

The GATS provoked concern that its rules might compromise the ability of governments to pursue sound regulatory and macroeconomic policies or might limit their freedom to achieve other domestic policy objectives. Most of these concerns seem to have been addressed. First, none of the GATS provisions prevent a member from taking measures for prudential reasons—for example, to protect investors or depositors or to ensure the integrity and stability of the financial system. Second, services supplied in the exercise of governmental authority, including activities conducted by a central bank or monetary authority or by any other public entity in pursuit of monetary or exchange rate policies, are excluded from the scope of the GATS. Third, even though a member's market access commitments oblige it to allow a certain degree of capital mobility—specifically, when the cross-border movement of capital is an essential part of the service itself and inflows of capital are related to commercial presence—the agreement allows a member to impose restrictions on current or capital transactions in the event of serious balance of payments or external financial difficulties or the threat thereof. Finally, the agreement allows a member to pursue other domestic policy objectives, through, for instance, directed lending programs, provided that the measures are neither discriminatory nor intended to restrict the access of suppliers to a market.

Source: Prepared by the volume editors, based on Mattoo (2000).

financial service sectors—banking, securities, and insurance—as well as in other services such as asset management and provision and the transfer of financial information.

The Next Round of Negotiations

In accord with the mandate contained in Article XIX of the GATS, negotiations on trade in services were launched in early 2001. The aim of these nego-

tiations is to achieve progressively higher levels of liberalization of trade in services across all sectors, including financial services. In these negotiations, there will be a need for developing countries to recognize the benefits of liberalization of financial services in helping to develop efficient and robust financial markets with foreign capital and expertise. Building an efficient financial system is a key to economic growth and development, and liberalization of financial services under the GATS will help coun-

Table 27.4 Market Access Commitments on Insurance (Life and Nonlife) under the GATS

Region	Full commitments on first three modes	Commitments on cross border supply (mode 1)		Commitments on consumption abroad (mode 2)		Commitments on commercial presence (mode 3)			
						Full, or limitations only on the legal form	Limitations		
		Full	Limited	Full	Limited		Number of suppliers only[a]	Foreign equity only	Number of suppliers and foreign equity
Africa	The Gambia	Gabon, The Gambia	Egypt, Ghana, Kenya, Nigeria, Tunisia	Egypt, Gabon, The Gambia, Lesotho, South Africa	Ghana, Kenya, Tunisia	The Gambia, Lesotho, Nigeria, Senegal, Sierra Leone, South Africa	Gabon, Mauritius, Morocco	Ghana, Kenya	Egypt
Asia and Pacific	Bahrain, Solomon Islands	Bahrain, Solomon Islands	India, Korea (Rep), Malaysia, Philippines, Qatar, Sri Lanka, Thailand, Turkey	Bahrain, Solomon Islands, Thailand	Brunei Darussalam, Hong Kong (China), Macau (China), Malaysia, Qatar, Sri Lanka, Turkey	Bahrain, Hong Kong (China), Indonesia, Israel, Macau (China), Solomon Islands, Turkey	Qatar	Korea	Brunei Darussalam, India, Malaysia, Pakistan, Philippines, Singapore, Sri Lanka, Thailand
Eastern Europe			Bulgaria, Czech Rep., Hungary, Slovak Rep., Slovenia		Czech Rep., Hungary, Slovak Rep., Slovenia	Poland, Romania	Czech Rep., Hungary, Slovak Rep.	Bulgaria	Slovenia

Latin America and the Caribbean	Guyana	Guyana	Argentina, Brazil, Colombia	Guyana	Argentina	Guyana, Panama, Paraguay	Argentina, Bolivia, Brazil, Chile, Colombia, Ecuador, Jamaica, Nicaragua, Peru, Uruguay, R. B. de Venezuela	Cuba, Mexico	Dominican Rep., Honduras

a. Unbound, discretionary licensing, reciprocity condition, or other limitations.

Source: Mattoo (2000).

Table 27.5 Market Access Commitments on Banking (Acceptance of Deposits and Lending of All Types) under the GATS

Region	Full commitments on first three modes	Commitments on cross border supply (mode 1)		Commitments on consumption abroad (mode 2)		Commitments on commercial presence (mode 3)			
							Limitations		
		Full	Limited	Full	Limited	Full, or limitations only on the legal form	Number of suppliers only[a]	Foreign equity only	Number of suppliers and foreign equity
Africa	Ghana, Kenya, Malawi, Mozambique, Sierra Leone	The Gambia, Ghana, Kenya, Malawi, Mozambique, Sierra Leone, Tunisia, Zimbabwe	Angola, Benin, Gabon, Morocco	The Gambia, Ghana, Kenya, Malawi, Mozambique, Sierra Leone, Tunisia, Zimbabwe	Benin, Gabon	Egypt, Ghana, Kenya, Lesotho, Mozambique, Nigeria, Senegal, Sierra Leone, South Africa	Angola, Benin, Gabon, Mauritius, Morocco, Tunisia	Zimbabwe	The Gambia, Morocco
Asia and Pacific	Papua New Guinea, Solomon Islands	Bahrain, Indonesia, Papua New Guinea, Qatar, Solomon Islands, United Arab Emirates	Israel, Kuwait, Malaysia	Bahrain, Hong Kong (China), Indonesia, Kuwait, Macau (China), Papua New Guinea, Philippines, Qatar, Solomon Islands, United Arab Emirates	Israel, Malaysia	Israel, Papua New Guinea, Solomon Islands	Hong Kong (China), Macau (China), Qatar, United Arab Emirates	Bahrain	India, Indonesia, Korea (Rep), Kuwait, Malaysia, Pakistan, Philippines, Singapore, Sri Lanka, Thailand

Eastern Europe		Romania	Czech Rep., Slovak Rep., Slovenia	Czech Rep., Romania, Slovak Rep., Slovenia	Bulgaria, Czech Rep., Poland, Romania, Slovak Rep.	Hungary, Slovenia		
Latin America and the Caribbean	Guyana, Haiti, Panama	Ecuador, Guyana, Haiti, Panama	Argentina, Ecuador, Guyana, Haiti, Jamaica, Panama, Paraguay		Argentina, Bolivia, Costa Rica, Guyana, Haiti, Jamaica, Panama, Paraguay	Chile, Colombia, Ecuador, El Salvador, Honduras, Nicaragua, Peru, Uruguay, R. B. de Venezuela	Mexico	Brazil, Dominican Rep.

a. Unbound, discretionary licensing, reciprocity condition, or other limitations.
Source: Mattoo (2000).

Table 27.6   (continued)

Participant	Market segment[a]				Phase-in date[b]	Limits on foreign equity or number of suppliers	Additional commit-ments, Reference Paper (RP)[c]	Additional commit-ments (other)[d]
India[h]	L	LD	[-]	[-]		Duopoly by service area; 25%	X	X
Indonesia[h]	L	[-]	I	[-]		Local PTT + 5 cooperators; I—duopoly; 35%	X	[-]
Israel[g,h]	[-]	[-]	I	[-]		74%	X	[-]
Jamaica	(L)	(LD)	(I)		09/2013	100%	X	[-]
Japan	L	LD	I	R		20% NTT/KDD; 100% other	X	[-]
Korea, Rep.	L	LD	I	R	For. eq.—2001	33% KT; 49% other (single investor limit—10% wire-based voice)	X	[-]
Malaysia	L	LD	I	[-]		Limited to current suppliers; 30%	[-]	X
Mauritius	(L)	(LD)	(I)	[-]	2004	100%	[-]	Considering introduction of RP
Mexico	L	LD	I	R		49%	X	[-]
Morocco	L	LD	I	[-]	2002	IAM: unbound; all others 100% at phase-in	X	[-]
New Zealand	L	LD	I	R		49.9% NZT (single investor limit only), 100% other	X	[-]
Norway	L	LD	I	R			X	[-]
Pakistan	[-]	[-]	[-]	[-]		Commercial presence: unbound	X	[-]
Papua New Guinea[h] **	[-]	[-]	[-]	[-]			X	[-]
Peru	L	LD	I	R	07/1999	100%	X	[-]
Philippines**	L	LD	I	[-]		40%		X
Poland	L	(LD)	(I)	(R)	2003	I (facilities based)—49% at phase-in; I (resale) and LD—49%; L—100%	X	[-]
Romania	(L)	(LD)	(I)	(R)	2003	100%	X	[-]
Senegal[e,h]	[-]	[-]	[-]	[-]		n.a.	X	[-]
Singapore	L	LD	I	[-]	04/2000	73.99% (49% direct; 24.99 indirect)	X	[-]
Slovak Rep.	(L)	(LD)	(I)	(R)	2003	100%	X	[-]
South Africa[h]	(L)	(LD)	(I)	(R)	2003	Duopoly at phase-in; 30%	X	[-]
Sri Lanka[e,h]	L	LD	I	[-]	I—01/2000, subject to tariff re-balancing	35% for international; 40 % other committed services; L and LD for WLL only—3 suppliers; I—duopoly	X	[-]

Switzerland	L	LD	I	R		100%	X	[-]
Thailand[f]	[-]	[-]	[-]	[-]		n.a.		Considering introduction of RP
Trinidad and Tobago[f]	(L)	(LD)	(I)	(R)	2010	100%	X	[-]
Tunisia	(L)	[-]	[-]	[-]		10% TT (2002), other 49%	[-]	[-]
Turkey (5)	(L)	(LD)	(I)	(R)	2006	49% at phase-in	[-]	X
United States	L	LD	I	R		20% radio licenses (direct only); 100% other	X	
R. B. de Venezuela	L	LD	I	[-]	*12/2000*	100%		[-]	X

Commitments submitted after Fourth Protocol

Albania	L rural; (L) urban	(LD)	(I)	(R)	2003	100%	X	[-]
Barbados	(L)	(LD)	(I)	(R)	2012	100%	X	[-]
China	(L)	(LD)	(I)	(R)	By service area, 12/2004– 12/2007	Joint venture required. 25% as of 12/2004; 35% as of 12/2006; 49% as of 12/2007	X	[-]
Croatia	(L)	(LD)	(I)	(R)	2003	100%	X	[-]
Cyprus[h]	[-]	[-]	[-]	[-]		n.a.	[-]	Decision taken in 1998 re: liberalization
Estonia	L	(LD)	(I)	(R)	2003	100%	X	[-]
Georgia	L	LD	I	R		100%	X	[-]
Jordan	(L)	(LD)	(I)	(R)	2005	100%	X	[-]
Kenya	L	LD	(I)	(R)	2003; (L) Nairobi	30%	X	[-]
Kyrgyz Rep.	L	(LD)	(I)	(R)	2003	100%	X	[-]
Latvia	(L)	(LD)	(I)	(R)	2003	100%	X	[-]
Lithuania	(L)	(LD)	(I)	(R)	2003	100%	X	[-]
Moldova	(L)	(LD)	(I)	(R)	2004	100%	X	[-]
Oman	(L)	(LD)	(I)	(R)	2004	70% as of 2001; 100% as of 2005	X	[-]
Suriname[g,h]	L	LD	I			40% public services; 100% nonpublic fixed and wireless nonvoice services; duopoly for public voice	X	[-]
Taiwan (China)	L	LD	I	R		Chunghwa Telecom 20% aggregate dir. and indir.; facilities-based 20% dir. and 60% aggregate dir. and indir.; 100% resale	X	[-]

(continued)

services and port services, where public monopolies are only gradually being privatized and more competition is being introduced. A third area, and one of growing importance, is multimodal transport, whereby goods pass from one country to another by various modes of transport in addition to ocean transport. Even though foreign multimodal transporters usually receive nondiscriminatory access to onward transport by road and rail, they frequently encounter difficulties in establishing their own inland transport operations. This can put them at a competitive disadvantage in situations where vertical integration provides benefits.

In 2000 maritime discussions were reinitiated as part of the broader negotiations on all services called for in GATS Article XIX. There are several reasons for believing that negotiations may be more successful this time. First, it may be possible to break the stalemate in maritime transport services by exploiting intersectoral negotiating tradeoffs. Second, it may be easier to negotiate commitments in the important area of multimodal transport when all transport sectors are being negotiated rather than maritime alone. Finally, and perhaps most important, unilateral liberalization in this sector is gathering steam as more and more countries appreciate that restrictions on maritime trade impose a significant cost on the whole economy (see WTO 1998c). It may therefore soon be possible to lock in the liberalization already achieved in an agreement under the GATS.

Liberalizing Trade in Air Transport Services

International air transport services are governed by an elaborate set of more than 3,500 bilateral agreements. These agreements typically specify the airlines of the parties that are allowed to fly on each international route between two countries, the capacity that can be provided by those designated airlines, and the extent to which capacity can be offered by airlines from third countries. In economic terms, they define country- and route-specific quotas. Most agreements only cover international traffic between two countries. Domestic air transport services are still generally protected from foreign competition.

The existing structure of bilateral agreements is inherently discriminatory, in that the agreements violate both the most-favored-nation (MFN) principle and the national treatment principle. Air

transport services are, to a large degree, excluded from the GATS. During the Uruguay Round, WTO members only negotiated certain complementary services (aircraft repair and maintenance, selling and marketing of air transport services, and computer reservation services). A GATS Annex on Air Transport specifically excludes from GATS rules the complex network of bilateral agreements on air traffic rights, and the MFN obligation has been suspended for the air transport sector.

Although precise estimates are hard to come by, empirical research suggests that there may be substantial gains from reforming the current international air transport regime in the direction of more open and competitive markets. Findlay and Nikomborirak (1999) report on work by Oum and Yu (1998) that analyzes differences in airlines' unit costs, decomposed into labor costs and operating efficiency. The latter might be affected by the extent of competition in markets, the characteristics of the overall management and control of the firm, the use of information technology systems, aircraft utilization planning, levels of employee skills, and so on. The results of Oum and Yu's analysis illustrate the possibility for developing economies to host internationally competitive carriers. Moreover, although input prices have traditionally been the most important determinant of competitiveness, efficiency improvements resulting from market liberalization and openness to foreign investment can yield significant reductions in airlines' unit costs.

Findlay and Nikomborirak (1999) also report on modeling work undertaken by the Australian Productivity Commission that examines the effects of market liberalization policies on services offered on routes to and from Australia. Among the estimated impacts of entry of another carrier were price decreases of 2.4–7.7 percent, increases in both Australian and foreign welfare, and an increase in total net passenger movements of nearly 4 percent.

Besides the beneficial effect on the sector's performance, there are several channels through which air transport liberalization may provide a positive stimulus to other sectors of the economy, notably tourism services. In the case of air cargo, more efficient service provision may translate into greater participation in international trade.

What are the possible approaches to sector reform? One route is from within the system of bilateral agreements. The increased proliferation in the 1990s of open skies agreements, which remove restrictions on access between and beyond the negotiating countries for their airlines, have been credited with leading to substantial market opening on selected routes, notably over the North Atlantic. This approach would, however, retain the discriminatory nature of the current system. Countries that do not enter into an agreement with a large trading partner risk diversion of traffic to third countries. Because most open skies agreements do not cover domestic traffic, foreign carriers are at a competitive disadvantage, since they are not able to draw on the extensive network maintained by domestic airlines. A series of open skies agreements is therefore unlikely to lead to a progressively more open and competitive system for international air transport.

A second route to reform would be to rely on regional agreements, which are likely to be associated with broader trade agreements, to foster sector reform. Examples of regional initiatives include the European Union agreement to establish a single market by 1997 and the Andean Pact Open Skies Agreement. The danger in regional approaches lies in the formation of blocs that lead to greater competition within the agreement area but raise barriers for airlines from outside the region.

The third approach, and, it can be argued, the most desirable one in the long run, would be to strengthen the GATS obligations with regard to air transport services and to negotiate market access concessions in a multilateral trading round. A first step might be to expand the coverage of services to include air freight and chartered services. A recent UNCTAD Expert Meeting on Air Transport Services observed that a large number of countries might wish to exclude the coverage of mode 1 (cross-border supply) but might be more open to negotiations on mode 3 (commercial presence). GATS coverage of the latter mode only would at least offer the benefits of the GATS in terms of MFN, market access, and national treatment for foreign investors in this sector.

As a final remark, it is important to stress that any reform route needs to be accompanied by appropriate mechanisms that address anticompetitive behavior of air transport services providers. Several characteristics of the sector highlight the potential for anticompetitive business practices. Major hubs are often dominated by the main national carriers, raising the possibility that foreign carriers might be denied access to airports or essential airport services. Frequent flier programs and long-term arrangements with travel agents may pose substantial entry barriers to foreign firms. Finally, the emergence of carriers' alliances, which often substitute for multinational mergers where these are restricted, has raised concerns about market concentration and cartel-like practices. Enforcement of competition policies in the international arena is necessarily difficult. Here again, the GATS may offer a small step forward—for example, by establishing a core set of procompetitive regulatory principles, such as already exist in the telecommunications sector.

Notes

Contributions to this chapter are as follows: "The Agreement," Bernard Hoekman; "The Current Pattern of Commitments," Rudolf Adlung and Antonia Carzeniga; "Financial Services: Past Negotiations and Issues for the Next Round," Masamichi Kono; "Telecommunications in the New Round," Lee Tuthill; "Maritime Negotiations in the WTO," Aaditya Mattoo; and "Liberalizing Trade in Air Transport Services," Aaditya Mattoo, based on input from Carsten Fink and on Findlay and Nikomborirak (1999).

1 It should be noted that GATS Article I states that the agreement applies to measures affecting trade in services, whereas Article XVII refers to all measures affecting the supply of services. It is not clear whether any significance should be attached to the distinction. In any case, it would seem that the set of measures affecting the supply of services cannot be narrower than that affecting trade in services.

2 MTN.GNS/W/164, September 3, 1993. The document warns that "the answers should not be considered as an authoritative legal interpretation of the GATS." It is, however, the basis on which many schedules of specific commitments have been drafted.

3 Often, limited forms of commercial presence are nonetheless necessary. Such forms may include local intermediary services suppliers for purposes of marketing subscriber takeup, local partners for billing and customer service functions, and presence of some localized facilities such as switches or leased line arrangements that may require on-site representatives or technicians.

4 Even though the GATS does permit members to seek temporary exemptions from the MFN obligations, the dominant view was that the continued suspension of the MFN rule would avert the need for many countries to take MFN exemptions that may be more difficult to negotiate away once explicitly listed.

5 The three relevant pieces of legislation are Section 19 of the Merchant Marine Act of 1920, Section 13(b)(5) of the Shipping Act of 1984, and the Foreign Shipping Practices Act of 1988. Even though specific action has rarely been taken, it has been claimed that the credible threat of doing so has induced an opening of foreign markets in some instances.

ally been more willing to liberalize mobile than fixed-line telecommunications services; mobile telephony has only recently been introduced, and there is thus no incumbent to protect. The entry restrictions sometimes benefit not only national firms but also foreign incumbents, as was the case with financial services in Malaysia. Other instruments, such as discriminatory subsidies or taxes, could be more easily targeted to achieve protection of the national firm.

Monopoly or oligopoly rents are sometimes seen as a means of helping firms fulfill universal service obligations through cross-subsidization. Governments, however, are increasingly devising means of achieving these objectives without sacrificing the benefits of competition. In some cases a form of "investment pessimism" leads to the belief that promises of oligopoly rents are necessary to finance new investment—although it is not clear why the market structure needs to be determined by policy, unless there are some initial investments the benefits of which may be appropriated by rivals. Finally, governments may seek to raise revenue (or rents for politicians and bureaucrats) by auctioning monopoly or oligopoly rights. This usually explains the promise of exclusive rights prior to privatization. Where competition would be feasible, granting exclusive rights amounts to indirect appropriation of consumers' surplus and may deny important dynamic efficiencies consequent on competition.

Ideally, governments would not resort to trade restrictions to pursue objectives that are better achieved through other means. In each of the cases listed above, entry restrictions are a second- or third-best instrument for achieving the objective in question but are chosen because of constraints such as inability to raise revenue without economic or political cost.

Are There Good Reasons to Limit Foreign Ownership, and What Are the Implications?

Most countries in the region maintain limits on foreign or private ownership, or both, but it is not easy to find a sound economic rationale for these restrictions. Insofar as the incentives to transfer technology, improve management, and so on are related to an owner's share in the profits, ownership limitations are bound to dampen those incentives and adversely affect firm performance. Governments are willing to bear this for three types of reasons:

1. If there are rent-generating restrictions on competition, the purpose of the observed limitations on ownership may be to balance the efficiency-enhancing and rent-appropriation aspects of foreign investment. This argument does raise the question of why rent appropriation cannot be prevented by ex ante auctions of equity or ex post taxation of profits.[4] (And, indeed, why do restrictions on competition continue to exist?)

2. Under a sort of "infant entrepreneur" rationale, foreigners are induced to form equity joint ventures so that local investors can learn by collaborating. As with all such arguments, it is difficult to judge whether the costs of protection are likely to be offset by the eventual benefits.

3. Probably most important is a purely political reluctance to allow foreign control of an essential service. These political concerns should be less strong if it is not one foreign monopolist but a number of competing foreign firms that provide the service.

In any case, there is so far no good analytical and empirical basis for evaluating the benefits and costs of ownership restrictions and how they interact with entry restrictions.

What Can the GATS Do?

The domestic political-economic forces that lead to protection may also dictate that it be obtained through inefficient instruments. Unlike the GATT, the GATS has created no hierarchy of instruments of protection, although the ranking of instruments in the cases of both goods and services is similar. Hence, quantitative restrictions, which have been discredited and outlawed as regards trade in goods, flourish in trade in services. When the rents accrue to foreigners, these quotas resemble voluntary export restraints. For instance, in the last round of negotiations countries sometimes conceded, and trading partners were content to receive, increased market access in the form of increased foreign ownership of existing domestic firms, rather than through allowing new entry.

Although it may not yet be politically feasible, or unambiguously desirable, to impose the same hierarchy of instruments in services as in goods, an attempt could nevertheless be made to create a legal presumption in favor of instruments such as fiscal measures that provide protection more efficiently.

The difficulty of switching to fiscal instruments of protection in services has probably been exaggerated. In the case of commercial presence, a number of fiscal instruments are possible, including entry taxes (or auctions of entry licenses), output taxes, and profit taxes. An *entry tax* increases the fixed costs of firms and lessens their willingness to enter the market; the market structure is therefore likely to be less competitive than in the absence of the tax. An *output tax* on foreign suppliers increases their marginal cost of providing a service and is similar in effect to a specific tariff. A *profit tax* is least likely to affect the economic decisions of firms, but if there are fixed costs of entry that must be covered by future profits, a profit tax would reduce the number of firms that could recover those costs. One or more of these fiscal instruments could help achieve outcomes superior to quotas, from a social welfare point of view. Ironically, the legal systems of many countries allow discrimination against foreigners through outright bans and entry quotas but make it difficult to impose discriminatory taxes. For instance, in the European Union a locally established foreign firm is treated in all respects like a European firm and may not be subject to any form of discrimination.

Precommitment to Future Liberalization

Policies that are believed in are most likely to succeed. The provision of many services, from finance to transport, requires highly specific sunk investments in assets that are not easily deployable for other uses. Investors' business plans are typically stretched out over long time periods, and many services providers expect to incur substantial losses in their first years of operation. It is therefore important that market liberalization programs be credible. Otherwise two sorts of problems can arise: (a) If there is significant uncertainty about policy, fewer investments will be made, and services providers will demand a premium on their returns on capital. (b) If it is possible to influence policy, services providers may behave strategically to manipulate policy choices in their own favor.

Credibility itself has two dimensions. One is to convince agents that current reforms will not be reversed. The other is to persuade them that future reforms will be carried out.

Under the GATS, many countries have bound the status quo. In principle, a clear GATS commitment not to restrict entry could add significantly to the contestability of markets. Unfortunately, even in relatively open markets, commitments are sometimes couched in language that diminishes their value. For instance, Chile's financial services schedule states that "a supplier of financial services operating through a commercial presence may be subject to evidence of economic need," and Philippines' telecommunications schedule notes that entry is subject to a "Franchise from the Congress of the Philippines" and a "Certificate of Public Convenience." It is far from clear whether such approval is contingent only on transparent and nondiscriminatory criteria such as technical or financial soundness or whether approval is a euphemism either for a restriction on the number of firms or for discrimination against foreign entrants. A priority in the next round would be to purge the schedules of such language.

One reason governments may be reluctant to liberalize immediately is a perceived need to protect incumbent suppliers from competition, because of infant industry–type arguments or to facilitate "orderly exit." The failure of infant industry policies in the past, and the innumerable examples of perpetual infancy, are in part attributable to governments' inability to commit themselves credibly to liberalize at some future date. The GATS offers a valuable mechanism for overcoming the credibility difficulty. Under the agreement, governments can make binding commitments to provide market access and national treatment at a future date. Failure to honor these commitments would create an obligation to compensate those who are deprived of benefits, making the commitment more credible than a mere announcement in the national context of intent to liberalize. A precommitment to liberalize can also instill a sense of urgency regarding domestic reform and efforts to develop the necessary regulatory and supervision mechanisms.

Several governments have taken advantage of the GATS to strike a balance between their reluctance to unleash competition immediately on protected national suppliers and their desire not to be held hostage in perpetuity either to the weakness of domestic industry or to pressure from vested interests. The most striking examples are in basic telecommunications, where a number of developing countries have bound themselves to introduce competition at precise future dates (Table 28.2). The use of the GATS as a mechanism for lending credibility to liberalization programs has been disappointing in other sectors.

BOX 28.1 SERVICES EXPORTS BY DEVELOPING COUNTRIES: POTENTIAL GAINS AND CURRENT BARRIERS

There are likely to be significant gains worldwide if restrictions on services exports from developing countries are eliminated. With greater liberalization, particularly in mode 4—movement of natural persons—many more developing countries could "export" at least the significant labor component of construction, distribution, environmental, and transport services, among others.

One of the most striking recent success stories in the areas of developing country services exports is the Indian software industry, which has emerged as a significant supplier to industrial country markets. Indian software exports grew from US$225 million in 1992–93 to US$1.75 billion in 1997–98 (a compound annual growth rate of approximately 50 percent).* This story has some noteworthy elements.

First, despite the growing importance of cross-border electronic delivery of software services, the movement of natural persons remains a crucial mode of delivery. Even though the share of onshore services (that is, at the client's site overseas) in total Indian software exports has been in continuous decline (in 1988, the percentage of on-site development was almost 90 percent), about 60 percent of Indian exports is still supplied through the temporary movement of programmers. [†]

Second, it cannot be assumed that other countries' trade policies will become progressively more liberal, particularly with regard to movement of persons. In the early 1990s the U.S. government introduced rules that obliged foreign workers to acquire temporary work visas (H1-B visas) and limited the number of visas issued during a year to 65,000. This contributed to the relative decline of onshore services by Indian firms (Heeks 1998). In 1998, in response to mounting labor shortages experienced in the U.S. information technology sector, the annual visa cap was raised to 115,000 for both 1999 and 2000.

Third, significant gains can be had from further liberalization. There are wide differences in the cost of software development and support: the average cost per line of code in Switzerland (the most expensive country) exceeds by more than 5

times that of India (the cheapest country), and average salaries are more than 11 times higher in Switzerland (Mattoo 1999). Even though differences in labor productivity imply that a lower average salary of programmers may not necessarily translate into a lower average cost per line of software code, by outsourcing programming activities, firms in industrial countries can save significantly on development and support costs. Against the background of a total market for software services worth (in 1997) about US$58 billion in the United States, US$42 billion in Europe, and US$10 billion in Japan, such cost savings could well be substantial (computed from WTO 1998b: table 3). Other gains from trade liberalization for importing countries include a more competitive market structure for software services, increased choice (because countries may develop a special expertise in certain development or support services), and greater diffusion of knowledge.

Health services is another area in which developing countries could become major exporters, either by attracting foreign patients to domestic hospitals and doctors or by temporarily sending their health personnel abroad. The Cuban government's strategy is to convert that country into a world medical power. SERVIMED, a trading company created by the government, prepares health tourism packages. During 1995–96, 25,000 patients went to Cuba for treatment, and 1,500 students went there for training; income earned from sales of health services to foreigners was US$25 million. Again, cost savings for patients and health insurers can be significant. For instance, the cost of coronary bypass surgery can be as low as 70,000 to 100,000 rupees in India, about 5 percent of the cost in industrial countries. The cost of a liver transplant in India is a tenth that in the United States (UNCTAD and WHO 1998).

A major barrier to consumption abroad of medical services is lack of portability of health insurance. For instance, U.S. federal or state government reimbursement of medical expenses is limited to licensed, certified facilities in the Unit-

BOX 28.1 (CONTINUED)

ed States or in a specific U.S. state. The lack of long-term portability of health coverage for retirees from OECD countries is also a major constraint on trade in health services. In the United States, for instance, Medicare, the program for retirees, covers virtually no services delivered abroad. Other nations may extend coverage abroad, but only for limited periods such as two or three months. This constraint is significant because it tends to deter some elderly persons from traveling or retiring abroad, and those who do retire abroad are often forced to return home to obtain affordable medical care. The potential effect of permitting portability could be substantial. If only 3 percent of the 100 million elderly persons living in OECD countries retired to developing countries, they would bring with them possibly US$30 billion to US$50 billion annually in personal consumption and US$10 billion to US$15 billion in medical expenditures (UNCTAD and WHO 1998).

Many different barriers constrain the movement of natural persons. The numerous formalities alone (for obtaining a visa, for example) make red tape related to FDI seem trivial by comparison. The most obvious barriers are explicit quotas or economic needs tests, such as requirements that employers take timely and significant steps to recruit and retain sufficient national workers in the specialty occupation and that no worker be laid off for a certain period preceding and following

the filing of any work permit or visa application.[‡] Qualification and licensing requirements and the regulations of professional bodies are other significant barriers. The entry of foreigners can be impeded by nonrecognition of their professional qualifications, burdensome licensing requirements, or the imposition of discriminatory standards. The requirement of registration with, or membership of, professional organizations can constitute an obstacle for a person wishing to provide a service on a temporary basis.

* See the National Association of Software and Service Companies (NASSCOM) Website, <http://www.nasscom.org>. These exports consist mainly of standardized coding and testing services.

† See <http://www.nasscom.org>. The dominance of on-shore delivery is attributable to, among other reasons, a reduction in information asymmetries with regard to the performance of programmers, the need for continuous client-developer interaction, and demands by Indian programmers to be sent abroad, in part to improve their skills and expose themselves to international markets (see Heeks 1998).

‡ Other barriers to movement of natural persons include double taxation, wage-matching requirements (that is, requirements that wages paid to foreign workers be similar to those paid to nationals in that profession, which eliminates the cost advantage for foreigners), and local training requirements (to replace foreign with national labor within a certain time frame).

Facilitating Reciprocity across Modes

A collective commitment to the use of appropriately designed formulas offers the best chance of linking different modes of delivery.[6] Such formulas can also help overcome concerns about free-riding that arise in an MFN-based system. But is it technically feasible to link concessions across modes? (See Sapir 1998; Thompson 2000.) One simple option is to take advantage of the current political pressure for accelerated liberalization in selected sectors, such as environmental services. This approach could be accepted on the condition that there be no gerry-

mandering: all countries would liberalize access in all modes, including the movement of individuals. Environmentalists and environmental services exporters could then be relied on to counter the opposition of employees and individual suppliers in the domestic environmental industry.

An alternative way of creating a link between modes is by requiring each country to provide increased "foreign labor content entitlements" to its domestic firms in relation to the country's increased exports of services (Mattoo and Olarreaga 2001). Entitlements would be global rather than bilateral, and the extent and pattern of use would be deter-

CARLO GAMBERALE
AADITYA MATTOO

29

DOMESTIC REGULATIONS AND LIBERALIZATION OF TRADE IN SERVICES

T RADE IN SERVICES, FAR MORE THAN TRADE IN GOODS, IS AFFECTED BY A VARIETY OF domestic regulations. A central task in multilateral trade negotiations has been to develop disciplines which ensure that such regulations support rather than impede trade liberalization. One basic discipline, the national treatment obligation, requires that regulations not discriminate in any way against foreigners. Trade, however, can be inhibited even by regulations that do not discriminate, such as certain standards and licensing requirements, and by the absence of procompetitive regulations. Although important initiatives have recently been taken to remedy these problems in the areas of accountancy and telecommunications, the overall disciplines on domestic regulations in the General Agreement on Trade in Services (GATS) remain weak. As we approach the next round of services negotiations, the question arises as to whether it is best to rely on further sectoral initiatives or whether it is possible to adopt a more general approach.

The diversity of services sectors and the difficulty of making certain policy-relevant generalizations have tended to encourage a sector-specific approach. We argue, however, that even though services sectors differ greatly, the underlying economic and social reasons for regulatory intervention do not, and that focusing on these reasons provides the basis for the creation of meaningful horizontal disciplines. Such a generic approach is to be preferred to a sectoral approach for at least three reasons: it economizes on negotiating effort; it leads to the creation of disciplines for all services sectors rather than only the politically important ones; and it reduces the likelihood that negotiations will be captured by sectoral interest groups.

An Overview of Regulation in Services

The economic case for regulation in services, as in goods, arises essentially from market failure attributable to three kinds of problems: natural monopoly or oligopoly, asymmetric information, and externalities. The social case for regulation is based primarily on considerations of equity. Figure 29.1 provides an overview of the main reasons for and the forms of regulation in different services sectors.

The existence of natural monopoly or oligopoly is a feature of the so-called locational services (UNCTAD and World Bank 1994). Such services require, first of all, specialized distribution networks: roads and rails for land transport, cables and satellites for communications, and pipes for water supply and sanitation and for energy distribution. They may also require specialized equipment for transmitting or receiving the service: railway stations and bus ter-

29.1 Approaches toward Domestic Regulation at the Multilateral and National Levels

Market failure	Services sector	Multilateral approach	Action required at national level
Monopoly; oligopoly	Network services: transport (terminals and infrastructure); environmental services (sewerage); energy services (distribution networks). Strengthen Article IX to deal with international cartels.	Generalize key disciplines in telecommunications Reference Paper to ensure cost-based access to essential facilities (roads, railroad tracks, terminals, sewers, pipelines, etc.).	Develop procompetitive regulation to protect consumer interests where competitive market structures do not exist.
Asymmetric information	Intermediation and knowledge-based services: financial services, professional services, etc.	Exercise nondiscrimination and generalization in applying the "necessity" test. Use the test to create a presumption in favor of choice of economically efficient policies for remedying market failure.	Strengthen domestic regulation to remedy market failure in an economically efficient manner.
Externalities	Transport, tourism, etc.		
Social objectives: universal service	Transport, telecommunications, financial, education, health.		Devise economically efficient means of achieving social objectives in competitive markets.

minals, seaports, airports, telephone exchanges. One reason for the tendency toward monopoly or oligopoly is the difficulty of duplicating networks and terminals, given space constraints. A second reason is the high barriers to entry associated with large initial investments. It must, however, be kept in mind that recent technological developments in areas such as telecommunications are leading to the emergence of relatively small optimal scales of production and are overturning conventional wisdom about the inevitability of monopoly.

Liberalization in locational services could imply two types of change. First, the monopoly itself needs to be delineated as narrowly as possible so that competition is introduced where feasible. For instance, in railways a monopoly track owner could sell track services to separate, competing operators of trains. Second, competition could be introduced for the right to provide the remaining monopoly services. Thus, the right to provide track services could be auctioned off to the firm that commits to supply the services at the lowest price. In the current context, the interesting issue arises when services that can be provided competitively must rely on services provided monopolistically—either by governments or by private firms. The challenge is to ensure

that all service providers, domestic and foreign, have access to the essential facilities that continue to be monopolistically controlled.

The problem of asymmetric information occurs in a wide range of intermediation and knowledge-based services (UNCTAD and World Bank 1994). Buyers are often inadequately informed about the true attributes of sellers. Thus, consumers cannot easily assess the competence of professionals such as doctors and lawyers, the safety of transport services, or the soundness of banks and insurance companies. In principle, the adequate dissemination of information could remedy the problem, but it may be too expensive to communicate the necessary information to individual buyers. In such situations, it may be easier to regulate suppliers than to educate consumers. The imposition of minimum regulatory conditions on suppliers reflects a certain uniformity of preferences among consumers about the quality of services. Thus, regulators ensure that all banks meet a certain threshold of financial soundness and professionals a certain threshold of competence (see Box 29.1). Regulating the output of a services industry, which is often invisible and customized, is usually more difficult than regulating inputs. Such regulation of

BOX 29.2 (CONTINUED)

ments) must take place on nondiscriminatory, transparent, and reasonable terms and at cost-oriented rates. The provisions regarding independent regulators require the regulatory body to be impartial, separate from, and not accountable to any services supplier.

To what degree do the Reference Paper's obligations bite? Can the paper live up to the expectation of ensuring effective market access? On the one hand, the regulatory principles lack precision in many respects and appear to leave room for discretionary decisionmaking by national regulators. It seems difficult, for example, to derive far-reaching obligations from vague language such as "reasonable" terms of interconnection or "appropriate measures" to prevent abusive business practices. Similarly, the obligation to provide interconnection at cost-oriented rates can only be limited in scope, as no reference is made to a specific methodology or definition of network cost. Thus, taken at its face value, it would seem that the Reference Paper prevents only the most egregious departures from procompetitive regulation (Bronckers and Larouche 1997).

On the other hand, two factors suggest that the Reference Paper's obligations have teeth. First, as already pointed out, several signatories of the agreement did not adopt the Reference Paper in full but excluded certain provisions. Arguably, these countries were concerned that their existing regimes would be inconsistent with the obligations set out in the paper. Second, the experience from two disputes pertaining to interconnection prices charged by the dominant incumbents in Mexico and Japan suggests that the prospect of WTO arbitration can contribute to the implementation of procompetitive regulation. In the case of Mexico, the United States initiated WTO dispute settlement proceedings and reserved its right to press its case even after the dominant Mexican carrier agreed to a reduction in interconnection fees. In the case of Japan, the United States threatened the initiation of a WTO complaint, and Japan subsequently agreed to lower interconnection charges substantially.

Although these two examples undoubtedly point to the relevance of the principles set out in the Reference Paper, one has to keep in mind that in both cases the lowering of interconnection rates was the immediate result of bilateral pressure applied by the United States. Moreover, the regulatory principles have not been critically tested, in the sense that so far no WTO panel has arbitrated on the basis of the Reference Paper.

important in sectors such as maritime, air transport, and communications services.[1] The current GATS provision in this area (Article IX) provides only for information exchange and consultation. Strengthened multilateral rules are needed to reassure small countries with weak enforcement capacity that the gains from liberalization will not be appropriated by international cartels. For instance, two obligations could be created. The first would require an end to the exemption from national competition law of collusive agreements that affect other countries. (Both the United States and the European Union currently exempt maritime conferences from the scope of their competition law.) The second would create a right of foreign consumers to challenge anticompetitive practices by shipping lines in the national courts of countries whose citizens own or control these shipping lines.

The second obligation is necessary to deal with the possibility of inadequate enforcement by public agencies and already has a precedent in the WTO rules on intellectual property and government procurement.

In all other cases of market failure, multilateral disciplines do not need to address the problem per se; rather, they should ensure that domestic measures for dealing with the problem do not unduly restrict trade. (The same is true for measures designed to achieve social objectives.) Such trade-restrictive effects can arise from a variety of technical standards, prudential regulations, and qualification requirements in professional, financial, and numerous other services (see Box 29.3), as well as from grants of monopoly rights to complement universal service obligations in such services as transport and telecommunications.

BOX 29.3 RULES FOR DOMESTIC REGULATIONS: THE EXPERIENCE WITH ACCOUNTANCY

John Hegarty

In the course of the Uruguay Round negotiations, accountancy services received significant attention. Accountancy makes a useful case study of how liberalizing trade in services requires attention to "behind-the-border" issues, in that the main barriers to trade derive from domestic regulations governing the sector.

After the Uruguay Round, in March 1995, the Council for Trade in Services established the Working Party on Professional Services (WPPS) to develop the disciplines necessary to ensure that specific regulatory measures did not constitute unnecessary barriers to trade. As a matter of priority, the WPPS was requested to make recommendations for multilateral disciplines in the accountancy sector. In December 1998 the council adopted the "Disciplines on Domestic Regulation in the Accountancy Sector" that had been submitted to it by the WPPS.

The disciplines on accountancy represent an important step forward in the definition of rules on domestic regulation under the GATS because they contain a binding "necessity test." Members are required to

> ensure that measures not subject to scheduling under Articles XVI or XVII of the GATS, relating to licensing requirements and procedures, technical standards and qualification requirements and procedures are not prepared, adopted or applied with a view to or with the effect of creating unnecessary barriers to trade in accountancy services. For this purpose, Members shall ensure that such measures are not more trade-restrictive than necessary to fulfil a legitimate objective. Legitimate objectives are, *inter alia,* the protection of consumers (which includes all users of accounting services and the public generally), the quality of the service, professional competence, and the integrity of the profession. ("Disciplines on Domestic Regulation in the Accounting Sector")

The necessity rule is without doubt the most substantive provision in the accountancy disciplines. The rest of the disciplines either add some limited value to existing GATS articles (such as Art. III, on transparency) or specify the application of the necessity test to types of measure. In some key cases, however, the specific rules contain language weaker than the necessity test.

For example, the provision on residency requirements says that members "shall consider" whether means less restrictive of trade could be employed to achieve the same policy objective, and the provision on qualification requirements states, "A Member shall ensure that its competent authorities *take account* of qualifications acquired in the territory of another Member, on the basis of equivalency of education, experience and/or examination requirements" (emphasis added). A proposal to create a presumption in favor of a test of competence as the least trade restrictive measure received little support.

The disciplines are also subject to three constraints that limit their impact. First, they apply only to those WTO members that have made commitments in the accountancy sector, not to all members. Second, they have no immediate application but enter into force only when formally integrated into the GATS, which requires waiting until the current negotiations have been concluded. Third, and most important, they do not apply to measures that are subject to scheduling under Articles XVI and XVII. In other words, a domestic regulation that has the effect of denying market access or national treatment is not automatically negated when the disciplines enter into force but must be addressed through future negotiations of specific commitments. This came as a disappointment to those who had hoped to see at least some "behind-the-border" issues dealt with by way of generally applicable rules.

There are several reasons for the relatively modest result in accountancy. The interest in these negotiations of those who had a real stake in liberalization was somewhat diminished when it became apparent that the more explicit barriers could not be addressed. To a significant extent,

(continued)

BOX 29.4 (CONTINUED)

was corporatized. TRAI was reconstituted in 2000, and its dispute resolution powers are now vested in a new quasi-judicial agency. The authority announced a decision on telephone tariffs that will substantially restructure telephone service prices over a three-year period, significantly improving incentives for investment in local networks. The regulator has also programmed an agenda of activities to address several other important regulatory matters, such as interconnection arrangements, the numbering plan, quality of service, business rules, and customer satisfaction.

For smaller countries, a different problem arises: the creation and operation of an efficient regulatory agency involves substantial fixed costs that could place a significant burden on resources. Apart from spectrum-monitoring equipment, computers, and programs, there is the cost of professional assistance for activities such as interconnection, cost estimation, and spectrum management. For example, the total cost of government in Dominica is US$41 million a year, whereas the budget of the U.S. telecommunications regulator, the Federal Communications Commission, runs to US$210 million a year. It is estimated that even a bare-bones regulatory authority is likely to cost about US$2 million each year, or 5 percent of Dominica's government budget.

In response to these problems, in May 2000 St. Lucia, Dominica, Grenada, St. Vincent and the Grenadines, and St. Kitts and Nevis set up, with World Bank support, the Eastern Caribbean Telecommunications Authority (ECTEL), the first regional telecommunications authority in the world. ECTEL is in the process of developing from a legal entity into a functioning institution. Although the member countries will retain their sovereign power over licensing and regulation, ECTEL will provide technical expertise, advice, and support for national regulations. In addition to the economies of scale in establishing a common regulator, there are at least three other advantages: the arrangement will promote the development of harmonized and transparent regulation in the region, allow for a greater degree of independence (and hence credibility) in regulatory advice, and enhance bargaining power in negotiations with incumbents and potential entrants. In fact, there is evidence that the creation of ECTEL, along with other reforms, has already prompted a decline in the prices of telecommunication services in the region. For example, the per-minute cost of a daytime call to the United States has fallen between 24 and 42 percent in these countries.

Source: Prepared by the volume editors, based on DeFreitas, Kenny, and Schware (2001).

Dealing with Asymmetric Information

The need for effective regulation of financial services needs no elaboration, particularly in light of the recent experiences of many countries. Again it is incumbent on the countries themselves to create adequate mechanisms for such regulation—something that is clearly necessary if a country is to benefit fully from liberalization (see Box 29.5).

Other areas in which the inadequacy of regulatory mechanisms for dealing with asymmetric information is a problem have received relatively less attention. For instance, in professional services, low standards and disparities in domestic training and examinations can become a major impediment to obtaining foreign recognition. Thus, inadequacies in domestic regulation can legitimize external barriers to trade. A further twist is that domestic consumers may actually prefer cheap, low-quality products. The question of how best to meet the needs of export markets given domestic preferences regarding quality is clearly an area in which much more research is needed.

Managing Conflicts between Efficiency and Equity

Trade policy affects the poor through three main channels: through the price of their consumption bundle; through demand for their labor and other assets they own, which has consequences for their income; and by bringing about changes in government revenue and therefore in the government's

BOX 29.5 FINANCIAL SECTOR LIBERALIZATION: THE NEED FOR POLICY COHERENCE

Stijn Claessens

Financial reform is an especially complicated subject. It is useful, to begin with, to distinguish three types of financial liberalization and the scope of each.

- *Domestic financial liberalization* allows market forces to work by eliminating controls on lending and deposit rates and on credit allocation and, more generally, by reducing the role of the state in the domestic financial system.
- *Capital account liberalization* removes controls on the movement of capital in and out of the country and does away with restrictions on the convertibility of currency.
- *Internationalization of financial services* eliminates discrimination in treatment between foreign and domestic financial services providers and removes barriers to the cross-border provision of financial services.

Internationalization has given rise to fears concerning the survival of local banks and financial companies, the loss of monetary autonomy, and the increased volatility of capital flows. Many of these concerns relate not just to internationalization of financial services but also to the processes of financial deregulation and capital account liberalization. The magnitude of the benefits and the costs of internationalization depend, to a great extent, on how internationalization is phased in with these other two types of financial reform and, in particular, with the strengthening of prudential regulation and supervision.

Many countries that have had successful experiences with opening up to foreign financial firms, including Brazil, Chile, Hungary, Ireland, Poland, Portugal, and Spain, also engaged in a process of domestic deregulation and reaped substantial gains (World Bank 2001a). The experience of the countries acceding to the European Union suggests that internationalization and domestic deregulation can be mutually reinforcing. Increased foreign entry bolstered the financial sector framework by creating a constituency for improved regulation and supervision, better disclosure rules, and improvements in the legal and regulatory framework for the provision of financial services. It also added to the credibility of rules. These benefits of opening up to foreign entry followed from both top-down actions on the part of government and bottom-up pressures from the market, as best international practices and experiences were introduced.

Although the two reform processes—internationalization and domestic financial deregulation—are mutually reinforcing, they are not sufficient in themselves. More than in other sectors, the gains and costs of financial reform depend on the regulatory and supervisory framework (Barth, Caprio, and Levine 2001). Experience shows that it is vital to strengthen the supporting institutional framework in parallel with domestic deregulation and internationalization. In the absence of such strengthening, foreign entry may entail risks. Foreign bank entry can destabilize local banks by drawing away the lowest-risk business—including large exporting firms—leaving local banks to venture farther out on the risk frontier. And several countries, especially in Africa, discovered with the failure of banks like BCCI and Meridien that a foreign name did not necessarily guarantee safety and soundness even when these foreign banks were operating in industrial economies or had some ownership links with reputable foreign sources.

The need for a supportive institutional framework is even more obvious when it comes to capital account liberalization. Experience in recent years, most recently in Asia, has shown that being able to achieve the potential gains, while avoiding the risks, of capital account liberalization depends to a great extent on whether domestic institutions and prudential authorities have developed sufficiently to ensure that foreign finance will be channeled in productive directions (Eichengreen 2001). Recent experience also shows the potential benefits of foreign financial institutions in stabilizing capital flows. Several countries with significant foreign presence, such

(continued)

as Argentina and Mexico, benefited from the access of these institutions to foreign capital during periods of economic difficulty (Dages, Goldberg, and Kinney 2000). More generally, studies show that diversity in ownership contributes to greater stability of credit in times of crisis (Barth, Caprio, and Levine 2000; La Porta, Lopez de Silanes, and Shleifer 2000). Insofar as foreign presence leads to a stronger regulatory and supervisory framework, it contributes to making capital account liberalization and internationalization mutually reinforcing.

ability to finance programs for the poor. The first step in the assessment of the impact of a change in trade policy on the well-being of the poor is to identify what the poor consume and what they own—type of labor, skills, and other assets.

If a country is a relatively inefficient producer of a service, liberalization and the resultant foreign competition are likely to lead to a decline in domestic prices and to improvements in quality. Insofar as the poor are consumers of these services, they are likely to benefit. But there is a twist: frequently, before liberalization, prices are not determined by the market but are set administratively and are kept artificially low for certain categories of end-users or certain types of services product. Thus, rural borrowers may pay lower interest rates than urban borrowers, and prices of local telephone calls and of public transport may be kept lower than the cost of provision. (Box 29.6 summarizes a study of the effect of financial liberalization on poor people's access to credit.) Sometimes the object is to ensure access for all consumers at the same price, irrespective of the cost of provision (for example, in transport and postal services). Or, the object may be to ensure cheaper access to, say, financial services for certain categories of user. This price structure is often sustained through cross-subsidization within public monopolies or through government financial support.

Unless special regulatory measures are taken, liberalization threatens these arrangements. Elimination of restrictions on entry implies an end to cross-subsidization because it is no longer possible for firms to make extranormal profits in certain market segments. New entrants may focus on the most profitable market segments, such as urban areas, where network costs are lower and incomes are higher. And privatization could mean the end of government support. The result is that even though the sector becomes more efficient and average prices decline, prices for certain key end-users may actually increase.

Despite these considerations, there is evidence of a positive relationship between competitive market structures and services expansion in sectors such as basic telecommunications. This is especially true in countries where initial conditions are feeble, as exemplified by low teledensity or by service rationing (long waiting lists for obtaining connections). Simply letting the market work can substantially improve access in an environment where services have been traditionally provided by inefficient public monopolies—even in the poorest countries and among low-income consumers. For example, women entrepreneurs in Bangladesh villages provide pay phone services at a profit, using mobile cellular technology. Even though rural villagers cannot afford a phone individually, they can afford one collectively (Lawson and Meyenn 2000).

These examples suggest that the important questions are these: In which sectors is there a conflict between efficiency and equity? How can the conflict be best addressed? What is the current situation? (If the status quo reflects redistribution in favor of vested interests—as, for example, the structure of telecommunications and transport prices often favors the urban middle class, and the pattern of directed lending programs favors the politically powerful—a move to the market can provide both efficiency and equity benefits. Precommitting to the market can serve as a device to preclude private capture.) A more general question is, how can distributive mechanisms achieve their goals in a world of unequal economic and political power? Which redistributive instruments lend themselves to capture by the politically powerful?

Ensuring Universal Service. Achieving the desirable social objective of universal service in an eco-

BOX 29.6 FINANCIAL LIBERALIZATION AND ACCESS TO CREDIT BY THE POOR

A study by Paul Mosley empirically estimates the impact of financial liberalization on access to rural credit in four African countries: Kenya, Lesotho, Malawi, and Uganda. Domestic financial liberalization via decontrol of interest rates and removal of credit subsidies has led to higher real interest rates but, except in Uganda, has not translated into a higher level of savings or increased access to rural credit. In Uganda average annual estimated credit disbursements to the agricultural sector showed a marginal increase, from US$116 million in the three years before liberalization to US$123 million in the three years after liberalization. In Malawi, by contrast, agricultural credit disbursements declined from US$121 million in the three years before liberalization to US$109 million in the three years after liberalization. Using sample survey data, Mosley found that between 1992 and 1997 the percentage of sampled households with access to rural credit rose from 13.1 to 25 percent in Kenya and from 9.2 to 21 percent in Uganda but that in Malawi the share declined from 12 to 8 percent.

It is also worth noting that access to credit by the poorest income decile remained unchanged in Kenya and Uganda but declined after liberalization from 1.9 to 0.9 percent in Malawi and from 2 to 1.9 percent in Lesotho. Commercial and foreign banks have been reluctant to move into informal lending despite the higher rates in that sector. Mosley observes that this is probably "due to high levels of subjective risk, supplemented with ignorance and a shortage of individuals able to act as go-betweens and present the financial results of microfinance institutions in a form digestible by commercial banks." Informal sector and rural lending is still carried out by traditional moneylenders, nongovernmental organizations, and government agencies.

Mosley's study also shows that financial reform in the forms of financial innovation in rural areas and development of financial institutions catering to the poor has had strong and significant effects in improving access to rural credit and lowering poverty. Some examples of successful microfinance institutions in Africa are PCEA Chogoria and the Rural Enterprise Program in Kenya and the CCEI/Gatsby Trust Scheme in Cameroon. Non-African examples include BancoSol in Bolivia and Bank Rakyat Indonesia. These microfinance institutions offer savings and credit services on commercial terms to marginal households and use peer pressure as a substitute for collateral in loan repayments and recovery. They have managed to sustain high loan recovery rates, cover costs, and make profits. Their lending rates lie in between those of commercial banks and informal moneylenders. Formal institutions can also mobilize deposits and allocate credit to small borrowers by forging links with informal and microfinance agents, thereby lowering information costs and developing community-based contract enforcement mechanisms. It should be noted that simply privatizing state microfinance agencies has proved disastrous, as illustrated by the collapse of Malawi's MRFC.

Source: Prepared by the volume editors, based on Mosley (1999).

---

nomically efficient way is a major challenge for national policymakers. The manner in which they pursue this objective is likely to have a profound effect on trade in a variety of areas, including financial, transport, telecommunications, health, and education services. The government can choose from a spectrum of policies that range from completely replacing the market to installing supportive policies that affect the market outcome (see Box 29.7).

Historically, governments have frequently relied on public monopolies to pursue (often unsuccessfully) the goal of universal service, either through cross-subsidization across segments of the market or through transfers from the government or from government-controlled banks. In addition to the inefficiencies created by monopolistic market structures, the burdens these obligations imposed on existing national suppliers are even now a significant impediment to liberalization in many coun-

BOX 29.7 PURSUING SOCIAL OBJECTIVES IN COMPETITIVE TELECOMMUNICATIONS MARKETS

Charles Kenny

There is growing evidence that private competitive markets can rapidly enhance the level of access to basic services. For example, in 1993 the Peruvian government embarked on a major reform of its telecommunications sector, supported by the World Bank. New laws enacted in 1993 and 1994 provided for the privatization of the two state-owned telecommunications utilities and the establishment of an independent regulator. The mobile telephone market was partially liberalized at once and is now fully competitive.

The telecommunications privatization contracts included substantial obligations to install public telephones in rural areas, supporting an increase in the number of public phones countrywide from 8,000 to 50,000 over the 1993–98 period. As the table shows, improvements were seen in many other areas, as well.

	1993	1998
Sector investments (millions of U.S. dollars)	28	2,099
Fixed lines		
Number	660,000	1,850,000
Penetration rate per 100 population (percent)	2.9	7.5
Mobile telephone lines		
Number	50,000	600,000
Penetration rate per 100 population (percent)	0.2	2.4
Towns with phone service (number)	1,450	3,000
Poor households in Lima with a telephone (percent)	1	21
Average waiting time for connection	118 months	45 days
Connection fee (U.S. dollars)	1,500	150

In 1999 a universal service levy of 1 percent charged on telecommunications operators' gross revenues was introduced to finance a telecommunications fund (FITEL) dedicated to meeting universal access objectives in areas that remained out of the reach of the network, as defined through socioeconomic studies and consultation with the local authorities and population. Funds were allocated through a competitive bidding process. The process encouraged operators to look for the best technology and other cost-savings practices, minimizing the need for subsidies. The choice of funding strategy can also support a level playing field among operators so that no operator is overcompensated or unfairly burdened by the funding mechanism.

The scheme in Peru was modeled on a similar universal access program in Chile, where just over US$2 million in public funds leveraged US$40 million in private investment to install telephones in 1,000 localities, at about 10 percent of the cost of direct public provision. Through a combination of sector liberalization and competitive provision of subsidized public access to areas not previously served, household ownership of a telephone in Chile increased from 16 to 74 percent between 1988 and 2000, and all but 1 percent of the remaining households were provided with public access to telephony.

Source: Wellenius (2001); World Bank (2001d).

tries. For instance, domestic banks saddled with bad debts because of past directed-lending programs are ill equipped to deal with foreign competition.

The current handicap of universal service obligations can in principle be imposed on new entrants, as well, in a nondiscriminatory way. Thus, such obligations were part of the license conditions for new entrants into fixed-network telephony and transport in several countries. Recourse to fiscal instruments, however, has proved more successful than direct regulation. For instance, in Chile government subsidies equivalent to less than 0.5 percent of total telecommunications revenue, allocated through competitive bidding in 1995, mobilized 20 times that amount of private investment for extending basic telephone services to rural areas (Wellenius 1997).

A third method is to fund the consumer rather than the provider (Cowhey and Klimenko 2001). Governments have experimented with various forms of vouchers in such areas as education and energy services. This last instrument has at least three advantages: it can be targeted more directly at those who need the service and cannot afford it; it avoids the distortions that arise from pricing services artificially low to ensure access; and it does not discriminate among providers.

Employment Effects of Trade Liberalization. Different modes of supply have different effects on factor markets. Cross-border trade and consumption abroad resemble goods trade in their implications. The effects of the movement of factors of production depend critically on whether the factors are substitutes for or complements to domestic factor services. Given the structure of factor prices in poor countries, liberalization can typically be expected to lead to an inflow of capital and skilled workers. Such inflows would tend to be to the advantage of the unskilled poor, increasing employment opportunities and wages.[3] Interestingly, it has been shown that even when foreigners compete with local skilled workers in a services sector, the productivity boost to the sector from allowing access to foreigners can lead to an increase in the demand for domestic skilled workers: the scale effect can outweigh the substitution effect (Markusen, Rutherford, and Tarr 2000).

Given these predictions, why are workers in developing countries sometimes skeptical about the benefits of liberalization? One concern is the possible reduction in employment in formerly public monopolies, which have frequently employed surplus labor. Alexander and Estache (1999) found, for example, that the privatization of electricity distribution in Argentina led to a 40 percent reduction in the work force after privatization. But there is also

evidence that pessimism may not always be justified. For example, a number of developing countries have managed to maintain or even increase employment in their liberalized telecommunications sectors. Since many developing countries have low teledensities (in the vicinity of 5 lines per 100 population), roughly 70 percent of telecommunications investment in developing countries is directed toward building wire line and mobile networks, which is labor-intensive and hence helps maintain or raise employment levels. Petrazzini and Lovelock (1996) found in a study of 26 Latin American and Asian economies that telecommunications markets with competition were the only ones that consistently increased their employment levels, while two-thirds of the countries with monopolies saw considerable declines in the telecommunications work force.[4] Nevertheless, there can be little doubt that many reform programs will require complementary policies to alleviate the social and economic costs of adjustment in factor markets.

Notes

1 For instance, recent World Bank research has shown that while maritime trade liberalization would lead to an average reduction in transport prices by 9 percent and to cost savings of up to US$850 million, the breakup of private carrier agreements would cause prices to decline by another 25 percent and would yield additional cost savings of up to US$2 billion on goods carried to the United States alone.

2 In many industrial country markets where fully competitive conditions have not been established, such as the telecommunications sector in the United Kingdom, the final price itself has been regulated.

3 Because the poor are likely to be unskilled, the question arises as to which services sectors they are likely to be employed in. Unfortunately, data on the skills composition of the work force in services sectors are available only for some OECD countries, and even there, at a rather aggregate level. Still, a certain pattern can be inferred: construction, distribution, and personal services tend to be unskilled labor–intensive, whereas communications, financial, and business services tend to be skilled labor–intensive.

4 In India the incumbent operator, the Department of Telecommunications, expanded its work force over the 1996–2000 period. In the face of competition, it was forced to improve its marketing strategy and expand its network, and it opened up thousands of public call offices all over the country.

Liberalization of services trade under the GATS framework is undertaken through horizontal (cross-sectoral) and sector-specific commitments with regard to market access and national treatment obligations for each of the four modes of supply. Countries have made a binding commitment to place no restrictions on market access (Article XVI) or on national treatment (Article XVII) for a mode of supply or have made a partial commitment by limiting market access and national treatment in line with various conditions listed in their schedule, or have left the entry "unbound" (that is, made no commitment).[4] A review of the GATS framework suggests that the provisions pertaining to movement of natural persons are sufficiently strong. A review of the first-round commitments in mode 4, however, indicates that liberalization in this mode has been very limited.

Assessing the GATS Framework

Several provisions and general disciplines within the GATS framework are pertinent to the movement of natural persons. Article III, on transparency, requires members to publish "all relevant measures of general application which pertain to or affect the operation of this agreement," including relevant international agreements to which the country is a signatory. Members are also required to inform the Council for Trade in Services of any new laws, regulations, and administrative guidelines or amendments that are relevant to their specific commitments, to respond to requests for specific information on any measures affecting the members' commitments, and to establish enquiry points for providing this information to other members. Article VI, on domestic regulation, requires members to ensure that in sectors where specific commitments are undertaken, requirements are based on objective and transparent criteria and do not in themselves constitute a restriction on the supply of the service. It also obligates members to undertake objective and impartial reviews of administrative decisions affecting services trade. Article VII, on recognition, grants members the discretion to recognize, in whole or in part, the education, experience, and licensing or certification of foreign services providers autonomously or by mutual agreement or harmonization. It also obligates members to apply the criteria or standards for authorization, licensing, or certification equally across all countries and

not to use the criteria as a "disguised restriction on trade in services." The article stresses the need for recognition based on multilaterally agreed criteria and common international standards and calls for sectoral negotiations on recognition (as have occurred in accountancy services).

A separate annex on the movement of natural persons defines mode 4 as covering "persons who are temporarily working in another member country. It is not applicable to individuals who are seeking access to the employment market of another member on a permanent basis or for citizenship or residency purposes." The annex covers independent and self-employed suppliers who are paid directly by their customers and natural persons employed by services suppliers in the host or home country or in a third-member country to supply a service. The annex states that countries can regulate entry and stay of natural persons provided they do not apply these measures in such a manner as to nullify or impair the benefits granted to members under their specific commitments.

Overall, the GATS framework addresses some of the most important regulatory barriers that constrain cross-border movement of labor in services. There are, however, two weak points in the GATS framework. The first is that important areas such as government procurement and subsidies that affect movement of natural persons either are not covered or are inadequately covered.[5] The second concerns the exception of measures related to public policy objectives. Regulatory interventions embodying market access and national treatment restrictions fall under Articles XVI and XVII, respectively. In all other cases such measures fall under Article VI, on domestic regulation. It is difficult to distinguish domestic regulations related to market access and national treatment provisions from regulations related to public policy objectives. Thus, market access and national treatment limitations can render Article VI disciplines ineffective (see Low and Mattoo 2000).

Assessing GATS Commitments on the Movement of Natural Persons

The GATS has failed to deliver sufficiently liberal commitments in mode 4. Horizontal and sectoral commitments filed by countries have been more limited for mode 4 than for the other modes of supply. The following discussion highlights the main problems with the nature and structure of commitments in this mode.

Limited Sectoral Coverage of Mode 4 Commitments. Mode 4 commitments are very limited in sectoral coverage. Sectors such as health services and legal and accountancy services where cross-border labor mobility is important have not been scheduled by many countries. Moreover, even where commitments have been made, they are subject to many market access and national treatment restrictions.

Limitations on Commitments.[6] Most countries have left their market access and national treatment obligations in mode 4 unbound in their sectoral schedules and have referred to their horizontal schedules. This amounts to virtually no sector-specific liberalization in mode 4. The horizontal commitments in mode 4 are in turn subject to many conditions and requirements relating to functional or hierarchical criteria, length of stay, labor market and economic needs tests, and the like. For instance, 100 countries have placed limitations on their horizontal commitments in mode 4, as against only 4 countries for mode 2. Moreover, the conditions are often not clearly specified.[7]

Table 30.1, which summarizes the commitments in selected services sectors where movement of natural persons is important, indicates that there are fewer full (no restrictions) commitments under mode 4 than for any of the other modes of supply. The percentages of partial commitments (commitments with limitations) and unbound commitments (no commitment) are far greater under mode 4 than for the other modes of supply.

The main conditions that are attached to commitments in mode 4 are:

- Entry restrictions for certain sectors and categories of personnel
- Limits on the duration of stay of natural persons
- Quantitative restrictions by numerical quotas for entry; specifications concerning the proportion of total employment that can be met by foreigners; specifications concerning the proportion of total wages
- Preemployment conditions and related requirements
- Economic, labor market, and management needs tests

- Requirements for technology and skill transfer (training local staff)
- Discriminatory tax treatment
- Requirement of government approval
- Requirement of work permits, residency, and citizenship in certain sectors
- Recognition of professional qualifications by the importing country
- Restrictions via minimum investment requirements.

Bias toward Higher-Level Services Personnel. The commitments in mode 4 are further limited because they are bound for only a small subset of services personnel. There is a clear bias in the horizontal commitments toward liberalizing the movement of higher-level services personnel. (Box 30.1 provides recent data on immigration of highly skilled and skilled workers to OECD countries.) Entry requirements are bound for three main categories of services providers: business visitors; personnel engaged in setting up commercial presence, such as intracorporate transferees (ICTs); and personnel in "speciality occupations." The commitments on ICTs come closest to full bindings. More than one-third of mode 4 entries refer to intracorporate transferees; of a total of 328 total entries, 239 relate to executives, managers, and specialists and 135 deal with ICTs. Only 17 percent of all horizontal entries cover low-skilled personnel. Sectoral commitments similarly facilitate the entry of only higher-level personnel in the professional, managerial, and technical categories, as specified in the horizontal schedules. There are, altogether, six entries for "independent contract suppliers" and for "other" services personnel, and there are very few commitments for qualified specialists. Moreover, these latter categories are not permitted to move in an individual capacity; they must be working for a specified duration for a juridical person in another country. Hence, liberalization in mode 4 is mainly for services providers at a higher level and is linked to commercial presence.

Structural Problems with Mode 4 Commitments. A fundamental problem with the structure of the mode 4 commitments is that there is no separation of temporary and permanent labor under the existing framework of commitments, even though the GATS is meant to cover only temporary labor flows in services. Most of the limitations which have been filed under mode 4 relate to general immigration administrative discretion, discriminatory practices, and reduced predictability.

Proposals for Liberalizing Movement of Natural Persons

If movement of natural persons is to be liberalized under the GATS, existing commitments in this mode have to be significantly improved in the current round of service sector negotiations. This can be realized through a two-pronged approach to negotiations: on a country-to-country level and on a multilateral level. Country-to-country negotiations concerning this mode will vary depending on the individual interests of the members concerned. Of broader significance is the need for multilateral discussion on ways to improve the structure and nature of the GATS framework and commitments concerning mode 4. The following discussion highlights the main issues for multilateral negotiations.

Improving the Structure of Commitments in Mode 4

Multilateral discussions should aim at supplementing the horizontal commitments in mode 4 with sector-specific commitments in this mode, especially in sectors such as professional and business services where mode 4 is important. These sectoral commitments must be detailed and specific in terms of the measures that are applicable to individual sectors and the services personnel categories relevant to each sector.

Countries need to make unambiguously worded and well-defined sectoral commitments with clearly outlined criteria for application of any limitations, for all subsectors within the sector that has been scheduled. All limitations, conditions, and exceptions should be clearly laid out in the sectoral schedules, for both market access and national treatment, rather than being broadly outlined in the horizontal schedules. Countries must also take steps to furnish information on these measures, in line with GATS Article III.

Specificity and detail will also require improved targeting of categories of service providers to whom the commitments and limitations are applicable. This can be done by introducing more disaggregated categories of services providers in the sectoral schedules that fit within the broad categories of intracorporate transferees, business visitors, specialists, and other persons referred to in the horizontal commitments. A finer classification of services personnel categories would facilitate clear and detailed sectoral commitments that are relevant to the particular sector or subsector under consideration and would reduce the scope for discretion and discrimination in implementing the commitments.

Horizontal Formula for Classification of Services Providers

Horizontal disciplines have an important role in liberalizing mode 4. Specific, detailed, and binding sectoral commitments can be meaningful only if the coverage, definitions, and criteria for provider categories, applicable measures, and associated criteria are common across all countries. All members should agree on the coverage of professionals and activities within the personnel categories that are included in the horizontal schedules (ICTs, business visitors, specialists, and other personnel) and must agree on the minimum criteria for determining whether an individual services provider fits into a particular category. There must be a broad consensus on the categories and subcategories and the conditions under which additional limitations such as economic needs tests and residency requirements may be allowed and on when such conditions should be barred altogether.

The multilateral discussions must also focus on expanding the categories of services providers covered by the horizontal commitments to remove the current bias toward higher-level personnel. It is important to include middle- and lower-level providers and to make the commitments more relevant to the interests of the developing countries with expertise in these categories. The coverage can be expanded in two ways: by explicitly introducing new categories such as technical support personnel (which would, for instance, include systems analysts and programmers in the case of software services), or by defining the coverage of the "other persons" and "specialists" categories. This expansion should allow for the inclusion of middle- and lower-level personnel in these latter categories by specifying relevant criteria and by modifying or removing certain conditions relating to skills, pre-employment, and job responsibilities that at present favor higher-level persons. The second option is likely to be easier to implement. In this context, common coverage and definition of these broader categories would help.

The need is thus for *complementarity rather than substitutability* between the sectoral and horizontal schedules. Neither set of commitments should dilute the other.

Broadening the GATS Framework on Movement of Natural Persons

It is also necessary to establish multilateral guidelines on some issues, to strengthen some of the current GATS provisions, and, overall, to broaden the reach of the GATS framework with respect to mode 4. The relevant issues to be addressed in this context include (a) the separation of temporary from permanent labor flows, (b) wage parity, (c) recognition, and (d) economic needs and other tests. It is important to note that for these norms to be effective, they must be supported by specific and detailed sectoral commitments and uniform horizontal commitments.

Separating Temporary from Permanent Labor Flows, and the GATS Visa. Multilateral discussion is required on the need to separate temporary from permanent movement of labor when a services sector has been scheduled. Temporary services providers should be treated separately from permanent migrants, outside the domain of immigration-related laws and labor market regulations and under a separate set of regulations. Alternatively, temporary services providers could be covered by a special subset of regulations within the overall immigration policy framework, with more liberal conditions for entry and stay. This would reduce the administrative burdens, delays, and costs they face in entering the foreign market and would make it easier to address issues such as social security, wage parity, and recognition for such personnel.

A separate class of visas, a "GATS visa," could be established for service professionals temporarily working overseas. This visa would be applicable to service providers who are covered by the sectoral and horizontal commitments filed by a member country and would help streamline the implementation of these commitments. This complementarity between the GATS visa and the commitment schedules is possible only if the recommendations outlined above regarding specificity, finer classification of provider categories, wider coverage of categories, and transparency are reflected in the commitments. Although the GATS visa need not be unrestricted in nature, any conditions attached to its issuance should not be more onerous and restrictive than those already specified in the commitments. This would require countries to make more generous and binding sectoral commitments in mode 4 that do not backtrack on the status quo. Once more liberal offers are forthcoming in mode 4, the GATS visa would facilitate uniformity in market access procedures, as opposed to the current situation of very divergent immigration standards and procedures across countries. There should also be multilateral guidelines governing the granting and use of the GATS visa, including guidelines on the time frame for issuance and procedures, costs, renewal, transferability of jobs, and treatment in terms of taxes, subsidies, and government procurement. The GATS visa should also include mechanisms for determining the status of applications, notifying delays, and questioning the grounds for rejection. Safeguard mechanisms can be introduced to prevent misuse of such visas, including more stringent requirements for first-time applicants and obstacles to transferring the visa to others and to permanent residence and citizenship status.

Introducing Norms for Addressing Wage Parity. The implications of wage parity conditions vary depending on sector-specific labor supply and demand conditions, as well as on the modalities by which wage parity conditions are implemented. It is thus difficult to establish a common approach to the use of wage parity conditions. Nevertheless, guidelines are required to establish (a) under what conditions (sectors, personnel categories, and local and economic conditions) wage parity may be permissible; (b) how wage parity conditions are to be implemented; and (c) how to link wage parity conditions to entry conditions and formalities.

It is proposed that in sectors in which the host country faces a severe shortage of personnel, wage parity conditions should not be imposed, as there is no immediate displacement effect on local labor. To ensure that exploitation of foreign labor does not occur, conditions can be imposed on other terms of employment, such as work hours, leave, overtime, and benefits. Guidelines on the remuneration package given to foreign workers can also be considered (depending on the period of time they are deputed abroad, sectoral conditions, and the employment level) in order to ensure a fair standard of living in the host country. This wage could be the reservation wage of the foreign services provider plus allowances for cost of living, taxes, savings, and such concerns, without requiring payment of a specific minimum wage or percentage of wages as is done at present. This would permit wages of foreign services providers to be below host-country wages but within a fair margin, allowing the home country to maintain its comparative advantage in mode 4 in that sector while also preventing the influx of foreign workers from massively driving down domestic wages in the sector in the host country. Specifics of the wage margin will depend on sector characteristics and should be decided mutually by the concerned countries under bilateral wage agreements and discussions between professional or industry associations in these countries. In sectors where there is likely to be local displacement, particularly in unskilled and semiskilled occupations, countries could consider grandfathering indigenous workers through wage subsidies. In both cases, the interests of labor unions and workers in the receiving countries could be addressed by using taxes and fees collected from foreign services providers to fund job training and to subsidize or relocate currently affected and potential future domestic services providers. It is likely that even the posttax or postfee receipts of the foreign services providers would exceed their reservation wages.

Multilateral discussions should also aim at delinking the wage parity condition from the visa issuance process. Wage parity should not be a cumbersome precondition for the issuance of visas. The earlier recommendation for specifying a maximum time frame for issuing GATS visas and notification requirements for delays and additional conditions should take into account delays caused by wage-related and labor certification requirements. Such delays and rejections should be open to challenge in the dispute settlement forum of the GATS.

Strengthening GATS Norms on Recognition. The GATS already contains a strong provision for recognition under Article VII. This provision needs to be strengthened by establishing detailed norms in certain areas and by facilitating mutual recognition agreements among countries.

- *Norms for nonaccredited sectors and activities.* In professional services such as software services where there are no formal accreditation or licensing procedures, norms are needed on the criteria to be used to accord recognition to professionals. These include criteria relating to minimum professional education, as sanctioned by a diploma, formal licensing or certification requirements, and minimum professional experience, which in turn should be reflected in the sectoral and horizontal commitment schedules. In addition, where countries have included recognition requirements in their commitment schedules, there should be mechanisms under the GATS to enable countries to engage in bilateral discussions to compare qualifications across home and host states and to assess the extent of equivalence based on bilaterally determined criteria.

- *Norms concerning equivalence of work-related and academic qualifications.* Consensus is required on how and when to accord equivalence between on-the-job experience and academic qualifications. Norms must be established that specify the kinds of jobs or positions and the kinds of academic qualifications that may be considered equivalent and substitutable for meeting entry requirements and sectors where such equivalence is difficult to establish. The latter will require the participation of professional bodies and associations in member countries to provide the criteria for equivalence, along with names of well-recognized training and higher education institutes in the respective countries, to better assess professional qualifications. GATS disciplines on recognition should further discourage differential treatment of the value of work experience and qualifications between foreign and domestic services sector professionals.

- *Norms concerning temporary licensing.* Disciplines governing licensing should allow for temporary licensing of foreign service professionals when such licensing procedures are lacking in the home country. The absence of such procedures should not constitute a barrier to the movement of professionals from these countries. Procedures could be developed for temporarily licensing engineers to practice in the specialty area. Multilateral discussion is required to determine these sectors and the associated procedures.

- *Norms concerning broad-based equivalence in recognition.* Multilateral discussions should focus on a system of granting recognition through broad-based equivalence of qualifications and standards. It would be useful to establish bridging mechanisms where there is a divergence of requirements and standards between home and host countries. The GATS framework should encourage discussions on a compensatory system of granting recognition, whereby local adaptation periods and aptitude tests for foreign services professionals can be used to offset differences among national systems and standards, such as those in the European Union.[8] Within this framework of broad-based equivalence, countries can bilaterally negotiate recognition agreements to suit their particular needs. There should also be mechanisms to facilitate regulatory cooperation among professional bodies in member countries to enable systematic exchange of information, mutual monitoring, and cooperative enforcement.

Introducing Norms for Economic Needs and Other Tests. Many countries have included conditions relating to economic needs tests in their commitment schedules, but the wording is usually vague. For instance, the EU requires the foreign services provider to have an "effective and continuous link" with the market, but it is not clear what is meant by this term.

The most far-reaching step in this regard would be to abolish the use of such measures as horizontal limitations. Any market access limitations involving this condition should be limited to sectoral commitments, but in line with certain multilateral guidelines so as to reduce the scope for discretion in the use of such tests. These guidelines include laying down clear criteria for applying the tests, establishing norms for the administrative and procedural formalities associated with the tests, and specifying how the results of the tests are to be used in restricting entry to foreign services providers (for example, translating the findings into quantitative limits on foreign personnel). Requirements and decisions made on the basis of such tests should be subject to challenge under the WTO's dispute settlement mechanism.

Consensus is required on the occupational categories that can be subject to such tests. These categories should be limited to as few as possible, and the market conditions (shortage of personnel; public policy objectives, and so on) under which these categories would be subject to economic needs and other tests should be defined. Highly qualified services professionals should be exempt from economic needs tests. At present, in some sectors such as software services, professionals are exempt from such tests only if their academic degree in a specialty is directly related to the employment, a practice that is discretionary. In lower-skilled and semi-skilled services activities, economic needs and other tests should not be applicable unless there is likely to be a disruptive effect on the host country labor market in that sector.

In addition to the areas mentioned above, disciplines are needed on subsidies and government procurement policies. Countries could be required to make explicit the existence of government procurement policies and subsidies in all relevant sectoral commitments schedules and to provide information on their nature, their magnitude, how they operate, and other relevant parameters. Where such policies are present and countries have scheduled commitments, any limitations on foreign services providers resulting from these policies should be clearly specified. These limitations could take the form of ceilings on the share of contracts or value of transactions to be procured from domestic sources, the number of local services persons employed, and the extent of preference to be accorded domestic contracts. In the case of subsidies, limitations could be filed on the maximum extent of subsidy as a share of total value of transactions in the sector. It is important that there be transparency in the use of these practices.

Conclusion

This chapter has highlighted the limited nature of liberalization that has occurred under the GATS framework for the movement of natural persons. Significantly more liberal commitments are required in this mode if developing countries are to exploit their comparative advantage in labor-intensive services. Several proposals have been made for improving the existing commitments and commitment structure and for improving the GATS framework by introducing multilateral norms on important regulatory aspects concerning this mode of services trade. Both approaches must be taken in conjunction: the multilateral norms would have little significance unless accompanied by the proposed modifications in the commitments, and the improved commitments will have greater relevance if there are broad principles to facilitate their implementation. The proposed changes in the GATS would also need to be supported by domestic measures and reforms at the individual country level to facilitate and to derive benefits from the liberalization of movement of natural persons. These domestic reforms include areas relating to standards and recognition, immigration and labor market policies, and tax policies. Most important, countries need to be more transparent about their domestic regulations. Without increased transparency on the part of individual countries, most of the proposed recommendations will not be enforceable or effective.

Notes

1 Movement of natural persons is defined in Article I.2 of the GATS as "[s]upply of a service . . . by a service supplier of a member through presence of natural persons of a member in the territory of any other member." It includes both services providers who are working overseas in an individual capacity and those who are part of a home, host, or third-country commercial establishment.

2 Certain restrictions on commercial presence, including the type of commercial entity (corporation, partnership) or a requirement for prior approval by host-country professional associations, are often meant to address issues such as professional liability and misconduct and national interest.

3 MFN is applicable to all services that have been scheduled by a member unless an MFN exemption has been taken. The principle of nondiscrimination is reflected in GATS Article XVII.3.

4 Market access limitations include limits on the number of services suppliers, the value of services transactions, the number of services operations or the quantity of the services output, the number of natural persons employed, foreign equity participation, and the type of entity or venture.

5 Article XIII exempts government procurement from the application of MFN, market access, and national treatment obligations. Article XV requires members to enter into negotiations and exchange information on subsidies to develop multilateral disciplines in this regard.

6 The discussion of this and the next point (on bias toward higher-level personnel) is based on a review of existing horizontal schedules of commitments.

7 Given the transparency provision in Article III, individual member countries can seek this information from other members, establish mechanisms and inquiry points to provide such information to other members, and seek recourse to the dispute settlement mechanism in case this provision is violated.

8 The General System of Directives of the EU permits professionals from other member countries who fall short in their qualifications and standards to qualify following a local training and adaptation period.

31

CATHERINE L. MANN

ELECTRONIC COMMERCE, THE WTO, AND DEVELOPING COUNTRIES

E LECTRONIC COMMERCE IS A SHORTHAND TERM THAT EMBRACES A COMPLEX AMALgam of technologies, infrastructures, processes, and products. It brings together whole industries and narrow applications, producers and users, information exchange, and economic activity in a global marketplace called the Internet. One of the best ways of understanding electronic commerce is to consider its basic elements and its impact on traditional transactions and marketplaces. This approach shows clearly how electronic commerce is intricately woven into the fabric of domestic economic activity and international trade.

Electronic commerce has three basic elements, not all of which are equally or universally developed within and among countries around the world:

- *Institutions and technologies that create the global network supporting the Internet marketplace.* Electronic commerce relies on a variety of technologies, some of which are well established (public phone network technology) and some of which are developing at breakneck speeds (for example, technologies to interconnect telecommunications,

cable, satellite, or other Internet "backbones" and "devices"). It also depends on institutions and firms such as Internet service providers (ISPs) to connect market participants, as well as end-user devices such as personal computers (PCs), television sets, and mobile telephones.

- *Services that connect the Internet marketplace to the traditional marketplace and further support the development of both.* Payment over the Internet through credit, debit, or Smart Cards or through other on-line methods link buyers and sellers in the virtual marketplace, who then complete their transactions (whether virtual or physical) through distribution and delivery systems. A range of new services (customer data management, network and device security systems, pricing and auction methods, and so on) augment and deepen the relationships between buyers and sellers.

- *Protocols, laws, and regulations that govern conduct and relationships.* Technical communications and interconnectivity standards, the legality and modality of electronic signatures, certification, and encryption, and disclosure, privacy, and content regulations all affect the conduct of activity in the Internet marketplace and the relationships between businesses, consumers, and government. These instruments may be developed and enhanced by both private and public intervention and interaction.

With these basic elements, electronic commerce leads to three kinds of innovations in traditional transactions and marketplaces:

merce and the financial sector of the economy. Electronic payments require an easy-to-use and secure payment vehicle. Although a number of countries are focusing on "cash on delivery" for tangible products, in the future a payment method that is on-line so as to accommodate products delivered digitally will be required. For business-to-business transactions, an easy-to-use electronic payments mechanism is essential for achieving the cost reductions promised by Internet-based commerce. At the same time, security for financial transactions is a sine qua non. Liberalization, along with appropriate regulation and supervision, will help bring international best practice, as well as global technologies, to bear to improve the functioning of the domestic financial sector.

Finally, *delivery logistics* (including customs) rounds out the set of services infrastructures that are key components in developing e-commerce. Speed is one of the most important characteristics of electronic commerce. Overnight delivery, just-in-time processing, and 24 (hour)/7 (day) operations are examples of how much faster and more precisely timed are economic activities in the e-commerce world. A country with inefficient distribution and delivery systems and without multimodal transport for international participation will be left behind in e-commerce. Government policies have a direct impact in these areas, and governments have the principal task of improving the efficiency and transparency of customs operations.

How should policymakers respond to these needs for domestic reforms? First, clear synergies exist between the elements of policy reform. Making substantial progress on only one element, such as telephone charges, will yield smaller rewards than expected because of the tight relationship between the three elements of e-commerce readiness. Second, exploiting the existing technology available worldwide has great advantages of interoperability and can jump-start the globalization of domestic producers. Finally, the greatest innovation, profit, and increase in economic well-being will be generated by private sector entrepreneurs serving market niches unique to the home country, since only domestic entrepreneurs are truly able to understand their own market. Even though domestic policy may favor international infrastructures and overseas innovation—in the recognition that network externalities and interoperability are important for creating the needed foundation for domestic initia-tives—domestic entrepreneurs and consumers will benefit in the long run.

Electronic Commerce on the WTO Agenda

In reviewing the services infrastructures that make electronic commerce possible, as well as the impact electronic commerce has on the traditional marketplace, it is clear that the WTO agenda has touched many aspects of what makes e-commerce develop successfully. It is also clear that much work is still to be done, both by countries themselves and through the WTO, to reap the benefits of e-commerce.

First, electronic commerce is clearly global from the very start, putting it directly within the purview of the WTO. Although traditional borders do still matter in the world of international trade, electronic commerce diminishes their importance. Companies with a Website are instantly international—whether or not they intended to be.

The electronic marketplace is currently free from explicit trade barriers (see Box 31.1). The absence of international tariffs or other barriers to electronic commerce transactions encourages people to investigate and then to continue to participate in the Internet marketplace, resulting in greater efficiency and economic benefits for its participants.

Yet the infrastructures that make electronic commerce possible are still burdened by a myriad of trade and investment barriers. The growth of global electronic commerce depends on continued liberalization of these infrastructures, many of which are already part of WTO commitments or are on the WTO agenda. For example,

- Computers and other information technology products are covered by the Information Technology Agreement (ITA) I and are under consideration for ITA II.
- Telecommunications is covered by the Basic Telecommunications Agreement, although rapid changes in communication technologies are blurring the lines between so-called facilities-based and value-added services.
- Financial services were addressed initially by the Financial Services Agreement (part of the GATS) but additional discussion of liberalization and regulation in this sector took place in other venues (the Bank for International Settlements and the IMF) in the aftermath of the financial crises of 1997.

BOX 31.1 THE ECONOMICS AND LAW OF DUTY-FREE ELECTRONIC COMMERCE

WTO members have decided that electronic delivery of products will continue to be free from customs duties. For the moment, this commitment is temporary and political, but there are proposals to make it durable and legally binding. Two aspects of the commitment are notable. First, only electronic transmissions are covered—goods ordered through electronic means but imported through normal channels are explicitly excluded. Second, the standstill applies only to customs duties; there is no mention of other forms of restriction. Most electronic commerce is already free of barriers, and so the objective is really to bind this existing openness and thus preclude the introduction of new barriers. But is duty-free electronic commerce the appropriate route?

Economic Implications

The exemption of one mode of delivery from taxation while others continue to be taxed is analogous to a preferential trading arrangement. As in such arrangements, there is a positive, trade-creating aspect and a negative, trade-diverting aspect. The latter arises when the tax-exempt mode is chosen simply to avoid the tax, even though it is less efficient than the taxed alternative. Although electronic delivery is frequently the most efficient means of delivery, it is conceivable that in some cases it will not be. For instance, given the current state of technology, it may be costlier in time and money to download films and music from the Internet than to acquire them in physical form. The welfare cost of undesirable trade diversion is the forgone tariff revenue, which has in fact been the main concern of developing countries. But while it is difficult to predict the revenue that could be raised through duties on products not now subject to such duties, as the table shows, the revenue consequences of diversion of physical trade into electronic channels are unlikely to be significant.

There is another, less obvious and more serious, problem with the proposal. Since it covers only electronic transmissions, it concerns for the most part what is currently regarded as trade in services. In its exclusive focus on customs duties, the proposal is not sufficiently sensitive to an important difference in trade regimes for goods and services. Quantitative restrictions, largely prohibited for goods, are allowed under the GATS (unless a member has committed not to use them) and remain a frequent instrument of protection for services, when feasible. For goods, an absence of customs duties would complement the ban on quotas and hence ensure free trade. But for services, banning only customs duties could force reliance on quotas. It may, of course, never be technically feasible to impose customs duties on services trade, in which case the proposed standstill is irrelevant. But if it were to become technically feasible to impose customs duties, there is no good reason why customs duties should be banned while quotas are allowed. Why would we want to prohibit the use of an economically superior instrument of protection while allowing the use of an inferior instrument?*

Legal Implications

The legal value of a commitment not to impose customs duties is not clear, given the existing structure of rules. Consider the two alternative possibilities:

- If a member has made a commitment in a particular sector to provide national treatment, all discriminatory taxes (including, by definition, customs duties) are already prohibited, and so the new commitment would add nothing.[†]
- If a member has not made a commitment to provide national treatment, that member remains free to impose discriminatory internal taxes other than customs duties, and, again, the new commitment has little value. (The proposal does not cover internal taxation.)

In sum, the strength of the proposal for duty-free treatment is that for a limited class of products (currently classified as goods but deliverable electroni-

(continued)

rect benefits from liberalizing the infrastructures on which these activities depend—are substantial. The three services sector infrastructures of communications, financial services, and delivery logistics are critical components for overall economic activity. Comprehensive liberalization of services could increase global gross domestic product (GDP) by 4 to 6 percentage points—twice that credited to the Uruguay Round—and raise the long-run global growth rate from 3.2 to 5.0 percent (see OECD 1997a; Hufbauer and Warren 1999). For the developing countries alone, GDP could increase by more than 1 percent as a result of the improvements in productivity derived from e-commerce.[4]

Although the transition to liberalization is almost never without cost, liberalization of services promises more comprehensive benefits because services are an input to production in virtually all sectors of the economy. In contrast, liberalization of selected goods sectors has a narrower conduit through which it can affect the overall economy. Many of the benefits of services sector liberalization result from greater efficiency within countries, but tightening the global links between the domestic and international markets for these services also contributes to the overall gains.

To the extent that the desire to be "e-commerce-ready" engages countries in a self-assessment of these services infrastructures, all the better. But the WTO process could be improved to do more to help countries reach these goals, which are consistent with the overall WTO objective of a less distortionary and more liberalized environment for international exchange.

Improving the WTO Process

The WTO has done a substantial amount of work with regard to electronic commerce, but the cross-cutting and rapidly evolving environment of electronic commerce exposes tensions within the organizing structure of the WTO (the GATT, the GATS, and the subcommittees), as well as in its members' operational methods (request-offer negotiations and negative versus positive commitments).[5] Nevertheless, the traditional WTO principles of nondiscrimination, transparency, and market openness remain valid and should be applied to electronic commerce. New rules are not necessary if the liberalizing *spirit* embodied in WTO agreements is honored.

The first tension is between the new marketplace and the *classification system for transactions* that is embodied in the WTO organizing structure. Should electronic commerce and digitized products be classified in the GATT, or the GATS, or both, or neither? The European Union strongly asserts that "all electronic transmissions consist of services" and that these products should therefore fall under the purview of the GATS (WTO 1999b). Most countries, including the United States, agree that services delivered over the Internet are covered by the GATS but that other products are more like a good or are a hybrid between a good and a service. (Electronic books are a much-cited example.).

More important, countries that made commitments in GATS schedules at the completion of the Uruguay Round might or might not have taken into consideration the "new marketplaces" (in time, geography, and information) made possible by the Internet. How these new marketplaces affect the degree of liberalization embodied in the commitments is a key issue. On the one hand, if e-commerce is "new," classifying these transactions or products under the GATS could make their treatment under the WTO less liberal because market access in the GATS exists only in sectors in which members have made specific commitments. On the other hand, the WTO could decide to sidestep the classification issue and require that members follow the course of most liberal treatment of these products, under either the GATT or the GATS, particularly when a specific transaction does not fit neatly within a negotiated GATS commitment. In some cases this could mean that electronic delivery of goods or services would be treated more favorably than other forms of delivery. For example, financial products or architectural services could be sold over the Internet even if the physical presence of a foreign bank or the licensing of foreign architects had not yet been scheduled for liberalization under the GATS. Rather than view this outcome with alarm, both industrial and developing countries should embrace it as a positive force, stimulating further the development of electronic commerce and encouraging deeper liberalization and deregulation throughout the economy.[6]

Governments do have a legitimate concern that their standards and regulations (for example, on pharmaceutical prescriptions, gambling restrictions, and the prudential regulation of banks) might be undermined by the more favorable treatment accorded to electronic commerce. Governments should therefore review how electronic commerce affects existing standards and regulations and should decide what combination of private sector response and public legislation will ensure the greatest benefits of electronic commerce for their citizens. This shows clearly, once again, how the Internet tightens the links between international and domestic policies.

A second issue relevant for developing countries and the WTO is *negotiating method*. This issue grows out of the synergies between the elements of e-commerce readiness. Because of these synergies, country delegations will begin emphasizing the "horizontal" approach to negotiations on electronic commerce. In the horizontal approach, negotiators seek to apply liberalizing measures, such as transparency and good governance in regulations, as well as consistency of ownership rules across sectors, to a broad range of services. For example, negotiators would seek to eliminate any discrimination across a particular mode of delivery—such as electronic commerce or rights of establishment—and across a range of services, such as financial services and small package delivery. This horizontal approach in negotiations is consistent with and in a formal way extends the liberalization bias engendered by electronic commerce.

A third question of particular relevance for the developing countries is the *WTO work program on electronic commerce*. To educate country delegations and to promote the cross-cutting nature of electronic commerce, a nonnegotiating working group should be set up in the WTO's General Council, rather than have the work fragmented throughout the WTO. Although input from the different councils and committees is important, the cross-cutting nature of electronic commerce means that leadership by the General Council is key. Close coordination of the work program under the General Council will help developing countries, particularly those with smaller negotiating staffs, participate more fully. Moreover, as discussed below, representatives from regional forums acting on behalf of their constituents should be recognized as another channel for broadening outreach and participation by countries that cannot be represented individually at all the meetings.

A final point is that *private sector participation* and the contribution of the private sector to the WTO work program are vital. Private sector participation has been the hallmark of all discussions of electronic commerce in regional forums, including the Asia-Pacific Economic Cooperation (APEC) and the Free Trade Area of the Americas (FTAA). The private sector is leading the way in setting global technological standards for electronic commerce, and it can also help resolve the technical aspects relevant to policymaking concerns in areas ranging from tax administration to privacy protection.

How Should Developing Countries Approach E-commerce in the WTO?

The technical and policy issues involved in electronic commerce are extremely complex, both within a country and among countries in the international arena. Leveraging human and administrative capital resources, both in negotiating and in nonnegotiating bodies, is a must, to keep up with e-commerce knowledge and to gain more traction in international negotiations. But WTO negotiations address more than just e-commerce. Can and should developing countries leverage their greater participation in global e-commerce into greater openness in sectors of their traditional interest?

Many developing countries are already members of regional groups such as the Association of Southeast Asian Nations (ASEAN), APEC, the Organization of American States (OAS), the Common Market of the South (MERCOSUR), and the Southern Africa Development Community (SADC). These groups have their own broad range of initiatives and are pursuing agendas for trade liberalization with more or less forward momentum or commitment. Countries in the region have found these groups to be good focal points for communicating concerns about e-commerce and government policies (for example, customs and telecommunications policies) and for comparing notes on how e-commerce is developing within their countries. The regional groups could do even more in this regard through their Websites to ensure that the full membership can gain insights from the leaders in the region.

In addition, some of these groups have forums for private sector interaction, such as the FTAA's Joint Private Sector Committee of Exports and APEC's Pacific Basin Economic Council. Venues of this kind could increase the potential for public-private investment partnerships to enhance the operations of the key service infrastructures. Such public-pri-

32

COMPLETING THE GATS FRAMEWORK

Safeguards, Subsidies, and Government Procurement

SERVICES NEGOTIATORS EMBARKED ON THE GATS 2000 SET OF DISCUSSIONS with much unfinished business left over from the Uruguay Round. More than a dozen years after the Uruguay Round's inception, the framework of GATS rules and disciplines is still very much under construction, with work outstanding on a number of key fronts. These include emergency safeguards, subsidies, government procurement, and domestic regulation. This essay focuses on the first three items on the unfinished, or "leftover," agenda for the GATS.

In the post-1994 period, little progress was made on this menu of leftover issues. In part, this reflects the focus on completing outstanding sectoral negotiations, particularly in the high-stakes areas of telecommunications and financial services. But it is also reflective of the technical complexity inherent in developing disciplines in hitherto uncharted waters and, in the case of government procurement, the fact that existing plurilateral disciplines already applied to services (and goods) under the Government Procurement Agreement (GPA).

The question of whether to include in the GATS a safeguard mechanism and subsidy disciplines was on the agenda of the Uruguay Round services negotiations. No consensus on developing rules was reached. Negotiators did, nonetheless, agree to explicitly provide for future work, that is, "negotiations on the question of emergency safeguard measures, the results of which would enter into force no later than three years after the WTO Agreement itself was to enter into force" (GATS Art. X), and "negotiations to develop multilateral disciplines on subsidies to avoid their distortive effects on trade in services" (GATS Art. XV). To date, neither mandate has been fulfilled. The Working Party on GATS Rules only recently agreed to extend the negotiating deadline on emergency safeguards to mid-March 2002, the third such extension since the end of the Uruguay Round.

Emergency Safeguards

For the purposes of this chapter, "safeguards" is used to describe a mechanism that can be invoked by governments, under specified conditions, to impose or increase protection in order to relieve, on a temporary basis, difficulties or pressures that have arisen as a result of liberalization commitments and obligations undertaken in trade agreements. The main features of a temporary safeguard are that it targets a specific product or industry, is applied on a most-favored-nation (MFN) basis, is of limited duration, is sometimes progressively liberalized over the period of its application, and in some cases is subject to demands for compensation from other members affected by the measure. Another key element of this type of measure is that increased imports resulting from the liberalization must be causing or threatening to cause "injury" to domestic producers of a like or directly competitive product. Examples of this type of safeguard can be found in GATT Article XIX, in the Agreement on Safeguards, in Article 5 of the Agreement on Agriculture, in Article 6 of the Agreement of Textiles and Clothing (ATC), and in numerous regional trade agreements, including the North American Free Trade Agreement (NAFTA) and most association agreements concluded between European Union members and other countries.

Historically, the existence of emergency safeguard measures in trade agreements was viewed a mechanism to help persuade domestic constituencies to accept greater liberalization. It provides some insurance for domestic industries fearing difficulties in adjusting to new competitive realities following liberalization. The historical record of emergency safeguards measures applied to goods trade in securing greater liberalization and facilitating adjustment is difficult to verify. The main role of safeguard clauses is to allow officials to address opposition to liberalization by pointing to the availability of a mechanism to suggest that "defensive" interests have been taken into account.

In the case of services, to date WTO members have not identified precise examples of potential circumstances where an emergency safeguard mechanism (ESM) might be required. Indeed, the discussions have largely been abstract. This may be symptomatic of the fact that with few exceptions (such as basic telecommunications), actual liberalization has been modest, with most bindings reflecting the regulatory status quo (and sometimes considerably less). Moreover, in view of the positive listing of scheduled commitments, the option of not making a commitment is always a negotiating possibility. Such regulatory freedom largely obviates adjustment pressures in sectors where countries may not deem domestic competitors capable of withstanding extra doses of competition.

The GATT Safeguards Paradigm and Trade in Services

The WTO Agreement on Safeguards is the most obvious template that might be used for services. It essentially imposes a two-part test: (a) imports must have increased in absolute quantities or rela-

tive to domestic production, and (b) imports must cause serious injury to a domestic industry producing like or directly competitive goods. In the services context, an initial problem is the definition of imports, given that there are four modes of service delivery. Thus, the first question is whether such an ESM could be designed to apply to what one would typically think of as "import" situations (cross-border trade) and whether it could (or should) be designed to apply to situations involving services supplied through any one of the other three modes of delivery.

Mode 1, cross-border trade, does not pose particular conceptual difficulties because there is an "import" in the traditional sense and the limitation on trade can take the form of constraining sales of foreign services suppliers in the importing country. For mode 2, the "import" transaction takes place in the exporter's market, and it is the customer who crosses the border to consume the service abroad. Any limitation on services trade would mean limiting the ability of the customer (rather than the supplier) to consume services abroad. In mode 3, the situation is even more complex since the transaction involves the establishment of the service supplier in the importing country. There is a dual dimension to the "importation" issue: the establishment of a commercial presence in a host country, and the sales or domestic operations of the established foreign supplier. The former may be dealt with via a limitation on foreign investment, but the latter cannot be conceptually considered as an "import." As regards mode 4, the application of the concept of "import" to movement of persons appears rather incongruous.[1]

Since the traditional purpose of an ESM is to provide short-term import relief to the domestic industry, the right to bring a complaint should be that of the "domestic industry." In the services context, the domestic industry could be composed of domestic services suppliers or foreign services suppliers that have established a commercial presence (or both). In this case, the question arises as to whether the term "domestic industry" should include all services suppliers located within the territorial limits of a country or whether the locally established services suppliers of foreign companies should be excluded. If locally established foreign services suppliers are excluded, negotiators must then consider the ramifications of classifying their services as "imports" and thereby possibly making them subject to what-

BOX 32.1 ASEAN PROPOSAL FOR A GATS EMERGENCY SAFEGUARD MECHANISM

The most detailed blueprint for a GATS safeguard clause submitted to date in the Working Party on GATS Rules (WPGR) came from the Association of Southeast Asian Nations (ASEAN) group. The ASEAN countries, led by Thailand, argued that services liberalization can have unforeseen consequences for national economies. Citing the example of the effects of financial liberalization in the recent Asian financial crisis, ASEAN countries have argued that countries should have recourse to an emergency safeguard to restrain foreign services providers.

The ASEAN proposal, which was presented to the WPGR in October 2000, uses the same standard as is applied to goods trade for establishing proof of injury to domestic industry for all four modes of supply. It would require a showing that the injury or threat thereof is caused by increased supply of services by foreign services suppliers. Countries that have shown skepticism about the need for a GATS safeguard mechanism have repeatedly argued that data for services industries, particularly in developing countries, are too incomplete and unreliable to establish either injury or causation. As a result, any safeguard could be prone to abuse and could result in repeated WTO challenges. The ASEAN proposal suggests that developing countries be granted more favorable treatment in the imposition of a safeguard. It would prohibit imposition of the safeguard against developing countries that have a small share of the market, and it would allow developing countries to impose safeguards for longer periods, depending on the severity of the measure imposed.

The ASEAN proposal describes three options for how a safeguard would be imposed for mode 3. The first, least restrictive, option would largely guarantee services suppliers who already have established a commercial presence in foreign countries the opportunity to maintain and expand their businesses, while restricting new entrants. The second option would prohibit expansion of business activities and additional capital investment of services providers by limiting the extension of rights. The third option would be even more restrictive, limiting businesses' acquired rights to those rights that have actually been exercised.

Other developing countries voiced concerns that a GATS ESM could most easily lend itself to imposing restrictions on the movement of natural persons, one of the modes of services delivery that many developing countries are keen to liberalize further in the current GATS round of talks. The ASEAN proposal speaks to this issue by including a provision that prohibits imposing the safeguard against temporary entry of natural persons from developing countries if these persons account for less than a certain percentage of the labor market.

---

a GATS ESM, have consistently identified as justifying the need for emergency safeguard provisions. Negotiating efforts could thus be directed to adapting in GATS (or in countries' schedules) provisions similar to those that currently govern the progressive liberalization of Mexico's financial markets under the NAFTA. Mexico, under the terms of NAFTA, is allowed to impose market share caps if the specific foreign ownership thresholds agreed to (25 percent for banks and 30 percent for securities firms) are reached before 2004. Mexico may have recourse to such market share limitations only once during the 2000–04 period and may only impose them for a three-year period. Under no circum-

stances may such measures be maintained after 2007 (Sauvé and Gonzalez-Hermosillo 1993). It is worth noting that Mexico has not made use of such provisions, even though the aggregate share of foreign participation in its financial system today significantly exceeds the thresholds described above (IMF 2000).

Subsidies

The question of subsidy disciplines, for which (unlike safeguards) a timetable for completing negotiations was not envisaged at the time the curtain fell on the Uruguay Round, has not given rise to the same degree of debate and discussion as that on a possible ESM. For this reason, deciding on the desirability or feasibility of introducing disciplines will require a more thorough identification phase to determine the extent to which subsidies exist in services industries and the circumstances in which they may result in adverse trade or investment effects. There may well be valid reasons to temper expectations on this front, as witnessed by the generally disappointing experience with attempts by the OECD Industry Committee to monitor industrial subsidies and the swiftness with which subsidy-related issues fell off the negotiating table in the recently abandoned negotiations on a Multilateral Agreement on Investment.

As with safeguards, determining the feasibility of subsidy disciplines will need to factor in the specificities of services trade. Although some guidance could come from the WTO's Agreement on Subsidies and Countervailing Measures (SCM), most experts agree that the SCM agreement is not a panacea. In particular, consideration of a countervailing mechanism would appear undesirable from both a policy and a conceptual viewpoint. The questions of export subsidies, which are prevalent in large infrastructure projects, and of investment incentives, which have recently proliferated beyond the OECD area to a number of emerging economies, may, however, deserve further consideration, particularly in the context of discussions on how best to enhance GATS provisions relating to commercial presence and to broaden the remit of the TRIMs agreement.

Article XV of the GATS calls on members to enter into negotiations on developing the necessary multilateral disciplines to avoid trade-distorting effects of subsidies and to address the appropriateness of countervailing procedures. The GATS does not currently define the term "subsidy." For our purposes, we can borrow the GATT definition of a subsidy as a financial contribution by a government that confers a benefit to a recipient. Comprehensive information is not available on the existence of subsidies in services trade, but anecdotal evidence suggests that sectors such as transport, utilities, audio-visual, tourism, and financial services typically benefit from some form of subsidization in a range of countries, both industrial and developing. Information and analysis regarding the impact of these subsidy practices on services trade and investment remain limited, however. Given the lack of available information, the discussion that follows is largely conceptual.

Existing GATS Disciplines on Subsidies

The existing GATS framework is not bereft of provisions applying to subsidies. It is generally accepted that subsidies are considered "measures" within the meaning of the GATS; thus, MFN obligations are applicable. National treatment applies to the subsidy practices of GATS signatories to the extent that a sector has been listed in a country's schedule of commitments. National treatment can exert a potentially strong discipline on the use of subsidies, as it requires that governments providing subsidies to domestic services suppliers also have to make them available to foreign providers operating in the country. Most GATS members have included limitations on national treatment that apply to all subsidy practices. Others have done so with respect to specific modes and specific sectors.[2] There is a debate as to whether the national treatment obligation extends across all modes of supply or whether members retain the freedom to discriminate between identical services delivered via a different mode on the grounds that such suppliers are not in "like" circumstances or are not "like service suppliers."

One can also note that services industries tend to be characterized by a higher degree of government ownership (particularly in developing countries), regulation, and intervention than goods-producing sectors. This tends to create large, entrenched service providers that can use cross-subsidization to extend into foreign markets from a highly protected home base. In such instances domestic regulatory conduct may have an effect similar to that of a trade-distorting subsidy, driving prices downward in the foreign market. The GATS contains provisions on monopolies and exclusive service providers (Art. VIII) and on business practices (Art. IX) that may be relevant to these circumstances.

The SCM agreement defines a subsidy as a financial contribution by a government or any public body located within the territory of a member that confers a benefit to the recipient. It adopts a "traffic light" approach to classifying subsidies (distinguishing between nonactionable, prohibited, and actionable subsidies) and prohibits export subsidies (see Box 18.3 in this volume). The first two elements of the SCM agreement could easily be extended to services; it makes little sense to expand the subsidy concept to regulatory measures, and the green-light carve-out approach would allow members to use subsidies in pursuit of social or noneconomic objectives (environmental protection, provision of services in remote or disadvantaged areas, regional development, national security, and the like). It could also deal with subsidies that are motivated by development objectives.

Matters are less straightforward regarding application of the ban on export subsidies. For mode 1 (cross-border supply), the situation is roughly comparable to trade in goods, and theoretically, the same prohibition could well be applicable. For mode 2, a domestic producer (of a like service) would have to claim that a foreign services provider received government assistance conditional on attracting a purchaser from the complaining country to consume the service abroad. Is this realistic? For instance, would a subsidy granted by a government to a local tourism authority to build large resort hotels to attract foreign tourists constitute a prohibited subsidy? How does such a situation differ from the subsidization of an aircraft repair facility that essentially services foreign aircraft companies?

The concept of an export subsidy is also confusing for mode 3. It is unlikely that a domestic government would provide a subsidy to a firm that is considering relocating or establishing a commercial presence in another jurisdiction. The existence of an export subsidy under such a scenario is highly improbable. On the other hand, investment incentives offered by host countries to attract investment from abroad may clearly have trade- and investment-distorting effects. Should the country with the most attractive package be brought before the WTO on charges of providing "unfair" subsidies? Countries often justify investment incentives as a form of economic (or regional) development assistance extended on grounds of market failure (information asymmetries, externalities), even though the trade implications of their actions can be apparent. Determining when investment incentives are trade-distorting and when they are legitimate for public policy reasons is not straightforward. An additional challenge with regard to investment incentives is the need to address them in the realm of goods trade, as well; ultimately, a coherent approach requires the same rules for both trade in goods and trade in services.

For mode 4, it is hard to think of credible examples in which export subsidies affect the movement of natural persons. It is more likely that an importing country would provide a subsidy (such as subsidized travel or relocation grants) to attract skilled workers to its territory. Policymakers are thus confronted with a situation like that under mode 3 (commercial presence) regarding investment or location incentives.

Similar complexity arises concerning the use of countervailing measures against subsidies that are deemed actionable. The SCM agreement requires, as preconditions for taking action, findings of (a) injury to the domestic industry of an importing country, (b) nullification or impairment of GATT benefits, or (c) "serious prejudice" to the interests of a member. The determination of injury caused by subsidization would be problematic for modes 2 through 4 because the traditional notion of imports does not readily apply. For mode 1, there would be implementation problems associated with measuring and observing trade data; the conceptual difficulty of defining "like services" and "like domestic services providers"; and practical enforcement difficulties, not least regarding electronic delivery. These problems parallel those arising in a safeguard context and are compounded by the difficulty of measuring the extent of subsidization. Given the intangible nature of many services transactions, calculating "per unit" subsidy rates poses formidable challenges.[3] It may be easier to apply a serious prejudice approach. According to the SCM agreement, serious prejudice is deemed to exist when the overall rate of subsidization exceeds 15 percent of the total funds invested in a new startup operation. This might be applied for mode 3, where the subsidization is given to entice the establishment of a commercial presence by a services provider.

Options for Moving Forward

Before embarking on the creation of disciplines, it is essential to determine whether trade-distorting subsidies are sufficiently pervasive to warrant rule-making, especially given the political difficulties countries with federal political systems confront in curtailing regulatory sovereignty in this area. The lack of progress to date reveals limited political appetite for forward movement (Sauvé and Wilkie 2000). A general notification and transparency provision along the lines of Article XXV of the SCM agreement might represent a useful starting point in determining the empirical significance of subsidies. It should be noted that the SCM agreement already provides scope for remedial action against unfair subsidization of services embodied in goods, creating possibilities for dealing with some of the potential concerns about trade-distorting subsidization in services.[4]

From a substantive standpoint, two issues may warrant further attention: (a) a prohibition on export subsidies, and (b) the issue of investment incentives in the context of establishment of a commercial presence. Export subsidies are intrinsically antithetical to fair trade. For the reasons mentioned above, their curtailment might only be workable for cross-border trade (mode 1), again raising the question of whether such a move could create distortions between modes of supply as firms circumvent the discipline by delivering the service via a different mode. As for the question of investment incentives, the relationship with existing GATS obligations pertaining to commercial presence, on the one hand, and the serious prejudice provision, on the other hand, suggest that not only could incentives be addressed incrementally but that new multilateral rules in this area could represent a useful complement to existing disciplines.

Government Procurement

Services are often the largest category of purchases by governments. This is increasingly so in countries that have been pursuing outsourcing and contracting strategies (Hoekman and Mavroidis 1997).[5] At present, comparable and disaggregated data on procurement of services are not available on a cross-country basis. In particular, data on expenditures by subcentral government entities are not comprehensive. Little is known regarding the policy stance taken toward procurement of services. Many countries maintain procurement regimes that afford various price and nonprice preferences to national suppliers, but in most cases there are no data on the extent to which such provisions are truly binding—for instance, with regard to local affiliates of foreign firms. Often, the latter firms will be treated as "domestic," so that the effect of discrimination may be minimal as long as establishment (or FDI) is the preferred mode of supply.

Services Procurement in Developing Countries

Developing country markets for services procurement are generally smaller than those of high-

income countries, not only in absolute size but also in relation to purchases of goods. Most developing economies also possess fewer national suppliers than industrial nations, reducing the scope for discriminating in favor of domestic industries. It also bears recalling that many expenditures by developing country governments are financed through official development assistance funds, both bilateral and multilateral. Official bilateral development aid is usually tied to procurement from the donor country, and recipient countries cannot subject purchases using such finance to international competition (Hoekman 1998b).

The economic effects of procurement discrimination will depend importantly on whether the products that are purchased are tradable. In the case of services procurement, many products will typically not be tradable. When trade is not feasible, a government's FDI policy stance becomes a key determinant of the effect of its discriminatory procurement policies. Indeed, problems of asymmetric information and monitoring costs often imply that governments will prefer to source from local firms, increasing the incentives for foreign firms to contest procurement markets through FDI. The intangible nature of many services implies that asymmetries of information are likely to influence the nature of contracting, increasing the likelihood of de facto discrimination, as purchasers often use the implicit promise of a long-term relationship to induce suppliers to deliver high-quality services in a timely fashion.

From a WTO perspective, two important issues flow from the following considerations: first, whether there are barriers to entry for prospective services suppliers through commercial presence, and, second, how entities decide who qualifies as a "local" bidder (using rules of origin in procurement agreements). An important determinant of the effect of a government's procurement practices will also derive from the host government's competition policy, the ambit and enforcement of which can determine whether the presence of a small number of suppliers is the result of artificial barriers to entry.

Policy and Negotiating Implications

In the context of ongoing services negotiations, the question arises whether existing stand-alone disciplines (the GPA, described in Chapter 40) should be incorporated into the GATS or whether a more general approach covering both goods and services is preferable. Stated differently, can a robust case be made for embedding disciplines on government procurement in the GATS? Disingenuous as the question may seem in the light of the GATS negotiating mandate to do precisely that, some of the above considerations begin to explain the skepticism that a number of experts have voiced regarding the desirability of such disciplines (Bosworth 2000; Evenett and Hoekman 2000). There are good grounds for believing that the domestic and foreign welfare effects of discriminatory procurement regimes may well be negligible and of a transient nature to the extent that domestic markets remain contestable. Commercial presence is typically the preferred route for contesting services procurement markets, in light of the natural advantages that flow from local establishment (Hoekman 1998b). For this reason a host country's foreign investment regime assumes crucial importance in maximizing the economic efficiency and domestic welfare gains from an open procurement regime.

Since the economic damage inflicted by discriminatory procurement policies depends on the contestability of markets, the optimal policy response should be to encourage open and competitive markets, promote investment regime liberalization, and vigorously enforce competition policy. Such a three-pronged policy course is one that many, although not all, countries can pursue unilaterally.[6] Priority attention should thus be given to the removal of barriers to entry and presence in markets. In negotiating terms, WTO members might be well advised to deploy greater efforts in enhancing market access and national treatment commitments under the GATS, particularly as regards mode 3 (commercial presence) than in developing GATS-specific disciplines on government procurement. They may also usefully think of the best ways of addressing investment-related matters more broadly in the WTO or of enhancing the "investment friendliness" of the GATS (Sauvé and Wilkie 2000).

Although trade and investment liberalization and an activist competition policy may ultimately obviate the need for multilateral procurement disciplines applicable to both goods and services, it is important to pay attention to the need to promote transparency in procurement as a means of reducing the scope for corruption and rent-seeking. This is, in fact, the approach that is currently being pursued by WTO members, suggesting once again that separate disciplines on government procurement of services in the GATS may well be of limited value and indeed perhaps unnecessary.

Conclusion

It is generally believed that the art of creating trade policy strikes a balance between "what policy makers practice and what economists preach" (Tharakan 1995). This is certainly true when considering the appropriateness of an emergency safeguard measure and of subsidy disciplines in services trade. The question of an ESM in services trade has been on the agenda for several years now. The debate has evolved but still appears somewhat elusive, as is reflected in the decision by GATS members to extend for a third time, to March 15, 2002, the deadline for completing negotiations on an ESM. The desirability of an ESM remains very much an open question, given the state of our knowledge of services trade. The test of "unforeseen circumstances" that is instrumental to the consideration of an ESM remains fragile simply because it is difficult to understand how it can be made operational via objective tests. Even if the desirability is accepted, one must consider the feasibility when it is apparent that there are several hurdles to overcome: modes of delivery, particularly commercial presence; the impact of technology; and the general paucity of the statistical information required for credible injury determinations—let alone the economics and the diversity of trade interests.

The chapter has reviewed, without advocating any particular course of action, the various options confronting the negotiating community. Still, the clear political expectation on the part of many developing countries that something concrete must arise from the current discussions suggests it is likely that the GATS will feature some form of ESM in future, even though the ultimate substantive provisions and operational modalities of such an instrument remain to be determined. We have outlined here possible proposals for a GATS ESM, ranging from a full-blown, GATT-like, instrument to a more cautious approach of experimentation in the financial services sector with a view to subsequent generalization.

The question of subsidy disciplines has not given rise to the same degree of debate and consideration as the question of safeguards. We have suggested that a more thorough identification phase is needed to determine the extent to which subsidies exist in services industries and result in adverse trade or investment effects. As is the case for safeguards, the feasibility of subsidy disciplines will need to factor in the special features of services trade and investment. Although the SCM agreement could provide some guidance, it is not a panacea. In particular, consideration of a countervailing mechanism would appear undesirable, from both a policy and a conceptual standpoint. The question of export subsidies and investment incentives, particularly in relation to the existing GATS obligations on commercial presence, might deserve further consideration.

Procurement regimes for services, even if they explicitly discriminate against foreign suppliers, are unlikely to have major repercussions for domestic or foreign welfare so long as markets are contestable. The priority issue from a developing country perspective may therefore lie more in removing barriers to access (that is, to trade) and to presence (investment) in goods and services markets and in enforcing domestic competition laws than in developing a GATS-anchored set of procurement disciplines. Even in the narrower confines of services trade, greatly expanding the market access and national treatment commitments under the GATS may largely obviate the need for a multilateral rule-making response. Moreover, market access is a precondition for foreign firms to contest procurement markets. If they are not permitted to access the market—which, in a procurement context practice, typically means establishing a commercial presence—procurement regimes and possible multilateral disciplines may well be of little consequence.

This is not to say there is no value in agreeing on any multilateral disciplines on procurement. There are significant potential gains from disciplines which ensure that procurement mechanisms become more transparent, thereby reducing the scope for corruption and rent-seeking. Even though procurement discrimination may have little impact on the efficiency of resource allocation in the long run, corruption and rent-seeking that strive to influence the allocation of procurement contracts are costly and inimical to the process of sustainable development. Any procurement disciplines that relate to process and transparency should be horizontal or across the board, as there is no compelling reason to treat procurement of services differently from procurement of goods (Hoekman and Mavroidis 1997). This latter consideration suggests yet another argument for resisting efforts to pigeonhole procurement disciplines under the GATS (all the more so because the GPA already covers services transactions, albeit on a plurilateral basis). Stronger returns on scarce negotiating efforts are likely to arise from ongoing attempts to agree on rules for transparency in public purchasing (Evenett and Hoekman 2000).

Notes

1 One could, however, argue that the use of an economic needs test represents a form of safeguard measure, since it relates directly to the capacity of the host country to absorb the additional entry of foreign personnel.

2 Examples are found in the schedules of Canada, the European Union, Japan, and the United States, among others.

3 It is also debatable whether it would be advisable to even contemplate a countervailing duty mechanism for services trade. Countervailing implies the use of a unilateral remedy to try to resolve what is inherently a bilateral or multilateral issue; at least two governments are involved, the one providing the subsidy and the complaining party.

4 An example of the latter can be found in the Illustrative List of prohibited export subsidies annexed to the SCM Agreement, which makes reference to transport and freight charges, as well as to the provision by governments of services more generally.

5 The analysis that follows draws on Hoekman (1998b) and Evenett and Hoekman (2000).

6 To date, only 87 of the WTO's 140 member governments possess a competition regime.

known as reservations or nonconforming measures) to either principle may be taken for services sectors on either a temporary or a permanent basis. These exceptions should be specified at the federal, state, or provincial level either at the time the agreement comes into force or within a specified period thereafter, and they are set out in the lists of reservations to a given agreement.

Rules and Disciplines

This section describes the approaches to services trade of Western Hemisphere subregional integration agreements in seven areas: domestic regulation, recognition, quantitative restrictions, denial of benefits, monopoly disciplines, general safeguards, and modification of schedules.

Domestic Regulation. According to the MERCO-SUR Protocol of Montevideo, national measures relating to qualification requirements and procedures, technical standards, and licensing requirements must be based on objective and transparent criteria and must not be more trade restrictive than is necessary to ensure the quality of the service (among other requirements). This is similar to the provisions of Article VI of the GATS. Neither NAFTA nor the NAFTA-type agreements contain an article on domestic regulation per se in their chapters on trade in services. Rather, the equivalent of the MERCOSUR discipline is contained in a more narrowly focused article related to the licensing and certification of professionals. In addition, the scope of the disciplines on domestic regulation in the services chapter of NAFTA-type agreements is also narrower, applying only to the cross-border supply of a service rather than to the supply of a service, as is the case with MERCOSUR and the GATS.[2] They do, however, contain separate chapters on technical standards covering goods and services and competition policy. Similarly, the Andean Community agreement on services does not contain disciplines on domestic regulation as such, but it partially addresses the issue through an article that binds members not to establish new measures that would increase the degree of nonconformity or would fail to comply with the liberalizing commitments contained in the agreement.

Recognition. All Western Hemisphere agreements encourage, but do not mandate, the recognition of the education, licenses, or certifications of providers of professional services (subject to exceptions). This stands in contrast to the GATS, which is neutral toward recognition. (That is, the GATS authorizes recognition but does not encourage or mandate it.) All the subregional agreements in the Western Hemisphere also contain an obligation to develop a generic blueprint aimed at defining procedures for assisting services professions to achieve mutual recognition of licenses and certifications. The encouragement of recognition agreements under Andean Community Decision 439 is somewhat overridden by the strong disciplines for moving toward harmonization of basic regulatory structures among members.

Quantitative Restrictions. All the subregional agreements covering services contain an article on nondiscriminatory quantitative restrictions, but the focus of the agreements differs. The MERCOSUR agreement prohibits the introduction of new nondiscriminatory quantitative measures in any scheduled commitment or sector. This prohibition mirrors a similar requirement of the GATS. The approach adopted in NAFTA and the NAFTA-type agreements requires a listing of quantitative restrictions on services in annexes, separating those that are discriminatory from those that are not, with subsequent notification to other parties to a given agreement of any new nondiscriminatory quantitative restriction that a party may adopt. To promote further liberalization, these top-down agreements request the parties to consult periodically with each other and to endeavor to negotiate the liberalization or removal of such restrictions.

Denial of Benefits. The GATS allows a member to deny the benefits of the agreement to the supply of a service and to a services supplier from or in the territory of a nonmember of the WTO. Under the WTO, a services supplier that is a juridical person is defined as any legal entity subject to majority ownership, effective control, and affiliation with another person. All subregional agreements in the hemisphere (with the exception of MERCOSUR) go further than the GATS, defining a services supplier not only as a legal entity under majority ownership or effective control but also as one that must conduct substantial business activities or operations in the territory of any of the member countries in order to benefit from a given agreement.

Monopoly Disciplines. These disciplines aim to ensure that monopoly suppliers do not abuse their market position or act in a way inconsistent with the specific commitments undertaken by countries in the context of specific agreements. In the Western Hemisphere some agreements contain disciplines on monopoly service providers and others do not. NAFTA, the Group of Three, and several of the bilateral agreements set out disciplines on monopoly practices with respect to both goods and services and extend those disciplines to state-owned enterprises as well. The agreement between the Dominican Republic and CARICOM not only contains a provision on monopoly and exclusive services suppliers but also envisages the future elaboration of a provision on anticompetitive business practices. The Andean Community has a separate agreement on competition (Decision 285), as does CARICOM (Protocol VIII). The other agreements in the hemisphere neither contain nor envisage provisions on competition, although MERCOSUR members are in the process of developing separate protocols on competition policy.

General Safeguards. In the Western Hemisphere only the CARICOM agreement includes an operational safeguard article at the time of writing. Several of the subregional agreements, including NAFTA and MERCOSUR, do not contain a general safeguard article for services trade.[3] Other agreements specify that general safeguards may be applied once future disciplines are developed on the subject, presumably when those being discussed at the unilateral level are finalized.

Government Procurement. Because of the large number of contracts tendered, government procurement is an important component of market access in services. At the subregional level, NAFTA broke new ground by including government procurement of services within the scope of the chapter on government procurement, requiring all federal agencies and several state enterprises to open public contracts to services providers in the three NAFTA member countries (under a positive list approach for entity coverage and a negative list approach for services coverage). Similar provisions are included in the Group of Three and in certain of the bilateral free trade agreements. The Andean Community agreement on services includes government procurement within its scope of application, although

it establishes no disciplines. If a separate instrument is not finalized before January 2002, members will be required to apply the national treatment principle for government procurement to the services sector. The MERCOSUR protocol does not include government procurement within its scope, but negotiations to develop a separate instrument in this area are in progress.

Modification of Schedules. Modification of national schedules is possible under the MERCOSUR agreement, subject to conditions similar to those set out in the GATS, which allows its members to modify or withdraw a commitment contained in their services schedules after a period of three years, subject to negotiating appropriate compensation. This is not the case for any of the top-down or NAFTA-type agreements because they do not contain schedules of commitments.

Investment

An important difference between the approaches to services liberalization taken by countries in the Western Hemisphere relates to the interplay between services and investment. MERCOSUR members, following the GATS approach, incorporated investment in services as one of the four modes of service delivery (mode 3, commercial presence). At the same time, MERCOSUR members have agreed to separate protocols on investment.[4] In contrast, NAFTA and the NAFTA-type agreements (with the exception of the Chile–Central America agreement) set out investment rules and disciplines for both goods and services in a separate chapter. These agreements guarantee the free entry of investments from other parties, albeit with country-specific reservations. CARICOM includes commercial presence as an integral part of the agreement. The Andean Community includes commercial presence as part of its services agreement but also has a separate agreement on investment (Decision 291).

Market Access

Because services do not face trade barriers in the form of border tariffs or taxes, countries restrict market access for services providers through discriminatory treatment contained in laws, decrees, and national regulations. Thus, the liberalization of trade in services implies modifications of national

Table 33.1 Specific Services Sectors Highlighted in the Subregional Integration Agreements of the Americas

Agreement	Trade in services	Temporary entry of business persons	Professional services	Telecommuni-cations	Financial services	Air transport	Land transport
MERCOSUR	Protocol of Montevideo	Annex to the protocol	n.a.	n.a.	Annex to the protocol	Annex to the protocol	Annex to the protocol
Andean Community	Decision 439	n.a.	n.a.	Decision 462	n.a.	n.a.	n.a.
CARICOM	Protocol II	n.a.	1995 and 1996 policy decisions[a]	n.a.	n.a.	Multilateral agreement[b]	n.a.
NAFTA	Chapter 12	Chapter 16	Annex to Chapter 12	Chapter 13	Chapter 14	n.a.	Annex to Chapter 12
Group of Three	Chapter 10	Chapter 13	Annex to Chapter 10	Chapter 11	Chapter 12	Annex to Chapter 10	n.a.
Bolivia-Mexico	Chapter 9	Chapter 11	Annex to Chapter 9	Chapter 10	Chapter 12	n.a.	n.a.
Costa Rica-Mexico	Chapter 9	Chapter 10	Annex to Chapter 9	n.a.	n.a.	n.a.	n.a.
Canada-Chile	Chapter H	Chapter K	Annex to Chapter H	Chapter I	n.a.	n.a.	n.a.
Chile-Mexico	Chapter 10	Chapter 13	Annex to Chapter 10	Chapter 12	n.a.	Chapter 11	n.a.
Mexico-Nicaragua	Chapter 10	Chapter 12	Annex to Chapter 10	Chapter 11	Chapter 13	n.a.	Annex to Chapter 10
Central America–Dominican Republic	Chapter 10	Chapter 11	Annex to Chapter 10	n.a.	n.a.	n.a.	n.a.
CARICOM–Dominican Republic	Annex II	Annex on temporary entry of business persons	Future	n.a.	n.a.	n.a.	n.a.
Chile–Central America	Chapter 11	Chapter 14	Annex to Chapter 11	Chapter 13	n.a.	Chapter 12	n.a.
Mexico–Northern Triangle	Chapter 10	Chapter 13	Annex to Chapter 10	Chapter 12	Chapter 11	n.a.	Annex to Chapter 10

n.a. Not applicable.
a. These decisions allow for the free movement among CARICOM countries of skilled persons who have university degrees, as well as of artists, sports persons, musicians, and media workers.
b. The CARICOM Multilateral Air Services agreement governs the operation of air services within the Caribbean Community.

33.1 Matrix of Possible Elements in Services Trade Agreements

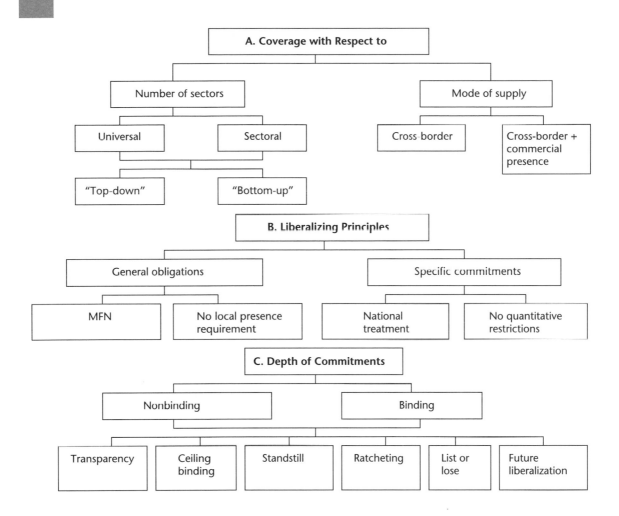

other members immediately and unconditionally. Many countries accord preferential treatment to some of their commercial partners in certain sectors, such as transport, telecommunications, recognition of professional qualifications, and other services. Exemptions to the MFN requirement may be included within the provisions of the agreement. However, a strong commitment to comply with this principle will reduce discriminatory treatment in international trade and will concurrently strengthen transparency in trade.[6]

- *No local presence requirement.* Many countries require a local presence (that is, an established trade presence) as a condition for foreign individuals or juridical persons wishing to provide services within their territory. This is usually the case with services that require close supervision to guarantee better consumer protection. This requirement may hinder international trade

because it may impose higher costs on foreign services suppliers who are not allowed to use the other modes of supply. Thus, allowing services providers to choose their preferred mode of supply can be expected to lower their costs and stimulate trade.

- *National treatment.* This principle stipulates that services and services providers from another country be accorded treatment no less favorable than that accorded to like services and services providers of national origin. Violations of the national treatment principle in the area of trade in services include a wide variety of situations ranging from nationality or permanent residence requirements to discriminatory practices with regard to fiscal measures, access to local credit and foreign exchange, limitations of the type of services that may be rendered by foreign suppliers, and many more.

- *No quantitative nondiscriminatory restrictions.* Technical considerations or market size may induce governments to establish quantitative nondiscriminatory restrictions on the rendering of given services. Such is the case in the allocation of radio and television frequencies, the number of banks allowed to operate in a given market, or the number of telecommunications companies authorized to provide cellular and basic telephony services in a given region within the country. These restrictions may also be associated with unfair business practices that may limit competition and allow for openly discriminatory actions in favor of a limited number of suppliers. Technology and other technical considerations permitting, a gradual elimination of these measures is a prerequisite for full liberalization of trade in services.

Depth of Commitments

The depth of the commitments undertaken in a trade agreement on services may vary substantially. An important determinant of the depth of commitments is the extent to which an agreement is binding. Most provisions in the GATS and NAFTA are binding, but cooperation groupings such as the Asia-Pacific Economic Cooperation (APEC) are based on voluntary, unilateral, and nonbinding commitments.

Members to an agreement have at their disposal several instruments for achieving different levels of commitments. The most important of these are presented below (organized from lower to higher levels of commitment).

Transparency. Transparency is normally the most basic or minimal level of commitment within a services trade agreement. It requires all members to the agreement to either directly inform the other parties of, or to set up national "inquiry points" to facilitate access to, all existing measures, at the level of the central or federal government and of state, provincial, or local governments, that may affect trade in services with respect to the disciplines developed for purposes of liberalization.

Lack of transparency in the design and enforcement of regulations constitutes one of the main impediments to services trade. Foreign investors, particularly those that are seeking to establish a commercial presence in the domestic market, are unlikely to commit resources in countries where it is unclear how the design and enforcement of regulation will affect their business activities.

Ceiling Binding. A long-established practice in merchandise trade agreements, the setting of a ceiling binding is also used for the adoption of commitments in trade in services. For instance, in the GATS schedule of commitments, countries may set up or indicate conditions and limitations on market access and national treatment that are not part of the existing legal or regulatory measures within the respective country. An example of such binding could involve establishing maximum screening quotas for foreign audiovisual programs, expressed as a cap on the daily percentage of programs, where the country involved reserves the freedom to operate below the quota.

The practice of binding above the regulatory status quo introduces a significant degree of uncertainty into foreign services providers' decisions to contest a foreign market through cross-border trade or commercial presence. Governments engage in this practice because it provides them not only with the flexibility to adjust their regulatory frameworks in the event of unforeseen circumstances (such as financial crises) but also with significant negotiating coinage in future services negotiations.

"Freeze" or "Standstill" on Existing Nonconforming Measures. This commitment, known as a "grandfather" clause, involves freezing the existing regime and measures up to a given date and undertaking a commitment not to make such measures more nonconforming in the future. It is used in agreements on trade in goods and in some agreements on trade in services (as in NAFTA, at the federal and provincial levels, and in the GATS with regard to MFN).

Ratcheting. In addition to a commitment to freeze existing measures, a moving floor of commitments can be established. Such a mechanism prevents countries from backsliding with respect to any unilateral liberalization implemented after the effective date of the freeze. If a given sector has been liberalized after the freeze date, a country that is party to the agreement cannot revert to a less liberal state for trade in the respective sector. This type of commitment, present in NAFTA-type agreements at the federal and provincial levels, is likely to have a positive effect on trade and investment in the member countries adopting it, as it signals to foreign services providers the countries' commitment not to introduce sudden regulatory changes that reverse previous liberalization initiatives.

"List or Lose." This type of commitment supplements the transparency commitment and speeds the process of liberalization. In the context of a negative list, or top-down, approach, the parties undertake to list all nonconforming measures to the agreed provisions of the agreement. Failure to include any nonconforming measure in the list is understood to eliminate the measure in question with respect to the other parties to the agreement. This is the approach adopted by NAFTA members with regard to the existing nonconforming measures at the federal or national level. Such an approach, however, was not implemented at the state or provincial level for those same countries.

Future Liberalization. This type of commitment involves establishing procedures and deadlines for advancing toward full liberalization of services trade among member countries.

Conclusion

The matrix developed above and set out schematically in Figure 33.1 is a highly simplified summary of the main components of a services trade agreement. In practice, the basic provisions presented in the figure are supplemented by additional disciplines in those areas, as discussed in the first part of this chapter: government procurement, domestic regulation and mutual recognition, subsidies, safeguards, business practices, and procedures for liberalizing the transit of business persons, among others.

On the basis of the three-tiered framework developed in this chapter, services negotiators might develop a menu of options regarding the liberalization of services trade and consider the pros and cons of each option. Ideally, a country involved in a negotiation on services trade would select elements affecting coverage, liberalizing principles, and depth of commitments so as to maximize the net benefits it expects to derive from an eventual agreement on services trade. The final combination that emerges from a negotiation will depend on the specific commercial interests of all the participating countries and their individual views on the advantages that more open and liberalized service markets can afford. A customized method of negotiation can thus be designed, and a series of commitments can be envisaged for countries that wish to advance in the liberalization of their services trade.

Notes

1 Under Article II of the GATS, the MFN principle can be the object of temporary exceptions with respect to specific services sectors. An annex to GATS Article II specifies the procedures under which such exemptions may be sought and the time period for such exemptions (in principle, not more than 10 years). The annex subjects MFN exemptions to periodic review and future negotiation. The GATS definition of MFN does not necessarily imply liberal or restrictive conditions of market access; it simply requires that the most favorable treatment given to any service supplier be accorded to all foreign services suppliers equally, in all sectors, and for all modes of supply. National treatment is a principle of a specific nature under GATS, resulting from the negotiating process and applying only to those sectors and modes of supply that participants incorporate specifically into their national schedules of commitments.

2 NAFTA-type agreements are structured so that the disciplines of the services chapter cover only cross-border trade in services (modes 1 and 2 of services supply, according to the GATS definition). As discussed below, commercial presence for services (mode 3 of service supply) is covered in a separate chapter on investment that encompasses disciplines relevant to both goods and services, and the movement of natural persons (mode 4 of services supply) is covered in a separate chapter on temporary entry for business persons. A business person means "a citizen of a Party who is engaged in trade in goods, the provision of services or the conduct of investment activities" (see NAFTA Article 1608).

3 The NAFTA agreement, the Group of Three, and the bilateral agreements that Chile has signed with Canada, Central America, and Mexico do not contain a general safeguard article, but they do contain an article on safeguards for balance of payments difficulties, in the case of disequilibrium in the current account.

4 Before concluding a Protocol on Services, MERCOSUR members elaborated two protocols containing comprehensive disciplines on investment: the Protocol of Colonia for the Reciprocal Promotion and Mutual Protection of Investment was signed on January 17, 1994, and the Protocol of Buenos Aires for the Promotion and Protection of Investments of Third States was signed on August 5, 1994. These two protocols, like the one on services, have not yet come into effect.

5 It should be noted that agreements on specific service sectors would not meet the conditions set out in Article V of the GATS, particularly with respect to the necessity for any preferential agreement to include "substantially all sectors," and thus probably would not be deemed compatible with WTO requirements.

6 An important question arising in the context of the MFN principle is how to treat the nexus between regional and multilateral initiatives aimed at liberalizing trade in services. Thus far, the GATS has dealt with this nexus through a very general standard—embodied in Article V—that establishes the requirements preferential trading arrangements must meet in order to be deemed consistent with the GATS. Specifically, Article V stipulates that an agreement providing for preferential, discriminatory treatment of trade in services must have "substantial sectoral coverage" (in terms of number of sectors, volume of trade, and modes of supply); provide for the elimination of "existing discriminatory measures"; and not result in "new or more discriminatory measures." The difficult questions of interpretation raised by the requirements contained in GATS Article V, coupled with the constraints on the availability of adequate data on services, make the implementation of Article V very difficult and weaken the potential contribution of regional arrangements toward the liberalization of services trade. For a detailed analysis of GATS Article V, see Stephenson (2000).

V

TECHNOLOGY AND INTELLECTUAL PROPERTY

Intellectual property has been defined as information that has economic value when put into use in the marketplace. The chapters in this part provide overviews of the economic rationales for protection of intellectual property and discuss issues and options relating to the implementation of the WTO Agreement on Trade-Related Aspects of Intellectual Property Rights (TRIPS).

International trade in goods embodying intellectual property rights (IPRs) grew steadily in the 1980s and 1990s, in part reflecting the increasing share of high-technology goods. Starting in the 1980s, a number of industrial country industries increasingly perceived inadequate enforcement of IPRs in importing countries as reducing their competitive

advantage. The United States used unilateral threats of sanctions to deal with perceived patent and copyright infringements in foreign countries and was an active proponent of multilateral disciplines in this area. Despite initial opposition by many developing countries, the WTO came to embody enforceable rules regarding ownership rights to intellectual property (IP). As IP is an element of domestic regulation, the TRIPS agreement is a prominent example of how multilateral cooperation in the trade area is being extended to include "behind-the-border" regulatory regimes—the subject of Part VI of this Handbook.

Implementation of the TRIPS agreement will involve substantial adjustments and costs for devel-

Table V.1 (continued)

Issue	Current status	Possible approaches
Patent protection for biotechnology inventions	The TRIPS agreement foresees future negotiations on the scope of patents for biotechnology inventions. No consensus, however, has emerged on the appropriate scope of protection in this sector.	Patenting rules for biotechnology inventions should ensure adequate developing country access to modern biotechnologies and should not restrict follow-on research. Revision of the TRIPS agreement in this area should be consensus-driven.
Copyright for Internet transmissions (electronic commerce)	No special TRIPS provisions exist on copyright protection for digital media. WIPO Copyright and Phonograms Treaties set out norms for protection and permit effective fair use exceptions.	Subject to retaining appropriate scope for fair use, treaties could be folded into the TRIPS agreement.
Extension of implementation deadlines	TRIPS provisions for least-developed countries come into effect in 2006. Thereafter, prolongations may be accorded upon "duly motivated requests." In Doha, LDCs were granted until 2016 to implement and enforce patents and trade secret provisions related to pharmaceuticals.	Implementation of TRIPS requirements should take into account the development implications of specific standards and be complemented by appropriate assistance.
Transfer of technology	TRIPS requires industrial countries to provide incentives for firms to transfer technology to LDCs. Doha clarifies that this is an obligation, not a best-endeavors commitment.	Industrial countries should identify and remove impediments to technology transfer and develop incentives to encourage it.

KAMAL SAGGI

34

INTERNATIONAL TECHNOLOGY TRANSFER AND ECONOMIC DEVELOPMENT

S UCCESSFUL INDUSTRIALIZATION, AND ECONOMIC DEVELOPMENT IN GENERAL, require that developing countries make the most efficient use of their scarce resources. By definition, developing countries lag behind the technology frontier and confront the issue of how best to bridge the technology gap. For this purpose, they need to rely on inflows of foreign technology, as well as indigenous research and development (R&D). But since technology can be imported, the need for domestic R&D can be questioned. Indeed, why not—following classical trade theory—simply purchase technology from those with comparative advantage in R&D?

The reason is that the prescription of specialization based on comparative advantage applies only under a stringent set of assumptions, many of which are not fulfilled in practice. For example, new technologies are rarely produced under conditions of perfect competition, and the market for technology is plagued by asymmetric information, making exchange difficult. As will be argued below, these aspects of the market for technology need to be taken into account to properly evaluate the histori-

cal policy initiatives of countries such as the Republic of Korea and Japan. Furthermore, the cumulative nature of innovation implies that technology acquisition is not a one-time decision but, rather, an ongoing process. Thus, a simple, dichotomous "make it or buy it" choice does not adequately capture the complexity of technology transfer.

A pressing concern for developing countries is that trade in technology is costly: successful exchange of technology requires investments on the part of buyers and sellers. In fact, the costs of technology transfer are themselves endogenous. An important aspect of a country's economic development is the reduction of such costs, enabling it to update its technological know-how continuously. Absorption of foreign technology can be facilitated by increasing the local stock of human capital and removing the regulatory and institutional constraints faced by entrepreneurs. As Parente and Prescott (1994) have shown, such barriers can help explain the income gap between industrial and developing countries.

In a recent paper Nelson and Pack (1999) interpret the debate about the causes of the "East Asian miracle" (the remarkable growth performance of many East Asian economies) as one between assimilationists and accumulationists. A somewhat oversimplified summary of this debate is that the latter view the accumulation of physical and human capital as both necessary and sufficient for the explosive growth of many Asian countries, whereas the assimilationists view accumulation to be only necessary and by no means sufficient. Instead, the assimila-

interestingly, productivity in domestic plants *declined* when foreign investment increased. In other words, Aitken and Harrison found evidence of negative spillovers from FDI; they suggested that foreign competition may have forced domestic firms to lower their output and thereby forgo economies of scale.[7] Nevertheless, the authors found that the net effect of FDI on the productivity of the *entire* industry was weakly positive.

Overall, several studies have cast doubt on the view that FDI generates positive spillovers for local firms. But such findings need not imply that host countries have nothing significant to gain (or must lose) from FDI. Domestic firms should be *expected* to suffer from an increase in competition; in fact, part of the benefit of inward FDI is that it can help weed out relatively inefficient domestic firms. Resources released in this process will be put to better use by foreign firms with superior technologies, by efficient new entrants (domestic and foreign), or by some other sectors of the economy. The point is that the reallocation of resources which accompanies the entry of foreign firms is a gradual process. Existing studies of spillovers may not cover a long enough period to be able to determine accurately how FDI affects turnover (entry and exit) rates. Such horizontal studies are further limited by their design, since they cannot clarify the linkages and spillovers that may result from FDI in industries *other* than the one in which FDI occurs. (See the further discussion below.)

A difficult challenge for the optimistic view regarding technology spillovers from FDI stems from the fact that under most circumstances multinationals would rather limit diffusion in the local economy. In fact, the theory of FDI is based on the idea that multinational firms are able to compete successfully with local firms precisely because they possess superior technologies, management, and marketing. Why, then, would multinationals not take concerted action to ensure that such advantages do not diffuse to local competitors? Part of the answer must be that such actions are costly and may even entail externalities between multinationals. Suppose that a costly action (such as litigation in local courts to enforce protection of intellectual property rights) can indeed help limit loss of knowledge capital for a multinational. A difficulty arises if all potential multinationals benefit from the curtailment of technology diffusion but the costs fall on only the one taking legal action. The public-

good nature of such actions suggests that developing countries hosting multinationals may indeed expect the rivalry among such firms to result in some degree of technology diffusion.

Despite weak econometric evidence regarding technology spillovers from FDI, there is strong support for the idea that FDI has a positive effect on economic growth in the host country. Using data from 46 developing countries, Balasubramanyam, Salisu, and Sapsford (1996) investigated the effect of FDI on growth. They found that the growth-enhancing effects of FDI were stronger in countries that pursued a policy of export promotion rather than import substitution, suggesting that trade policy is an important determinant of the effects of FDI. Furthermore, in countries with export-promoting trade regimes, FDI had a stronger effect on growth than did domestic investment. Both findings relate well to the results of Borensztein, de Gregorio, and Lee (1998), who found that FDI contributed *more* to domestic growth than did domestic investment. These authors, however, also found that FDI was more productive than domestic investment only if the host country had a minimum threshold stock of human capital. The latter result underscores the point that if a country's absorptive capacity remains unchanged, increased outward orientation or openness toward FDI will not necessarily lead to a higher growth rate.

In summary, although microeconometric studies have not provided much support for the hypothesis that *competitors* of multinationals enjoy spillovers from their technology transfer, studies using aggregate FDI data find that FDI contributes to growth in developing countries, even more than does domestic investment, so long as the host country has adequate absorptive capacity. We now turn to an alternative channel of technology spillovers that has not been explored by rigorous microeconometric studies.

Vertical Technology Transfer

It is useful to distinguish between technology transfer between potential competitors (horizontal technology transfer) and between suppliers and buyers (vertical technology transfer). Most of the existing literature has tended to focus on horizontal transfers and particularly on attempts to identify technology spillovers from multinational firms to local firms.

Vertical technology transfer has been documented in Asian economies, where firms from industrial countries have chosen to buy firms' output in order to sell the products under their own names (Hobday 1995). For example, companies such as Radio Shack and Texas Instruments have commissioned firms in developing countries to produce components or entire products, which are then sold under the retailer's name. Rhee, Ross-Larson, and Pursell (1984: 61), summarizing the results of extensive interviews in Korea in the late 1970s, report:

The relations between Korean firms and the foreign buyers went far beyond the negotiation and fulfillment of contracts. Almost half of the firms said they had directly benefited from the technical information foreign buyers provided: through visits to their plants by engineers or other technical staff of the foreign buyers, through visits by their engineering staff to the foreign buyers, through the provision of blueprints and specifications, through information on production techniques and on the technical specifications of competing products, and through feedback on the design, quality and technical performance of their products.

The knowledge transfers involved were multifaceted: not only manufacturing knowledge was transferred but also exact sizes, colors, labels, packing materials, and instructions to users. It has also been found that in the later 1970s many importing firms from industrial countries maintained, in Korea and in Taiwan (China), for example, very large staffs who spent considerable time with local manufacturers assisting them in meeting the importers' specifications (Keesing 1982). Motivated by this evidence, Pack and Saggi (1999) developed a model that explores the interdependence between production of manufactures in developing countries and marketing in industrial countries. In their model, a buyer from an industrial country can transfer technology to producers in a developing country in order to outsource production. Since firms in developing countries often lack the ability to successfully market their products internationally, technology leakage in the developing country market actually benefits the industrial country firm, since it increases competition among developing country suppliers. An interesting implication of their analysis is that fully integrated multinational firms may be more averse

to technology diffusion than firms that are involved in international arm's length arrangements.

More recent evidence regarding vertical technology transfer is provided by Mexico's experience with the *maquiladora* sector and the automobile industry. Mexico started the maquiladora sector as part of its Border Industrialization Program designed to attract foreign manufacturing facilities along the U.S.-Mexico border. Most maquiladoras began as subsidiaries of U.S. firms that shifted labor-intensive assembly operations to Mexico because of its low wages relative to the United States. The industry evolved over time, however, and the maquiladoras now employ sophisticated production techniques, many of them imported from the United States. In the automobile industry, one of Mexico's most dynamic sectors, FDI resulted in extensive backward linkages: within five years of initial investments by U.S. firms, there were hundreds of domestic producers of parts and accessories. U.S. firms and other multinational firms transferred technology to these Mexican suppliers: industry best practices, zero-defect procedures, production audits, and so on were introduced to domestic suppliers, improving their productivity.

With our discussion of international technology transfer in hand, we now discuss policies that have been implemented in several countries with respect to international technology transfer.

Government Policies Related to Technology Transfer

In countries that until recently emphasized import-substituting industrialization (ISI)—including most countries in Africa, Latin America, and Southeast Asia—imports embodying new products or reflecting the cost advantages of new processes were discouraged by tariffs and quotas. As a result of this protection, local producers were not compelled by competition to develop new technology. The unprofitability of exports under ISI regimes implied that firms had little interest in inventing new products or processes which would allow them to compete on world markets.

In contrast, in countries that adopted more outward-oriented development strategies, technology acquisition has been a major concern of governments. Even when domestic markets were protected in Japan, Korea, and Taiwan (China), penetration of export markets required the acquisition of knowledge about new processes and products. The greater export orientation in these economies generated a strong demand for technology that has been satisfied in several ways. Japan, Korea, and Taiwan all limited FDI while encouraging other modes of technology transfer, particularly licensing. In fact, it is often overlooked that, regardless of their orientation toward international trade, few countries practiced laissez-faire in the market for technology, and governments often discriminated between the different modes of technology transfer.

The experiences of Japan and Korea have been studied widely in order to draw policy lessons. Ozawa (1974) provides a detailed account of the role imported technology and local R&D (aimed at facilitating absorption of foreign technology) played in Japan's technological development. The Ministry of International Trade and Investment (MITI) was actively involved in Japan's acquisition of foreign technology: it limited competition between potential Japanese buyers, it restricted FDI until 1970 and never greatly liberalized it, and it encouraged the diffusion of acquired technology. MITI even insisted that foreign firms share their technology with local firms as a precondition for doing business in Japan. In contrast to their restrictive policies toward FDI, Japanese government agencies aggressively encouraged licensing of foreign technology.

A similar story can be told about Korea's experience with inflows of foreign technology. A central theme of Korean policy has certainly been the general discouragement of FDI combined with a very liberal policy toward technology licensing (Moran 1998). Furthermore, Korea encouraged its firms to export by providing them with subsidized loans conditional on export performance. One possible consequence of such policies may have been the improvement in productivity that resulted from the vertical technology transfers discussed earlier.

In contrast to Japan and Korea, the Chinese government, which has been particularly interventionist in technology transactions, has encouraged FDI in the form of joint ventures. After maintaining a closed economy for many years, China opened its doors to foreign investment in the late 1970s. It correctly views FDI not merely as a supplement to domestic investment but as a major source of new technology and a fully developed marketing capability. Yet its insistence on joint ventures may restrict foreign firms from adopting their most preferred mode of entry.

As is clear from the above discussion, several successful Asian countries enacted restrictive investment policies and sought foreign technology through licensing arrangements and joint ventures. What, if any, is the rationale behind such policies? An immediate explanation is that these policies simply reflect protectionism: large public firms or hitherto protected private firms fearing competition from multinational firms secured protection for themselves. Although that argument certainly carries weight, a benign interpretation may also be possible. A favorable case for restrictions on FDI can be made by pointing out that the market for technology is subject to many failures: it must contend with asymmetric information (sellers know more about the technology than do potential buyers) and imperfect competition (technology is usually sold after some invention has been patented). By prohibiting FDI and placing other restrictions on the conduct of foreign firms, government policies in many countries effectively weakened those firms' bargaining position. In Japan MITI actively restricted many local firms from participating as potential buyers of foreign technology to improve the bargaining position of the others.

But what explains the policy preference for joint ventures and technology licensing over FDI? Such policies may reflect a perception that licensing and joint ventures lead to more local involvement and therefore greater technology spillovers to local agents. A recent paper by Blomström and Sjöholm (1999), however, casts doubt on this viewpoint. Using plant-level data for 1991 for Indonesian establishments, the authors find that the degree of foreign ownership did not affect either the productivity of firms that received foreign equity or the extent of spillovers to the domestic sector. Yet their results are puzzling: they also find that plants with no foreign investment were less productive than those that received foreign investment. Perhaps the results suggest some sort of threshold effect: beyond a certain degree of foreign ownership, additional foreign equity may not affect productivity or spillovers.

Regarding the mode of technology transfer, several empirical studies have found that multinationals transfer technologies of new vintage through direct investment, preferring to license or transfer their older technologies via joint ventures (see Mansfield and Romeo 1980; Smarzynska 2000). Such studies cast further doubt on the preference for licensing and joint ventures over direct investment. The motivation for transferring older technologies could be strategic in that multinationals, wishing to prevent the dissipation of their technological advantages, are wary of transferring key technologies to their joint venture partners. Or it could simply be that the transactions costs of transferring new technologies via the market are higher, thus motivating internalized transfers by multinational firms. For example, asymmetric information problems are likely to be more severe for cutting-edge technologies; buyers in developing countries may have very little information about their value.

From a technology owner's perspective, FDI and arm's length arrangements such as licensing are alternative channels for extracting rents on the basis of technology; each has its advantages and disadvantages. There is, of course, no guarantee that what is perceived as an advantage by a technology owner is so viewed by developing country firms. In fact, in many instances the interests of the two parties may be diametrically opposed. For example, licensing contracts often involve many restrictions regarding exports to third markets, rights of ownership of improvements that the licensee may make to the licensed technology, the purchase of inputs produced by the licensor, and so on. Such restrictions suggest that licensors attempt to use their bargaining power to secure favorable licensing contracts. In this light, policy interventions, as in the case of Japan, might be motivated by a desire to shift the terms of licensing contracts in favor of local firms.[8]

Many countries still do not allow free entry of multinational firms and often express preferences with regard to type of FDI: entry of a soft drink giant such as Pepsi or Coca-Cola is viewed differently from entry of an automobile manufacturer such as General Motors or Ford. Unfortunately, other than the usual political-economy explanations for why certain industries are able to secure protection while others fail to do so, there is little in the literature that helps us understand such policies. Although it is possible that spillovers to the local economy are higher when FDI is drawn to particular sectors, there is little empirical evidence to support this argument. Clearly, the viewpoint that the type of FDI matters is closely related to the idea of industrial targeting in general, and the pitfalls of government attempts to correctly identify "high spillover" industries are all too well known to need further discussion here.

Despite the subtle policy interventions outlined above (many of which occurred in the past), in recent years government policies across the world have become more liberal toward foreign investment. Economic reform in many formerly communist countries has added to the list of countries vying for FDI. With the growing success of nations that utilized international trade in goods and services and in technology to facilitate their convergence toward Western levels of per capita income, government policy has become more liberal. Most countries are now eager to attract FDI, and many have concluded bilateral investment treaties (BITs) with important source countries: as of 1999, over 1,600 BITs had been negotiated, compared with about 400 at the beginning of 1990 (UNCTAD 1997). This trend amounts to an almost complete reversal of attitudes in many developing countries that had been strongly averse to permitting investments by multinational firms. Many governments have increasingly recognized that multinational firms serve as conduits of superior technology, as well as of management techniques. This realization stems from the success of countries such as Malaysia, Singapore, and Thailand that rely heavily on FDI and from a quest for the sources of their success, which include international technology transfer and local investments in infrastructure and education that facilitate absorption of technology.

Coupled with the increasing adoption of bilateral treaties is the proliferation of the use of fiscal and financial incentives in both industrial and developing countries to lure FDI. Such overly optimistic policies carry dangers of their own and may reduce welfare in host countries. A case for such policies can be made on the basis of the positive externalities from FDI, but, as noted earlier, convincing evidence on this front is missing.

Conclusion

It has become a staple of development thinking that the transfer of technology from industrial to developing countries is an important component of sustained growth. Yet the possibility of such technology transfer need not imply that domestic R&D in developing countries is redundant. Despite the usual neoclassical assumption that technology diffuses freely, a precondition for successful absorption of technology by developing countries is that they be involved not only in technology adaptation but also in some technology creation of their own.[9] In the absence of such activities, the efficient absorption of new technologies (generated at an ever-increasing pace in the industrial countries) will become progressively more difficult.

Indigenous R&D cannot take place without an adequate stock of human capital. The accumulation of human capital through the education of a country's labor force builds the general foundation needed for successful R&D. In fact, the R&D that needs encouragement during the early stages of development may be quite incremental in nature. Historical experience shows that to be innovators themselves, countries must first learn to absorb foreign technologies and adapt them to local conditions. Empirical evidence demonstrates that even pure imitation within the same country requires significant investments in R&D (Mansfield, Schwartz, and Wagner 1981). The magnitude of such investment is surely no smaller in the international context, where technological diffusion is more difficult.

There is some evidence for the view that government policy in countries such as Japan and Korea may have played a role in the countries' technological development. Since we do not have the proper counterfactual experiments, we cannot know how successful these countries might have been in the absence of government intervention. Existing evidence, however, leaves little doubt that certain fundamentals, such as adequate human capital, have to be in place before an economy can absorb foreign technologies effectively. In addition, an outward orientation—not necessarily to the extent of the use of export performance requirements—facilitates absorption of foreign technology. By contrast, as evidenced by the experience of countries that vigorously pursued import substitution, insisting on domestic technological development in isolation has proved to be a costly and ineffective development strategy.

While much of the explicit international trade in technology occurs through FDI, historical experience shows that many countries have preferred licensing and joint ventures. Empirical evidence supporting the idea that such modes of technology transfer lead to more learning by local firms is scant or completely missing. On the contrary, empirical evidence has shown that *newer* technologies are more likely to be transferred via FDI than through licensing or joint ventures.

Recently, several countries have reversed their attitude of hostility toward FDI in that they have implemented policies such as tax holidays designed to attract FDI. If the case for such policies rests on positive spillovers from FDI to domestic firms, that case may be rather weak. Several studies have failed to find positive spillovers from FDI to firms competing directly with subsidiaries of multinationals. These studies require careful interpretation, however, since FDI spillovers may be vertical rather than horizontal.

Notes

1 Of course, international technology transfer also occurs through channels that do not involve firms or governments: ideas disseminate by way of scientific and technical literature and communication between researchers. We do not discuss these channels of knowledge diffusion, since it is virtually impossible to assess their magnitude.

2 For example, empirical microeconomic studies often find low levels of total factor productivity in developing country firms even when they employ equipment identical to that in industrial countries (Pack 1987).

3 In a seminal contribution, Teece (1976) demonstrated that on average, the costs of technology transfer from a home plant to a foreign one, within the same firm, constitute 20 percent of the total investment cost of a new plant. These costs, which may be as high as 60 percent of the total cost of a project, arise from the divergent technological capabilities of the parties exchanging technology, even though they are part of the same firm.

4 Since these payments only record the *explicit sale* of technology, they provide no clue about the importance of technology transfer through FDI in relation to imitation, reverse engineering, and trade in goods.

5 Usually, technology spillovers are viewed as unintentional technology transfers. Alternatively, a firm may have the option of curtailing spillovers to other firms but simply may not find it worthwhile to do so.

6 A self-selection problem may also plague plant-level studies: the more productive plants may be the ones that attract foreign investment.

7 A recent paper by Djankov and Hoekman (2000) also found negative spillover effects of FDI for domestic firms in Czech industry.

8 An explicit recognition of the opposing interests of the two parties suggests that strategic considerations might play an important role in determining the outcomes of licensing negotiations. Strategic considerations are relevant because multinationals arise mostly in oligopolistic industries where strategic decisionmaking is essential.

9 For an extended discussion of the need for domestic capability to successfully absorb foreign technology, see Pack and Saggi (1997).

35

JAYASHREE WATAL

IMPLEMENTING THE TRIPS AGREEMENT

I NTELLECTUAL PROPERTY (IP) CAN BE LOOSELY DEFINED AS CREATIONS OF THE human mind, and intellectual property rights (IPRs) as legal rights governing the use of such creations (see Box 35.1). The Agreement on Trade-Related Aspects of Intellectual Property Rights, (TRIPS), which came into effect with the establishment of the WTO on January 1, 1995, is the most comprehensive international agreement on intellectual property to date. This is not only because of the breadth of the subject matter covered but also on account of its near-universal applicability. The TRIPS agreement must be implemented by the 144 current members (as of January 2002) of the WTO and will apply to future members. When fully implemented, the agreement will unambiguously strengthen protection of intellectual property rights almost worldwide, a feat not achieved by any single international treaty up to now.

The TRIPS agreement covers all major IPRs, including some new areas and rights not before addressed by international law or, in some cases, even by national laws of many industrial countries. Its implementation will necessitate changes in the IPR laws of all WTO members, without exception. Undoubtedly, however, the more important changes are those in the relevant laws, regulations, and procedures of developing countries, where many sectors of economic and social activity, such as agriculture, health, education, and culture may be affected. In addition, future ways of doing business may change in some of these sectors in some developing countries on account of increased awareness of and evolving attitudes toward IPRs (Watal 2000a).

Following the entry into force of the TRIPS agreement, new international IP instruments have been found to be necessary to keep up with technological developments. Some of these have been introduced by the World Intellectual Property Organization (WIPO), in particular, in relation to the Internet. In recent years, developing country members of the WTO have proposed several changes, not least to bring under the TRIPS agreement the issues of traditional knowledge and genetic resources.

Key Provisions of the TRIPS Agreement

The provisions of the TRIPS agreement can be broadly divided into five main categories: standards, enforcement, dispute settlement, general provisions and principles, and transitional arrangements.

Standards

The TRIPS Agreement sets out the minimum standards of protection to be provided by WTO mem-

BOX 35.1 AN OVERVIEW OF INTELLECTUAL PROPERTY RIGHTS

At the broadest level, intellectual property has traditionally been divided into *industrial property*—inventions and identifying marks that are useful for industry and commerce—and *artistic and literary property*, or works of culture. This distinction reflected a perception that cultural creations differed fundamentally from functional commercial inventions. The distinction has, however, been considerably blurred in the age of information technology and digital products.

There are four primary forms of industrial property rights.

1. A *patent* awards an inventor the right to prevent others from making, selling, importing, or using the protected invention without authorization for a fixed period of time within a country. In return, society requires that the application be published in sufficient detail to reveal how the technology works, thereby increasing the stock of public knowledge. The minimum period of protection required under the TRIPS agreement is 20 years from the date an application is filed. Many countries recognize *utility models* or *petty patents*, which award rights of shorter duration to small, incremental innovations requiring some investment in design and development.

2. *Rights to industrial designs* protect the aesthetic aspects of a functional article. The TRIPS agreement requires that designs be protected for a minimum period of 10 years.

3. *Trademarks* and *service marks* protect rights in a distinctive mark or name used to distinguish a product, service, or firm. Their fundamental objective is to reduce consumer search costs and eliminate consumer confusion over product quality and origin. A related device is *geographical indications*, which certify that products such as wines, spirits, and foodstuffs were made in a particular place and embody the quality or reputational characteristics of that location.

4. Artistic, musical, and literary works are protected by *copyright*, which grants exclusive rights to the particular expression of the work for a period of time, typically the life of the creator plus 50 years (in some countries such as the United States and members of the European Union, 70 years). Copyright covers only expressions rather than ideas and therefore provides thinner protection than patents. Rights extend to the reproduction, display, performance, translation, and adaptation of the works. Examples of copyrighted works include books, films, music, and computer software. The primary limitation on copyright protection stems from the fair-use doctrine, which defines the conditions under which copying for limited purposes is permitted.

The TRIPS agreement requires that computer programs be protected at least by copyright, on the principle that software code is a literary expression. Countries may vary in the degree to which reverse engineering of computer programs is permitted under the fair-use doctrine or other limitations.

Because computer programs may constitute a commercially useful process, a number of industrial countries permit firms to patent them. This policy is pushing patent protection into new areas, including methods of doing business. Another evolution is the tendency toward awarding patents for biotechnological research tools.

For some technologies, sui generis, or special, protection regimes exist. One such case is the design of integrated circuits. These are more than literary expressions but the inventive step is often minimal, suggesting a compromise between patent and copyright. Indeed, a 10-year protection term is provided and requires only originality in terms of being the product of original intellectual efforts. Another is plant breeders' rights (PBRs), which permit developers of new, distinctive, and genetically stable seed varieties to prevent others from marketing and using these varieties for a fixed term. Many countries limit these rights through exceptions permitting farmers to use seeds for subsequent replanting and researchers to use the seeds for further breeding.

Although not literally IPRs, a related area of business regulation is the definition of the bound-

BOX 35.1 (CONTINUED)

aries of protection for proprietary *trade secrets*. A production process or formula may be kept secret within the firm, but if a competitor learns the confidential information through legitimate reverse engineering, the originator has no rights to exclude its use. Unfair competition includes such activities as carrying on industrial espionage,

inducing employees to reveal trade secrets, and encouraging defection of technical employees to produce their own versions of a product based on proprietary information. Definitions of unfair competition vary considerably across countries.

Source: World Bank (2001a).

bers in each of the main areas of intellectual property. The IP areas covered are patents and the protection of plant varieties; copyright and related rights (that is, the rights of performers, producers of sound recordings, and broadcasting organizations); undisclosed information (trade secrets and test data); trademarks; geographical indications; industrial designs; and the layout designs of integrated circuits.

With the notable exception of the moral rights of authors under copyright, the substantive provisions of the main international IP conventions of the WIPO (the Paris and Berne Conventions) are incorporated by reference into the TRIPS agreement and have to be complied with. Also mentioned are the Rome Convention and the so-called Washington Treaty on Integrated Circuits. There is no mention in the TRIPS agreement of the international treaty for the protection of plant varieties, known by its French acronym, UPOV.

The main elements of protection for each IPR are generally defined in terms of the subject matter that is to be protected or that can be excluded; the preconditions for such protection; the rights accruing on protection and the permissible exceptions to those rights; and the minimum duration of protection. Generally, IPRs give creators exclusive rights over the use of their creations for a fixed duration of time. In some cases, however, IPRs are valid indefinitely, as long as the conditions for their protection continue to be met, as is true for trademarks, geographical indications, and trade secrets. In the case of plant variety protection, the TRIPS agreement only obliges, at the minimum, an "effective" sui generis (special) regime. Test data submitted for regulatory approval of new pharmaceutical or agricultural chemical products need to be protected against "unfair commercial use." Overall, these standards are generally closer to the pre-TRIPS IPR standards typ-

ically available in industrial countries than those in developing countries. Important limitations on the scope of IPRs, such as "fair use," "compulsory licenses," "government use," and other limited exceptions that are widely available under national laws, are also included in the TRIPS agreement.

Enforcement

The second main category of provisions deals with domestic procedures and remedies for the enforcement of IPRs. For the first time in international IP law, detailed provisions on civil and administrative procedures and remedies, provisional measures, special requirements related to border measures, and criminal procedures are laid out. These provisions specify the minimum procedures and remedies that must be available so that rightsholders can effectively enforce their private rights in domestic judicial, quasi-judicial, or administrative institutions, in accordance with certain general principles. The TRIPS agreement requires that procedures for the enforcement of IPRs be effective and constitute a deterrent to further infringement, but it creates no obligation to distinguish the enforcement of IPRs from the enforcement of law in general—say, by instituting a separate judicial system or through any redistribution of resources.

Dispute Settlement

The TRIPS agreement makes disputes between WTO members about compliance with the agreement's obligations subject to the WTO's dispute settlement procedures. This feature distinguishes the TRIPS agreement from previous international IP law and may, indeed, have been one of the reasons for bringing the subject of intellectual property into the Uruguay Round. It is important to note that for a period of five years, up to 2000, nonviolation-type complaints could not have been brought under the TRIPS agreement. At the Fourth Ministerial Conference of the WTO, held in Doha in November 2001, it was agreed that this period would be prolonged so that the issue of the scope and modalities of such complaints could be examined further in the TRIPS Council and a report made to the next ministerial conference.

General Provisions and Principles

The TRIPS agreement provides for certain basic principles, such as nondiscrimination between domestic and foreign IPR holders (national treatment) and among foreign IPR holders (most-favored-nation, or MFN, treatment), and it contains some general rules on acquiring and maintaining IPRs. It also permits members to adopt certain measures to meet specified policy objectives, including protection of public health and nutrition, provided that the measures are consistent with the agreement's provisions. As a minimum standards agreement, the TRIPS agreement allows members to provide more extensive protection of intellectual property if they so wish. Members are also free to determine the appropriate method of implementing the provisions of the agreement within their own legal system and practice. Thus, the TRIPS agreement does not call for global harmonization of IPR laws. More specifically, it leaves countries free to determine their own national "parallel import" policies with regard to the import of goods that are put on the market legitimately by rightsholders in another market.

Transitional Arrangements

The obligations under the TRIPS agreement apply equally to all members, but developing countries have a longer period to phase them in. Industrial country members had to comply with all of the provisions of the agreement as of January 1, 1996. For developing countries and transition economies the corresponding date of compliance was generally January 1, 2000, and for least-developed countries (LDCs) it was January 1, 2006. (At the Doha ministerial conference, the date for LDCs was extended to 2016 with respect to pharmaceutical products.) Under the agreement, the transition period can be extended only for LDCs. Special transition rules apply where a developing country does not provide, as of 1995, product patent protection for a given area of technology—for example, pharmaceuticals, chemicals, or certain biotechnological inventions. In that case, the country may postpone the formal introduction of such protection to January 2005. However, subject to certain conditions, exclusive marketing rights (EMRs) for eligible pharmaceutical and agricultural chemical product inventions must be made available by all such WTO members, with effect from January 1, 1995, for a period of five years from the date of the marketing approval, or less if the patent decision is made earlier.

Legislative Options for Implementation of the TRIPS Agreement in Developing Countries

Contrary to a widespread perception, by the time the TRIPS agreement entered into force, many developing countries already had IPR laws and procedures that met a number of their TRIPS obligations. Only in the areas of layout designs of integrated circuits, plant variety protection, test data, and, perhaps, the protection of geographical indications for wines and spirits did the agreement necessitate entirely new laws, in many developing countries and in some industrial countries. Significant changes in the existing laws of some developing countries were required with respect to patents and copyright and related rights. In general, relatively marginal adjustments were required in laws and procedures in other areas, including enforcement (other than at the border, in some cases). Many developing countries, particularly in East Asia and Latin America, implemented the TRIPS agreement, in full or in large part, before the transition periods expired. The number of WTO members that were not already providing patent protection to pharmaceutical products at the entry into force of the agreement was less than 20, and of these, only a few—notably, Egypt, India and Pakistan—are waiting until 2005 to do so.

The TRIPS agreement leaves some degree of legislative leeway in implementation. Apart from allowing WTO members to determine the best way of implementing the agreement within their own legal systems and practice, some provisions give countries room to deliberately select a legislative option. For instance, the obligation on textile designs in the TRIPS agreement can be met through industrial design law or through copyright law. In addition, the text of the TRIPS agreement is dotted with "may" provisions that are clearly optional. Finally, many terms used in the agreement are not defined: "inventions," "new," "inventive step," "microorganisms," "essentially biological," "effective," "unreasonably," and "legitimate," to mention just a few. These must be interpreted at the national level (Watal 2000a).

From this plethora of legislative options, it is possible to isolate the most important ones that are to be exercised by developing countries:

- Standards to be set on the criteria of patentability, including how far to go on biotechnological inventions in general and plant inventions in particular
- The grounds on which to allow compulsory licenses or government use of patents
- Whether to allow parallel trade
- How to implement the provisions regarding test data.

The TRIPS agreement calls for respecting the three universally recognized criteria for patentability: novelty, inventive step or nonobviousness, and industrial applicability or utility. These, and other issues relating to scope of patents, are not defined further under the agreement, and historically, different countries have followed different standards. Some countries, for example, grant patents for gene sequences with no known utility or for trivial inventions that may be excluded elsewhere. Many other countries exclude patents on scientific principles, computer software per se, and methods of doing business. Throughout the 1990s, however, standards in the United States, the European Union (EU), Japan, and Australia have converged to a large extent, particularly in the area of biotechnological inventions. Indeed, some developing countries such as the Republic of Korea and Singapore have adopted similar standards in this sector. Some developing countries, including Brazil and Argentina, have specifically excluded genes and computer programs from patent protection. On plant variety protection, many developing countries have opted to follow UPOV 1978, either fully or in conjunction with some provisions of UPOV 1991.

The TRIPS agreement does not restrict the grounds for the grant of compulsory licenses for patents. The grounds in industrial country laws, even after TRIPS implementation, range from "public interest" in Germany to "demand for that product not being met on reasonable terms" in the United Kingdom and similar provisions in Australia and New Zealand. Developing countries have tried to retain even greater flexibility in this area. Some developing countries, notably Brazil, have included the ground of "nonworking" of the patent locally. Discrimination in the enjoyment of patent rights between locally produced and imported products is, however, prohibited under the TRIPS agreement, rendering "local nonworking" controversial as a ground for compulsory licenses.[1] As noted below, the Doha ministerial conference clarified several TRIPS provisions that can be used for public health purposes, including compulsory licenses. In line with the Berne Convention, exceptions to copyright are defined broadly under the TRIPS agreement. National laws on copyright and related rights allow compulsory licenses in certain situations, contain other specific exceptions, and even permit free use as a part of the concept of fair use. Dispute settlement bodies may further define the limits to these exceptions, as recent panel reports on the EU-Canada patent dispute concerning the "Bolar" provision (WT/DS/114/R) and on the EU-U.S. copyright dispute (WT/DS/160/R) have done.[2] In both cases there were two disputed measures, and in both decisions one measure was ruled to be compatible with the TRIPS agreement and the other was found to be inconsistent.

National policies on parallel trade vary widely. The United States generally gives the rightsholder the right to prevent parallel imports of patented or copyrighted products but is more open to such imports under trademarks. Japan permits the rightsholder in the exporting jurisdiction to take steps to prohibit such parallel sales—for example, by requiring "implied consent" through the use of labels or by other means. European countries generally give the rightsholder the right to prevent parallel imports from within the EU but prohibit such imports from outside, at least in the area of trademarks. New Zealand allows parallel imports in all copyrighted products, while Australia allows them in selected products such as books, semiconductor chips, and sound recordings. It is difficult to generalize about developing countries' policies. Brazil limits the right of the rightsholder to prevent parallel imports under its industrial property laws, but Argentina clearly extends such a right. South Africa recently passed legislation to allow parallel imports of medicines, at the discretion of the health minister, and India's draft patent law would also allow parallel imports.

Test data is an area that was difficult to negotiate and that has been subject to widely varying interpretation. There are two separate obligations: to keep such data secret, and to protect the data against unfair commercial use. Some assert that the second obligation calls for market exclusivity for a certain period—say, five years—for the developer of test data for new pharmaceutical and agricultural chemical products when test data were submitted after considerable effort (Kirk 1997). Others claim that this provision allows for the use of the test data by authorities to approve subsequent equivalent products (Correa and Yusuf 1998). If the U.S.-Argentina dispute of May 2000 (WT/D/22), which is at the stage of bilateral consultations, is eventually resolved by a panel or Appellate Body, the outcome should throw more light on this issue.

Economic Implications of IPRs

IPRs can be broadly classified in two categories according to their economic function. (a) Some types of IPRs, notably patents and copyright, serve to bridge the gap between the social value and the private value of innovation. (b) Others, such as trademarks and geographical indications, merely distinguish the origin and quality of goods and services. Economists have been more fascinated by the first category.

If private innovators cannot appropriate the returns to their innovation, they will not produce the socially optimal level of innovative activity. But the social value of innovation lies in its widespread diffusion and there is thus a tradeoff between the incentives for creativity and innovation and those for diffusion (Besen and Raskind 1991). Intellectual property, however, is not the only means of appropriating the returns from innovation. Several studies have shown that IPRs are particularly important for generating and protecting creativity and innovation where considerable expenditure of time and resources is required to generate products or processes that, once produced, are quick, cheap, and easy to imitate. (Pharmaceutical products, computer programs, music recordings, and films are examples.) Other industries that are less susceptible to imitation or are subject to rapidly changing technologies predominantly use lead time, trade secrets, learning advantages, and sales and service differences as the primary means of appropriability (Levin and others 1987). A broader scope of protection does not necessarily lead to greater amounts of socially beneficial innovation. It has been argued that patent protection can bring with it practices that may lead to socially wasteful patent races and duplicative research or to blocking patents. This may obstruct further innovation and thus hinder rather than stimulate technological and economic progress (Merges and Nelson 1990; Mazzoleni and Nelson 1998). Concerns have been expressed regarding cumulative research and development (Scotchmer 1991) in general and "platform" or enabling technologies (such as gene sequences and telecommunication standards) in particular. The debate has thus revolved around how to achieve a balance between rewarding current efforts at innovation and encouraging further innovation. Competition law that safeguards against anticompetitive practices has an important role in this regard.

There is a substantial and growing body of literature on the economic impact of stronger IPR protection in developing countries, as measured through empirical studies (Maskus 2000a). Unfortunately, few studies have yielded clear-cut results. Nevertheless there are indicators that stronger patent regimes:

- Could lead to increased global trade—specifically, exports from OECD countries to developing countries (Maskus and Penubarti 1995).
- Could attract more foreign direct investment (FDI) for host countries, particularly in sectors such as pharmaceuticals (Mansfield 1994).
- Could lead to increased licensing of technologies to, and possibly more local production through, FDI in developing countries (Maskus 1998).
- May lead to pharmaceutical research and development (R&D) more appropriate to the needs of developing countries—although it is too early to tell (Lanjouw and Cockburn 2000).
- Contribute to higher growth rates. Stronger patents in open economies have been shown to raise growth rates by 0.66 percent, on average (Gould and Gruben 1996). The strength of IPRs may decline as incomes increase from very low levels and then rise at the highest income levels. Trade openness and market freedom may affect this trend positively (Maskus 2000a).

On the other hand, there are studies showing that:

- Stronger IPRs may not significantly reduce the North-South technology gap, although utility models could be an important source of technical change and information diffusion (Park, 2000).
- In India prices of patentable medicines could, depending on assumptions, rise by as much as 250 percent. Compulsory licenses could significantly reduce prices, although not to prepatent levels. Price controls, applying India's present policy, could reduce patented drug prices by only about 40 percent (Watal 2000b).
- Product differentiation and the availability of substitute medicines in the therapeutic category do play an important role in reducing such price effects (Fink 2000). In India, even in the absence of patents, new drug markets are fairly concentrated, and market share has been gained through brand loyalty established by trademarks (Watal 1995).

More empirical analysis is needed on the economic implications of the policy options available to developing countries under the TRIPS agreement, such as compulsory licensing or parallel trade, to supplement recent work (Scherer and Watal 2001). Some observers have long felt that compulsory licenses at reasonable royalties do not necessarily impede technological progress or lower the rate of innovation (Scherer 1977). Yet there remains opposition, particularly by the research-based pharmaceutical industry, to the use of this policy instrument (see <www.phrma.org>), as, for example, in the case of HIV/AIDS medicines in South Africa and Thailand (see <www.cpt.org>; see also Box 36.1 in this volume). The economic case for parallel trade is less clear, and the interests of various groups of developing countries are likely to differ significantly.

There are few studies that document how changes induced specifically by the TRIPS agreement in developing countries would affect future exports, whether of generic products after patent expiry or of domestically owned IP products. Nor are existing studies on technology transfer able to distinguish clearly between increases in licensing payments stemming from higher costs and those resulting quantitative or qualitative increases. More important, there has been no empirical evidence on the relationship between stronger IPRs and the level of domestic creativity and innovation in developing countries. There is mixed descriptive evidence on the U.S. Patent and Trademark Office Website concerning the increased filing of patents by developing countries in the United States in recent years, suggesting that greater local inventive activity in some countries is coinciding with changes in patent laws or strategies. As far as major diseases are concerned, a primary challenge is to develop mechanisms for encouraging the required R&D (see Box 35.2).

Dispute Settlement to Date

The TRIPS Agreement was the outcome of difficult North-South and intra-North negotiations, reflecting strong economic interests both of the rightsowners and of those benefiting from weaker levels of protection for IPRs. This conflict of interest was partly resolved through "constructive ambiguity," with each side interpreting the agreement according to its own convenience. Interpretation of ambiguous clauses in certain ways in national laws may be one means of asserting victory in past negotiating battles—the more so as there are no official records of the negotiations and there are areas where the text is unclear and liable to differing interpretations. North-South disputes on the TRIPS agreement have only begun to surface in the WTO in many of these controversial areas, largely because developing countries had up to the end of 1999 to implement most of the provisions of the Agreement. Nevertheless, some North-South disputes already arose in the transition period. Some important ambiguities were clarified in the Doha Ministerial Declaration on the TRIPS agreement and public health, which clearly asserts members' right to use to the fullest extent the flexibility available in the TRIPS agreement.

Up to January 2002, WTO members had invoked the dispute settlement procedures 24 times, in 20 distinct cases. In the overwhelming majority of the complaints (16 of the 24), the United States was the complainant. The EC was the complainant in 6 cases, Canada in 1, and Brazil in 1. Up to 1999, there were 5 complaints against developing countries and in May 2000, 2 more were added. Of the 24 complaints, 9 (including 2 against a developing country) were settled by mutual agreement, 7 were decided by panels (3 of them at the appellate level), and the remaining 8 are pending. Three of the 8 pending complaints are more than three years old. Of the 20 distinct cases, 10 relate primarily to patents or

BOX 35.2 COMBATING DISEASE WORLDWIDE: FOSTERING THE REQUIRED R&D

A critical task facing the global economy is to develop mechanisms that encourage research aimed at developing treatments for diseases which are common in poor countries and, at the same time, achieve widespread distribution of those treatments at affordable prices. The issue has become prominent because of the severe epidemic of HIV/AIDS, in particular in Sub-Saharan Africa, South Asia, and Southeast Asia. But HIV/AIDS is not the only disease plaguing poor nations; malaria, tuberculosis, and other maladies are equally debilitating. In fact, HIV/AIDS is unusual in that it affects both rich and poor countries. Pharmaceutical firms therefore have incentives to develop HIV/AIDS medicines for sufferers in high-income economies, and what is being debated is how to transfer these medicines to poor countries. In contrast, malaria and other diseases endemic to impoverished nations are "neglected" in that they attract little research and development (R&D). For example, the World Health Organization (WHO 1996) has estimated that of the US$56 billion spent globally on medical R&D in 1994, less than 0.2 percent was spent on tuberculosis, diarrheal maladies, and pneumonia, and virtually all of this research was carried out by public agencies and military authorities. R&D on antimalarial vaccines and drugs is meager. Some research is going on under the auspices of the Multilateral Initiative on Malaria, involving the United Nations Development Programme (UNDP), the World Bank, and WHO, and by the Medicines for Malaria Venture, a public–private sector cooperative initiative. Funding for the Multilateral Initiative comes to perhaps US$3 million per year, and Medicines for Malaria is soliciting support from foundations in the hope of raising US$30 million per year. These amounts are inadequate for the job, given the costs of developing and testing new drugs.

There are two main reasons for this low rate of R&D. Most important, the low purchasing power in poor companies gives pharmaceutical companies insufficient incentives to introduce new drugs into those markets. A second reason is that in the past many developing countries did not recognize or enforce patent protection for pharmaceutical products. Regarding the latter problem, the TRIPS agreement requires that developing WTO member countries provide patents for new pharmaceutical products by 2005 at the latest (by 2016, for least-developed countries). There is concern, however, that the provision of product patents in pharmaceutical products could confer considerably greater market power on rightsholders by delaying the entry of generic competitors for new products. Then such firms might reduce sales or output in particular markets, supporting higher monopolistic prices in key medical therapies.

Considerable pressure has been exerted on pharmaceutical companies to provide drugs to poor countries at marginal production cost (or less). For example, Merck & Co. recently announced that it would cut the prices of two AIDS-controlling drugs in Africa by 40 to 55 percent, adding to sharp price cuts announced a year earlier. Abbott Laboratories offered to sell its two AIDS drugs, Norvir and Kaletra, at prices that would earn the company no profit. Many other firms, including the Bristol-Myers Squibb Co. and GlaxoSmithKline PLC, have announced similar price cuts. These research-intensive firms have three concerns about low-cost distribution programs. First, provision at marginal cost adds nothing to their ability to cover the costs of R&D. Second, while they may be willing to supply their medicines cheaply, they wish to retain the exclusive distribution rights inherent in patents. Indeed, this preference underlay the recent lawsuit by several firms against the South African government, challenging the constitutionality of its 1997 Medicine and Related Substances Control Act. Third, drug manufacturers are concerned that the availability of far cheaper medicines in poor countries could erode their ability to sustain higher prices in rich countries.

Under Article 68 of Brazil's Industrial Property Law (Law 9.279/96), foreign firms must manufacture patented drugs within Brazil before three years have elapsed from the grant of the patent. Failure to meet these "working requirements"

BOX 35.2 (CONTINUED)

could result in an order by the Brazilian authorities to local firms to manufacture generic substitutes under compulsory license—a threat that recently faced the makers of the AIDS drugs Efavirenz (Merck & Co.) and Nelfinavir (Roche). This issue was raised by the United States at the WTO, but a bilateral settlement was arrived at, and the case was withdrawn.

In economic terms, to address effectively the diseases endemic to poor countries through development of and access to new treatments requires separation of the dynamic incentives for R&D from the need for widespread distribution at low cost. Because paying for the required R&D is beyond the means of poor countries, any comprehensive solution to the problem requires significant increases in assistance from industrial countries and financial support from multilateral organizations and private donors. These monies would be used for two purposes. An immediate task would be to build effective health care delivery systems in poor countries, where health infrastructures are weak. The second task would be to provide incentives for firms to engage in R&D in new and effective vaccines and medicines. Most likely, these incentives would involve purchase by governments or international public agencies of bulk amounts of targeted drugs from manufacturers at negotiated prices and the dis-

tribution of the drugs to designated countries at low cost, while preventing backflow of cheap medicines to higher-income nations. If such negotiations are unfeasible or ineffective, it may be advisable to establish a system of royalties under which countries could acquire licenses to produce and distribute the drugs. For this system to be effective, small countries without production facilities may need to be given the right to import drugs from generic producers in third countries.

Ganslandt, Maskus, and Wong (2001) estimate the annual cost of such an international strategy at between US$8.2 billion and US$12.1 billion. While this commitment would represent a substantial portion of current aid funding (which amounted to US$84.9 billion in 1999), it would correspond to only 0.03 to 0.05 percent of the OECD's 1998 GDP. Indeed, if the US$12.1 billion were paid by the United States, the European Union, and Japan it would come to only US$13.50 per person per year. For a final perspective, the US$12.1 billion may be compared with the anticipated loss in South African GDP, if the current epidemic continues unchecked, of US$22 billion in 2010.

Source: Prepared by the volume editors, based on Ganslandt, Maskus, and Wong (2001).

EMRs (5 of these concern pharmaceuticals), 3 to copyright, 3 to trademarks, and 4 predominantly to enforcement. (See "Update of WTO Dispute Settlement Cases," available at <www.wto.org>.)

Some have suggested that retaliation by withdrawal of concessions under the TRIPS agreement could be more effective and beneficial than conventional trade retaliation (Subramanian and Watal 2000). Indeed, Ecuador's request for such retaliation against the EU in the *Bananas* dispute was recently granted by the Dispute Settlement Body after WTO arbitration (see WT/DS27/ARB/ECU, available at <www.wto.org>).

Proposals and Prospects for Reform of the TRIPS Agreement

In the preparations for the WTO ministerial meetings at Seattle in 1999 and Doha in 2001, there were more proposals for reform of the TRIPS agreement by developing countries than by the original *demandeurs*, certain industrial countries. This is a reflection of the perception by many developing countries that, in both mercantilist and real terms, they were losers from this agreement. Thus, some developing countries, backed by some important nongovernmental organizations in industrial countries, have

2000b). FDI often embodies efficiency advantages through superior technologies, management skills, and marketing. The subsequent diffusion of this knowledge into the broader economy is a complex process. Intellectual property rights could enhance that diffusion by ensuring greater contract certainty between enterprises and suppliers and by providing more protection for commercializing technologies in local markets. Furthermore, enterprises would experience stronger incentives to train managerial and technical workers because workers would feel more constrained against misappropriating trade secrets. At the same time, IPRs raise imitation costs, thereby limiting diffusion of technologies, at least temporarily. Learning by honest means could be slowed if the system raised the costs of inventing around patents. Finally, legal restrictions on defection of skilled workers would engender conflict between the objectives of training and diffusion.

That IPRs could play a positive role is suggested by Park and Ginarte (1997), who focus on the relationship among patents, investment in capital and in research and development (R&D), and growth. They found no direct correlation between patent strength and growth, but there was a strong and positive impact of patents on physical investment and on R&D spending, which in turn raised growth performance. Thus, it seems clear that IPRs and FDI work jointly to raise productivity and growth.

Turning to licensing, survey results point to the importance of IPRs in persuading enterprise managers to transfer their most advanced technologies (Mansfield 1995). There is practical evidence from China to support these arguments (Maskus, Dougherty, and Mertha 1998). When interviewed, managers of many foreign enterprises expressed great reluctance to locate R&D facilities in China, citing fear of misappropriation and patent infringement. Nearly all reported that their enterprises transfer technologies that are at least five years behind global standards or bring in technologies that will be obsolete within a few years. Foreign enterprises are also reluctant to license advanced technologies to unrelated enterprises.

Domestic Innovation

Traditionally, developing countries have established IPR systems that favor information diffusion through low-cost imitation of foreign products and technologies, in the belief that domestic invention and innovation were insufficiently developed to warrant protection. But inadequate IPRs can stifle technical change even at low levels of economic development. This is because much innovation is aimed at local markets and may suffer infringement that capitalizes on local familiarity. These investments are costly and may only be made when risks of unfair competition and trademark infringement are small. Adequate and enforceable IPRs also help reward creativity and risk-taking by new enterprises and entrepreneurs.

In the overwhelming majority of cases, invention in developing nations involves minor adaptations of existing technologies, but the cumulative effect of these small inventions can be critical for growth in knowledge and activity. Moreover, to absorb knowledge and know-how in advanced technologies requires considerable investment in such factors as process control and product quality maintenance. These investments tend to have high social returns in developing economies because they are crucial for raising productivity toward global norms (Evenson and Westphal 1997).

An example of this process is that protection for utility models, which are patents of short duration awarded to small, incremental inventions, has been shown to improve productivity in technology-follower countries. In Brazil utility models were important in permitting domestic producers to gain a significant share of the farm machinery market by adapting foreign technologies to local conditions. Utility models in the Philippines encouraged successful adaptive invention of rice threshers.

In perhaps the most systematic study, Maskus and McDaniel (1999) considered how the Japanese patent system affected postwar Japanese technical progress, as measured by increases in TFP. The system was designed to encourage incremental and adaptive innovation and diffusion of knowledge. Provisions included early disclosure of, and opposition proceedings to, patent applications; an extensive system of utility models; and narrow claim requirements in patent applications. The authors found that this system promoted the development of large numbers of utility model applications for incremental inventions, which were based in part on laid-open prior applications for invention patents. In turn, utility models had a strongly positive impact on real TFP growth over the period.

Innovation through product development and entry of new firms seems to be stifled by weak trademark protection in poor nations. A recent survey of trademark use in Lebanon provided evidence on this point (Maskus 2000c). Firms in the apparel industry wish to design clothing of high quality and style aimed at Middle Eastern markets. Attempts to do so have been frustrated by trademark infringement in Lebanon and in neighboring countries. In the food products sector, legitimate firms suffer from considerable misappropriation of their trademarks. Similar difficulties plague innovative producers in the cosmetics, pharmaceuticals, and metal products sectors. The essential point is that local product development and entry of new firms may be restrained by trademark infringement targeted largely at domestic enterprises.

Similar problems exist in China (Maskus, Dougherty, and Mertha 1998). According to anecdotal information, trademark infringement significantly and negatively affects innovative Chinese enterprises. Many examples were cited in interviews of the difficulties facing Chinese producers of their own brands of consumer goods, such as soft drinks, processed foods, and clothing. The establishment of brand recognition in China requires costly investments in marketing and distribution channels. Enterprises that achieve this recognition find their trademarks applied to counterfeit products that are of lower quality and damage the reputation of the legitimate enterprise. This situation probably has an important deterrent effect on enterprise development in China and effectively prevents interregional marketing, which would permit the attainment of economies of scale.

Copyright industries such as publishing, entertainment, and software are likely to be dominated by foreign enterprises (which can absorb temporary losses and can afford to deter infringers) and by pirate firms. Thus, lower-quality copies are widely and cheaply available, but the economy's domestic cultural and technological development is slowed. For example, Lebanon has a small film and television industry that believes it could successfully export to neighboring economies if they had stronger copyright protection. In China the domestic software industry has grown rapidly in the area of particular business applications that do not suffer much from copying but has faced obstacles in developing program platforms. In short, domestic commercial interests in stronger copyrights have emerged and are playing a role in promoting enforcement.

Building Markets and Improving Quality

Intellectual property rights not only promote R&D and product innovation; they also encourage the development of interregional and international distribution and marketing networks that are important for achieving firm-level scale economies. Weak IPRs limit incentives for such investments because rightsowners cannot prevent their marketing outlets from debasing the quality of their products, nor can they readily deter counterfeiting of their trademarks. IPRs permit effective monitoring and enforcement of activities throughout the supply and distribution chains, giving both innovators and distributors an incentive to invest in marketing, services, and quality guarantees.

Quality assurance is critical for safeguarding the interests of consumers. Widespread sale of counterfeit products can ruin reputations achieved at considerable cost, especially for new enterprises, and the problem can be overcome only at additional cost. In principle, effective trademark enforcement both raises the average quality of products over time and provides a wider range of qualities from which consumers may choose.[1] This process is particularly important in food products, beverages, cosmetics, and medicines, where counterfeit products can be hazardous. Indeed, field research in China suggests that despite the advantages to poor consumers of having access to low-cost product knockoffs and unauthorized copies of entertainment products, these consumers are becoming resentful that market saturation by unauthorized goods diminishes the range of legitimate goods available (Maskus, Dougherty, and Mertha 1998).

In a related vein, inadequate copyrights cannot support the complex contracts that allocate rights in modern creative industries. Poor copyright enforcement is thought to be a critical factor in the inability to create music industries in Sub-Saharan Africa, despite the abundance of musical talent, for it retards the establishment of collection societies and recording facilities. In contrast, India has long had a system of effective copyright protection, which is thought by many observers to have been important in developing and protecting its successful film and software industries.

Complementary Policies

As suggested earlier, the benefits just listed are unlikely to emerge to a significant degree unless other market and policy conditions complement the intellectual property system. Thus, policymakers need to take a broad view of how to promote innovation, learning, and dynamic competition. The following collateral policy approaches are most important in securing such gains.

Human Capital Development

Perhaps the most important complementary factor is a strong commitment to education, training, and skills development. The positive role of educational attainment in economic growth is well established empirically. An economy with an abundance of skills will probably invest more in innovation and product development, but such investment is more likely where IPRs are protected.

There are other arguments as well. IPRs have stronger stimulative effects in countries with an adequate endowment of skills than in countries that are scarce in skills. One reason is that a nation with a greater supply of technical and managerial skills is more capable of successfully adapting, and managing, foreign technology to local conditions. Teece (1977, 1986) found that the costs of transferring technology decline with increases in the local supply of technical and professional workers. Moreover, strengthened IPRs reduce these transfer costs, as licensors and licensees operate in an environment of freer information flows and greater certainty (Arora 1996; Yang and Maskus 2001).

Finally, economies with stronger educational attainment and skill endowments are better able to diffuse technical information into competitive uses through honest means of discovery and competition. Nelson and Pack (1999) point to the importance of learning and technical adaptation among enterprises as critical in fostering structural change in East Asian economies. While this may have happened in an environment of permissive imitation and copying, the abundant formation of human capital was an important factor underlying the process. With the advent of stronger IPRs it becomes yet more important to build a sound basis of education and skills for competitive purposes.

Factor Market Flexibility

Tightened intellectual property protection is likely to raise pressures for structural adjustment in many economies. Counterfeit production and piracy will be reduced significantly over time by trademark and copyright enforcement. The task of reallocating people currently engaged in such activity toward legitimate business will be easier, the more flexible is the labor market in terms of internal migration and employment costs. Field evidence suggests that a significant share of counterfeit firms are able to continue producing similar goods legitimately under licensing agreements after IPRs are enforced (Maskus 2000c). In this sense, adjustment may be less difficult than anticipated. Net job losses in formerly infringing firms could, however, be significant in countries with extensive reliance on counterfeiting. Countries may wish to establish training and assistance programs for displaced workers.

It is also important to foster flexibility in the market for technical and managerial personnel, which are important conduits for learning technologies and adapting them to new uses. In doing so, due recognition of the role of appropriate nondisclosure requirements in protecting trade secrets is in order.

The issue of capital markets may be more one of scale than of flexibility. The ability of local entrepreneurs to undertake R&D and to commercialize new products is greatly lessened in an environment of limited capital. Countries may wish to liberalize restrictions on capital flows, recognizing that foreign investors may be willing to take risks on new enterprises.[2] Establishing venture capital markets may be appropriate in some circumstances. It is also advisable to move toward market allocation of investment and away from public direction of capital.

Technology Infrastructure

While IPRs constitute an important stimulus for technology acquisition and adaptation, they may be usefully supplemented by programs to promote technical change. Industrial countries and many higher-income developing countries have extensive systems of support in this area. Such programs range from public assistance for basic R&D in universities and research institutes to extension services in agricultural science. They also provide incentives for commercializing the results of public research and encouraging collaborative research ventures among private firms and between private and public enterprises for the development of new technologies and products. Such models might be usefully adopted in many developing countries if tailored to specific circumstances and implemented in a transparent and procompetitive manner. There is, however, an opportunity cost to allocating scarce budgetary resources to R&D programs. For example, the social returns in the least-developed countries would probably be small in relation to those from further improvements in primary education and in other pressing development areas.

Technology development processes could benefit in many countries from the use of incentives to bring publicly sponsored inventions to the marketplace. According to survey evidence, public research institutes in developing countries often develop useful inventions that fail to be commercialized (UNCTAD 1995b). This problem is common, for example, in China's state-run science academies (Maskus, Dougherty, and Mertha 1998). Finding mechanisms under which public agencies and private enterprises can cooperate in such commercialization could bring a number of new technologies to the market, with benefits for consumers. Intellectual property protection plays an important role in sorting out the appropriate claims to the associated economic returns.

Low levels of R&D spending may be associated with such factors as an inadequate environment for risk-taking, taxation systems that do not recognize R&D as a business cost, and weak information about technological opportunities. Policies could aim to remove such impediments. This observation would pertain especially to ensuring competitive prospects for small and medium-size enterprises, which remain the source of much innovation in both industrial and developing countries.

Interestingly, R&D activity by local enterprises is an important conditioning factor for effectively absorbing technologies transferred from abroad. For example, Dougherty (1997) found that in Chinese manufacturing enterprises, TFP growth induced by foreign licensing contracts was significantly higher where domestic enterprise partners were engaged in R&D programs of their own.

Open Market Access

Economies that are more open to trade and FDI experience a growth premium, relative to closed economies, from strengthening their IPRs (Gould and Gruben 1996). One reason is that stronger property rights create market power, which is more easily abused in economies that are not open to for-

eign competition. Thus, to strengthen IPRs while maintaining closed markets is to work at cross-purposes. For example, a patent has more power in the presence of an import quota on similar goods, which narrows consumer substitution choices. Competitive markets help limit the effective scope of IPRs to their intended function—to foster investment through competition between enterprises, but not to prevent fair entry.

There are additional reasons why IPRs and open markets are complementary. Openness improves a country's access to available international technologies, intermediate inputs, and producer services, all items that can raise domestic productivity. The evidence demonstrates that such flows are deterred by weak patent rights and trade secrets (Maskus 2000a). In addition, a critical purpose of IPRs is to encourage investment in improved product quality, which is essential for breaking into export markets. Similarly, IPRs can support marketing investments that raise product demand and permit economies of scale.

These observations support certain policy prescriptions as countries strengthen their IPRs. First, it is important to continue efforts to liberalize restrictions on trade, investment, and services. Second, while authorities should remain vigilant about the potential for licensing abuses, the common practice of inspecting all proposed licensing contracts and requiring costly modifications and disclosure clauses serves mainly to limit access to advanced technologies. Thus, it seems advisable to adopt a more open stance toward technology agreements and to replace technology-monitoring offices with reliance on competition rules.

Industrial countries stand to gain considerably from a stronger global IPR regime. In turn, they should carry out their obligations to provide liberal access to their own markets. If IPRs are to support more advanced production structures in developing countries, those countries cannot be denied the ability to compete abroad. In this context, countries adopting new regimes have a long-term interest in promoting free trade in goods in which their own emerging intellectual property advantages will support exports. For example, developing countries could build advantages in such goods as textiles and apparel, handicrafts, local cultural products, and processed foods. To ensure such gains, developing countries should push their richer counterparts to implement the agreement on phasing out the Multifibre Arrangement, to avoid the use of protectionist technical product standards, to liberalize agricultural protection, and to exercise restraint in the use of antidumping restrictions.

Competition Policy

Competition rules are used to discipline anticompetitive practices in the use of IPRs. The essence of IPRs is to define the boundaries within which an inventor enjoys exclusive rights to the use of her creation. To abuse an intellectual property right is to try to extend one's exploitation beyond the limitations established. Claims that a rightsholder has engaged in anticompetitive activity are often complex and require significant judicial and legal expertise in their interpretation.

Several developing countries and countries in transition have recently upgraded or adopted competition regimes, but this area is open to considerable reform. Article 40 of the Agreement on Trade-Related Aspects of Intellectual Property Rights (TRIPS) invites nations to consider the intimate linkages between intellectual property protection and competition policy. It is instructive to set out the major issues in order to understand the tradeoffs and complexities they pose.[3]

Regulating Monopoly Prices

The danger of monopoly pricing is rarely the focus of competition policy per se and is more often the subject of price regulation for purposes of public health. Box 36.1 provides examples of two cases in which governments have taken action. Competition policy tends to ignore the pricing decisions of firms protected by IPRs, since property rights permit firms to extract some portion of consumer surplus as the reward for innovation. Firms set prices that take account of market substitutes, which are rarely absent in a competitive economy. In that context, the proper role of policy is to ensure that products and technologies face effective competition within the relevant market.

BOX 36.1 PHARMACEUTICAL POLICIES AND THE TRIPS AGREEMENT

In response to the TRIPS agreement, South Africa and Brazil recently introduced laws bearing directly on their ability to react to price increases that may emerge from patents. The greatest spur to these attempts to limit patent rights came from a desire to procure AIDS drugs at affordable prices in order to manage an enormous health care crisis. Both laws are controversial, and the Brazilian legislation briefly became the subject of a WTO dispute.

South Africa's Medicines Law

In November 1997 South Africa enacted significant amendments to its Medicine and Related Substances Control Act that permit the health minister to revoke pharmaceutical patent rights in South Africa if the associated medicines are deemed too expensive. The amendments further empower the minister to order compulsory licensing if the patentee engages in abusive practices, defined basically as failure to sell a drug in adequate amounts to meet demand or refusal to license the product on reasonable terms so that

domestic firms may meet demand. They also permit parallel importation (imports of original or generic versions without the authorization of the South African patent holder) of drugs and allow the health minister to override regulatory decisions concerning the safety and registration of medicines. The law requires pharmacists to employ generic substitution (prescribe generic versions of patented drugs) unless the doctor or patient forbids it; sets limits on pharmacy markup rates; and bans in-kind inducements from drug manufacturers to physicians.

Although it may be a heavy dose of regulation, South Africa's law is probably consistent with the TRIPS agreement (Abbott 2000). While some legal scholars claim that patent rights necessarily extend to an ability to preclude parallel imports, the bulk of opinion is that TRIPS Article 6 provides full latitude for each country to choose its own policy on exhaustion of a patent—the point of distribution (national, regional, or international) at which the rights of an IPR holder to control further sales are exhausted. Beyond this issue, TRIPS

BOX 36.1 (CONTINUED)

Article 31 provides ample grounds under which compulsory licenses may be issued, subject to certain conditions (Watal 2001). In particular, licensing may be compelled when a prospective user has not been able to obtain a license from the patent holder on reasonable commercial terms within a reasonable period of time, so long as market-based compensation is paid. Compulsory licenses may be issued without observing even these constraints in cases of national emergency. Finally, the price-control provisions of the South African amendments do not seem to be restrained by the TRIPS agreement, which does not address domestic health regulation.

Brazil's Industrial Property Law

Law 9279, which came into force in 1997, updated most aspects of Brazil's industrial property regime to comply with the TRIPS agreement. It provides patents for pharmaceutical products as required, but it permits the issuance of compulsory licenses in cases where patent holders choose to supply the market through imports rather than through local production. That is, the law does not recognize imports as a method of meeting its requirement of "working" in the Brazilian market.

The legislation explicitly defines "failure to be worked" as "failure to manufacture or incomplete manufacture of the product" or "failure to make full use of the patented process." Although the Brazilian industrial property law refers to all patents, its most aggressive use is aimed at transferring production of AIDS drugs to domestic firms and government agencies in order to reduce their prices below those on the U.S. and European markets. Media reports indicate that this active intervention has dramatically reduced treatment costs in Brazil.* In combination with prevention programs and effective methods of distribution and clinical treatment, the country has limited AIDS mortality to far lower levels than those in Sub-Saharan Africa.

In early 2001 the United States issued a complaint at the WTO about Brazil's "working" requirements. The case was suspended shortly thereafter, in part because of pressure brought to bear on the U.S. government by advocates of inexpensive access to essential medicines for developing countries.

* "Look at Brazil," *New York Times* (January 28, 2001).
Source: World Bank (2001c).

The South African and Brazilian cases reflect widespread concern that the implementation of patent protection in poor countries could keep new medicines out of reach for those most in need. It should be noted that the TRIPS agreement cannot require that countries patent drugs that were available on the market before patents were introduced, while pharmaceutical companies may choose not to take out patents in poor economies, thereby providing room for governments to procure generic versions. Developing countries, however, were sufficiently worried about the potential impact of patents on future drugs that they pushed for some relief at the WTO ministerial meeting in Doha, Qatar, in November 2001. An important outcome of that meeting was an agreement by WTO members that the least-developed countries could put off implementing patent protection for an additional

14 years, as well as a statement that nothing in the TRIPS agreement could be used to prevent those countries from taking whatever steps are necessary to procure essential medicines at low cost in the event of medical emergencies. Thus, the Doha agreement essentially permits the least-developed countries to ignore patent rights in drugs for the foreseeable future.

Interpreting Licensing Agreements

Alleged abuses relate most often to selling practices and licensing restrictions. A vast literature exists on the competitive effects of market power created by patents, trademarks, and protected know-how (OECD 1989).[4] There are few concrete guidelines in the area because of the complicated nature of markets for information and technology. Vertical licensing agreements, for example, may ensure that distributors maintain downstream product quality, which aids competition, but tie-in sales of unrelated products to technology purchasers could extend the scope of the initial property right and harm competition.

Among the potential competitive problems that arise from the exploitation of IPRs are, first, cartelization of horizontal competitors through licensing agreements that fix prices, limit output, or divide markets. Competitors may be licensees or licensors, either in the market for the product or technology itself or in extended markets. For example, patent-pooling and cross-licensing agreements between competing licensors may reduce competition in downstream product markets that use the licensed technologies as key inputs, particularly where the agreements set prices or restrict territories and fields of use.

Competition agencies find it difficult to set rules covering such licensing agreements. Rather, the focus has been on whether an agreement could cartelize a significant share of a market, requiring a definition of "significant market" and identification of competing products and technologies. Concerns also arise over agreements that require resale price maintenance of distributors' prices. Such agreements could fix prices in ways that would not be necessary for monitoring and enforcing quality. It is evident that such risks are greater the more regulated is entry into distribution contracts—a common situation in many developing countries.

A second concern is the exclusionary effects of license agreements. Such agreements could prevent other firms from competing by raising entry barriers. For instance, tie-in sales could grant a licensor a dominant position in the market for the tied good. (Potential competitors would be forced to enter the markets for both the technology and the tied good.) Similar problems emerge where licensees are required to use only the licensor's current and future technologies. A third concern arises where licensors, either individually or in patent pools, hamper the development of competing technologies through exclusive grant-back provisions and exclusivity arrangements in future technology purchases. Again, competition policy must assess the potential anticompetitive impacts of such arrangements if there is to be intervention.

Another general class of problems relates to attempts to acquire market power by purchasing exclusive rights to competing technologies and products. Such efforts effectively are horizontal mergers, which may be analyzed in terms of their effect on current and future market concentration. A final problem is nonprice predation, in which IPRs may be used to bring bad-faith litigation and opposition proceedings in order to exclude and harass competitors. This may be particularly troublesome where potential rivals are small and new and so have insufficient resources to defend themselves against extensive litigation. Other forms of entry deterrence may be practiced as well, and the burden of competition authorities is to distinguish predation from legitimate enforcement of IPRs. For example, firms may refuse to license technologies in particular markets or to certain firms, which could be construed either as a legitimate business practice or as unfair competition.

Thus, there are complex relationships between IPRs and their potential abuse. Competition authorities must develop the capability to distinguish various forms of behavior in terms of potential impacts on static and dynamic competition. It is therefore probably advisable for countries developing competition rules to adopt the U.S. "rule of reason" approach rather than attempt to codify rules covering specific actions, as in the EU approach.

Perhaps most important is the recognition that the anticompetitive effects of licensing and sales agreements depend critically on market structure. In many developing economies entry of new competitors is made difficult by monopoly distributor laws, lack of parallel imports, general trade and investment protection, and inadequate financial markets. Thus, it is important to consider the wider relationship of business regulation to the development of stronger IPRs.

Treatment of Parallel Imports

Parallel imports are goods brought into a country without the authorization of the patent, trademark, or copyright holder after those goods were placed legitimately in circulation elsewhere. Note that these goods are legitimate copies, not pirated copies or knockoffs.

Parallel imports are regulated by the territorial exhaustion of IPRs. Under national exhaustion, rights end on first sale within a nation, but IPR owners may prevent parallel trade with other countries. Under international exhaustion, rights are exhausted on first sale anywhere, and parallel imports are permitted. A third option is regional exhaustion within a group of countries.

The TRIPS agreement recognizes, in Article 6, the prerogative of each country to set its own regulations covering parallel imports. This treatment was critical in securing the adherence to TRIPS of numerous developing countries, which maintain the right to set specific exhaustion regimes.

Exhaustion policies vary widely, even among industrial economies. With few exceptions, the European Union (EU) adopts exhaustion in all fields of intellectual property within the EU but bars parallel imports coming from outside its territory. The United States maintains a "common-control exception" in the case of parallel imports of trademarked goods. This principle permits trademark owners to block parallel imports except when both the foreign and U.S. trademarks are owned by the same entity or when the foreign and U.S. trademark owners are in a parent-subsidiary relationship. In addition, blocking parallel imports requires a demonstration that the imports are not identical in quality to original products and may cause confusion among consumers. Owners of U.S. patents and copyrights are protected from parallel imports. Australia deregulated parallel imports in copyrighted compact disks in 1998.

Few developing countries restrict parallel trade. Some nations substitute laws mandating a sole national distributor for products imported under trademark or copyright, effectively banning parallel imports. In other countries parallel imports are widely seen as a useful policing device against price collusion arising from territorial restraints, and parallel exports are viewed as a channel for penetrating foreign markets.

This wide divergence in policies toward parallel imports suggests that there is no clear answer to whether such imports are beneficial or harmful in welfare terms. Three arguments are advanced in favor of permitting parallel trade: (a) Restrictions on parallel imports amount to nontariff barriers to goods that have legitimately escaped the control of IPR owners. (b) Parallel imports could play an important policing role against abusive price discrimination and collusive behavior; because the colluding firms could be foreign, the loss to consumers from the firms' behavior is not balanced by a gain in local profits. (c) Government enforcement of territorial rights invites rent-seeking, and

it is better to rely on private enforcement of contractual exclusive territories while permitting parallel trade.

Among the arguments made in favor of controlling parallel imports is that price discrimination need not be harmful and, under certain circumstances, can raise economic well-being (Varian 1985). Banning parallel trade would result in international price discrimination, or one price set per market. By contrast, full parallel trade would force uniform pricing by the IPR holder, subject to differences in transport and marketing costs. Economies with inelastic demand would face higher prices under price discrimination than under uniform pricing, harming consumers. Countries with elastic demand—typically, developing economies—would enjoy lower prices under price discrimination. Indeed, in the presence of parallel trade, foreign rightsholders may choose not to supply such countries because local demand might be insufficient (Malueg and Schwartz 1994). Thus, restricting parallel imports could lower welfare in developing economies through higher prices and reduced product availability.

Most developing countries, however, oppose restricting parallel trade (Abbott 1998b). In part, this reflects a concern that domestic prices of pharmaceuticals could actually be higher for imported goods under price discrimination. Furthermore, many nations see opportunities for being parallel exporters and achieving export and industrial growth through that channel, seeing little likelihood that their markets will go unserved.

Whether price discrimination harms or helps particular nations depends on circumstances. Malueg and Schwartz (1994) argue for banning parallel imports on the grounds that perfect price discrimination would result in a net expansion of global output and would increase global welfare, while ensuring that goods are provided to low-price markets. Maskus and Chen (2000) point out that parallel imports may be most beneficial within a regional trade agreement, where transport costs are low, but that they could be costly otherwise. Parallel imports might also be restrained on the ground that they free-ride on the investment, marketing, and service costs of authorized distributors. If this is a serious problem, markets may suffer slower rates of product introduction.

A final point is that parallel imports could disrupt national price-control systems in pharmaceuticals

(Box 36.2). In terms of current global social policy, this issue arises most dramatically in efforts to transfer treatments for HIV/AIDS and other diseases to the least-developed nations at low prices. In the absence of restraints on parallel exports of these treatments, pharmaceutical companies are reluctant to participate. Thus, an effective system of restrictions is called for in this area.

BOX 36.2 DIFFERENTIAL PRICING

Differential pricing, also called tiered pricing or equity pricing, is a system in which prices of identical goods increase with ability to pay, usually measured by per capita income. It is discussed most frequently in the area of medical drugs and vaccines. For example, under a differential pricing scheme for HIV/AIDS drugs or malaria vaccines, prices in poor countries would be set at far lower levels than in rich countries. Differential pricing often exists within countries as well, through procurement mechanisms. Bulk purchases by governments or health care institutions can achieve considerable discounts for eligible patients in relation to prices charged on open markets to uncovered patients. (In the latter case the price differences may not be related to levels of patient income, if higher-income individuals are more likely to be included in the purchasing programs.) For differential pricing to be sustained, restraints against reselling the drugs must be in place, which is often difficult.

Differential pricing is not the same as the standard economic concept of price discrimination, under which products are priced higher (or lower) in countries or to consumers with less (or more) elastic demand. Price discrimination is a profit-maximizing strategy that should emerge naturally within segmented markets where reliable information about demand exists. Differential pricing, by contrast, reflects a conscious decision by firms and governments to organize prices for the purpose of distributing critical goods, particularly essential medicines, to poor consumers at low cost.

Price discrimination would, in principle, support a pricing structure that correlated highly with differential pricing under the following assumptions: demand becomes more inelastic as per capita income rises; demand may be perfectly revealed; firms may set prices without restraint; and markets are fully segmented. Empirical analysis, however, finds little evidence that prices of medicines are related to per capita income; indeed, they are often higher in developing than in industrial countries (Scherer and Watal 2001). Four primary factors seem to explain the fact that prices in developing nations are often higher (and prices in industrial countries lower) than might be anticipated on the basis of tiered pricing. First, many developing countries retain high tariffs and taxes on medicines, and local distribution systems may be monopolized and inefficient. Second, drug manufacturers may find it more profitable to sell low volumes of branded drugs at high prices to the relatively wealthy in developing countries than at low prices in high volumes to the poorer segments. Third, because of price controls and monopsony purchasers in higher-income economies, prices may be effectively limited there. Fourth, despite the scope for segmenting markets through transport costs, restraints on parallel imports, and differences in packaging and trademarks, countries may be effectively integrated in other ways. Specifically, reference pricing systems (under which prices in one country are controlled according to some average of prices in other countries) and concerns that consumers in high-income economies would demand similar price advantages provide an incentive for firms to refuse significant price cuts in poor countries. These processes likely form a major impediment to differential pricing, which would otherwise be in the interests of pharmaceutical companies.

To be sure, some differential pricing exists at the international level. It is well documented that this strategy works for vaccines, where large differences in per-unit prices exist between industrial countries and poor countries. Numerous pharmaceutical companies now provide antiretroviral drugs to the poorest countries at steep discounts (see Box 35.2, in this volume). To date,

BOX 36.2 (CONTINUED)

this system has relied on bilateral negotiations between particular countries and firms, so the coverage of the price cuts in poor countries remains small.

Many analysts believe that differential pricing must be at the core of international attempts to distribute medicines to the low-income countries and that mechanisms must be found to establish and sustain such pricing tiers (Maskus 2001). Accomplishing this will require action on a broad international front. A consensus must be reached on which drugs are to be included in a system of tiered pricing and which countries would qualify for steep discounts under the program. Developing countries need to relax import constraints on medicines, improve their distribution and health care systems, and establish guarantees that funds allocated for drug purchases will be managed efficiently and that program drugs will not be diverted outside targeted markets. Higher-income and middle-income developing economies need to prevent parallel imports of the program drugs, which means that extensive monitoring and labeling systems are required. Industrial countries need to forgo including

prices of program drugs in poor countries in their reference lists for price controls. Finally, agreement has to be reached on a mechanism for procuring drugs from pharmaceutical firms for cheap distribution. Most likely this would involve bulk purchasing programs, which could be carried out by procurement agencies for individual governments, groups of governments, or international organizations, in order to negotiate price cuts. Where the target drugs are patented, such purchasing programs could be complemented by a licensing regime in which royalties would be paid to the patent holder to permit local production and distribution in poor countries. These licenses would in many cases have to permit imports from licensed producers in third markets because small nations could not efficiently produce the drugs themselves.

A system of this kind could not be financed without considerable assistance from the rich countries and international development institutions. Thus, it would require a substantive increase in aid budgets, perhaps buttressed by tax incentives for firms that donate drugs to poor countries.

Facilitating Technology Transfer

Governments in many developing countries remain doubtful that the intended benefits of the TRIPS agreement, especially in terms of additional technology transfer on reasonable terms, will be forthcoming. TRIPS Articles 66 and 67 commit industrial nations to use best efforts to identify measures they could take to encourage such transfers, in particular to the least-developed countries, and to promote mechanisms to build a sound and viable technological base in the recipient countries. To date, those best efforts have been nil, generating concerns that technology exporters do not intend to employ TRIPS in a manner that would be seen as equitable by technology importers. Rather, concerns are mounting that firms owning critical technolo-

gies for the management of important public health and environmental problems could choose to use TRIPS to support highly restrictive licensing arrangements or not to license the technologies at all (Watal 2000a).

This omission could induce an effort to roll back some of the TRIPS standards. To forestall this, an important initiative for enterprises and agencies in industrial countries to undertake in the near term would be a program to make the technology transfer commitments more effective. Such a program could remove any impediments to outward transfers that persist in the industrial economies. It could also envision a fund for providing considerably more technical and financial assistance to poor countries in the implementation and administration of IPRs. Competition authorities in the industrial countries

37

PROPRIETARY PROTECTION OF GENETIC RESOURCES AND TRADITIONAL KNOWLEDGE

THE AGREEMENT ON TRADE-RELATED ASPECTS OF INTELLECTUAL PROPERTY Rights (TRIPS) brought many aspects of intellectual property (IP) into prominence in the developing world. This increased consciousness has prompted developing countries to explore the use of IP to protect the vast repositories of genetic resources that they house and to exploit the potentially significant economic benefits of these resources. A number of circumstances in the 1990s contributed to highlighting the possible importance of such protection.

First, the basic physical reality confers an advantage on developing countries. These countries, it is estimated, are home to about 90 percent of the world's genetic resources and traditional knowledge (Wilson 1992).[1] More than 90 percent of the world's research and development activity, however, takes place in the industrial countries (Sachs 2001). The picture of a gene-rich, technology-poor South and a technology-rich, gene-deficient North creates the potential for mutually beneficial bargains between the two groups.

Second, and following from the first point, the North has a strong economic and ecological interest in ensuring the preservation of genetic resources. Developments in biotechnology increase the prospects of companies in the North that are interested in better harnessing the South's gene pool. A number of research and other institutions in industrial countries have entered into contracts with developing countries for searching out genetic resources ("bioprospecting"). The best-known example is the contract signed in 1991 between Merck & Co. and Costa Rica's Instituto Nacional de Biodiversidad (INBio) under which Merck paid INBio US$1 million to provide a limited number of documented plant samples for isolation, as well as plant and insect extracts for use in the drug discovery process.[2]

Meanwhile, serious concerns have emerged about the loss of global biodiversity, which could have catastrophic consequences.[3] Although the estimates vary greatly, a consensus seems to be emerging that large-scale destruction of biodiversity is occurring, with potentially serious consequences for humankind. For example, it is estimated that the biodiversity-rich tropical rain forests and moist forests are being cleared at the rate of 1.8 percent of their area per year, which translates into the loss each year of an area of forest the size of the state of Florida (FAO 1995). Wilson (1992) estimates that deforestation is leading to a loss of about 2.7 percent of the species in these forests every decade, and with the rate of deforestation accelerating, the biodiversity loss could be enormous. A median estimate is that there are approximately 10 million species in the world, and the current extinction rate of species is about 5 percent per decade (Raven and McNeely 1998). At that rate, about 50,000 species could be lost each year, of which only 70,000 have been recognized and named, and about two-thirds of living species would be lost over the course of the 21st century. Wilson (1992: 280) has warned, "Clearly we are in the midst of one of the great extinction spasms of geological history."

In a curious inversion of the accusations of piracy of conventional forms of intellectual property rights (IPRs) leveled against developing countries in the 1980s and 1990s, the gene rich South had similar complaints against the gene-importing North. In a number of prominent incidents companies in the North turned out to be involved in the use—without remuneration—of plants or resources found in developing countries. The term "biopiracy" began to acquire resonance. In some instances the practice led to the development of a patented product, fueling the perception that developing countries were doubly disadvantaged: not only were their resources being used without remuneration, but the resulting end product came with a higher price tag attached because of the ensuing monopoly.[4]

Finally, in the preparations for the Seattle ministerial meeting of trade ministers in late 1999, a number of developing countries raised the issue of protection of traditional knowledge. Bolivia, Colombia, Ecuador, and Nicaragua specifically proposed that the Seattle conference establish a mandate for the next round of trade negotiations to (a) carry out studies, in collaboration with other relevant international organizations, in order to make recommendations on the most appropriate means of recognizing and protecting traditional knowledge as the subject matter of intellectual property rights; (b) on the basis of these recommendations, initiate negotiations with a view to establishing a multilateral legal framework that would grant effective protection to expressions and manifestations of traditional knowledge; and (c) complete this legal framework in time for its inclusion as part of the results of the current round of trade negotiations (WTO, WT/GS/W/362).[5]

This chapter addresses the following questions: What is the subject matter under discussion, and what are its potential benefits? Why do we need a mechanism for international cooperation in relation to genetic resources—or, to put it differently, what is the market failure that warrants corrective social action? What are the main considerations that should underlie a system of proprietary protection for traditional knowledge and genetic resources, and what are the practical difficulties associated with implementing a cooperative scheme? What are the main options facing developing countries in the period ahead as they consider international cooperation on this issue? What, realistically, are likely to be the economic payoffs to developing countries for their genetic resources? Finally, what future actions should developing countries be considering to realize their objectives?

The Subject Matter and Its Value

Developing countries are seeking to protect two related but distinct resources: traditional or indigenous knowledge, and genetic resources, which include seeds, endoplasm, rare animal and plant species, and parts of plants and animals. The former refers typically to practices in farming and agriculture that have been devised and refined over long periods of time and can be clearly attributed to human actions.[6] The latter, by contrast, are not usually the product of human invention or creativity but are typically found in nature. The real importance of genetic resources lies in the encoded genetic information that is proving to be valuable in developing medicines and pharmaceutical products to cure human diseases and for raising agricultural productivity.

Why is it important to protect indigenous knowledge and genetic resources? First, there is the economic benefit. Plants and other organisms are natural biochemical factories and yield many products that enhance human welfare. Leaving aside the fact that a large proportion of the world's population—in China, India, and Brazil, for example—depends on plants for medicine, the modern drug industry is founded on genetic resources. It is estimated that more than 100 drugs in international commerce are derived from plants. For instance, of the top 20 drugs sold (with a market value of US$6 billion) in the United States in 1988, 2 were taken directly from natural resources, 3 were semisynthetic, 8 were synthetics with chemical structures modeled on natural compounds, and 7 had their pharmacological activity defined as a result of

indigenous communities? Conceptually, the right should be awarded to those who have had a key role in accumulating knowledge or preserving resources. How would this be determined, given that the current state of science may not enable germ plasm to be assigned to any particular site? How are rights to be assigned if new varieties draw from a large number of sources of germ plasm?

3. How would the right be acquired? Broadly, there are two options. Under the first option, they could be acquired, as in the case of copyright, as soon as certain legal conditions are met, with minimum formalities. This approach offers administrative ease and simplicity. The second option, similar to that taken in the main areas of property rights protection, such as patents and trademarks, is to require some kind of formal registration before the right is acquired. This approach would be more complicated but does provide clarity and legal and business security. Formal registration delineates the private and public domain in a practical, clear manner.

4. There is likely to be a thorny transitional issue of what to do with traditional knowledge already in the public domain and with genetic resources already acquired under the previous regime that did not require any form of compensation.[10]

One of the main points of opposition to the grant of proprietary rights for genetic resources in industrial countries is likely to be the long-standing principle in IP law that such rights cannot be granted for things found in nature; rights are granted only for human creations or inventions. In general, the essential common prerequisite for granting proprietary protection is novelty or distinctiveness, under a doctrine of nonobviousness or inventive step (as in patents) or one of sufficient level of creativity (copyright and industrial design) or distinctive feature (trademarks). Thus, protection depends on the newness of the knowledge and information generated (Cottier 1998).[11]

Options for International Cooperation

It is clear that the protection of genetic resources will require international cooperation on a number of fronts: resource management, science, technology transfer, finance, and so on (see Reid 1998).[12] It is also generally understood that a number of dis-

parate actors—individuals, local communities, nongovernmental organizations, governments, international institutions, research centers, and pharmaceutical, agricultural, and other firms—will need to be brought together in the search for ways and means of achieving the common goal of protecting biodiversity.

The issue in a trade context is a narrower one: whether there needs to be international cooperation, possibly in the form of an international agreement such as the TRIPS agreement, to accord proprietary protection for traditional knowledge and genetic resources. Clearly, the role of such an agreement would be to complement the other vital efforts described above. Before embarking on such a path, developing countries may need to consider the options for international cooperation. There are three possible variants, which are discussed next.

Option I: Negotiation of a Full-Fledged International System of IPR Protection

The most ambitious path would be to seek a full-fledged international agreement on the protection of genetic resources. Theoretically, this is the most appealing, but there are significant practical difficulties of a legal and political nature. The legal problems, outlined above, have to do with designing a system of sui generis protection that is easy to implement. The political problems are related to the resistance to be expected from industrial countries that are reluctant to embrace any new system of protection, especially one that goes against the grain of entrenched legal precepts that see only creation, not preservation, as susceptible to proprietary protection.

Option II: Using and Strengthening the Existing International Framework

A less ambitious approach would be to work within the parameters set by the CBD and to rely on contractual arrangements between industrial country companies and developing countries to regulate access to the use of genetic resources. The advantage of this approach is its simplicity and the fact that it has precedents in practice. Its disadvantages are twofold.

First, voluntary cooperation, although welcome, cannot be guaranteed in all instances, and the terms of such cooperation will necessarily be influenced by whether prior rights to such resources exist. If these rights are internationally recognized, and if infringements are credibly punishable, the reward for maintaining the resources will be higher than it otherwise would be. In the absence of such rights, bargaining power is asymmetric, and this could skew any bioprospecting contracts in favor of the companies.

Second, and more seriously, the contract cannot bind third parties (those that are not parties to the contract). Thus, if a company in a country other than the host country makes unremunerated use of genetic resources, the owner of the resource will have no legal recourse, and biopiracy will prevail.

Moving along the spectrum of the pure contractual route, but in the direction of strengthening it, would be the suggestions made by the World Wide Fund for Nature. These would require that patent applications in the field of biotechnology (a) disclose the country of origin of biological samples used in the research leading to the invention that is the subject of the application and (b) include a statement of compliance with all national laws relating to access to genetic resources and to any bioprospecting arrangements entered into by the prospective patentee. Furthermore, countries of origin and local communities would have an opportunity to oppose the grant of a patent where there is a perception of noncompliance with national laws. One could go even further and require that the TRIPS agreement incorporate an obligation on all countries that the prospective patentee obtain the prior informed consent of the country from which genetic resources are obtained as a precondition for the grant of the patent (or at least that such consent be obtained before the commercialization of the patent).[13]

Option III: A Global Biocollection Society

Yet another form of international cooperation that is a halfway house between the pure contractual approach and the full-fledged proprietary protection route is a scheme proposed by Drahos (2000) to establish a global biocollection society (GBS), possibly under the auspices of the World Bank. Membership would be open on a voluntary basis to companies and to groups with claims to traditional knowledge and genetic resources. The GBS would act as the repository for community registers of indigenous knowledge and as the custodian of these registers, under strict obligations of confidentiality. It could also assist in negotiations between companies and groups over the use of genetic resources, set standards for such contracts, and provide a dispute resolution mechanism.

The advantage of this proposal is that it would avoid the need to negotiate an international treaty on intellectual property rights for genetic resources. It could also create an incentive for pharmaceutical companies to join because the transactions costs of dealing with the GBS would be lower than those associated with national bureaucracies administering national laws.

How Much Will the Effort Be Worth?

A key question is, what economic benefits will, realistically, flow to developing countries for the genetic resources that they possess? The initial expectations sparked by the early contracts between INBio and Merck have been to some extent belied. There is skepticism about the likely economic benefits, stemming both from theoretical considerations and from experiences with bioprospecting contracts.

Simpson, Sedjo, and Reid (1996) argue strongly that the marginal value of genetic resources is likely to be small because of the real possibility of redundancy in discoveries and because identical drugs or drugs with similar clinical properties can be isolated from different species. The number of presently untested species is high, and no one tree or genetic resource is likely to be the unique repository of the valuable code: if one tree holds the potential for an important cure, another tree that evolved in response to the same environmental stresses is likely to have similar properties.

Stone (1998) asserts that the contentiousness over the equitable sharing of the fruits of genetic resources is almost certainly disproportionate to the likely booty. Estimates of the value of an average species vary widely, from US$44.0 to US$24 million. Simpson, Sedjo, and Reid (1996) calculate that the median value of the world's top 18 biodiversity hot spots is about US$2 per hectare, although for some areas of western Ecuador it might be US$20 per hectare. Others, using a different methodology, conclude that the world's 3 billion hectares of tropical forest are worth, on average, US$0.9 to US$1.32 per hectare as pharmaceutical mines (Mendelsohn and Balick 1995). In the case of the well-publicized agreement between Merck and INBio, the contract involved the payment of a fixed sum of US$1 million plus a contingent fee—a royalty—estimated at between 2 and 3 percent of the value of any eventual discovery. There has been no real rush of pharmaceutical firms to mimic the Merck-INBio agreement, which is not known to have generated anything for Merck to date. The jury thus seems to be out on the practical value that developing countries can expect to appropriate from possessing genetic resources.

Estimates of the likely benefits will clearly have to condition developing countries' stance in any multilateral negotiations on protection of genetic resources. In any future bargaining a hard-headed assessment of the likely gains in this area should inform what developing countries are willing to give up in such areas as other IPR issues. For example, Cottier (1998) implicitly argues that industrial countries' willingness to accept developing country demands on genetic resources should in turn induce developing countries to reconsider their opposition to extending patent protection to biotechnological inventions.[14] Whether this is a bargain worth making remains to be seen, and more research on the economic value of genetic resources needs to underpin policy positions.

The Agenda for Developing Countries

Irrespective of the form that international cooperation takes, developing countries that are hosts to genetic resources have to strengthen their own legal and institutional frameworks for protecting traditional knowledge and genetic resources. (The CBD requires countries to protect biodiversity.) The first step, to enact legislation, is being undertaken in a number of countries (see <www.biodiv.org>). The next step would be to create a registration system for compiling all forms of knowledge and resources that could, in principle, be protected.

This compilation could proceed at both the national and international levels. INBio has established an elaborate biodiversity inventory—through the development and management of biological, ecological, taxonomic, and related systematic information on living species and systems found in Costa Rica (Sittenfield and Lovejoy 1998). This information lists not only the species but also where they may be collected without damaging ecosystems. India has pioneered legislation for the registration of traditional knowledge and the establishment of a National Community Gene Fund that has the goal of supporting the conservation and sustainable use of genetic resources, thereby benefiting farming and other rural communities.[15]

Developing countries must demonstrate that their actions at the national level to protect genetic resources and traditional knowledge are workable and that they do indeed lead to flows of resources to individuals and communities that serve to increase the incentives to protect these resources. This will strengthen developing countries' case for seeking to replicate internationally their systems of domestic protection.

Finally, work needs to be intensified in national and international fora, including the World Intellectual Property Organization, on resolving the difficult legal issues concerning the creation of a proprietary system for protection of traditional knowledge and genetic resources.

Notes

1 South America is reported to have the largest concentration of plant species: Colombia, Peru, and Ecuador between them have 40,000 species on just 2 percent of the Earth's surface.

2 The contract also included a contingency or royalty payment that would be triggered in the event of commercially profitable exploitation of the resources provided. There have been similar contracts between the National Cancer Institute in the United States and organizations in Madagascar, the Philippines, Tanzania, and Zimbabwe for provision of samples. INBio has also signed agreements with a major U.K. technology licensing firm, the British Technology Group, to isolate and test a compound that could potentially eliminate a nematode which plagues banana and other crops, and with Cornell University and the Bristol-Myers Squibb Co. to test and identify chemical compounds developed from insect extracts for use in treating malaria.

3 Throughout this chapter the terms "genetic resources" and "biodiversity" are used interchangeably, although the two are not formally identical. Biodiversity is a measure of the genetic variation contained within the Earth's biological resources (plants, animals, fish, bacteria, insects, and so on). It increases with the number of distinct species. Many species have critical masses or thresholds: once their population falls below a critical number, they are doomed to extinction. Biodiversity is thus not related simply to the quantity of biological resources but also to their distribution in relation to the threshold levels. Beyond these levels, additional quantities of resources contribute little to biodiversity (Heal 1998).

4 The neem tree, traditionally used in India for pest control, medical therapies, and other purposes, was the subject of a patent by a chemical company. Cottier (1998) describes the case of the collection in Kenya by Western companies of bark and leaves from the *Acacia nilotica* tree and the subsequent use of these materials in the development of patentable products.

5 The African group of countries also proposed the inclusion of this issue in the next round of trade negotiations (WT/GC/W/302).

6 Several examples of socially useful practices have been catalogued in the literature. Among them is the practice of cutting 30-to-40-day-old sorghum or calatropis plants and placing them in irrigation channels to control termite attack in light, dry soils (Gupta 1998).

7 Artemisin, the only drug effective against all strains of malaria, was discovered because the Chinese use it to treat fever. Taxol, derived from western yew, has anticancer properties. Michellamine B, a novel compound from a vine found in Cameroon, has promise as an anticancer, anti-HIV drug.

8 The ability of modern biotechnology to transfer genes across organisms renders feasible the development of a wide array of genetically engineered plants and animals that have significant economic and therapeutic value. Thus, the returns to maintaining a rich and biodiverse system are probably large because improvements in biotechnology and natural genetic information will be complements in production.

9 More than 130 countries have signed the convention. A notable exception is the United States, which had concerns about the possible dilution of traditional intellectual property rights protection as an outcome of the CBD.

The principle that genetic resources are the common heritage of humankind was a central tenet of the International Undertaking on Plant Genetic Resources and of the Food and Agriculture Commission on Plant Genetic Resources, both established in the 1980s. Under this regime, countries that restricted access to such resources were criticized, as happened in the case of Ethiopia, which in 1977 placed an embargo on the export of its coffee germ plasm. Although the intent of these initiatives was to ensure widespread availability of genetic resources for agriculture and industry, it gave the source country little benefit for its use and hence provided little incentive for conservation. These international agreements on plant genetic resources embodied the notion of farmers' rights arising from their past, present, and future efforts to conserve and improve plant genetic resources. They envisaged the right to equitable compensation for their use that would come out of a fund to which countries would

voluntarily contribute. To date, not much by way of contribution to this fund has been forthcoming.

10 The CBD grandfathers seed collections that were already in existence before 1994.

11 The one exception is in the field of undisclosed information or trade secrets, where requirement of novelty is not a precondition for obtaining protection. A common approach in the past has been for environmental nongovernmental organizations and governments of rich countries to persuade developing country governments to protect habitats, including tropical forests, that are rich in genetic resources. There has been some success—governments have established parks and preserves—but this effort has been inadequate, and the protection is haphazard (Sedjo 1992).

12 For example, the pilot phase of the Global Environment Facility provided financial support for conservation in developing countries in return for actions by them to protect biodiversity that had national and global benefits.

13 The pharmaceutical industry is increasingly involved in the transfer of chemical extracts rather than samples of plants and animals. A strict reading of the CBD suggests that the requirement of prior informed consent (in Art. 15.5) applies to genetic resources and not to chemical extracts, although the convention allows countries to take measures to manage their biological resources that would also apply to such extracts.

14 Article 27.3 of the TRIPS agreement allows countries to exclude most biotechnological inventions from patent protection. This article is currently under review. Some industrial countries are keen to see the exception narrowed, which would force developing countries to extend the scope of protection for most biotechnological inventions.

15 At the international level, a Clearing House Mechanism under the CBD and the System-wide Information Network on Genetic Resources within the centers of the Consultative Group on International Agricultural Research provide a framework for data collection and exchange of information. In principle, these networks could become nuclei for the international registration of plant genetic rights.

The underlying notion is that the community of living authors and performers should benefit from the use of works and performers of their predecessors that are no longer protected because the term of protection has expired. Such a remuneration right can be established by legislation in favor of an authors' and performers' fund administered by a foundation or nonprofit corporation. The entity should be largely managed and administered by the authors' and performers' organizations themselves. Collecting societies, where they exist, can collect the remuneration in the same way as they do for the use of protected works and performances. The money would not be distributed according to the individual distribution schemes but would be forwarded to the foundation or corporation. For developing countries, this is an attractive proposal.[6] Of course, nothing prevents the extension of this proposal to include expressions of folklore, which would then attract a similar right of remuneration.

The Digital Environment: The WIPO Copyright Treaty

The emergence of global information networks like the Internet and electronic commerce raises a number of key issues in the field of copyright:

- The use of computers requires that works be transformed from their traditional material form into digital form. Digitization has two main advantages: transmission of a digitized work occurs without any degradation (every copy is perfect), and copies of such a work can be made quickly and cheaply. Unfortunately, these advantages also mean that copyright may be infringed with ease and on a scale previously unknown.

- Material stored or made available for access on hosts or transmitted through the Internet may be the subject of copyright owned by a third party who has not consented to these activities.

- To protect their works against these first two risks, authors have often resorted to technical protection measures. These measures usually operate at one of two levels: access control and copy control.[7] They remain effective, of course, only if their unauthorized circumvention is prohibited.

- With works in digital form, it is easy to remove any rights management information. If this is done, it may become difficult to prove copyright ownership.

These issues are addressed in the WIPO Copyright Treaty (WCT), adopted on December 20, 1996, at the Diplomatic Conference on Certain Copyright and Neighboring Rights Questions under the auspices of the World Intellectual Property Organization (WIPO). The WCT confirms an author's exclusive right, in the digital environment, to reproduce his or her work in any manner or form (Agreed Statement Concerning Article 1.4).[8] It is also understood that the storage of a protected work in digital form in an electronic medium constitutes a reproduction of that work. The WCT grants an exclusive right to authors to authorize making their works available through interactive, on-demand services (Art. 8). The relevant act of exploitation is making the work available to the public: the act "commences, and is completed by providing public access to the work" (Hugenholtz 2000). For the first time in an international instrument, the WCT recognizes that in a digital environment any new rights with respect to digital uses of works would, for the rights to be effective, require the framework support of provisions dealing with technical measures of protection and electronic rights management information. To this end, the WCT obliges contracting parties to provide adequate legal protection and effective remedies against the circumvention of measures protecting the rights of authors (Art. 11), and to provide, under certain conditions, adequate remedies against the removal or alteration of electronic rights management information (Art. 12).[9]

Related Rights: Performers

Since 1961, performers of musical works have been protected within the framework of the International Convention for the Protection of Performers, Producers of Phonograms and Broadcasting Organizations (the Rome Convention). For historical reasons, this protection was weak; performers do not have exclusive rights but should merely be able to prevent certain acts from being performed in respect to their recorded performances or should be able to prevent their live performances from being recorded or broadcast. The TRIPS agreement similarly states that performers should "have the possibility of preventing" a limited number of acts (Art. 14.1).

Like the WCT, the WIPO Performers and Phonograms Treaty (WPPT) addresses issues relating to the protection of performers' rights in the digital context, and it greatly enhances their position. For the first time, it grants performers certain exclusive rights of authorization in respect to their live and recorded performances. For their live performances, performers have the exclusive right to authorize the broadcasting and communication to the public of such performances and their recording (fixation) (Art. 6). For their recorded performances, performers have the exclusive right to authorize the reproduction of these performances (Art. 7), their distribution (Art. 8), their rental (Art. 9), and their being made available so that "members of the public may access them from a place and at a time individually chosen by them" (Art. 10).[10] Performers are also entitled to remuneration for broadcasting and communication to the public of commercial recordings of their performances (Art. 15) and (another first) are given moral rights on similar terms to those extended to authors (Art. 5)—that is, paternity and integrity rights.

Developing countries seeking international protection of expressions of folklore can benefit from an important step forward in the WPPT. Unlike the Rome Convention, which limits the definition of "performers" to those who perform "literary or artistic works" (Art. 3), the WPPT extends the definition to apply also to those who perform "expressions of folklore" (Art. 2). Certain expressions of folklore, such as folk tales, folk poetry, folk songs, instrumental folk music, folk dances, and folk plays, live through performance. To the extent that these performances are protected against unauthorized recording and broadcasting and communication to the public, the expressions of folklore being performed are indirectly protected. This is a fairly efficient means for their indirect protection (Ficsor 1997).

The WPPT grants coextensive rights to the producers of sound recordings (Arts. 11–15). Obviously, they do not enjoy any moral rights in respect of their recordings. If the balance between authors (including composers), performers, and producers of sound recordings in the WCT and the WPPT is maintained and is not disturbed by the existence of "iron triangles" of the sort described above, they could be used to make multinational record companies into "partners and not predators," helping foreign direct investment, as well as domestic investment by local musicians, to contribute toward alleviating poverty.

The Crafts Industry

The importance of the crafts industry is often trivialized, but the U.S. International Trade Commission has estimated that it generates US$30 billion annually worldwide, and some analysts have estimated the amount as double that. A study commissioned by the Policy Sciences Center of the crafts industry in India, the largest such industry in the world, estimated the annual revenue of this industry at US$5.6 billion. It employs 9 million to 10 million artisans (Liebl and Roy 2000).

As in the music industry, the absence of effective enforcement of property rights creates significant potential opportunity costs for developing countries and indigenous peoples. The experience of the Kwakiutl Indians of western Canada is an excellent example (Chartrand 1996). For over a century, Kwakiutl women have knitted sweaters with a traditional thunderbird motif. In the mid-1980s two Japanese businessmen visited the Indian reservation, purchased some sweaters, and mass-produced copies for sale in Asia. Apparently, US$100 million worth of sweaters was sold. The Kwakiutl were outraged; all they had received was payment for a handful of sweaters. This incident fueled a movement for the protection of the rights of indigenous peoples in Canada.

A preferable alternative scenario would have been for the Kwakiutl to have registered the thunderbird design and negotiated a licensing agreement with the Japanese businessmen. Under such a license, they could have been paid royalties that probably would have been calculated as 20 percent of gross income, or US$20 million for the tribe. This is a good example of how, by asserting the intellectual property rights of indigenous peoples, multinational corporations can become "partners" instead of "predators."

There are limitations to copyright protection in this context, as is illustrated by two Australian cases. In *Yumbulul v. Reserve Bank of Australia* (1991, 2 I.P.R. 481), representatives of the Galpu clan unsuccessfully sought to prevent the reproduction by the Reserve Bank of the design of a Morning Star pole on a commemorative banknote. A member of the clan had created the pole, having obtained the necessary knowledge and authority through initiation and revelatory ceremonies. The clan claimed that he owed the clan a communal obligation to prevent the design of the pole from being used in a manner that was culturally offensive. The trial judge ruled that the artist had successfully disposed of his intellectual property right through a binding agreement. The judge did lament that "Australia's copyright law

respect to wines and spirits enjoy additional protection (Art. 23). Members of the WTO have agreed to enter into negotiations to raise the level of protection for individual geographical indications (Art. 24). Some developing countries have argued in the TRIPS context that the work mandated in respect to the establishment of a notification and registration system of geographical indications for wines should be extended to other products recognizable by their geographical origins, such as handicrafts and agro-food products.[17]

Ethnobotanicals

Genetic resources and traditional knowledge are another important potential source of revenue for developing countries and indigenous peoples, and this is an area in which intellectual property protection can play an important role. Two examples are illustrative.

Neem. For hundreds of years, people in India have made use of a natural fungicide in the bark of the neem tree. Recently, a pharmaceutical company went to India, identified the active ingredient in the bark, patented that active ingredient, and then offered it for sale to Indians. This caused an uproar in the country. The registration of the patent for neem in the European Patent Office was challenged, and the Technical Board of Appeal eventually found in favor of the applicants for revocation of the patent. The board ruled that since the properties of neem tree bark had been known for many years in India, the patented invention did not satisfy the absolute novelty requirement of the European Patent Convention.[18]

Lycopene. For centuries, the Amazonian Indians in Ecuador have used *tamate,* a small, cylindrical tomato found in the jungle, for its cancer-fighting properties. A multinational pharmaceutical company went to Ecuador, isolated the active ingredient, lycopene, patented it, and now sells it as one of the cutting-edge products in cancer treatment.

In neither case did the country or its indigenous peoples receive any benefit from what should have been their industrial property rights to these items of traditional knowledge. (The phrase "industrial property" includes patents, utility models, "petty patents," trade secrets, and the like.) A closer look at the two examples shows that any protection of the

industrial property rights of indigenous peoples with respect to their traditional knowledge should involve, first, protection *against* acquisition of industrial property rights by "outsiders" as the result of an appropriation of traditional knowledge and, second, protection *under* industrial property of the traditional knowledge of indigenous peoples for their own benefit.

Protection against Exploitation of Industrial Property

Where protection against exploitation of industrial property is concerned, two complementary approaches can be taken. The first is to establish a notification requirement for patentability. For example, at the third session of the Standing Committee on the Law of Patents (SCP) of the WIPO, the Colombian delegation proposed the inclusion of a provision to this effect in the (then draft) Patent Law Treaty. The proposal stated that where it appears that an invention which forms the subject of a patent application is based on genetic resources that are part of a country's "biological and genetic heritage," a copy of the contract affording access to the genetic resources in the country of origin should be filed (SCP/3/10). Unfortunately, the proposal was rejected for relating to a substantive requirement of patentability and so not falling within the scope of the treaty, which is concerned with formal requirements (procedures and documentation) only. The prospects of a similar proposal succeeding at an international trade negotiation round are slim, given the strong opposition to such a requirement by pharmaceutical companies and the governments of countries with strong pharmaceutical industries.

The second approach is to prevent the unauthorized (improper) acquisition of industrial property rights (especially patents) over traditional knowledge by documenting and publishing traditional knowledge as searchable prior art, should the holders of the traditional knowledge concerned want this. (An example of such an approach is the World Bank's Indigenous Knowledge Program.) Once such knowledge becomes part of the prior art, that mere fact destroys the novelty of any invention based on such knowledge. Even if a patent is obtained, it may be revoked on this ground. This procedure may involve an application launched by the holders concerned (which would involve substantial legal costs) or by a rival pharmaceutical company that wants to exploit the knowledge for its own gain, and at its own cost. (See the further discussion in the next section.)

Protection for Exploitation of Industrial Property

Economically, the main aim of the second aspect of protection is to secure revenue for indigenous peoples through the exploitation of their ethnobotanical knowledge. Again, two approaches are possible: through patents and through transfer of technology.

Patents. Holders of traditional knowledge can be given access to the industrial property system to enable them to obtain patents (or utility models or "petty patents" where provision is made for these), where appropriate. A basic problem with doing so is that a patent protects active ingredients that have been isolated and tested. Such isolation and testing may cost hundreds of millions of dollars and are out of reach for most developing countries, let alone their indigenous peoples. Another problem is that it may not be possible to obtain a patent because the novelty of the invention may have been destroyed by the local community's own prior use of the invention.[19]

Transfer of Technology. A variety of approaches to transfer of technology can be considered. For these to be effective, there must be an organized body of knowledge and an identifiable entity to administer transfers. One approach is illustrated by the contract signed in 1991 between Merck & Co. and the non-profit organization Instituto Nacional de Biodiversidad (INBio) in Costa Rica. Under the terms of the agreement, Merck received about 10,000 plant samples over a two-year period and was supplied with information about their traditional use. Merck paid a reported US$1.35 million to INBio for the samples and agreed to pay a royalty ranging between 2 and 3 percent (Blakeney 2000). If one of the samples becomes a billion dollar drug, this implies US$20 million to US$30 million in royalties.

A problem with this approach is that if the royalties are paid to an official body, they may disappear into the general state revenue account and not benefit the relevant communities or individuals. An alternative approach relies on the law relating to the protection of trade secrets: the trade secret is disclosed (licensed) to someone in exchange, among

other things, for an undertaking of confidentiality and for remuneration (usually, a royalty). The Policy Sciences Center is experimenting with a trade secret approach for communities to use so that they can derive revenue from ethnobotanical knowledge. For example, the center has made a grant to the nongovernmental organization Otro Futuro in Venezuela to assist it in helping the Dhekuana Indians develop an archive and atlas and to protect their intellectual property rights in resources ranging from myths, stories, legends, and music that can be copyrighted to ethnobotanicals that can be patented. The problem is that up until now the Dhekuana had perceived property in all these categories as being communally owned by 12 tribes inhabiting about 2 million square acres. The experiment involves establishing a community foundation in which the tribes would be represented on the board of directors and in which the property rights for copyright and patent could be vested. (Another option is to establish a for-profit corporation; see Norchi 2000.) Ethnobotanical knowledge would be protected by being treated as a trade secret by the community foundation, not to be disclosed to a pharmaceutical company or others unless such "outsiders" agree to pay royalties to the foundation.

This approach is not free from pitfalls, either. Trade secret protection usually depends on the legal rules of each country, and international attempts at harmonization have not been very successful. The TRIPS agreement, for example, simply states, "Natural and legal persons shall have the possibility of preventing information lawfully within their control from being disclosed to, acquired by, or used by others without their consent in a manner contrary to honest commercial practices" (Art. 39.2).[20] The protected information should be secret in the sense that it is not, as a body or in the precise configuration and assembly of its components, generally known among or readily accessible to persons within the circles that normally deal with the kind of information in question; that it has commercial value because it is secret; and that the person lawfully in control of the information has taken reasonable steps, under the circumstances, to keep it secret. A problem with ethnobotanical knowledge is that often the steps to keep the information secret may not be sufficient under existing common or civil law rules; secrecy often flows only from the fact that, because of customary law and practices, few people have access to the information (Gervais 2001).

intellectual property–related issues—full information. The preceding discussion suggests the following policy options that might be pursued at the international level by developing countries.

Copyright and Related Rights

- In the interest of developing their music industries, developing countries should seek the incorporation of the WIPO "Internet treaties" into a future trade agreement, in the same way that the TRIPS agreement incorporates the substantive provisions of the Berne Convention.
- Similarly, the incorporation of the WIPO Performers and Phonograms Treaty (WPPT) will establish an international regime for the indirect protection of expressions of folklore.
- Although the sui generis protection of nonoriginal databases (those that do not meet the requirement of originality in copyright law) is important for the protection and exploitation of ethnobotanical knowledge, one should be mindful of the possible negative effects of a strong exclusive-rights regime on the scientific and education sectors. The International Bureau of the WIPO has commissioned a study of such impacts, and the findings from this study should be considered carefully.

Trademarks and Geographical Indications

- The protection of geographical indications could be strengthened. Developing countries can argue strongly for extending a notification and registration system of geographical indications for wines to other products that can be recognized by their geographical origins and that are economically and culturally important to these countries, such as handicrafts and agrofood products.

Patents

- A good case can be made for the introduction of an authorized access requirement. Where it appears that an invention which forms the subject of a patent application is based on genetic resources that are part of a developing country's "biological and genetic heritage," a copy of the contract affording access to the genetic resources in the country of origin should be filed.
- This requirement can be transformed into a (lesser) notification requirement to fit a "compensatory liability" regime. Disclosure of access and utilization of such resources can be mandated, with disclosure triggering an obligation to pay "reasonable compensation."

Unfair Competition

- As an alternative to an exclusive-rights regime for the protection of nonoriginal databases, developing countries can consider arguing for the adoption of an expropriation model of protection.
- As an alternative to extending the protection of geographical indications, developing countries can seek strengthened protection against misleading the public as a form of unfair competition.
- To protect ethnobotanical knowledge against unauthorized misappropriation, trade secret protection at the international level needs to be strengthened.
- As an alternative to the protection of ethnobotanical knowledge by a notification requirement of patentability, a compensatory liability regime can be introduced, bolstered by a disclosure requirement.

Notes

This chapter was supported by the Policy Sciences Center, a nongovernmental organization founded by Harold D. Laswell, Myres S. McDougal, and George Dession at the Yale Law School in 1948; by the World Bank's Development Grant Facility for Culture; by the government of the Netherlands; and by the Swedish International Development Agency.

1 The sector of the international music recording trade known as World Music emerged as a distinct category in the 1980s (Collins 2000). It began with the growing interest in the popular music of Africa, such as the jugu music, maringa, and Afrobeat of anglophone West Africa, the mbalax and electro-griot music of francophone West Africa, the soukous of Central Africa, the mbawanga and chimurenga music of southern Africa, and rai music from Algeria and Morocco. Today World Music includes, in addition to its popular African music component, Cuban, Latin American, Arabic, Indian, Eastern European, and Asian popular and folk styles.

2 Article 15.4 forms part of the Stockholm (1967) and Paris (1971) Acts of the convention. According to the intention of the revision conference, this article implies the possibility of granting protection to expressions of folklore (Ficsor 1997).

3 Sometimes, of course, works that appear to be expressions of folklore can be traced back to their original authors, allowing them or their successors in title to recover royalties. This occurred with "El Condor Pasa," a famous song of the 1970s.

4 An interesting exception to this general observation has been noted in respect to the traditional Onge people of the

Andaman Islands in the Bay of Bengal (Norchi 2000). Songs are composed for certain occasions, and their performance may be requested again later. Only the original composer is then allowed to sing the song. Should anyone else try to do so without the composer's permission, that act is treated as theft.

5 An example is the "life plus 70" rule (copyright ceases to subsist 70 years after the death of the author) introduced for Europe by Article 1(1) of Council Directive 93/98 of October 29, 1993, harmonizing the terms of protection of copyright and certain related rights (1993 O.J. L290/9).

6 Some may argue that this proposal amounts to a new form of (indirect) taxation, which may make its adoption politically difficult in countries such as the United States (Gervais 2001).

7 Examples of access control are the use of passwords and encryption; an example of copy control is the use of software which limits the number of copies that can be made of a digital work.

8 The inclusion of temporary ("ephemeral") copies within the reproduction right had the potential of defeating the entire treaty (Vinje 1997). Even this agreed statement, unlike the other agreed statements, was adopted not by consensus but by majority vote.

9 The general obligation in Article 11 gives contracting parties an important degree of flexibility, when drafting their domestic legislation, to choose the types of technological measure that should be protected, the types of sanctions that should be imposed, and the actual activities that should be targeted. The provision in Article 12 reflects general agreement on the need to protect certain types of information attached to works in order to provide some security for their identification and tracking in open information networks (Reinbothe, Martin-Prat and Von Lewinsky 1997).

10 This right is subject to the impairment test also found in respect to the limited (copyright) rental right in the TRIPS agreement (Art. 11).

11 A certification mark, in terms of the Trade Marks Act 1995 (Cth), is a sign used, or intended to be used, to distinguish goods or services dealt with or provided in the course of trade and certified in relation to quality, accuracy, or some characteristic (such as origin, material, or mode of manufacture) from other goods or services dealt with or provided in the course of trade, but not so certified (sec. 169). Certification marks symbolize and promote the collective interests of certain groups of traders; by preventing traders whose goods do not comply with the certification process from using the mark, the integrity of those traders whose goods are certified is maintained (Wiseman 2001).

12 Goods may include a wide range of items, such as fabrics, boomerangs, coolamons, nets, traps, seed and shell necklaces, didgeridoos, musical recordings, sticks, and sculptures. Services may include activities such as theatre, dance, concerts, and educational and tourism programs (Wiseman 2001).

13 The Policy Sciences Center is assisting the Indian commissioner for handicrafts to implement a certification system for products labeled "handmade in India."

14 The special protection of well-known marks is based on article 6 bis of the Paris Convention, as extended by Articles 16.2 and 16.3 of the TRIPS agreement. This protection will be further extended by the adoption of the Joint Recommendation concerning Provisions on the Protection of Well-Known Marks by the Assembly of the Paris Union for the Protection of Industrial Property and the General Assembly of the WIPO, September 20–29, 1999. The recommendation clearly raises the level of protection beyond that of the TRIPS agreement and extends the scope of the substantive subject matter by also dealing, for example, with business identifiers and domain names (Kur 2000).

15 A "false indication" is one that does not correspond to the facts; it is an indication relating to a geographic area for goods not originating in that area. An indication is false only where this association/connotation is understood by the public in the country where the indication is used for such products (Baeumer 1997).

16 Although this definition is based on that of an "appellation of origin" in the Lisbon Agreement, it is broader in one respect: the TRIPS agreement protects goods that derive a reputation from their place of origin without their having a quality or other characteristic that is due to that place (Baeumer 1997).

17 See, for example, the communication submitted by Kenya, on behalf of the African Group, to the General Council of the WTO in preparation for the 1999 ministerial meeting in Seattle (WT/GC/W/302, August 6, 1999).

18 Essentially, the novelty of an invention is destroyed if it has been disclosed anywhere and in any manner or form (Art. 52).

19 Whether such prior use would actually destroy the novelty of the invention for which a patent is sought depends on the patent law of the country in which protection is sought. Under the U.K. Patents Act of 1977, for example, use can be the basis of a challenge to novelty if it effects a public release equivalent to publication (Cornish 1999). The question is whether a skilled worker, by observation or analysis, could discover and reproduce the invention; see *Stahlwerk Becker's Patent* (1919) 36 R.P.C. 13 (HL).

20 The phrase "a manner contrary to honest commercial practices" connotes "at least practices such as breach of contract, breach of confidence and inducement to breach, and includes the acquisition of undisclosed information by third parties who knew, or were grossly negligent in failing to know, that such practices were involved in the acquisition."

21 The use of the expression "secret information" as opposed to "undisclosed information" in the TRIPS agreement does not imply any difference in substance; it merely indicates that the rightful holder of the information must take certain measures or must behave in a certain way to keep the information unknown to third parties (Art. 6, note 6.01).

22 The "rightful holder" of secret information is the natural or legal person who is lawfully in control of such information (Art. 6, note 6.03).

23 It has been argued that traditional intellectual property models, as supplemented by classic trade secret law, often fail to

afford those who produce the current most commercially valuable information goods enough lead time to recoup their investments. The risk of market failure inherent in this "state of chronic under-protection tends to keep the production of information goods at suboptimal level" (Reichman 1994).

24 Section 301 of the U.S. Trade Act of 1974, as amended, allows (and sometimes requires) the U.S. government to take unilateral retaliatory actions against alleged unfair trading practices of partner countries. Since 1988, the U.S. Trade Representative has been required to identify foreign countries that deny adequate and effective protection of intellectual property rights or deny fair and equitable access to U.S. intellectual property holders.

TRADEMARKS, GEOGRAPHICAL INDICATIONS, AND DEVELOPING COUNTRIES

T RADEMARKS ARE WORDS, SIGNS, OR SYMBOLS THAT IDENTIFY A BRAND WITH A certain product or company. A consumer buying a can with the Coke or Pepsi logo knows that when she opens the can she is going to taste a carbonated soft drink with a certain cola flavor. Similarly, a traveler booking a flight on Lufthansa usually has a good idea about the safety record of the airline, the comfort of the seating area, the in-flight service, the punctuality of arrivals and departures, and so on. In short, trademarks offer customers the assurance of purchasing what they intend to purchase. Geographical indications—or appellations of origin—fulfill a very similar purpose. They identify a product or service with a particular location. A tea lover ordering a cup of Darjeeling tea anywhere in the world wants to be assured that the leaves used to make the tea are indeed from the Darjeeling region in India.

Trademarks and geographical indications belong to the wider family of intellectual property rights (IPRs) and as such receive legal protection against unauthorized use by third parties. Trademarks, like other IPRs, can be registered by businesses and individuals in special depositories created by governments. Registration prevents the coexistence of confusingly similar marks and serves as proof of ownership in the case of, for instance, legal disputes. Although trademark laws and registration offices can be found in virtually every country, national regimes often differ markedly regarding the scope of protection, the requirements for names and symbols that can be protected, guidelines for avoiding confusing marks, registration costs, the legal means available for fighting infringement, and other important details. Since trademark laws and regulations differ from country to country, a firm entering a foreign market may find that its trademark is not protected abroad. To address this issue, intergovernmental treaties have been negotiated to protect the trademark rights of foreign firms. Most prominently, the WTO Agreement on Trade-Related Aspects of Intellectual Property Rights (TRIPS) requires nondiscrimination—national treatment and most-favored-nation treatment—with regard to intellectual property protection and defines minimum standards of protection that the trademark laws of member countries have to meet.

Since its inception, the TRIPS agreement has been criticized for being detrimental to the interests of developing countries in terms of transferring rents to intellectual property–owning firms in the industrial world, restricting access to essential products such as life-saving drugs, and creating burdensome implementation requirements. Most of the controversy around TRIPS, however, has focused on innovation-type IPRs, notably patents, copyright, and plant breeders' rights, rather than on trademarks or geographical indications.[1]

This chapter reviews the general economic rationale for trademark protection and its role in developing countries, assesses the obligations of developing countries under the TRIPS agreement in this area, and discusses the interests of developing countries in future multilateral negotiations. We conclude that trademark protection fosters efficient allocation of resources, promotes business development, and may enhance export performance. The potential negative effects of TRIPS-consistent trademark regimes are likely to be small, especially compared with some other forms of intellectual property covered by the agreement. Although the development of a business-friendly trademark regime is primarily a challenge for domestic reform, compliance with the TRIPS standards of protection can benefit developing economies. The discussion mainly focuses on trademarks, but most of the arguments are also applicable to geographical indications. We deal explicitly with geographical indications only when there are considerations specific to this type of intellectual property.

The Economics of Trademark Protection

The basic economic rationale for trademark protection goes back to Akerlof's (1970) seminal insight regarding the failure of markets to provide for an efficient allocation of resources if consumers are unable to assess the quality of products offered to them. In this situation, information asymmetries between sellers and buyers prevent some transactions in high-quality goods from occurring, leading to inefficiencies. Trademarks offer a way around this dilemma. As producers of goods and services develop a reputation for quality over time, consumers can use brand names to distinguish between a premium-quality product and a low-end product.

Alternatively, brand names allow for easy identification of goods that are examined and compared by governments or private consumer groups with the aim of disseminating information about product reliability, safety records, and other quality aspects. Consumers may be willing to pay a premium for branded goods, regardless of their quality, in order to minimize search costs. For this system to work, consumers must be able to clearly associate the good or service with its producer. If competitors were able to free-ride on the trademark

holder's good reputation by offering products with inferior characteristics bearing the same brand name, consumers would be willing to pay less for brand-name products because of the risk of receiving fakes, and the trademark holder would, from a social point of view, underinvest in developing products with desirable characteristics such as quality and safety.

There is a key difference between protection of trademarks and protection of IPRs that seek to stimulate creative and inventive activity—patents, copyright, plant breeders' rights, and so on. Higher quality induced by trademark protection is clearly a private good. Better physical or functional features of a product or a greater extent of ancillary pre- and after-sale services are rival in consumption. By contrast, one person's consumption of a new technology or artistic expression induced by patent or copyright protection does not diminish another person's consumption of the same technology or artistic expression; thus, these products can be thought of as public goods (Arrow 1962). From a social welfare perspective, preventing free-riding—as all forms of IPRs do—is clearly desirable when it concerns reputation for quality. It is only second best, however, in the case of a public good such as the formula for a new drug or the lyrics of a new song, which, ideally, should be made available at marginal cost to the public at large. This fundamental difference is reflected in the fact that patents and copyright receive protection for only a limited time period (20–50 years), whereas trademarks can endure forever, provided they remain in use.[2]

A closely related difference between the two forms of IPRs is that patents and copyright expressly grant monopolies—albeit limited in scope—whereas trademarks can, in theory, coexist with perfectly competitive markets. Trademarks alone do not prevent firms from imitating a competing good or service, be it a low-end or a premium-quality product, as long as it is sold under a different brand name. In this regard, geographical indications are somewhat different because they do prevent firms from outside a given region from producing a perfect substitute if production relies on immobile, region-specific inputs (such as favorable climatic conditions, in the case of agricultural produce). In practice, however, aside from selected luxury products (for example, Roquefort or Parmesan cheese), geographical indications typically do not pose a significant obstacle to interregional competition.

Advertising-intensive consumer products (so-called status goods) constitute a special group within the category of products bearing trademarks. In the case of status goods, the mere use or display of a particular branded product confers prestige on its owners, apart from any utility derived from the product's function and physical characteristics (Grossman and Shapiro 1988a). Since in this case the brand name plays a central role in firms' product differentiation strategies, it is no surprise to find that owners of well-known brands often register up to 40 or more different trademarks to deter competing firms from entering their "brand space." Market research reports regularly put the value of well-known brands at billions of dollars. For instance, according to Interbrand, a consultancy, the Mercedes brand is worth about US$22 billion. Brand affiliation is also surprisingly stable; of the 25 top-selling consumer goods brands in the 1960s, 16 are still among the top 25 today (Evans and Wurster 2000: 150).

In the case of status goods, brand ownership can confer substantial market power on producers, but this does not necessarily imply that firms generate supernormal profits. Since the potential supply of trademarks is limitless, as long as entry is otherwise unrestricted the resulting market structure for many status goods industries can be characterized as monopolistically competitive—witness the intense competition between a relatively small number of brand-name sports shoe producers around the world.

A further twist in the case of status goods is that their perceived value often stems from their exclusivity—in other words, from the fact that only a select group of consumers enjoys them. If trademark protection were not enforced, imitation would allow consumers with less discerning tastes to enter the "exclusive club." Hence, illegitimate producers can impose an externality on trademark holders by preventing legitimate firms from offering their customers the prestige associated with a small, select network of users. This externality may dilute the market power of premium-good producers and lower their incentives to invest in reputation (Grossman and Shapiro 1988b).

While the basic role of trademark protection is to provide incentives for firms to invest in quality and reputation, there are other benefits associated with secure trademark rights. First, in the absence of counterfeiting, legitimate producers can more easily expand sales, allowing them to achieve economics of scale. Second, trademarks contribute to greater product safety—crucial in pharmaceutical and food industries—since the goods can easily be traced back to producers that can be held responsible; branded products are thus more likely to meet mandatory health and safety standards. Legitimate producers may also have a greater incentive to fight black-market producers if the latter free-ride on established brands. Third, trademarks may encourage innovative activity. A firm that has developed a solid reputation for high-quality goods is likely to invest continuously in upgrading its product portfolio to maintain its competitive edge. Whether protection of trademarks alone provides a sufficient incentive for engaging in research and development (R&D) activities depends, however, on the extent to which firms can appropriate their innovative efforts through trade secrets or simply by being the first in the market. For many industries, other forms of intellectual property protection are likely to be necessary if the firm is to appropriate R&D efforts, and, indeed, companies that own a valuable brand name usually also show a strong portfolio of patents and other types of IPRs.[3]

A concern that frequently arises in the context of intellectual property ownership is the potential for anticompetitive practices by titleholders. As mentioned above, this concern is arguably less severe for trademarks than for patents and copyright because trademarks do not expressly grant market power. Nonetheless, owners of strong brands can create market entry barriers, most prominently through vertical restraints in licensing agreements with distributors and retailers—witness the government argument in the prominent U.S. antitrust case against Microsoft. Appropriate competition policy remedies are necessary to counter such practices if indeed they are found to be detrimental to consumers.[4]

Trademarks in Open Economies

The basic proposition that trademark protection improves economic efficiency by helping to resolve information asymmetries is strongest in international markets because asymmetries of information are likely to be more pronounced when producers and consumers are located in different countries. Economic research has demonstrated the importance of reputation in determining trade patterns between countries (see, for example, Rauch 1999). Developing

39.1 Global Demand for Trademarks and Patents

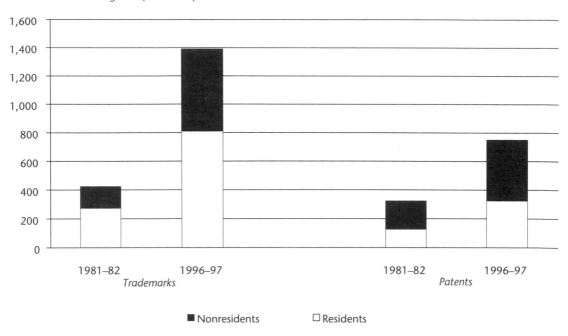

Number of worldwide grants (thousands)

■ Nonresidents ☐ Residents

Note: For various reasons, numbers should be considered orders of magnitude only. First, the number of countries included in the two different periods differed because of political changes. Second, the availability of protection, the strength of protection, and the quality of the administrative system for intellectual property rights differ significantly across countries. In some countries, for example, firms may be deterred from filing a trademark or patent because enforcement is weak or because it takes several years to complete the application process. Finally, in some developing countries the collection of industrial property statistics is unreliable, and reporting practices to the World Intellectual Property Organization (WIPO) are not consistent across countries.
Sources: Braga, Fink, and Sepulveda (2000); authors' estimates from WIPO data.

when it stood at around 64 percent, but it was still larger than for patents, where little more than 40 percent of grants went to domestic residents. This pattern is also borne out in Figure 39.2, which compares trademark and patent grants in 1997 in low- and middle-income countries with grants in high-income countries. Remarkably, more than half of trademark grants in developing countries went to domestic residents. Although this share is somewhat lower than in the high-income group, it suggests that developing country firms do not use the trademark system much less intensively than their industrial country counterparts.

International Agreements on Trademarks

Nations have long protected the trademark rights of foreigners and have cooperated to facilitate the cross-border registration of trademarks. Most prominently, the Paris Convention of 1883, to which 162 countries are signatories, establishes minimum standards of protection and priority filing rights, which offer trademark holders a time period of six months to file their titles abroad once they have registered them domestically. Firms residing in countries that are members of the 1891 Madrid Convention, currently encompassing 68 states, can substantially reduce the transactions costs involved in registering trademarks in multiple countries by filing a single international application and designating the countries where they seek protection. Similarly, the Lisbon Treaty of 1958, with 20 signatories, provides for an international registration mechanism for geographical indications.

The WTO TRIPS agreement goes beyond the pre-existing IPR conventions. It sets more stringent international standards for trademark protection in selected areas and, for the first time in an international treaty, establishes enforcement principles that WTO members are required to meet. The specific TRIPS provisions on trademarks require members to establish registration procedures that are trans-

 **39.2** Nationality of Trademark and Patent Title Holders by Country Income Group, 1997

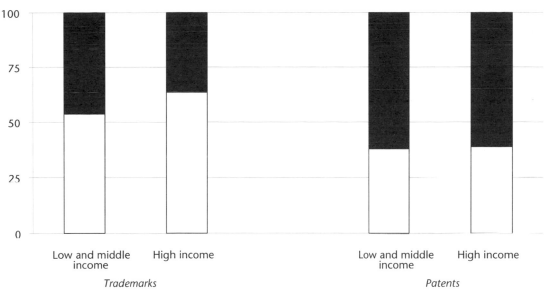

Percentage of grants

Trademarks — Low and middle income / High income

Patents — Low and middle income / High income

Note: The definition of income groups follows the World Bank classification. In the case of patents, countries of the former Soviet Union were excluded because the reported data appear to include grants for utility models.
Source: Authors' estimates from WIPO data.

parent and independent of the characteristics of goods and services for which protection is requested. Countries must also extend protection to internationally recognized trademarks in order to prevent their speculative registration and fraudulent use. It is important to recognize, however, that in many countries the trademark standards negotiated under TRIPS were already part of pre-TRIPS law and jurisprudence (Watal 2001).

On geographical indications, the TRIPS agreement calls for protection against use that would mislead the public or constitute an act of unfair competition. A stronger form of protection is provided for wines and spirits, for which the use of translations or expressions such as "kind" or "type" is prohibited. (For example, wine sold as "Chablis-type wine, made in Chile" would be in violation of the agreement.) The agreement calls for the establishment of a multilateral system of notification and registration of geographical indications for wines and spirits, although little progress has been made in this area to date.

The Final Declaration of the WTO's Doha ministerial meeting reaffirms the agenda on geographical indications built into the TRIPS agreement. It sets a formal deadline for completing the negotiations on the above-mentioned system of registration by 2003, when the Fifth Ministerial Meeting is to be held. WTO members still disagree, however, on the issue of extending to other products the higher level of protection currently granted to wine and spirits, as called for under TRIPS.[9]

With regard to enforcement, TRIPS sets general standards on, among other things, enforcement procedures, the treatment of evidence, injunctive relief, damages, and provisional and border measures. At the same time, Article 41.5 makes clear that countries do not need to "put in place a judicial system for the enforcement of intellectual property rights distinct from that for the enforcement of law in general, nor does it affect the capacity of members to enforce their law in general."

The Benefits and Costs of Trademarks under TRIPS for Developing Countries

The potential benefits associated with legally binding disciplines on trade-related measures under the WTO have to do with overcoming domestic political economy constraints, enhancing the credibility of

7 It must be kept in mind that while obtaining a trademark can be relatively inexpensive, marketing it may require significant resources.

8 Several caveats need to be pointed out. First, new registrations are a flow figure, which may not necessarily correspond to the stock of trademarks in force. Second, the number of grants is unlikely to be proportional to the "economic value" of the underlying intellectual property titles. Finally, although the statistics consider all domestically incorporated firms as domestic residents, it is possible that these firms are partially or fully owned by foreigners.

9 So far, the discussions have been marked by divisions between the EU (the trade bloc that hosts the largest number of geographical indications) and "new world" countries such as Argentina, Australia, Canada, Chile, and the United States, which are mostly "consumers" of such indications and thus favor relatively lax standards of protection.

10 In one dispute, the European Union challenged the TRIPS-consistency of a U.S. law regarding the use of trademarks in connection with businesses or assets confiscated in Cuba. The other dispute was brought by the United States against the European Union's alleged lack of protection of trademarks and geographical indications for agricultural products and foodstuffs (see <www.wto.org>).

11 Its success can be attributed to two factors. First, the prevention of "cybersquatting" is in the interest of all countries and cannot readily be remedied by purely domestic enforcement. Second, the Internet is a radically new phenomenon, with few entrenched interests, the promise of large economic benefits, and a user community that is inherently "global" and therefore likely to respect international arbitration.

"BEHIND-THE-BORDER" AND REGULATORY ISSUES

VI

As tariffs and quotas became less important in OECD countries as the result of rounds of multilateral trade negotiations, differences in national regulatory regimes became more apparent. Policies that were put on the table for possible negotiation of rules included government procurement, product standards, inward foreign investment, competition law, labor standards, and environmental norms. The WTO now includes disciplines in some of these areas—in procurement (albeit only for signatories of the relevant agreement) and in product standards. In others there are as yet no disciplines, although all have advocates. Calls for multilateral action range from coordinated application of national policies to the harmonization of domestic regulatory regimes.

The chapters in this part discuss the principal "behind-the-border" regulatory issues that have come up in the WTO context and provide an introduction to the key questions that are likely to be prominent on the multilateral negotiating agenda in the coming decades. Simon J. Evenett, in Chapter 40, discusses issues surrounding government procurement. Product standards and related regulation are the topic of Chapter 41, by John S. Wilson. Bernard Hoekman and Kamal Saggi, in Chapter 42, review the pros and cons, from developing countries' standpoint, of multilateral rules for investment policies. Similarly, Chapter 43, by Peter Holmes, looks at the case for rules on competition policies and anticompetitive behavior. In Chapter 44, Simon

SIMON J. EVENETT

40

MULTILATERAL DISCIPLINES AND GOVERNMENT PROCUREMENT

THE GROWTH OF TOTAL SPENDING BY CENTRAL AND LOCAL GOVERNMENTS WAS ONE of the most profound economic changes of the 20th century (Tanzi and Schuknecht 2000). Although a large portion of that growth was devoted to higher transfer payments, governments and state-owned entities of all types spent considerable sums on goods and services produced by the private sector.

Throughout much of the post–World War II era, discrimination against foreign suppliers was rife. It was driven in part by the prevailing Keynesian macroeconomic orthodoxy, which emphasized that the smaller is the share of each dollar of government expenditure spent on goods produced abroad (imports), the larger is the increase in national income caused by a rise in government expenditure. Governments could reduce this share—what economists call the marginal propensity to import—by refusing to buy goods from abroad. More important rationales are nationalism and outright protectionism: claims that "our money" should be spent on "our goods" to secure "jobs at home." Because of such considerations, government procurement was initially excluded from the GATT; Article III

(national treatment) does not apply to procurement. It was not until the completion of the Tokyo Round of multilateral trade negotiations, in 1979, that a code of conduct for central government procurement was introduced into the GATT. The code bound only its signatories, and most GATT contracting parties did not join. During the Uruguay Round, the coverage of the agreement was expanded to include services and additional government entities. Membership, however, remains limited mostly to OECD countries.

A number of factors explain the greater acceptance by OECD nations of international rules on national procurement practices. Since the mid-1970s, government budgets in these countries have come under increased pressure. Spending by welfare states on health, education, and pensions has grown considerably. Faced with the choice of raising taxes or cutting nonwelfare spending, governments came to place greater emphasis on cuts. One way to reduce nonwelfare spending is to stimulate competition between firms that bid for government contracts, and allowing foreign suppliers to bid helps achieve this goal.

A second, related factor has been the widespread privatization of state-owned enterprises. Without governments standing behind them, these enterprises know that poor management decisions will not be "bailed out" by the state; that is, they face what economists refer to as a "hardening of the budget constraint." But the owners of newly privatized firms also know that their profits will not be entirely taxed away by the state. These two changes

417

entrepreneurs to set up production facilities in the nation with the procurement ban depends on policies toward FDI. Therefore, the long-term consequences of a procurement ban are a function of domestic competition and FDI policies.

Procurement Discrimination in Auctions

Many government purchases are transacted not through markets but through bidding by suppliers for a contract. Each firm typically bids a price for completing the contract, given what it thinks other firms are bidding. Economists have found that outright bans on foreign bids unsurprisingly reduce the competition faced by each domestic bidder, which then all submit higher bids. The government then finds itself choosing from a range of higher bids, and the overall cost of the contract rises. Thus, there is a strong presumption against forms of discrimination that exclude foreign bidders (McAfee and McMillan 1989). Similarly, any measure that increases the cost of one group of bidders results in that group raising its bids (or perhaps not bidding at all). The other bidders, facing less competition, raise their bids, too. Again, government's procurement costs rise. In simulations of auctions, Deltas and Evenett (1997) found that such cost discrimination against foreign firms can raise procurement costs significantly, but less than outright prohibitions on foreign bidding.

One form of discrimination that is used by many developing countries—price preferences—can actually lower procurement costs. McAfee and McMillan (1989) demonstrated this result in an analysis of optimal procurement auctions. The significance of this result is that it undermines the presumption that a cost-minimizing procurement official would always choose not to discriminate against any bidder, domestic or foreign. To understand the intuition underlying McAfee and McMillan's result, it is important to bear in mind two points. First, in most analyses of auctions, if one supplier raises its bid, then other suppliers have an incentive to raise their bids too. Second, price preferences only inflate the actual bids of foreign suppliers when domestic and foreign bids are compared. If a foreign supplier's inflated bid is still the lowest, the government awards the contract to that foreign supplier but only pays the amount of the actual bid.

McAfee and McMillan's insight was to show that foreign firms make their bids knowing that a price preference will be used to inflate those bids. They respond to high price preferences by lowering their bids and reducing their profit margins. If the probability of a foreign firm being the low bidder is high, raising price preferences might actually reduce procurement costs. If the foreign firms have, on average, lower costs than domestic firms, an increase in price preferences from zero will always reduce procurement costs because the probability that a foreign firm will still win the contract is so high.

Both McAfee and McMillan (1989) and Deltas and Evenett (1997) found in simulations of auctions that the possible cost reductions resulting from price preferences were very small (often less than 1 percent). Worse still, Deltas and Evenett found that if the government accidentally chose the wrong rate of price preference, these cost reductions quickly became cost increases—even with small errors. This is particularly important because policymakers do not typically have access to all the relevant information (including the actual probability distributions of the costs of the domestic and foreign firms) needed for choosing the optimal price preference. Even if they did, political factors would probably "encourage" them to choose a higher-than-optimal price preference. Deltas and Evenett's simulations imply considerable gains in the expected profitability of domestic firms from even modest (5–10 percent) price preferences. In practice, the likely procurement cost reductions are very small and, given the realities of policymaking, will almost certainly never be realized. This form of procurement discrimination is bad policy, too. Still, when the three forms of procurement discrimination are compared, price preferences tend to have the least adverse effect. Cost discrimination is more distortive than price preferences but less distortive than outright bans on bids from foreign suppliers. Unfortunately, the current plurilateral WTO agreement on procurement bans price preferences but imposes much weaker disciplines on the other two forms of procurement discrimination—the more distortive ones (Hoekman 1998b).

The WTO Agreement on Government Procurement

The WTO Government Procurement Agreement (GPA), which entered into force on January 1, 1996, is a plurilateral agreement that binds only signatories (Hoekman and Kostecki 2001). At the time of writing, the GPA had only 26 members: Austria, Belgium, Canada, Denmark, the European Union (as an entity), Finland, France, Germany, Greece, Hong Kong (China), Ireland, Israel, Italy, Japan, the Republic of Korea, Liechtenstein, Luxembourg, the Netherlands, Norway, Portugal, Singapore, Spain, Sweden, Switzerland, the United Kingdom, and the United States. Although China, Iceland, the Kyrgyz Republic, Latvia, Panama, and Taiwan (China) are negotiating accession (in some cases as part of general WTO accession), the current membership of the GPA is limited to high-income countries.

GPA Principles and Disciplines

The GPA establishes a framework of rights and obligations regarding parties' national procurement laws, regulations, and procedures. Governments are required to apply the principle of national treatment to the products, services, and suppliers of other parties to the GPA and to abide by the most-favored-nation (MFN) rule, which prohibits discrimination among goods, services, and suppliers of other parties. The agreement emphasizes transparency of laws, regulations, procedures, and practices regarding government procurement. Five annexes to the GPA specify, for each member, which government authorities (central government, subcentral governments, and other state bodies such as utilities) are covered and which purchases of goods and services are subject to multilateral disciplines. Only those transactions that exceed certain threshold levels are affected. Although a common threshold of SDR 130,000 was established for central government entities, thresholds for purchases of construction services and procurement by noncentral government entities are often higher (see Hoekman and Kostecki 2001).

All goods purchases are subject to GPA disciplines unless a nation secured exemptions during the negotiation of the agreement (or during subsequent accession to the agreement). By contrast, only those services listed in the annexes are covered by the GPA. Thus, as in the General Agreement on Trade in Services (GATS), a "positive list" approach to coverage was taken. Indeed, there is a very close correspondence between GATS specific commitments and the coverage of the GPA. Although nondiscrimination (MFN and national treatment) lies at the core of the GPA, effectively banning price preferences, many members have conditioned their commitments on market access to that offered by other members of the GPA (Hoekman and Mavroidis 1997). This insistence on reciprocal access to procurement markets reduces the benefits of enhanced competition in domestic procurement contracts.

In addition to nondiscrimination, the GPA has two other important features: measures to improve transparency in the procurement process, and enforcement provisions. The agreement contains numerous provisions on the procurement process, covering the use of selected and invited tendering, the nature of technical specifications used in tenders, and the criteria for awarding contracts. For example, Article VI enjoins nations from creating "unnecessary" obstacles to trade when setting specifications and calls for the use, "where appropriate," of performance rather than design standards. Contracts must be awarded to the supplier that is deemed capable of undertaking the contract and that has submitted the lowest bid or that best meets the evaluation criteria laid out in the original tender. Essentially, the second requirement prohibits a procuring entity from refusing to award a contract to a supplier on grounds that were not specified in the tender. The effectiveness of this requirement depends critically on the breadth of the evaluation criteria in the tender.

Transparency-related provisions emphasize publication of tenders and notification of regulations to the WTO. Ex post transparency norms are relatively weak. The GPA allows a government to refuse to award a contract on "public interest" grounds, which are not defined. Once a contract award has been made, the procuring entity does not have to provide an explanation to the losing bidders; an explanation is required only when a member government intervenes on behalf of a bidding firm under the GPA's enforcement procedures.

The enforcement provisions of the GPA are particularly noteworthy. Recognizing that aggrieved bidders desire rapid and effective redress, the GPA mandates that members establish impartial domestic arbitration procedures capable of making swift decisions. Complainants are allowed to invoke the provisions of this WTO agreement in making their case in a domestic arbitration procedure. In addition to these domestic procedures, members are allowed to bring cases to the WTO dispute settlement body. The effectiveness of this domestic dimension to enforcing an international trade agreement depends crucially on the manner in

BOX 40.1 (CONTINUED)

Estimates of the Social Gain from GPA Membership

Entities involved	Billions of rupees	As percentage of GDP	As percentage of fiscal deficit[a]
Central government only	67.5	0.34	8.4
Including state governments	90.3	0.45	11.3
Including public sector enterprises	340.6	1.70	42.5

a. Using the budgeted fiscal deficit of the central government for 1999–2000.

The government is currently using preferential treatment in government purchases as a tool of industrial policy. In keeping with the spirit of reform, there is no need to continue with the preferential treatment of PSEs. Discontinuing preferential treatment for the small-scale sector, however, may not be feasible politically. The indirect subsidy to this sector is not very large; in 1999 the share of purchases by the procurement agency from the small-scale sector was no more than 8 to 10 percent of total purchases. If these purchases involved a price preference of 15 percent (which, in fact, they do not), the total "subsidy" to the small-scale sector would be about 1.2 to 1.5 percent of total expenditure. This could easily be paid out as an explicit subsidy through a suitable mechanism. The other sectors receiving preferential treatment are very small, and exceptions for them could be sought.

Source: Prepared by the volume editors, based on Srivastava (2000).

the agreement falls short of its potential for two reasons. First, the GPA bans price preferences, the least (economically) costly and most transparent form of procurement discrimination. Provisions on cost or entry discrimination are far more opaque and allow for the use of local content criteria by developing countries in awarding contracts. Tightening up on cost and entry discrimination and channeling protectionist use of policies toward observable price preferences would improve the rules of the game from an efficiency perspective and would provide a focal point for negotiators (Hoekman and Mavroidis 1997).

Second, the provisions for disciplining bribery and corruption are too weak. A reformed GPA might require signatories to delegate contract award decisions to independent public servants or agencies (where possible); to take steps to protect whistleblowers; and to create an independent auditing or investigative office, which could be located in the legislative rather than the executive branch of government. These steps would complement tougher penalties for graft by public officials and restrictions on postretirement employment opportunities for officials.

As mentioned, the GPA has few developing country members. In part, this reflects a desire to be able to apply policies of discrimination and a concern that the gains from membership will be limited (Hoekman 1998b). Since the late 1990s, discussions in the WTO have begun to focus on transparency, as opposed to market access. At the 2001 ministerial meeting of the WTO in Doha, agreement was reached to launch negotiations on transparency in government procurement in 2003. Although not explicitly linked to efforts to reduce corruption and bribery, transparency in procurement practice is intended to have this effect.

In setting priorities for reform efforts, a good case exists for tackling bribery and corruption first and discrimination second (Evenett and Hoekman 2000). Graft probably always reduces welfare, under any circumstances. By contrast, when the quantity demanded by the government is initially below the domestic industry's output, procurement discrimination merely reshuffles sales from foreign to domestic firms in markets and has no consequences for national welfare. If political pressures are such that the elimination of procurement discrimination is not feasible, the WTO should be geared toward making discrimination as transparent as possible. This may involve encouraging price preferences on foreign bids instead of adopting measures that increase the costs, or reduce the number, of foreign supplies. More generally, the focus should be on increasing the transparency of procurement practices of WTO members.

Notes

I thank Bernard Hoekman for helpful comments and suggestions. Any remaining errors are mine.

1 If the country imposing a ban on foreign procurement is large, its action may affect the terms of trade. If the ban raises the relative price of, say, steel and the nation was exporting steel, the ban will raise the relative price of steel for all purchasers—including foreigners—who will then buy less. Thus, the procurement ban would be equivalent to an export tax. If the nation was importing steel before the ban was imposed, the increase in the relative price of steel reduces total (government plus private sector) domestic demand and thus reduces imports of steel. Note, however, that most developing nations are unlikely to be able to affect their terms of trade in this manner.

2 SAROK uses the wholesale price as the market price. Imports refers to goods procured directly from overseas with foreign currency, not imported goods procured in the domestic market with local currency.

requirements. Among the most important costs are those associated with mandates that industry retest and recertify products that have already been tested for conformity with similar standards in multiple markets. This results in higher costs to consumers and marks a key point at which trade policy intersects with standards systems and regulation.

In principle, standards and regulations are directly aimed at overcoming market failures. Indeed, they may be the least trade-restricting policies available for regulatory purposes. Under some circumstances, standards may expand trade. In consequence, it is not clear that the trade impacts of technical barriers are inefficient or that they should be the subject of

multilateral negotiations. Total removal of technical regulations to trade would not necessarily achieve efficiency gains sufficient to overcome losses from reduced social protection.

The historical record does show, however, that in practice countries may regulate for purposes other than social protection. Technical regulations may discriminate against foreign suppliers, both in their design and in their outcomes, and may be used to gain strategic trade advantages for domestic firms over foreign competitors. Standards are often nontransparent and in some cases needlessly force firms to duplicate testing and certification costs. Regulations may be drafted to exclude both domestic and

BOX 41.1 SPS MEASURES: THE KENYA FISH EXPORTS CASE

In January 1998 the European Union (EU) banned the importation of fresh fish and fish products from Kenya, Mozambique, Tanzania, and Uganda, to safeguard EU consumers from the risk of cholera. The ban was still in effect in July 2000. This action was taken without regard to the disciplines of the WTO Sanitary and Phytosanitary Measures (SPS) agreement, which provides that if a member is to apply SPS measures, it has to prove scientifically that the product in question poses a real threat to the health of consumers. The agreement requires that assessment of the risk be carried out on the basis of techniques developed by relevant international organizations (if these exist). This is to ensure that such action is not based merely on fears or conjecture but that there is sufficient scientific evidence. Even after the risk assessment has been conducted and sufficient evidence has been gathered, an opportunity must be given to the exporter to put in place measures that eliminate the health risk, and a timeframe for compliance must be set. In the case of the African fish, the EU made it clear that the ban was not based on scientific evidence but was, rather, motivated by the lack of a credible system in Kenya to safeguard the products from possible contamination. The EU clearly stated that if this were not changed, the products would be shut out of the EU market.

Fish is a leading nontraditional export, and in 1994 Kenya exported fresh fish worth US$50 million, representing about 2 percent of the country's total commodity exports. There were, moreover, fears that the ban could be extended to fresh fruits and vegetables, another of Kenya's leading nontraditional exports. The EU imposes controls that subject imported fruits and vegetables to 10 percent sampling for microbial control, and this requirement is already affecting Kenya's exports of the products. This development is disturbing considering that in these areas Kenya has a comparative advantage. (The EU has agreed to extend by one year the July 2000 deadline for imposing new maximum pesticide residue levels on horticultural exports from the African, Caribbean, and Pacific countries covered by the Cotonou Convention.)

The EU action caused considerable losses in the fish industry. The Kenyan Ministry of Health, which is the competent authority, needed to embark immediately on an action plan to address the concerns raised by the EU. The SPS measures and quality assurance procedures outlined by the EU have to be strictly adhered to in order to restore confidence. This requires capacity building both by the Kenya Bureau of Standards, where the sampling of food exports for contamination takes place, and by the Ministry of Health.

Source: Prepared by the volume editors, based on Mwega and Muga (2000).

foreign entrants into a particular market, so as to support entrenched monopolies. Finally, standards may be stronger than necessary for achieving optimal levels of social protection, thus imposing excessive costs on consumers and reducing net welfare.

A process for rationalizing costly technical regulations can therefore be beneficial. Such rationalization involves ending discriminatory treatment, removing duplicative testing requirements, recognizing that foreign standards could achieve the same level of social or consumer protection as domestic standards, making regulation more transparent, and scaling regulations at levels that do not impose excessive costs on consumers and firms.

Quantifying the Trade Effects of Technical Barriers and Standards

There is considerable interest among policymakers in empirical work on the impacts of technical regulations on trade. This interest reflects the belief that regulations often constitute important nontariff barriers to trade and that their use is proliferating. Many observers claim that the trade-restricting effects of technical regulations in industrial countries are particularly costly for exporters in developing nations. These arguments arise from anecdotal examples and case studies.

Several recent studies have related trade flows to measures of a country's standards. Swann, Temple, and Shurmer (1996) and Moenius (1999) discussed the multiplicity of economic hypotheses about trade and standards and note that standards can increase or reduce trade. Swann, Temple, and Shurmer regressed U.K. net exports, exports, and imports over the period 1985–91 on counts of voluntary national ("idiosyncratic") and international standards recognized by the United Kingdom and Germany. Standards counts were taken from the PERINORM database and were matched with the three-digit Standard Industrial Classification (SIC) of the industry they applied to. The authors concluded that U.K. standards had a positive effect on both exports and imports; the standards served both to signal quality abroad and to raise import demand in the United Kingdom. Swann, Temple, and Shurmer also concluded that German standards reduce U.K. exports, perhaps suggesting a protective impact. Finally, they found that idiosyncratic standards increased trade more than did international ones. They hypothesized that the

smaller effect of international standards might reflect a tradeoff between more trade, based on higher economies of scale, and less trade, associated with reduced product variety.

Otsuki, Sewadeh, and Wilson (2000) estimated the impact of changes in the EU standard on aflatoxin levels in food using trade and regulatory survey data for 15 European countries and 9 African countries between 1989 and 1998. The results suggest that the implementation of new aflatoxin standards in the EU would have a negative impact on African exports of cereals, dried fruits, and nuts to Europe. The EU standard, which would reduce health risk by approximately 1.4 deaths per billion a year, could decrease African exports by more than 60 percent, or US$ 670 million, as compared with regulation based on an international standard.

There is suggestive evidence that standards often act to raise costs and thereby serve to restrain trade. The OECD (1999b) found that the costs of meeting differing standards and technical regulations in its member nations, along with the costs of testing and certification, can amount to between 2 and 10 percent of overall product costs. Research stimulated by the EU Single Market program in the mid-1980s illustrated how significant such standards-induced trade barriers can be. A typical example was building tiles, where voluntary industry standards differed by EU country. Spain was found to be the lowest-cost producer of such tiles, average prices being between 40 and more than 100 percent lower than prices charged by producers in countries such as Germany, France, and the Netherlands (Hoekman and Kostecki 2001). Such price differences were the result of a combination of differing standards and government procurement regulations. In France nonstandard tiles could not be used in public works (about 40 percent of the market), and private firms were hesitant to use nonstandard tiles because insurance companies tended to require that buildings meet industry standards. Pasta is another example; Italy's pasta purity laws required that pasta be made of durum wheat, a high-quality type produced in the south of the country. This increased the cost of pasta in comparison with that in other EU countries, where pasta tended to consist of a mix of wheat qualities.

It has been estimated that over 60 percent of U.S. exports are subject to health, safety, and related standards in their destination markets. Government-issued certificates were required for 45 per-

BOX 41.2 (CONTINUED)

Steel. Because of objections by Australia and New Zealand to the use of untreated wooden dunnage, an Indian steel company was forced to use treated wood or wood substitutes. These were not only more expensive but also in short supply. Australia and New Zealand also require fumigation of containers, involving an additional cost of US$400 per container.

Packaging, Marking, and Language Barriers. In some European markets texturized yarn must be supplied in equal-length packages, creating additional costs for exporters. German norms for engineering products are problematic in that technical regulations are rarely made available in English. Indian exporters must employ translators, and the translations may not be accepted by German authorities, generating additional uncertainty for exporters.

* A process standard might alternatively stipulate that all mango pulp must be processed using a specific method. Economists usually argue that product standards are more efficient regulatory tools than process standards, since product standards allow heterogeneous firms to choose the technology that minimizes the resource costs of achieving a specific regulatory target, while process standards do not. It has also been

pointed out, however, that in the context of food safety regulations, process standards can sometimes be the optimal regulatory option; that is, a hazard analysis and critical control point (HACCP) system, which includes flexible process standards designed to reduce microbial contamination in food, might be superior to specific product standards, given the expense of microbiological tests and the recurrent nature of the pathogen hazard. The costs of enforcement and the degree of administrative discretion in enforcement are also important considerations in any evaluation of the relative efficiency of process or product standards.

† According to Article 2.1.1.20 of the OIE International Animal Health Code, which deals with the import of milk and milk products from countries considered infected with foot-and-mouth disease (FMD) or rinderpest, the veterinary authorities of exporting countries are required to produce international sanitary certificates attesting that these products originate from herds or flocks that were not subject to any restrictions due to FMD at the time of milk collection and that the products have been processed to ensure the destruction of the FMD virus according to the procedures laid down in the article.

Source: Prepared by the volume editors, based on Cardona and others (2000).

Agreement on Technical Barriers to Trade (TBT), and the Agreement on Sanitary and Phytosanitary Measures (SPS). The TBT agreement addresses "product characteristics or the related processes and production methods" reflected in technical regulations and requires that these regulations conform to basic principles of transparency and nondiscrimination. Relevant international standards developed by bodies such as the ISO—if they exist—must be used as the basis for technical regulations unless this would be inappropriate because of climatic, geographic, or technological factors.

A principal objective of the WTO SPS agreement is to minimize the negative effect on trade from the adoption and enforcement of SPS measures. WTO members are encouraged to adopt internationally recognized standards but are free to apply stricter standards. The agreement recognizes the rights of

importing countries to implement SPS measures that diverge from international norms (if these exist) but requires that they provide scientific justification for such measures and apply risk assessment mechanisms. International SPS standards are developed by several organizations, including the Office Internationale des Epizootic (OIE), international and regional organizations operating within the framework of the International Plant Protection Convention (IPPC), and the Codex Alimentarius Commission.[1]

WTO Enquiry Points and Notifications

To increase the transparency of technical regulations and SPS measures, WTO members are required to establish enquiry points that are responsible for providing answers to all reasonable questions from interested members and for making available relevant documents on the standards that apply. They must also notify new and proposed standards to the WTO SPS and TBT committees. As of 1999, as shown in Table 41.1, three-quarters of developing country WTO members had established enquiry points under the SPS agreement, whereas 92 percent of high-income members had done so.

In the first five years of WTO operations, notifications based on the SPS agreement rose substantially, reflecting increased concerns about food, animal, and plant safety (Figure 41.1). Since SPS measures normally remain valid once enacted, the cumulative number of active measures has grown rapidly. Note that the number of notifications based on the SPS agreement is, in general, increasing both in high-income and in middle- and low-income countries.

Table 41.1 Total Number of Countries That Have Established SPS Enquiry Points

Country group	1995	1999
Middle and low Income		
Number of countries	78	98
Number of countries with SPS enquiry points	49	74
Percentage of total	63	76
High income		
Number of countries	34	36
Number of countries with SPS enquiry points	28	33
Percentage of total	82	92

Source: World Bank calculations, based on WTO data.

41.1 Number of Notifications under the SPS Agreement by Region, 1995–99

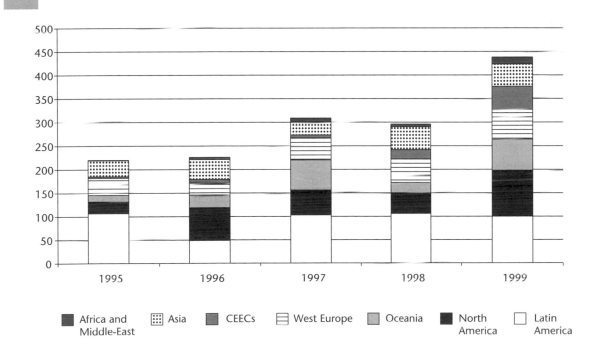

Legend: Africa and Middle-East | Asia | CEECs | West Europe | Oceania | North America | Latin America

Source: Wilson (2000a): 7.

BOX 41.3 MOVING FORWARD: A PROPOSAL

What is most needed in the standards area from a development perspective is a framework to support national capacity building and improve the design of international standards. An action plan to bridge the standards divide and address the problems confronting developing countries in *voluntary* standards requires support for infrastructure modernization and enhanced access for those countries to standards-development activities. There is currently no coordinated international framework for addressing critical development needs in this area. A global effort is required to develop a framework for a targeted financial assistance plan for modernizing the standards infrastructures of low-income countries and enhancing developing countries' capacity to participate in international standards-development activities. Innovative ways of achieving this goal, including the use of global information technology networks, should be explored.

In addition efforts should focus on promoting trade expansion through regulatory reform and removal of mandatory technical barriers that are discriminatory. Such efforts are in the long-term economic interest of both industrial and developing countries. One way forward is for developing countries to endorse the wider use of "supplier's declaration of conformity" to regulatory requirements. A systematic review of products subject to mandatory government testing and certification that can be moved to "declaration of conformity status" should be undertaken. A multilateral global conformity agreement could then be developed on the basis of this list for negotiation and agreement at the WTO or in another, more appropriate forum. It is critical that developing countries benefit from and participate in such an agreement. A plan to provide technical assistance and funds to support mechanisms such as post-market surveillance systems in developing countries must be part of the effort.

In agricultural trade (food products) the lack of progress toward harmonized, internationally accepted standards has the potential for seriously eroding the gains made through removal of traditional trade barriers. The wide range of differing sanitary and phytosanitary standards imposed by importers—standards that lack a foundation in sound science and are not based on risk assessments—is particularly costly to developing countries dependent on agricultural exports. A concerted effort to accelerate the creation of appropriate international standards would help support continued expansion of agricultural and horticultural trade and reduce the number of SPS-related disputes and problems that exporters from developing countries confront.

42

BERNARD HOEKMAN
KAMAL SAGGI

MULTILATERAL DISCIPLINES AND NATIONAL INVESTMENT POLICIES

I N THE PAST 50 YEARS, LITTLE HAS BEEN DONE TO NEGOTIATE MULTILATERAL DISCI-plines on policies that affect factor movement. With the exception of the General Agreement on Trade in Services (GATS), there are no disciplines in the WTO on policies pertaining to labor and capital movement. Some WTO members have argued that there is a need to negotiate multilateral rules for investment policies, such as the right of establishment and national treatment for foreign investors. In part, these arguments have to do with market access objectives. In many sectors the preferred mode of supplying a market may be through foreign direct investment (FDI), not exports. If FDI is restricted by the host country, foreign firms have an interest in rules that enhance or guarantee their market access. Another line of argument emphasizes the potential payoffs to developing countries of signing on to multilateral rules as a commitment device—as a mechanism to implement rules that governments want to adopt but are constrained from adopting because of political-economy factors (Markusen 2001; Moran 1998). Yet another rationale for considering rules in this area is to ensure that investment policies do not distort the mode of supply choice of firms (Feketekuty 2000; Low and Mattoo 2000). For developing countries, a policy of great interest in this regard is locational subsidies (tax concessions) offered by high-income country governments to attract or retain FDI.

Bora, in Chapter 19 in this volume, discusses the implementation of the Agreement on Trade-Related Investment Measures (TRIMs) negotiated in the Uruguay Round. This agreement basically prohibits measures that are inconsistent with the GATT's national treatment principle (Art. III GATT) and its ban on the use of quantitative restrictions (Art. XI GATT). The GATS goes further by including establishment and national treatment for investors as commitments that signatories may decide to make for specific services industries. An important issue for WTO members is whether to extend the trading system through general rules regarding investment policies, and, if so, what form such rules might take. The 1996 WTO ministerial meeting in Singapore led to the creation of a working group on trade and investment with the mandate of examining the relationship between trade and investment policies. At the 2001 ministerial meeting, in Doha, agreement was reached to initiate negotiations on investment policies at the 2003 WTO ministerial meeting, if consensus exists on the modalities of such negotiations.

This chapter surveys the main arguments that have been suggested for why developing countries should support the creation of a multilateral agreement on investment. As in other areas, the answer may vary depending on country circumstances. A key chal-

BOX 42.1 (CONTINUED)

FDI is a direct instrument of development and growth. Since growth strategy should vary from country to country depending on factor endowment, technology, and so on, FDI policy ought to be country-specific to some extent. In the Indian context, for example, this translates mostly into sectoral prioritization. Infrastructural problems continue to be India's biggest bottleneck, followed by the poor quality of the services sector and shortcomings in the agriculture sector—lagging modernization and availability of critical inputs. The priorities for FDI in India are, accordingly, relatively straightforward: the infrastructure sector (energy, transport and communications, cement, and so on) comes first, followed by the services sector (including the financial and insurance industries) and agricultural machinery, chemicals, and fertilizers.

An effective prioritization scheme does not require a complex system of regulations and incentives. Reform should aim for simplicity—for example, the removal of many of the arbitrarily set caps on foreign equity in different sectors. Any prioritization scheme carries the danger of allowing costly discretion for too long, and a timetable must be set for removal of the restrictions. This is where multilateral rules can help. There is a yawning gap between FDI approvals and actual inflows in India. Since liberalization in 1991, the ratio of actual to approved FDI has been no more than 25 percent An alarming absolute decline in FDI in India since 1998 suggests that the existing incentive packages and vows of commitment are not enough to attract foreign investors. Further assurance and security for foreign investors are needed and might be obtained from WTO rules.

Such rules should revolve around a most-favored-nation (MFN) code of conduct aiming at gradual, time-bound removal of restrictions on FDI, with defined prioritization deadlines for different developing countries and with safeguard provisions that allow for well-defined temporary deviations from free foreign entry, but on grounds of industry-specific ills only, not on account of balance of payments or other problems.

Source: Prepared by the volume editors, based on Das (2000).

International Spillovers

Investment-related policies may rationally attempt to shift rents (profits) from source to host countries through measures that effectively tax investors. The opportunity for this arises because FDI usually occurs in imperfectly competitive markets, and such policies can therefore give rise to spillovers. The same is true for policies that encourage FDI. Clearly, both types of policies can provide a basis for international cooperation. What follows focuses primarily on incentive policies, as these are most obviously potentially detrimental to developing countries. Distortions created by imperfect competition call for competition policies (see Chapter 43, by Holmes, and Chapter 44, by Evenett, in this volume).

From an individual country's perspective, incentives to attract FDI may be justified if FDI generates positive externalities. An example is when FDI generates technological spillovers for local firms, thereby making more efficient use of national resources.[3] There exists a large literature that tries to determine whether host countries enjoy such spillovers. Spillovers may arise when local firms adopt technologies introduced by multinational enterprises through imitation or reverse engineering; when workers trained by a multinational transfer information to local firms or start their own firms; and when derived demand (both upstream and downstream) from multinationals leads to local provision of services or inputs that are also used by local firms.

The empirical support for positive spillover effects is ambiguous (see Chapter 34, by Saggi, in this volume). Nevertheless, if governments believe that there exists a solid economic case for promoting inward FDI via incentives because of positive externalities, countries may find themselves in a bidding war for attracting FDI.[4] This can be to the detriment of the parties involved if it leads to excessive payment to the investor—that is, transfers that exceed the social value of the expected spillovers. The proliferation in the use of incentives for FDI suggests that this is an important possibility and that there may be a case for international cooperation to ban or discipline the use of fiscal incentives.

Clearly, a key issue here is whether fiscal incentives are effective. The empirical evidence on this issue, too, is far from clear. Many studies have concluded that incentives for inward FDI do not play an important role in altering the global distribution of FDI (Wheeler and Mody 1992; Caves 1996). Others conclude that incentives do have an effect on location decisions, especially for export-oriented FDI (see Guisinger and associates 1985; Hines 1993; Devereux and Griffiths 1998).[5] When incentives do not distort the global allocation of FDI, they basically end up as transfers to multinationals. It is precisely when such incentives fail to attract FDI that developing countries have the most to gain from committing to not using them. The case for cooperation under these circumstances is based mainly on distributional grounds.

If incentives do affect FDI, there may be an efficiency case against competition for FDI. It must be recognized, however, that competition for FDI via incentives may actually help ensure that FDI goes to those locations where it is most highly valued. Incentive competition may act as a signaling device that improves the allocation of investment across jurisdictions by ensuring that FDI moves to where it has the highest social return. It can do so in situations where investors locate in countries or regions in which the social return to FDI is lower. In such situations governments should apply incentive policies on a nondiscriminatory basis.

In practice, locational competition is generally not driven by information asymmetries that can lead to FDI not flowing to countries where social returns are highest. This is the case, in particular, for efforts by high-income countries to retain or attract FDI that would be more efficiently employed in developing countries. Labor unions and groups representing the interests of local communities may oppose plant closures and efforts by firms to transplant facilities. Similar motivations underlie the use of trade policy instruments such as antidumping by industrial countries. It is important, therefore, to distinguish

between competition for FDI between developing countries, which may be efficient, and locational incentives used by industrial nations. The latter are much more likely to be inefficient because they attract or retain industries that otherwise would locate in developing countries. Such incentive policies, as well as complementary policies that protect industries which cannot compete (examples are restrictive rules of origin in regional agreements and antidumping), are prime candidates for discipline through international negotiations (Moran 1998).

The foregoing suggests there are valid reasons to question the rationale for a multilateral agreement that seeks to discipline all incentives. If incentives fail to alter the global allocation of FDI, restricting their usage has mainly distributional consequences. In this case unilateral action to cease granting incentives is the optimal policy. If incentives *are* effective in altering location decisions, a case may exist for subsidy freedom, since countries may be able to signal important information to potential investors. Developing countries, however, have an unambiguous incentive to push for multilateral disciplines on industrial country policies that have the effect of keeping firms from relocating to developing countries. A key need is to increase information on the use of incentives and analysis of their effects.

Spillovers due to Regional Integration

Some regional integration agreements (RIAs) extend the reach of national treatment to investors from partner countries. Examples include the European Union (EU), where freedom of investment is a basic principle; the North American Free Trade Agreement (NAFTA); and various association agreements that the EU has concluded with neighboring countries. Insofar as RIAs lead to discrimination between insiders and outsiders in FDI policies, they impose negative externalities over and above whatever investment "diversion" occurs because of the preferential liberalization of trade barriers (see Chapter 55, by Hoekman and Schiff, in this volume). Eliminating this discrimination can be a powerful argument in favor of multilateral rules. An important empirical question is whether such discrimination occurs and how large it is. This is difficult to determine, as doing so requires careful and detailed assessments of the applicable legislation on both a horizontal and a sectoral basis. Some agreements—for example, the EU and some of the agreements the

FDI is therefore critical in identifying reform priorities and determining how multilateral rules and agreements may assist in meeting the objectives that are defined. Undertaking such analysis will require information on existing policies—including policies in partner countries—and assessments of their effects.

Notes

1 In the case of other domestic policy distortions, the optimal policy is well known: remove the distortions at the source, if necessary through appropriately designed regulatory intervention that is applied on a nondiscriminatory basis (i.e., that applies equally to foreign and domestic firms). Thus, the adoption of low and uniform tariffs is preferable to the use of investment policies to offset the effects of high protection. This point of view is implicit in the WTO, which not only aims at progressive liberalization of trade but also prohibits the use of most TRIMs.

2 Investment measures have tended to be concentrated in specific industries, with automotive, chemical and petrochemical, and computer industries leading the list (Moran 1998). Local content requirements are most important in the auto industry; export requirements are more important in the computer industry. In chemicals and petrochemicals, local content requirements and export requirements are employed extensively.

3 The use of the word "spillovers" is somewhat unfortunate, since productivity improvements are unlikely to be costless and automatic.

4 Government officials are often not convinced of the inefficacy of incentives, as illustrated by the use of such instruments by many countries.

5 Fiscal incentives are found to be unimportant for FDI geared toward the domestic market. This type of FDI is more sensitive to the extent to which it will benefit from import protection.

6 See Markusen (2001) for a discussion of the credibility case for an investment agreement and Fernandez and Portes (1998) for an analysis of how international agreements may support credibility.

The International Centre for the Settlement of Investment Disputes (ICSID), which operates under the aegis of the World Bank, is responsible for applying the convention. The ICC has a Court of Arbitration. UNCITRAL has adopted a set of arbitration and conciliation rules that can be used in the settlement of commercial disputes.

7 See Henderson (1999) for a comprehensive analysis of the OECD-based MAI negotiations.

PETER HOLMES

43

TRADE, COMPETITION, AND THE WTO

T HIS CHAPTER LOOKS AT THE TRADE AND COMPETITION DEBATE, WHICH HAS BEEN a preoccupation for more than 50 years. Studies and policy experience show that although the case for some form of multilateral rules is in principle clear, there is extensive debate about how their introduction might be effectively brought about, what the institutional locus of any rule-making effort should be, and how international norms might be enforced.

Background

The topic "trade and competition policy" was put on the WTO agenda at the Singapore ministerial meeting in 1996, and a decision was made to set up a working group on this interface. The working group is not a negotiating forum, but its work has influenced the attitudes of WTO members toward the possibility of negotiations, and its reports give a valuable account of the evolution of the debate.[1]

Concerns about competition and trade have a long pedigree. Adam Smith, in the *Wealth of Nations*, had already denounced the monopolistic power of the East India Company, which he argued hurt both India and the United Kingdom. Smith presciently drew attention to the significance of international anticompetitive behavior in the services sector and to the symbiotic role of private and public actors.[2] Before World War II, international cartels had a high profile, and after the war the 1947 Havana Charter of the abortive International Trade Organization (ITO) included, in Article 46.1, a requirement that members police international restrictive behavior:

Each Member shall take appropriate measures and shall co-operate with the Organization to prevent, on the part of private or public commercial enterprises, business practices affecting international trade which restrain competition, limit access to markets, or foster monopolistic control, whenever such practices have harmful effects on the expansion of production or trade and interfere with the achievement of any of the other objectives set forth in Article 1.[3]

The Havana Charter contained no general obligation to adopt a competition law. The ITO as an organization would have been called on to investigate any complaints not resolved by consultation and to report its recommendations for action. The Havana Charter allowed for intergovernmental cooperation and also provided a means for dealing with disputes in the services sector. Although the debate has moved a long way from the Havana Charter in many respects, it is striking that the aims

police all export cartels. Even the EU, desirous as it is to see enhanced cooperation, has some problems with a commitment to police the anticompetitive behavior of its firms in export markets. There are also, of course, governments that in fact want their firms to be able to make monopoly profits.

The competition policy community itself has shown strong political reticence. Discussions at the OECD revealed that competition specialists do not want their turf taken over by trade officials. The debate often focuses on vertical restraints; trade officials sometimes demand that exclusive distribution systems be allowed and that parallel imports be banned, and this is opposed by competition officials, who do not have a market access perspective (see Box 43.1). As discussed below, however, the emphasis of the discussions and recent proposals has moved away from market access.

BOX 43.1 WHY COMPETITION POLICY SHOULD NOT BE SEEN THROUGH A MARKET ACCESS LENS

Bargaining over market access concessions has been a time-honored and highly effective means of lowering border barriers in multilateral trade negotiations. Unsurprisingly, when the view emerged that inadequate competition policy enforcement could undermine the expected market access gains from trade reforms, some began to argue that international disciplines on competition policies were necessary to ensure market access.

This viewpoint—which for some time had considerable currency among leading U.S. policymakers—arose out of frustration on the part of U.S. exporters over their attempts to gain access to the Japanese market. From the mid-1980s on, many U.S. trade policy analysts argued that Japanese authorities had tolerated anticompetitive business practices by Japanese firms, in particular through vertical integration between producers and distributors. A vast legal and economic literature grew up on whether Japan's markets were relatively more closed than other nations' markets, with little agreement emerging. (Evenett and Suslow 2000 survey much of this debate.)

Unlike trade reform, where reduction in border barriers typically improves both access to domestic markets and the domestic allocation of resources, there are numerous instances in which prohibiting horizontal and vertical agreements between firms might enhance market access at the expense of economic efficiency. For example, a manufacturer may sign a long-term exclusive contract with a supplier that effectively shuts out foreign suppliers from competing for the manufacturer's business. The manufacturer may forgo the benefits from competition among suppliers in order to encourage one supplier to undertake relationship-specific investments (such as the purchase of special machines or the cost of tailoring parts to the manufacturer's particular needs). Without a long-term contract, the supplier would be unwilling to undertake such commitments. The benefits of such relationship-specific investments would be lost if long-term contracting with suppliers were banned on the grounds of preserving foreign market access.

The potentially divergent effects on market access and economic efficiency of certain competition policy decisions suggests that the former may not be a good proxy for the latter—unlike the case of most negotiations over border barriers. This explains the view of most competition authorities that any multilateral initiatives on competition policy ought to be evaluated solely in terms of their effects on economic efficiency and not on market access (Hoekman 1997). There may be other explicit goals for competition policy (for example, black empowerment in South African law), but many consumer groups argue that broad "public interest" provisions in competition laws are easily captured and distorted by producer interests.

Summing up, national competition enforcement should not focus on market access. (This is not because other aims such as redistribution are unimportant but because competition policy is rarely the best instrument for achieving them.) During 1997–2000, a clear consensus emerged in the WTO Working Group that competition policies and international competition policy initiatives should not be evaluated in terms of their effects on trade flows.

Is there an assurance paradox that can be solved through a binding multilateral agreement? Even if there were maximum goodwill, international antitrust enforcement is in large part a public good. Any country that offers to take other countries' interests into account without an assurance that others will do the same incurs a cost. But is it the case that everyone is likely to be willing to adopt effective antitrust enforcement if others agree to do the same? As noted above, certain interests oppose more effective international enforcement. Nevertheless almost all governments see the desirability of competitive markets. The fact that there are real differences of opinion does not mean that agreement is impossible, but it helps in understanding why it has not yet been reached.

Can a WTO regime be devised that offers greater benefits than costs for all members? If so, what form would it take? What is clear from the discussions is that the idea of an international agency reporting on and eventually policing international competition issues is not even being discussed at the WTO. The EU would like all (or nearly all) WTO members to have their own competition law and calls for the creation of stronger modalities for cooperation, not a global equivalent of its Competition Directorate. Unlike the abortive ITO, the WTO has a judicial arm but no executive. Bringing in the WTO essentially means bringing in the Dispute Settlement Body (see Chapter 9, by Delich, in this volume).

Fox (1999) argues that the international competition issue should be split, with a general WTO obligation that members have a competition law ensuring that market access is not unreasonably impaired, and with other matters left to other fora. Many analysts have argued that there are such substantial differences in philosophy between jurisdictions (and between trade and competition officials) that any substantive rules on competition law would risk forcing a single option in a domain where opinions are divided and would even risk the subordination of efficiency considerations in vertical restraint to market access considerations (Hoekman and Holmes 1999; Marsden 2000). But as discussions have proceeded at the WTO and the OECD, there has been a clarification of what is commonly agreed and what is not. There is a consensus that nondiscrimination and transparency are key disciplines that everyone should respect. What remains to be agreed is not whether these principles should be made to apply, but how. Whereas in 1995

the EU could be said to have seriously sought to achieve convergence on substantive as well as procedural issues at the WTO, its aims are now much more modest: it is unimaginable that the EU would propose that everyone adopt a WTO competition code so specific as to rule out any of the existing provisions of U.S. law.

Developing Countries

A WTO agreement that obliged members to have a competition law of some kind would clearly primarily affect developing economies that do not have a competition law, as well as those such as Hong Kong (China), which argue that their own open trade regimes are sufficient to guarantee fully competitive markets.[5] As discussed in Box 43.2, the latter argument is not compelling.

Why would developing countries need a WTO competition code when they could adopt domestic laws unilaterally? The tally of countries with competition laws shows that the number has been increasing every year. Competition policy is spreading in Sub-Saharan Africa, and there is a growing recognition of the need for vigorous competition policy to assist the transition from economies dominated by parastatals. South Africa has been in the vanguard of promoting the use of competition policy as a way of achieving both economic and social ends, to make industry more competitive in export markets and to deconcentrate power. Developing countries are also increasingly aware of international cartels and anticompetitive practices regarding distribution. The Consumer Unity & Trust Society (CUTS) recently examined an interesting case in which the Indian subsidiary of Unilever was found to be abusing its control of the distribution system in neighboring Bhutan.[6] In this case the Bhutan authorities were able to take effective action by insisting that Unilever allow a second distributor to carry its products.

Although there is little empirical evidence on the link between competition and growth (Tybout 2000), technical assistance and voluntary adoption of laws should not be controversial. There is an interesting precedent in the treatment of basic telecommunications in the General Agreement on Trade in Services (GATS), where negotiators produced a reference paper laying down regulatory and competition principles that countries could sign on to à la carte but had to stick to once agreed (see Box

BOX 43.2 FREE TRADE AND COMPETITION POLICY

It is sometimes asserted that, in the absence of government-sponsored barriers to trade and investment, national competition policy cannot improve the allocation of resources in a small economy. Over 30 years ago, Bhagwati (1968) showed that if a monopoly producer in a small, open economy was exposed to unimpeded competition from abroad, the monopolist would be unable to charge a price above the world price. More important, the monopolist would expand output until the marginal cost of production equaled the world price—the outcome that would prevail in a competitive market. Thus, competition from abroad could not only tame but actually eliminate domestic market power. If this theoretical proposition were borne out in the empirical literature, it would call into question the rationale for certain national competition policies. For example, there would be no need to worry that a merger of two domestic firms would result in excessive market power, as any attempt to do so would be frustrated by overseas rivals willing to sell at the world price of the commodity in question.

Empirical studies have certainly borne out the claim that trade reform helps reduce the exercise of market power by domestic firms (Feenstra 1996; Tybout 2000). It has not been shown, however, that eliminating tariffs eliminates domestic market power. Even if such findings did emerge, they would only apply to markets in which the goods are tradable. Although it could be argued that open foreign direct investment regimes could inject competitive pressures into nontradable sectors, EU and U.S. antitrust experience demonstrates that even in competitive economies, some markets remain vulnerable to anticompetitive practices. Thus, the available empirical evidence suggests that trade liberalization is not a perfect substitute for an active competition policy, although it is an important and powerful procompetitive policy.

29.2, by Carsten Fink, in this volume). A similar quasi-voluntary approach could be pursued in the competition area. Better international cooperation in antitrust could also be a positive attraction. "Positive comity" would not go very far, but a real commitment to sharing information and expertise where cartels are discovered in industrial countries could be a major benefit, which could only be taken up by a country that has a competition law.

One of the most sensitive issues in this area is the potential abuse of patents. The WTP Agreement on Trade-Related Aspects of Intellectual Property Rights provides a right for host and importing countries to control patent abuses through competition law—a little used provision that should be reaffirmed and strengthened in any competition agreement.

The Positions of the Major Players

In the 1990s the United States claimed that Japan's competition laws were operating in a manner that was biased against U.S. imports. By 1996, however, the United States had lost interest, and the demand that trade and competition should be on the post-Singapore WTO agenda came essentially from the EU.

The EU has made a point of incorporating into nearly all its recent preferential trade agreements with Central and Eastern European countries (CEECs) competition provisions that ban "(i) all agreements between undertakings, decisions by associations of undertakings and concerted practices between undertakings which have as their object or effect the prevention, restriction or distortion of competition; and (ii) abuse by one or more undertakings of a dominant position in the territories of the Community or of [the partner country] as a whole or in a substantial part thereof, *if they may* affect trade between the two partners."[7] The agreements declare that the meaning of these terms shall be that used in the EU under what are now Articles 81 and 82 (formerly Articles 85 and 86 of the European Community treaty). The full wording of this and equivalent agreements has been widely seen as dictation by the EU of the form of domestic competition policy its partners should have. In fact, the wording of the agreement technically leaves the associates free to achieve this end by their own means, but the CEECs' relationship with the EU means that the latter can make such demands, largely due to the carrot-and-stick of EU membership. The 1999 EU–South Africa Free Trade Agreement contains similar provisions but does not spell out detailed competition policy criteria.[8] The EU-Mexico Free Trade Agreement (2000) contains equivalent provisions.[9]

The EU is thus creating a web of bilateral agreements, including agreements with the United States—which is doing the same. The EU, however, is arguing that having so many overlapping and possibly inconsistent agreements is inadequate and inefficient. The United States maintains that given the different interests and capacities of different parties, this approach is inevitable.

The European Commission would like to see a generalization of the provisions it has been putting into its trade agreements introduced into the WTO. The bilateral agreements of the form referred to above are feasible only if a state has a competition law. The EU would like a basic agreement on the need for domestic competition law in WTO members, although its proposals provide for opt-outs (see also Garcia Bercero and Amarasinha 2001).

What we are proposing is to introduce, into the WTO, provisions that require its members to adopt certain minimum standards and core principles as it relates to their domestic competition laws and regulations and to respect certain requirements of international co-operation between competition authorities. The establishment of a domestic competition policy and a competition authority with sufficient enforcement powers remain the basis, in the absence of which a country would not be able to address anti-competitive practices of a domestic or international character. What we are aiming at is therefore, somewhat similar to what we did in the TRIPs Agreement, namely the establishment of a certain number of basic principles for inclusion in domestic laws. (Mogens 2001)

The EU is thus asking in some ways for more in a WTO agreement than was provided in the Havana Charter, but it insists that its aims are modest:

More specifically, we suggest that WTO negotiations should focus on three key issues:

core principles of domestic competition law and policy; 2) co-operation between competition authorities, including both specific cases and more general co-operation and exchange of information; and 3) technical assistance and capacity-building for the reinforcement of competition institutions in developing countries. (Mogens 2001)

However, in a communication of June 29, 2001, the EU suggested, "Individual developing countries may . . . wish to reserve their judgement on the costs and benefits of such an agreement. In this connection, a possible option to explore could be to provide for the possibility for developing countries to decide, at the conclusion of negotiations, whether they wish to subscribe to the competition agreement."[10]

The European Commission argues strongly that the adoption of common core principles, including nondiscrimination and transparency, should not conflict with other development objectives. But the commission also suggests that if countries do want to exclude sectors from competition rules or from national treatment provisions, they should be free to do so, subject only to the proviso that exclusions must be transparent and hence predictable for economic actors—the model perhaps being similar to some of the elements in the GATS, referred to above. The EU places great stress on the benefits of a common framework for cooperation, which it argues would be helped by some agreement on common principles. It stresses, however, that the obligation to undertake cooperation will be "voluntary" in that the strict obligation will be to consider requests, not to act on them, although there could be an obligation to explain any refusal. This gets around the problem of onerous procedural obligations, but it leaves open the complaint that the EU can also refuse assistance to developing countries, even though the EU's aims are said to include "responding to the longstanding developing country concerns about the importance of assistance by 'home' competition authorities in those cases in which foreign firms may be engaged in anticompetitive practices with an impact on developing country markets."[11]

One solution is that the obligation to offer cooperation could be asymmetrical. Here we can also see a possible parallel with GATS, where countries may decline to open up sectors but are required to apply policies on a most-favored-nation (MFN) basis.

The Clinton administration in the United States, however, argued strongly for more bilateral and voluntary cooperation *outside* the WTO. The ICPAC report of April 2000 highlighted the global dimension of antitrust and the weaknesses of existing arrangements but firmly argued against WTO involvement:

> At this juncture, the majority of the Advisory Committee believes that the WTO as a forum for review of private restraints is not appropriate. Given the possible risks, and the lack of international consensus on the content or appropriateness of rules or dispute settlement in this area, this Advisory Committee believes that the WTO should not develop new competition rules under its umbrella.[12]

Most economists with a disinclination toward harmonization will have an instinctive sympathy for this position. There is, nevertheless, an inconsistency in it: the ICPAC report shows that the voluntary approach is not delivering.

The U.S. view has evolved under President Bush. In mid-2001 U.S. Trade Representative Robert Zoellick stated:

> In competition policy, U.S. trade and anti-trust authorities recognize the significance of the issue. Therefore, we are working to understand more clearly what the EU seeks, and are discussing with the EU how it can accommodate the concerns of the United States and other countries.[13]

But doubts remain:

> What is not clear to us, however, is how competition obligations based on the core principles should be assessed; for example, the important question of how dispute settlement might operate or whether other forms of oversight such as peer review might be more satisfactory.[14]

The EU responds that only the consistency of laws with agreed core principles, not cases and enforcement, should be subject to the Dispute Settlement Body, and it favors peer review. The EU does have something to offer the United States: enhanced cooperation on antitrust enforcement. The EU might have to be ready to exchange confidential information with the United States, although whether this is a priority for the latter will have to be determined.

Developing countries are divided. South Africa and some Latin Americans are favorably inclined, but Asian countries are more skeptical. Officially, India has argued that while it recognizes the multilateral dimension of competition policy and supports the work of UNCTAD, it wants to see some of the basic systemic issues of the WTO sorted out before new areas are included in negotiations. There are, however, influential counterviews within India.[15]

Meanwhile, in October 2001, the OECD held its first Global Competition Forum, along the lines suggested by the ICPAC. The forum was attended by 30 OECD members and 26 nonmember governments (including India), as well as selected business and consumer groups. The mandate of this group is dialogue and exchange of experience regarding best practice and modes of cooperation; it is not expected to address trade issues per se.[16]

Conclusion

The Doha Ministerial Declaration calls for negotiations on competition to be launched at the Fifth WTO Ministerial Conference, in 2003, if consensus can be reached on the modalities of negotiations. The EU has an increasing number of countries on its side now that it has become more flexible and has moved well away from its initial focus on market access. It is ready to discuss opt-outs or phase-ins for developing countries that do not have the inclination or the capability to introduce a competition law. It will, however, have to seriously consider going beyond its present offer on export cartels. And it will probably have to make concessions on other topics—for example, on antidumping, which has to be seen as an issue distinct from competition in this context.[17]

There is perhaps a deal that would interest developing countries, under which those countries that agree to have a competition law would obtain significant additional rights, above all in terms of cooperation. This is more likely to involve discussion and exchange of information than an attempt to address really sensitive matters such as multijurisdictional review of mergers. No country is likely to give up the right to review cases, but there are things that can usefully be done even here—for example, agreeing on ways to define relevant markets.

The key challenge for developing countries is to ensure that negotiations strengthen the competitive disciplines in global markets and that progress is made toward addressing their needs and recognizing national capacity constraints.

Notes

I thank numerous friends and colleagues at the World Bank, the WTO secretariat, and the European Commission for their advice and assistance for this chapter. The chapter draws heavily on an earlier collaboration with Bernard Hoekman and benefited greatly from his editorial assistance.

1 On the pros and cons, see the 2001 report to the WTO General Council of the WTO Working Group on the Interaction between Trade and Competition Policy (WT/WGTCP/5, October 8, 2001).

2 See Smith (1976 edition), vol. 2, ch. 7, pt. 2: 87–103.

3 Available at <http://www.globefield.com/havana.htm#CHAPTERV>.

4 Some U.S. experts believe that repealing the U.S. Webb-Pomerene Act, which allows export cartels, would have no impact, as any adverse effects affecting only foreigners are legal in any case in the United States—and, indeed, elsewhere.

5 This is the strongly held position of the Hong Kong government, but it is contested by the Hong Kong Consumer Council.

6 See <http://www.cuts-india.org/7-update.htm>. The CUTS Website, <http://www.cuts.org>, contains comprehensive material on competition policy in developing countries.

7 EU-Polish Association Agreement, <http://158.169.50.70/eur-lex/en/lif/dat/1993/en_293A1231_18.html>.

8 Available at <http://europa.eu.int/comm/trade/bilateral/saf.htm>.

9 Available at <http://europa.eu.int/comm/trade/bilateral/mexico/fta.htm>; see Article 39 and Annex XV.

10 "Draft Communication from the EC and its Member States: A WTO Competition Agreement and Development," June 29, 2001.

11 Ibid.

12 Available at <http://www.usis.it/file2000_02/alia/a002280a.htm>.

13 In a statement of July 17, 2001, after meeting Pascal Lamy; see <http://usinfo.state.gov/topical/econ/wto/pp0717a.htm>.

14 Ibid.

15 See "Let's Be Proactive on Multilateral Competition Policy," available at <http://www.cuts-india.org/>, "Viewpoint."

16 See <http://www.oecd.org/daf/clp/global_forum.htm>.

17 For a full discussion of why antidumping and competition policy are different, see Lawrence (1998).

Table 44.1 Economies with Firms Convicted of Price Fixing by the United States or the European Commission during the 1990s

Economy	Cartel
Angola	Shipping
Austria	Carton board, citric acid, newsprint, steel heating pipes
Belgium	Ship construction, stainless steel, steel beams
Brazil	Aluminum phosphide
Canada	Carton board, pigments, plastic dinnerware, vitamins
Denmark	Shipping, steel heating pipes, sugar
Finland	Carton board, newsprint, steel heating pipes
France	*Aircraft*, cable-stayed bridges, carton board, citric acid, ferry operators, *methionine*, newsprint, *plasterboard*, seamless steel tubes, shipping, sodium gluconate, stainless steel, steel beams
Germany	*Aircraft*, graphite electrodes onboard, citric acid, aluminum phosphide, lysine, *methionine*, newsprint, pigments, *plasterboard*, seamless steel tubes, steel heating pipes, vitamins
Greece	Ferry operators
India	Aluminum phosphide
Ireland	Shipping, sugar
Israel	Bromine
Italy	Carton board, ferry operators, newsprint, seamless steel tubes, stainless steel, steel heating pipes
Japan	Graphite electrodes, lysine, *methionine*, seamless steel tubes, shipping, sodium gluconate, sorbates, thermal fax paper, vitamins
Korea, Rep. of	Lysine, *methionine*, shipping
Luxembourg	Steel beams
Malaysia	Shipping
Mexico	Tampico fiber
Netherlands	Carton board, citric acid, ferry operators, ship construction, sodium gluconate, tampico fiber
Norway	Carton board, explosives, ferrosilicon
Singapore	Shipping
South Africa	Diamonds, newsprint
Spain	*Aircraft*, carton board, stainless steel, steel beams
Sweden	Carton board, ferry operators, newsprint, stainless steel
Switzerland	Citric acid, laminated plastic tubes, steel heating pipes, vitamins
Taiwan (China)	Shipping
United Kingdom	*Aircraft*, carton board, explosives, ferry operators, newsprint, pigments, *plasterboard*, seamless steel tubes, shipping, stainless steel, steel beams, sugar
United States	*Aircraft*, aluminum phosphide, bromine, cable-stayed bridges, carton board, citric acid, diamonds, ferrosilicon, graphite electrodes, isostatic graphite, laminated plastic tubes, lysine, maltol, *methionine*, pigments, plastic dinnerware, ship construction, shipping, sorbates, tampico fiber, thermal fax paper, vitamins
Zaire	Shipping

Note: Italics denote that the product is currently under investigation.
Source: Levenstein and Suslow (2001): table 1.

Table 44.2 Cross-Border Mergers and Acquisitions in Latin America and Asia Pacific, 1991–98

	1991	1992	1993	1994	1995	1996	1997	1998	Sum 1994-8
Latin America									
Inward FDI	3.9	10.4	13.7	30.1	32.8	45.9	69.2	73.8	251.8
Inward cross-border M&A				14.8	11.4	22.3	43.8	41.3	161.5
% with majority stakes	24.4	59.3	27.9	21.1	53.1	50.2	58.4	75.9	
% of Inward FDI				49.2	34.8	48.6	63.3	56.0	
Outward FDI	0.7	5.1	3.4	8.5	7.3	5.8	15.1	9.4	46.1
Outward cross-border M&A				8.5	2.8	5.2	7.2	7.0	30.7
% with majority stakes	17.7	89.2	65.7	29.2	75.6	80.7	59.5	71.4	
% of Outward FDI				100.0	38.4	89.7	47.7	74.5	
Asia and Pacific									
Inward FDI	6.4	21.2	33.5	68.6	73.3	92.4	101.6	96.5	432.4
Inward cross-border M&A				44.0	38.6	55.5	48.4	27.1	213.6
% with majority stakes	5.0	8.8	15.3	12.9	7.7	7.1	27.6	51.0	
% of Inward FDI				64.0	52.7	60.1	47.6	28.1	
Outward FDI	4.3	16.9	23.4	69.3	42.7	51.9	47.4	22.8	234.1
Outward cross-border M&A				23.8	21.6	26.9	33.5	9.6	115.4
% with majority stakes	31.8	59.1	21.8	27.8	29.4	19.9	42.1	34.5	
% of Outward FDI				34.3	50.6	51.8	70.7	42.1	
Developing Economies									
Inward FDI	41.7	51.1	72.5	95.6	105.5	129.8	148.9	179.5	659.3
Inward cross-border M&A	13.8	38.2	64.5	67.2	70.3	88.3	108.1	79.3	413.2
% with majority stakes	18.2	31.8	18.4	18.9	18.4	23.1	41.8	66.7	
% of Inward FDI	33.2	74.7	88.9	70.4	66.6	68.0	72.6	44.2	
Outward FDI	8.3	22.7	34.9	42.5	45.6	49.2	61.1	33.0	231.4
Outward cross-border M&A	5.4	22.7	27.4	33.4	25.1	35.1	41.7	18.0	153.3
% with majority stakes	31.8	65.8	27.4	27.4	34.1	29.4	42.0	49.2	
% of Outward FDI	64.6	100.0	78.6	78.5	55.0	71.5	68.3	54.5	
Industrial Economies									
Inward FDI	114.8	120.3	138.9	141.5	211.5	195.4	233.1	480.6	1262.1
Inward cross-border M&A	71.4	83.7	97.8	129.1	167.0	186.2	232.9	478.6	1193.8
% with majority stakes	65.2	73.6	56.2	74.9	76.6	76.4	82.0	77.3	
% of Inward FDI	62.2	69.6	70.4	91.3	79.0	95.3	99.9	99.6	
Outward FDI	189.8	180.0	205.8	241.5	306.5	283.5	359.2	731.7	1922.4
Outward cross-border M&A	79.9	99.2	134.9	163.0	212.2	239.3	299.3	540.0	1453.8
% with majority stakes	59.3	59.3	44.0	61.5	62.4	63.6	72.6	76.6	
% of Outward FDI	42.1	55.1	65.5	67.5	69.2	84.4	83.3	73.8	

Note: M&A, mergers and acquisitions.
Source: Kang and Johansson (2000); UNCTAD (2000c).

borders. Brazil, by contrast, exempts from merger review any proposed commercial transaction between firms with no corporate presence within its borders.

The diversity of notification requirements, differences in the deadlines for making merger review decisions, and the presence or absence of judicial review add considerably to the cost of undertaking international mergers and also increase the probability of different and inconsistent decisions being made by national antitrust authorities. In the 1990s the magnitude of these transactions costs became a source of concern for the International Bar Association, as well as for policymakers. Several sensible proposals for reducing these costs were made (see ICPAC 2000: ch. 4). In the remainder of this section I focus on the potential for resource misallocation due to multijurisdictional merger reviews. (I abstract from the associated transactions costs.)

There are two potential types of resource misallocation that merger reviews can generate. First, a proposed merger that improves the global allocation of resources may be vetoed by at least one antitrust authority. Second, a proposed merger that distorts the global allocation of resources may be allowed to proceed. In the first case the potential for improving resource allocation is forgone; in the second case actual resource allocation is adversely affected. The following three features of national enforcement—call them the "international antitrust trinity"—can generate these inefficient outcomes.

- *Multiple veto.* Each nation has the right to veto a proposed transaction.
- *National standards.* Each nation evaluates a proposed merger in terms of its effects on firms and consumers within its borders only.
- *No compensation scheme.* Each nation makes a decision on whether to allow a given merger without reference to any other merger or policy matter that might be of importance to the nations reviewing the merger.

The *multiple veto* feature of national merger review has already been discussed. The *standards* adopted by each nation can differ and need not focus on the effect of the merger on the sum of consumer and producer surplus within a nation. Suppose that a proposed merger affecting only two nations is reviewed using standards that place far more weight on producer interests than on consumer welfare. It would not be surprising if such a merger were permitted by both nations—especially if the merged entity's additional market power increased its profits by more than enough to compensate (in the eyes of the reviewing authorities) for any consumer welfare losses. In this case a proposed merger that—as measured by the traditional microeconomic standard—distorts the global allocation of resources is permitted.

The *absence of any compensation mechanism* is what differentiates multijurisdictional merger review from many other areas of international cooperation and negotiation, including trade reform. Antitrust officials and practitioners are reluctant to make tradeoffs across cases in the same way that tradeoffs across sectors occur during trade negotiations. Consequently, any merger that has significant adverse effects in one jurisdiction is likely to be rejected, even though the benefits created by the merger in other jurisdictions could more than offset the harm done. Thus, a merger that improves the global allocation of resources might never come about, having been vetoed by at least one jurisdiction. Essentially, the effects of international mergers spill over national borders, and, in the absence of any compensation scheme, mergers that could in principle improve the global allocation of resources will not take place.

It is useful to keep this trinity in mind when assessing international initiatives on competition policy. One class of proposals advocates procedural cooperation between national antitrust authorities, in part to encourage the convergence of substantive standards for evaluating mergers. Another set of proposals calls for internationally agreed minimum standards. Yet another argues for explicit harmonization of standards, which could be accomplished through the adoption of common regional, plurilateral, or multilateral norms.

Even if a common standard were adopted, it need not be based on, or be consistent with, the efficiency standard advocated by microeconomists. Furthermore, even if efficiency were adopted as the common standard, the resource misallocation created by the two other elements of the trinity—multiple veto and lack of a compensation mechanism— would remain. The sources of resource misallocation go far deeper than the adoption of conflicting merger review standards by nations.

However politically infeasible it may seem at present, the logic of these arguments suggests that only a supranational decisionmaker able to consider the aggregate efficiency effects of a merger in all affected jurisdictions can avoid the resource misallocation created by national merger review. (A national decisionmaker with a cosmopolitan viewpoint, to which other nations defer, could also fulfill this role.) Such a decisionmaker would consider only the aggregate impact of a merger on resource allocation, irrespective of the distribution of welfare gains and losses in different national markets. Since, of course, the distribution of gains and losses is a primary reason why national competition authorities differ in their assessments of mergers, such a supranational arrangement may well have to involve the creation of structural adjustment funds as well. These could mitigate the effects of decisions under which certain states lose while the aggregate welfare of the group of nations improves.

Although supranational decisionmaking is rather unlikely in the near or medium term, the point is that a supranational solution might overcome the inefficiencies created by the international antitrust trinity and do so far more effectively than the other proposals outlined above.

National Anticartel Policies in an Integrating World

Private cartels attempt to raise profits through agreements to restrict the quantity supplied to a market, to fix prices, or to rig bids. Such agreements distort the allocation of resources away from the competitive norm, and for this reason many nations have passed laws that restrict or ban agreements likely to cartelize markets within their jurisdictions. By contrast, many nations often exempt firms from anticartel laws with respect to attempts to cartelize overseas markets, presumably on the grounds that no harm is done to domestic consumers. An interesting question is whether the effectiveness of national anticartel laws is compromised in a multicountry world.

National anticartel laws have a dual purpose: to punish cartels that are found to exist, and to deter cartels from forming in the first place. The effectiveness of the deterrent depends critically on the severity of the punishment and on the probability of assembling sufficient credible evidence of cartelization. The following three factors undermine the deterrent provided by national anticartel law in a world of many jurisdictions (Evenett, Levenstein, and Suslow 2001):

- Difficulties in collecting evidence abroad, interviewing witnesses overseas, and extraditing persons from other jurisdictions.
- Lessened attractiveness of national corporate leniency or amnesty programs to firms that fear applications for leniency in one jurisdiction will leave them exposed to investigations and potential punishment in other jurisdictions. This is particularly worrisome because such programs have been instrumental in encouraging firms to "defect" from a cartel agreement and to supply evidence of wrongdoing by other firms to state authorities—and rarely are cartel members successfully prosecuted without a former member turning state's evidence.
- "Multimarket effects" that increase the incentive to collude. Fines for cartelization are a function of the cartel's effects within a single jurisdiction, without taking into account the enhanced profits derived from cartelizing other nations' markets, as well.

Practitioners have recognized the difficulties created by the first two factors, but the third factor has received little attention in policy circles, although it has been extensively analyzed in the economics literature. Only a few jurisdictions have taken steps to overcome the first set of difficulties, principally through signing bilateral cooperation agreements on antitrust matters (for example, an agreement in 2000 between Australia and the United States) or by invoking mutual legal assistance treaties (as in the case of the United States and Canada).[4] What more could be done to enhance the deterrent posed by national cartel laws in a multijurisdictional world?

A first option would be to extend the set of existing cooperation agreements on antitrust matters to include more nations. A slightly different variant might be to negotiate regional, plurilateral, or even multilateral agreements that permit signatories to request other signatories to collect evidence, interview persons, and consider extraditing those charged with cartelization. Yet another possibility would be to agree on minimum standards for cooperation between jurisdictions and then allow nations to tailor cooperative agreements to their specific needs.

A second option, which could easily build on the first, would be to allow for the simultaneous application of corporate leniency in multiple jurisdictions. In addition, nations could agree on a minimum degree of leniency for successful petitioners and minimal conditions for such leniency. Each nation would retain its own leniency program, and there would be no pooling of sovereignty. A more ambitious variant would be for a group of nations to agree to establish a common leniency program, whereby firms would apply to a single body for leniency in all of the jurisdictions that are parties to the agreement. This would avoid the difficulties created by inconsistent leniency decisions being made by multiple antitrust authorities.

A third option would be to establish a panel that would estimate the pecuniary gains a cartel has made from all the markets in which it has been found to operate. Such a panel could be entirely advisory, suggesting fines that each jurisdiction could impose and doing so in such a way that total fines equal or exceed the total gains from cartelizing many markets. Panels could be formed on a case-by-case basis, and their membership would draw from the professional economic and antitrust communities.

In sum, much can be done to enhance the effectiveness of national anticartel laws against international cartels without creating a new supranational agency or pooling national sovereignty. Much could also be accomplished regionally, plurilaterally, or through organizations such as the OECD. Nations with more aggressive anticartel regimes could move ahead more quickly, taking the steps outlined above in cooperation with like-minded nations.

Conclusion

In determining a policy stance with respect to international competition policy matters, decisionmakers are well advised to give primary consideration to efficiency, not market access. This chapter has discussed why national antitrust laws may perform suboptimally in an integrating world economy from an efficiency perspective. The reasons differ for cartel and merger policies, illustrating that the general debate over trade and competition policy needs to be replaced by specific analyses of the problems faced by national enforcement of different aspects of antitrust laws. These analyses point to markedly different reform options for the two types of antitrust policies considered here. While there is in principle a case for supranational approaches to merger review, nations need not pool sovereignty for the sake of fighting international cartels.

Although the analysis in this chapter is economic in nature, it must be borne in mind that the principal practitioners of antitrust law are lawyers, who are typically attuned to operating in a single jurisdiction. Given differences across nations in legal traditions and procedures, legal practitioners, when dealing with other jurisdictions, place much emphasis on procedural cooperation. Such cooperation may over time enhance trust in foreign jurisdictional procedures and practitioners and is arguably the first step in forging new approaches to international competition policy. This form of procedural cooperation is to be encouraged and should not be confused with the skepticism expressed above about the efficiency-enhancing effects of procedural cooperation aimed at convergence of national standards for merger review.

Notes

1 For the purpose of this chapter, I use the terms "competition policy" and "antitrust policy" interchangeably. In other words, the discussion of competition policies is confined to the elements of antitrust policy—policies toward mergers, acquisitions, takeovers, cartels, vertical restraints, monopolization, and anticompetitive practices.

2 This pickup in anticartel enforcement started in the United States with the reform of its corporate leniency program, which grants amnesties to qualifying firms that come forward with evidence of cartelization. The sizable fines imposed by U.S. authorities have not gone unnoticed by other nations and have provided a pecuniary incentive for enhanced anticartel enforcement elsewhere. For a discussion of the enforcement record against international cartels in the 1990s, see Evenett, Levenstein, and Suslow (2001).

3 See Tavares (2001) for an account of how various Latin American initiatives on competition policies are affecting the implementation of antitrust enforcement in that region.

4 Waller (2000) describes the extensive and fruitful cooperation between the United States and Canada in these matters and contrasts it with the absence of any sustained cooperation on cartel enforcement between the European Commission and the U.S. Department of Justice.

SIMON TAY

45

TRADE AND LABOR

Text, Institutions, and Context

I N THE RUN-UP TO THE 1996 WTO MINIS-
TERIAL MEETING IN SINGAPORE, THE
United States and the European Union (EU) supported a "social clause" that would amend the WTO
to permit countries to impose trade measures to
ensure that minimum labor standards were met by
their trading partners (Leary 1996). Much heated
debate resulted, largely along North-South lines,
with many nongovernmental organizations
(NGOs) and federations of unions supporting the
introduction of such a social clause. The final statement from the Singapore meeting recognized the
reality of lower wage costs in developing countries
as a legitimate advantage and designated the International Labour Organization (ILO) "the competent body to set and deal with [labor] standards"
(WTO 1996: 4). This was reaffirmed at the Doha
ministerial meeting in 2001. Box 45.1 summarizes
some of the key labor standards at issue.

To date, efforts to link labor rights to trade within
the WTO have been stymied. Nevertheless, the idea
of using trade measures and sanctions to promote
and protect labor rights resurfaces regularly, both in
the WTO and outside it (Rodrik 1997). In the ILO,

where sanctions have not traditionally been acceptable, efforts
have been made to curb child
labor and other abuses through
trade measures. Unilateral
efforts by cities and states to
connect trade and economic
measures to labor and human
rights have also been
increasing.[1] This has been most
noticeable in the case of Myanmar, where a number of human
rights abuses, including forced
labor, have been reported.[2]

In 1999 the ILO developed a convention (No.
182) against the worst forms of child labor that
potentially has implications for trade. This highlights the real possibility that treaties in this area
may come into conflict with the WTO, with no clear
priority between conflicting international rules and
institutions. The Vienna Convention on the Interpretation of Treaties provides that the most recent
and most specific treaty should prevail. In the area
of trade and labor this could lead to rapid changes
in international law and policy and to inconsistency.

In the run-up to the Seattle ministerial meeting in
1999, there were signs that it would no longer be
possible for the WTO to continue to exclude labor
standards. Labor issues have featured prominently
on the U.S. agenda, as a result of lobbying by unions
and other interest groups.[3] In Europe labor protection has been a concern for many countries, especially regarding child labor. This chapter considers
the connections between trade and labor. The current debate in the WTO is a beggared choice
between, on the one hand, ignoring the interdependence between trade and economic issues and
the protection and promotion of human dignity

BOX 45.2 TRADE AND LABOR STANDARDS: THREE DEBATES

Commonly expressed complaints about limited adherence to core labor standards (CLSs) and the alleged effects on foreign economies focus on the operations of export-processing zones (EPZs), international wage spillovers, and the putative "race to the bottom" in labor standards.

Export-Processing Zones
Core labor standards may be introduced across most of the economy but waived or weakened in the export sector. Questions then arise as to the effects of EPZs on wages and whether export-specific exemptions from CLSs constitute an export subsidy. The available evidence (Maskus 1997) indicates that firms in EPZs tend to pay higher wages than firms outside the zones. There are a number of reasons for this. Take the case of an EPZ in an economy that has a large informal sector with low wages, a small formal sector with higher wages, and substantial unemployment. Exempting from tariffs imports that are intermediate goods in EPZ production in order to attract labor-intensive assembly operations will raise the demand for low-skilled labor. Favorable tax treatment and subsidies to fixed costs within EPZs are likely to attract foreign capital, further expanding labor demand and raising wages in and outside the area. To the extent that workers are then trained and acquire skills, employers are likely to seek to retain them, putting further upward pressure on wages in the EPZ.

Comparative Advantage and International Wage Spillovers
Organized labor interests in high-wage countries are often concerned about the effects on their own labor markets of limited CLSs in low-wage countries. Differences in labor standards, however, will have negligible implications for employment, wages, and wage inequality in high-wage countries. For example, less than 5 percent of children working in developing countries are engaged in export sectors, and their contribution to output is small (although in particular sectors, such as carpets, footwear, and apparel, child labor is more prevalent). Wage and income inequality have increased since the 1980s in the

EU and the United States, but although this increase has coincided with the opening of markets to international trade, the correlation does not necessarily imply causation. Changes in technology, demographics, regulation, and unionization rates could also be responsible for these labor market trends (Richardson 1995). It is misleading to ascribe differences in wages across countries (or changes in these differences) to differential labor standards. Policy changes that weaken labor standards are not necessarily correlated with lower wages in poor countries, larger volumes of low-priced exports from those countries, and, ultimately, downward wage pressure in the importing countries.

Competitive Impacts on Standards
Another common complaint is that competition will reduce standards in the higher-standard (OECD) countries—that there will be a "race to the bottom" in labor standards. This claim has two variants: (a) there is a danger that standards will decline to low levels worldwide, or (b) the competition in standards may be concentrated among low-wage nations, preventing countries that would otherwise move toward higher standards from doing so. The simple argument that competition can push standards toward their lowest levels is wrong on its face; it presumes that the lowest standards will prevail as market outcomes. It is unlikely that, accounting for global income levels and technologies, African or South Asian labor standards would prevail in international competition. Moreover, it is questionable that integrated markets must see convergent labor standards. Open economies can sustain high standards through some combination of higher taxes, lower wages, and exchange rate devaluation.

The Empirical Evidence on Labor Standards and Trade
The empirical evidence suggests that differential CLS levels have little effect on exports and export prices. OECD (1996), a study relating measures of export performance to indicators of labor standards, found no relationship between the two. The study detected no effects of differences in

BOX 45.2 (CONTINUED)

core labor standards on U.S. import prices in sectors such as textiles and apparel, nor was there any indication that export prices for handmade carpets are lower in countries in which use is made of child labor. Rodrik (1996) econometrically related basic measures of labor standards across countries to international trade flows, using data such as country ratification of ILO conventions covering core labor standards and an indicator of enforcement problems in child labor standards. He, too, was unable to determine any relationship in the data or to find any suggestion of a positive statistical relationship between low labor standards and flows of FDI from the United States to particular countries. Indeed, there was some evidence that FDI is lower than expected in countries with low labor standards.

Aggarwal (1995) notes that it is common in developing countries for labor standards to be lower in less export-oriented sectors and in non-traded goods than in export-oriented industries, including even textiles and carpeting. Within all manufacturing, workers in firms with high export-output ratios tend to receive higher wages and benefits than those in less export oriented firms. Aggarwal found no association between U.S. FDI and poor labor standards in developing countries. In fact, she concludes that U.S. FDI is not concentrated in countries or sectors with low labor standards and that countries with weaker labor standards do not have higher import penetration rates in the United States than countries with stronger labor standards.

Such evidence will not satisfy those who are concerned about the impacts of differences in labor standards (or of EPZs) on competitiveness. The studies can be criticized for their inability to measure CLS effectively, given the inherent difficulties with data in this area. Further criticisms are that the studies did not adequately control for other significant impacts on trade and FDI and that they are static (cross-sectional). Many observers, for example, point to the rapid increases in manufactured exports from EPZs in China, where CLSs are not fully respected (although it is not known whether this fact explains export growth).

Source: Prepared by the volume editors, based on Maskus (1997).

(see Revesz 1992; Stewart 1992; Esty 1996), perceptions of a "race to the bottom" persist.

"Psychic" or "Moral" Spillovers

Some argue that as economic interdependence increases, so does concern about moral issues such as the treatment of our fellow human beings. They see the growth of the world economy and world trade as being in tandem with the promotion of human rights, both being post–World War II phenomena. In human and labor rights the international community has been increasingly willing to take action against violators. This is especially true where the abuses are gross and large scale (Steiner and Alston 1996).

By and large, developing countries that have been accused of violations do not seek to justify them in the name of sovereignty. They agree that there is a core of basic labor and human rights that have to be observed, such as the prohibition against slavery and other forms of forced labor, but they question the effectiveness of trade sanctions in resolving such evils. As an alternative, they propose assistance and the transfer of resources to promote and enable solutions. For example, a common rebuttal regarding child labor is that banning the goods produced, without further action, may lead to factory closures and to the child workers being abandoned to street life as prostitutes or to criminal behavior. The common defense against the "moral spillover" argument is thus most often a debate not about morality itself but about the effectiveness of using trade measures to address moral issues.

Unilateralism, Compulsion, and Protectionism

Although unilateral actions per se are not illegal under international law, such measures can be a form of compulsion, practiced by larger and richer states against less powerful countries. Moreover,

- Greater transparency and timely public access to WTO documents
- Policy discussions with civil society, especially NGOs and other groups working on social concerns[5]
- Arrangements for access and participation of NGOs and experts in the dispute settlement process
- Increasing dialogue and cooperation between the WTO and international environmental bodies such as the secretariats of multilateral environmental agreements, the United Nations Environment Programme (UNEP), and the ILO
- Increasing coordination between economic and trade agencies and their environmental and labor counterparts at the national level.

By such means, coordination between trade and social policies could be increased.[6] This would better achieve the first-best solution of reconciling the differing concerns at the level of the production of goods rather than in their trade. The increased cooperation between different institutions would allow for better understanding. This path could be pursued both at the international level and within national governments.

There is also a need for support and mediation on social concerns outside the WTO, especially with regard to extending assistance and resources to help countries strengthen labor rights protection. The WTO as an institution faces several limitations in dealing directly with these issues. It lacks expertise, will, and culture, and some developing countries view it with skepticism as representing certain Northern countries' interests in promoting freer trade. The prospect of discussions in the WTO appears to be threatening because it could lead to new, binding rules. Finally, and perhaps most important, the WTO has no strong mechanism or principles regarding assistance.[7] Efforts to deal with contentious issues of social concern may be better received and more effectively implemented if they are carried out through other institutions. What the WTO must then do is to be open to greater exchange, improved access, and better coordination with these other entities and processes.

The above recommendations should be seen as achievable and effective in the short to medium term. A more positive agenda for coordination and cooperation in the longer run may be tentatively sketched as follows (Runnals and Tay):

- Accept the equality of multilateral agreements on labor rights with those on trade rules, and work toward their congruence. Unilateral measures should be avoided.
- Recognize that efforts at the state level must be emphasized in order to achieve a "first-best" reconciliation of trade and social concerns in the production and manufacture of goods. Such a reconciliation should be sought both in policies and in institutions such as trade ministries and labor unions.
- Emphasize cooperation and assistance to facilitate compliance with labor obligations, especially in developing countries and in vulnerable sectors such as small and medium-size enterprises. Trade sanctions and measures to restrict or prohibit market access should be avoided.
- Recognize the appropriate role of specialized fora on labor issues and increase their dialogue and coordination with the WTO. Proposals for amendment of the WTO or for the creation of new international institutions should be put aside, at least for the short to middle term.
- Change habits, culture, and outlook within the WTO in areas that would benefit labor concerns as well as improve governance in general.

WTO members have taken steps to address some of these issues. For example, WTO documents have been made much more accessible to academics and the public in the past few years. This improvement has taken advantage of Internet technology, as well as the interest of NGOs that follow the WTO process, such as the International Center for Trade and Sustainable Development. More can and should be done to create a more positive context in which the WTO and the international community can deal with the intersections between trade and social concerns and foster better coordination and cooperation.

Conclusion

Controversies among nations over labor rights protection are likely to continue. Recent incidents and cases, such as the treatment of Myanmar by the ILO, have further polarized discussion. In approaching new issues, the initial reaction of many people and institutions is, understandably, to avoid changes in paradigms. ("If it ain't broke, don't fix it.") This is especially so for the WTO, which many have adjudged a success in its field. But there are also those who believe that something *is* broken, who embrace change, and who see a need for vast and dramatic changes in the WTO and other international institutions. These groups share a common viewpoint, even if analyses of what, more precisely, is broken and what the remedy is continue to be debated.

Countless agendas and counteragendas have arisen, and more will come up. There are no easy solutions. There may, however, be points on which broader agreement can be reached. The WTO does not stand in isolation; it stands within a wider international community that has dynamic concerns other than trade, including labor and human rights. The trade organization was transformed in the Uruguay Round to shoulder new issues outside the traditional purview of trade in goods. In many instances, it did not take in these new areas in entirety but, as with investment policy and intellectual property rights, strove to find and deal with the nexus of these issues with trade.

A similar approach may be used for labor rights. It is wrong to call for the WTO to displace the ILO in protecting workers. But it would be equally wrong to ignore the legitimate economic, social, and political imperatives that call for improved dialogue, better coordination, and mutually supportive policies and institutions in the international community. A new context for improved coordination and exchange is needed before and for deciding on an agenda. Such a context can and should be the foundation for progress on these issues.

Notes

I thank Gary Sampson, Daniel Esty, Veena Jha, Martin Khor, Beatrice Chaytor, Halina Ward, and James Cameron for inputs to the paper, and Will Martin, Patrick Low, Kym Anderson, Bijit Bora, and Mari Pangestu for feedback from the World Bank–Pacific Economic Cooperation Council (PECC) seminar.

1 Some such efforts by cities in the United States have been successfully challenged and set aside by federal courts as an intrusion on national foreign policy.

2 The action taken against Myanmar was decided by the ILO in the Resolution on the Widespread Use of Forced Labour in Myanmar, 87th Session of the ILO International Labour Conference, June 1999, available at <http://www.ilo.org/public/english/standards/relm/ilc/ilc87/com-myan.htm>. For a report on the measure, see "Burma Barred from ILO Meetings and Technical Aid," ILO News, ILO U.S. Branch Office, at <http://us.ilo.org/news/focus/998/FOCUS-3.html>.

3 In January 1999 and again in July 1999 the U.S. government proposed that the WTO establish a working group on trade and labor. See the U.S. proposal on labor rights, WT/GC/W/139, 1999, International Centre for Trade and Sustainable Development (ICTSD).

4 See the UNDP *Human Development Report* series.

5 Pursuant to Article V.2 of the Marrakesh Agreement that established the WTO, the General Council in mid-1986 adopted guidelines for arrangements on relations with NGOs. For a general discussion of NGOs in the WTO, see Esty (1999).

6 The WTO has of late come to recognize the need for coordination and to take steps accordingly. For instance, the Committee on Trade and the Environment has granted observer status to 20 intergovernmental organizations concerned with the environment, including the secretariat of the Convention on International Trade in Endangered Species of Wild Fauna and Flora (CITES). A number of symposia with NGOs have also been held since 1994.

7 The general preference for developing countries is at best a vestigial principle in the WTO. There have been some calls for assistance to least-developed countries, but they have focused on technical assistance and training for trade matters and trade facilitation rather than broader developmental assistance and resource transfers.

BOX 46.1   BASIC PRINCIPLES OF ENVIRONMENTAL REGULATION

Environmental problems can be usefully divided into two types: domestic, in which the damage is contained within the borders of a country, and transboundary, in which the damage affects more than one country. Dealing with the latter generally requires international cooperation. The emergence of global environmental problems such as global warming and ozone depletion has led to a growing recognition of the interdependence of the global environment and to the conclusion of around 200 multilateral environmental agreements.

At both the domestic and international levels, a widely accepted principle of environmental policy is that "the polluter pays": public policy should seek to ensure that firms pay not only the direct cost of production but also the social cost of the pollution they generate. The marginal social cost associated with a unit of pollution will vary across countries. Countries may have very different preferences regarding environmental protection, reflecting differences in the absorptive capacity of their ecosystems, in income levels (wealth), and in culture. Thus, the "polluter pays" principle is entirely consistent with the existence of widely different environmental standards among countries.

The manner in which environmental policy is implemented varies greatly from country to country. Some countries make efforts to ensure that polluters do pay according to an estimate of the costs that they impose on society, while others fail to enact such policies, thereby providing their producers with an implicit subsidy. This subsidy does not arise from countries' adoption of lower standards but from their failure to ensure that polluters bear the cost of the chosen standard. Like all subsidies, the welfare cost of such a policy is borne principally by the country providing the subsidy (it is the country's own environment that is polluted), and the welfare benefit accrues primarily to consumers in other countries who receive goods or services at lower prices.

Production and consumption activities in one country may have detrimental impacts on other countries. Such negative spillovers or externalities may be physical (air and water pollution, acid rain) or intangible (mistreatment of animals, consumption of ivory). In such cases there is a basis for cooperation and negotiation. Unilateral trade policy, however, is not the appropriate instrument for dealing with the externality; standard economic theory requires that externalities be addressed at the source. This means either that the producer or consumer must bear the real costs of the activity, or that property rights must be assigned that give owners an incentive to manage and price resources appropriately. Trade sanctions cannot offset an environmental externality efficiently because they affect both consumers and producers of a good and usually have an impact on only a part of total production or consumption.

Only if international trade itself were the problem would intervention in trade be the appropriate policy response, but that is a rare occurrence. For example, there might be a ban on international trade in harmful products as a supplement to domestic bans if moving the products were dangerous. But if the concern is about international transport, it is the transport that should be taxed (made to pay its full social cost), not the trade; that is, the aim is to encourage cleaner forms of transport, not to prevent goods from moving.

Although environmental policies may reduce the ability of enterprises located in countries with high standards to compete with those operating in nations with low standards, this is exactly what the policy aims at. If high standards are what a society wants, the result should be the contraction of the affected activities. Restricting imports makes no sense, as it promotes the domestic activities that the environmental policy is attempting to constrain. This, of course, is one reason why domestic industries may seek to "level the playing field" through trade policy—it is one way of avoiding part of the impact of environmental regulation. More generally, if consumers prefer environmentally friendly goods, they should be willing to pay for them.

Source: Prepared by the volume editors, based on McCulloch, Winters, and Cirera (2001) and Hoekman and Kostecki (2001).

gating GMO from non-GMO crops during cultivation, transport, and any subsequent industrial production, entailing unnecessary costs. The irony is that when developing countries raised similar questions regarding ecolabeling of textiles and footwear, their arguments were dismissed on the grounds that consumer preferences should be catered to. Interestingly the issue of consumer preference has not been given much emphasis in discussions on GMOs.[3]

Trade Law versus Environmental Law: A Crisis of Legitimacy

Trade negotiators seek to extract better terms of trade and to open other countries' markets while keeping their own as closed as possible. The focus is on national or regional, not global, welfare. In the case of the environment, the concept of international society is not metaphorical but real. Attempts to introduce nonconsensual politics through instruments such as trade barriers goes against the grain of environmental politics. To accommodate differences in development and in domestic environmental regimes, the Rio Declaration, adopted at the UN Conference on Environment and Development (the "Earth Summit") in 1992, embraced the principle of common but differentiated state responsibility.[4] This creates an incongruity: although the focus in the trade policy–WTO context has been on disciplining sovereign rights to impose tariff barriers, members now seek to resurrect sovereign rights to erect these barriers for environmental purposes.

A crisis of legitimacy arises because the consensual character of environmental law is being overturned by recourse to nonconsensual trade disputes, often in an incoherent way, depending on the economic stakes. When substantial commercial interests are involved, as in the case of GMOs, the effects on the environment may be examined only in a cursory manner. Elected developing country governments have voiced concern that nonelected NGOs representing limited constituencies may have a greater influence on trade disputes than governments do.[5] The trade and environment debate is increasingly straitjacketed into North-South lines.

Developing Country Positions

In general, industrial countries place high political priority on the inclusion of environmental and sustainable development considerations in trade negotiations. This reflects the fact that any negotiating agenda that does not pay adequate attention to the environment will fail to generate political support in industrial countries. Developing countries are less than enthusiastic, to say the least. They worry about a resurgence of protectionism and the use of unilateral measures under the guise of environmental concerns and are fearful that accommodating the use of trade-restrictive measures for nontrade purposes may spill over into other areas such as labor standards. They also perceive the current trade and environment debate as lacking balance. Proposals by industrial countries focus on accommodating measures that restrict trade, as opposed to measures that promote trade (Jha and Vossenaar 2001). A recent assessment by the UN General Assembly of progress in implementing Agenda 21, the environmental action plan adopted at Rio de Janeiro in 1992, showed that little headway has been made on so-called supportive measures, such as finance, access to environmentally sound technologies, and capacity building. This engenders skepticism concerning the sincerity of industrial countries about advancing sustainable development objectives on the basis of the principle of common but differentiated responsibilities. Doubts often expressed by industrial countries about the extent to which such supportive measures can be specified in WTO agreements aggravate the problem.

At the risk of oversimplification, the developing country position on trade and environment could be summarized as follows. Environment and sustainable development are important policy objectives, but there is no convincing evidence that existing trade rules stand in the way of legitimate environmental policies and the promotion of sustainable development. Compatibility between trade and the environment is the rule; conflict is the exception. Where conflicts have arisen, GATT Article XX has proved sufficient for dealing with them while at the same time providing the checks and balances to avoid abuse. The CTE has made an important contribution to enhancing understanding of trade and environment linkages, and this process continues. Finally, environmental and development objectives should be achieved through supportive measures and international cooperation, as well as through better coordination at the national and multilateral levels. All this leads to the position that it is premature to engage in negotiations on trade and environment.

examine whether existing instruments, such as the prior informed consent (PIC) procedure, are sufficient from the perspective of developing countries to prevent environmental damage from such imports, in particular with regard to product coverage and procedures.

Dispute Settlement

The contours of the trade and environment debate have been affected by panel and Appellate Body (AB) decisions, some of which were quite controversial. (See the submission by Pakistan, WT/GC/W/162.) Several suggestions for reform of the dispute settlement mechanism have arisen as a response to the perceived political nature of dispute resolution on trade and environment matters.[10] This section reviews aspects of the *Shrimp* case and a number of proposals for rectifying some of the imbalances created by the panel in this case.[11]

In 1997 India, Malaysia, Pakistan, and Thailand requested the establishment of a WTO panel to consider U.S. trade restrictions on shrimp imports. Under the authority of the Endangered Species Act (ESA), the United States had imposed embargoes on the import of shrimp from a number of its trading partners for the purpose of protecting the sea turtle population. The ESA makes access to U.S. shrimp markets conditional on certification that a country has adopted conservation policies that the United States considers comparable to its own with respect to regulatory programs and incidental taking of turtles. The United States unsuccessfully argued that this trade measure satisfied Article XX(g), which allows trade restrictions if needed to conserve an exhaustible natural resources. The panel rejected the U.S. argument on the basis of its interpretation not of Article XX(g) but of the chapeau to Article XX. The panel found that the U.S. measure constituted unjustifiable discrimination between countries where the same conditions prevail. The United States appealed the panel's reasoning. The AB found fault with the panel's interpretation and took Article XX(g) into consideration. It decided, however, that although the embargo served an environmental objective that is recognized as legitimate under the article, the measure was applied in a manner that constituted arbitrary and unjustifiable discrimination between WTO members, contrary to the requirements of the chapeau of Article XX.

The AB made several determinations in this case on the interpretation and application of Article XX(g). The means-to-an-end relationship between the trade measure and the policy of conserving an exhaustible, endangered species, sea turtles, was observably close and real, and therefore the measure was one "relating to" the conservation of an exhaustible natural resource. The AB also determined that the imposition of the embargo was an even-handed measure, in that it was implemented in conjunction with restrictions on domestic harvesting of shrimp, as required by Article XX(g).

In justification of the wider meaning to be given to "natural resource" in Art XX(g), the AB cited the UN Convention on the Law of the Sea (UNCLOS), the Convention on International Trade in Endangered Species of Wild Fauna and Flora (CITES), and other bilateral and multilateral actions to protect living natural resources. It also cited GATT 1947 panel rulings that fish was an "exhaustible natural resource." In taking this view, the AB held that XX(g) covers both living and nonliving natural resources. According to the defendants in the case, the AB extended further the ruling in the *Gasoline* case (relating to U.S. imports of gasoline from Venezuela and other countries), opening the way for a country to adopt national measures operating beyond its legal jurisdiction to protect the environment and conserve "natural resources" and then to enforce these measures through trade barriers, provided this is preceded by a process of getting targeted countries to negotiate with it on bilateral, regional, or multilateral environmental agreements.

In the *Shrimp* case, however, the AB went on to rule that the U.S. embargo was applied in a manner that would constitute a means of both unjustifiable and arbitrary discrimination between countries where the same conditions prevail, contrary to the requirements of the chapeau of Article XX. The body reasoned that unjustifiable discrimination includes the application of a trade measure, such as the U.S. embargo, that does not allow for any inquiry into the appropriateness of the regulatory program for the conditions prevailing in the exporting countries. The failure to engage in serious negotiations to conclude bilateral or multilateral agreements or to undertake cooperative efforts for the conservation of sea turtles before enforcing the embargo, and the unilateral application of that embargo, further underscored its unjustifiability. Furthermore, that same rigidity and inflexibility applied to the certification procedures adopted by the United States, and this amounted to arbitrary discrimination.

The AB stated that "perhaps the most conspicuous flaw in this measure's application relates to its intended and actual coercive effect on the special policy decisions made by foreign governments, Members of the WTO." An interesting question would be to examine whether most, if not all, trade measures would fall into this category of measures with "intended and actual coercive effect."

The AB also ruled, "It is not acceptable in international trade relations for one WTO member to use an economic embargo to require other WTO members to adopt essentially the same comprehensive regulatory program, to achieve a certain policy goal, as that within that member's territory, without taking into consideration different conditions which may occur in the territories of those other members." As there is little environmental justification for harmonization of regulatory regimes, the "same conditions prevail" test may be difficult to meet. Added to this is the issue of the "appropriateness" of the regulatory programs of the importing countries when applied to the exporting countries.

Following this interpretation, there were several suggestions by developing countries on the scope of the functions. Many developing countries expressed the view that as long as no consensus has been achieved in the CTE on the interpretation of Article XX, the AB should not interpret rules in such an evolutionary manner as to overturn the existing consensus. According to Pakistan's proposal to the General Council (WT/GC/W/162), it is necessary to clarify the relevant provisions of the Dispute Settlement Understanding (DSU) to make clear that the responsibility for clarifying or modifying the provisions of the WTO agreements clearly rests with WTO members and that it would not be appropriate for the AB to usurp these functions under the guise of interpreting law on the basis of contemporary developments. Pakistan added that the AB should defer to the General Council for making modifications in the relevant rules, as the member countries consider appropriate.

Amicus Curiae Briefs. The defendants in the *Shrimp* case also claim that the AB ruling regarding the admission of amicus curiae briefs opens the way for NGOs to file briefs before the WTO Dispute Settlement Body, for these briefs to be brought to the attention of the dispute panels by the WTO secretariat or by any of the parties to the dispute, and for the panels to take notice of such briefs. It is feared that while this ruling would help NGOs get "environment and sustainable development" reflected in the WTO process, it would in the course of time enable other interests and pressure groups, whether of industry or of labor, to use this route as well. Furthermore, many international environmental NGOs are funded by corporate donors, and this method of indirect influence may now increase. NGOs from developing countries appear to be more interested in transparency in the negotiating processes and in the proposals submitted for negotiation.

With the *Shrimp* dispute, a question has arisen as to whether panels should take account of amicus briefs submitted to them by public interest groups or NGOs. The relevant applicable provisions of the DSU (Article 13.2) suggest that panels may seek information from any relevant source and may consult experts to obtain their opinions on certain aspects of the matter at hand. Pakistan has noted that this does not appear to suggest that the AB can accept unsolicited briefs; Article 13.2 should therefore be clarified to state that panels and ABs should not take account of unsolicited information. Many developing countries take the view that amicus curiae briefs and greater NGO participation more generally would unnecessarily distort the balance in favor of industrial countries that can more easily fund the participation of NGOs. They have also pointed out that inclusion of NGO opinions and inputs should be done through national coordination; there is no need to internationalize essentially national conflicts.

The Role of the Appellate Body. According to the DSU, the AB is only expected to examine issues of law covered by the panel report. In the *Shrimp* case the AB examined de novo the facts of the case and made a finding on legal issues that had not been addressed by the panel. Pakistan has proposed that in all such cases the AB should be required to remand the case to the panel for reexamination. It has also suggested that to avoid unnecessary delays in the settlement of the dispute as a result of such remands, the panel should complete its examination within a period of one month.

Although the shrimp decision appears to have broadened the scope of measures that would be clearly considered acceptable under the chapeau of

VII

THE TRADING SYSTEM AND DEVELOPING COUNTRIES

S ince the entry into force of the agreement establishing the WTO, it has become clear that many governments and civil society groups in developing countries have been disappointed with the outcome of the Uruguay Round, in terms both of market access payoffs and of the implementation of certain WTO agreements. There is also a widespread perception that efforts to negotiate additional disciplines on domestic regulatory policies in the WTO may divert attention from more critical development-related priorities.

A major theme of much of the criticism is that more attention should be focused on ensuring that multilateral rules support the development of low-income countries—i.e., that the rules are not inappropriate for their institutional capacities and constraints. Expanding the set of players involved in domestic trade policy formulation and the preparation of negotiating positions can help achieve this objective, in the process enhancing the "ownership" of eventual agreements. Participation is another necessary condition—but is not sufficient, as noted in Chapter 47, by Diana Tussie and Miguel F. Lengyel. Many developing countries have inadequate (or no) representation in Geneva, which impedes their active engagement in negotiations and in the day-to-day functioning of the WTO. Options have been identified that would allow poor countries to expand their representation in Geneva at relatively low cost; for example, Blackhurst, Lyakurwa, and Oyejide (2000) propose transfer of national representatives from other UN bodies to Geneva and more intense cooperation by members

were, many failed to maintain official representation in Geneva.

To a large extent the situation was reversed at the beginning of the 1990s. The developing country share of GATT membership rose from 66 percent in 1983 to 74 percent by the late 1990s. Of the 44 new members added since 1982 (37 in 1987 alone), 43 were developing countries and, more recently, transition economies (Michalopoulos 1999a). More significant, however, is the relatively active role that many developing countries played in the Uruguay Round negotiations, not only fully participating in the exchange of concessions but also advancing, on an individual or group basis, a positive agenda of their own. This historic shift in policy and preferences reflected a myriad of domestic and international, economic and political, developments. Decreasing returns from and fatigue with import substitution, together with the fall of the Berlin Wall, led to the de-ideologization of trade and closer integration into the world economy. Developing countries began to swim with rather than against the current. The previously downplayed issue of market access gained increasing salience, and multilateral trade negotiations became more relevant as an instrument for securing such access. A greater awareness of the importance of a rules-based system for anchoring import regimes and protecting export interests emerged in many developing countries. Stepping up participation was necessary on all counts.

At the same time, industrial countries started to see the engagement of developing countries in multilateral trade talks through new lenses. The minimal size of developing countries' markets had previously been perceived as not being worth the effort of pressing for greater access. The result was a situation in which developing countries had negligible obligations and liberalization in sectors of export interest to them was disproportionately small (Tussie 1987; Oyejide 2000; Ricupero 2000). GATT Article XVIII, section B, and the Enabling Clause left developing countries with very little that needed to be done to internalize the results of negotiating rounds into domestic policy. In other words, trade negotiations had at best a marginal impact on the domestic policy process in these countries.

By the mid-1980s, the picture had changed significantly. Several developing countries became major exporters of manufactured goods, even in those sectors in which it had been assumed they lacked comparative advantages. Furthermore, as competition among the major trading players intensified, the continued opening and greater contestability of developing countries' markets became a more highly valued goal. Finally, the United States was firmly determined to extend the GATT into services and other new areas and was no longer willing to accept free-riding of developing countries on such issues as intellectual property. To sum up, either out of conviction or because of fears of closing markets and the implications of conditional most-favored-nation (MFN) treatment, developing countries abandoned their former defensiveness and embraced a much more participatory attitude. Their strategic dilemma turned from whether to engage in the multilateral trading system to choosing an appropriate strategy of participation, focusing on what commitments to make and on how to micromanage a bloated trade agenda.

The challenges of inclusion soon proved to be highly demanding. Developing countries learned in the early stages of the Uruguay Round that greater participation did not translate automatically into leverage, as they found it difficult to decisively influence the process of agenda setting and to shape the final outcome of negotiations. Similarly, with the expansion of the agenda through the inclusion of very complex and slippery issues (services, intellectual property, technical barriers, and sanitary and phytosanitary standards), many developing countries' capacity for analysis and for turning such analysis into sound negotiating positions was overtaxed (Tussie and Glover 1993). "A pro-active, constructive approach was frequently out of reach for many countries because of resource and research capacity constraints" (Chadha and others 2000: 432–33).

The impact of these difficulties on the results of the Uruguay Round should not be underestimated. A balanced negotiating outcome would have required an agenda that reflected the interests of all stakeholders as evenly as possible, as well as consistent participation by developing countries. Various assessments agree that in such circumstances the outcome would have been tilted more against industrial countries' interests. To be sure, developing countries did not leave the negotiations empty-handed: the inclusion of agriculture, the commitment to phase out the restrictions on textiles, and the creation, with the birth of the WTO, of a much stronger dispute settlement mechanism than the one existing under the GATT can be deemed important gains. Yet these were more than offset by concessions: a more restrictive approach toward special and differential treatment, commitments made in the intellectual property and services agreements, the binding of many developing country tariffs, and new disciplines on subsidies and customs valuation, to mention the most significant ones. Furthermore, the very creation of the WTO added new challenges for effective participation. The greatly expanded trade agenda called for additional institutional capacity in member governments. In addition, in contrast to the GATT, the WTO accommodated ongoing negotiations, demanding constant involvement. Finally, while the new dispute settlement mechanism is an asset, it gave rise to a need to finance and develop expertise on international trade law in order to take full advantage of it. Given the level of technical expertise required, questions have been raised about developing countries' capacity to bring cases efficiently as complainants and to protect their interests as defendants. Even though some technical assistance is available from the WTO secretariat, it is not intended to assist developing countries on specific cases. External legal counsel usually comes from an international law firm or consultant, at considerable cost, although the creation of the Advisory Centre on WTO Law in 2001 provides some access to subsidized legal assistance (see Chapter 9, by Delich; see also Weston and Delich 2000).

The Post–Uruguay Round Situation

Six years after the entry into force of the WTO, developing countries face new challenges and priorities related to their participation in multilateral negotiations. There is a broad consensus that market access has not improved as much as expected. Agriculture products continue to face high protective tariffs, as do the classic footwear, clothing, textiles, and steel sectors, even after allowing for the Generalized System of Preferences. In agriculture tariffs peaks have proliferated to the point of reaching 350 percent in important export products, some of them particularly sensitive for developing countries. Industrial countries' trade policies continue to obstruct export diversification and reduce incentives for processing commodities, with serious implications for export growth of products with greater value added, and commitments on subsidies limit the scope for implementing support policies for growth and exports (Lengyel and Tussie 2000).

These by now rather classic North-South agenda items do not exhaust the complex menu on the table. Following the failure to launch a new round of negotiations in Seattle, the intricate issue of trade in services became the engine of WTO negotiations in 2000. Complexity is related to several factors: negotiations are proceeding simultaneously at the multilateral and regional levels; they involve several sectors of great importance for the domestic economy and, therefore, different producer interests; and the results spill over into other areas such as intellectual property rights and foreign direct investment. The weaving of negotiating positions has become highly complex, both technically and politically. As countries diversify their exports across products and markets, it becomes more difficult for them to concentrate their bargaining resources in a few selected areas. With the expansion of the negotiating agenda, occasions for friction expand as well, making it virtually impossible to pursue a single-issue strategy. Argentina was among the early learners of this lesson: it "discovered this [during the Uruguay Round] when, in spite of its efforts to concentrate on agriculture, it was drawn into bilateral disputes over intellectual property" (Tussie and Glover 1993: 231–32), with painful tradeoffs between these sectors.

At the same time, thinly disguised forms of administered protection have flourished. Both industrial and developing countries are resorting to safeguards, countervailing duties, and, especially, antidumping measures to protect producers operating in their domestic markets. In other words, as multilateral negotiations reduce conventional barriers, trade relief policies are being used and abused. This question goes far beyond the North-South agenda, branching out into South-South relations. Indeed, in tandem with regional trade agreements, an undercover war of mutually paralyzing trade relief measures has mushroomed. Many developing countries have actively applied trade relief measures on "sensitive" sectors precisely against neighbors that, because of geographic proximity, are able to benefit most from trade liberalization. The South-South dimension has also emerged in the context of investment policies, against the backdrop of a potential race to the bottom over incentives. As countries compete to attract investments, transnational corpo-

BOX 47.1 (CONTINUED)

the Quad into consultation. On the basis of these discussions, on July 17, 1986, a draft was submitted on behalf of Colombia and Switzerland to the PrepCom. Further discussions indicated that the Café au Lait draft had come to command the explicit support of nearly 50 GATT members. A revised draft (W/47/Rev. 2, July 30, 1986) provided the basis for the Punta del Este declaration and the launch of the Uruguay Round. By resolving the impasse on services, the Café au Lait group had prevented the GATT bicycle from toppling over and had successfully expressed the voice of smaller developing countries in setting the negotiating agenda.

In good measure, the success of the Café au Lait reflected the strategies that the group employed. An issue-based focus gave the group a simplicity of structure that presented a marked contrast to the traditional blocs of developing countries, with their infinite log-rolling and shopping lists of demands. The Café au Lait, in all its versions, also enjoyed a flexibility of agenda that equipped it to work as a negotiating coalition rather than purely a proposal-making one. The flexibility of the Jaramillo-led agenda derived from the investigative process from which it emerged. Common interests and the emphasis on research created a virtuous cycle that strengthened intragroup coherence and won external legitimacy for the group. Furthermore, in overcoming the North-South divide, the Café au Lait was unprecedented. The group was also particularly appropriate for the consensus-based

culture of the GATT. The Café au Lait group presented itself as a bridge-building coalition engaged in mediation-type diplomacy in the space provided by the EU-U.S. rift on services and the extremes of the U.S. position versus the G-10. Its alternative name, Friends of the New Negotiations, was indicative of this positive stance. It is not entirely surprising that the path of issue-based diplomacy pursued by the G-20/Café au Lait was subsequently taken up with fervor by the Cairns Group of agricultural exporters.

While the Café au Lait group successfully demonstrated a new pattern of coalition diplomacy to developing countries and highlighted the weaknesses of the bloc-type diplomacy of the G-10, it is noteworthy that its attempts to continue its activities in the Uruguay Round did not yield any visible results. The group survived in various versions—the Hotel de la Paix Group, the Friends of Services Group, the Rolle Group—but it had minimal visibility and minimal successes to its credit. Whether the Café au Lait represents a new and lasting style of coalition diplomacy or merely a one-time success that relied primarily on external conditions remains an open question. Nevertheless, the sharp policy reversals that the group produced in the traditional bloc diplomacy of developing countries and the example it gave of successful issue-based diplomacy make the coalition a landmark in the stance of developing countries in multilateral trade negotiations.

Source: Based on work presented in Narlikar (2000).

of the WTO decisionmaking process predated the Seattle meeting. The process, as during the GATT period, moved on the basis of consensus, arrived at through formal and informal consultations, much like an "old boys' club." It worked well when players were few and issues were fairly straightforward, but over the past 15 years it seems to have gone into slow motion. The image of past success, nonetheless, led to unrealistically high expectations on the part of both new entrants and new activists. The result is that high expectations now coexist uneasily with decreasing returns. The diversity of interests

and objectives currently represented, albeit faultily, in the WTO makes it difficult to reach consensus over the broad range of issues.

The grievances of many developing countries with this system mounted following the conclusion of the Uruguay Round, particularly regarding the constraints the agreements imposed on these countries' real possibilities of influencing the agenda-setting process. Although developing countries played an active role in the period leading up to the Seattle meeting, submitting over half of the more than 250 specific proposals on the agenda, they claimed that their proposals were not given due weight. The "green-room" practice fueled the disenchantment, underpinning the claims of a "democratic deficit" and a lack of transparency during the Seattle meeting. The "green room" is the name given to the traditional method used in the GATT/WTO to expedite consultations; it involves the Director General and a small group of members, numbering between 25 and 30 and including the major trading countries, both industrial and developing, as well as a number of other countries that are deemed to be representative. The composition of the group tends to vary by issue, but there is no objective basis for participation. This procedure worked when most developing countries were quiet bystanders. After the significant concessions made in the Uruguay Round, developing countries felt entitled to be included in the green-room process, and on several occasions they submitted declarations stating that they would not adhere to any consensus reached without their effective participation. Although the subsequent ministerial meeting, in Doha, was more inclusive and open to all members, the issue of effective participation remains a key one.

Perceptions of inequities in the WTO decision-making system implicitly call into question other facets of governance, specifically, the failure to balance the costs and benefits arising from trade negotiations. "The end result has been an absence of 'ownership' of many agreements, and a general suspicion of the WTO" (Chadha and others 2000: 434). One reason for this has been the costs associated with the implementation of certain WTO agreements (see Chapter 48, by Finger and Schuler, in this volume).

To be sure, the WTO is not an international organization intended to "govern" the global economy, or even international trade relations, as a whole. It does, however, perform some functions of governance at an international level by providing a forum for trade rule-making (legislative function); protecting trade opportunities; fostering transparency in the trading system; and enforcing rules through a dispute settlement system (judicial function). In addition, there are other functions not attributed formally to the WTO that are subject to an intense international debate as to whether they should be put under its purview. Examples include the supply of international public goods and the subjection of markets to social objectives. Given the scope of the recent questioning of WTO governance, efforts to pursue new trade negotiations on a comprehensive basis will probably have to go hand in hand with a streamlining of the decisionmaking process that pays due attention to the requirements of efficiency and legitimacy. Unless these worries are addressed, new negotiations will add to the frustration.

Enhancing Participation

Improving developing countries' participation involves two central dimensions. First, improving skills and institutional capacity to analyze, take stock of, and manage the workings of existing agreements is a precondition for designing adequate positions in follow-up negotiations. Second, a reform of the WTO decisionmaking system is needed to allow developing countries to increase their voice in the affairs of the organization. On the first front, there is no doubt that efforts must be made at the national level, particularly in view of the ever-finer heterogeneity of developing countries' interests. Gone are the times when multilateral bargaining could be broadly articulated by a grand coalition of developing countries. The need for each country to do its own homework in following issues, to attend all meetings, and to have teams in capitals doing extensive background research and providing adequate instructions on all matters cannot be dismissed. The acquisition of sufficient knowledge about how the system works, of technical skills, and of an adequate institutional capacity should be priorities. This is particularly so given that the WTO is a member-driven organization with a very small secretariat, leaving a great part of the analysis of issues and development of positions to members.

Enhanced capacity to participate also requires an effort to overcome the lack of coordination and the turf wars at the national level that usually plague developing countries. Coordination problems stem from various sources, "including differences regarding the location of real compared to nominal authority with respect to the articulation and implementation of trade policy as well as differences in terms of which institution has the responsibility for trade policy and which government agency has the power to negotiate and sign international agreements" (Oyejide, 2000: 23). The need for coordination is pressing not only among government agencies but also between them and business. In most developing countries business tends to follow negotiations at the WTO from a considerable dis-

- How much will implementation cost?
- What are the development problems in this area?
- Does the WTO agreement correctly diagnose the development problems?
- Does the WTO agreement prescribe an appropriate remedy?

"Appropriate," in the last question, refers both to correct identification of the problem and to recognition of the capacities (resource constraints) of developing countries. To lend specificity to the discussion of the scope and cost of the investments that may be involved in implementing WTO commitments, we review (primarily) World Bank project experience with customs reform, with application of SPS standards, and with the installation of systems of intellectual property rights (IPRs). In each of the three areas, we outline basic WTO obligations and examine how implementation might be managed so as to best help developing countries use trade as a vehicle for development. On the basis of this discussion, we offer some recommendations that may help avoid future implementation problems. This effort must include binding commitments by industrial country members to furnish technical assistance to developing country members that request it. In the Uruguay Round developing countries took on *bound* commitments to implement the agreements in exchange for *unbound* commitments of assistance. This should be avoided in future negotiations.

Customs Valuation

The WTO Customs Valuation agreement addresses only *valuation*—only one part of the customs process. In addition to providing information on how much customs reform might cost, we argue in this section that given the initial situation in many developing countries, changing the valuation process without undertaking overall customs reform is not likely to improve the predictability of the customs process. Likewise, changing the customs valuation process would not significantly lessen the possibility of using the customs process as a nontariff barrier.

Scope and Content of the Customs Valuation Agreement

The Uruguay Round Customs Valuation agreement establishes the transaction value of the shipment in question as the primary basis for customs value and prescribes a hierarchy of methods for determining that value. The first, basic option is to use as the customs value the transaction value of *the* imported merchandise—the price actually paid or payable for the specific shipment. The agreement lists items (add-ins) that must be included in the price actually paid or payable, such as packing costs and the cost of tools, dies, and molds provided by the buyer. The second alternative is to use the transaction value of *identical* merchandise sold for export to the same country of importation, at or about the same time, for which a transaction value can be determined. The third, fourth, and fifth options are also attempts to come as close as operationally possible to the transaction value of the specific shipment. The agreement also contains a rogue's gallery of methods that may not be used, such as the selling price of competing domestic products, or the selling price of the goods in the market of the exporting country or in another export market.

Presumed Administrative Environment

The valuation process the Uruguay Round agreement imposes is one that complements the customs systems in place in most of the advanced trading countries (both developing and industrial). That system is based on the generalized use of electronic information management and on built-in incentives for compliance by importers. Trade in these countries takes place in large-scale lots, and duty rates are generally low. In this context, departure from routine business practice (for example, retrieval of additional information in response to a valuation inquiry) is costly. Importers themselves normally conduct the valuation process, including the application of the add-ins and take-outs needed to comply with the rules. In Norway a paperless customs declaration system operates around the clock; clearance takes 15 minutes, on average, and is almost always completed well before the goods arrive. About 85 percent of declarations pass through the system without being stopped for further investigation (WCO 1999). Investigation and verification of the importer-submitted customs value do not normally cause physical delay of the shipment; instead, the importer posts a customs bond sufficient to cover the amount at issue. Financial institutions in many developing countries do not offer such bonds.

Developing Countries' Customs Practices and Problems

Customs practices in many developing countries differ significantly from those in the more advanced trading nations. The differences often involve basic concepts, not just differences in details or efficiency.

Physical Control. Effective customs administration has both physical and administrative dimensions. Physical control has to do with keeping track of what passes into and out of the country. In many poorer countries, traditional smuggling—goods sneaked across the border, away from recognized ports—is a significant problem. At a duty rate of 50 percent, the avoided duty on the number of television sets one person can transport on a bicycle-jitney can come, in a poor country, to a year's wages. Where physical control systems are lax, smuggling need not even involve clandestine overland trails or secret moonlit beaches; goods often move through ports without coming under the supervision of customs authorities.

Administrative processes. Customs processes in poorer countries exhibit many interacting weaknesses: excessive procedures that are not codified (often, not even a published schedule of current tariff rates is available); poorly trained officials; a civil service system that does not pay a living wage, leaving officials dependent on side payments for performing their functions; and ineffective provision for appeal. Cunningham (1996), in an assessment of several least-developed countries that are considering customs reform, observed that systems and procedures seem to have evolved so as to maximize the number of steps and approvals needed—to create as many opportunities as possible for negotiation between traders and customs officials. It should be evident from this brief account of customs problems in poor countries that valuation is only an inch in a whole yard of customs operations that need improvement.

Reform Experience in Developing and Transition Economies

We present in this section a digest of our review of World Bank projects bearing on customs reform. Table 48.1 contains a tabulation of the cost of customs reform projects in a sampling of countries. Reform projects have included the following elements (few projects covered them all):

- *Computerization,* including the introduction of computerized customs systems and of systems for warehouse inventory control and statistical reporting
- *Improvements in valuation procedures*
- *Cargo controls* to speed up processing and eliminate fraudulent or incorrect valuation
- *Refitting of customs buildings* in order to permit the use of UNCTAD's ASYCUDA customs software
- *Administrative reforms,* including creation of a new division responsible for customs valuation and tariff classification; recruitment and training of staff; establishment of an appeals tribunal; and reduction of the discretion exercised by customs officers
- *Provision of antismuggling and drug interdiction equipment,* ranging from X-ray equipment and gas chromatographs to communications equipment
- *Training of management and staff* in basic management, customs procedures, and computer operations; establishment of staff training schools
- *Screenings for drug interdiction*
- *Legislative reforms,* including revision of laws, formal accession to the Harmonized System Convention, and measures to increase transparency.

The reforms we reviewed cover 16 major categories of activities ranging from rewriting legislation, through training in auditing procedures, to physical security in customs warehouses and policing of smuggling and of traffic in illicit drugs. Combinations of these components may involve a cost in the neighborhood of US$10 million for one country.

Sanitary and Phytosanitary Standards

The SPS agreement recognizes the right of governments to restrict trade when necessary to protect human, animal, or plant life or health, but it limits exercise of that right to measures that do not unjustifiably discriminate between countries with the same conditions, and that are not disguised restrictions on trade. The agreement further obligates members to impose such restrictions only to the extent necessary to protect life and health, and on the basis of scientific principles. Restrictions are not to be maintained if scientific evidence to support them is lacking. The last point implies that SPS measures can be put in place only on the basis of patent, the patented process, the patented product, or the product or products directly made from the patented process.)

- What exceptions to those rights are permissible (for example, compulsory licensing may be required).
- How long the protection lasts (WTO 1999: 214 f).[2]

The TRIPS agreement, like the SPS agreement, builds on standards set forth in relevant international conventions such as the 1967 Paris Convention for the Protection of Industrial Property and the 1989 Washington Treaty (the Treaty on Intellectual Property in Respect of Integrated Circuits, sometimes labeled the ICIP Treaty).

Extension of IPR Obligations

The TRIPS agreement requires each WTO member to adhere to the provisions (with a few exceptions) of the international IPR conventions, whether or not the member is a party to those conventions. This in itself was a significant widening of obligations for many countries. For example, the coverage of integrated circuits was an extension even for some industrial countries.[3] Under the TRIPS agreement, WTO members must consider unlawful—if not authorized by the rightsholder—the import, sale, or other commercial distribution of the integrated circuit design, of integrated circuits containing that design, and of articles that contain such integrated circuits.

As another example, the Rome Convention, which establishes rights of performers, producers of sound recordings, and broadcasters, has few signatories, particularly among developing countries. The TRIPS agreement, however, creates obligations for governments to allow recording companies from one country to attack unauthorized reproduction and sale of their products within another country. In some areas the TRIPS agreement has broader coverage than the relevant international convention. For example, it goes beyond the Berne Convention by requiring copyright protection for certain computer programs and computerized databases, and it contains the first multilateral obligations concerning industrial designs (e.g., textile designs).

The enforcement provisions of the TRIPS agreement require that a member provide civil as well as criminal remedies for infringement of IPRs. They also obligate members to provide means by which rightsholders can obtain the cooperation of customs authorities to prevent imports of infringing goods. Although it is impossible to predict how the process of application and interpretation through the WTO dispute settlement mechanism will play out, a number of legal experts believe that there is sufficient "wiggle room" in the agreement that developing countries could—within a good-faith implementation of their obligations—strike a balance between the interests of second-comers and the need to promote innovation and investment (see Reichman 1998 and references cited therein). This would, however, require a considerable departure from the balance that has been institutionalized in the industrial countries' IPR law. That balance, many experts argue, is tipped toward the interests of commercialized producers of knowledge—and tipped past the point of optimality even for the communities of interests that make up industrial country societies.[4]

Yet the tendency of the WTO is to give the benefit of the doubt to established standards. Finding grounds for moving away from such standards is particularly difficult in the area of intellectual property rights, which are, after all, an existential matter of legal definition, not a scientific matter of empirical estimation.

How to Do It

Even for an individual country, it would be nigh on impossible to provide objective guidelines on how to strike the optimal balance between legal incentives to create and the costs incurred by users and potential second-comers as a result of protecting IPRs. Systems in place have to be seen as the outcome of accepted (e.g., democratic) political processes, not of scientific calibration. It would be even more difficult to adjust this balance to different levels of economic development. Analysts have so far built up little knowledge about the impacts of various forms of IPRs on economic development, much less about the effects of different degrees of any of these forms.[5]

Our review of World Bank projects in support of IPRs again shows a considerable range of needed reforms—new legislation (e.g., to extend IPR protection to plant varieties), improvement of administrative structures (capacity to review applications, including the introduction of computerized information systems and extensive training for staff), and better enforcement. Some information on the associated costs is reported in Table 48.3.

Table 48.3 World Bank Projects Related to Intellectual Property Rights

Country	Project description	Cost (millions of U.S. dollars)
Brazil, 1997–2002	Training for staff administering IPR laws (component of science and technology reform project)	4.0
Indonesia, 1997–2003	Improvement of IPR regulatory framework (component of information infrastructure development project)	14.7
Mexico, 1992–96	Establishment of agency to implement industrial property laws (component of science and technology infrastructure project)	32.1

Lessons Learned

The following are the main points that emerge from our review.

A need for reform. In the areas we have covered—customs administration, sanitary and phytosanitary standards, and intellectual property rights—there was no shortage of World Bank projects to review. Developing countries are willing to borrow money to finance improvements in these areas. It is evident that they themselves see a need for reform.

The message from industrial countries: "Do it my way!" The content of the obligations imposed by the WTO agreements on customs valuation, SPS, and intellectual property rights can be summed up as the advanced countries saying to the others, "Do it my way!" The Customs Valuation agreement imposes on all countries a system in use in the leading industrial countries; the TRIPS and SPS agreements explicitly establish as the WTO standard international conventions developed in large part by the industrial countries.

Although the SPS agreement appears to allow countries to retain indigenous systems, doing so is not a real alternative. In defending trade-related actions, the systems recognized by international conventions have the legal benefit of the doubt; an indigenous system must prove itself. The developing countries do not have the necessary resources to defend their systems, and so the only effective option for a country that retains an indigenous system of standards is not to apply standards at the border at all.[6] The WTO's free-rider problem has not gone away; it has been swapped for a *forced*-rider problem, and the burden has been shifted from the industrial countries to the developing countries.

For the advanced countries whose systems are compatible with international conventions (or vice

versa), the WTO adds no more than an obligation to apply their domestic regulations fairly at the border. This includes not discriminating among transactions involving different countries and not unnecessarily impeding international transactions. Countries that at present apply their own indigenous standards have the additional—and far larger—obligation to apply the internationally sanctioned standards in their domestic economies. Although new WTO areas such as SPS and IPRs aim at the trade-related aspects of their subject matter, their implementation by developing countries requires, first of all, the establishment of such systems, or the conversion of indigenous systems to those recognized by international conventions.

A related lesson is that the scope of what the WTO regulates is narrower than the scope of what must be done to make development sense out of implementation. Customs valuation versus customs reform is an example: it helps little to change customs valuation procedures if containers still sit on the dock for 60 days.

Inappropriate diagnosis and inappropriate remedies. One effect of the "do it my way!" nature of the agreements is to intensify the ownership problem. This characteristic also returns us to our initial questions. From a development perspective:

- Do the WTO agreements appropriately identify the problems faced by developing countries?
- Given countries' needs and their resource bases, do the agreements provide the most effective remedies?

The Customs Valuation agreement provides neither appropriate diagnosis nor appropriate remedies. It addresses only a small part of most developing countries' problems with customs

BOX 48.1 COSTS OF IMPLEMENTING THE WTO AGREEMENTS: THE JAMAICAN EXPERIENCE

This box provides some (conservative) estimates of the cost to Jamaica of implementing selected WTO agreements.* The estimates do not take into account the need for and cost of ancillary investments and reforms that may be required to support implementation.

Agreement on Trade-Related Aspects of Intellectual Property Rights (TRIPS)

Implementation of the TRIPS agreement in Jamaica will require an initial public sector investment of at least US$1 million. This is associated with upgrading and modernization of the domestic intellectual property rights (IPRs) system. Modernization involves:

- Revision of existing laws (on, for example, trademarks and patents)
- Enactment of new laws on layout designs, geographical indications, plant varieties, and so on
- Development of proper administrative structures and officers to implement intellectual property (IP) procedures and policies as required by the legislation and the government.

A new Intellectual Property Office (JIPO) will administer the laws required by the TRIPS agreement. Approximately US$437,500 was already allocated to the existing IPR structures; another US$875,000–US$1.25 million will be required to develop the JIPO so that it covers all TRIPS areas. The estimated costs required for establishing the JIPO come to about US$775,000 a year over five years, after which the office is expected to be nearly self-sufficient. An additional estimated US$250,000 is needed to jump-start the implementation of major enforcement programs, including border controls; these are likely to be recurring costs.

Agreement on Sanitary and Phytosanitary Measures (SPS)

Implementation of the SPS agreement will require a total of US$7.6 million. This includes revision of current laws and regulations to make them WTO-compliant (US$200,000); establishment of an Agriculture Health and Food Safety Authority to administer and coordinate SPS activities (US$6 million); upgrading and equipping of existing laboratories in areas such as pest identification, pesticide

residue analysis, and microbiology, and provision of training in lab methodology, quality management, and use of equipment (US$500,000); conduct of pest surveys, surveillance, and monitoring (US$250,000); establishment of an enquiry point (US$150,000); creation and strengthening of inspection facilities at ports of entry and exit to serve all the agencies involved in the certification of food imports and exports, with provision for additional staff, training, and equipment to detect high-risk materials in shipments (US$500,000); and funding for participation in international standard-setting meetings, working groups, and the Committee on SPS Measures (US$30,000). Many of these costs will be recurring.

Customs Valuation

The estimated initial cost of implementing the WTO Customs Valuation agreement is US$840,000, most of which is needed for training (US$120,000), computing equipment and databases (US$50,000), and increased staffing (US$600,000). Staffing costs will be recurring.

Conclusion

These are very rough estimates and are quite conservative. Nevertheless, they illustrate that for a small developing country the implementation of the WTO agreements can be a substantial undertaking that requires both technical and financial assistance. Implementation of the TRIPS, SPS, and Customs Valuation agreements narrowly defined—that is, excluding ancillary and complementary investments to improve customs and standards institutions, and ignoring all costs for businesses—will require at least US$10 million. These financial resources are in addition to what is already budgeted by the government or allocated by donor countries as overseas development assistance to Jamaica.

* The cost estimates were originally made in Jamaican dollars and were converted to U.S. dollars at the rate of US$1 = J$45.

Source: Prepared by the volume editors, based on a paper prepared by the Ministry of Foreign Affairs and Foreign Trade, Jamaica.

Notes

This chapter draws heavily on Finger and Schuler (2000).

1 One critic argues that "these [are] not 'minimum' standards of intellectual property protection in the classical sense of the term; rather, they collectively expressed most of the standards of protection on which the developed counties could agree among themselves" (Reichman 1998: 603).

2 The TRIPS agreement provided the following transition periods: industrial countries, until January 1, 1996; developing countries and transition economies, up to January 1, 2000; least-developed countries, up to January 1, 2006. The transition period for a least-developed country may be extended on a "duly motivated" request by the country. Developing countries that currently provide patent protection to processes and not to products—for example in the food, chemicals, and pharmaceutical sectors—can delay until January 1, 2005, the application of the obligation to protect products. Even here, governments must ensure that inventions made between 1995 and 2004 will be able to gain patent protection after January 1, 2005.

3 This treaty is not yet in force; thus far, it has only nine signatories, of which only one has ratified.

4 Reichman, for example, asserts that "the logical course of action for the developing countries in implementing their obligations under the TRIPS Agreement is to shoulder the pro-competitive mantle that the developed countries have increasingly abandoned" (Reichman 1998: 606). Templeman (1998) argues that there is no public justification for the level of intellectual property protection defined by industrial countries' laws.

5 Abbott (1998a: 501), in his introduction and summary in an issue of the Journal of International Economic Law devoted to the TRIPS agreement, notes this lack of understanding of the impact of IPRs on economic development.

6 We are not arguing here that the iron fist imposes the wrong standards. Our concern is to remove the velvet glove of comforting rhetoric from that fist.

7 Matthew Stillwell of the Center for International Environmental Law pointed this out to us.

8 The experiences we have reviewed were in fairly large and more advanced developing countries; the costs could be higher in least-developed countries of a similar size that begin farther from the required standards, and they may be lower in much smaller countries.

right to exclude or graduate specific developing countries from GSP benefits. During the first 10 years of the scheme (1968–78), less than 11 percent of eligible imports actually received GSP treatment. A decade later, in 1988, only 27 percent of all dutiable imports was granted preferential access.

The benefits derived by developing countries from the GSP have thus been quite small in relation to the total exports of developing countries, and they have been heavily concentrated in a few beneficiaries. Up to the mid-1980s, three economies—Hong Kong (China), the Republic of Korea, and Taiwan (China)—accounted for about 45 percent of total GSP gains. This concentrated nature of GSP benefits remained unchanged through the early 1990s, as 6 to 12 of the largest beneficiaries claimed 71 to 80 percent of the total.

Both of the key components of S&D provisions have been criticized in the literature (Wang and Winters 1997). It has been argued that the component which grants greater flexibility to developing countries in their use of trade policy instruments is counterproductive because these "market-distorting" measures impose a self-inflicted cost on developing countries' own economies, while nonreciprocity may prelude their use of the GATT/WTO framework as an "agency of restraint." The GSP component does not provide, it is argued, a stable and reliable basis for investment, and it promotes production and trade inefficiencies in the beneficiary countries. These criticisms foreshadowed developments regarding S&D treatment during the Uruguay Round negotiations, in particular.

The Uruguay Round

The launch statement that began the Uruguay Round in September 1986 contained an explicit understanding that developing countries would be accorded S&D treatment in the negotiations in accordance with the terms of the 1979 Framework Agreement. But the adoption of the "single undertaking" as the guiding principle for the round ensured that the agreements coming out of the negotiations would radically change the form and content of most of the key elements of the second dimension of S&D provisions. In particular, the agreements had the effect of reducing the scope of many of the existing S&D provisions, and the surviving provisions were reformulated essentially in the form of longer time periods within which developing countries were to implement the new agreements. In other words, the intent of the Uruguay Round agreements is that developing countries should eventually meet virtually the same set of standards as industrial countries on a broad range of market access issues.

Thus, many post–Uruguay Round S&D provisions are expressed in terms of transition periods and differences in threshold levels. That is, the Uruguay Round agreements specify how soon and to what extent industrial and developing countries should meet their obligations. Some of the agreements add nonmandatory offers of technical assistance to help developing countries fulfill their commitments. The implied eventual convergence in standards of behavior for industrial and developing countries applies, in particular, in such areas as the use of quantitative trade restrictions, offers of special assistance to producers, tariff binding, and reciprocity.

For example, the use by developing countries of quantitative restrictions for dealing with balance of payments problems has been constrained by the imposition of more stringent rules and procedures. A schedule for removing existing quantitative restrictions has to be publicly announced, and there is an explicit preference for price-based measures for curtailing imports. Where the use of quantitative import restrictions is justified, they must be limited in duration and be applied on a nondiscriminatory basis. Similarly, the right of developing countries with per capita income equal to or greater than US$1,000 to use export subsidies has been sharply curtailed, as they are required to eliminate export subsidies by 2003.

Several Uruguay Round agreements appear to preserve some of the old S&D treatment provisions. For instance, the Agreement on Technical Barriers to Trade includes a statement that developing countries are not required to use international standards which are not appropriate for their needs or which may hinder the preservation of indigenous technology. Similarly, the provisions on safeguards exempt a developing country's exports from countervailing measures as long as its share of total imports of the product is 4 percent or less. Most provisions for S&D treatment of LDCs survived the changes introduced in the Uruguay Round; perhaps the single most important S&D provision to survive without modification is the GSP. But the Uruguay Round did nothing to eliminate or even reduce many of the limitations (including the unilateral nature of the scheme) that have traditionally curtailed the benefits derivable from the GSP.

It may be concluded, therefore, that in general the Uruguay Round essentially reduced S&D treatment for developing countries to extended transition periods over which developing countries would assume the same levels and scope of obligations as industrial countries. But the setting of transition periods and threshold levels appears haphazard and ad hoc and is not closely linked to objective criteria reflecting differences in levels of development or a country's institutional and human capacity. In the light of experience with implementation following the Uruguay Round, the transition periods and threshold levels appear to have been excessively optimistic in many cases.

Redefining Special and Differential Treatment

The deficiencies associated with post–Uruguay Round S&D treatment provisions suggest the need for a careful rethinking of the concept—of its justification, form, and content. The absence of such rethinking during the Uruguay Round probably led to the patchwork nature of the post–Uruguay Round S&D provisions. For example, the adoption and wholesale use of transition periods appear not to have been carefully thought through. The transition periods are probably meant to reflect the costs of changes in trade policy rules for an economy. But there are typically at least three different types of cost: the costs of adjustment, of implementation, and of compliance. Some policy changes (e.g., tariff rate reduction) may be associated with minimal implementation and compliance costs, although the adjustment cost could be high if the reduction is large and is implemented quickly. A long transition (implementation) period could be a way of reducing (or perhaps spreading out) the adjustment cost. By comparison, a policy change that mandates increased protection of intellectual property rights could be associated with high costs of implementation, compliance, and adjustment, to the extent that it involves human and institutional capacity building for implementation and compliance, in addition to the cost of adjustment. In such a case the use of a transition period may, by itself, be neither wholly adequate nor appropriate for taking account of the full costs associated with the policy or rule change.

It is obvious that the limited duration of the transition periods used to reflect S&D "concessions" in many Uruguay Round agreements renders them both inadequate and inappropriate as a basis for building capacity for enhanced production and trade in low-income countries.

Redefining S&D treatment also requires multilateral agreement regarding the classification of WTO member countries and the measurable development, trade, and other parameters that should be used in this categorization. Currently, the WTO appears to recognize (implicitly, at least) three categories of countries in its membership: industrial, developing, and least developed. The WTO indirectly defines the least-developed countries by adopting the UN list. This list, however, is defective for at least two reasons. First, it is based on income and hence does not necessarily reflect trade competitiveness, with which the WTO is (or should be) concerned. Second, it excludes several very low income countries. This may be why the agreement on subsidies expands the UN list to include other countries with per capita income of up to US$1,000. As for "developing countries," the WTO has no specific definition. In practice, it falls back on an implicit self-designation arrangement that permits countries to so describe themselves.

An explicit categorization of WTO member countries based on a multilaterally agreed set of measurable criteria could also address the questions of which countries are eligible for S&D treatment and which countries should be graduated out of which S&D provisions, and when. The Uruguay Round agreement on subsidies offers an example. By categorizing beneficiaries according to per capita income, it was able to express the graduation threshold in terms of measurable economic indicators (such as exceeding a specified per capita income over three consecutive years or achieving a specified export share) rather than by assigning a transition period. Thus, a solution to the problems associated with country categorization and graduation could be the adoption and generalization of the principle used in the agreement on subsidies. As an alternative, the WTO might consider adopting the World Bank's classification of countries as low income, middle income, and high income. This method has at least two advantages: it is determined in a transparent way, and it is widely accepted. The income based indicator could be supplemented by a measure of trade competitiveness (for example,

tries, and questions of ownership and the setting of priorities.

The "first-wave" response can be dated to the second half of the 1990s. It focused on three initiatives. The first, launched in May 1996 at UNCTAD IX in Midrand, South Africa, was the Joint Integrated Technical Assistance Programme for Selected Least-Developed and Other African Countries (JITAP). The second initiative was taken in December that year in Singapore, at the First WTO Ministerial Conference, which adopted the Comprehensive and Integrated WTO Plan of Action for LDCs. The plan envisaged closer cooperation between the WTO and other multilateral and bilateral agencies assisting LDCs in the area of trade. To implement the Plan of Action, a high-level meeting convened by the WTO in October 1997 launched the Integrated Framework for Technical-Related Assistance, Including Human and Institutional Capacity Building to Support Least-Developed Countries in their Trade and Trade-Related Activities (the Integrated Framework, or IF). Finally, a separate initiative designed to help African countries prepare for future WTO negotiations emerged, encompassing a variety of interventions, including UNCTAD's positive agenda program.

The "second-wave" response, dating from around mid-2000, followed reviews of the experience of the JITAP and the IF. It apparently has broader objectives and a much wider scope than the initiatives in the first wave. It is concerned with "mainstreaming trade" as an integral part of the overall development and poverty reduction effort. In other words, it is more explicit in its recognition of trade as a major engine of enterprise development, diversification, economic growth, and poverty reduction. Consequently, it is focused on assisting the countries concerned to identify and prioritize structural supply-side constraints, including insufficient human, institutional, and productive capacity and inadequate trade-related infrastructure. It is significant that the second-wave response emerged in the context of a renewed effort by major international financial institutions such as the World Bank and the IMF, and by the development community as a whole, to pursue a more inclusive policy agenda aimed at addressing entrenched poverty and the marginalization of the poorest countries in the new global economy.

This chapter reviews the main issues encompassed by the first and second waves of responses. The latter holds the key to a sustainable integration of African countries into the global economy and to their more effective participation in the WTO. These goals will require complex interventions, demanding a coherent approach from African policymakers, development partners, and other actors. To the extent that regional markets and regional integration constitute a springboard for enhancing integration in the global economy, there is a need to make specific provisions in these interventions to support the development of intra-African trade.

The "First Wave": The JITAP, the IF, and Assistance with Preparations for Future Negotiations

In April 1994, 30 African countries signed the Marrakech Agreement that established the WTO, even though only a handful of African countries had been active participants in the Uruguay Round negotiations and in the multilateral trading framework established by the GATT. By 1998, 10 more African countries had joined the WTO, and 5 others were at various stages of accession. The 40 African members of the WTO constitute nearly a third of the entire membership. This surge in the interest of African countries in the multilateral trading system reflected the fact that several of them had undertaken significant liberalization of their national economies as part of economic reforms under adjustment programs supported by the World Bank and the IMF. It further reflected a basic perception that with the increasing globalization of the world economy, the disciplines of the WTO agreements provide a framework for stable and predictable market access and for safeguarding national trading and related interests.

It was clear from the start, however, that participation in the WTO framework and in international trade would require building up the necessary capacity. Shortly after the Marrakech meeting, in October 1994, African trade ministers meeting in Tunis adopted a Framework for Action for the Implementation of the Uruguay Round Agreements by African Countries. The framework was substantially concerned with the identification of capacity-building needs for the development and management of trade policy, including the implementation of the Uruguay Round agreements, participation in the WTO framework, and the promotion of exports. The JITAP, the IF, and UNCTAD's positive agenda interventions emerged during the second half of the 1990s as responses to these concerns. Each of these responses is briefly described below.[2]

The JITAP

The JITAP was established as a collaborative venture by the three Geneva trade agencies in cooperation with interested international donors. As has been noted, the Geneva trio had over the years acquired substantial expertise in providing technical assistance for various aspects of trade-related capacity building as part of their respective mandates. Indeed, the JITAP was conceived as a vehicle for utilizing this expertise by adopting a systematic approach and a framework for donor and interagency coordination. To enhance the sustainability of JITAP interventions, much emphasis was placed on human resource development, institutional capacity building, and strengthening of export supply capabilities.

Eight countries—Benin, Burkina Faso, Côte d'Ivoire, Ghana, Kenya, Tanzania, Tunisia, and Uganda—were initially selected for JITAP projects. The objectives of the JITAP were put into effect through a series of interconnected activities aimed at building national capacity to understand the WTO agreements and their development implications for each beneficiary country, including their implications for trade negotiations; adapting the national policy and regulatory framework to the WTO agreements; and enhancing the country's capacity to take advantage of the WTO agreements through improved export readiness. Although the JITAP concept was launched in 1996, it only took off two years later, following the establishment of a Common Trust Fund to finance program activities and the receipt of pledges to the fund from 13 donor countries, amounting to US$8.2 million of the estimated funding needs of US$10.3 million over four years. The fund is managed by the ITC and is supervised by a steering group of representatives of donors, beneficiaries, and the secretariats of the ITC, UNCTAD, and the WTO. In 1999 the three agencies implementing the JITAP delivered just under US$3 million of activities.[3]

The IF

The JITAP concept of interagency coordination in the delivery of trade-related capacity-building interventions also underlies the IF's activities. The Geneva trio, along with the World Bank, the IMF, and the UNDP, constitute the six core organizations collaborating in the delivery of trade-related capacity-building assistance under the IF. The IF is the product of the expressed desire of WTO member states "to foster an integrated approach to assist least-developed countries in enhancing their trading opportunities."[4]

As noted above, the IF was established at the high-level meeting organized by the WTO in October 1997 to put into effect the Comprehensive and Integrated WTO Plan of Action for the Least-Developed Countries adopted in Singapore in December 1996. The main assumption underlying the IF is that each LDC has a different set of initial conditions and therefore specific trade-related capacity-building requirements. Accordingly, it was emphasized right from the start that the interventions envisaged under the IF must be demand-driven to ensure the relevance and country ownership of the capacity-building process. Each participating country was therefore required to carry out a needs assessment for trade-related technical assistance.

The IF adopted a methodology based on a standard questionnaire that was designed to help countries carry out the needs assessment exercise with the assistance of any, some, or all of the six agencies. Following the completion of the needs assessment exercise, the six agencies were to cooperate in preparing a provisional program of trade-related technical assistance that responded to the needs which had been identified. The provisional program, which became known as the integrated response, was to be discussed and agreed on with the LDC concerned. Each of the six agencies would then assume responsibility for implementation of those aspects of the integrated response that fell within its competence and specialization. By mid-1999, 40 of the 48 LDCs had completed the needs assessment exercise.[5]

To facilitate implementation of the integrated response, it was further expected that the exercise would culminate in the scheduling of a trade sector roundtable meeting with donors, typically in the context of a World Bank Consultative Group Meeting or a UNDP Roundtable Meeting. The purpose of these meetings was to give development partners an opportunity to endorse a multiyear program of trade-related technical assistance and to pledge support for elements of the program. By mid-1999,

Assessment

It is too early to assess the second-wave response, since implementation has hardly begun. A few positive elements, however, that have emerged from the reviews of the JITAP and the IF could potentially bridge the major gaps evident in the first-wave response.

JITAP II. The effort that is to be made in JITAP II to strengthen the role of ministries of trade as the focal point for trade policy is to be welcomed. The experience of several developing countries in East Asia, Latin America, and elsewhere has shown the need for such a corporate framework to manage the trade policy process; to oversee policy issues concerned with multilateral and regional trade agreements, including compliance and negotiation; and to facilitate coordination with other institutions concerned with national economic management, with a view to ensuring that supply-side constraints are adequately addressed.

In this regard, human resources development and training for trade-supporting services are essential. The JITAP II proposal for a stronger involvement of local universities and business schools to complement other activities aimed at strengthening the network of trainers, if acted on, will be a significant contribution. There is considerable scope for intercountry cooperation in this area in promoting high-quality regional centers of excellence to fulfill training, advisory, analytical, and research functions. These could be developed from within existing institutions.

JITAP II further proposes to address relevant regional integration elements by including as criteria for the extension of the program to other countries such factors as the role of a country with respect to regional integration; the country's potential to benefit from the program; proximity to regional clusters; and possibilities for regional synergies and economies of scale at the implementation stage.

IF II. The IF was originally an unfunded mandate, and donors and agencies differed in the priority to be given it. Situating it at the center of a beneficiary country's program of assistance with development partners provides a more solid basis for establishing the link between trade and development, on the one hand, and development strategy and poverty reduc-

tion, on the other. If IF II takes off as expected, the proposed trade chapter of the PRSPs would include the identification and prioritization of trade-related capacity requirements, from infrastructure to human resources, within a coherent policy framework.

It has been suggested that, ultimately, mainstreaming trade will give greater visibility to the linkages between trade and all other related policy areas, including health, education, and general social conditions (see Fried 2000). This would require governments to reflect on how they can most efficiently use the limited resources they are able to devote to trade. In this regard, it is to be hoped that in the reassessment of the use of resources, such constraints as the understaffing of the WTO missions of African countries in Geneva and cases of complete nonrepresentation would be resolved in a decisive manner (see Blackhurst, Lyakurwa, and Oyejide 2000). By the same token, it would require development partners to reexamine development assistance priorities to ensure that they are sending a coherent message across their various assistance mechanisms and institutions. The World Bank, in particular, as the lead agency in the mainstreaming exercise, faces a major challenge to ensure that it becomes more proactive in engaging national trade policymakers to determine the nature and extent of trade-related technical assistance and capacity building needed by a country.

Conclusion

This chapter has revisited the question of trade-related capacity building for enhanced African participation in the international economy. It has suggested that the first-wave response to this question during the second half of the 1990s led to greater sensitization in African countries on international trade issues, including participation in the WTO. The JITAP and the IF, however—as the main instruments of capacity-building interventions— were constrained by serious deficiencies. The JITAP was limited to just a few countries and was not able to deliver projects to enhance competitiveness and overcome constraints on the supply side, including those in production and infrastructure. The IF itself never actually took off. Issues related to intraregional trade policy were mostly ignored.

Still, by the time of the Seattle ministerial conference in 1999, there was much evidence that the effort given to technical assistance to prepare African countries for trade negotiations had paid off. In Seattle African countries exhibited an unprecedented degree of preparedness and greater awareness of the issues at stake. At the next ministerial meeting, in Doha, they played an active role. Technical assistance for trade negotiations is an ongoing activity that will call for improved coordination among the various partners involved.

Mandated reviews of the JITAP and the IF during 2000 resulted in a second-wave response concerned with mainstreaming trade as an integral part of the overall development and poverty reduction effort. For the JITAP, specifically, the review resulted in a commitment to extend JITAP II to an additional 10 to 15 countries, given the demand for its accelerated and integrated mode of trade-related capacity-building interventions. It was further proposed that one of the criteria for selecting the additional countries should be their role in regional integration processes. For the IF, the centerpiece of the new arrangements is to place trade-related technical assistance within the framework of a country's national PRSP process. This is expected not only to ensure that trade takes its rightful place in policy terms but also to create a viable framework for making available the resources required to foster the necessary skills, institutions, and infrastructure for the effective integration of IF-eligible countries into the world economy. IF II will require complex interventions, demanding a coherent approach from African policymakers, development partners, and other actors.

Notes

An earlier version of this paper was presented at the African Economic Research Consortium (AERC) Seminar on Assistance in the Preparation of African Countries for the WTO Trade Negotiations, Geneva, March 9, 2001. The author may be reached at <David.Luke @ties.itu.ch>.

1 See, for example, the Framework for Action for the Implementation of the Uruguay Round Agreements by African Countries adopted at a meeting of African trade ministers in Tunis, October 1994 (available from the Organization of African Unity), and OECD (1999b).

2 It should be noted that the regular trade-related technical cooperation activities of the Geneva agencies and of other bilateral and multilateral donors continued outside the framework of the three initiatives.

3 See, for example, UNCTAD, "Review of Technical Co-operation Activities," TD/B/47/2/Add.1, 2000, and ITC, "JITAP Mid-term Evaluation, Management Response," November 16, 2000.

4 See WTO, "Singapore Ministerial Declaration," WT/Min (96)/DEC, 1996, para. 14.

5 See WTO, "High Level Meeting on Integrated Initiatives for Least-Developed Countries, Trade Development, Outcome and Follow-up, Report of the Director-General," WT/MIN (98)/2, 1998, and WTO, Sub-Committee on Least-Developed Countries, "Note on the Meeting of 12 July 1999," WT/COMTD/LDC/M/16, 1999.

6 See WT/COMTD/LDC/M/16, 1999.

7 See also WTO, "Review of the Integrated Framework: Communiqué from Heads of the Six Core Agencies," WT/LDC/SWG/IF/2, July 12, 2000: 2.

8 See ITC, "JITAP Mid-term Evaluation, Management Response," November 16, 2000.

9 See WT/LDC/SWG/IF/2, July 12, 2000.

10 See WTO, Sub-Committee on Least-Developed Countries, "Integrated Framework—Proposal for a Pilot Scheme," WT/LDC/SWG/IF/13, February 16, 2001.

VIII

TRADE POLICY QUESTIONS AND GUIDELINES

T he chapters in this part are more normative than most of the others in this
Handbook in that they offer rules of thumb for policy. These policy recommendations are not abstract
or absolute; they are based on extensive country
experience, and in many instances they do not so
much give formulas as point toward asking specific
questions and determining the situation that applies
in a given context. As emphasized in other parts of
the Handbook, trade reforms must be accompanied
by many other, complementary, actions. What
these are will depend on the country concerned.
Although each country must determine its own priorities, taking into account the prevailing institutional capacity constraints, the rules of thumb that
are proposed for trade policies are quite robust in
the sense that they help guide policymakers away
from narrow and piecemeal approaches that are
likely to be inefficient. Chapter 51, by Constantine

Michalopoulos, Maurice Schiff, and David Tarr, outlines these general rules.

One area of policy advice that is particularly controversial—despite many years of research and cross-
country experience—is the design of the tariff
structure. Chapter 52, by David G. Tarr, on arguments for and against uniformity in the structure of
the tariff, comes out strongly in favor of a single tariff rate for all goods. Although not all may agree with
this recommendation, it is important to understand
the arguments as to why uniformity makes for good
economic policy. It is also important to note that uniformity does not necessarily mean free trade. A preference for uniformity has implications for the pursuit
of multilateral tariff negotiations, which can be used
both to reduce the dispersion in tariffs and to reduce
the average level of tariffs. Countries that have uniform tariffs cannot play the WTO game of trading
concessions on tariffs for specific goods; they must

What is the impact of status quo trade policies on the poor? It is important to determine the effect on the poor of the existing pattern of protection and subsidization. Such effects may be positive or negative and may affect particular products consumed by the poor or the incomes of a significant number of the poor, throughout the country or in a particular region. Taxes or supports for important food staples or inputs to agriculture, in particular, should be identified and their incidence examined. In those cases where the structure of protection is not beneficial to the poor, there is a prima facie case for reform. In cases where some of the poor benefit, an assessment should be made of the relative magnitude of their potential losses and the economywide gains from reform.

Are there nontariff barriers for reasons other than for health, safety, and the environment? To the extent that significant nontariff barriers are present, there is again a prima facie case for reform, starting with conversion to tariffs. This reform is likely to benefit the poor more than the nonpoor, since license recipients typically collect rents and (almost by definition) are unlikely to be poor, and the competition for licenses wastes resources that could be used productively.

What is the average tariff, and how dispersed is it? The more the dispersion, the greater the difference in treatment of different sectors and segments of society is likely to be, and the greater the urgency of reform. Dispersion, which is often generated by exemptions and tariff escalation, will lead to high effective rates of protection and is likely to entail significant inefficiencies.

Is there discrimination against agriculture? The overall policy stance affecting agriculture should be determined, starting with an assessment of the effective rate of protection for this sector compared with manufacturing. (See Schiff and Valdés 1992 for a description of a methodology for doing this.) Agriculture is of great importance for poverty reduction because the rural poor are likely to account for a large share of the country's poor.

How well do critical service markets function? Do the poor have access to important ancillary services such as transport? Do policies discriminate against foreign suppliers and lead to high-cost, low-quality domestic supply? Is entry possible in labor-intensive sectors such as tourism and back-office services? Does competition prevail in key backbone sectors such as transport, finance, and communications? Is appropriate procompetitive regulation in place?

How efficient is the customs service? How long does it take to clear a container or air freight shipment? How does this compare with the norms in neighboring countries and with best practice? How large are "unofficial" trade facilitation payments? Is there a functioning drawback and temporary admission mechanism?

The overall analysis of the trade regime should yield a preliminary judgment on the desirability of trade reform. This judgment should then be reviewed in light of the potential short-term effects of trade reform on the poor and on other groups in society that are likely to experience serious adverse effects. If there are possible negative effects, it is important to identify the relevant products and sectors early on, to make it possible to design arrangements for dealing with the adverse impacts of the reform and to develop strategies for building consensus in support of reform. It must be recognized that there will always be groups that lose from trade reform; by definition, trade policy is an instrument through which income gets redistributed in the economy. In many cases those that lose will not be the poor but those who benefit from the scarcity rents that are created by restricting trade.

Strong government commitment to the reform is critical. The government should attempt to explain the desirability of the reform and obtain support from some parts of civil society. Achieving a broad consensus may be a difficult task. The benefits from reform are likely to be dispersed, uncertain, and spread over time, whereas the private costs of sectors that will be facing increased competition from imports will be obvious, near term, and likely to be concentrated in powerful political groups.

It might appear tempting to design a trade reform by identifying sectors that are important to the poor—either on the consumption side or on the income side—and singling out these sectors for differentiated cuts in protection. If, for instance, many poor people produce maize, as in Mexico, it might seem sensible to exclude this product from a tariff reduction. There are at least two problems with this approach; one is fundamental, and the other has to do with political economy. The fundamental problem is that trade policy is a single instrument, and a basic principle of economic policy formulation is that a single instrument cannot be expected to address multiple targets. The political-economy problem is that once a highly differentiated trade regime is adopted, it is essentially impossible to stop special interests from building a case that their sector deserves special treatment for one reason or another. Returning to the example of maize, if we decide to maintain or raise protection, we are likely to find that there is another important group of poor people for whom maize is an important expenditure item.

A better approach is to concentrate on developing two different sets of instruments—one (trade policy) focused on providing the incentives appropriate for the efficient production and use of goods and services, and another (distributional policy) focused on alleviating poverty. With this assignment of instruments, trade policy can be designed using the simple, comprehensible guidelines for trade policy formulation. A set of distributional instruments will necessarily have a much wider range of dimensions, including expansion of access to education, the provision of safety nets, and investments in the infrastructure needed to provide people in poorer regions with access to the markets and other amenities enjoyed by relatively advantaged people.

Complementary Policies

As has been emphasized in other chapters in this Handbook, trade policy reform and institutional strengthening must be implemented in the context of a variety of complementary policies. Some of these are general, and some are focused on making the trade policy reform more likely to benefit the poor.

Macroeconomic Policy

Macroeconomic stabilization and a competitive exchange rate are essential for supporting greater integration into world markets. Exchange rate depreciation at the outset of major trade reform programs will facilitate adjustment. Great care must be taken to avoid real exchange rate appreciation at a time of import liberalization. As appreciation is largely determined by macroeconomic and fiscal policies, it is important that these are managed so as to be consistent with the trade reform.

Markets

If markets are not competitive or are missing, trade reforms may not benefit the poor. Critical obstacles to the operation of market signals must be identi-

fied. Questions that should be posed include the following:

- In agriculture, are prices passed on to farmers, or are there government or private intermediaries that make large profits on the sale of farm products or farm inputs?
- More generally, is the reform likely to destroy existing markets that are significant for the poor? Will it make it possible for poor consumers to obtain new goods? (For further discussion, see Winters 2000a; McCulloch, Winters, and Cirera 2001.)
- Are there serious impediments of various kinds (legal, cultural, and infrastructural) to labor mobility? Labor market restrictions, such as prohibitions on firing workers, often spawn an informal labor market sector, with the poor concentrated there. Reduction in the restraints in the labor market, especially combined with trade reform, can result in an expansion of the formal sector and an increased demand for labor in that sector. This can have a strong impact on poverty reduction, since it will allow the poor to move out of the informal sector and into the formal sector.
- Are there serious financing obstacles to participation in trade? In the long run developing an effective financial system is a key to development. In the short run trade-focused instruments such as the use of back-to-back letters of credit may alleviate some of the most pressing obstacles to trade.
- Are there serious obstacles to setting up a business? Competition may be impeded because it is difficult to obtain a license to start a new business or to make an investment. Or foreign investment may be impeded. The reduction in barriers to entry, especially those imposed by governments at various levels, can be expected to improve competition and allow entrepreneurs to sell new, cheaper imports to the poor or to provide services necessary to bring goods to market. The latter is particularly important in cases in which reform affects entities that provide ancillary services to the poor and that may cease to do so after reform occurs. An example would be the provision of transport, storage, and distribution services to farmers by a marketing board. If there are barriers to entry into such services activities, or if entry is unlikely to occur because the market cannot sustain operations, continued government involvement may be necessary.

BOX 51.1 (CONTINUED)

Liberalization often is not yet locked in, is subject to reversal, and is often seen as donor driven, without strong national ownership. The consequence is that private agents remain hesitant to invest. WTO tariff bindings are generally much higher than actual rates, so there is room for much greater use of this commitment mechanism. Reciprocal free trade agreements with countries outside Africa and harmonization of trade and investment policies along subregional lines would also help.

3. *Integrate further trade reforms with national "business plans" for economic diversification.* Trade reforms need to be accompanied by measures that lay a stable base for investment and production: effective and honest tax and customs administrations, functioning commercial courts, reliable infrastructure, and a working financial system. Failure to effect these measures has blunted the investment response to first-generation trade reforms in most African countries. With Africa ranked among the world's riskiest places to do business, even retaining domestic savings becomes a challenge. In 1990 flight capital accounted for almost 40 percent of private wealth in Africa, compared with 6 percent in East Asia and 10 percent in Latin America. Investment booms everywhere have been led by domestic capital, so the first order of business is for governments to provide a safe and profitable environment that will persuade their citizens to invest at home. While some countries, such as Mauritius and Uganda, have steadily improved their risk ratings, others, including Kenya and Zimbabwe, have seen sharp declines.

The cost of doing business in Africa is high partly because of its economic sparseness and the distance of much of its production from the sea, but weak business services are also a major impediment. An efficient Nacala rail line and port could save Malawi the equivalent of 3 percent of its GDP. Road transport in Africa may be twice as costly as in Asia, in part because of unofficial tolls. Restrictive agreements help explain why air transport tariffs and handling charges can be twice those for comparable

flights in other regions. International telephone charges and Internet connections are among the world's costliest. Ugandan firms lose an average of 91 days a year because of power outages.

4. *Mainstream regionalism in a new way.* Despite past failures and the lackluster implementation of existing schemes, the case for Africa's economic integration remains compelling. Alternative approaches are needed, however. One is to stress an outward orientation, or open regionalism, and a flexible design for jointly implementing specific projects. Since African economies are very small, both individually and as subgroups, the potential welfare gains from freer trade within Africa may be limited. Creating an economic space in which investors can produce for regional as well as global markets may provide better growth opportunities than simply removing barriers to trade among African countries themselves. This approach may serve as a building block for eventual market integration while being less political.

5. *Create a platform for effective African participation in multilateral forums such as the WTO.* Such forums are essential for underpinning the credibility of reforms and for enforcing "appropriate" global standards, which are becoming prerequisites for accessing markets in industrial countries. But African countries also need to help shape these standards and to negotiate for the dismantling of restrictive trade practices that inhibit export diversification. Agriculture, processed goods, and textiles and clothing are particularly important. In order to be effective at the WTO, it will be essential to pool expertise.

6. *Base all this on consultative processes.* Any business plan requires a supportive, mutually accountable relationship among business, labor, and government. Much of East Asia's success has been attributed to active interactions between the state and business. Poor communication, and outright mistrust, between these groups limit growth in many African countries. Consultative groups should begin by focusing on regulations that affect the entire private sector, but they can also serve as

BOX 51.1 (CONTINUED)

agents of restraint on government behavior, to ensure support for proexport policies. The government needs to be accountable for services standards, and business for performance. In many countries closer consultation will be needed in the new era of globalization, democracy, and participatory politics.

Source: Prepared by the volume editors based on World Bank (2000a): ch. 7.

DAVID G. TARR

52

ARGUMENTS FOR AND AGAINST UNIFORM TARIFFS

An effective trade policy is central to the integration of developing countries into the international economic system and the growth that integration will generate. Trade policy, together with the exchange rate, forms the transmission mechanism through which international trade affects domestic resource allocation, the efficient and competitive restructuring of industry and agriculture, access to new and diverse technologies, improved incentives to exporters, and reduction of smuggling, rent-seeking, and corruption in customs. Tariff policy is the centerpiece of trade policy in a market system. Tariffs are, with very few exceptions, the only acceptable policy tool for protection under the GATT/WTO. They are superior to alternative instruments of protection such as nontariff barriers (NTBs)—that is, quotas, licenses, and technical barriers to trade (TBTs)—because they are less likely to lead to rent-seeking and corrupt practices, and because tariffs limit the exercise of domestic monopoly power where it exists, whereas NTBs do not.

WORLDWIDE EXPERIENCE IN THE PAST 50 YEARS DEMONSTRATES THE BENEFITS OF open trade regimes. The OECD countries brought trade barriers down through successive WTO negotiations and experienced sustained growth in trade and incomes. Many developing country governments initially took a different stance and attempted to promote industrialization behind high protective barriers. But in the past 10 years or so, the balance of opinion has shifted in these countries as well, with the growing evidence that high rates of protection significantly depress economic development, and that open trade regimes are more conducive to growth. Moreover, virtually all recent development success stories have been based on strong growth of industrial exports. Exporters have not been disadvantaged in these successful economies, either because there were low barriers to imports—as in Chile, Hong Kong (China), and Singapore—or because regimes were developed to provide incentives to exporters comparable to import-competing sectors despite the protection, as in the Republic of Korea, Mauritius, and Taiwan (China).[1]

This chapter examines the arguments for and against a uniform tariff structure. Arguments against uniformity have to do with terms of trade; promotion of "strategic" or infant industries or restructuring of industries; revenue or balance of payments considerations; and the utility of tariffs as a negotiating tool at the WTO. Arguments in favor of uniformity include political-economy considerations, administrative convenience, and reduction of smuggling and corruption in customs. We maintain that tariff uniformity is the best choice, in practice.

In many circumstances in which tariffs are second-best policy instruments—for raising public revenues or coping with balance of payments problems, for example—a uniform tariff rate is the most practical and efficient alternative. If a country is interested in using the tariff as a bargaining instrument in multilateral negotiations, it is immaterial whether the tariff is uniform or differentiated; the issues are the country's capacity to use the tariff as a bargaining instrument and what it will bargain for. Differentiated tariff protection in support of infant or restructuring industries is typically ineffective at addressing the alleged market failure problem: governments are not very good at picking winners, and there are serious dangers that the policy will be overwhelmed by requests for protection from vested interests irrespective of economic merits.

A uniform tariff conveys a number of advantages, the most important of which is that if the tariff is uniform, the gains to industry lobbying are much smaller (and may be negative), creating a free-rider problem for the lobbying industry and dramatically reducing the incentive to lobby for protection. This means that (a) the level of protection is likely to be lower (the recent experience of Chile is a dramatic case in point); (b) there is a direct saving of resources because of the reduced lobbying; (c) the reduction in the gains from lobbying for protection provides a vastly improved signal to valuable entrepreneurial talent, which will thus be encouraged to create better and cheaper products; and (d) the reduction in resources devoted to lobbying will result in less corruption in government, and this may have positive spillover effects on other dimensions of government activity.

Arguments for Tariffs and for Nonuniform Tariffs

There are several arguments in favor of government intervention through tariffs. Some of these support tariffs as first-best policies and call for nonuniform tariffs. The reasons given are (a) to exploit a monopsony position and thereby improve the terms of trade, and (b) to maximize benefits from a "strategic" application of protection. Often, governments wish to pursue other objectives than the pursuit of real income, or there may be constraints on the use of first-best instruments to achieve those objectives.[2] Other justifications for tariffs are (c) as instruments for temporary protection of a specific "infant" or restructuring industry, (d) to raise budgetary revenue, (e) to reduce imports as a remedy for balance of payments problems, and (f) as bargaining tools to extract concessions from trading partners. First-best policies in the pursuit of these objectives are subsidies (objective c), indirect taxes (objective d), and devaluation and other macroeconomic policies (objective e).[3] When the first-best policies are not available, we argue below that low and uniform tariffs are preferable to a high and varied tariff structure.

Tariffs to Exploit Monopsony Power

One generally accepted theoretical reason for a country to impose tariffs on individual products is in order to exploit its monopsony power and thereby improve its terms of trade. If a country is large enough that it imports a significant share of the world's supply of a particular product, a tariff on that product could lower the price the country must pay to world suppliers. Consistent with this argument, the government could impose tariffs at different levels on different products to exploit the monopsony power it possesses, and the "optimal" tariff on each product would be different.

Although the theory is valid, in practice there are very few products in which the typical developing country possesses sufficient monopsony power for this argument to be relevant. Even then, the tariffs would typically be quite small (1 to 10 percent) because the share of world imports would have to be large indeed to allow high tariffs. Furthermore, the actual tariffs for most countries are typically larger than the values optimal tariffs could reasonably be expected to take. For all practical purposes, tariff policy can be established without reference to this basically theoretical issue.

Tariffs to Gain Strategic Advantage

In recent years a number of arguments have been developed justifying tariffs on the basis of strategic considerations in industries with excess profits that are highly concentrated globally. Among others, Brander and Spencer (1985) developed models showing that in the presence of an international oligopoly, tariffs could increase a country's welfare by enabling excess profits to be shifted from foreign to domestic firms. Krugman (1992) showed that given the existence of increasing returns to scale in the firm, protection to allow domestic firms to gain initial competitive advantage at the expense of foreign firms could be reinforced by internal economies of scale and would allow domestic firms to appropriate excess profits.

Despite its popularity among theorists in the 1980s, today strategic trade theory is not regarded as a significant policy choice. There is doubt as to whether excess profits really exist (except in the very short term) in many industries worldwide and whether they are not easily dissipated by new entrants or by utilization of excess capacity. Eaton and Grossman (1986) have shown that the policy conclusions of strategic trade policy models can be completely reversed, depending on assumptions about which little is known. For example, whether firms compete in price or in quantity will reverse the optimal policy conclusion from subsidizing an industry to taxing the industry. One of the principal authors of this literature has concluded that the risks of following strategic trade theory far outweigh the possible gains (Krugman 1989, 1992); a country might make small gains in some circumstances, but the measures are more likely to be misapplied and to lead to large losses. Given that a typical developing country seldom has a manufacturing firm competing in international markets dominated by only a few firms with excess profits, the potential scope for strategic trade policy is inherently limited.

Infant Industry and Restructuring Protection

The use of tariffs to effect welfare improvements over the longer run has been defended most often on infant industry grounds. The infant industry argument posits that certain industries are initially uneconomic but that they may become competitive (at world prices) in the long run because costs may decrease over time through learning-by-doing effects. Market failures stemming from gains that are external to the firm may prevent the development of industries that exhibit positive discounted present values. For example, a firm may be unwilling to invest in technical know-how that may become freely available to other firms; that is, the activities of an individual firm could generate externalities that cannot be captured by the firm. (If there were no externalities, the firm would be willing to make the investments, and there would be no need to depart from laissez-faire policy.) Similar

arguments have been made in the context of economies in transition, where it is argued that if some firms in the process of restructuring are given protection for a time, they will be able to increase their productivity and become viable in the longer term. A firm may be faced with imperfections in its markets for inputs that raise its costs—for example, because an inefficient banking sector prevents it from obtaining credit.

The argument, then, is that temporary tariffs may be necessary to protect these infant and restructuring industries so that they can generate benefits for the economy as a whole. Under the infant industry argument for protection, the optimum tariff structure would not normally be uniform because protection would be accorded only to specific industries affected by market failure or externalities but would not be warranted for other industries. But as Baldwin (1969) has explained, a tariff will not typically address the market failure problem and therefore is not better than laissez-faire policy. Consider, for example, the case of the inability of the firm to appropriate the gains from investment in technical know-how. A duty raises the domestic price of a product and, from the viewpoint of the domestic industry as a whole, makes some investments in knowledge more profitable. But the individual entrepreneur still faces the same externality problem as before—the risk that other firms in the same industry will copy, without cost to themselves, any new technology discovered by the firm and will then drive the product's price or factor prices to levels at which the initial firm will be unable to recover the costs of acquiring knowledge (Baldwin 1969: 298).

Thus, a tariff does not correct the problem. Indeed, it has been shown more generally that the best intervention is a policy which attacks the problem at the source (Bhagwati and Srinivasan 1969). In this case, the appropriate interventions directed at the source of the distortion, which could be imperfect appropriability, labor turnover, or capital market imperfections, are not tariffs but rather measures such as provision of information, patent protection, or more effective use of instruments to allow collateral.[4] Sometimes a government may argue that the whole manufacturing sector is an infant. Although protection is unlikely to be the appropriate response, if any protection is offered for this purpose, a uniform tariff would be called for, not a diverse structure.

Revenue Considerations

Trade taxes are not optimal instruments for achieving a revenue objective because they significantly distort production and consumption choices. Preferred instruments for raising revenue are taxes such as income taxes or commodity taxes (excise taxes, value-added taxes, and so on), which, since they are applied neutrally to domestically produced and imported goods, impose less distortion or inefficiency costs. The use of tariffs to raise revenue presupposes that other trade-neutral tax instruments are not available or cannot be used beyond existing levels; in other words, domestic taxes have to be taken as given either because the tax base cannot be enlarged rapidly enough or because marginal costs of increased domestic tax collection are very high (Corden 1974; Balassa 1989; Mitra 1992).

One of the best-known arguments for a nonuniform structure is the inverse elasticity rule. If the economy is characterized by only final goods (ignoring rent-seeking, administrative, and smuggling costs), the most efficient way to generate tax revenue is to impose higher tariffs on the goods with the lower elasticity of demand (Ramsey 1927). This causes the least distortion, since it diverts the least resources. The simplicity of this rule has appeal for theoretical economists. The rule becomes exceedingly complex in practice, however, because of substitution effects between goods and the presence of intermediate goods and of goods that cannot be effectively taxed. Application then requires not just the own-elasticities but a complete set of cross-elasticities of demand, including the substitution elasticities with untaxed goods such as household leisure and underground economy goods. In fact, this information is never available, so that information requirements make the application of Ramsey-type rules impractical. We know of no country that has actually tried to implement them. A still more important reason to avoid Ramsey-type rules for diverse tariffs is that lobbying is likely to lead to the application of tariffs which depart from uniformity in economically inefficient ways. We return to the lobbying argument below.

Balance of Payments Considerations

Tariffs are sometimes employed to deal with a balance of payments problem, but, again, they are not the best instrument. A balance of payments problem is a macroeconomic problem, and the optimal response is to attack the problem directly through macroeconomic tools—that is, through a combination of actions to reduce domestic spending (expenditure reduction) and to encourage exports and discourage imports (expenditure switching). Expenditure reduction can be achieved through fiscal or monetary tightening, which reduces domestic absorption for any given level of output. Expenditure switching, which is best accomplished through depreciation of the real exchange rate, raises the domestic price of tradables in relation to nontradables, thereby encouraging exports and discouraging imports. Across-the-board import surcharges are often applied for balance of payments reasons; this has the same effect in reducing imports as does exchange rate depreciation, but it fails to achieve the beneficial effects on the export side. The optimal tariff structure, given that it is a surrogate for a devaluation (without export incentives), must be uniform, inducing resources to flow into import-competing industries in general rather than into any particular import-competing industry.

Tariffs as a Negotiating Tool and WTO Accession

Finally, countries may use tariffs as a bargaining tool to extract concessions from trading partners in multilateral trade negotiations within the context of the WTO. For countries applying for WTO membership, the future level and structure of tariffs are important elements of the accession negotiations. The WTO, however, does not focus on the actual level of tariffs (the "applied rate") but on the "bound" rate. The bound rate is the maximum legal level of the tariff for each individual tariff line that a country may not exceed without either renegotiating the tariff or providing compensation by reducing the tariff level for other products. (Michalopoulos treats this issue in some depth in Chapter 8, on WTO accession.) In summary, it is unwise for acceding countries to use tariffs as a bargaining tool, since experience has shown that this is likely to delay accession. More generally, if a country were to succeed in negotiating a structure of high bound rates, it may have gained a pyrrhic victory: by negotiating such a structure, it would create an opening for domestic interests to exert political pressure for additional protection in the future. The government would lose the "political cover" that legally binding WTO commitments offer against

no effective opposing lobbying influence advocating tariffs on these intermediates. The result is low tariffs on intermediates and high tariffs on selected final goods—a situation known as tariff escalation.

The tariff escalation that characterizes the trade regimes of many countries, both industrial and developing, causes problems of inefficient resource allocation. In the long run this escalating tariff structure that tends to favor production of final goods at the expense of intermediates encourages assembly-type activities while discouraging production of intermediate goods. The result is that because an intermediate goods industry does not exist today to lobby for equal protection, incentives are established that hinder its eventual creation.

It is well known that Chile has a uniform tariff, but there are quite a few other economies with tariff structures that are uniform or at least close to uniform. Estonia and Hong Kong (China) have uniform tariffs because they practice free trade. Bolivia and the Kyrgyz Republic have virtually uniform tariff schedules of 10 percent. Singapore has a simple tariff average of 0.5 percent and a standard deviation of less than 3 percent. A number of other countries, including Brunei Darussalam, Ecuador, Honduras, and Mexico, have tariff averages under 13 percent and small variances (under 6 percent).

At the other end of the spectrum are countries such as Bangladesh and India, with tariff averages of 84 and 56 percent and tariff variances of 26 and 24 percent, respectively. Korea, Mexico, South Africa, and Turkey have more than 10,000 tariff headings, while most other countries average about 6,000 tariff headings. A large number of economies have granted exceptional levels of protection to a limited number of products. The list—Cameroon, Canada, China, Egypt, the European Union, Hungary, India, Indonesia, Israel, Nepal, Nicaragua, Norway, Saudi Arabia, the Solomon Islands, Turkey, and the United States—includes some of the poorest countries but also some of the most prominent OECD members.

Conclusions and Practical Steps

The above analysis strongly suggests that there is little economic justification and there are many dangers in providing differentiated tariff protection to various sectors of industry and agriculture. At the practical level, the arguments for a diverse tariff structure rest on the ability of governments to (a) "pick the winners"—that is, to identify the candidates that are most likely to meet the conditions justifying intervention—and to choose and maintain the appropriate level for the tariff, subsidy, or other policy variable; (b) be immune to pressures from vested groups that inevitably arise once willingness to grant special status is established; and (c) prevent any protection granted from becoming permanent. The empirical evidence in both industrial and developing countries during the past three decades casts doubt on most governments' ability to meet these conditions. Moreover, the economy must provide its most talented members with the incentive to engage in entrepreneurial activities such as starting or expanding firms, developing new products, and lowering costs. If tariffs, subsidies, or tax exemptions differ greatly by sector, talented people will find it more profitable to engage in the socially wasteful activity of lobbying the government for these privileges. Endorsement of a more general approach—with little differentiation in the level of assistance—thus emanates from a wider skepticism about the practical merits of targeting of any kind (Krugman 1989, 1992; Westphal 1990). Experience therefore indicates that the best industrial policy is for the government to provide a stable macroeconomic and regulatory environment conducive to business development, with neutral incentives for all firms and industries. Some practical steps suggested by the above arguments are discussed next.

Concertina Approach. If a uniform tariff structure is to be put in place sequentially, priority should be given to reducing the highest rates. (For further discussion, see Chapter 53, by Panagariya, in this volume.) The costs in the form of inefficiencies in resource allocation rise more than proportionately with the height of the tariff. As a consequence, the greatest gains will come from reductions in the maximum rates. In addition, very high tariffs may be prohibitive of imports, so that there will be revenue gains from reductions in the rates. Reductions of the high rates will also reduce smuggling, corruption, and rent-seeking disproportionately.

Simultaneously raising the low rates (as suggested by Hatta 1977) is more controversial, especially with respect to intermediate and capital goods (see Neary 1997). If there is no duty drawback or its equivalent in place, increasing the tariff on intermediate goods imposes a tax on the exportable goods that use the intermediate, so that because of the tariffs, too few resources are devoted to exports.[8] Moreover, it may be argued that raising tariffs on imports of raw materials and intermediates penalizes "technology" imports that are critical for increasing productivity. Against these potential costs, one must weigh the fact that permitting tariff-free imports of intermediates and capital goods penalizes the development of intermediate and capital goods industries in relation to final goods sectors and represents a forgone opportunity to raise revenue. And with a diverse tariff structure, the political-economy, corruption, and smuggling problems persist.[9]

Duty Drawback and Temporary Admission. To reduce the added antiexport bias created by raising tariffs on intermediate and capital goods, many countries employ mechanisms that allow exporters duty free access to imported intermediates. These mechanisms include duty drawback procedures, temporary admission, and export-processing zones. Coupled with effective duty-free access to imported intermediates for exporters, the welfare tradeoff from raising tariffs on intermediate and capital goods is much more likely to be positive.

As noted in Chapter 18, by English and De Wulf, in this volume, the principal problem with duty drawback schemes is that their administration can be very costly and can lead to cumbersome procedures and delays. Moreover, these schemes do not remove all the antiexport bias of tariffs.[10] Given the recognized need to provide duty-free access to imported inputs to exporters, in countries where the capacity to administer duty drawback schemes is weak "temporary admission," should be offered (as opposed to zero tariffs on intermediates). Temporary admission guarantees duty-free access to imported intermediates, and to the extent that the government bureaucracy can administer the program, it imposes tariffs on imported inputs destined for the domestic market, thereby encouraging the development of domestic intermediate goods industries. Temporary admission and zero tariffs on intermediates both provide tariff-free access to intermediates for exporters, but temporary admission diminishes tariff escalation in comparison with zero tariffs on intermediates.

In general, raising tariffs on intermediates poses a conflict between the need to provide balanced protection to intermediates and final goods (that is, to reduce effective protection on final goods) and the need to reduce antiexport bias. Duty drawback appears to resolve the conflict, but it does so at the expense of creating administrative complexity. In addition, any scheme that exempts intermediates from tariffs could reduce the incentive for real import liberalization, which is the first-best policy choice (see Cadot, de Melo, and Olarreaga 2000). Low uniform tariffs, in general, are the best policy and are best combined with duty drawback or temporary admission, depending on administrative competence and the level of the tariff. In many countries it will also be important to obtain technical assistance for institutional development of duty drawback and temporary admission mechanisms.

Multiple Tariff Bands (Tariff Simplification): Not Identical with Tariff Uniformity. It is sometimes argued that for administrative convenience the tariff structure should be simplified into three to five tariff bands. For example, with five tariff bands, tariffs could be 0, 10, 20, 30, or 40 percent (or 0, 5, 10, 15, or 20 percent), but values in between would be prohibited. It should be clear that tariff simplification is not tariff uniformity and that simplification will allow very high rates of effective protection. An important point is that such a system suffers from virtually all the problems of a diverse structure, including encouragement of lobbying for high protection by industry groups, and will encourage misclassification by customs authorities, in comparison with a uniform system.[11]

If, however, tariff simplification is used as a vehicle for moving toward low and uniform tariffs by limiting the number of tariffs and reducing both tariff levels and the dispersion of the tariff structure in the process, then it is a very useful step. More generally, a tariff structure that is low and has a small standard deviation will convey many of the same benefits of a low uniform structure. For example, with a sufficiently small standard deviation, there will be little gain from lobbying or incentives for corruption and, in customs, for misclassification. But tariff simplification by itself, without reduction of the level or dispersion of the tariff structure, will convey relatively small benefits from lower administrative costs.

The Tariff Level. OECD countries have, on average, reduced their tariffs on manufactures to less than 5 percent, although a few peaks, notably in agriculture, textiles, and leather products, remain. The main problem in most countries is agriculture, where, as a result of the tariffication following the Uruguay Round, tariff schedules are quite high, reflecting the previously high supports and protection. If revenue from a tariff is needed, countries

owners of factories specialized in the production of import-competing goods to those specialized in export goods. This may be politically costly. Finally, the reallocation of resources induced by trade liberalization may itself bring with it short-run real costs.

The presence of these costs automatically gives rise to the notion that tariff reductions should be balanced according to some criterion: the cost of one's own liberalization must be balanced by the benefits from liberalization by one's trading partners. The obvious criterion for achieving this balance with respect to the terms of trade cost is to ensure that the terms of trade are unchanged in the postliberalization equilibrium. This would effectively allow each country to benefit from the efficiency gains resulting from its own liberalization without redistribution of income across countries. From the viewpoint of small developing countries, this may not be a major issue, since their own liberalization has little impact on the terms of trade. But for large economies such as the United States, the European Union (EU), and Japan, it is important and plays out in the form of demands for reciprocity.

As for the long-run income distribution effects, unless one is faced with the conservative welfare function such that any movement away from the existing equilibrium is seen as harmful, there is no presumption that the effects of trade are harmful. Indeed, to the extent that most developing countries are exporters of labor-intensive goods, trade liberalization is likely to improve income distribution by raising the return to labor at the expense of capital. Finally, phasing in liberalization over a number of years can minimize the adjustment costs. Starting with the Kennedy Round, this has been the approach under the GATT and the WTO. In the case of multilateral liberalization, these costs are likely to be especially low, since the simultaneous liberalization by partner countries allows export industries to expand rapidly to absorb the resources released by import-competing industries.

In this chapter I discuss the main approaches to trade liberalization that have been taken in past multilateral negotiating rounds and their relative merits.

Sectoral Approaches

Conceptually, two types of sectoral approaches can be distinguished. First, one or more sectors may be identified, and all members may liberalize imports within those sectors. This is sometimes called a "zero for zero" approach. Second, each member may seek liberalization from its major trading partners in its sectors of comparative advantage in return for its own liberalization of sectors of comparative disadvantage.

The first approach has guided much of the liberalization of trade in services during and since the Uruguay Round. Member countries have identified broad sectors such as financial services and telecommunications and have bargained market access within them. The approach was also applied to trade in goods during the first WTO ministerial meeting, held in Singapore. At that meeting, a group of countries signed the Information Technology Agreement (ITA), under which they committed themselves to complete free trade in a set of technology products.

For liberalization of trade goods, this sectoral approach is not particularly attractive. There are two problems. First, there is some concern that under this approach, the sectors that are liberalized first will be those in which economically powerful nations have export interests. Sectors in which developing countries enjoy comparative advantage, such as textiles and clothing, will be taken up last. This view is certainly supported by the fact that, on balance, industrial countries are exporters and developing countries importers of the products covered by the ITA. In addition, even in services, negotiations in sectors in which developing countries have an overwhelming advantage have not been opened.

The second drawback of this approach is that initially it is likely to lead to a lower level of welfare. The sectors that will be picked initially are likely to be those with lower tariffs to begin with. Economic theory suggests that under plausible assumptions, the elimination of relatively low tariffs without a simultaneous reduction in the high tariffs leads to reduced welfare globally, as well as in individual countries. Such a policy change engenders a reallocation of resources from less distorted to more distorted sectors.

Under the second sectoral approach, all industrial products are made part of the negotiation, but members negotiate with their partners sector by sector. In principle, this approach can be expected to yield an efficient outcome. Each member will seek liberalization in sectors and countries where its exports face the highest barriers. In turn, its trading partners will seek access to its most protected sectors. Thus, the bargain is biased in favor of lowering the highest tariffs.

The approach may become administratively complex if trade patterns happen to be such that each country exports goods to one set of countries but imports them from an entirely different set of countries. For instance, if India's exports go mainly to the United States while its imports come from the EU, bilateral negotiations between India and its two trading partners become difficult. One suspects that under the current structure of trade and tariffs, this is not a significant problem (although this has not been empirically verified). Goods subject to high tariffs in developing countries are largely imported from industrial countries and evenly distributed over the latter. Conversely, major exports of developing countries face high barriers in all industrial countries; examples include agricultural products and apparel.[2]

Across-the-Board Approaches and Tariff Reduction Formulas

Rather than negotiate on a sector-by-sector basis, member countries may adopt an across-the-board approach such that all tariffs are rolled back according to a prespecified formula. Of course, even in a sector-by-sector approach, some previously agreed rule must be used to ensure a balance in the bargain (that is, reciprocity). The formulas discussed below are therefore relevant for the sector-by-sector approach as well.

Perhaps the simplest rule to follow is the reduction in all tariffs by a fixed percentage. For example, the member countries may agree to roll back all (or a subset of) existing tariffs by 50 percent. Formally, we can set

$$(53.1) \qquad \frac{dt_i}{t_i} = b$$

where b is a constant between 0 and 1, t_i is the initial tariff rate in sector i, dt_i is the change in t_i, and dt_i/t_i is the proportionate *reduction* in the initial rate. This approach has the advantage that within a country it leads to a larger absolute reduction in high tariffs and a smaller absolute reduction in low tariffs, which must broadly promote efficiency. More protected sectors are liberalized more, and effective protection of any particular sector is

unlikely to rise because input tariffs decline proportionately more than output tariffs. If the countries engaging in liberalization have equal levels of tariffs and are also of equal size, this approach will lead to balanced reductions in tariffs across the countries.

The bargain will be unbalanced, however, if either of these conditions is violated. For instance, if two countries are of equal size but one has an average tariff of 50 percent and the other an average tariff of 5 percent, a 50 percent reduction in the tariff leads to a 25 percentage point reduction by the former but only 2.5 percentage points by the latter. Such liberalization leads to a deterioration of the terms of trade of the first country. Likewise, if both countries have 50 percent tariffs but one country is 10 times the size of the other, a 50 percent reduction by the former leads it to give greater market access than it receives and hence results in a deterioration of its terms of trade.

There are various approaches that attempt to correct for these differences in initial tariffs and country size. The simplest approach is to define liberalization in terms of the tariff revenue forgone. For example, we can set the proportionate reduction in tariff equal to

$$(53.2) \qquad \frac{dt_i}{t_i} = \frac{f}{\left(t_i \cdot p_i \cdot M_i\right)} = \frac{f}{\left(t_i \cdot V_i\right)}$$

where f is a constant, p_i is the border price, M_i is the quantity of imports, and V_i is the value of initial imports at the world price. We can think of f as a measure of market access given by the country undertaking liberalization. An advantage of tariff reductions according to (53.2) is that the formula takes into account both the initial tariff rate and the size of the country in the world market. To achieve the same level of liberalization, f, a country that imports larger volumes of good i and imposes a higher initial tariff on the latter has to liberalize proportionately less to achieve the same level of liberalization. Alternatively, if the initial level of tariff in a sector is low, the credit given for a given percentage reduction in the tariff is also low.

Tariff reductions according to (53.2) are defensible from the viewpoint of balancing the bargain between member countries, but for a given level of imports this formula implies a lower proportionate reduction in the tariff whenever the initial tariff is high. From an efficiency standpoint, this may not be a desirable outcome. For instance, if final goods are subject to high tariffs and inputs to low tariffs, this

JOSEPH F. FRANCOIS
WILL MARTIN

54

BINDING TARIFFS: WHY DO IT?

BORN OUT OF THE EXPERIENCE OF ESCA-
LATING TARIFFS IN THE PERIOD BETWEEN
the two world wars, the multilateral trading system is
a set of rules that restricts the damage governments
can impose through unbridled use of the range of
policy instruments otherwise available to them. In
most cases multilateral trade rules do not prescribe
precisely what countries must do. Rather, they tend
to operate by imposing limits on the values and
types of protection that are allowed and by forcing a
degree of transparency in trade regimes. Like Ulysses
tied to the mast, governments are then able to listen
to the siren call of protectionist lobbies while pleading an inability to actually respond. Tariffs are
prohibited from varying across suppliers by most-
favored-nation (MFN) requirements, and their variation across commodities and over time is limited by
schedules of tariff bindings (concessions). The
application of nontariff barriers is limited, or even
prohibited, by GATT rules. Contingent protection,
through fair trade and safeguard actions, is also (at
least in theory) limited by related WTO/GATT disciplines. Other rules apply to balance of payments
actions, licensing requirements, and trade-related
investment measures. In the
Uruguay Round market access
bindings were also introduced
for the services sectors.

Because the multilateral system centers on bindings, tariff
negotiations in the WTO are not
actually about applied tariff
rates but, rather, about the
underlying bound rates. For this
reason, an important feature of
the policy landscape left by the
Uruguay Round agreements is
tariff bindings on industrial and
agricultural goods. Because tariff bindings are commitments not to raise tariffs above a certain level,
their actual relevance depends on how far bound
rates are above actual applied rates. In the case of
OECD industrial tariffs, there is a close correspondence between applied and bound rates. This is not
the case for developing countries. In particular, for
many developing countries (and also for Australia),
the industrial tariff landscape now features bound
rates that are often well above applied rates. For the
poorest developing countries, tariffs are often still
completely unbound.

Bindings are vital to the process of securing trade
agreements. If an agreed tariff reduction could easily
be reversed unilaterally, any liberalization offer
would have to be weighed against the probability of
backsliding. Exporting firms, which provide much of
the political support for multilateral trade liberalization, are likely to be unenthusiastic about tariff cuts
they expect to be short-lived. Bindings themselves are
considered so important that countries agreeing to
bind previously unbound tariffs are given "negotiating credit" for the decision. This is true even if the
tariff is bound above the currently applied level.

In this chapter we examine the issue of tariff bindings and its relationship to the assessment of tariff negotiations. We first examine the post–Uruguay Round tariff landscape to get a general sense of the differences between bound and applied rates and the implications that new reductions in bound rates (especially for developing countries) will have for applied rates. This is followed by a discussion of the implications of bindings, in terms of real income gains and security of market access.[1]

Industrial Tariff Bindings: An Empirical Overview

Under the Uruguay Round, the share of developing country imports of industrial products subject to tariff bindings rose from 13 to 61 percent (Blackhurst, Francois, and Enders 1996). This rise was mainly the result of commitments by Latin American countries to apply ceiling bindings on 100 percent of their tariff lines, and commitments made by Asian developing economies. Some tariff bindings predate the end of the Uruguay Round. Chile was the only developing country that offered to bind 100 percent of its tariff lines in the context of the Tokyo Round, while Costa Rica, El Salvador, Mexico, and the República Boliviariana de Venezuela bound 100 percent of their tariff lines on their accession to the GATT during the period 1986–91. Among Asian developing economies, Indonesia bound more than 90 percent of its tariff lines during the Uruguay Round. India, the Republic of Korea, Malaysia, the Philippines, Singapore, and Thailand bound between 60 and 89 percent; Sri Lanka and Zimbabwe bound less than 15 percent.

Table 54.1 presents summary data on bindings and applied rates for industrial products in 29 economies. These data reflect the tendency of developing country tariffs to be unbound, or to be bound well above applied rates. Where developing economies had bound all or a significant portion of tariffs prior to the end of the Uruguay Round (as had Chile, Costa Rica, El Salvador, Mexico, and the República Boliviariana de Venezuela), the Uruguay Round tariff commitments often reflected a decline in ceiling rates rather than necessarily in applied rates. For these reasons, implementation of Uruguay Round tariff commitments by developing countries has involved virtually no further declines in current applied tariffs. This means that, to the extent that reductions have

occurred since the end of the Uruguay Round, they have been undertaken for reasons unrelated to WTO commitments.

More detailed data are presented in Table 54.2, which presents the number of unbound tariff lines (as a percentage of the within-category total) by economy and GATT/WTO multilateral tariff negotiation (MTN) category. These data are drawn from the WTO Integrated Data Base (IDB). What is clear is that for many individual product categories, substantially all trade remains unbound across developing countries, except in Latin America. This applies, for example, to transport equipment, miscellaneous manufactures, fisheries products, metals, and wood products. For many developing economies in the IDB, over 60 percent of trade remains unbound in most product categories; these economies include Cameroon, Chad, Gabon, India, Macau (China), Malaysia, the Philippines, Senegal, Sri Lanka, Thailand, Tunisia, Turkey, and Zimbabwe.

What is important for future industrial tariff negotiations is the current level of ceiling bindings vis-à-vis applied rates and the limited coverage of bindings. Taken together, the combination of bound and applied rates means that developing countries will, collectively, be able to reduce bound rates, or introduce them for the first time, while having to make only modest (and in many cases no) changes in applied rates. Hence, for industrial tariffs the relevant scenarios for many developing countries in the next round are likely to involve little or no real reductions in applied tariffs. This will be true whether or not developing countries take an active part in future industrial tariff negotiations. As in previous rounds, there is a good chance that only OECD countries and some middle-income developing countries will actually be forced to reduce industrial tariffs as part of any upcoming industrial tariff negotiations. The only way to avoid such an outcome may be to make particularly large cuts in the highest tariff bindings, in order to close the current gap between bound and applied rates, or to otherwise redefine the negotiation benchmark (perhaps focusing directly on applied rates) for the purpose of defining negotiation parameters.

Bindings and the Security of Market Access

Although the perception is that new bindings did not have much effect on the applied rates of many developing countries during the Uruguay Round,

Table 54.2 (continued)

Region	1 Wood, pulp, paper, and furniture	2 Textiles and clothing	3 Leather, rubber, footwear, and travel goods	4 Metals	5 Chemicals and photographic supplies	6 Transport equipment	7 Nonelectric machinery	8 Electric machinery	9 Mineral products and precious stones and precious metals	10 Manufactured articles not elsewhere specified	11 Fish and fish products
Africa											
Cameroon	100.00	99.64	100.00	100.00	100.00	100.00	100.00	100.00	100.00	100.00	100.00
Chad	100.00	100.00	100.00	100.00	100.00	88.81	100.00	100.00	100.00	100.00	100.00
Senegal	83.00	64.40	74.20	99.00	97.00	27.50	14.80	2.50	94.10	96.20	56.10
South African Customs Union	0.82	0.24	2.29	0.17	0.29	0.27	0.00	0.45	6.11	2.06	84.38
Tunisia	64.77	6.65	60.00	74.58	62.25	51.23	47.82	54.76	89.35	56.05	95.80
Zimbabwe	86.70	93.20	80.00	94.00	93.90	80.80	79.80	96.60	97.30	93.00	66.70
Eastern Europe											
Hungary	0.54	1.34	0.00	0.00	3.81	27.50	1.39	9.22	2.39	4.65	61.72
Poland	0.00	0.62	0.00	0.00	0.37	42.62	0.59	0.00	0.60	4.29	95.33

Source: WTO Inegrated Data Base.

other rules-based constraints on protection can be analyzed qualitatively in a similar way.

We begin by representing the underlying distribution of protection in the absence of a tariff binding by a distribution such as that depicted in Figure 54.1. In general terms, we motivate our representation by the political process, which leads to uncertainty about the pattern of protection over time. In this context, there are numerous political models that can be invoked here to drive the underlying probabilities related to a particular government orientation toward trade (see, for example, Stahl and Turunen-Red 1995). What is important for the present discussion is not the choice of a particular political submodel but the resulting characterization of trade policy as subject to uncertainty. Formally, therefore, we simply assume that the expected level of the tariff is m_0 in the absence of a binding on the tariff rate applied and that the distribution of protection can be characterized by its mean and variance.

Under these circumstances, a tariff binding reduces both the average rate of protection and the variability of protection. The exact relationship between changes in tariff bindings and actual protection depends on a number of factors, including the underlying variability of protection and the gap between the tariff binding and the average rate of protection. Because it eliminates the highest rates of protection, which are the ones that inflict the greatest costs on the economy, even a tariff binding that is substantially above the average rate of protection can greatly reduce the cost of protection, as is shown in the next section.

The Welfare Implications of Bindings

What are the welfare implications of bindings? To explore this issue, we use Figure 54.2 for the case of a small country. (See Francois and Martin 2001 for a more formal treatment.) In the figure, the line labeled "Import demand" represents the compensated aggregate import demand curve. With a fixed tariff, the welfare cost of protection is defined by the Harberger triangle *cab* under the excess demand curve. Alternatively, consider symmetric variations around this tariff level, with a higher tariff yielding a higher domestic price, P_h, in one time period and a lower one, P_L, in another. The welfare cost of the higher tariff is *cfg*, and that of the lower tariff is *cde*. The reader can verify that the average of these areas (the expected cost of protection) exceeds the cost of protection under a fixed tariff. Clearly, therefore, the expected cost of protection *for a given average tariff level* is higher in our example than when that tariff is certain. This benefit of bindings is separate from

54.1 Implications of a Tariff Binding for the Applied Rate of Protection

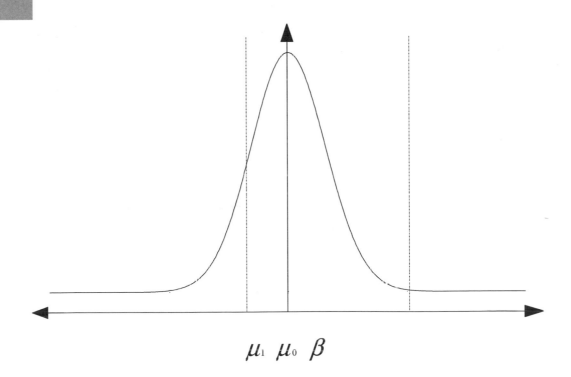

$$\mu_1 \ \mu_0 \ \beta$$

54.2 Welfare Implications of Tariff Bindings for a Small Country

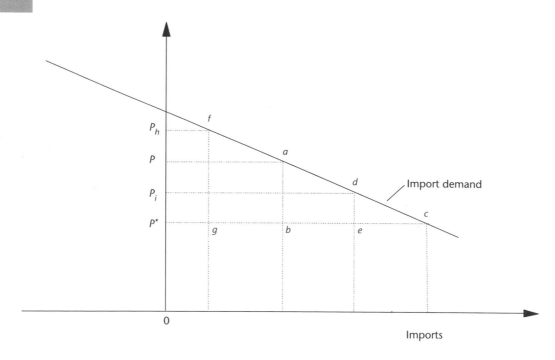

the investment-related benefits of reduced uncertainty (discussed briefly below). It follows from the geometric aspect of the welfare costs of price distortions. The expected benefits of reduction in uncertainty will be magnified, for small countries, when preferences reflect risk aversion.

By similar arguments, benefits related to secured market access conditions in export markets can be identified. These benefits depend critically on the nature of the security. Consider again a small exporter, with the excess import demand curve again represented in Figure 54.2. We now assume away home import policy variance and focus instead on uncertainty in foreign market access conditions. Free trade is represented by price line P^*. We again assume symmetric variations in protection, this time as reflected in market access conditions for exports.

Exports are determined by the terms of trade and by import demand, as reflected in the intersection of the world price line for importables. If protection in export markets is low, terms of trade are relatively favorable, and trade occurs along world price line P_L. Alternatively, with high protection in export markets, terms of trade are given by P_h. The welfare costs of these two states, compared with free trade, are $P_h P^* cf$ and $P_L P^* cd$, respectively.

What are the implications of price stability through bindings? Clearly, if market access can be secured at the lower level of protection, P_L, the move is welfare improving. As the current example of China's accession to the WTO and the countersituation of unsecured MFN treatment in the U.S. market have highlighted, secure MFN access (that is, secured access at the "best available rate") is better than unsecured access. Consider also, however, a stabilized level of protection at the mean level P. In the present example, if we compare the welfare effects of the varied states (in terms of shifting terms of trade effects) with the fixed state P, in the absence of risk aversion, variable terms of trade are preferred. The reader can verify this by adding the relevant squares and triangles under the excess demand curve. Again, this is analogous to well-known results in the price stabilization literature, this time for demand agents (that is, the importer). The actual welfare implications of bindings on the part of trading partners will depend critically on the elasticity of demand, possibilities for consumption smoothing, and relative risk aversion.

Commercial policy stability in both import and export markets is analogous to commodity price stabilization. For a small country, the benefits follow from the imposition of own-security. There may also be benefits from foreign market access security, but whether this happens hinges on the nature of commercial policy security on the export market side (and the rents that may be generated in export markets), as well as on the relative risk aversion of home economic agents. Thus, the national welfare benefits of reducing commercial policy uncertainty are much more evident for securing one's own policies than for securing partners' policies.

Yet another set of effects is likely to follow from a generally improved commercial policy environment (see Francois 1997). In the case of Mexico this is emphasized by Kehoe (1999) and by Young and Romero (1994), who stress the linkages between the terms attached to foreign capital and the conditions for access of the domestic economy to the global economy. Basically, the conditions for international capital lending reflect a number of factors, including the security provided by outside obligations (such as Mexico's accession to the GATT in 1986 and to the North American Free Trade Agreement in 1993). As elements are added that reduce the underlying sources of commercial policy uncertainty, the price of capital for a given country on world markets (inclusive of risk premiums) shifts accordingly. Arguably, when we view bindings at a macro level, this effect may be the most important vis-à-vis the expected costs of protection discussed above. It serves to reduce uncertainty for foreign investors about the ability of an economy to link itself with the global economy and hence to generate returns that can ultimately be repatriated.

Conclusions

This chapter has examined the issue of tariff bindings and their relationship to applied tariff rates. A key feature of multilateral negotiations is the focus on tariff bindings. Since the inception of the GATT system in 1947, trade liberalization under the GATT has been based on the introduction of tariff bindings that have increasingly constrained the range and variability of protection rates. The ramifications of this process are clearest for the OECD countries, where tariffs on industrial products are now relatively stable, at rates dramatically below the levels observed through the mid-20th century. The process is not as far along, however, in the case of agriculture, where effective GATT disciplines are new, or in that of industrial tariffs of developing countries.

For many developing countries, tariff bindings on industrial tariffs are still well above applied rates (and the same is true for almost all countries in the case of sensitive agricultural products). High tariff bindings allow substantial room for applied tariff rates to vary below the level of the binding. Even so, bindings may reduce both the average applied tariff and the variability of the applied rate of protection. In this sense, bindings increase the security surrounding market access conditions. While the importance of the security and certainty of market access has long been recognized in the policy process, little attention has been devoted to these issues in analyses of the benefits of WTO negotiations. These analyses are therefore likely to understate the gains from binding tariff commitments under the WTO.

Note

1 A more formal examination of the relationship between bound and applied rates is found in Francois and Martin (2001).

BERNARD HOEKMAN
MAURICE SCHIFF

55

BENEFITING FROM REGIONAL INTEGRATION

THE WORLD HAS WITNESSED A VERITABLE EXPLOSION OF REGIONAL INTEGRATION agreements (RIAs) in the past 15 years (see Box 55.1). More than half of world trade now occurs within actual or prospective trading blocs, and nearly every country in the world is a member of one or more RIAs. RIAs take many forms. The most common are the free trade area (FTA)—where trade restrictions among member countries are removed but each member maintains its own trade policies toward nonmembers—and the customs union, an FTA whose members adopt a common external trade policy. Deeper forms of integration include common markets—customs unions that also allow for the free movement of factors of production—and economic unions, which involve some degree of harmonization of national economic policies.

Because, by definition, RIAs involve discrimination against nonmembers (they result in preferential liberalization among partner countries only), they are inconsistent with the most-favored-nation (MFN) rule, the fundamental principle of the WTO. Given the prevalence of regional trade arrangements and the historical importance of trade agreements as instruments of foreign policy and, sometimes, nation-building, the WTO does not prohibit RIAs. Instead, it imposes on members disciplines designed to minimize "opportunistic" behavior that is aimed primarily not at integration but at discrimination against non-members. This is done by requiring that WTO members notify new RIAs to the WTO, that they do not raise barriers to trade against the rest of the world, and, most important, that they eliminate barriers to trade on substantially all intraregional trade in goods.[1] The last requirement is intended to ensure that the RIA has integration as its goal.

The WTO disciplines can be regarded as rules of thumb intended to minimize the negative implications of regional integration for the multilateral trading system. For historical reasons related to the creation of the European Economic Community in the 1950s, GATT/WTO rules on regionalism have never been effectively enforced. The Doha Development Agenda of 2001 launched negotiations on the rules applying to regionalism. The issues that arise in this context, which are discussed extensively in the literature, include technical trade policy measures such as the use of rules of origin (discussed elsewhere in this volume) and the procedures used to ascertain whether individual RIAs satisfy WTO rules.

This chapter takes the perspective of an individual country and asks what types of RIAs are likely to be most beneficial to developing nations. To a large extent, this depends on the form and coverage of the RIA and on the identity of the partner countries. Since many, if not most, developing countries pur-

BOX 55.1 SELECTED MAJOR REGIONAL INTEGRATION AGREEMENTS AND DATES OF FORMATION

Europe

European Union (EU). Formerly European Economic Community (EEC), European Community (EC). *1957,* Belgium, France, Germany, Italy, Luxembourg, Netherlands; *1973,* Denmark, Ireland, United Kingdom; *1981,* Greece; *1986,* Portugal, Spain; *1995,* Austria, Finland, Sweden.

European Economic Area (EEA). *1994,* EU, Iceland, Liechtenstein, Norway.

Euro-Mediterranean Economic Area (Euro-Maghreb). Bilateral agreements: *1995,* with Tunisia; *1996,* with Morocco.

EU Bilateral Agreements with Eastern Europe. *1994,* with Hungary, Poland; *1995,* with Bulgaria, Czech Republic, Estonia, Latvia, Lithuania, Romania, Slovak Republic, Slovenia.

North America

Canada-U.S. Free Trade Area (CUSFTA). *1988,* Canada, United States.

North American Free Trade Area (NAFTA). *1994,* Canada, Mexico, United States.

Latin America and the Caribbean

Andean Pact. *1969* (revived in 1991), Bolivia, Colombia, Ecuador, Peru, the República Bolivariana de Venezuela.

Central American Common Market (CACM). *1960* (revived in 1993), El Salvador, Guatemala, Honduras, Nicaragua; *1962,* Costa Rica.

Common Market of the South/Mercado Común del Sur (MERCOSUR). *1991,* Argentina, Brazil, Paraguay, Uruguay.

Group of Three (G3). *1995,* Colombia, Mexico, República Bolivariana de Venezuela.

Latin American Integration Association (LAIA). Formerly Latin American Free Trade Area (LAFTA), *1960* (revived in 1980), Argentina, Bolivia, Brazil, Chile, Colombia, Ecuador, Mexico, Paraguay, Peru, Uruguay, República Bolivariana de Venezuela.

Caribbean Community and Common Market (CARICOM). *1973,* Antigua and Barbuda, Barbados, Jamaica, St. Kitts and Nevis, Trinidad and Tobago; *1974,* Belize, Dominica, Grenada, Montserrat, St. Lucia, St. Vincent and the Grenadines; *1983,* The Bahamas (part of the Caribbean Community but not of the Common Market).

Africa

Cross-Border Initiative (CBI). *1992,* Burundi, Comoros, Kenya, Madagascar, Malawi, Mauritius, Namibia, Rwanda, Seychelles, Swaziland, Tanzania, Uganda, Zambia, Zimbabwe.

East African Cooperation (EAC). *1967* (formerly East African Community, EAC; broke up in 1977 and recently revived), Kenya, Tanzania, Uganda.

Economic and Monetary Community of Central Africa (CEMAC). *1994* (formerly Union Douanière et Economique de l'Afrique Centrale, UDEAC); *1966,* Cameroon, Central African Republic, Chad, Congo, Gabon; *1989,* Equatorial Guinea.

Economic Community of West African States (ECOWAS). *1975,* Benin, Burkina Faso, Cape Verde, Côte d'Ivoire, The Gambia, Ghana, Guinea, Guinea-Bissau, Liberia, Mali, Mauritania, Niger, Nigeria, Senegal, Sierra Leone, Togo.

Common Market for Eastern and Southern Africa (COMESA). *1993,* Angola, Burundi, Comoros, Djibouti, Egypt, Ethiopia, Kenya, Lesotho, Malawi, Mauritius, Mozambique, Rwanda, Somalia, Sudan, Swaziland, Uganda, Zambia, Zimbabwe.

Indian Ocean Commission (IOC). *1984,* Comoros, Madagascar, Mauritius, Seychelles.

Southern African Development Community (SADC). *1980* (formerly known as the Southern African Development Coordination Conference, SADCC), Angola, Botswana, Lesotho, Malawi, Mozambique, Swaziland, Tanzania, Zambia, Zimbabwe; *1990,* Namibia; *1994,* South Africa; *1995,* Mauritius; *1998,* Democratic Republic of the Congo, Seychelles.

Economic Community of West Africa (CEAO). *1973* (revived in 1994 as UEMOA), Benin, Burkina Faso, Côte d'Ivoire, Mali, Mauritania, Niger, Senegal.

West African Economic and Monetary Union (UEMOA, or WAEMU). *1994,* Benin, Burkina Faso, Côte d'Ivoire, Mali, Niger, Senegal, Togo; *1997,* Guinea-Bissau.

Southern African Customs Union (SACU). *1910,* Botswana, Lesotho, Namibia, South Africa, Swaziland.

(continued)

BOX 55.1 (CONTINUED)

Economic Community of the Countries of the Great Lakes (CEPGL). *1976,* Burundi, Rwanda, Democratic Republic of the Congo.

Middle East and Asia
Asia-Pacific Economic Cooperation (APEC). *1989,* Australia, Brunei Darussalam, Canada, Indonesia, Japan, Republic of Korea, Malaysia, New Zealand, Philippines, Singapore, Thailand, United States; *1991,* People's Republic of China, Hong Kong (China), Taiwan (China); *1993,* Mexico, Papua New Guinea; *1994,* Chile; *1998,* Peru, Russian Federation, Vietnam.
Association of Southeast Asian Nations (ASEAN). *1967,* Indonesia, Malaysia, Philippines, Singapore, Thailand; *1984,* Brunei Darussalam;

1995, Vietnam; *1997,* Myanmar, Lao People's Democratic Republic; *1999,* Cambodia. (ASEAN members created a free trade area in 1992.)
Greater Arab Free Trade Area (GAFTA). *1998,* Bahrain, Egypt, Iraq, Jordan, Kuwait, Lebanon, Libya, Morocco, Oman, Qatar, Saudi Arabia, Sudan, Syria, Tunisia, United Arab Emirates, Yemen.
Gulf Cooperation Council (GCC). *1981,* Bahrain, Kuwait, Oman, Qatar, Saudi Arabia, United Arab Emirates.
South Asian Association for Regional Cooperation (SAARC). *1985,* Bangladesh, Bhutan, India, Maldives, Nepal, Pakistan, Sri Lanka.

Source: World Bank (2001b).

sue regional integration strategies in parallel with WTO membership and multilateral negotiations, the question of how such parallel paths can be best pursued is also addressed.

Economic Aspects

The development impacts of RIA membership depend importantly on the countries that are involved, the type of agreement, and its substantive coverage. Recent research suggests that of particular importance to developing countries are whether large industrial countries are members of the agreement, the extent of sectoral exclusions, and the degree to which the RIAs involve "deeper integration"—that is, extend beyond preferential elimination of barriers to trade in goods. In order to understand the economic effects of RIAs, a few definitions are in order.

Trade creation takes place when a member country of the RIA (Country 1) increases its imports from its partner country (Country 2) without a reduction in Country 1's imports from the rest of the world (ROW). This occurs because with the removal of tariffs between member countries, Country 2's products become cheaper than those of Country 1. The increase in (cheaper) imports results in an increase in consumption and a reduction in output in Country 1. Trade creation is beneficial.

Trade diversion takes place when imports from the ROW are replaced in Country 1 by more expensive imports from Country 2. Why would Country 1 import more expensive goods from Country 2? Because goods from Country 2 do not pay the import tariff, while ROW goods do. Trade diversion is typically harmful.

Transfers occur between member countries of the trade bloc because removal of tariffs between them means that exports obtain better prices in the partners' markets (a positive transfer), while the costs of imports net of tariffs increase (a negative transfer).

Trade Creation and Diversion and the Type of RIA

Assume that Mexico imports either from the United States or from Japan and applies a 20 percent tariff on all imports. For a given product, the United States sells at a price of $100 and Japan sells at a price of $110. With the 20 percent tariff, the cost to the Mexican consumer is $120 for the good from the United States and $132 for the product from Japan. Consumers import from the cheaper source—from the United States, not Japan. Now assume that Mexico forms an RIA with the United States, along the lines of the North American Free Trade Agreement (NAFTA). Tariffs on imports from the United States fall to zero, and consumers now pay $100. This is a case of trade creation because the

United States was already the cheapest source and has become even cheaper, replacing more expensive domestic output and raising consumption as well. Note that the consumer price must fall for trade creation to take place. Since the United States was the only source of Mexican imports to begin with, having an RIA with the United States is identical to unilateral trade liberalization by Mexico and is beneficial.

Assume now that the good is exported by the United States at $110 and by Japan at $100. With the 20 percent tariff, the cost to consumers is $120 for the good from Japan and $132 for that from the United States. The good is imported exclusively from Japan at $120. After Mexico forms an RIA with the United States, the cost of imports from the United States is $110, which is lower than the $120 consumer cost for imports from Japan. Consumers switch their source of imports from Japan to the United States. But although the United States is the cheapest source for consumers, it is not the cheapest source for Mexico as a whole. The reason is that although the consumer cost of imports from Japan is $120, the true cost for Mexico is only $100. The $100 is the cost in scarce foreign exchange that Mexico pays for imports from Japan, while the additional $20 associated with the 20 percent tariff is simply a transfer from consumers to the government and is not a cost to the nation. To put it differently, before entering the RIA, Mexico paid $100 to the foreign supplier, and after entering the RIA, it pays $110. Thus, Mexico loses $10 per unit of import. This is the cost of trade diversion from a cheaper to a more expensive source. Another way of showing this result is that the consumer price fell by $10 (from $120 to $110), but the government lost $20 in tariff revenue, so the net loss is $10.

Note that trade diversion occurred because the 20 percent tariff is higher than the 10 percent difference in cost between the U.S. and the Japanese good. If the tariff were lower— say, 5 percent—the cost of Japan's imports would be $105, still lower than the U.S. price of $110 free of tariff. Consumers would have continued to import from Japan, the cheapest source, and trade diversion would not have occurred. This example points to an important lesson: RIAs should lower their external trade barriers because that reduces the extent of trade diversion. Another reason for so doing is that reducing external trade barriers makes possible the classical gains from trade. Note also that the welfare impact of an

RIA is ambiguous a priori and depends on whether trade creation or trade diversion dominates. Of course, even an RIA that is dominated by trade diversion and has a negative welfare effect can be turned into a beneficial RIA by lowering external trade barriers sufficiently.

In the example above, imports were from either Japan or the United States but not from both. This is relevant for a small country facing imports of a similar good from two large exporters. Countries, however, may import the good from more than one source; this is particularly likely to be the case when a small country imports from another small country and from the ROW. For instance, assume that Mali imports from Côte d'Ivoire and from the ROW. Say that the world price for a given product is $100 and Mali charges an import tariff of 20 percent, or $20. Thus, the import price paid by consumers in Mali (and faced by its producers) is $120. Côte d'Ivoire's supply of exports to Mali is not horizontal at $120, as is the case for the ROW. Rather, it is upward sloping: an increase in Côte d'Ivoire's supply of exports to Mali implies a higher (marginal) cost of production because Mali is a large buyer of Côte d'Ivoire's exports (although it is a small buyer of ROW exports). In equilibrium, Côte d'Ivoire also sells at $120 because it cannot sell at a price above that of the ROW. (The analysis that follows is presented graphically in the appendix to this chapter.)

Assume now that Mali forms an RIA with Côte d'Ivoire. As long as Mali continues to import from the ROW, the consumer price remains $120. Since the consumer price remains unchanged, no trade creation takes place. Before the RIA, the Mali government obtained $20 in tariff revenue for each unit imported from Côte d'Ivoire, and Côte d'Ivoire exporters obtained $100. After the RIA, Mali no longer charges a tariff on Côte d'Ivoire imports and Côte d'Ivoire obtains $120 for its exports. In other words, Mali now loses tariff revenue and pays $20 more for its imports from Côte d'Ivoire. This amounts to a transfer of income from Mali, the importing country, to Côte d'Ivoire, the exporting country. Note that this occurs even if the quantity of imports from Côte d'Ivoire remains unchanged (that is, even if Côte d'Ivoire's supply of exports is vertical or perfectly inelastic), in which case there is no trade diversion.[2]

It is likely, however, that Côte d'Ivoire's exports to Mali will increase after Mali's import tariff is

North may increase policy credibility, investment, and growth, this is unlikely to happen in the absence of complementary domestic policy reforms.

The benefits from RIAs in terms of larger markets, greater competition, and the realization of economies of scale will depend in part on the extent to which the RIA involves deeper integration; that is, to what degree it extends to services markets and regulatory regimes that determine the conditions of competition prevailing in the regional market. Since industrial partner institutions are generally superior to those found in developing countries, a North-South RIA is likely to provide more benefits from deep integration.[3] However, in the case of services industries and services sector regulation, as well as institutions that protect competition and property rights, a good case may exist for regional harmonization and cooperation between neighboring countries. Thus, South-South agreements can also be effective mechanisms for regulatory reform and cooperation and may generate more appropriate standards. Examples include common competition, regulatory, or intellectual property agencies (such as patent offices)—all institutions with the potential for economies of scale or scope if a regional approach is taken, as opposed to the creation of multiple regulatory agencies in individual countries. But this does not normally require a preferential trade arrangement.

Two final arguments in favor of North-South RIAs can be mentioned. First, endowment differences are usually larger between members of a North-South RIA than between members of a South-South RIA. Developing countries are therefore likely to exploit their comparative advantages better in a North-South RIA than in a South-South one. Second, a crucial determinant of long-term growth is the absorption of knowledge and technology. Since these assets are mainly produced in high-income countries, liberalization that occurs in the context of a North-South RIA is likely to generate more growth than opening up through a South-South RIA.

Political Aspects

Many RIAs have been driven by political rather than economic goals. These political objectives include security, governance, democracy, and human rights. The clearest example is that of European integration, whose founding fathers sought to create a framework within which Franco-German wars would no longer be possible. With this motive in mind, the Economic Coal and Steel Community (ECSC) was founded in 1951, and the European Economic Community (EEC) in 1957. European integration has continued to deepen and expand over the years. Other RIAs based in part on political objectives include the Common Market of the South (MERCOSUR) and the Association of Southeast Asian Nations (ASEAN).

An RIA can enhance security because it increases the level of trade between member countries and, in so doing, increases familiarity between the people of the member countries and lessens the degree of misconceptions. Increased economic integration also makes wars more costly. Thus, security issues provide a rationale for discriminating against nonmembers and limiting trade preferences to member countries. If this is the case, external tariffs should be chosen optimally in order to maximize the security objective. The optimal level of external tariffs will fall over time, especially if the RIA results in deeper integration. The reason is that with the formation of the RIA, trade between member countries increases, and so does security. As the level of security rises, the security benefits from additional trade decrease, and so do the optimal tariffs. The same dynamics arise if the RIA involves deep integration—this type of cooperation will also increase security and, over time, reduce the optimal level of external protection.

Other RIAs with a "security" dimension are those that may have been created as a form of protection against a regional hegemon. An example is the Gulf Cooperation Council (GCC), established in part to counterbalance regional powers (Iran and Iraq). One reason why Central and Eastern European countries wanted to conclude free trade agreements with the European Union was a desire to reduce the possible exercise of Russian hegemony. Latin America provides another example: in 1996 a rumor of a coup in Paraguay led to a joint statement by the presidents of the four MERCOSUR countries that democratic institutions were necessary for maintaining membership in the group. This statement is said to have eliminated the threat. Democracy is an explicit condition of the association agreements between MERCOSUR and both Chile and Bolivia.

RIAs can therefore be vehicles for pursuing democracy and governance objectives. Using RIAs to lock in changes in political institutions is likely to be more effective in North-South than in South-South RIAs. The reasons include the demonstrated track record and the high value placed on democracy and human rights in most high-income countries; indeed, high-income nations may make entry into the club conditional on the reform of political institutions. The likelihood of effective enforcement of governance criteria is also higher. In the case of North-South agreements the costs of a breakdown of cooperation will be higher for developing country members than under a South-South agreement, as the preferential access to industrial markets is worth more. In addition, there may be financial and technical assistance transfers associated with North-South agreements that are tied to the pursuit and attainment of governance objectives.

Although an RIA can generate political and security benefits, especially when these were part of the objectives for setting up the RIA, it may also worsen security. This is most likely to happen where the distribution of transfers is asymmetric. For instance, in the United States in the 19th century, the North was more developed than the South. It produced manufactures and "exported" them to the South, while the South exported agricultural products. The North dominated the Congress in the 1830s and was able to pass a law raising tariffs on imports of manufactures, resulting in a large income transfer from the South to the North. This was called the "tariff of abominations" in South Carolina, which refused to collect it. The issue played an important role in the genesis of the Civil War (Adams 1993).

In the 1960s Kenya, Tanzania, and Uganda formed the East African Community (EAC). Kenya had a more developed manufacturing sector than the other two, and the RIA resulted in large income transfers from Tanzania and Uganda to Kenya. The EAC ultimately fell apart. Similarly, in the Central American Common Market (CACM) in the late 1960s, the more developed El Salvador benefited from income transfers from Honduras. Honduras asked to renegotiate its share of tariff revenues, but El Salvador refused, and Honduras left the CACM. Another example is that of Pakistan before East Pakistan secured its independence (as Bangladesh) in 1971. West Pakistan was more developed and had highly protected industries. East Pakistan had to pay high protected prices for imports, but the revenues were spent mostly on West Pakistan. Between 1948, when Pakistan became independent, and 1971, East Pakistan's income per capita fell by about a third in

relation to that of West Pakistan. Finally, war ensued, and Bangladesh became an independent nation.

Such tensions and potential conflicts can be minimized by lowering external trade barriers. This can be done independently in a free trade agreement but not in a customs union, where the country that benefits from the large transfers may not want to agree to a reduction in the common external tariff.

WTO Rules

As mentioned above, the WTO imposes several disciplines on RIAs between member countries, requiring that agreements liberalize substantially all trade and do not result in higher external barriers. Despite the creation of a single Committee on Regional Trade Agreements (CRTA) to review RIAs notified to the WTO, a major problem has been inability to achieve a consensus in the WTO on whether specific RIAs comply with WTO rules. The reason for this is that the CRTA, like all WTO bodies, operates by consensus. In addition, there has been relatively little use of dispute settlement procedures to contest the operation or design of RIAs, although a 1996 case brought by India suggests that there is scope to do so.[4]

The Doha Development Agenda provides for the launching of negotiations on WTO rules, including those relating to preferential trading arrangements. This raises the question as to what might be done to strengthen WTO disciplines. Economists sometimes argue that a necessary condition for preferential liberalization to be deemed multilaterally acceptable is that the volume of imports by member countries from the rest of the world not decline on a product-by-product basis after the implementation of the agreement. The evidence to date suggests that although the intensity of intraregional trade increased in the last century, the propensity of regions to trade with the rest of the world, expressed as a percentage of regional GDP, has also expanded. Global integration, measured by trade flows and capital flows, does not appear to have been affected negatively by regional integration efforts since World War II (World Bank 2000c).

No one knows, however, what would have happened without RIAs. More important, the trade volume test is a flawed one in that it does not guarantee that nonmembers will not be hurt by a RIA. A more appropriate measure of the impact of a RIA on non-imports from the partner and because of the lower tariff rate.

The partner gains *EFGJ*, which is less than the home country loss of *EFGI* by the triangle *GIJ*. The reason for the net loss of triangle *GIJ* for the RIA members as a whole is the trade diversion, $Q_2 - Q_1$. This amount was previously imported from the ROW at a cost of P_W but is now produced at a higher marginal cost.

Notes

This chapter draws on the results of a World Bank research project on regional integration, much of which was summarized in World Bank (2000c), and on parts of chapter 10 of Hoekman and Kostecki (2001). See both of these sources and the Website <www.world bank.org/trade> for additional references to the literature.

1 Article XXIV of the GATT allows FTAs and customs unions if (a) trade barriers after integration do not rise, on average (Article XXIV.5); (b) all tariffs and other regulations of commerce are removed on substantially all intraregional exchanges of goods within a reasonable length of time (Article XXIV.8); and (c) the arrangements are notified to the WTO Council. Article V GATS similarly requires that integration agreements have substantial sectoral coverage, in terms of the number of sectors, volume of trade affected, and modes of supply; that they provide for the absence or elimination of substantially all measures violating national treatment in sectors where specific commitments were made in the GATS; and that they do not result in higher trade barriers against third countries.

2 Many analysts equate trade diversion with income transfers. As this example shows, they are not necessarily the same, and income transfers can occur even in the absence of trade diversion.

3 By deep integration is meant measures beyond the border that increase the degree of competitiveness of each of the economies with respect to suppliers from the other members. This includes harmonization or mutual recognition of standards and regulations (for example, regarding production, sanitary standards, and so on).

4 As noted by Hoekman and Kostecki (2001), a rare example was a case brought by India against Turkey in 1996. India contested Turkey's imposition of quotas on imports of textile and clothing products, which were required because Turkey had entered into a customs union with the European Union. A WTO panel found that Turkey's measures were inconsistent with GATT Articles XI and XIII and rejected Turkey's assertion that its measures were justified by GATT Article XXIV. On appeal, the Appellate Body upheld the panel's conclusion on the illegality of the quotas but found that the legal interpretation of Article XXIV by the panel was erroneous; the Appellate Body stated that a panel should first ascertain whether an RIA complies with Article XXIV before considering other GATT provisions.

APPENDIXES

Table A.1 Trends in Average Tariff Rates for Developing and Industrial Countries, 1980–99
(unweighted; percent)

Economy	1980	1981	1982	1983	1984	1985	1986	1987	1988	1989	1990	1991	1992	1993	1994	1995	1996	1997	1998	1999
Developing economies																				
Albania	44.4																	15.9		
Algeria					22.6	21.7	27.0	23.1	23.8	24.6			22.9	24.8					24.2	
Antigua and Barbuda							12.0			15.0						12.0			9.0	
Argentina			28.0			35.0	23.3	27.0	27.0	25.0	20.5	12.2	11.8	10.9		10.5	11.2	11.3	13.5	11.0
Bahamas, The	29.8							32.3									32.0			
Bahrain		1.7							7.1		3.0						4.0			7.7
Bangladesh				99.9			81.8		102.2	94.0		88.6	71.0	50.0	42.0	27.4		24.6	23.8	22.2
Barbados							17.3				22.0					17.0		9.7	13.6	
Belarus																		12.3	12.6	13.0
Belize							17.3				20.0					17.0	9.8		9.2	
Benin						48.3	47.5	37.4		37.8	42.0	40.3	40.0	41.6			13.1	12.3	11.0	
Bolivia						12.1	20.0	20.0	19.0	17.0	16.0	10.0	10.0	9.8	9.8	9.7	9.7	9.7	9.7	9.0
Botswana																30.0	11.1			
Brazil	44.0	49.0		48.0	48.0	49.0	51.0	51.0	41.0	35.0	32.2	25.3	21.2	14.2	11.9	11.1		11.8	14.6	13.6
Brunei Darussalam															2.7					
Bulgaria													17.9			21.0	32.2	16.6	17.6	
Burkina Faso								60.8									32.2	32.2	31.1	
Burundi	37.9						37.0		36.9					7.4						
Cambodia																	35.0			
Cameroon								32.0						18.8	18.4		18.1			
Cape Verde																	24.1	20.0		
Central African Rep.							32.0									18.6		7.0		
Chad																	15.8	15.8		
Chile					35.0	20.0	20.0	20.0	15.0	15.0	15.0	11.0	11.0	11.0	11.0	11.0		11.0	11.0	10.0
China			49.5				38.1	39.5			40.3		42.9	39.9	36.3		23.6	17.6	16.8	

Colombia																		11.8
Congo, Dem. Rep.	23.6																	11.6
Congo, Rep.	23.8				22.4	22.4	20.7	24.7	20.7		34.1	20.6	17.6	17.6		17.6	11.7	11.7	11.6
Costa Rica		21.1	32.0	21.1	16.4				15.0	11.2	20.6		9.9	9.9		15.7	8.0	7.2
Côte d'Ivoire	30.8	28.7	27.2	26.3	26.6	26.4	26.0	23.3	25.0	30.6	25.8	23.6	22.0	20.0	21.4	19.2	9.2	10.7
Cuba		17.1		29.7				11.7	12.2	11.9	11.9	13.4	10.9	10.7	8.4			
Cyprus					12.1	12.1	10.3	11.7	10.4	5.0	4.8	7.7	7.3	6.9				
Czech Rep.			6.2	6.2	6.2		5.3	4.8	15.0				9.0	6.8				
Dominica				31.9	28.0													
Dominican Rep.			37.7		37.1		28.0		17.8	17.8	14.5							
Ecuador					28.0			9.3	11.9	12.3	11.3	11.3	11.3	11.6				
Egypt, Arab Rep.	47.4			42.8	42.8	33.5	42.2		28.3	28.1	35.5	26.8	20.5					
El Salvador			23.0	21.1	16.0		13.1	10.1	10.2	9.2	8.0	5.7	0.0					
Estonia								5.5	0.1	0.0	0.0							
Ethiopia	29.0			29.6			16.3	28.8										
Fiji									12.4									
Gabon								18.6	20.4	13.5	20.4	20.6						
Gambia, The									13.5	12.5	13.6							
Ghana	43.3	30.0	30.0	23.0	17.0	17.0	17.0	17.0	17.5	15.0	12.5	8.5						
Grenada			27.2		25.0					9.3								
Guatemala			22.8	16.0	13.0			10.8	12.0	11.4	11.4	12.0	8.4	7.6				
Guinea	76.4		8.9		8.2	13.0		10.8		14.3	14.3	16.4						
Guyana			17.4	20.0		20.0		17.0	10.0				10.4					
Haiti	27.7		11.6															
Honduras								10.0	9.7									
Hong Kong (China)	0.0	0.0	0.0	0.0	0.0	0.0	0.0	0.0	0.0	0.0	0.0	0.0	0.0	0.0	8.1			
Hungary	74.3	24.0	15.0	12.6		8.5	8.5	15.2	14.3	14.3	13.3	12.4						
India		37.0	100.0	98.8	81.8	79.2	53.0	47.8	47.8	38.7	35.0	30.0	32.2					
Indonesia	29.0	27.0	31.5	27.0	20.6	20.3	20.0	19.4	13.2	13.2	9.5	10.9						
Iran	20.7		20.7		25.2													

(continued)

Table A.1 (continued)

Economy	1980	1981	1982	1983	1984	1985	1986	1987	1988	1989	1990	1991	1992	1993	1994	1995	1996	1997	1998	1999
Trinidad and Tobago	23.8								17.3	17.0		18.6	18.7			18.7		9.1	9.2	
Tunisia			26.4		27.8	27.2	24.5	24.0	26.0	27.1	27.4	27.7	27.5		27.0	30.0			29.9	
Turkey				40.0	22.0	24.7	31.4	26.6	22.7					26.7				13.5	12.7	8.2
Uganda							30.0	19.9							17.1		12.8	13.2		
Ukraine																9.1		10.1	10.0	
United Arab Emirates		1.2					4.5										4.0			
Uruguay		47.0				38.0	40.0	29.1	27.5		23.0	21.5	18.2	17.0	14.7	9.3	9.5	10.0	12.2	4.6
Venezuela, R. B. de					28.0	28.0		32.9	32.9	30.6	19.0	16.0	16.4	15.7	11.8	13.4		11.9	12.0	12.6
Vietnam													11.0		12.7					15.1
Western Samoa																	9.0			
Yemen		26.0						16.2									20.0			
Yugoslavia, FR	12.0					11.8	11.8	11.8		11.8										
Zambia								29.9						25.9	26.9	23.8	13.6	13.6	6.8	
Zimbabwe				10.0			8.7	8.9		10.1				17.2	17.2	15.6	25.0	24.0	22.2	21.8
Industrial economies																				
Australia										14.2		12.9	10.4	9.8	9.6	6.5	6.1	5.6	5.3	5.0
Canada										9.1	8.8			8.7	8.6		6.4	5.8	4.8	4.6
European Union									8.7	8.7	8.7			7.7	7.6	6.8	6.7	6.2	6.0	5.6
Iceland				8.5			6.0			3.8				3.7			4.1		4.1	4.0
Japan			11.0						7.1	6.9		6.3	6.3	6.3	6.3	6.3	5.9	5.7	5.5	5.2
New Zealand										14.5			8.7	8.5			7.2	5.4	4.5	3.8
Norway									6.0	5.7				6.1		5.9	5.5	4.4	4.0	3.3
Switzerland										4.4				4.2	4.1		0.0	0.0	0.0	0.0
United States	9.8								6.6	6.3	6.3	6.3	6.3	6.4		5.9	5.8	6.6	5.2	4.8

566

Average, developing economies (129)	27.6	23.1	30.0	30.5	29.7	27.2	26.6	24.7	23.4	23.8	23.2	24.3	21.5	19.4	18.7	16.1	14.9	13.7	13.1	11.3
Average, industrial economies (23)	9.8	11.0	8.5		6.0	7.1	8.2	7.9	8.5	7.9	6.8	7.2	6.3	5.3	5.0	4.4	4.0			

Note: Blanks indicate not available. All tariff rates are based on unweighted averages for all goods in ad valorem rates, or applied rates, or most-favored-nation (MFN) rates, whichever data are available over a longer period.

Sources: WTO, Integrated Data Base CD-ROM (2000), and *Trade Policy Review—Country Reports* (various issues, 1990–2000); UNCTAD, *Handbook of Trade Control Measures of Developing Countries, Supplement, 1987,* and *Directory of Import Regimes.* 1994; Dean, Desai, and Riedel (1994); Finger, Ingco, and Reincke (1996); World Bank, *World Development Indicators* (various years, 1998–2000); OECD, *Indicators of Tariff and Non-Tariff Trade Barriers* (1997b); Inter-American Development Bank, "Statistics and Quantitative Analysis Data" (1998).

Table A.2 (continued)

Region	Economy	Year	Tariff rate (unweighted, percent)			Net FDI inflow (millions of U.S. dollars)		
			All goods	Agri-culture	Manu-factures	1997	1998	1999
7	Australia	1998	5.3	1.2	5.8	7,732	6,345	5,422
7	Canada	1999	4.6	4.6	4.5	11,761	21,705	25,061
7	European Union	1999	5.0	10.0	4.2	128,574	248,615	305,058
7	Iceland	1999	4.0	10.8	2.5	149	148	66
7	Japan	1999	5.2	11.0	3.7	3,200	3,192	12,741
7	New Zealand	1999	3.7	2.0	4.0	2,623	745	−1,063
7	Norway	1999	3.3	9.7	2.6	3,627	3,599	6,577
7	Switzerland	1998	0.0	0.0	0.0	6,636	7,500	3,413
7	United States	1999	4.8	8.7	4.3	105,488	186,316	275,533
Average/total								
1–6	Developing economies (96)	1993–99	13.1	17.0	12.4	194,014	189,155	223,166
7	Industrial economies (23)	1998–99	4.0	6.4	3.5	269,790	478,165	632,808
1	East Asia (15)	1994–99	9.8	13.9	9.4	88,412	83,488	92,915
2	South Asia (5)	1996–99	27.7	26.3	28.0	4,889	3,668	3,183
3	Sub-Saharan Africa (26)	1993–99	16.5	19.2	16.0	7,409	3,954	4,934
4	Middle East and North Africa (11)	1995–99	14.4	20.8	13.2	8,426	9,776	11,806
5	Transition Europe (15)	1996–99	9.6	15.7	7.8	20,630	21,235	23,128
6	Latin America and the Caribbean (24)	1995–99	10.1	13.8	9.5	64,248	67,034	87,200

Sources: WTO, Integrated Data Base CD-ROM (2000), and *Trade Policy Review* (various issues, 1993–2000); World Bank, *World Development Indicators 2000;* UNCTAD, *World Investment Report 2000.*

Table A.3 Tariff Escalation in Developing and Industrial Countries, 1994–2000
(unweighted average; percent)

Region	Economy	Year	Agricultural products[a]			Industrial products[b]		
			First stage	Semi-processed	Fully processed	First stage	Semi-processed	Fully processed
1	China	1997	19.3	34.3	29.2	7.4	13.3	19.3
1	Fiji	1996				5.0	10.0	22.5
1	Indonesia	1998	4.7	4.4	13.9	3.8	7.9	11.6
1	Korea, Rep.	1999	49.9	93.2	31.8	3.4	7.8	8.0
1	Malaysia[b]	1997				1.0	7.0	11.9
1	Papua New Guinea	1999				16.2	2.9	10.4
1	Philippines	1998	14.3	20.3	23.2	3.5	7.1	11.1
1	Solomon Islands[b]	1998				29.0	15.4	25.6
1	Thailand[a]	1999	43.5	48.0	38.0			
2	Bangladesh[a]	1999	16.1	23.0	29.2	17.6	20.7	24.1
2	India	1997	25.4	29.9	42.8	23.6	35.4	36.4
2	Myanmar	1996	7.4	6.7	10.9	4.3	3.7	6.0
2	Sri Lanka[b]	1994	30.0		40.0	20.0	15.6	22.5
3	Burkina Faso[a, b]	1997	31.8	32.6	33.4	28.5	35.7	29.0
3	Cameroon[a, b]	1994	23.9	23.0	25.0	20.0	15.0	21.0
3	Côte d'Ivoire	1994				18.1	21.6	26.2
3	Guinea[a,]	1998	17.4	18.5	18.1	16.8	16.6	16.1
3	Kenya[a]	1999	16.4	24.7	24.7	15.2	17.9	18.6
3	Madagascar	1998	4.9	8.3	7.6	1.1	6.7	7.7
3	Mali	1999	14.5	15.2	18.0	4.7	7.4	12.8
3	Mauritius[b]	1994				14.8	17.2	39.5
3	Nigeria[b]	1999				25.0	24.0	31.0
3	South Africa[a, b]	1997	12.4	10.9	15.6	4.9	18.6	13.8
3	Tanzania[a, b]	1999	18.5	25.0	23.0	13.3	13.3	18.3
3	Togo	1997	12.6	10.6	15.2	6.2	11.8	15.1
3	Zambia[a, b]	1997	18.3	18.2	21.0	14.4	9.5	16.5
4	Bahrain[a, b]	2000	4.8	2.8	11.2	5.0	6.2	9.0
4	Cyprus	1998	24.3	32.3	26.8	0.8	5.6	4.6
4	Egypt, Arab Rep.	1997	33.0	36.9	44.5	24.2	29.5	39.5
4	Israel[a, b]	1999	12.0	7.0	24.5	12.8	4.1	8.4
4	Malta	1999	2.5	6.4	9.3	5.4	7.3	8.5
4	Morocco	1997	48.0	51.6	83.0	22.0	35.6	30.3
4	Tunisia[a, b]	1994	35.4	33.7	43.0	32.0	31.3	34.6
4	Turkey	1997	35.1	43.7	64.7	0.5	6.7	5.8
5	Bulgaria	1998	20.1	26.3	32.3	8.4	12.8	17.3
5	Czech Rep.	1998	4.9	16.4	18.6	0.6	4.6	5.6
5	Hungary	1999	20.8	39.4	39.1	2.6	5.8	8.8
5	Latvia	1999	8.0	18.9	17.5	1.1	1.3	3.4
5	Poland[a]	1999	16.5	22.5	44.9	5.6	9.8	11.2
5	Romania	1999	57.9	110.0	158.4	25.9	16.9	17.1
5	Slovak Rep.	1999	4.6	15.4	17.3	0.6	4.3	5.1
6	Argentina	1998	10.0	13.9	16.0	7.7	12.0	15.3
6	Barbados	1999	22.7	16.9	18.4	11.0	6.9	13.8
6	Bolivia	1998	10.0	10.0	10.0	10.0	10.0	9.3
6	Brazil	2000	9.5	13.2	15.6	8.9	11.9	15.8

(continued)

Table A.4 (continued)

Region code	Economy	Coverage ratio of NTBs[a]		
		1984–87	1988–90	1991–93
4	Iran	99.3		
4	Jordan	12.9		
4	Kuwait	3.8	3.5	
4	Libya	10.3		
4	Morocco	27.6		
4	Oman	3.6		
4	Qatar	1.3		
4	Saudi Arabia	5.4	3.9	
4	Syria	36.6		
4	Tunisia	76.2	63.7	32.7
4	United Arab Emirates	1.0		
4	Yemen	28.7		
5	Cyprus	32.2		
5	Romania	0.0		
5	Turkey	97.2	96.4	
5	Yugoslavia, FR	27.7	29.2	
6	Argentina	31.9	16.1	0.2
6	Bahamas, The	0.1		
6	Bolivia	25.0	2.0	
6	Brazil	35.3	3.2	1.5
6	Chile	10.1	10.6	0.1
6	Colombia	73.2	73.8	1.7
6	Costa Rica	0.8		
6	Ecuador	59.3	63.6	
6	El Salvador	19.2		
6	Guatemala	7.4		
6	Guyana	16.0		
6	Haiti	30.8		
6	Jamaica	6.6		
6	Mexico	12.7	6.3	3.9
6	Nicaragua	27.8		
6	Paraguay	9.9		1.8
6	Peru	53.4		
6	Trinidad and Tobago	23.4		
6	Uruguay	14.1		
6	Venezuela, R. B. de	44.1	11.9	2.4
7	Australia		3.4	0.7
7	Canada		11.1	11.0
7	European Union		26.6	23.7
7	Iceland			3.9
7	Japan		13.1	12.2
7	New Zealand		14.1	0.4
7	Norway		26.6	23.7
7	Switzerland		12.9	13.5
7	United States		25.5	22.9

Average				
1–6	Developing economies (80)	29.8	32.7	8.1
7	Industrial economies (23)		16.7	12.4
1	East Asia (10)	23.2	7.1	3.6
2	South Asia (5)	47.6	33.6	20.4
3	Sub-Saharan Africa (26)	32.7	47.1	8.8
4	Middle East and North Africa (15)	27.3	41.9	21.1
5	Transition Europe (4)	39.3	62.8	
6	Latin America and the Caribbean (20)	25.1	23.4	1.7

Note: Blanks indicate not available.

a. Includes additional quantitative restrictions in the form of all types of licenses and import authorizations, quotas, import prohibitions, advance import deposits, foreign exchange restrictions, fixed customs valuations, and state trading monopolies. Calculated as percentage of products within a category affected by an NTB applied to a tariff line.

Sources: UNCTAD, *Directory of Import Regimes, 1994,* and *Handbook of Trade Control Measures of Developing Countries, Supplement, 1987;* OECD, *Indicators of Tariff and Non-Tariff Barriers* (1997b).

Table A.6 Tariff Peaks and Preference Margins, Canada, 1999
(unweighted; percent)

Tariff peak in HS 2-digit product		Number of 6–digit lines	MFN tariff	LDC	GSP	Mexico	Chile	CAR
01	Live animals	4	198.8	0	0	0	0.25	0.25
02	Meat and edible meat offal	10	109.9	0.6	0.17	0.17	0.6	0.6
04	Dairy products; birds' eggs; honey	26	197.5	0.31	0.03	0.05	0.5	0.54
06	Live tree & other plant; bulbs, cut flowers	1	15.2	0.47	0.47	0.51	0.6	1
08	Edible fruit and nuts; melons	1	16.6	0	0	0	0	0
10	Cereals	3	70.2	0	0	1	0.69	0.53
11	Prod mill indust; malt; starches	7	85.3	0.14	0.02	0.14	0.07	0.14
12	Oil seed, oleagi fruits; misc grain	1	18.3	0	0	0	0	0
13	Lac; gums, resins and other veg	1	74	0	0	0	0	0
15	Animal/veg fats and oils and prod	8	28	0.8	0.57	1	1	1
16	Prep of meat, fish or mollusks	5	68.7	0.59	0.14	0.22	0.5	0.66
17	Sugars and sugar confectionery	1	16.6	0	0	0	0	0
18	Cocoa and cocoa preparations	2	85.5	1	0.18	1	0.73	1
19	Prep of cereal, flour, starch/milk prod	3	54.5	0.96	0.26	0.87	0.96	1
20	Prep of vegetable, fruit, nuts prod	2	19.4	0	0	0.77	0.48	1
21	Miscellaneous edible preparations	4	48.9	0.97	0.37	0.77	0.83	1
22	Beverages, spirits and vinegar	3	26.7	0.67	0.27	1	1	1
23	Residues and waste from food indust	2	30.3	0.29	0	0.4	0.5	0.5
24	Tobacco and manufactured	1	17.6	0	0	1	1	1
33	Essential oils & resinoids, perf	1	18	1	0.74	1	0.57	1
35	Albuminoidal subs; modified starches	2	18	0	0	0	0.5	0.5
39	Plastics and articles thereof	5	16.7	1	0.36	0.7	0.72	1
40	Rubber and articles thereof	7	16.8	1	0.37	0.85	1	1
42	Articles of leather; saddlery, travel pr	3	16.6	1	0.42	0.72	1	1
43	Furskins and artificial fur thereof	2	19.2	1	0.34	0.61	1	1
51	Wool, fine/coarse animal hair nes	7	16.5	0.87	0.41	1	1	0
52	Cotton	66	17.3	0.15	0.06	0.62	0.62	0
53	Other vegetable textile fibers and yarns	2	16	1	0.13	1	1	0
54	Man-made filaments	34	19	0.01	0	1	1	0
55	Man-made staple fibres	68	19	0.1	0.03	1	1	0

56	Wadding, felt and nonwoven, yarns etc.	22	16.9	0.39	0.16	0.77	0.77	0
57	Carpets and other textile floor coverings	14	18.9	1	0.47	0.77	0.77	0
58	Special woven fab; tufted tex fab, etc.	31	17.9	0.34	0.11	0.65	0.65	0
59	Impregnated, coated, cover/laminated	13	17.8	0.9	0.33	0.73	0.73	0
60	Knitted or crocheted fabrics	16	18	0.38	0.12	0.65	0.65	0
61	Art of apparel and clothing access	114	23.3	0.07	0.02	0.62	0.62	0
62	Art of apparel and clothing access	116	22.4	0.09	0.04	0.66	0.66	0
63	Other made-up textile articles	52	22.1	0.14	0.06	0.68	0.68	0.03
64	Footwear, gaiters and articles	23	20.8	0.12	0.07	0.7	0.67	0
65	Headgear and parts thereof	4	18.7	0.61	0.12	1	1	0
67	Prepr feathers & down; art flower nes	4	21.3	1	1	1	1	1
68	Art of stone, plaster, cement, asbestos	1	21.3	0	0	1	1	1
70	Glass and glassware	7	16.6	0.46	0.22	0.73	1	1
85	Electrical mech equip parts, sound pr	3	16.7	0	0	0	0	0
86	Railw/tramw locom, rolling stock, etc.	7	15	1	0.55	0.92	1	1
89	Ships, boats and floating structures	10	22.5	1	0.04	0.74	1	1
91	Clocks and watches and parts nes	6	18.6	1	0.5	1	1	1
94	Furniture; bedding, mattress, cushion	2	21	0	0	0.77	1	1
95	Toys, games and sports requisites nes	1	16.4	0.13	0.06	0.84	1	1
96	Miscellaneous manufactured articles	4	17.5	0.68	0.34	0.76	1	1

Note: nes, not elsewhere specified; CAR, Caribbean Community; GSP, Generalized System of Preferences; LDC, least-developed countries; MFN, most-favored-nation. Tariff peaks are defined as MFN duties that exceed 15 percent.
Sources: OECD and WTO tariff files.

Table A.7 Tariff Peaks and Preference Margins, European Union, 1999
(unweighted; percent)

Tariff peak in HS 2-digit product	Number of 6-digit lines	MFN	LDC	GSP	ACP
01 Live animals	7	38.2	0.06	0	0.3
02 Meat and edible meat offal	41	71	0.08	0	0.1
03 Fish & crustacean, mollusk nes	17	18.7	1	0.1	1
04 Dairy prod; birds' eggs; honey	25	59.1	0.12	0.01	0.06
06 Live tree & other plant; bulb, cut flowers	2	16.9	1	0.18	1
07 Edible vegetables and roots and tubers	12	25.4	0.79	0.15	0.66
08 Edible fruit and nuts; melons	8	20.2	0.66	0.12	0.64
09 Coffee, tea, mat and spices	2	16	0.5	0.69	1
10 Cereals	14	75.6	0.06	0	0.06
11 Prod mill indust; malt; starches	31	38.2	0.17	0.02	0.2
12 Oil seed, oleagi fruits; misc grain	1	74.4	0.15	0	0.16
13 Lac; gums, resins and other veg	1	17.8	1	0.3	1
15 Animal/veg fats and oils and prod	8	56	0.6	0.19	0.51
16 Prep of meat, fish or mollusks	22	23.5	0.68	0.2	0.67
17 Sugars and sugar confectionery	9	37.6	0.14	0.03	0.21
18 Cocoa and cocoa preparations	1	24	0.25	0.1	0.25
19 Prep of cereal, flour, starch/ milk prod	13	34.1	0.37	0.11	0.39
20 Prep of vegetable, fruit, nuts prod	42	26.1	0.88	0.15	0.88
21 Miscellaneous edible preparations	8	19.2	0.95	0.28	0.78
22 Beverages, spirits and vinegar	12	35.7	0.71	0.33	0.77
23 Residues and waste from food indust	6	71.4	0.06	0.03	0.11
24 Tobacco and manufactured	8	56.2	1	0.39	1
29 Organic chemicals	3	33.9	1	0.33	0.53
35 Albuminoidal subs; modified starches	2	24.9	1	1	1
38 Miscellaneous chemical products	2	45.9	0.5	0	0.33
56 Wadding, felt and nonwoven, yarns, etc.	2	21.1	1	0.15	1
64 Footwear, gaiters and articles	13	18.2	1	0.3	1
87 Vehicles o/t railw/tramw roll stock, pts	5	16.3	1	0.44	1

Note: nes, not elsewhere specified; ACP, African, Caribbean, and Pacific (Lomé Convention) countries; GSP, Generalized System of Preferences' LDC, least-developed countries; MFN, most-favored-nation.
Sources: OECD and WTO tariff files.

Table A.8 Tariff Peaks and Preference Margins, Japan, 1999
(unweighted; percent)

Tariff peak in HS 2-digit product		Number of 6-digit lines	MFN tariff	LDC	GSP
02	Meat and edible meat offal	9	39.31	0.13	0.13
03	Fish & crustacean, mollusk nes	4	15	0	0
04	Dairy prod; birds' eggs; honey	25	28.99	0.05	0.05
07	Edible vegetables and roots and tubers	1	15.8	0	0
08	Edible fruit and nuts; melons	11	19.81	0.15	0.09
09	Coffee, tea, mat and spices	5	17.81	0.49	0.11
10	Cereals	1	63.38	0	0
11	Prod mill indust; malt; starches	28	23.24	0.11	0.06
12	Oil seed, oleagi fruits; misc grain	1	19.1	0	0
15	Animal/veg fats and oils and prod	2	26.99	0	0
16	Prep of meat, fish or mollusks	4	20.69	0.05	0.05
17	Sugars and sugar confectionery	11	71.25	0.05	0.05
18	Cocoa and cocoa preparations	6	22.77	0.49	0.18
19	Prep of cereal, flour, starch/milk prod	13	21.91	0.15	0.04
20	Prep of vegetable, fruit, nuts prod	32	22.69	0.23	0.06
21	Miscellaneous edible preparations	7	22.35	0.19	0.11
22	Beverages, spirits and vinegar	16	38.65	0.39	0.16
24	Tobacco and manufactured	2	18.63	0	0
29	Organic chemicals	2	20	1	1
35	Albuminoidal subs; modified starches	2	23.31	1	1
38	Miscellaneous chemical products	1	80.83	1	1
41	Raw hides and skins (other than fur)	10	26.08	1	0.57
42	Articles of leather; saddlery, travel pr	5	15.52	0.2	0.1
43	Furskins and artificial fur thereof	8	16.25	0.47	0.47
53	Other vegetable textile fibres and yarns	4	16	1	1
58	Special woven fab; tufted tex fab, etc	4	17.9	1	0.5
60	Knitted or crocheted fabrics	3	15.7	1	0.5
64	Footwear, galters and articles	16	36.24	0.81	0.4

Note: nes, not elsewhere specified; GSP, Generalized System of Preferences; LDC, least-developed countries; MFN, most-favored-nation.
Sources: OECD and WTO tariff files.

Table A.9 Tariff Peaks and Preference Margins, United States, 1999
(unweighted; percent)

Tariff peak in HS 2-digit product description		Number of 6-digit lines	MFN tariff	LDC	GSP	Mexico	ATP	CAR
02	Meat and edible meat offal	2	19.2	0	0	1	0	0
04	Dairy prod; birds' eggs; honey	2	20.9	0.38	0	0.25	0.38	0.38
07	Edible vegetables and roots nes	10	20.56	0.88	0.18	0.9	1	1
08	Edible fruit and nuts; melons	5	16.66	0.8	0.18	0.74	0.8	0.8
11	Prod mill indust; malt; starches	1	16.3	1	0	1	1	1
12	Oil seed, oleagi fruits; misc, etc.	3	77.95	0	0.33	0.67	0	0
15	Animal/veg fats and oils and prod	4	19.92	0.5	0.25	0.5	0.5	0.5
19	Prep of cereal, flour, milk prod	2	16.79	0.84	0.5	0.63	0.84	0.84
20	Prep of vegetable, fruit, nuts	11	28.67	0.55	0.11	0.56	0.55	0.55
21	Miscellaneous edible prep	1	19.8	0.74	0	0.43	0.74	0.74
24	Tobacco and manufactured	7	73.48	0.14	0.09	0.96	0.14	0.14
28	Inorgn chem; compds of prec	1	15.1	1	1	1	1	1
29	Organic chemicals	4	16.75	1	1	1	1	1
30	Pharmaceutical products	1	30	0	0	0	0	0
42	Articles of leather; saddlery	1	20	0	0	0.6	0.13	0.13
51	Wool, fine/coarse animal hair	4	20.45	0	0	1	0	0
52	Cotton	10	18.34	0	0	1	0	0
54	Man-made filaments	27	16.37	0	0	1	0	0
55	Man-made staple fibres	56	16.27	0	0	0.97	0	0
56	Wadding, felt and nonwoven, yarn	1	15.2	0	0	1	0	0
58	Special woven fab; tufted fabrics	15	18.47	0	0	1	0.07	0.2
60	Knitted or crocheted fabrics	5	18.58	0	0	1	0	0
61	Art of apparel and & clothing access	58	19.5	0	0	0.85	0.02	0.05
62	Art of apparel and clothing access	41	18.85	0	0	0.83	0.02	0.14
64	Footwear, gaiters and parts, etc.	12	27.77	0.01	0.01	0.57	0.01	0.01
69	Ceramic products	4	17.63	0.09	0.09	0.27	1	1
70	Glass and glassware	4	16.16	1	0.08	0.42	1	1
82	Tool, implement, cutlery, spoons	1	15.23	1	0.65	0.65	1	1
86	Railw/tramw locom, rolling stock	7	17.2	1	1	1	1	1
87	Vehicles o/t railw/tramw roll stock	5	25	1	0	1	1	1
96	Miscellaneous manufactures	2	20.66	0.78	0.57	1	0.78	0.78

Note: nes, not elsewhere specified; ATP, Andean Trade Preferences Act; CAR, GSP, Generalized System of Preferences; LDC, least-developed countries; MFN, most-favored-nation.
Sources: OECD and WTO tariff files.

Table A.10 Comparison of MFN Applied Tariffs of Labor-Intensive Products, Selected Countries, 1997–99
(unweighted; percent)

Region code	Economy	Year	Industrial product	Textiles and clothing	Footwear	Average	Protection ratio
Developing economies							
1	China	1997	16.5	27.7	25.0	27.6	1.7
1	Hong Kong (China)	1999	0.0	0.0	0.0	0.0	1.0
1	Indonesia	1998	9.7	14.9	16.8	14.9	1.5
1	Korea, Rep.	1999	7.6	10.4	11.5	10.4	1.4
1	Myanmar	1997	5.1	11.2	5.3	11.0	2.2
1	Philippines	1998	9.2	17.8	22.2	18.0	2.0
1	Singapore	1998	0.0	0.0	0.0	0.0	1.0
2	India	1997	35.2	44.1	45.0	44.1	1.3
3	Egypt	1997	35.0	52.4	61.8	52.7	1.5
3	Madagascar	1998	6.9	17.3	10.0	17.0	2.5
3	Mali	1999	10.4	19.7	21.1	19.7	1.9
3	Morocco	1997	32.1	47.1	50.0	47.2	1.5
4	Bulgaria	1998	15.2	23.4	25.8	23.6	1.6
4	Cyprus	1998	4.8	9.6	10.3	9.6	2.0
4	Czech Rep.	1998	5.0	7.5	9.3	7.6	1.5
4	Estonia	1998	0.0	0.0	0.0	0.0	1.0
4	Hungary	1999	7.4	9.3	9.5	9.3	1.3
4	Latvia	1999	2.5	7.4	9.7	7.5	3.0
4	Malta	1999	7.9	10.1	10.0	10.1	1.3
4	Romania	1999	17.5	24.6	25.5	24.7	1.4
4	Slovak Rep.	1999	4.6	7.3	7.9	7.4	1.6
4	Turkey	1997	5.8	9.9	23.6	10.5	1.8
5	Argentina	1998	13.6	20.9	26.6	21.1	1.6
5	Bolivia	1998	9.6	10.0	10.0	10.0	1.0
5	Brazil	1998	14.8	20.7	27.0	20.9	1.4
5	Chile	1999	10.0	10.0	10.0	10.0	1.0
5	Colombia	1998	10.9	18.5	19.2	18.6	1.7
5	Costa Rica	1999	5.4	12.6	15.4	12.7	2.4
5	Ecuador	1999	11.0	18.6	19.2	18.6	1.7
5	El Salvador	1997	7.1	18.7	18.5	18.7	2.6
5	Guatemala	1999	7.0	20.9	23.3	20.9	3.0
5	Mexico	1998	12.4	22.2	33.6	22.8	1.8
5	Nicaragua	1998	4.9	11.2	13.1	11.3	2.3
5	Paraguay	1998	11.1	19.0	21.0	19.0	1.7
5	Peru	1998	13.0	17.8	20.0	17.9	1.4
5	Uruguay	1998	12.0	20.9	22.6	21.0	1.8
Industrial economies							
6	Australia	1998	5.8	16.2	13.1	16.0	2.8
6	Canada	1999	4.5	11.4	14.8	11.6	2.6
6	European Union	1999	4.2	9.4	10.0	9.4	2.2
6	Japan	1999	3.7	8.6	19.1	9.1	2.5
6	New Zealand	1999	4.0	8.3	11.6	8.6	2.2

(continued)

to a partner divided by the share of world exports to the partner. It is calculated as:

$$T_{ij} = (x_{ij}/X_{it})/(x_{wj}/X_{wt})$$

where x_{ij} and x_{wj} are the values of country i's exports and of world exports to country j and where X_{it} and X_{wt} are country i's total exports and total world exports, respectively. An index of more (less) than unity indicates a bilateral trade flow that is larger (smaller) than expected, given the partner country's importance in world trade.

Intraindustry Trade

Some analyses of factors influencing the success or failure of efforts to promote industrialization and growth conclude that a growing level of intraindustry trade (IIT) plays an important positive role. Intraindustry exchange produces extra gains from international trade over and above those associated with comparative advantage because it allows a country to take advantage of larger markets. By engaging IIT, a country can simultaneously reduce the number of similar products it produces while increasing the variety of goods available to domestic consumers. The IIT index ranges between zero and one, with larger values indicating a greater level of trade between firms in the same industry. Higher IIT ratios suggest that net gains from specialization in different products are being exploited and that the participating country is increasing its integration into the world economy. IIT is calculated as:

$$IIT_{jk} = 1 - [\text{sum}_i | X_{ijk} - M_{ijk}| / (X_{ijk} + M_{ijk})]$$

where X_{ijk} and M_{ijk} represent exports and imports of products from industry i in country j to and from country k. The computation is generally confined to manufactured goods defined at the Standard Industrial Trade Classification (SITC) three-digit level.

Revealed Comparative Advantage Index

Measures of revealed comparative advantage (RCA) have been used to help assess a country's export potential. The RCA indicates whether a country is in the process of extending the products in which it has a trade potential, as opposed to situations in which the number of products that can be competitively exported is static. It can also provide useful information about potential trade prospects with new partners. Countries with similar RCA profiles, such as those in Africa, are unlikely to have high bilateral trade intensities unless intraindustry trade is involved. RCA measures, if estimated at high levels of product disaggregation, can focus attention on other nontraditional products that might be successfully exported. The RCA index of country i for product j is often measured by the product's share in the country's exports in relation to its share in world trade:

$$RCA_{ij} = (x_{ij}/X_{it}) / (x_{wj}/X_{wt})$$

where x_{ij} and x_{wj} are the values of country i's exports of product j and of world exports of product j and where X_{it} and X_{wt} refer to the country's total exports and world total exports. A value of less than unity implies that the country has a revealed comparative disadvantage in the product. Similarly, if the index exceeds unity, the country is said to have a revealed comparative advantage in the product.

Export Specialization Index

The export specialization (ES) index is a slightly modified RCA index in which the denominator is usually measured by specific markets or partners. It provides product information on revealed specialization in the export sector of a country and is calculated as the ratio of the share of a product in a country's total exports to the share of this product in imports to specific markets or partners rather than its share in world exports:

$$ES = (x_{ij}/X_{it}) / (m_{kj}/M_{kt})$$

where x_{ij} and X_{it} are export values of country i in product j and total exports of country i, respectively, and where m_{kj} and M_{kt} are the import values of product j in market k and total imports in market k. The ES is similar to the RCA in that a value of the index less than unity indicates a comparative disadvantage and a value above unity represents specialization in this market.

Export Diversification (or Concentration) Index

Export diversification is held to be important for developing countries because many developing countries are often highly dependent on relatively few primary commodities for their export earnings. Unstable prices for these commodities may subject a developing country exporter to serious terms of trade shocks. Since the covariation in individual commodity prices is less than perfect, diversification into new primary export products is generally viewed as a positive development. The strongest positive effects are normally associated with diversification into manufactured goods, and its benefits include higher and more stable export earnings, job creation and learning effects, and the development of new skills and infrastructure that would facilitate the development of even newer export products. The export diversification index (DX) for a country is defined as:

$$DX_j = (sum \ |h_{ij} - h_i|) \ / \ 2$$

where h_{ij} is the share of commodity i in the total exports of country j and h_i is the share of the commodity in world exports. The related measure used by UNCTAD is the concentration index, or Hirschman index (H), which is calculated using the shares of all three-digit products in a country's exports:

$$H_j = sqrt \ [\ sum \ (x_i \ / \ X_t)^2]$$

where x_i is country j's exports of product i (at the three-digit SITC classification) and X_t is country j's total exports. The index has been normalized to account for the number of actual three-digit products that could be exported. Thus, the maximum value of the index is 239 (the number of individual three-digit products in SITC revision 2), and its minimum (theoretical) value is zero, for a country with no exports. The lower is this index, the less concentrated are a country's exports.

Export Similarity Index

Many countries have an unusual pattern of export specialization in relation to the rest of the world. Often, some product exports, typically manufactures, have grown more rapidly than the average of world exports. It is not clear, however, to what extent these results reflect a common tendency among countries and to what extent the results are driven by the performance of individual countries. The export similarity index (XS) provides useful information on distinctive export patterns from country to country. It is defined as:

$$XS \ (j, k) = sum \ [min \ (X_{ij}, X_{ik}) * 100]$$

where X_{ij} and X_{ik} are industry i's export shares in country j's and country k's exports, which usually include a group of countries or competitors. The index varies between zero and 100, with zero indicating complete dissimilarity and 100 representing identical export composition. This measure is subject to aggregation bias (as the data are more finely disaggregated, the index will tend to fall) and hence embodies a certain arbitrariness due to product choice (see Noland 1997 for details).

Trade Complementarity Index

The trade complementarity index can provide useful information on prospects for intraregional trade in that it shows how well the structures of a country's imports and exports match. It also has the attraction that its values for countries considering the formation of a regional trade agreement can be compared with others that have formed or tried to form similar arrangements (see Michaely 1996 for details). The index of trade complementarity (TC) between countries k and j is defined as:

$$TC_{ij} = 100 - sum \ (|m_{ik} - x_{ij}| \ / \ 2)$$

where x_{ij} is the share of good i in the global exports of country j and m_{ik} is the share of good i in all imports of country k. The index is zero when no goods are exported by one country or imported by the other and 100 when the export and import shares exactly match.

Changes in Global Demand for Major Exports

The index of global demand changes is a constant market share analysis of export performance in a country due to the relative favorable or unfavorable changes in global demand prospects. It indicates how rapidly a country's recent exports would grow relative to world trade if the country just maintained its current market for these products. This approach isolates the influence of change in global demand for specific goods from any changes in the country's market shares or from diversification into

facturing sectors. Each data set has undergone extensive quality control and has been examined for anomalies.

Production Data

The production data are collected by UNIDO and OECD through the joint annual collection program for general industrial statistics and are published in the UNIDO annual commercial publication, the *International Yearbook of Industrial Statistics*. UNIDO provides internationally consistent data by collecting annual data directly from all non-OECD member countries through its country questionnaire. The OECD collects data for its member states and provides the information to UNIDO. The data are usually obtained from industrial census statistics and then compiled into ISIC categories. The industrial data cover only the manufacturing sector and are published at two different levels of detail. The three-digit level of aggregation covers 28 manufacturing sectors; the four-digit level covers 81 manufacturing sectors. For each sector, the data on production report yearly values in thousands of U.S. dollars for total output, value added, gross fixed capital formation, and average wages. Values for the other variables—number of enterprises, total number of employees, and number of female employees—are expressed in units. The data published by UNIDO are not complete across all years or industries; missing observations are reported as a dot or a blank.

Trade Data

The trade data are collected and organized by the United Nations Statistical Department and are reported in the COMTRADE database. For the purpose of the Trade and Production Database, the data are first downloaded in the SITC rev. 2 classification and are then transformed into the ISIC classification. This process utilizes the concordance filters developed by the OECD and yields two slightly different concordance tables, one for exports and one for imports. These tables do not follow a one-to-one correspondence, but matching is achieved through a method that involves a series of carefully estimated weights. The Trade and Production Database is balanced and reports values for imports and exports. Data on mirrored exports (exports calculated using import data reported by partner countries) are also provided.[7] The World Bank's WITS system was used to mirror missing trade data. To make the database manageable, the trade flows are aggregated according to World Bank regions and by income level. The database also reports data on trade flows for particularly interesting markets such as the EU, Japan, and the United States, as well as world totals, producing a total of 34 regional groups.[8]

The trade data are quite complete; there are very few country periods for which data are missing. When the data are not available, the missing observations are reported as dots or blanks. All trade values are reported in thousands of U.S. dollars.

Tariff Data

The tariff data utilized in the database originate from two sources: the WTO and UNCTAD. The WTO tariff data are from published *Trade Policy Review* (TPR) reports and from the Internet version of the IDB. The published TPR data, consisting of tariff averages in ISIC (2) nomenclature, were coded manually by Bank staff into the database. The raw data were converted to ISIC (2) using a concordance developed in the WTO Trade Policy Review Division. The tariff averages may include ad valorem equivalents; in cases where no ad valorem equivalent was available, the ad valorem part of compound duties was used, but only for those duties for which the ad valorem part is always lower than or equal to the total value of the duty. In addition, only out-of-quota duties have been retained in the calculations.

The IDB data are expressed in HS nomenclature at the national tariff line level (that is, more detailed than the six-digit level). The tariff data may contain ad valorem equivalents if these were provided by the reporting country, and, depending on how the data are submitted by the reporting country, in-quota duties may have been included in the averages. Conversion of the IDB information from the HS to the ISIC and the calculation of tariff averages were undertaken by the World Bank. The methodology employed and the soundness and accuracy of the results are obviously not the responsibility of the WTO. The ISIC concordance and the methodology for calculating tariff averages used by the Bank for the IDB data are not strictly comparable to the methodology behind the tariff averages and the ISIC conversion published by the WTO Trade Policy Review Division.

Tariff data are also available through the TRAINS database maintained by UNCTAD. TRAINS is a comprehensive computerized information system at the HS-based tariff line level that covers tariff, paratariff, and nontariff measures, as well as import flows by origin, for more than 100 countries. In the best cases the TRAINS data begin in the late 1980s. UNCTAD reports the tariff data utilizing the six-digit HS classification. The conversion from the HS classification into ISIC was achieved using a one-to-one concordance table. TRAINS data are far from complete. Although there are only a few countries for which no tariff data are available, the time-series are quite sparse.

The Trade and Production Database may include tariff data for a particular country from UNCTAD and the WTO. Discrepancies may occur due to differences in the concordances and methodologies used by the WTO Trade Policy Review Division, the World Bank in converting the raw data in the WTO IDB files, and UNCTAD. For example, UNCTAD calculates the simple averages using as the denominator only the actual number of dutiable lines, but the WTO Trade Policy Review Division includes all lines. When filtering the IDB tariffs, we followed the TPR approach. The tariff data reported in the Trade and Production Database are most-favored-nation simple averages at the three- or four-digit level of the ISIC.

Input-Output Tables

Input and output tables are based on the Global Trade Analysis Project (GTAP) database, version 4. The GTAP database utilizes data from the early 1990s in constructing its input and output tables. Only one table is provided for each country in the database. The GTAP aggregates some countries in regions; those countries therefore have the same input and output tables.[9] Those interested in how the GTAP constructs each particular input/output table may refer to the GTAP database or consult the GTAP Website, <www.gtap.org>. The tables reported in the Trade and Production Database are aggregated at the three-digit level of the ISIC classification. To facilitate the use of the tables within the database, the data reflecting input and output have been broken down into two tables. The first table reports the share of output from each manufacturing sector that is sold to other industrial sectors, and the second table reports the value of intermediate inputs from each

manufacturing sector that is required to produce one unit of output in each manufacturing sector. Using this GTAP data, the Trade and Production Database provides an intermediate import-share table that demonstrates the import share of intermediates utilized by each sector in each country. These tables are available only in EXCEL format.

Problems and Special Considerations

The data in the Trade and Production Database have been grouped and organized to facilitate the use of the database for a large number of purposes. The database is not designed to produce quick answers but rather to assist researchers in the lengthy and cumbersome exercise of collecting and organizing data. In order to give the researcher the maximum degree of flexibility, the data have not been changed beyond the adaptations described above. Nevertheless, a few points need to be emphasized. Monetary data are not deflated and are expressed in thousands of U.S. dollars. If the data were not supplied in U.S. dollars, the common practice was followed of using the yearly average exchange rate to convert the domestic currency to the dollar.[10] Caution should also be used when analyzing data gathered from Germany (GER).[11] To produce a consistent time series, data on Germany before and immediately after unification are constructed as the sum of the Federal Republic of Germany (DFA) and the Democratic Republic of Germany (DDR). Especially for the years immediately after unification, it is possible that some data on the DDR were not reported, thus producing a sudden shift in the time-series. The production data from UNIDO are subject to differences in national classifications, and assumptions are needed to convert from the national (country-specific) industrial classification into the ISIC classification. For example, similar industries may be allocated to slightly different ISIC sectors in different countries, or data from industries of the same size may be too small to be reported in some countries, while they may be fully reported in others. These kinds of problem are generally most pronounced at the more disaggregated level.[17]

A common issue in trade data is the presence of the label "not classified" for a trade partner. This is the case when the country does not know, or does not wish to disclose, the origin or the destination of a trade flow. The Trade and Production Database deals with this issue by reporting data on "not clas-sified" countries as separate observations instead of allocating them to any region. Nevertheless, the "not classified" value may be negative due to con-cordance aggregation between the SITC and the ISIC classifications. In this case, the negative value is split across all regions according to weights cal-culated on the basis of existing documented trade. This problem affects only a minimal part of the data and is equivalent to assuming that exports or imports not classified by country of destination or origin are distributed to each region using as weight the documented trade flows.[13] In the even rarer case that, after the transformation from SITC to ISIC, the documented trade flows with the regions turns out to be negative, the value of "not classified" is diminished by the amount of the sum of those negative values, and the negative values are set to zero. These operations are performed only on the data aggregated by region and income level. To give maximum flexibility to researchers, the reallo-cation of the negative values is not performed in the ASCII file reporting country-by-country trade flows.

Another recurring issue with trade data, as dis-cussed in detail by Feenstra (1996) and by Hanson and Feenstra (2001), is the existence of entrepôts—that is, countries where transits of trade flows take place but that are not the origin or the final destina-tion of the flows. In many cases the country of ori-gin (O) reports the entrepôt (T) as the destination of the shipment. Meanwhile, the entrepôt country does not report the import, and the final importer (F) reports the original exporter (O) as the origin. This creates a surplus (between O and T) and a deficit (between O and F). In the example above, country (F) reports an import from (O) that is not reported (as an export to F) by country (O), creat-ing a discrepancy. The researcher should keep this in mind when analyzing entrepôts such as Hong Kong (China), Macau (China), Singapore, and the Netherlands. For this reason, trade data also include values of mirrored exports.[14] In many cases there are huge discrepancies that are attributable to rea-sons such as transport costs, different product clas-sifications, entrepôts, and poor accounting methods. It is advisable to use mirrored exports only where there are serious doubts about the capa-bility of the reporting country in managing the col-lection of records on trade flows.[15]

Notes

1 The Trade and Production Database is also available at <www.worldbank.org/research/trade>. It is provided on an "as is" basis.

2 Feenstra (1996) covers U.S. imports from 1972 to 1974. Feen-stra, Lipsey, and Bowen (1997) covers trade, production, and tariff data from 1970 to 1992, but production data are only available for OECD countries. It does include nontariff barriers (coverage ratios), which are excluded from the Trade and Pro-duction Database. Feenstra (2000) covers only trade, but at a much higher level of product disaggregation than the one fol-lowed here.

3 For more information on UNIDO's industrial databases, see <http://www.unido.org/doc/50215.htmls>.

4 For more information on the COMTRADE database and other products of the United Nations Statistical office, see <http://esa.un.org/unsd/pubs>.

5 For more information on WTO products, see <http://www.wto.org>. For more information on UNCTAD's TRAINS database, see <http://www.unctad.org/trains/index.htm>.

6 For more information on the GTAP dataset, see <http://www.gtap.agecon.purdue.edu/>.

7 Generally, import data are of better quality than export data, for fiscal reasons. Mirrored data, however, need to be used with caution, as noted by Yeats (1995).

8 Because of rounding errors and aggregation issues, there may be very slight differences (usually less than 0.01 percent) between the sums of the different regions and totals. Users should be aware of these possible discrepancies.

9 If the input and output tables are not country-specific, the name of the region is also reported in each table.

10 The researcher should keep this practice in mind and treat with caution cases where there has been a large and sudden change in the exchange rate.

11 In other databases the country code identifying Germany may be DEU instead of the one used here, GER.

12 Note that the four-digit codes starting with 312 are commonly collapsed into the three-digit category 311.

13 Negative values were encountered in less than 0.01 percent of the observations.

14 Mirrored data are available from 1980 to 1998. Many coun-tries failed to report trade data before 1980 and for 1999, pro-ducing incomplete results for those years.

15 In some cases, however, mirrored exports may be considered more precise than exports because trade flows are usually bet-ter recorded at entrance (imports). Therefore, mirrored exports contain useful and utilizable information, on a bilateral basis, where the partner countries have good customs administra-tions.

Glossary of Trade-Related Terms

ACP African, Caribbean, and Pacific countries, a group of mostly former European colonies.

Actionable subsidy A type of subsidy that is not prohibited under WTO rules but against which a member may respond by imposing a countervailing duty.

Administered protection See Contingent protection.

Ad valorem An ad valorem duty (tariff, charge, and so on) is based on the value of the dutiable item and expressed in percentage terms: for example, a duty of 20 percent on the value of automobiles.

Advisory Centre on WTO Law Entity based in Geneva that provides legal counseling on WTO law and dispute settlement to developing and transition countries that are WTO members on a subsidized basis, depending on the income level of the requesting government; 72 WTO members are eligible to request assistance.

AGOA (African Growth and Opportunities Act) U.S. legislation providing duty-free access for a large number of products for 35 African economies.

Aggregate measure of support Measure of the total support given to an activity as a result of policies such as production subsidies and market price support policies. Used in the WTO Agreement on Agriculture.

Antidumping Trade policy used by importing governments to counteract dumping, for example by imposing duties or negotiating price increases.

Appellate Body WTO body that hears appeals against the findings of dispute settlement panels.

ASYCUDA Automated System for Customs Data. A computerized customs management system developed and implemented by UNCTAD that covers most foreign trade procedures and handles manifests and customs declarations, accounting procedures, transit and suspense procedures.

Binding See Tariff concession.

Border tax adjustment Fiscal measure compensating, in whole or in part, for the different treatment either between imports and similar domestic products or between exports and similar products sold on the domestic market. For example, refunds of domestic indirect taxes on goods destined for export; or charges on imports similar to the taxes levied on like domestic products. Also see Duty drawback.

Cairns Group Coalition of developing and industrial country exporters of agricultural commodities formed in the Uruguay Round to negotiate stronger multilateral disciplines on agricultural trade policies.

Capacity building In a trade context, activities supported by the donor community aimed at strengthening the ability of stakeholders in developing countries to develop national trade policy, undertake analysis, and identify their interests in international trade negotiations.

Cartel Arrangement between firms to control a market—for example, to fix prices or limit competition between members of the cartel.

Ceiling binding Often used to describe a situation where there is a large difference between the tariff that is actually applied and the level at which the tariff is bound in GATT (the "ceiling").

C.I.F. Cost, insurance, and freight. The cost of a good delivered to the importing country's port.

The Glossary draws on material in Finger and Olechowski (1987) and the glossary maintained by Professor Alan Deardorff on his home page: http://www-personal.umich.edu/~alandear/glossary/. Chapter 55 contains a listing of acronyms of regional trade agreements. Many of the terms are discussed further in the accompanying CD-ROM on applied trade policy for developing countries.

CITES Convention on International Trade in Endangered Species of Wild Fauna and Flora. Establishes rules for trading such species, up to and including a complete ban on all trade.

Codex Alimentarius Commission The "food code"—an international set of standards, codes of practice, and guidelines and recommendations relating to food quality and safety, including codes governing hygienic processing practices, recommendations relating to compliance with standards, limits for pesticide residues, and guidelines for contaminants, food additives, and veterinary drugs. The Codex Alimentarius Commission is the body responsible for compiling the standards.

Compensatory adjustment Measure taken, after withdrawing a (tariff or other) concession, to compensate for such withdrawal (GATT Art. XXVIII).

Competition policy Legislation and regulations designed to protect and stimulate competition in markets by outlawing anticompetitive business practices such as cartels, market sharing, or price fixing.

Computable general equilibrium (CGE) models Mathematical characterizations of the economy, used to predict the impact of policy changes, taking into account both direct effects as well as indirect effects that work through labor and other markets.

Concertina approach Method of reducing tariffs by lowering the highest rates first, then the next highest, and so forth.

Content, domestic or local Rules establishing a minimum proportion (by value or volume) of a product that must be domestically or locally produced in order to obtain a benefit (for example, a tariff concession).

Contestability A market is contestable if new suppliers can enter it easily. The threat of such entry is a discipline on the incumbent suppliers and can prevent prices from rising far above costs, because any excess profits will be rapidly followed by entry.

Contingent protection Trade barriers that are imposed if certain circumstances (contingencies) are met. Examples include antidumping or countervailing duties (to offset subsidies) and safeguards. Also called administered protection.

Copyright Instrument to protect the rights of authors of original works (print, audio, video, film, software) from unauthorized copying and use. Generally for the life of the author, plus 50 years.

Cotonou Agreement Partnership agreement between the EU and the ACP countries signed in June 2000 in Cotonou, Benin. Replaces the Lomé Convention. Its main objective is poverty reduction, "to be achieved through political dialogue, development aid and closer economic and trade cooperation."

Counter trade Form of barter committing the exporter to offset the value of his exports, in whole or in part, by imports from his trading partner. Also see Offset requirement.

Countervailing duty Duty levied on imports of goods that have benefited from production or export subsidies. The duty is intended to offset the effect of the subsidy.

Credit (for autonomous liberalization) Mechanism through which developing countries are granted recognition in WTO talks for unilateral liberalization of the trade regime that has occurred in the period before negotiations commence. Past efforts by developing countries to establish such a mechanism were not successful.

Customs duty Charge levied on imports and listed in an importing country's tariff schedules. Duties may be specific or ad valorem or a combination of the two (ad valorem with a specific minimum or the greater of the two).

Customs union A group of countries forming a single customs territory in which (1) tariffs and other barriers are eliminated on substantially all the trade between the constituent countries for products originating in these countries, and (2) there is a common external trade policy (common external tariff) that applies to nonmembers.

Customs valuation Establishment, according to defined criteria, of the value of goods for the purpose of levying ad valorem customs duties on their importation.

Decoupling Action to ensure that subsidies to producers (usually farmers) are unrelated to production so as to provide no incentive to increase production; in contrast, simple subsidies per unit of output tend to increase production.

Deep integration Intergovernmental cooperation in designing and applying domestic policies such as taxes, health and safety regulations, and environmental standards. May involve either harmonization of policies or mutual recognition; generally occurs in the context of regional integration agreements.

Deficiency payment Direct monetary payment by government to producers to compensate for the difference between the market price of a good and a higher guaranteed price for that good in the case of, say, low international commodity prices.

Degressivity Mechanism to ensure that the application of a measure gradually becomes less severe over time. For example, a tariff set at 50 percent that is reduced by 10 percentage points each year and becomes zero in year 5.

Differential and more favorable treatment See Special and differential treatment and Enabling clause.

Dispute Settlement Body WTO body that is responsible for dealing with disputes between WTO members. Consists of all WTO members meeting together to consider the reports of dispute settlement panels and the Appellate Body.

Domestic content See Content.

Dumping A form of price discrimination by which the export price of the product exported from one country to another is less than the comparable price, in the ordinary course of trade—that is, including transport and related costs—for the like product when destined for consumption in the exporting country (GATT Art. VI). Also defined as sales below the estimated cost of production. The margin of dumping is the difference between the two prices.

Duty drawback scheme A duty drawback scheme (often administratively demanding) is a form of border tax adjustment whereby the duties or taxes levied on imported goods are refunded, in whole or in part, when the goods are re-exported. The idea is to reduce the burden on exporters while maintaining tariffs for revenue or protective purposes. See also Temporary admission.

Economic needs test Measure requiring a demonstration that an import (of goods but more usually natural service providers) cannot be satisfied by local producers or service providers.

Effective rate of protection A measure of the protection afforded by an import restriction calculated as a percentage of the value added in the product concerned. Takes into account the protection on output and the cost-raising effects of protection on inputs.

Emergency action See Safeguard action.

Enabling clause 1971 GATT Decision on "Differential and More Favorable Treatment, Reciprocity and Fuller Participation of Developing Countries". One of the so-called Framework agreements, it enables WTO members, notwithstanding the nondiscrimination requirements, to "accord differential and more favorable treatment to developing countries, without according such treatment to other contracting parties." See also Generalized system of preferences.

Escape clause Clause in a legal text allowing temporary derogation from its provisions under certain specified emergency conditions. See also Safeguard Action (GATT Art. XIX.)

Europe Agreement Free trade agreement between the EU and various Central and Eastern European countries.

Everything but Arms A 2001 EU initiative to grant least developed countries duty- and quota-free access for their exports.

Exchange control Restrictions imposed by a government or central bank over the holding, sale, or purchase of foreign exchange. Typically used when the exchange rate is fixed and the central bank is unable or unwilling to enforce the rate by exchange-market intervention.

Exhaustion Policy stance of a country regarding parallel imports of goods protected under intellectual property rights. Under national exhaustion, rights end upon the first sale of the good within a nation, and right holders may prevent unauthorized imports of the goods concerned. Under international exhaustion, rights end upon the first sale anywhere in the world, after which parallel imports are permitted.

Export-processing zone (EPZ) A designated area or region in which firms can import duty-free as long as the imports are used as inputs into the production of exports. Traditional EPZs are fenced-in industrial estates specializing in manufacturing for exports. Modern ones have flexible rules that may permit domestic sales upon payment of duties when leaving the zone. EPZs generally also provide a liberal regulatory environment for the firms involved as well as infrastructure services.

Export promotion A strategy for economic development that emphasizes support for exports through removal of anti-export biases created by policy. May be associated with policies such as duty drawbacks, export subsidies, marketing support, or matching grants for exporters.

Externality Occurs when the action of one agent (person, firm, government) affects directly other agents, making them better or worse off. Beneficial effects are called positive externalities; harmful ones negative externalities.

Fast track A procedure under which the U.S. Congress agrees to consider implementing legislation for

Government procurement Purchasing, leasing, rental, or hire purchasing by government entities or agencies.

Graduation Concept linking the rights and obligations of a developing country to its level of development. Referred to in the WTO Trade Policy Review Mechanism. Generally used in the context of GSP and similar types of preferential treatment of low-income countries as a mechanism or set of criteria to determine when countries cease to be eligible for preferences.

Grandfather clause A clause exempting signatories from certain treaty obligations for legislation or regulations that were adopted before accession to the treaty and that are inconsistent with the treaty.

Gray-area measure Measure whose conformity with contractual obligations is unclear: for example, voluntary export restraints under pre-WTO rules of the GATT.

Green room Used to describe discussions in the WTO among a subset of countries, generally the major OECD members and a small number of developing countries.

GTAP The Global Trade Analysis Project, based at Purdue University in the United States. It provides data and models for computable general equilibrium modeling.

Harmonized System (HS) "Harmonized Commodity Description and Coding System". Nomenclature developed by the World Customs Organization for customs tariffs and international trade statistics.

HIPC Heavily Indebted Poor Countries Initiative. An agreement among official creditors to help the most heavily indebted countries to obtain debt relief.

Impairment Damage to, or weakening of, benefits accruing under contractual rights and obligations. (GATT Art. XXIII).

Import substitution Theory of and approach to development that focuses on providing domestic substitutes for all imported manufactures via trade protection and various types of industrial policies.

Infant industry Infant industry arguments suggest that new (non-traditional) industries must be protected from import competition while they are establishing themselves. This is a so-called second-best argument in that it does not address the fundamental market failures that cause industries to fail to develop (such as financial market imperfections).

Integrated Framework for Trade-related Technical Assistance (IF) Joint activity and donor-financed trust fund managed by six agencies—IMF, International Trade Centre (Geneva), UNCTAD, UNDP, World Bank, and WTO—to work with LDCs to undertake diagnostic studies aimed at assisting countries to identify key constraints to better integration into the world economy and to provide follow-up trade-related technical and financial assistance.

Intra-industry trade Trade in which a country both exports and imports goods that are classified to be in the same industry.

Labeling Requirement, either mandatory or voluntary, to specify whether a product satisfies certain conditions relating to the process by which it was produced or its characteristics.

Least developed country (LDC) A country that satisfies a number of criteria established by the United Nations that together imply a very low level of economic development. As of 2002, the UN had classified 49 countries in the LDC group. Used in the WTO Subsidies Agreement, where LDCs are granted differential treatment.

Licensing (of imports or exports) Practice requiring approval to be granted by the relevant government authority, or by a body designated by such authority, as a prior condition to importing or exporting.

Automatic licensing Where approval is freely granted—for example, licensing for keeping statistical records.

Nonautomatic licensing Where approval is not freely granted. This may be used as a restriction itself, or it may be used to administer a quota. The license may be subject to certain conditions: for example, a requirement to export; the use to which the imported good is to be put; the purchase of a specified quantity of the domestically produced like product; or the availability on the domestic market of the domestically produced like product.

Discretionary licensing Nonautomatic licensing (see above).

Linking scheme An import-licensing requirement that forces an importer to purchase specified amounts of the same type of product from domestic producers before they can apply for import licenses. An example is a two-tier quota allocation system for licenses in which obtaining a license to buy or sell on a market is linked to the amount bought or sold in a second market.

Local (or domestic) content requirements See Content.

Lomé Convention This agreement was between the EU and the ACP countries on trade concessions (GSP treatment), development aid, and general cooperation. Replaced by the Cotonou Agreement in 2000.

MAI Multilateral Agreement on Investment. Effort by the OECD in the late 1990s to establish a set of disciplines on investment-related matters. Negotiations failed and were suspended in 1998.

Market access Refers to the conditions under which imports compete with domestically produced substitutes. These are determined by the extent to which foreign goods are confronted with tariffs, discriminatory taxes, and other regulations.

Matching grant Subsidy that is conditional on a co-payment or contribution by an industry or enterprise.

Maximum (minimum) price system (for imports) Price(s) decreed by the authorities of the importing country and above (below) which price(s) imports may not enter the domestic market. Actual import prices below the decreed minimums trigger a protective action, such as the imposition of additional duties or of a quantitative restriction. Different terms are used in different countries and different sectors: basic import price, minimum import price, reference price, and trigger price.

Markup In economics, a measure of the difference between the unit price of a good and its marginal cost of production. In WTO terms sometimes used to indicate the extent to which an applied tariff exceeds the bound rate.

Mercantilism An economic philosophy of the 16th and 17th centuries that international commerce should primarily serve to increase a country's financial wealth, especially of gold and foreign currency. To that end, exports are viewed as desirable and imports as undesirable unless they lead to even greater exports. In a WTO context, the term is often used to describe the quid pro quo nature of bargaining over trade policies.

Mixing regulation Describes two kinds of practices: (1) regulation specifying the proportion of domestically produced content in products offered for sale on the domestic market; (2) regulation specifying, for any imports of a given product, the quantity of a domestically produced like product that must be purchased by the importer.

Mode of supply Term used in the GATS context to identify how a service is provided by a supplier to a buyer.

Most favored nation (MFN) principle MFN is the "normal," non-discriminatory tariff charged on imports of a good. In commercial diplomacy, exporters seek MFN treatment that is, the promise that they will be treated as well as the most favored exporter. Called normal trade relations in the United States.

Multifiber Arrangement (MFA) "Arrangement Regarding International Trade in Textiles." Negotiated as a temporary exception to the GATT in 1973. Regulates trade in certain textile products between signatories by means of negotiated bilateral quotas. Superceded by the WTO Agreement on Textiles and Clothing in 1995, which specifies that all quotas are to be abolished by 2005.

Mutual recognition The acceptance by one country of another country's certification that a product has satisfied a product standard. Often based on formal agreements between countries if the standards are mandatory.

National treatment Principle that foreign goods, services, and persons (investors), once they have entered a country and satisfied any formalities that are required, are treated in exactly the same way as national goods, services, or persons. In particular, they face the same internal taxes and no additional restrictions.

Necessity test Procedure to determine whether a policy restricting trade is necessary to achieve the objective that the measure is intended to attain.

Negative list In an international agreement, a list of those items, entities, products, and so on to which the agreement will *not* apply, the commitment being to apply the agreement to everything else. Contrasts with positive list.

Nominal rate of protection The proportion by which the (tariff-inclusive) internal price of an import exceeds the border or world price. See also Effective rate of protection.

Noneconomic objective Describes situations where a policy objective is other than the efficient allocation of resources. In the trade policy setting, it refers to the view that a restriction on imports may serve a purpose that goes beyond the restriction of trade itself. In general desired changes in output, consumption, and so forth can be achieved at lower economic cost through other types of policies.

Nontariff barrier (NTB) A catchall phrase describing barriers to international trade other than the tariffs—for example, quotas, licensing, or voluntary export restraints.

Nontariff measure Any government action with a potential effect on the value, volume, or direction of trade. Also see Nontariff barrier.

Nonviolation Procedure under WTO disputed settlement provisions under which a WTO member argues that actions by another member, even though allowed under WTO rules, nullify or impair benefits expected under the agreement.

Normal value Price charged by an exporting firm in its home market. Used to compare with the price charged by the firm on an export market to determine if there is dumping. (GATT Art. VI). See also Dumping.

Nullification Negation of benefits accruing under the WTO as a result of actions taken by a member. See also Dispute Settlement Body and Panel.

Offset requirement Requirement, stipulated by the authorities of the importing country, that exporters to that country compensate for their exports by, say, purchasing products of the importing country or investing in the importing country. Also see Counter trade.

Orderly marketing arrangement See Voluntary export restraint.

Origin rule Criterion for establishing the country of origin of a product. Often based on whether production (processing) leads to a change in tariff heading (classification) or on the level of value added in the country where the good was last processed.

Panel In WTO, a group of three independent experts nominated by the WTO secretariat from a roster approved by members that is responsible for determining the validity of allegations brought by one WTO member against another claiming nullification or impairment of rights or obligations (that is, violation of WTO rules and disciplines).

Parallel imports Trade that is made possible when a good that is protected under intellectual property provisions (patents, copyrights) is sold in different countries for different prices. A parallel import comprises arbitrage activity and occurs when traders import the good from a lower-price market into a higher-price country.

Para tariff Charges on imports that act as a tariff but are not included in a country's tariff schedule. Examples include a statistical tax, stamp fees, and so forth.

Partial equilibrium analysis The study of one market in isolation, assuming that anything that happens in it does not materially affect any other market.

Patent A right granted to its owner to exclude all others from making, selling, importing or using the product or process described in the patent for a fixed period of time, generally 20 years. To be patentable, inventions have to be novel, non-obvious, and be useful or have industrial applicability.

Phytosanitary regulation Pertaining to the health of plants. See SPS measure.

Plurilateral agreement In WTO, an agreement to which membership is voluntary, dealing with an issue that is not covered by the WTO. In 2002 there were two plurilateral agreements—on civil aircraft policies and government procurement.

Positive list In an international agreement, a list of those items, entities, products, and so on to which the agreement *will* apply, with no commitment to apply the agreement to anything else.

Poverty Reduction Strategy Paper (PRSP) Document describing a country's macroeconomic, structural and social policies, and programs to promote growth and reduce poverty, as well as associated external financing needs. PRSPs are prepared by governments through a participatory process involving civil society and development partners, including the World Bank and the IMF, and provide the basis for concessional lending and debt relief under the enhanced HIPC Initiative.

PPM Production and processing method. Used in instances where trade policy action by a country is motivated by a desire to ensure that imports have been produced in a way that satisfies a national or international production or process norm. Often these norms will be environmental in nature.

Precautionary principle Policy under which measures are motivated by the possibility that use of certain technologies (for example, biotechnology, genetically modified organisms, and pesticides) could be harmful to human or animal health and safety or the environment, although there is no certainty to that effect.

Predatory pricing Action by a firm to lower prices so much that rival firms are driven out of business, after which the firm raises prices again to exploit the resulting monopoly power.

Preference Preferential treatment. In GATT terms, this represents a derogation, in the sense of treatment that is more favorable than MFN. See also Generalized System of Preferences and Special and Differential Treatment.

Preshipment inspection Mechanism under which goods are inspected and certified in the country of origin by specialized inspection agencies or firms. Often used by importing governments to combat over- or underinvoicing of imports by having the value of consignments determined by independent entities (firms).

PRSP See Poverty Reduction Strategy Paper.

Price discrimination The practice of charging different customers different prices for the same good in order to exploit their different degrees of enthusiasm for it—for example, lower off-peak fares exploit workers' need to travel in the rush hour, while allowing less urgent personal travel to take place at other times. When this occurs internationally and the lower price is charged for export, it is called dumping.

Price undertaking Commitment by an exporter to either raise prices or reduce sales in a market as a way of settling an antidumping suit brought by import-competing domestic firms. Generally has an effect analogous to a quota.

Principal-supplier rule Rule, in bilateral negotiating procedures, according to which an import concession on a specific product is to be negotiated only with the country that is actually or potentially the major supplier of that product. Note that the WTO MFN rule requires that the concession be extended to all other members.

Prisoner's dilemma A situation where agents with perfect information that act rationally (that is, pursue their "selfish" best interests) are confronted with a set of payoffs (or rewards) in which not cooperating is the dominant strategy, even though cooperation would in principle increase their joint payoffs.

Producer subsidy equivalent A measure of the aggregate value of the gross transfers from consumers and taxpayers to farmers due to policy measures. Also called producer support estimate.

Protocol of accession Legal document recording the conditions and obligations under which a country accedes to an international agreement or organization.

Quad Refers to the participants in the Quadrilateral meetings—that is, Canada, the European Union, Japan, and the United States.

Quantitative restriction or quota Measure restricting the quantity of a good imported (or exported). Quantitative restrictions include quotas, nonautomatic licensing, mixing regulations, voluntary export restraints, and prohibitions or embargoes.

Global Quota Quota specifying the total volume, or value, of the product to be imported (exported) without regard to the country or countries of origin (destination) of the product.

Bilateral quota Quota applied to imports from (exports to) a specific country.

Quota by country Quota that not only specifies the total volume, or value, of the product to be imported (exported), but also allocates the trade between the various countries of origin (destination).

Quota rent The economic rent received by the holder of a right to import under a quota. Equals the domestic price of the imported good, net of any tariff, minus the world price, times the quantity of imports.

Real exchange rate The nominal exchange rate adjusted for inflation. Unlike most other real variables, this adjustment requires accounting for price levels in two currencies. The real exchange rate is: $R = EP^*/P$ where E is the nominal domestic-currency price of foreign currency, P is the domestic price level, and P^* is the foreign price level. Equivalent to the real price of foreign goods; that is, the quantity of domestic goods needed to purchase a unit of foreign goods. Also defined as the relative price of traded goods in terms of non-traded goods.

Reference price See Maximum (minimum) price system.

Remedy Legal term to describe a measure recommended by a WTO dispute settlement panel that aims to bring the policies of a member found to have violated WTO rules or disciplines into compliance with its obligations.

Rent-seeking Refers to activities that use resources to obtain incomes through transfers but which do not increase national income. Such activities result in an extra cost to society (the loss of income from the diversion of resources away from productive towards rent-seeking activities) beyond the distortionary costs associated with measures that give rise to the rents.

Request-offer procedure Negotiating procedure based on the tabling, by each party, of a list of concessions requested of other parties, followed by an offer list of the concessions that could be granted if its request were met.

Restrictive business practice Measures by business enterprises to limit access to markets and restrain competition (such as the formation of a cartel).

Retaliation Imposition of a trade barrier in response to another country's increasing its level of trade restrictions.

Revealed comparative advantage (RCA) The ratio of a country's exports of a good to the world's exports of that good divided by that country's share of exports of manufactures in the world exports of manufactures. The index for country i good j is $RCA_{ij} = 100(X_{ij}/X_{wj})/(X_{it}/X_{wt})$ where X_{ab} is exports by country a (w = world) of good b (t = total for all goods). A value of the index above (below) one, is interpreted as a revealed comparative advantage (comparative disadvantage) for the good.

Rollback The phasing out of measures inconsistent with the provisions of an agreement.

Round In the WTO context, a multilateral trade negotiation. There have been eight rounds: Geneva (1947), Annecy (1949), Torquay (1950–51), Geneva (1955–56), Dillon (1960–61), Kennedy (1963–67), Tokyo (1973–79), and Uruguay (1986–94). A ninth multilateral negotiation was launched in Doha, Qatar, at the end of 2001.

Rule of origin See Origin rule.

Safeguard action Emergency protection to safeguard domestic producers of a specific good from an unforeseen surge in imports (GATT Art. XIX), to protect a country's external financial position and balance –of payments (GATT Art. XII, XVIII:B), or to protect an infant industry in a developing country (GATT Art. XVIII:A or C). See also Escape clause.

Sanitary and phytosanitary (SPS) measure A technical requirement specifying criteria to ensure food safety and animal and plant health. Many international SPS standards are set by the FAO/WHO. See also Codex Alimentarius Commission.

Second-best argument (for protection) Any argument for protection that can be countered by pointing to a less costly policy that would achieve the same desired result. Also refers to rationales for protection to partially correct a distortion in the economy when the first-best policy for that purpose is not available. For example, if domestic production generates a positive externality and a production subsidy to internalize it is not available, then a tariff may be second-best optimal.

Selectivity Application of a rule, regulation, or trade action on a discriminatory basis to certain countries.

Shallow integration Reduction or elimination of border barriers to trade. Contrasts with deep integration.

Special and differential treatment The principle in WTO that developing countries be accorded special privileges, either exempting them from some WTO rules or granting them preferential treatment in the application of WTO rules.

Special drawing right International payment facility administered by the IMF. Also used as an international unit of accounting, defined in terms of the five most important national currencies in international trade.

Special safeguard In the WTO Agreement on Agriculture, a protectionist measure that can be triggered automatically by a decline in prices or an increase in imports.

Specific commitment Under the GATS, technical term describing the commitments made by WTO members on national treatment and market access for service sectors.

Specific tariff A specific duty (tariff, import tax) expressed in terms of a fixed amount per unit of the dutiable item. For example, $1,000 on each imported vehicle or $50 on each ton of wheat.

Specificity A policy measure that applies to one or a subset of enterprises or industries as opposed to all industries.

SPS See Sanitary and phytosanitary measure.

Standard Rule, regulation, or procedure specifying characteristics that must be met by a product (such as dimensions, quality, performance, or safety). When these put foreign producers at a disadvantage, they may constitute a nontariff barrier. See also Technical barrier to trade.

State trading Trade by a government agency or enterprise or by an enterprise to which the government has granted exclusive or special privileges in respect of international trade. State trading does not necessarily involve a monopoly or quantitative restriction of trade and does not require state ownership (GATT Art. XVII).

Standstill A commitment not to take any new trade restrictive or distorting measure.

Strategic trade policy The use of trade policies to alter the outcome of international competition in a country's favor, usually by allowing its firms to capture a larger share of industry profits.

Structural adjustment Process of reallocating resources and changing the structure of production and employment of a national economy to reflect changing economic policies or trading conditions.

Subsidy Assistance granted by government to the production, manufacture, or export of specific goods, and taking the form either of direct payments, such as grants or loans, or of measures having equivalent effect, such as guarantees, operational or support services or facilities, and fiscal incentives.

Sunset clause Provision in a legal instrument limiting the duration of validity of a particular measure or policy.

Tariff See Customs duty.

Tariff binding In GATT context, commitment by countries not to raise particular tariff items above a specific or bound level. Also referred to as ceiling bindings. The so-called schedule of tariff concessions of each WTO member is annexed to its protocol of accession. See also Ceiling binding.

Tariff equivalent Measure of the protective effect of an NTB—the tariff that would have the exact same effect on imports as the NTB.

Tariff escalation Occurs if the tariff increases as a good becomes more processed. Escalation discourages imports of more processed varieties of the good (discouraging foreign processing activity) and offers domestic processors positive levels of effective protection. For example, low duties on tomatoes, higher duties on tomato paste, and yet higher duties on tomato ketchup.

Tariff peaks Tariffs that are particularly high, often defined as rates that exceed 15 percent or the average nominal tariff by a factor of more than three.

Tariff rate quota (TRQ) Measure under which a good is subject to a MFN tariff, but a certain quantity (the "quota") is admitted at a lower, sometimes zero, tariff. TRQs are mainly applied to agricultural trade and can be seasonal.

Tariffication Procedure of converting NTBs into their tariff equivalents. In the Uruguay Round, all industrial countries' agricultural NTBs were tariffed and bound.

Technical barrier to trade Trade-restrictive effect arising from the application of technical regulations or standards such as testing requirements, labeling requirements, packaging requirements, marketing standards, certification requirements, origin-marking requirements, health and safety regulations, and sanitary and phytosanitary regulations.

Technical regulation A mandatory requirement or standard specifying the characteristics that an imported product must meet. Usually aimed to protect public health or safety. See Technical barrier to trade.

Temporary admission Customs regime under which firms may import intermediates duty free if used in export production, and are required to document ex post that imports have been used for this purpose. See also Duty drawback.

Terms of trade The price of a country's exports relative to the price of its imports.

Total factor productivity (TFP) A measure of the output of an industry or economy relative to its inputs. The term and its abbreviation often refer to the growth of this measure.

Trade capacity The supply-side ability (capacity) of a country to benefit from the opportunities offered by the world market and MFN or preferential access to markets.

Trade creation Occurs when liberalization results in imports displacing less efficient local production and/or expanding consumption that was previously thwarted by artificially high prices due to protection.

Trade diversion Occurs when a trade reform discriminates between different trading partners and a less efficient (higher cost) source displaces a more efficient (lower cost) one. Can arise whenever some preferred suppliers are freed from barriers but others are not.

Trade integration Process of reducing barriers to trade and increasing participation in the international economy through trade. Also used to describe efforts to integrate trade policy and strengthening of trade-related institutions into a country's overall development strategy.

Trade Policy Review Mechanism WTO mechanism for periodic review of the trade policies and practices of members.

Trade promotion authority See Fast track.

Trade-related Investment Measure Policy used by governments to influence the operations of foreign investors by establishing specific performance standards relating to trade. Examples are export performance requirements and local content rules (mandating that investors use a certain proportion of domestic inputs in their production).

Trade-related Technical Assistance Services financed and/or provided by donors and development agencies to strengthen trade-related institutions and build trade capacity in developing countries. See also Integrated Framework.

Trademark Distinctive mark or name to identify a product, service, or company.

Transaction value Used for customs valuation purposes—the price of a good actually paid or payable.

Transparency Clarity, openness, predictability, and comprehensibility (used in regard to individual trade-related regulations and operation of institutions).

Atinc, Tamar Manuelyan. 1997. "Sharing Rising Incomes: Disparities in China." World Bank, Washington, D.C.

Australia, Department of Foreign Affairs and Trade. 1999. *Global Trade Reform: Maintaining Momentum.* Canberra.

Australia, Industries Assistance Commission. 1981. *Passenger Motor Vehicles and Components: Post-1984 Assistance Arrangements.* Canberra.

———.1984. *Local Content Schemes: A Technical Analysis.* Working Paper. July. Canberra.

Australia, Industry Commission. 1997. *The Automotive Industry.* Vols. 1 and 2. Report 58. May 26. Canberra.

Azam, Jean-Paul, and Shantayanan Devarajan. 1997. "The CFA Franc Zone in Africa: A Symposium." *Journal of African Economies* 6 (1, March): 1–2.

Baeumer, Ludwig. 1989. "Considerations concerning a Definition of Geographical Indications." Presented to the WIPO Symposium on the International Protection of Geographical Indications, Santenay, France, September 9–10.

———. 1997. "Protection of Geographical Indications under WIPO Treaties and Questions concerning the Relationship between Those Treaties and the TRIPS Agreement." Presented to the WIPO Symposium on the International Protection of Geographical Indications in the Worldwide Context, Eger, Hungary, October 24–25.

Bagwell, Kyle, and Robert W. Staiger. 1999. "An Economic Theory of GATT." *American Economic Review* 48 (1): 216–48.

Bajaj, Harbans L. 1995. "Managing Contracts for Power Projects." Presented at the International Conference on Contract Management in the Construction Industry, New Delhi.

Balassa, Bela. 1989. "Tariff Policy and Taxation in Developing Countries." Policy Research Working Paper Series 281. World Bank, Washington, D.C.

Balasubramanyam, V. N. 1991. "Putting TRIMs to Good Use." *World Development* 19: 1215–24.

Balasubramanyam, V. N., M. Salisu, and D. Sapsford. 1996. "Foreign Direct Investment and Growth in EP and IS Countries." *Economic Journal* 106: 92–105.

Baldwin, Richard E. 1994. *Towards an Integrated Europe.* London: Centre for Economic Policy Research.

———. 2001. "Regulatory Protectionism, Developing Nations, and a Two-Tier World Trade System." In Keith E. Maskus and John S. Wilson, eds., *Quantifying the Trade Effect of Technical Barriers: Can It Be Done?* Ann Arbor: University of Michigan Press.

Baldwin, Richard E., and Anthony Venables. 1997. "International Economic Integration." In Gene M. Grossman and Kenneth Rogoff, eds., *Handbook of International Economics,* vol. 3. Amsterdam: North-Holland.

Baldwin, Robert. E. 1969. "The Case against Infant Industry Protection." *Journal of Political Economy* 77: 295–305.

———. 1992. "Assessing the Fair Trade and Safeguards Laws in Terms of Modern Trade and Political Economy Analysis." *World Economy* 15 (2, March): 185–202.

Baldwin, Robert, and J. David Richardson. 1972. "Government Purchasing Policies, Other NTBs, and the International Monetary Crisis." In H. English and K. Hay, eds., *Obstacles to Trade in the Pacific Area.* Ottawa: Carleton School of International Affairs.

Barajas, Adolfo, Roberto Steiner, and Natalia Salazar. 1999. "Foreign Investment in Colombia's Financial Sector." IMF Working Paper WP/99/150. Washington, D.C.

Bardhan, Pranab. 1997. "Corruption and Development: A Review of the Issues." *Journal of Economic Literature* 35: 1320–46.

Bardsley, P., and P. Cashin. 1990. "Underwriting Assistance to the Australian Wheat Industry: An Application of Option Pricing Theory." *Australian Journal of Agricultural Economics* 34 (3): 212–22.

Barfield, Claude E. 1996. "Regionalism and US Trade Policy." In Jagdish Bhagwati and Arvind Panagariya, *The Economics of Preferential Trade Agreements.* Washington, D.C.: AEI Press.

Barro, Robert J., and Xavier Sala-i-Martin. 1995. *Economic Growth.* New York, McGraw-Hill.

Barth, James R., Gerard Caprio, Jr., and Ross Levine. 2001a. "Bank Regulation and Supervision: What Works Best?" Presented at the 13th Annual World Bank Conference on Development Economics, Washington, D.C., May 1–2.

Barth, James R., Gerard Caprio, Jr., and Ross Levine. 2001b. "The Regulation and Supervision of Banks around the World: A New Database." Policy Research Working Paper Series 2588. World Bank, Development Research Group, Washington, D.C.

Belderbos, R., and P. Holmes. 1995. "The Economics of Matsushita Revisited." *Anti-Trust Bulletin* 40 (winter): 825–57.

Ben-David, Dan. 1993. "Equalizing Exchange: Trade Liberalization and Income Convergence." *Quarterly Journal of Economics* 108 (3): 653–79.

Benjamin, Nancy, and Xinshen Diao. 2000. "Liberalizing Services Trade in APEC: A General Equilibrium Analysis with Imperfect Competition." *Pacific Economic Review* 5 (1).

Bergman L., C. Doyle, J. Gual, L. Hultkrantz, D. Neven, L. Roller, and L. Waverman. 1998. *Europe's Network Industries: Conflicting Priorities—Telecommunications.* London: Centre for Economic Policy Research.

Besen, Stanley M., and Leo J. Raskind. 1991. "An Introduction to the Law and Economics of Intellectual Property." *Journal of Economic Perspectives* 5 (1): 3–27.

Bhagwati, Jagdish N. 1968. *The Theory and Practice of Commercial Policy.* International Finance Section, Department of Economics. Princeton, N.J.: Princeton University.

———. 1971. "The Generalized Theory of Distortions and Welfare." In Jagdish N. Bhagwati, Ronald W. Jones, Robert A. Mundell, and Jaroslav Vanek, eds., *Trade, Balance of Payments and Growth: Papers in International Economics in Honor of Charles P. Kindleberger.* Amsterdam: North-Holland.

———. 1987. "Directly Unproductive Profit-Seeking (DUP) Activities." In John Eatwell, Murray Milgate, and Peter Newman, eds., *The New Palgrave: A Dictionary of Economics,* 845–47. New York: Stockton Press.

———. 1988. *Protectionism.* Cambridge, Mass.: MIT Press.

———. 1998. "Powerful Reasons for the MAI to Be Dropped Even from the WTO Agenda." *Financial Times* (October 22).

Bhagwati, Jagdish N., and Robert E. Hudec, eds. 1996. *Fair Trade and Harmonization: Prerequisites for Free Trade?* 2 vols. Cambridge, Mass.: MIT Press.

Bhagwati, Jagdish, and Arvind Panagariya. 1986. *The Economics of Preferential Trade Agreements.* Washington, D.C.: AEI Press.

Bhagwati, J., and T. N. Srinivasan. 1969. "Optimal Intervention to Achieve Non-Economic Objectives.", *Review of Economic Studies* 36: 27–38.

———. 1999. "Outward-Orientation and Development: Are Revisionists Right?" Yale University Economic Growth Center Discussion Paper 806. New Haven, Conn.

Bienaymé, Marie-Hélène. 1989. "The Possible Content of a New Treaty on the Protection of Geographical Indications at the Multilateral Level (Part I)." Presented to the WIPO Symposium on the International Protection of Geographical Indications, Santenay, France, September 9–10.

Biggs, Tyler. 1999. "A Micro-Econometric Evaluation of the Mauritius Technology Diffusion Scheme." RPED Discussion Paper. World Bank, Regional Program on Enterprise Development, Washington, D.C.

Blackhurst, Richard. 1991. "Trade Policy Is Competition Policy." Paper prepared for the OECD, Paris.

———. 1998a. "Capacity Building in Africa for Enhanced Participation in the WTO." Prepared for the dissemination conference of the AERC collaborative research project on Africa and the world trading system. African Economic Research Consortium, Nairobi. Processed.

———. 1998b. "The Capacity of the WTO to Fulfill Its Mandate." In Anne O. Krueger, ed., The WTO as an International Organization. Chicago: University of Chicago Press.

———. 2001. "Reforming WTO Decision-Making: Lessons from Singapore and Seattle." In Klaus Deutsch and Bernhard Speyer, eds., World Trade Organization Millennium Round: Freer Trade in the Twenty-first Century. London: Routledge.

Blackhurst, R., J. Francois, and E. Enders. 1996. "Market Access and Developing Countries." In Will Martin and L. Alan Winters, eds., The Uruguay Round and the Developing Economies. Cambridge, U.K.: Cambridge University Press.

Blackhurst, Richard, William Lyakurwa, and Ademola Oyejide. 2000. "Options for Improving Africa's Participation in the WTO." World Economy 23 (4): 491–510.

Blakeney, Michael. 1998. "Communal Intellectual Property Rights of Indigenous People in Cultural Expressions." Journal of World Intellectual Property 1 (6): 985–1002.

———. 2000. "The Protection of Traditional Knowledge under Intellectual Property Law." European Intellectual Property Review 22 (6, June): 251–61.

Blejer, Mario, and Adriene Cheasty. 1990. "Fiscal Implications of Trade Liberalization." In Vito Tanzi, ed., Fiscal Policy in Open Developing Economies, 66–81. Washington, D.C.: IMF.

Blomström, Magnus. 1986. "Foreign Investment and Productive Efficiency: The Case of Mexico." Journal of International Economics 15: 97–110.

———. 1989. Foreign Investment and Spillovers. London: Routledge.

Blomström, Magnus, and Hakan Persson. 1983. "Foreign Investment and Spillover Efficiency in an Underdeveloped Economy: Evidence from the Mexican Manufacturing Industry." World Development 11 (6): 493–501.

Blomström, Magnus, and Fredrik Sjöholm. 1999. "Technology Transfer and Spillovers: Does Local Participation with Multinationals Matter?" European Economic Review 43 (4–6): 915–23.

Bora, B., and S. Guisinger. 1997. "Impact of Investment Liberalization in APEC." Flinders University, Adelaide, Australia. Processed.

Bora, B., and I. N. Neufeld. 2000. "Tariffs and the East Asian Crises." UNCTAD, Trade Analysis Branch, Geneva. Processed.

Bora, B., and R. Pomfret. 1995. "Manufacturing Policies." In R. Pomfret, ed., Australia's Trade Policies. Melbourne: Oxford University Press.

Bora, Bijit, Peter J. Lloyd, and Mari Pangestu. 2000. "Industrial Policy and the WTO." World Economy 23 (4, April): 543–59.

Borensztein, E., J. de Gregorio, and J. W. Lee. 1998. "How Does Foreign Direct Investment Affect Economic Growth?" Journal of International Economics 45: 115–35.

Borrell, Brent. 1997. "Policy-Making in the EU: The Bananarama Story, the WTO, and Policy Transparency." Australian Journal of Agricultural and Resource Economics 41 (June): 263–76.

Bosworth, Malcolm. 2000. "Comment." In Pierre Sauvé and Robert M. Stern, eds., GATS 2000: New Directions in Services Trade Liberalization, 211–17. Washington, D.C.: Brookings Institution Press and Harvard University.

Botsch, Andreas. 1995. "Labor Standards and the Multilateral Trade and Investment System." In Rajah Rasiah and Norbert von Hoffman, Social and Environmental Clauses and Free Trade. Bonn, Germany: Friedrich Ebert Stiftung.Bovard, James. 1991. The Fair Trade Fraud: How Congress Pillages the Consumer and Decimates American Competitiveness. New York: St. Martin's Press.

Braga, Carlos Prima. 1996. "Trade-Related Intellectual Property Issues: The Uruguay Round Agreement and Its Economic Implications." In Will Martin and L. Alan Winters, eds., The Uruguay Round and the Developing Economies. Cambridge, U.K.: Cambridge University Press.

Braga, Carlos A. Primo, Carsten Fink, and Claudia Paz Sepulveda. 2000. Intellectual Property Rights and Economic Development. World Bank Discussion Paper 412. Washington, D.C.

Brander, J. A. 1995. "Strategic Trade Policy." In Gene M. Grossman and Kenneth Rogoff, eds., Handbook of International Economics, vol. 3. Amsterdam: North-Holland.

Brander, J., and B. Spencer. 1985. "Export Subsidies and International Market Rivalry." Journal of International Economics 18: 83–100.

Bronckers, Marco C. E. J., and Pierre Larouche. 1997. "Telecommunications Services and the World Trade Organisation." Journal of World Trade 31 (3): 5–48.

Brookes, Martin, and Saki Wahhaj. 2000. "The Shocking Effect of B2B." Goldman Sachs Global Economics Paper 37. Global Economics Week (February 3).

Brown, Drusilla K., and Robert M. Stern. 2001. "Measurement and Modeling of the Economic Effects of Trade and Investment Barriers in Services." Review of International Economics 9 (2, May): 282–86.

Brown, Drusilla K., Alan V. Deardorff, and Robert M. Stern. 1996. "Modeling Multilateral Liberalization in Services." Asia-Pacific Economic Review 2: 21–34.

Brown, Drusilla K., Alan V. Deardorff, Alan K. Fox, and Robert M. Stern. 1996. "The Liberalization of Services Trade: Potential Impacts in the Aftermath of the Uruguay Round." In Will Martin and L. Alan Winters, eds., The Uruguay Round and the Developing Economies. Cambridge, U.K.: Cambridge University Press.

Bruton, H. J. 1998. "A Reconsideration of Import Substitution." Journal of Economic Literature 36: 903–36.

Buffie, Edward. 2001. Trade Policy in Developing Countries. Cambridge, U.K.: Cambridge University Press.

Buigues, P., A. Jacquemin, and A. Sapir, eds. 1995. European Policies on Competition, Trade and Industry. Cheltenham, U.K.: Edward Elgar.

Burtless, Gary, Robert Z. Lawrence, Robert E. Litan, and Robert J. Shapiro. 1998. Globaphobia: Confronting Fears about Open Trade. Washington, D.C.: Brookings Institution Press.

Cadot, Olivier, Jaime de Melo, and Marcelo Olarreaga. 2000. "Can Duty Drawbacks Have a Protectionist Bias?" World Bank, Washington, D.C. Processed.

Djankov, Simeon, and Bernard Hoekman. 2000. "Foreign Investment and Productivity Growth in Czech Enterprises." *World Bank Economic Review* 14 (1): 49–64.

Dollar, David. 1992. "Outward-Oriented Developing Economies Really Do Grow More Rapidly: Evidence from 95 LDCs, 1976–1985." *Economic Development and Cultural Change* 40: 523–44.

Dollar David, and Aart Kraay. 2001. "Growth *Is* Good for the Poor." Policy Research Working Paper Series 2587. World Bank, Development Research Department, Washington, D.C. Processed.

Domberger, Simon, Christine Hall, and Eric Ah Lik Lee. 1995. "The Determinants of Price and Quality in Competitively Tendered Contracts." *Economic Journal* 105: 1454–70.

Donovan, D., and Y. H. Mai. 1996. "APEC Trade Liberalisation: The Impact of Increased Capital Mobility." *Australian Commodities* 3: 520–26.

Dornbusch, Rudiger, and Sebastian Edwards. 1994. "Exchange Rate Policy and Trade Strategy." In Barry P. Bosworth, Rudiger Dornbusch, and Raúl Labán, *The Chilean Economy: Policy Lessons and Challenges,* ch. 2. Washington, D.C.: Brookings Institution Press.

Dougherty, Sean M. 1997. "The Role of Foreign Technology in Improving Chinese Productivity." MIT Science and Technology Initiative, Beijing. Processed.

Drahos, Peter. 2000. "Indigenous Knowledge, Intellectual Property and Biopiracy: Is a Global Bio-Collecting Society the Answer?" *European Intellectual Property Review* 22 (6, June): 245–50.

———. 2001. "Negotiating Intellectual Property Rights: Between Coercion and Dialogue." Presented to the Ninth Annual Conference on International Intellectual Property Law and Policy, Fordham University School of Law, New York, April 19–20.

Drake, William, and Kalypso Nicolaides. 2000. "The Information Revolution and Services Trade Liberalization after 2000." In Pierre Sauvé and Robert M. Stern, eds., *GATS 2000: New Directions in Services Trade Liberalization.* Washington, D.C.: Brookings Institution Press and Harvard University.

Drechsler, L. 1990. "A Note on the Concept of Services." *Review of Income and Wealth* 36 (3): 309–16.

Dutz, Mark. 2001. "Pre-Shipment Inspection." PREM Note 53. World Bank, Washington, D.C.

Dyer, Geoff. 2001. "Patentes: Un ministro desafiante." *Clarin* (February 12). Buenos Aires.

Eaton, J., and G. Grossman. 1986. "Optimal Trade and Industrial Policy under Oligopoly." *Quarterly Journal of Economics* 101: 383–406.

Ebrill, Liam, Janet Stotsky, and Reint Gropp. 1999. *Revenue Implications of Trade Liberalization.* IMF Occasional Paper 180. Washington, D.C.

Edwards, Sebastian. 1989. "Exchange Rate Misalignment in Developing Countries." *World Bank Research Observer* 4 (1, January): 3–21.

———. 1993. "Openness, Trade Liberalization and Growth in Developing Countries." *Journal of Economic Literature* 31 (3, September): 1358–93.

———. 1998. "Openness, Productivity and Growth: What Do We Really Know?" *Economic Journal* 108: 383–98.

Edwards, Sebastian, and Daniel Lederman. 1998. "The Political Economy of Unilateral Trade Liberalization: The Case of Chile." NBER Working Paper 6510. National Bureau of Economic Research, Cambridge, Mass.

Ehrenberg, D. 1995. "The Labor Link: Applying the International Trading System to Enforce Violations of Forced and Child Labor." *Yale Journal of International Law* 20: 361–417.

Ehrlich, Paul R., and Edward O. Wilson. 1991. "Biodiversity Studies: Science and Policy." *Science* 253 (August 16): 758–62.

Eichengreen, Barry. 2001. "Capital Account Liberalization: What Do the Cross-Country Studies Tell Us?" *World Bank Economic Review* 15 (3): 341–65.

Elbadawi, Ibrahim, and Nader Majd. 1996. "Adjustment and Economic Performance under a Fixed Exchange Rate: A Comparative Analysis of the CFA Zone." *World Development* 24: 939–51.

Elbehri, A., M. Ingco, T. Hertel, and K. Pearson. 1999. "Agriculture and WTO 2000: Quantitative Assessment of Multilateral Liberalization of Agricultural Policies." World Bank, Washington, D.C. Available at <http://wbln0018.worldbank.org/trade/decagridoc.nsf>.

Esty, Daniel C. 1996. "Environmental Regulation and Competitiveness: Theory and Practice." In Simon S. C. Tay and Daniel C. Esty, eds., *Asian Dragons and Green Trade: Environment, Economics, and International Law.* Singapore: Times Academic Press.

European Commission. 2001. "EU Approves 'Everything But Arms' Trade Access for Least Developed Countries." Press Release, February 26. Brussels.

Evans, Gareth J. 1993. *Cooperating for Peace: The Global Agenda and Beyond.* Sydney, Australia: Allen and Unwin.

Evans, Philip, and Thomas Wurster. 2000. *Blown to Bits: How the New Economics of Information Transforms Strategy.* Boston, Mass.: Harvard Business School Press.

Evenett, Simon J., and Bernard M. Hoekman. 2000. "Government Procurement of Services and Multilateral Disciplines." In Pierre Sauvé and Robert M. Stern, eds., *GATS 2000: New Directions in Services Trade Liberalization,* 143–64. Washington, D.C.: Brookings Institution Press and Harvard University.

Evenett, Simon J., and Valerie Y. Suslow. 2000. "Preconditions on Private Restraints on Market Access and International Cartels." *Journal of International Economic Law* 3 (4): 593–631.

Evenett, Simon J., Margaret C. Levenstein, and Valerie Y. Suslow. 2001. "International Cartel Enforcement: Lessons from the 1990s." *World Economy* 24 (9, September): 1221–45.

Evenson, Robert E., and Larry E. Westphal. 1997. "Technological Change and Technology Strategy." In Hollis Chenery and T. N. Srinivasan, eds., *Handbook of Development Economics,* vol. 3. Amsterdam: North-Holland.

Faini, Riccardo, and Jaime de Melo. 1990. "Adjustment, Investment and the Real Exchange Rate in Developing Countries." *Economic Policy* (October): 492–519.

FAO (Food and Agriculture Organization). 1995. *The State of the World's Forests.* Rome.

Feenstra, Robert C. 1996. "U.S. Imports, 1972–1994: Data and Concordances." NBER Working Paper 5515. National Bureau of Economic Research, Cambridge, Mass.

———. 2000. *World Trade Flows, 1980–1997.* March. University of California, Davis. Processed.

Feenstra, Robert C., Robert E. Lipsey, and Harry P. Bowen. 1997. *World Trade Flows, 1970–1992 with Production and Tariff Data.* NBER Working Paper 5910. National Bureau of Economic Research, Cambridge, Mass.

Feketekuty, G. 2000. "Assessing and Improving the Architecture of GATS." In Pierre Sauvé and Robert M. Stern, eds., *GATS 2000:*

New Directions in Services Trade Liberalization, ch. 4. Washington, D.C.: Brookings Institution Press and Harvard University.

Fernandez, Raquel, and Jonathan Portes. 1998. "Returns to Regionalism: An Analysis of the Nontraditional Gains from Regional Trade Agreements." *World Bank Economic Review* 12: 197–220.

Ficsor, Mihály. 1997. "Attempts to Provide International Protection for Folklore by Intellectual Property Rights." Presented to the UNESCO-WIPO World Forum on the Protection of Folklore, Phuket, Thailand, April 8–10.

Fikentscher, W., and U. Immenga, eds. 1995. *Draft International Antitrust Code*. Baden-Baden, Germany: Nomos.

Findlay, Christopher, and Deunden Nikomborirak, 1999. "Air Transport." Paper prepared for East Asian Conference on Options for the WTO 2000 Negotiations, Manila, July 19–20. Available at http://www1.worldbank.org/wblep/trade/wto2000_region_work.html#EASTASIA.

Findlay, R. 1978. "Relative Backwardness, Direct Foreign Investment and the Transfer of Technology: A Simple Dynamic Model." *Quarterly Journal of Economics* 92: 1–16.

Finger, J. M. 1969. "Substitution and the Effective Rate of Protection." *Journal of Political Economy* 77 (6, December): 972–75.

———. 1974. "GATT Tariff Concessions and the Exports of Developing Countries: United States Concessions at the Dillon Round." *Economic Journal* 335: 566–75.

———. 1975. "Tariff Provisions for Offshore Assembly and the Export Earnings of Developing Countries." *Economic Journal* (June): 365–71.

———. 1976a. "Effects of the Kennedy Round Tariff Concessions on the Exports of Developing Countries." *Economic Journal* 86 (341): 87–95.

———. 1976b. "Trade and Domestic Effects of the Offshore Assembly Provision in the United States Tariff." *American Economic Review* 66 (4, September): 598–611.

———.1979. "Trade Liberalization: A Public Choice Perspective." In Ryan C. Amacher, Gottfried Haberler, and Thomas D. Willett, eds., *Challenges to a Liberal International Economic Order*. Washington, D.C.: American Enterprise Institute for Public Policy Research.

———. "Policy Research." *Journal of Political Economy* 89: 1270 71.

———. 1982. "Incorporating the Gains from Trade into Policy." *World Economy* 5 (December): 367–77.

———. 1986. "Ideas Count, Words Inform." In R. H. Snape, ed., *Issues in World Trade Policy*. London: Macmillan.

———. 1991a. "Development Economics and the GATT." In Jaime de Melo and André Sapir, eds., *Trade Theory and Economic Reform—North, South, and East: Essays in Honor of Béla Balassa*. Cambridge, Mass.: Basil Blackwell.

———. 1991b. "The GATT as International Discipline over Trade Restrictions: A Public Choice Approach." In Roland Vaubel and Thomas D. Willett, eds., *The Political Economy of International Organizations: A Public Choice Approach*. Boulder, Colo.: Westview.

———. 1991c. "That Old GATT Magic No More Casts Its Spell (How the Uruguay Round Failed)." *Journal of World Trade* 25 (2): 19–22.

———, ed. 1993. *Antidumping: How It Works and Who Gets Hurt*. Ann Arbor: University of Michigan Press.

———. 1998. "GATT Experience with Safeguards: Making Economic and Political Sense of the Possibilities That the GATT Allows to Restrict Imports." Policy Research Working Paper Series 2000. World Bank, Development Research Group, Washington, D.C.

———. 1999. Statement made at the Workshop on Developing Countries and the New Round of Multilateral Trade Negotiations, Harvard University, November 5–6.

———. 2001. "Implementing the Uruguay Round Agreements: Problems for Developing Countries." *World Economy* 24 (9, September): 1097–1108.

Finger, J. M., and Dean DeRosa. 1980. "The Compensatory Finance Facility and Export Stabilization." *Journal of World Trade Law* 14 (January–February): 14–22.

Finger, J. M., and Bernard Hoekman. 1999. "Developing Countries and a New Trade Round: Lessons from Recent Research." World Bank, Washington, D.C. Processed.

Finger, J. M., and M. Kreinin. 1976. "A New International Economic Order: A Critical Survey of the Issues." *Journal of World Trade Law* 16 (6, November): 493–512.

Finger, J. Michael, and Tracy Murray. 1993. "Antidumping and Countervailing Duty Enforcement in the United States." In J. Michael Finger, ed., *Antidumping, How It Works and Who Gets Hurt*. Ann Arbor: University of Michigan Press.

Finger, J. Michael, and Julio Nogués. 2002. "The Unbalanced Uruguay Round Outcome: The New Areas in Future WTO Negotiations." *World Economy* 25 (3, March): 321–40.

Finger, J. Michael, and Andrzej Olechowski, eds. 1987. *The Uruguay Round: A Handbook for the Multilateral Trade Negotiations*. Washington, D.C.: World Bank.

Finger, J. Michael, and Ludger Schuknecht. 2001. "Market Access Advances and Retreats: The Uruguay Round and Beyond." In Bernard Hoekman and Will Martin, eds., *Developing Countries and the WTO: A Pro-Active Agenda*. Oxford, U.K.: Basil Blackwell.

Finger, J. Michael, and Philip Schuler. 1999. "Implementation of Uruguay Round Commitments: The Development Challenge." Policy Research Working Paper Series 2215. World Bank, Development Research Group, Washington, D.C.

———. 2000. "Implementation of Uruguay Round Commitments: The Development Challenge." *World Economy* 23 (4, April): 511–25.

Finger, J. M., and L. A. Winters. 1998. "What Can the WTO Do for Developing Countries?" In Anne O. Krueger, ed., *The WTO as an International Organization*. Chicago: University of Chicago Press.

Finger, J. M., and A. J. Yeats. 1976. "Effective Protection by Transportation Costs and Tariffs: A Comparison of Magnitudes." *Quarterly Journal of Economics* (February) 90 (1, February): 169–76.

Finger, J. M., H. Keith Hall, and Douglas R. Nelson. 1982. "The Political Economy of Administered Protection." *American Economic Review* 72 (3, June): 598–611.

Finger, J. Michael, Merlinda D. Ingco, and Ulrich Reincke. 1996. "The Uruguay Round: Statistics on Tariff Concessions Given and Received." World Bank, Washington, D.C.

Finger, J. M., Ulrich Reincke, and Adriana Castro. 2002. "Market Access Bargaining in the Uruguay Round: Rigid or Relaxed Reciprocity?" In Jagdish N. Bhagwati, ed., *On Going Alone. The Case for Relaxed Reciprocity in Freeing Trade*. Cambridge, Mass.: MIT Press.

al Biodiversity: Converging Strategies. Durham, N.C.: Duke University Press.

Heeks, R. 1998. "The Uneven Profile of Indian Software Exports." Working Paper 3. Institute for Development Policy and Management. University of Manchester, U.K.

Helleiner, Gerald K., ed. 2001. Non-Traditional Exports and Development in Sub-Saharan Africa: Experience and Issues. Helsinki: World Institute for Development Economics Research.

Henderson, David. 1999. The Multilateral Agreement in Investment: A Story and Its Lessons. Wellington: New Zealand Roundtable. Available at < www.nzbr.org.nz >.

Henson, Spencer, Rupert Loader, Alan Swinbank, Maury Bredahl, and Nicole Lux. 2000. "Impact of Sanitary and Phytosanitary Measures on Developing Countries." Centre for Food Economics Research, Department of Agricultural and Food Economics, University of Reading, U.K.

Herin, Jan. 1986. "Rules of Origin and Differences between Tariff Levels in EFTA and in the EC." AELE Occasional Paper 13. Geneva.

Hertel, Thomas W. 2000. "Potential Gains from Reducing Trade Barriers in Manufacturing, Services and Agriculture." Federal Reserve Bank of St. Louis Review 82: 77–99.

Hertel, Thomas, and Will Martin. 2000. "Liberalising Agriculture and Manufactures in a Millennium Round: Implications for Developing Countries." World Economy 23 (4, April): 455–69.

Hertel, T., K. Anderson, J. F. Francois, and W. Martin. Forthcoming. "Agriculture and Non-agricultural Liberalization in the Millennium Round." In M. D. Ingco and L. A. Winters, Agriculture and the New Trade Agenda from a Development Perspective. Cambridge and New York: Cambridge University Press.

Hill, H., and P. Arthukorala. 1998. "Foreign Investment in East Asia." Asian Pacific Economic Literature 12 (2): 23–50.

Hill, T. P. 1977. "On Goods and Services." Review of Income and Wealth (23): 315–38.

Hindley, Brian, and Alasdair Smith. 1984. "Comparative Advantage and Trade in Services." World Economy 7: 369–90.

Hines, J. R. 1993. "Altered States: Taxes and the Location of FDI in America." NBER Working Paper 4397. Cambridge, Mass.: National Bureau of Economic Research.

Hirschman, Albert O. 1958. The Strategy of Economic Development. New Haven, Conn.: Yale University Press.

———. 1981a. Essays in Trespassing: Economics to Politics and Beyond. Cambridge, U.K.: Cambridge University Press.

———. 1981b. "Three Uses of Political Economy in Analyzing European Integration." In Albert O. Hirschman, Essays in Trespassing, ch. 12. London: Cambridge University Press.

Hobday, Michael. 1995. Innovation in East Asia: The Challenge to Japan. Cheltenham, U.K.: Edward Elgar.

Hodge, J. 2000. "Liberalising Communications Services in South Africa." Development Southern Africa 17 (3, September): 373–87.

———. 2001. "Estimating the Cost of Services Protection in a Developing Economy: The Case of South Africa." In Robert M. Stern, ed., Services in the International Economy. Ann Arbor: University of Michigan Press.

Hodge, J., and H. Nordas. 1999. "Trade in Services: The Impact on Developing Countries." Report to Norwegian Foreign Ministry. Processed.

Hoekman, Bernard. 1993. "Rules of Origin for Goods and Services." Journal of World Trade (August): 82–99.

———. 1995. Trade Laws and Institutions: Good Practices and the World Trade Organization. World Bank Discussion Paper 282. Washington, D.C.

———. 1996. "Assessing the General Agreement on Trade in Services." In Will Martin and L. Alan Winters, eds., The Uruguay Round and the Developing Economies. Cambridge, U.K.: Cambridge University Press.

———. 1997. "Competition Policy and the Global Trading System." World Economy 20: 383–406.

———. 1998a. "Preferential Trade Agreements." In Robert Z. Lawrence, ed., Brookings Trade Forum: 1998, 299–320. Washington, D.C.: Brookings Institution Press.

———. 1998b. "Using International Institutions to Improve Public Performance." World Bank Research Observer 13 (2): 249–69.

———.2000. "The Next Round of Services Negotiations: Identifying Priorities and Options." Federal Reserve Bank of St. Louis Review 82: 31–47.

———. 2002. "Strengthening the Global Trade Architecture for Development." World Trade Review 1: 23–46.

Hoekman, Bernard, and Carlos A. Primo Braga. 1997. "Protection and Trade in Services: A Survey." Open Economies Review 8: 285–308.

Hoekman, Bernard, and Peter Holmes. 1999. "Competition Policy, Developing Countries and the WTO." World Economy 22 (6, August): 875–94.

Hoekman, Bernard, and Michel M. Kostecki. 2001. The Political Economy of the World Trading System: The WTO and Beyond. 2d ed. New York: Oxford University Press.

Hoekman, Bernard, and Michael P. Leidy. 1992. "Holes and Loopholes in Regional Trade Arrangements and the Multilateral Trading System." In Kym Anderson and Richard Blackhurst, eds., Regional Integration and the Global Trading System, 325–60. New York: St. Martin's Press.

Hoekman, Bernard, and Will Martin, eds. 2001. Developing Countries and the WTO: A Pro-active Agenda. Oxford, U.K.: Blackwell Publishers.

Hoekman, Bernard, and Aaditya Mattoo. 2000. "Services, Economic Development and the Next Round of Negotiations on Services." Journal of International Development 12 (2, March): 283–96.

Hoekman, Bernard, and Petros Mavroidis. 1994. "Competition, Competition Policy, and the GATT." World Economy 17: 121–50.

———, eds. 1997. Law and Policy in Public Purchasing: The WTO Agreement on Government Procurement. Ann Arbor: University of Michigan Press.

———.2000. "WTO Dispute Settlement, Transparency and Surveillance." World Economy 23 (4): 527–42.

Hoekman, Bernard, and Patrick A. Messerlin. 2000. "Liberalizing Trade in Services: Reciprocal Negotiations and Regulatory Reform." In Pierre Sauvé and Robert M. Stern, eds., GATS 2000: New Directions in Services Trade Liberalization. Washington, D.C.: Brookings Institution Press and Harvard University.

Hoekman, Bernard, and Kamal Saggi. 1999. "Assessing the Case for WTO Disciplines on Investment Related Policies." Journal of Economic Integration 15: 588–610.

Hoekman, Bernard, H. L. Kee, and Marcelo Olarreaga. 2001. "Markups under Domestic and Foreign Entry." Background paper for World Development Report 2001. World Bank, Washington, D.C.

Hoekman, B., P. Low, and P. Mavroidis. 1998. "Regulation, Competition Policy, and Market Access Negotiations: Lessons from the Telecommunications Sector." In Einar Hope and Per Maeleng, eds., *Competition and Trade Policies,* 115–140. London: Routledge.

Hoekman, Bernard, Francis Ng, and Marcelo Olarreaga. 2001. "Eliminating Excessive Tariffs in the QUAD and Least Developed Country Exports." Policy Research Working Paper Series 2604. World Bank, Washington, D.C.

Hoff, Karla, and Joseph E. Stiglitz. 2000. "Modern Economic Theory and Development." In Gerald M. Meier and Joseph E. Stiglitz, eds., *Frontiers of Development Economics: The Future in Perspective.* New York: Oxford University Press.

Holmes, P., J. Kempton, and F. McGowan. 1996. "International Competition Policy and Telecommunications: Lessons from the EU and Prospects for the WTO." *Telecommunications Policy* 20 (10): 755–67.

Honglin Zang, K., and J. Markusen. 1999. "Vertical Multinationals and Host-Country Characteristics." *Journal of Development Economics* 59: 233–52.

Hope, Einar, and Per Maeleng, eds. 1998. *Competition and Trade Policies.* London: Routledge. Available at <http://www.southcentre.org/publications/competition/toc.htm#TopOfPage>.

Hudec, Robert E. 1978. *Adjudication of International Trade Disputes.* London: Trade Policy Research Centre.

———. 1987. *Developing Countries in the GATT Legal System.* London: Trade Policy Research Centre.

———. 1990. *The GATT Legal System and World Trade Diplomacy.* 2d ed. Salem, N.H.: Butterworths.

———. 1993. *Enforcing International Trade Law.* Salem, N.H.: Butterworths.

Hufbauer, Gary Clyde, and Kimberly Ann Elliott. 1993. *Measuring the Costs of Protection in the United States.* Washington, D.C.: Institute for International Economics.

Hufbauer, Gary Clyde, and Tony Warren. 1999. "The Globalization of Services: What Has Happened? What Are the Implications?" Working Paper 99-12. October. Institute for International Economics, Washington, D.C.

Hugenholtz, P. Bernt. 2000. "Caching and Copyright: The Right of Temporary Copying." *European Intellectual Property Review* 22 (10): 482–93.

Hull, Cordell. 1948. *The Memoirs of Cordell Hull.* New York: Macmillan.

Ianchovichina, Elena, W. Martin, and E. Fukase. 2000. "Modelling the Impact of China's Accession to the WTO." Prepared for the Third Annual Conference on Global Economic Analysis, Monash University, Adelaide, Australia, June 27–30. Available at < www.monash.edu.au/policy/conf2000.htm >.

Ianchovichina, Elena, Aaditya Mattoo, and Marcelo Olarreaga. 2001. "Unrestricted Market Access for Sub-Saharan Africa: How Much Is It Worth and Who Pays for It?" Policy Research Working Paper Series 2595. Washington, D.C., World Bank.

Ianchovichina, Elena, Robert McDougall, and Thomas Hertel. 1999. "A Disequilibrium Model of International Capital Mobility." Presented at the Second Annual Conference on Global Economic Analysis, Ebberuk, Denmark, June 20–22.

ICPAC (International Competition Policy Advisory Committee) 2000. "Final Report." Available at <http://www.usdoj.gov/atr/icpac/finalreport.htm>

ICRIER (Indian Council for Research on International Economic Relations). 1999. [Sectoral reports on health services, legal services, accountancy services, construction and engineering services, and software services.] Prepared for the Ministry of Commerce, New Delhi.

ILO (International Labour Organization). 1998. *Labor and Social Issues Relating to Export Processing Zones.* Geneva.

IMF (International Monetary Fund). 1999. *Annual Report on Exchange Arrangements and Exchange Restrictions, 1999.* Washington, D.C.

IMF. 2000. *International Capital Markets: Developments, Prospects and Key Policy Issues.* World Economic and Financial Surveys. September. Washington, D.C.

IMF. Various issues. *Direction of Trade Statistics.* Washington, D.C.

Ingco, Merlinda, John Nash, and others. Forthcoming. "Agriculture, the New Trade Agenda, and the WTO Round: Creating A Trading System for Development." World Bank, Washington, D.C.

ITCB (International Textiles and Clothing Bureau). 1999. "Experience with the Implementation of the ATC: Main Areas of Concern, Article-by-Article." April. Geneva.

Jackson, John H. 1997. *The World Trading System.* 2d ed. Cambridge, Mass.: MIT Press.

Janow, Merit E. 2000. "Transatlantic Cooperation on Competition Policy." In Simon J. Evenett, Alexander Lehmann, and Benn Steil, eds., *Antitrust Goes Global: What Future for Transatlantic Cooperation?* 29–56. Washington, D.C.: Brookings Institution Press and Harvard University.

JETRO (Japanese External Trade Relations Organization). 2001. White Paper, "Foreign Direct Investment 2001: Accelerated Corporate Realignment through Mergers and Acquisitions." Tokyo.

Jha, Veena, and René Vossenaar. 2001. "Breaking the Deadlock: A Positive Agenda on Trade, Environment and Development?" In Gary P. Sampson and W. Bradnee Chambers, eds., *Trade, Environment, and the Millennium.* 2d ed. Tokyo: United Nations University.

Jones, P., and J. Hudson. 1996. "Standardization and the Costs of Assessing Quality." *European Journal of Political Economy* 12: 355–61.

Junta del Acuerdo de Cartagena. 1995. "Proyecto de resolución sobre criterios y procedimientos para fijar requisitos específicos de origen (REOS)." August. Lima.

Kalirajan, Kaleeswaran, Greg McGuire, Duc Nguyen-Hong, and Michael Schuele. 2001. "The Price Impact of Restrictions on Banking Services." In Christopher Findlay and Tony Warren, eds., *Impediments to Trade in Services: Measurement and Policy Implications.* London and New York: Routledge.

Kanbur, Ravi. 2001. "Economic Policy, Distribution and Poverty: The Nature of Disagreements." Cornell University, Ithaca, New York. Processed. Available at <http://www.people.cornell.edu/pages/sk145>.

Kang, Nam-Hoog, and Sara Johansson. 2000. "Cross-Border Mergers and Acquisitions: Their Role in Industrial Globalization." STI Working Paper 2000/1. OECD, Paris.

Kapur, Devesh, and Richard Webb. 2000. "Governance-Related Conditionalities of the International Financial Institutions." Group of 24 Discussion Paper 6. Available at <http://www.ksg.harvard.edu/rodrik/g24-kapurwebb.pdf>.

Karsenty, Guy. 2000. "Just How Big Are the Stakes? An Assessment of Trade in Services by Mode of Supply." In Pierre Sauvé and Robert M. Stern, eds., *GATS 2000: New Directions in Services*

Malan, Rian. 2000. "In the Jungle." *Rolling Stone* (May 25).

Malueg, David A., and Marius Schwartz. 1994. "Parallel Imports, Demand Dispersion, and International Price Discrimination." *Journal of International Economics* 37: 167–96.

Mann, Catherine. 1999. *Is the U.S. Trade Deficit Sustainable?* Washington, D.C.: Institute for International Economics.

Mann, Catherine, and Sarah Cleeland Knight. 2000. "Electronic Commerce in the World Trade Organization." In Jeffrey Schott, ed., *The WTO after Seattle*. Washington, D.C.: Institute for International Economics.

Mann, Catherine L., Sue E. Eckert, and Sarah Cleeland Knight. 2000. *Global Electronic Commerce: A Policy Primer*. Washington, D.C.: Institute for International Economics.

Mansfield, Edwin. 1994. *Intellectual Property Protection, Foreign Direct Investment, and Technology Transfer*. International Finance Corporation Discussion Paper 19. Washington, D.C.: World Bank.

———. 1995. *Intellectual Property Protection, Direct Investment, and Technology Transfer: Germany, Japan, and the United States*. International Finance Corporation Discussion Paper 27. Washington, D.C.: World Bank.

Mansfield, E., and Anthony Romeo. 1980. "Technology Transfer to Overseas Subsidiaries by U.S. Based Firms." *Quarterly Journal of Economics* 95: 737–49.

Mansfield, E., M. Schwartz, and S. Wagner, 1981. "Imitation Costs and Patents: An Empirical Study." *Economic Journal* 91: 907–18.

Manual on Statistics of International Trade in Services. 2000. Prepared by the Commission of the European Union, the IMF, the OECD, the United Nations, UNCTAD, and the WTO.

Marko, M. 1998. "An Evaluation of the Basic Telecommunications Services Agreement." CIES Policy Discussion Paper 98/09. Centre for International Economic Studies, University of Adelaide, Australia.

Markusen, James R. 1983. "Factor Movements and Commodity Trade as Complements." *Journal of International Economics* 13: 341–56.

———. 1989. "Trade in Producer Services and in Other Specialized Intermediate Inputs." *American Economic Review* 79 (1): 85–95.

———. 1995. "The Boundaries of Multinational Enterprises and the Theory of International Trade." *Journal of Economic Perspectives* 9: 169–89.

———. 2001. "Multilateral Rules on Foreign Direct Investment: The Developing Countries' Stake." *Review of International Economics*. 9 (2): 287–302.

Markusen, James R., Thomas F. Rutherford, and Linda Hunter. 1995. "Trade Liberalization in a Multinational Dominated Industry." *Journal of International Economics* 38: 95–17.

Markusen, James, Thomas Rutherford, and David Tarr. 2000. "Foreign Direct Investment in Services and the Domestic Market for Expertise." Policy Research Working Paper Series 2413. World Bank, Washington, D.C.

Marsden, P. 2000. "The Divide on Verticals." In Simon J. Evenett, Alexander Lehmann, and Benn Steil, eds., *Antitrust Goes Global: What Future for Transatlantic Cooperation?* Washington, D.C.: Brookings Institution Press.

Martin, W. 1996. "The Abolition of the Multi-Fiber Arrangement and Its Implications for Fiber Markets." Prepared for the conference, "The WTO and the Uruguay Round Agreement: Implications for South Asian Agriculture," Katmandu, April.

Martin, Will, and Devashish Mitra. 2001. "Productivity Growth and Convergence in Agriculture and Manufacturing." *Economic Development and Cultural Change* 49 (2, January): 403–22.

Martin, Will, and Mari Pangestu. Forthcoming. *Options for Global Trade Reform: A View from the Asia-Pacific*. New York: Cambridge University Press.Martin, W., and P. Urban. 1984. "Modeling Producer Response under Support Price and Stabilization Schemes." Paper presented to the 28th Annual Conference of the Australian Agricultural Economics Society, Sydney.

Martin, Will, and L. Alan Winters, eds. 1996. *The Uruguay Round and the Developing Economies*. Cambridge, U.K.: Cambridge University Press.

Martin, Will, and K. Yagashima.1993. "Concerted Trade Liberalization and Economic Development in the Asia-Pacific Region." Background paper for *East Asia's Trade and Investment: Regional and Global Gains from Liberalization* (Washington, D.C.: World Bank, 1994). World Bank, International Economics Department, Washington, D.C.

Martinez de Prera, Josefina. 2000. "Revenue-Neutral Tariff Reform: Welfare Effects of Uniform Tariffs in 13 Developing Countries." Ph.D. dissertation, University of Colorado, Boulder. Available at < http://ussub.colorado.edu/~martindp />.

Mashayeki, M. 2000. "Trade-Related Investment Measures." In UNCTAD, *Positive Agenda and Future Trade Negotiations*. Geneva.

Maskus, Keith. 1997. "Should Core Labor Standards Be Imposed through International Trade Policy?" Policy Research Working Paper 1817, World Bank, Washington, D.C.

———. 1998. "The Role of Intellectual Property Rights in Encouraging Foreign Direct Investment and Technology Transfer." *Duke Journal of Comparative and International Law* 9 (1): 109–61.

———. 2000a. *Intellectual Property Rights in the Global Economy*. Washington, D.C.: Institute for International Economics.

———. 2000b. "Regulatory Standards in the WTO: Comparing Intellectual Property Rights with Competition Policy, Environmental Protection and Core Labor Standards." World Bank, Washington, D.C. Available at <http://www1.worldbank.org/wbiep/trade/TradePolicy.html# TRIPS>

———. 2000c. "Strengthening Intellectual Property Rights in Lebanon." In Bernard Hoekman and Jamel Zarrouk, eds., *Catching Up with the Competition: Trade Opportunities and Challenges for Arab Countries*, 251–84. Ann Arbor: University of Michigan Press.

———. 2001. "Options for Raising Access to Essential Medicines: Report to Working Group 4 of the Commission on Macroeconomics and Health." World Health Organization, Geneva.

Maskus, Keith E., and Yongmin Chen. 2000. "Vertical Price Control and Parallel Imports: Theory and Evidence." Policy Research Working Paper Series 2461. World Bank, Washington, D.C.

Maskus, Keith E., and Mohamed Lahouel. 2000. "Competition Policy and Intellectual Property Rights in Developing Countries." *World Economy* 23: 595–611.

Maskus, Keith E., and Christine McDaniel. 1999. "Impacts of the Japanese Patent System on Productivity Growth." *Japan and the World Economy* 11: 557–74.

Maskus, Keith, and Mohan Penubarti. 1995. "How Trade-Related Are Intellectual Property Rights?" *Journal of International Economics* 39: 227–48.

Maskus, Keith E., and John S. Wilson. 2001. *Quantifying the Impact of Technical Standards to Trade: Can It Be Done?* Ann Arbor: University of Michigan Press.

Maskus, Keith E., Sean M. Dougherty, and Andrew Mertha. 1998. "Intellectual Property Rights and Economic Development in China." Presented at the Southwest China Regional Conference on Intellectual Property Rights and Economic Development, Chongqing, September 16.

Maskus, K. E., T. Otsuki, and J. S. Wilson. 2000. "Quantifying the Impact of Technical Barriers to Trade: A Framework for Analysis." Policy Research Working Paper Series 2512. World Bank, Washington, D.C.

Masuyama, S., D. Vanderbrink, and S. Y. Chia. 1997. *Industrial Policies in East Asia*. Nomura Institute and Institute of Southeast Asian Studies, Tokyo Club Foundation for Global Studies.

Mathis, J. 2000 "Towards a Positive Agenda for Multilateral Negotiations on Competition Policy: Interests of Developing Countries." In UNCTAD, *Positive Agenda and Future Trade Negotiations*. Geneva.

Mattoo, Aaditya. 1999. "Financial Services and the WTO: Liberalization Commitments of the Developing and Transition Economies." Policy Research Working Paper Series 2184. World Bank, Washington, D.C.

————. 2000. "Developing Countries in the New Round of GATS Negotiations: Towards a Pro-active Role." *World Economy* 23 (4): 471–89.

————. Forthcoming. "Shaping Future Rules for Trade in Services: Lessons from the GATS." In Takatoshi Ito and Anne Krueger, ed., *Trade in Services*. Cambridge, Mass.: National Bureau of Economic Research.

Mattoo, Aaditya, and Marcelo Olarreaga. 2001. "Reciprocity across Modes of Supply in the World Trade Organization: A Negotiating Formula." Policy Research Working Paper Series 2373. World Bank, Washington, D.C.

Mattoo, Aaditya, and Ludger Schuknecht. 2000. "Trade Policies for Electronic Commerce." Policy Research Working Paper Series 2380. World Bank, Development Research Group, Washington, D.C.

Mattoo, Aditya, and Robert Stern. Forthcoming. *India and the WTO*.

Mattoo, Aaditya, and Arvind Subramanian. 1998. "Regulatory Autonomy and Multilateral Disciplines." *Journal of International Economic Law* 1: 303–22.

Mazzoleni, Robert, and Richard R. Nelson. 1998. "The Benefits and Costs of Strong Patent Protection: A Contribution to the Current Debate." *Research Policy* 27: 273–84.

McAfee, R. Preston, and John McMillan. 1989. "Government Procurement and International Trade." *Journal of International Economics* 26: 291–308.

McCulloch, Neil, L. Alan Winters, and Xavier Cirera. 2001. *Trade Liberalization and Poverty: A Handbook*. London: Centre for Economic Policy Research.

McDougall, Robert, Aziz Elbehri, and Truong P. Truong. 1998. "Global Trade, Assistance, and Protection: The GTAP 4 Data Base." Center for Global Trade Analysis, Purdue University, West Lafayette, Ind.

McGuire, Greg. 1998. *Australia's Restrictions on Trade in Financial Services*. Staff Research Paper. Productivity Commission, Canberra.

McGuire, Greg, and Michael Schuele. 2001. "Restrictiveness of International Trade in Banking Services." In Christopher Findlay and Tony Warren, eds., *Impediments to Trade in Services: Measurement and Policy Implications*. London and New York: Routledge.

McGuire, Greg, Michael Schuele, and T. Smith. 2001. "Restrictiveness of International Trade in Maritime Services." In Christopher Findlay and Tony Warren, eds., *Impediments to Trade in Services: Measurement and Policy Implications*. London and New York: Routledge.

McKibbin, Warwick, and P. J. Wilcoxen. 1996. "The Role of Services in Modeling the Global Economy." *Asia-Pacific Economic Review* 2: 2–13.

Mehta, P. 2000. "Taming Unilever in Bhutan." Consumer Unity & Trust Society (CUTS), Jaipur.

Mendelsohn, R., and M. J. Balick. 1995. "The Value of Undiscovered Pharmaceuticals in Tropical Forests." *Economic Botany* 49 (2): 223–28.

Merges, R. P., and R. R. Nelson. 1990. "On the Complex Economics of Patent Scope." *Columbia Law Review* 90 (4, May): 839–916.

Messerlin, Patrick A. 2001. *Measuring the Costs of Protection in Europe: European Commercial Policy in the 2000s*. Washington, D.C.: Institute for International Economics.

Messerlin, Patrick, and Karl Sauvant. 1990. *The Uruguay Round: Services in the World Economy*. Washington, D.C.: World Bank.

Michaely, Michael. 1996. "Trade Preferential Agreements in Latin America: An Ex-Ante Assessment." Policy Research Working Paper Series 1583. World Bank, Washington, D.C.

Michaely, Michael, Demetris Papageorgiou, and Armeane M. Choksi. 1991. *Liberalizing Foreign Trade: Lessons of Experience in the Developing World*, vol. 7. Oxford, U.K.: Blackwell.

Michalopoulos, Constantine. 1998a. "Developing Countries' Participation in the World Trade Organization." Policy Research Working Paper Series 1906. World Bank, Washington, D.C.

————. 1998b. "WTO Accession for Countries in Transition." *Post-Soviet Prospects* 6 (3. June).

————. 1999a. "The Developing Countries in the WTO." *World Economy* 22 (1, January): 117–43.

————. 1999b. "The Integration of Transition Economies into the World Trading System." Policy Research Working Paper Series 2182. World Bank, Washington, D.C.

————. 1999c. "Trade Policy and Market Access Issues for Developing Countries: Implications for the Millennium Round." Policy Research Working Paper Series 2214. World Bank, Washington, D.C.

————. *Developing Countries and the WTO*. New York: Palgrave.

Michalopoulos, Constantine, and L. Alan Winters. 1997. "Summary and Overview." In Peter D. Ehrenhaft and others, eds., *Policies on Imports from Economies in Transition*. Studies of Economies in Transformation 22. Washington, D.C.: World Bank.

MITI (Ministry for Industry and Trade), Japan. 1999. *1999 Report on the WTO Consistency of Trade Policies by Major Trading Partners*. Tokyo, Industrial Structure Council, MITI.

Mitra, Pradeep. 1992. "The Coordinated Reform of Tariffs and Indirect Taxes." *World Bank Research Observer* 7 (2): 195–218.

————. 1994. "Protective and Revenue Raising Trade Taxes: Theory and Application to India." *Economic Studies Quarterly* 45 (3): 265–87.

Mochebelele, Motsamai. 1998. "Trade in Services: Potential and Prospects for the Economy of Lesotho." Prepared for CAPAS regional meeting, Mauritius, December 7–9. Processed.

Approach." *American Journal of International Law* 94 (2, April): 335–47.

PECC (Pacific Economic Cooperation Council). 1995. *Survey of Impediments to Trade and Investment in the APEC Region.* Singapore.

Petri, Peter A. 1997. "Foreign Direct Investment in a Computable General Equilibrium Framework." Prepared for the conference "Making APEC Work: Economic Challenges and Policy Alternatives," Keio University, Tokyo, March 13–14.

Petrazzini, B. A., and P. Lovelock. 1996. "Telecommunications in the Region: Comparative Case Studies." Presented at the International Institute for Communication Telecommunications Forum, Sydney, Australia, April 22–23.

Phillips, David A. 2001. "Implementing the Market Approach to Enterprise Support: An Evaluation of Ten Matching Grant Schemes." World Bank, Washington, D.C. Processed.

Pinheiro A. 2000. "The Brazilian Privatisation Experience: What's Next?" Prepared for the Global Development Network Conference, Tokyo, December 10–13.

Pistor, Katharina. 2000. "The Standardization of Law and Its Effect on Developing Economies." Group of 24 Discussion Paper 4. Available at <http://www.ksg.harvard.edu/rodrik/g24-pistor.pdf>.

Poapongsakorn, N. 2000. "The Thai Automotive Industry." Prepared for the PECC-ASEAN Auto Project, School of Advanced Management Technology, Manila.

Porges, A. 2000. "The Banana War: Whose Market Access?" World Bank, Washington, D.C. Processed.

Preeg, E. 1994. "Traders in a Brave New World: The Uruguay Round and the Future of the International Trading System." Center for Strategic and International Studies, Washington, D.C. Processed.

Productivity Commission. 1998. *Inquiry into the Automotive Industry.* Canberra: Australian Government Publishing Service.

Pursell, Garry. 1999. "Export Policies and Institutions in Developing Countries: The Role of the World Bank." World Bank, Washington, D.C. Processed.

———. 2001. "The Australian Experience with FDI and Local Content Programs in the Auto Industry." *Journal of World Trade* [..].

Rajapathirana, S., C. Lusthaus, and M. Adrien. 2000. "Review of the Integrated Framework for Technical Assistance for Trade Development of Least Developed Countries." World Bank, Washington, D.C. Processed.

Ramachandran, Vijaya. 1993. "Technology Transfer, Firm Ownership, and Investment in Human Capital." *Review of Economics and Statistics* 75: 664–70.

Ramos, Raul, and Juan Rosellón. 1991. "La economía elemental de las reglas de origen." *El Trimestre Económico* 481–96.

Ramsey, F. P. 1927. "A Contribution to the Theory of Taxation." *Economic Journal* 37: 47–61.

Rauch, J. E. 1999. "Networks versus Markets in International Trade." *Journal of International Economics* 48: 7–35.

Ravallion, Martin. 1999. "Protecting the Poor in Crisis." PREM Note 12. World Bank, Washington, D.C.

Ravallion, Martin, and Dominique van de Walle. 1991. "The Impact on Poverty of Food Pricing Reforms: A Welfare Analysis for Indonesia." *Journal of Policy Modeling* 13 (2): 281–99.

Raven, John. 2000. *Trade and Transport Facilitation: An Audit Methodology.* Washington, D.C.: World Bank.

Raven, Peter H., and Jeffrey A. McNeely. 1998. "Biological Extinction: Its Scope and Meaning for Us." In Lakshman D. Guruswamy and

Jeffrey A. McNeely, eds., *Protection of Global Biodiversity: Converging Strategies.* Durham, N.C.: Duke University Press.

Rege, Vinod. 1999. "Developing Country Participation in Negotiations Leading to the Adoption of the WTO Agreement on Customs Valuation and Preshipment Inspection: A Public Choice Analysis." *World Competition* 22 (1, March): 37–117.

Reichman, Jerome H. 1994. "Legal Hybrids between the Patent and Copyright Paradigms." *Columbia Law Review* 94: 2432–558.

———. 1998. "Securing Compliance with the TRIPS Agreement after US v India." *Journal of International Economic Law* 1 (4, December): 603–06.

———. 2000. "Of Green Tulips and Legal Kudzu: Repackaging Rights in Subpatentable Invention." *Vanderbilt Law Review* 53: 1743–98.

———. 2001. "IPR as Related to Crafts in India: Compensatory Liability Legislation." Presented to the Crafts Workshop, India, World Bank, Washington, D.C., January 9.

Reichman, J. H., and Pamela Samuelson. 1997. "Intellectual Property Rights in Data?" *Vanderbilt Law Review* 50: 51–166.

Reid, Walter V. 1998. "Halting the Loss of Biodiversity: International Institutional Measures." In Lakshman D. Guruswamy and Jeffrey A. McNeely, eds., *Protection of Global Biodiversity: Converging Strategies.* Durham, N.C.: Duke University Press.

Reinbothe, Jörg, Maria Martin-Prat, and Silke Von Lewinsky. 1997. "The New WIPO Treaties: A First Résumé." *European Intellectual Property Review* 4: 171–76.

Revesz, R. 1992. "Rehabilitating Interstate Competition: Rethinking the 'Race to the Bottom' Rationale for Federal Environmental Regulation." *New York University Law Review* 67: 1210–54.

Rhee, Yung Whee, Bruce Ross-Larson, and Garry Pursell. 1984. *Korea's Competitive Edge: Managing Entry into World Markets.* Baltimore, Md.: Johns Hopkins University Press.

Rhodes, Sylvia A. 2000. "The Article 21.5/22 Problem: Clarification through Bilateral Agreements?" *Journal of International Economic Law* 3 (3, September): 553–58.

Richardson, J. David. 1995. "Income Inequality and Trade: How to Link, What to Conclude." *Journal of Economic Perspectives* (9, Summer): 33–56.

Richardson, Martin. 1991. "The Effects of a Content Requirement on a Foreign Duopsonist." *Journal of International Economics* 31: 143–55.

———. "Content Protection with Foreign Capital." *Oxford Economic Papers* 45: 103–17.

Ricupero, Rubens. 1998. "Integration of Developing Countries into the Multilateral Trading System." In Jagdish Bhagwati and Matthias Hirsch, eds., *The Uruguay Round and Beyond: Essays in Honor of Arthur Dunkel.* Ann Arbor: University of Michigan Press.

———. "A Development Round: Converting Rhetoric into Substance." Presented at John F. Kennedy School of Government symposium, "Efficiency, Equity and Legitimacy: The Multilateral Trading System at the Millennium," Harvard University, Cambridge, Mass., June 1–2.

Rivera-Batiz, L., and P. Romer. 1991. "International Integration and Endogenous Growth." *Quarterly Journal of Economics* 106: 531–56.

Robinson, Sherman, Zhi Wang, and Will Martin. 2002. "Capturing the Implications of Services Trade Liberalization." *Economic System Research* 14 (March).

Rodriguez, Francisco, and Dani Rodrik. 2001. "Trade Policy and Economic Growth: A Skeptic's Guide to the Cross-National Evidence." In Ben S. Bernanke and Kenneth Rogoff, eds., *NBER Macroeconomics Annual 2000*. Cambridge, Mass.: MIT Press.

Rodriguez-Clare, A. 1996. "The Division of Labour and Economic Development." *Journal of Development Economics* 49: 3–32.

Rodrik, Dani. 1987. "The Economics of Export-Performance Requirements." *Quarterly Journal of Economics* 102: 633–50.

———. 1996. "Labor Standards in International Trade: Do They Matter, and What Do We Do about Them?" Overseas Development Council, Washington, D.C. Processed.

———. 1997. *Has Globalization Gone Too Far?* Washington, D.C.: Institute for International Economics.

———. 1998. "Why Do More Open Economies Have Bigger Governments?" *Journal of Political Economy* 106 (October): 997–1032.

———. 1999. *Making Openness Work: The New Global Economy and the Developing Countries*. Washington, D.C.: Overseas Development Council.

———. 2000a. "Can Integration into the World Economy Substitute for a Development Strategy?" June. Harvard University, Cambridge, Mass. Processed.

———. 2000b. "Institutions for High-Quality Growth: What They Are and How to Acquire Them." *Studies in Comparative International Development* 35 (3, fall): 3–31.

Rollo, Jim, and L. Alan Winters. 2000. "Subsidiarity and Governance Challenges for the WTO: Environmental and Labour Standards." *World Economy* 23 (4): 561–76.

Romer, David. 1993. "Openness and Inflation: Theory and Evidence." *Quarterly Journal of Economics* 108 (4, November): 870–903.

Rose, Nancy L. 1985. "The Incidence of Regulatory Rents in the Motor Carrier Industry." *RAND Journal of Economics* 16 (3, autumn): 299–318.

Rose-Ackerman, Susan. 1999. *Corruption and Government*. Cambridge, U.K.: Cambridge University Press.

Sachs, Jeffrey. 2001. "A New Paradigm for Development." In Roger B. Porter, Pierre Sauvé, Arvind Subramanian, and Americo Beviglia-Zampetti, eds., *Efficiency, Equity, and Legitimacy: The Multilateral Trading System at the Millennium*. Washington, D.C.: Brookings Institution Press and Harvard University.

Sachs, Jeffrey, and Felipe Larraín. 1999. "Why Dollarization Is More Straitjacket Than Salvation." *Foreign Policy* (fall): 80–92.

Sachs, Jeffrey, and Andrew Warner. 1995. "Economic Reform and the Process of Global Integration." *Brookings Papers on Economic Activity* 1: 1–118.

Safadi, R., and S. Laird. 1996. "The Uruguay Round Agreements: Impact on Developing Countries." *World Development* 24 (7): 1223–42.

Sampson, G. 1987. "Safeguards." In J. Michael Finger and Andrzej Olechowski, eds., *The Uruguay Round: A Handbook for the Multilateral Negotiations*. Washington, D.C.: World Bank.

———. 1999. "Trade, Environment and the WTO." Overseas Development Council, Washington, D.C.

Sapir, André. 1997. "The Political Economy of EC Regionalism." *European Economic Review* 42: 717–32.

———. 1998. "GATS 1994–2000." *Journal of World Trade* 33: 51–66.

Sartar, S. 2000. "Privatisation and Beyond: The Indian Experience in Infrastructure Services." Prepared for the Global Development Network Conference, Tokyo, December 10–13. Processed.

Satapathy, C. 1994. "Valuation of Goods Traded Internationally, with Special Reference to Implementation of GATT Agreement in Developing Countries." University of Bath.

———. 2000. "Implementation of WTO Agreement on Customs Valuation." *Economic and Political Weekly* (Mumbai, India) 35 (25, June 17–23).

Sauvé, Pierre, and James Gillespie. 2000. "Financial Services and the GATS 2000 Round." In Robert E. Litan and Anthony M. Santomero, eds., *Brookings-Wharton Papers on Financial Services: 2000*, 412–52. Washington, D.C.: Brookings Institution Press.

Sauvé, Pierre, and Brenda Gonzalez-Hermosillo, 1993. "Implications of the NAFTA for Canadian Financial Institutions." *C. D. Howe Commentary*, no. 44 (April). Toronto: C. D. Howe Institute.

Sauvé, Pierre, and Robert M. Stern. 2000. *GATS 2000: New Directions in Services Trade Liberalization*. Washington, D.C.: Brookings Institution Press and Harvard University.

Sauvé, Pierre, and Christopher Wilkie. 2000. "Investment Liberalization in GATS." In Pierre Sauvé and Robert M. Stern, eds., *GATS 2000: New Directions in Services Trade Liberalization*, 331–63. Washington, D.C.: Brookings Institution Press and Harvard University.

Scherer, F. M. 1977. *The Economic Effects of Compulsory Patent Licensing*. Monograph Series in Finance and Economics. New York: New York University.

———. 1994. *Competition Policies for an Integrated World Economy*. Washington, D.C.: Brookings Institution Press.

———. 2000. *Competition Policy: Domestic and International*. Cheltenham, U.K.: Edward Elgar.

Scherer, F. M., and J. Watal. 2001. "Post-TRIPS Options for Access to Patented Medicines in Developing Countries." Harvard University, Cambridge, Mass. Processed.

Schiff, Maurice, and Alberto Valdés. 1992. *The Plundering of Agriculture in Developing Countries*. Washington, D.C.: World Bank.

Schive, Chi. 1990. *The Foreign Factor: The Multinational Corporations' Contribution to the Economic Modernization of the Republic of China*. Stanford, Calif.: Hoover Institution Press.

Schott, Jeffrey J., and Johanna W. Buurman. 1994. *The Uruguay Round: An Assessment*. Washington, D.C.: Institute for International Economics.

Schott, J. J., and J. Watal. 2000. "Decision-making in the WTO." *International Economics Policy Briefs* 00-2 (March).

Scollay, R. 1996. "The Closer Economic Relations Agreement." In B. Bora and C. Findlay, eds., *Regional Integration and the Asia Pacific*. Melbourne: Oxford University Press.

Scotchmer, Suzanne. 1991. "Standing on the Shoulders of Giants: Cumulative Research and Patent Law." *Journal of Economic Perspectives* 5 (1, winter): 29–41.

Sedjo, Roger A. 1992. "Property Rights, Genetic Resources, and Biotechnological Change." *Journal of Law and Economics* 35 (April): 199–213.

Sharer, Robert, and others. 1998. "Trade Liberalization in IMF-Supported Programs." *World Economic and Financial Surveys*. Washington, D.C.: IMF.

Shatz, Howard J., and David G. Tarr. 2000. "Exchange Rate Overvaluation and Trade Protection: Lessons from Experience." Policy Research Working Paper Series 2289. World Bank, Washington, D.C.

Shiells, Clint, Robert Stern, and A. Deardorff. 1986. "Estimates of the Elasticities of Substitutions between Imports and Home

USITC (U.S. International Trade Commission). 1987. "Standard-ization of Rules of Origin." Report to the Committee on Ways and Means of the U.S. House of Representatives. Washington, D.C.

———. 1997. *The Dynamic Effects of Trade Liberalization: An Empir-ical Analysis.* Investigation 332-375. Publication 3069. October. Washington, D.C.

———. 1998. *Global Assessment of Standards Barriers to Trade in the Information Technology Industry.* Publication 3141. Novem-ber. Washington, D.C.

Valles, Cherise, and Brendan McGivern. 2000. "The Right to Retal-iate under the WTO Agreement: The Sequencing Problem." *Journal of World Trade* 34 (2): 63–84.

Van, P. H., and H. Y. Wan. 1999. "Emulative Development through Trade Expansion: East Asian Evidence." In A. Woodland and J. J. Piggott, eds., *International Trade Policy and the Pacific Rim.* Sydney: Macmillan.

Vandermerve, S., and M. Chadwik. 1989. "The Internalisation of Services." *Service Industries Journal* 9: 79–93.

Varian, Hal R. 1985. "Price Discrimination and Social Welfare." *American Economic Review* 75: 870–75.

Vaubel, R. 1986. "A Public Choice Approach to International Organization." *Public Choice* 51: 39–57.

Verikos, George, and Keven Hanslow. 1999. "Modeling the Effects of Implementing the Uruguay Round: A Comparison Using the GTAP Model under Alternative Treatments of International Capital Mobility." Presented at the Second Annual Conference on Global Economic Analysis, Ebberuk, Denmark, June 20–22.

Vermulst, Edwin A. 1994. "Rules of Origin as Commercial Policy Instruments? Revisited." In Edwin A. Vermulst, Jacques Bour-geois, and Paul Waer, eds., *Rules of Origin in International Trade: A Comparative Study,* 433–84. Ann Arbor: University of Michigan Press.

Vermulst, Edwin, Jacques Bourgeois, and Paul Waer, eds. 1994. *Rules of Origin in International Trade: A Comparative Study.* Ann Arbor: University of Michigan Press.

Vinje, Thomas C. 1997. "The New WIPO Copyright Treaty: A Happy Result in Geneva." *European Intellectual Property Review* 5: 230–36.

Vogel, David. 1995. *Trading Up: Consumer and Environmental Regu-lation in a Global Economy.* Cambridge, Mass.: Harvard Univer-sity Press.

Vossenaar, Rene. 1999. "Process and Production Methods: Sizing up the Issues from the South." In Halina Ward and Duncan Brack, eds., *Trade, Investment and the Environment.* Washing-ton, D.C.: Brookings Institution Press.

Vousden, Neil. 1990. *The Economics of Trade Protection.* Cam-bridge, U.K.: Cambridge University Press.

Waller, Spencer Weber. 2000. "Anti-Cartel Cooperation." In Simon J. Evenett, Alexander Lehmann, and Benn Steil, eds., *Antitrust Goes Global: What Future for Transatlantic Cooperation?* Wash-ington, D.C: Brookings Institution Press.

Walmsley, Terrie Louise. 1999. "Incorporating International Capi-tal Ownership into the GTAP Mode: Results for Asia-Pacific Trade Liberalisation." Presented at the Second Annual Confer-ence on Global Economic Analysis, Ebberuk, Denmark, June 20–22.

Wang, Z. K., and L. Alan Winters. 1997. "Africa's Role in Multilat-eral Trade Negotiations: Past and Future." *Journal of African Economies* 7 (supp. 1).

Ward, H. 1996. "Common but Differentiated Debates: Environ-ment, Labour, and the World Trade Organization." *Internation-al and Comparative Law Quarterly* 45 (July): 592–632.

Warr, P. G. 1978. "The Case against Tariff Compensation." *Aus-tralian Journal of Agricultural Economics* 22 (2, August): 85–98.

Warren, Tony. 2001a. "The Application of the Frequency Approach to Trade in Telecommunications Services." In Christopher Findlay and Tony Warren, eds., *Impediments to Trade in Services: Measurement and Policy Implications.* London and New York: Routledge.

———. 2001b. "Quantity Impacts of Trade and Investment Restrictions in Telecommunications." In Christopher Findlay and Tony Warren, eds., *Impediments to Trade in Services: Mea-surement and Policy Implications.* London and New York: Rout-ledge.

Warren, Tony, and Christopher Findlay. 2000. "How Significant Are the Barriers? Measuring Impediments to Trade in Services." In Pierre Sauvé and Robert M. Stern, eds., *GATS 2000: New Directions in Services Trade Liberalization.* Washington, D.C.: Brookings Institution Press and Harvard University.

Watal, Jayashree. 1995. "MNEs, Market Structure and Price Com-petition in Patentable Drug Markets in India." Presented at the seminar on Technology and Globalization, Institute for Eco-nomic Growth, Delhi, April 3.

———. 1998. "The TRIPS Agreement and Developing Countries: Strong, Weak or Balanced Protection?" *Journal of World Intellec-tual Property* 1 (2, March): 281–307.

———. 2000a. *Intellectual Property Rights in the World Trade Orga-nization: The Way Forward for Developing Countries.* New Delhi: Oxford University Press.

———. 2000b. "Pharmaceutical Patents, Prices and Welfare Losses: A Simulation Study of Policy Options for India under the WTO TRIPS Agreement." *World Economy* 23 (5, May): 733–52.

———. 2001. *Intellectual Property Rights in the WTO and Develop-ing Countries.* The Hague: Kluwer Law International.

Watson, Peter. 2000. "Export Processing Zones: Has Africa Missed the Boat? Not Yet!" World Bank, Washington, D.C. Processed.

WCO (World Customs Organization). 1999. "Survey of Customs Reform and Modernization: Trends and Best Practices." Avail-able at <www.wcoomd.org/frmpublic.htm>.

Wellenius, Bjorn. 1997. "Telecommunications Reform: How to Succeed." Public Policy for the Private Sector Note 130. World Bank Group, Finance, Private Sector, and Infrastructure Net-work, Washington, D.C.

———. 2001. "Chile: Extending Telecommunications to Rural Areas." World Bank, Washington, D.C. Processed.

Weston, Ann, and Valentina Delich. 2000. "Settling Trade Disputes after the Uruguay Round: Options for the Western Hemi-sphere." LATN Working Paper 10. Latin American Trade Net-work, Buenos Aires.

Westphal, L. E. 1990. "Industrial Policy in an Export-Propelled Economy: Lessons from South Korea's Experience." *Journal of Economic Perspectives* 4: 41–60.

Whalley, John. 1996. "Developing Countries and System Strength-ening in the Uruguay Round." In Will Martin and L. Alan Win-ters, eds., *The Uruguay Round and the Developing Economies.* Cambridge, U.K.: Cambridge University Press.

———. 1999. "Special and Differential Treatment in the Millenni-um Round." Centre for the Study of Globalisation and Regionalisation (CSGR) Working Paper N 30/99. May. University of Warwick, Coventry, U.K.

Wheeler, David, and Ashoka Mody. 1992. "International Investment Decisions: The Case of U.S. Firms." *Journal of International Economics* 33: 57–76.

Whichard, Obie. 2002. Measurement and Classification of Service Sector Activity: Data Needs for GATS 2000." In Robert M. Stern, ed., *Services in the International Economy*. Ann Arbor: University of Michigan Press.

Whish, R., and D. Wood. 1994. "Merger Cases in the Real World: A Study of Merger Control." OECD, Paris.

White, Howard, and Edward Anderson. 2000. "Growth versus Distribution: Does the Pattern of Growth Matter?" Institute of Development Studies, University of Sussex. Brighton, U.K. Processed.

WHO (World Health Organization). 1996. *The World Health Report 1996. Fighting Disease, Fostering Development*. Geneva.

———. 2000. *The World Health Report 2000. Health Systems: Improving Performance*. Geneva.

Wilson, E. O. 1992. *The Diversity of Life*. Cambridge, Mass.: Belknap Press of Harvard University.

Wilson, J. S. 1995. *Standards and APEC: An Action Agenda*. Washington, D.C.: Institute for International Economics.

———. 1999. "The Post-Seattle Agenda of the WTO in Standards and Technical Barriers to Trade: Issues for the Developing Countries." Washington, D.C.: World Bank.

Wilson, John. 2000a. "The Development Challenge in Trade, Sanitary and Phytosanitary Standards." Prepared for the WTO Committee on Sanitary and Phytosanitary Standards. June.

Wilson, J. S. 2000b. "Technical Barriers to Trade and Standards: Challenges and Opportunities for Developing Countries." World Bank, Washington, D.C. Processed.

Wilson, J. S. 2001. "Standards, Regulation, and Trade: Recommendations from a Development Perspective." Background paper for *World Development Report 2002*. World Bank, Washington, D.C.

Winham, Gilbert R. 1986. *International Trade and the Tokyo Round Negotiation*. Princeton, N.J.: Princeton University Press.

———. 1998. "Explanations of Developing Country Behavior in the GATT Uruguay Round Negotiation." *World Competition Law and Economics Review* 21 (3): 109–34.

Winters, L. Alan. 1997. "Assessing Regional Integration Agreements." June. World Bank, Washington, D.C. Processed.

———. 1998. "Regionalism versus Multilateralism." In Richard Baldwin, Daniel Cohen, André Sapir, and Anthony Venables, eds., *Market Integration, Regionalism and the Global Economy*. London: Centre for Economic Policy Research.

——— 1999 "Regionalism and the Rest of the World." World Bank, Washington, D.C. Processed.

———. 2000a. "Trade and Poverty: Is There a Connection?" In B. Ben-David, H. Nordstrom, and L. A. Winters, *Trade, Income Disparity and Poverty*, 43–49. Geneva: WTO.

———. 2000b. "Trade Policy as Development Policy: Building on Fifty Years' Experience." *Proceedings of the High-Level Round Table on Trade and Development, 10th United Nations Conference on Trade and Development, Bangkok, February*. Available at <http://www.unctad-10.org/index_en.htm>.

WIPO (World Intellectual Property Organization). 1997. *Asian Regional Round Table on Implementation of the Agreement on Trade-Related Aspects of Intellectual Property Rights, Singapore, January 15–17*. Geneva.

———. 1998. *Intellectual Property Reading Material*. No. 476 (E): March. 2d ed. Geneva.

Wiseman, Leanne. 2001. "The Protection of Indigenous Art and Culture in Australia: The Labels of Authenticity." *European Intellectual Property Review* 23 (1, January): 14–25.

Wolf, M. 1984. " Two Edged Sword: Demands of Developing Countries and the Trading System." In Jagdish N. Bhagwati and John Gerard Ruggie, eds., *Power, Passions, and Purpose: Prospects for North-South Negotiations*. Cambridge, Mass.: MIT Press.

Woo, Yuen Pau, and John S. Wilson. 2000. *Cutting through Red Tape: New Directions for APEC's Trade Facilitation Agenda*. Vancouver, B.C.: Asia Pacific Foundation of Canada.

World Bank. 1992. *The East Asian Miracle: Economic Growth and Public Policy*. New York: Oxford University Press.

———. 1995. "ARE: Egypt into the Next Century." Report 14048-EGT. May. Washington, D.C.

———. 1996a. "Container Transport Services and Trade: Framework for an Efficient Container Transport System." Report 15303-CHA. Washington, D.C.

———. 1996b. *World Development Indicators 1996*. Washington, D.C.

———. 1997. "Ethiopia Export Development Strategy." Processed. World Bank.

———. 1998. *Assessing Aid: What Works, What Doesn't, and Why*. New York: Oxford University Press.

———. 1999. *World Development Indicators 1999*. Washington, D.C.

———. 2000a. *Can Africa Claim the 20th Century?* Washington, D.C.

———. 2000b. "India: Policies to Reduce Poverty and Accelerate Sustainable Development." Report 19471-IN. Washington, D.C.

———. 2000c. *Trade Blocs*. Washington, D.C.

———. 2000d. *World Development Indicators 2000*. Washington, D.C.

———. 2000e. *World Development Report 2000/01: Attacking Poverty*. New York: Oxford University Press.

———. 2001a. *Finance for Growth: Policy Choices in a Volatile World*. World Bank Policy Research Report. New York: Oxford University Press.

———. 2001b. *Global Economic Prospects and the Developing Countries 2001*. Washington, D.C.

———. 2001c. *Global Economic Prospects 2002: Making Trade Work for the World's Poor*. Washington, D.C.

———. 2001d. "Information and Communications Technology Sector Strategy Paper." Washington, D.C. Available at <http://www.worldbank.org/html/fpd/notes/205/205summary.html>.

Worldscope. 1998. "Corporate Financial and Ownership Indicators." Bethesda, Md.

WTO. 1994a. *Compilation of Horizontal Commitments, All Sectors*. Geneva.

———. 1994b. *Country-wise Schedules of Commitments*. Geneva.

———. 1996a. "Japan: Taxes on Alcoholic Beverages. Report of the Appellate Body." Available at <http://www.wto.org/english/tratop_e/dispu_e/distab_e.htm>.

———. 1996b. *Trade Policy Review: Korea*. Geneva.

———. 1997a. *Opening Markets in Financial Services and the Role of the GATS*. Special study. Geneva.

———. 1997b. "A Review of Statistics on Trade Flows in Services." WTO Council for Trade in Services. Geneva.

———. 1997c. *WTO Annual Report 1997*. Geneva.

———. 1998a. "Japan: Measures Affecting Consumer Photographic Film and Paper, Report of the Panel, 31 March." Available at <http://www.wto.org/english/tratop_e/dispu_e/distab_e.htm>.

————. 1998b. "Presence of Natural Persons." Background note. WTO Council for Trade in Services. Geneva.

————. 1998c. "WTO Adopts Disciplines on Domestic Regulation for the Accountancy Sector." WTO Working Party on Professional Services. Geneva.

————. 1999a. "Indonesia—Certain Measures Affecting the Automobile Industry: Report of the Panel." WT/DS54/R, WT/DS55/R, WT/DS59/R, WT/DS64/R. Geneva.

————. 1999b. "Preparations for the 1999 Ministerial Conference." Job (99)/479/Rev. 3. Geneva.

————. 1999c. "Technical Note on the Accession Process." WT/ACC/7. March. Geneva.

————. 2000a. "Communication from Mauritius on Behalf of the African Group." Doc. Ref. S/CSS/W/7. Geneva.

————. 2000b. International Trade in Services. Geneva.

————. 2000c. "World Trade in 1999." WTO Secretariat. Geneva.

————. Various issues. Trade Policy Review. Geneva.

————. Various years (1997, 1998). Miscellaneous Documents on Professional Services. Working Party on Professional Services. Geneva.

WTO Secretariat. 1999. Guide to the Uruguay Round Agreements. The Hague: Kluwer Law International.

Yang, Guifang, and Keith E. Maskus. 2001. "Intellectual Property Rights and Licensing: An Econometric Investigation." Weltwirtschaftliches Archiv 137: 58–79.

Yeats, Alexander. 1995. "Are Partner Country Statistics Useful for Estimating 'Missing' Trade Data?" Policy Research Working Paper Series 1501. World Bank, Washington, D.C.

Young, L., and J. Romero. 1994. "A Dynamic Dual Model of the North American Free Trade Agreement." In Joseph F. Francois and Clinton R. Shiells, eds., Modeling Trade Policy: Applied General Equilibrium Assessments of North American Free Trade. Cambridge, U.K.: Cambridge University Press.

Youssef, H. 1999. "Special and Differential Treatment for Developing Countries in the WTO." TRADE Working Paper 2. South Centre, Geneva.

Yu, E. S. H., and C. C. Chao. 1998. "On Investment Measures and Trade." World Economy 21 (Global Trade Policy Issue): 549–61.

Zeiler, Thomas W. 1992. American Trade and Power in the 1960s. New York: Columbia University Press.

Zutshi, B. K. 1998. "Bringing TRIPs into the Multilateral Trading System." In Jagdish Bhagwati and Matthias Hirsch, eds., The Uruguay Round and Beyond: Essays in Honor of Arthur Dunkel. Ann Arbor: University of Michigan Press.

Index